ENDANGERED WATER SNAKES

Northern Copperbelly Water Snake, *Nerodia erythrogaster neglecta*
Lake Erie Water Snake, *Nerodia sipedon insularum*

(Reproduced from a watercolor by David M. Dennis, 1994.)

CAPTIVE MANAGEMENT AND CONSERVATION OF AMPHIBIANS AND REPTILES

Edited by James B. Murphy, Kraig Adler, and Joseph T. Collins

Foreword by Gerald Durrell

1994

Society for the Study of Amphibians and Reptiles

Series Editor's Note

The frontispiece to this volume depicts two taxa of water snakes, both of them described and named by Roger Conant. The Lake Erie Water Snake (*Nerodia sipedon insularum*) was once abundant and widespread throughout the islands of western Lake Erie, but in recent years populations have declined dramatically due to habitat loss caused by shoreline development and by active eradication by islanders. The Northern Copperbelly Water Snake (*Nerodia erythrogaster neglecta*) has a larger range, from western Tennessee to Michigan, but its distribution is not continuous and the snake persists only in scattered pockets of swamp-forest habitat which are threatened by drainage of wetlands, housing developments, and similar activities. Accordingly, the United States Fish and Wildlife Service has proposed both taxa for Federal listing as threatened species (see *Federal Register*, volume 58, number 158, pages 43857–43863, 18 August 1993). The Fish and Wildlife Service estimates that less than 2,000 adults of each of these snakes remain in the wild. Federal listing will give these snakes added protection from the two factors most threatening to their survival: collection and habitat loss. Copies of this frontispiece are being donated to various wildlife agencies as an aid in the conservation effort.

The Society is very grateful to David M. Dennis for drafting the watercolor from which this frontispiece is reproduced. For his assistance in producing this drawing, we also thank Richard B. King. David Dennis also drafted the headpieces to the individual chapters.

Contributions to Herpetology, Volume 11

Kraig Adler, *Editor*
Timothy D. Perry, *Associate Editor*

Volumes in the *Contributions to Herpetology* series can be purchased from the Publications Secretary, Robert D. Aldridge, Department of Biology, St. Louis University, 3507 Laclede, St. Louis, Missouri 63103, USA (*telephone*: area code 314, 658-3900 or 658-3916; *fax*: area code 314, 658-3117). A list of all Society publications, including those of The Ohio Herpetological Society and the *Catalogue of American Amphibians and Reptiles*, is printed at the end of this book; additional copies of this list are available from Dr. Aldridge. *Contributions* are published irregularly and ordered by separate subscription, although Society members receive a substantial pre-publication discount. Authors who wish to have manuscripts considered for publication in the *Contributions* series should contact the Editor: Kraig Adler, Cornell University, Section of Neurobiology and Behavior, Seeley G. Mudd Hall, Ithaca, New York 14853-2702, USA.

Members of the Society receive a quarterly technical journal (*Journal of Herpetology*) and a quarterly newsletter (*Herpetological Review*). Currently, dues are US$25.00 for students, $40.00 for all others, world-wide; institutional subscriptions are $70.00. Additional $25.00 for airmail delivery outside the USA. Society members receive substantial discounts on *Herpetological Circulars, Facsimile Reprints*, and on books in the *Contributions* series. The *Catalogue* is available by separate subscription. Apply to the Society's Treasurer, Karen L. Toepfer, P.O. Box 626, Hays, Kansas 67601-0626, USA. Overseas customers can make payments in USA funds or by International Money Order. All persons may charge to MasterCard or VISA (include account number and expiration date).

Library of Congress Catalog Number: 94-67894. ISBN: 0-916984-33-8.
Production specifications are given at the end of this book.

TABLE OF CONTENTS

REPRODUCTIVE BIOLOGY

MODEL PROGRAMS FOR AMPHIBIANS

MODEL PROGRAMS FOR REPTILES

MODEL PROGRAMS FOR REPTILES (continued)

FUTURE DIRECTIONS

SPECIAL TECHNIQUES

INDEX

FOREWORD

EVERY HERPETOLOGIST I EVER MET BEGAN LIFE AS A MINI-ZOOKEEPER, SURROUNDED by snakes, tortoises, frogs, lizards and the like. That the young herp enthusiasts matured into competent and productive biologists is evident from the contents of this book. But also evident is the new found maturity of herpetology itself as a discipline.

Growing up happens fast when a youngster must face unpleasant aspects of "the real world." Certain real world conditions—pollution, loss of natural habitat and over-exploitation of species—have finally been widely accepted as serious threats to biodiversity in general and to herpetofauna in particular. At risk is the very existence of species that give so much joy to people who keep, breed and study them in captivity. Herpetophiles, once content with isolated success in the zoo or lab or at home, are responding to the situation by collaborating with other biologists on difficult husbandry and reproduction cases and with conservationists on breeding for release-to-the-wild programmes. Those studying genetics, behaviour and physiology are concerned with wild as well as captive populations and they apply results to species survival and recovery strategies. Most importantly, people from all sectors of the herpetological community are communicating with each other on behalf of the animals they so love.

Nearly twenty years ago Princess Anne, Patron of the Jersey Wildlife Preservation Trust, opened our new Reptile Breeding Centre. In a note to us later, she wrote "I hope the herpets are happy." With the 1991 symposium, on which this book is based, and with the book itself, which includes numerous interesting and valuable chapters, conservation of amphibians and reptiles has come of age. If they could speak, I think the herpets would say to Princess Anne, "Yes, things are looking up."

GERALD DURRELL

London, 18 June 1994

INTRODUCTION

IN JUNE 1978, THE SOCIETY FOR THE STUDY OF Amphibians and Reptiles sponsored a landmark symposium on the reproductive biology and diseases of captive reptiles as part of its twenty-first annual meeting, held at Arizona State University in Tempe. At that time, the captive management of reptiles as a field was in its infancy and many of the papers dealt with large, charismatic taxa such as giant tortoises, sea turtles, green iguanas, boid snakes, and crocodilians. Several environmental parameters, including temperature and light, were addressed at this conference, as were reproductive strategies, ethology, and artificial methods for inducing reproduction. A major portion of the program dealt with veterinary techniques and procedures. The symposium was published by the SSAR in 1980, in a volume edited by James B. Murphy and Joseph T. Collins.

Today, more than a decade and a half later, circumstances have dramatically changed. The symposium "Captive Management and Conservation of Amphibians and Reptiles," sponsored by the SSAR and the Herpetologists' League and held in conjunction with their joint meeting at Pennsylvania State University in August 1991, reflected these changes in three major ways. First, due to increased and mostly human pressures on ecosystems throughout the world, a number of conservation efforts have been undertaken that incorporate captive breeding programs, some of which are operating in the country of origin. What is particularly reassuring about these programs is that increased collaboration between biologists in various disciplines is an important component that has contributed substantially to the breadth and success of these endeavors, a point emphasized by Gerald Durrell in his foreword to this book. Second, the evidence for global decline of amphibian populations has reemphasized the need to adapt and devise husbandry techniques for these creatures. Thus, the symposium was expanded from the scope of its 1978 precursor to encompass the status of captive amphibian programs. Finally, because a wealth of information is now available dealing with disease processes as well as veterinary techniques and procedures, these topics received less emphasis.

This book is based on the 1991 symposium, although additional authors were invited to contribute chapters on topics that could not be included among the oral presentations. This expansion of the original scope was done in order to produce a volume of more comprehensive coverage, both in terms of topical areas and taxonomic groups.

Future Studies

Symposia reflecting advances in captive management programs should be convened regularly to assess progress and provide a forum for discussion. But what form should symposia take in the future?

If one reviews the contents of this book, gaps and trends are evident. Relatively few chapters deal with amphibian topics, and indeed few sustained, long-term captive programs exist. Virtually no programs have been implemented for taxa within such families as the Amphiumidae, Leiopelmatidae, Pelobatidae, Myobatrachidae, Brachycephalidae, Rhinodermatidae, Centrolenidae, and Microhylidae. Reports on reproduction in other families are limited to a few genera.

More chapters in this volume deal with reptiles, yet there are significant gaps in coverage. Chelonians are gaining popularity in captivity and there are some well-designed and successful programs. Management initiatives for squamates are haphazard, and those for the lizard families Pygopodidae, Xantusiidae, Dibamidae, Xenosauridae, Anguidae, and Anniellidae are virtually non-existent. There is only one captive reproduction of an amphisbaenian known to us. Some primitive snake species, all within the family Boidae, have enjoyed widespread popularity for many years and have been reproduced regularly, but members of the families Uropeltidae, Leptotyphlopidae, Anomalepidae, Typhlopidae, and most of the Colubridae have not been reproduced in captivity.

The absence of specialized feeding requirements may explain why certain species are chosen for captive management. Most of them are maintained on diets of laboratory rodents, crickets, or other easily obtainable food items. In fact, some species of colubrids (i.e., in the genera *Lampropeltis*, *Elaphe*, and *Pituophis*), several boids, and one or two lizard species are produced in such numbers that these captive reptiles may now be viewed as laboratory colonies or "domestic reptiles."

Expanded programs for crocodilian captive management have increased, but financial incentives drive the process. The recent conservation directions in New Zealand outlined by Cree et al. with tuataras (this volume, page 377) expands our understanding of their biology dramatically.

Opportunities exist for persons who recognize this disparity of coverage and are motivated to fill in the gaps by designing comprehensive management protocols for the neglected species, many of which represent endangered or threatened taxa. This can be done through inference by investigating the biology of closely related, but better known, species, or by learning more about their habits in nature. There are too many instances where the only information available on the habits of a particular species is a brief note buried in the literature, but sometimes such notes are valuable clues. Marginally effective or unproductive efforts should be critically evaluated and either eliminated or revised. Given this situation, serious amateurs and researchers with varied opportunities, backgrounds, and expertise can contribute significantly to conservation initiatives by using captive management models as a tool. The beneficiaries of such a holistic approach would be the animal treasures which we all admire and value.

Dedication

The 1991 symposium was dedicated to Roger Conant, Director Emeritus of the Philadelphia Zoo. (For biography, see the chapter by Kraig Adler, this volume, page 17) This book is also dedicated to Dr. Conant, in recognition of his many contributions to the growth of herpetology in North America, including the development of captive management programs for amphibians and reptiles and the education of several generations of nascent herpetologists who were introduced to the field by reading one or more of his many books.

Acknowledgments

We take this opportunity to thank the many persons involved in arranging the 1991 symposium. The Organizing Committee, representing the SSAR and the Herpetologists' League, included Edmund D. Brodie, Jr., William S. Brown, Joseph T. Collins, J. Whitfield Gibbons, Linda E. Maxson, Joseph C. Mitchell, and James B. Murphy; Kraig Adler served as committee chairman. We thank Joseph R. Bailey, the late C. J. McCoy, Edmond V. Malnate, Sherman A. Minton, Norman J. Scott, Jr., Margaret M. Stewart, Robert O. Wagner, and Ermi Zhao for serving as symposium moderators and Joseph R. Bailey, Roger K. Conant, and M. Graham Netting for their contributions to a reception and ceremony honoring Roger Conant that were ably arranged by Joseph C. Mitchell.

The considerable costs of the symposium, which involved several speakers from overseas, were underwritten by generous donations sent in honor of Roger Conant. The many persons and organizations who contributed are listed elsewhere in this volume (pages 13–14), but we wish to single out for special recognition Philippe de Vosjoli, Harry Foster, and Brian E. Smith. Part of these funds have been used to support the cost of publication of this volume. We also acknowledge the SSAR for its financial support toward publication costs.

We thank Gerald Durrell, the noted British zoologist, explorer, and author of numerous books on animals and the founding director of the Jersey Wildlife Preservation Trust located on Jersey Island in the English Channel, for contributing the foreword to this volume. David M. Dennis, the well-known natural history artist at Ohio State University, whose artwork has graced many SSAR books, kindly painted the watercolor from which the frontispiece to this book has been reproduced.

For their aid in reviewing one or more manuscripts for this volume, we thank Paul Andreadis, Jonathan Ballou, David A. Blody, J. Kevin Bowler, Donal M. Boyer, Bayard H. Brattstrom, Peter Brazaitis, William S. Brown, James J. Bull, Gordon M. Burghardt, Jonathan A. Campbell, Fred Caporaso, Theodore Case, David Chiszar, Justin D. Congdon, William E. Cooper, David Crews, Martha L. Crump,

Herbert C. Dessauer, Philippe de Vosjoli, Ellen Dierenfeld, C. Kenneth Dodd, Jr., Maureen A. Donnelly, David Duvall, Michael A. Ewert, Gary W. Ferguson, Henry S. Fitch, Joseph P. Flanagan, Nat B. Fraser, James C. Gillingham, Ronald R. Goellner, Patrick T. Gregory, Louis J. Guillette, Timothy R. Halliday, Robert W. Henderson, Jack Herbert, Raymond B. Huey, R. Howard Hunt, John B. Iverson, Robert G. Jaeger, James Harvey Johnson, Richard Jones, Robert H. Kaplan, Paul A. Klein, Michael W. Klemens, Robert Lacy, Paul Licht, Harvey B. Lillywhite, Kenneth McCloud, Sean McKeown, Lyndon A. Mitchell, Kenneth A. Nagy, Steven Pakes, F. Harvey Pough, Peter C. H. Pritchard, Hugh Quinn, David T. Roberts, Richard A. Ross, Terri L. Roth, Richard D. Sage, Norman J. Scott, Jr., Larry G. Talent, Carol R. Townsend, Ronald L. Tremper, Duane Ullrey, Paul A. Verrell, Brian Viets, Laurie J. Vitt, Kentwood D. Wells, and Christen Wemmer. In addition, we thank Jo Gayle Howard and John Shadduck for their advice concerning reviewers. Johnny R. Arnett and Ian Swingland kindly assisted with other editorial matters.

The individual editors of this volume would like to recognize several persons and institutions for their assistance.

James B. Murphy: The herpetology staff at the Dallas Zoo, specifically Donal Boyer, Clay Garrett, David Roberts, Lyndon A. Mitchell, and Winston Card; Dallas Zoo employees Warren Iliff (former director), Richard Buickerood (current director), and Ronald Kagan (former general curator); the Dallas Zoological Society; and especially Gina Jurik of the Dallas Zoo for so masterfully handling the myriad duties of management of the editorial review process.

Kraig Adler: Dawn Potter for keyboarding part of the text and for handling the numerous details of page proofs; Timothy D. Perry and Lindy Costello for formatting the text and readying it for the press; undergraduate members of the Cornell Herpetological Society, Sarah J. Klinowski, Luis R. Padilla, Vincent T. Marshall, Bryan L. Stuart, Tristan K. Weinkle, and Kevin C. Zippel, for reading and critiquing the proofs; and Cornell University for its administrative support for the editorial processing of this book.

Joseph T. Collins: Suzanne L. Collins, for her cooperation and support during the editing of the manuscripts making up this volume; Philip S. Humphrey, director of the University of Kansas Natural History Museum, for his forebearance of Collins's herpetological pursuits; and Sarah Taylor for her diligence in managing the editorial process.

The editors of this volume would furthermore like to thank the following persons for stimulating discussions with one or more of them about the interface among zoos, academic institutions, and conservation organizations: David Barker, John L. Behler, Judith A. Block, David A. Blody, Edmund D. Brodie, Jr., Jonathan A. Campbell, Charles C. Carpenter, David Chiszar, Roger Conant, Harry W. Greene, John D. Groves, Stephen H. Hammack, Richard D. Hudson, Elliott R. Jacobson, William W. Lamar, the late Hobart F. Landreth, Dale L. Marcellini, Russell A. Mittermeier, R. Andrew Odum, Nikolai Orlov, Ray Pawley, the late Louis J. Pistoia, George B. Rabb, Richard A. Ross, Frank L. Slavens, and Brian E. Smith.

JAMES B. MURPHY
KRAIG ADLER
JOSEPH T. COLLINS

27 July 1994

Addresses of the Volume Editors

James B. Murphy, Department of Herpetology, Dallas Zoo, 621 East Clarendon Drive, Dallas, Texas 75203, USA.

Kraig Adler, Section of Neurobiology and Behavior, Cornell University, Seeley G. Mudd Hall, Ithaca, New York 14853-2702, USA.

Joseph T. Collins, Natural History Museum, University of Kansas, Lawrence, Kansas 66044-2454, USA.

PATRONS

The Society gratefully acknowledges support from these individuals and organizations whose aid has made possible the publication of this book

BENEFACTORS

AMERICAN FEDERATION OF HERPETOCULTURISTS
(Philippe de Vosjoli)

IN HONOR OF AMY S. BRIDEGAM
(Brian E. Smith)

DETROIT ZOOLOGICAL SOCIETY
(Steve Graham, Charles M. Hammond)

DOCENT COUNCIL OF THE ZOOLOGICAL SOCIETY OF PHILADELPHIA
(Roberta DeVries, the late Ruth Zantzinger)

HOUGHTON MIFFLIN COMPANY
(Nader F. Dareshori, Harry Foster)

ZOOLOGICAL SOCIETY OF PHILADELPHIA
(The late William V. Donaldson, John D. Groves, Wilbur Amand)

FRIENDS OF THE SOCIETY

Individuals

KRAIG ADLER
In honor of JAMES D. ANDERSON
MARY L. ANDERSON
RUDOLF G. ARNDT
DOROTHY O. and JOSEPH R. BAILEY
AARON M. BAUER
The late CHARLES M. and MARTHA R. BOGERT
CHARLES C. CARPENTER
In honor of ISABELLE HUNT CONANT
C. KENNETH DODD, JR.
ARTHUR C. ECHTERNACHT
VINCENT D. VON FRESE
HAJIME FUKADA
BARNEY GARDNER
TERRY E. GRAHAM
BILLIE B. and DAVID L. HARDY
VICTOR H. HUTCHISON
SALLY KREBS
EDMOND V. MALNATE
MADGE R. and SHERMAN A. MINTON
JOSEPH C. and WENDY H. MITCHELL
PAUL E. MOLER
DANIEL H. MORENO
JOHN J. MORIARTY

Individuals (continued)

M. GRAHAM NETTING
RAYMOND NOVOTNY
RAY PAWLEY
RALPH PFINGSTEN
RODOLFO RUIBAL
C. ROBERT SHOOP
HOBART M. SMITH
LUCILLE F. and WILLIAM H. STICKEL
ARTHUR STUPKA
SAMUEL S. SWEET
FRANKLIN J. TOBEY, JR.
DAVID B. and MARVALEE H. WAKE
FRANK T. WATROUS
ROBERT G. WEBB
DANIEL C. WILHOFT
The late JOHN G. and PHYLLIS G. WILLIAMS

Organizations

HERPETOLOGY ON-LINE NETWORK
IDAHO HERPETOLOGICAL SOCIETY
MINNESOTA HERPETOLOGICAL SOCIETY
ONTARIO HERPETOLOGICAL SOCIETY
PHILADELPHIA HERPETOLOGICAL SOCIETY
TUCSON HERPETOLOGICAL SOCIETY
VIRGINIA HERPETOLOGICAL SOCIETY

Captive Management and Conservation of Amphibians and Reptiles

The Remarkable Career of Roger Conant

Kraig Adler*

Introduction

Most herpetologists and herpetoculturists in North America, including teenagers and our most senior scientists, have been influenced in one way or another by Roger Conant. More than any other American herpetologist active today, he has had an even broader impact on the public at large, through his many books, radio and television programs, his consultantship to the Boy Scouts of America, and many other educational activities. Thus, it was only fitting to honor Roger in 1991, with the symposium about captive management and conservation of amphibians and reptiles on which this book is based.

His Early Life and Career

Roger Conant was born in Mamaroneck, New York, on 6 May 1909, and later lived some of his boyhood years in Philadelphia where he was destined to spend most of his professional life. His interest in reptiles began at the age of 12 when he attended a summer boy scout camp in Connecticut and caught his first water snakes. Two of his camp counselors were undergraduate students of that beloved teacher at Cornell University, Albert H. Wright. Wright had inspired them to pursue an interest in herpetology and they, in turn, encouraged young Conant. They even let him assist in the capture of a copperhead. He was hooked on snakes! Likewise, his interest in the boy scouts has also continued throughout his life. As a teenager, Roger became so knowledgeable about snakes that he regularly lectured to boy scout troops and other groups for US$5 a talk. This supported his hobby and enabled him to save some money for college. He managed to attend the University of Pennsylvania but had to drop out after two years due to financial circumstances stemming from the Great Depression.

Since Roger had always been interested in zoos, he worked for a year at a private zoo near Middletown, New Jersey, but soon he got a critical break. In 1929, at the age of 19, he became Curator of Reptiles at the Toledo Zoological Park in Toledo, Ohio. Here, unlike his other offer from the St. Louis Zoo where he would have been a lowly assistant, at Toledo he could develop his own program, albeit a modest one at first. The original collection of reptiles was quite small and was kept in an all-weather building that housed an assortment of animals. It took only half an hour each day to curate, so he had many other duties, mostly in the giraffe house. The collection grew, of course, and had to be moved to the pachyderm house, where it was displayed in an assemblage of cages in the lobby. This collection required half a day's work for him to maintain, but soon he began to design the zoo's new reptile house which was opened in 1934. By then, Roger was General Curator (in effect, director) of the zoo.

The Toledo period also represented Roger's graduate-level training, for besides the zoo experience, Ann Arbor was nearby with its constellation of herpetologists at the University of Michigan: Alexander G. Ruthven, E. C. Case, Helen T. Gaige, and Frank N. Blanchard, together with their many students including Howard K. Gloyd. Gloyd became Roger's close friend and a lifelong colleague. Association with this group established exacting standards for Roger and set his career off in a scientific direction. Today's major zoos have scientific programs, but this was not the normal situation in the 1930s. Zoos in those days were little more than menageries, not the conservation and research or-

---

*Section of Neurobiology and Behavior
Cornell University
Ithaca, New York 14853-2702, USA

Opposite page: Roger Conant studying a specimen of *Agkistrodon contortrix* in his laboratory at the University of New Mexico (1983).

ganizations that the better ones have become in the last few decades. Roger's first papers, beginning in 1929, were notes on captive specimens, field trips, animal health, and zoo educational programs, but soon this changed to include more academic subjects.

The second edition of the book, "The Herpetology of Michigan" by Alexander G. Ruthven, Crystal Thompson, and Helen T. Gaige, had been published a year before Conant's arrival in Toledo and it impressed upon Roger the value of having such a wealth of up-to-date information all under one cover. Since there was nothing like it for Ohio, he decided to produce one himself. At that time, Charles F. Walker, then associated with the Ohio State Museum, was monographing the amphibians of Ohio, so Roger restricted his plans to cover only the reptiles. He had facilities at the zoo for a fluid-preserved reference collection—in a makeshift museum in the basement of the administration building—but there was still the problem of transportation to collect specimens throughout the state. This was not a simple problem during the Depression years. Cars, and even gasoline at 20 cents a gallon, were expensive.

FIGURE 2. Preserving a specimen of *Lampropeltis getula* found dead on the road, Delmarva Peninsula of southern Delaware (May 1936).

FIGURE 1. As a very young Curator of Reptiles, Toledo Zoo, holding a specimen of *Elaphe obsoleta lindheimeri* (spring or summer 1929).

In 1929, Roger was bitten by a specimen of *Crotalus mitchellii* and, due to a bungling doctor, he lost his left thumb. The doctor forgot to give him a tetanus shot and he suffered through five weeks of lockjaw, during which he had to be heavily sedated and remained unconscious. But Roger turned misfortune into opportunity. The State of Ohio recompensed him for the loss of his thumb with a payment of US$1,100, of which he promptly spent $800 to purchase a car. Thus did he finance his expeditions to all parts of Ohio, which resulted in a large collection of museum specimens and his book, "The Reptiles of Ohio" (published 1938; second edition with revisionary addenda in 1951), which was called "a landmark in the development of herpetology in the Eastern United States" by Karl P. Schmidt.

Roger was one of the first to use the spot-mapping technique that is now so widespread and which he perfected. His maps showed the exact locations for individual specimens, rather than simple county records as in "The Herpetology of Michigan," and he related species distributions to physiographic regions which permitted a more fundamental understanding of their ranges in terms of geological history and current environments. He assembled life history data into a useful synthesis and he never exaggerated information for effect, which unfortunately was a device used in some other reptile books of the day. His monograph thus became the standard for state herpetologies and his basic plan is still the one used today. The book also put Conant on the herpetological map. (Conant's years of collecting reptiles in Ohio have been delightfully recorded in his booklet, "Herpetology in Ohio—Fifty Years Ago," issued in 1982.)

The Philadelphia Zoo Years

By 1935, Conant had published more than a dozen papers, including several carefully researched taxonomic papers on snakes. With his well-earned reputation he won a position as Curator of Reptiles at the Philadelphia Zoo, where he spent the next 38 years. He added the titles of Public Relations Counsel and Membership Secretary in 1936, and he served as Director from 1967 until his retirement six years later.

FIGURE 3. As Curator of Reptiles, Philadelphia Zoo (early 1940s).

FIGURE 4. Collecting water snakes in the Mississippi Delta, near Port Sulphur, Louisiana (March 1948).

Philadelphia had been the first American zoo to exhibit a collection of reptiles—in 1874—and Roger inherited an old building that had once housed the bird collection and thus was far from satisfactory for amphibians and reptiles. Only in 1972 did the zoo open a new facility. This was designed by him, of course, and incorporated many modern exhibition features that have been widely imitated. In the naturalistic tropical river display, for example, the lights dim on schedule, followed by thunder and lightning, and then an ecological message is heard about the importance of rain storms in tropical ecosystems.

Under Roger's tutelage, the Philadelphia Zoo was involved in some of the earliest captive breeding programs. The zoo was also particularly successful in developing the right combination of environments and diets for a wide range of species, thus establishing longevity records for many species of reptiles. He edited the zoo's publications—*Fauna* and *America's First Zoo*—for a total of 28 years. He also wrote and conducted a weekly radio show, "Let's Visit the Zoo," for the Philadelphia affiliate of the National Broadcasting Company, beginning in 1936 and for more than 33 years. He made frequent appearences on television.

During the same period, Roger's lifetime association with the Boy Scouts of America led to his production of their merit badge pamphlets on reptiles (editions in 1944, 1958, 1972, and 1976). He wrote similar articles on reptiles for various National Audubon Society publications, *Canadian Nature*, *Nature Magazine*, and many others that were directed at young people.

Roger's research during his time at the Philadelphia Zoo focused on water snakes. This interest eventually took him to Mexico during 1949–1967 where, with his wife Isabelle Hunt Conant, an outstanding wildlife photographer, he spent a collective total of one year in the field on numerous trips supported by grants from the United States National Science Foundation. The Conants collected in all parts of Mexico, including Baja California, the Mexican Plateau, and along the Guatemalan border in Chiapas.

The "Field Guide"

Following some preliminary correspondence, in 1951 Roger Tory Peterson visited the zoo to ask Roger to write the volume on amphibians and reptiles for the field guide series that bears his name. Conant was a logical choice for the task because of his prominence as a herpetologist and because he had written the booklet "Reptiles and Amphibians of the Northeastern States" (first edition published in 1947) which emphasized field identification based on photographs and thumbnail descriptions of key species characteristics. Many of the photographs were taken by Isabelle. In reality, the proposed field guide required a team and Roger and Isabelle were perfect for the job. The photographs alone required a herculean effort, since the Conants set out to illustrate every species and most subspecies found in North America east of the 100th meridian (which passes through central Nebraska). At one time or another they had specimens of almost every one of them alive at the zoo or at their home, and they often had to keep them alive and healthy for a very long time for Isabelle's photography and hand coloring.

Color photography then was not very reliable without costly equipment so Isabelle photographed in black-and-white, then brown-toned the prints in her darkroom and hand colored each one with watercolor dyes. Any error required her to start all over again, for the dyes were permanent. For his part, Roger laid out the book, wrote the text, and assembled the detailed distribution maps. In typical Conant fashion, the descriptions of species and their key identification characteristics are models of succinctness. The range maps, which summarize an enormous body of data, were not just up-to-date but, in fact, were well ahead of the published literature. As with all of Roger's publications, there was painstaking attention to detail and accuracy. The result, published in 1958, was a resounding success, an information- and illustration-packed, cloth-bound volume of 384 pages and 40 color plates—all for only US$3.95!

FIGURE 5. The Conants working in the shelter of their camper parked near the source of the Río Nazas in Durango, Mexico (September 1960).

The second edition appeared in 1975, but covered more territory since the companion volume on western North America, by Robert C. Stebbins, published in 1966, did not extend as far as the 100th meridian. It came as far east as the eastern borders of the Rocky Mountain states, thus creating a huge gap in the coverage of the two volumes, including the rich herpetofauna of the Big Bend region of Texas. Roger's new edition, therefore, had to add many more species and was appropriately retitled "Eastern and Central North America."

The third edition of the "Field Guide" appeared in 1991 and continued the high standards of the previous versions. Joseph T. Collins joined Roger and assisted in updating the text and the distribution maps. With Isabelle's untimely death in 1976, Tom R. Johnson was selected to rework the illustrations and add some new ones. Together, these three editions represent the most widely used title in all of herpetology. Half a million copies have been sold to date. (The story of how Isabelle and Roger put together the first edition is wonderfully told, often with highly amusing anecdotes, in a series of articles by Roger Conant that appeared in the *Bulletin of the Chicago Herpetological Society* in 1991 and 1994.)

Post-Retirement Activities

In 1973, because of Isabelle's declining health, Roger took early retirement from the zoo and moved to Albuquerque where he was given a courtesy position as Adjunct Professor of Biology at the University of New Mexico. Freed from his administrative duties at the zoo, Roger could devote much more time to herpetology. The second edition of his "Field Guide" appeared in 1975. There were numerous other papers on a wide variety of subjects, including the Pine Barrens of New Jersey, kinosternid turtles, semiaquatic amphibians and reptiles of the Chihuahuan Desert, reproductive biology of reptiles, a new *Agkistrodon*, and several others on his favorite animals, the water snakes.

Isabelle died in 1976. Up to that time she had been actively involved in nearly all of Roger's projects, as photographer, artist, field collector, data analyst, and editor. There was now an enormous void in Roger's personal and professional life and within weeks of Isabelle's death he visited Howard K. Gloyd, his old colleague, who then lived in Tucson, Arizona. As early as 1932, they had conceived a joint plan to monograph the snakes of the genus *Agkistrodon*, and had published several papers on the subject over the period 1934–1943. But by the late 1940s each had heavy administrative duties and the project languished. It was rejuvenated, first, when HK (as Gloyd was called by his closest friends) moved to Tucson in 1958 and again, in 1976, when Roger agreed to reenter the collaboration, for by this time HK was terminally ill and could not complete the book by himself.

This was an immense project, including detailed scale counts on more than 6,200 specimens and a bibliography of nearly 2,000 entries. HK had completed a large part of the research and preliminary writing, but much had to be revised and updated, and by then HK's energies were gone. He died in 1978. It was Roger who completed the task of rewriting, assembled the maps and all the color photographs, and saw this mammoth book through the press, with the essential assistance of HK's widow, Kathryn, who in 1979 became Roger's wife. The book, published by the Society for the Study of

FIGURE 6. The Conants demonstrating their technique for obtaining photographs for use in the "Field Guide" (middle to late 1960s).

Amphibians and Reptiles (SSAR) in 1990, is 620 pages long with 53 plates, and was soon hailed by reviewers as the definitive treatment of the four Asian and American genera making up the *Agkistrodon* complex. As one reviewer, Jonathan A. Campbell, remarked: "This book is one of the few herpetological works that can truly be considered a 'classic' from the date of its first appearance." As part of his work in completing this book, Roger visited Costa Rica and, together with Kathryn, also went to Japan, China, Taiwan, Thailand, Malaysia, Indonesia, India, and Sri Lanka, in order to learn more about these snakes in their native habitats.

Other Activities and Honors

Roger was never content only to do his own research, but gave freely of his time to numerous organizations to support and develop the discipline. He served as Secretary and, later, President of the American Society of Ichthyologists and Herpetologists (ASIH). He chaired the important ASIH committee which began the standardization of common names for the amphibians and reptiles of the United States and Canada (published in 1956). He also served on the Board of Directors of SSAR. He was the editor of the zoo section for *Parks and Recreation* magazine for 20 years and served as Secretary and also President of the American Association of Zoological Parks and Aquariums (AAZPA), an organization now recently re-named the American Zoo and Aquarium Association.

FIGURE 7. During his active retirement years (November 1988).

The AAZPA honored Roger in 1989 with its R. Marlin Perkins Award for being a model of professional excellence for the rest of the zoo community. Indeed, his example of combining serious research with the more usual duties of a zoo curator had a significant influence in transforming the roles of zoo personnel and in helping to bridge the gulf that then separated curatorial staff from their academic colleagues at universities and museums. The National Recreation and Park Association presented him with its Distinguished Service Award, and the Herpetologists' League designated him its Distinguished Herpetologist Lecturer in 1983. The University of Colorado conferred upon Roger the honorary degree of Doctor of Science at its commencement ceremonies in 1971.

These are but a few of the numerous honors accorded Roger for his lifetime of service and achievement, but they do not begin to measure the impact that he has had on countless young people, which may well be his most important legacy. Through his personal example and many activities—books, Boy Scout pamphlets, radio and television shows, and articles in animal-oriented magazines—Roger Conant has inspired generations of youngsters to become professionals or take a serious interest in animals through conservation, husbandry, or other activities.

Roger also took the time to encourage those who made visits to see him at the zoo or who had the temerity to write. The latter numbered in the many thousands. He was always helpful, always courteous, always detailed in his reply, and always willing to write back again and again. Surely the administration and his poor secretaries had little conception of the impact that this humble zoo employee had on the development of herpetology in North America.

It should also be recorded that Roger's books on reptiles stimulated the early development of SSAR's predecessor organization, The Ohio Herpetological

Society (OHS), and influenced the careers of many of the authors in this volume, including the three editors. His book, "The Reptiles of Ohio," became a kind of bible for amateur herpetologists in Ohio in the late 1950s and provided a framework for them to do serious field research. Roger was also an unofficial adviser during OHS's foundation period beginning in 1958. Thus, when the society, as SSAR, celebrated its silver anniversary in 1982, it was only fitting that Roger should take his rightful place, front and center, when the group photograph of early officers was taken.

FIGURE 8. With early officers of The Ohio Herpetological Society (now Society for the Study of Amphibians and Reptiles), gathered for the society's 25th annual meeting in Raleigh, North Carolina (August 1982). *From left*: Kraig Adler, Ray E. Ashton, Jr., Paul M. Daniel, Stephen G. Tilley, David M. Dennis, Barry D. Valentine, Roger Conant, Corson J. Hirschfeld, Joseph T. Collins, Ronald A. Brandon, and Henri C. Seibert.

Happily, Roger's work continues to inspire us yet today, for he is one of those rare persons who somehow retain their creative potential and work ethic well beyond the age of 80. He is now, at the age of 85, completing his memoirs, which when published will provide example and encouragement to new generations of budding herpetologists and herpetoculturists for many years to come.

Roger Conant's Herpetological Books and Monographs

1938. The Reptiles of Ohio [first edition]. Amer. Midl. Nat., 20: 1–200.
1939. What Snake Is That? D. Appleton-Century, New York and London. x, 163 pages, 32 plates (with William Bridges.)
1951. The Reptiles of Ohio (second edition). Univ. Notre Dame Press, Notre Dame, Indiana. 284 pages.
1958. A Field Guide to Reptiles and Amphibians of the United States and Canada East of the 100th Meridian [first edition]. Houghton Mifflin, Boston. xviii, 366 pages, 40 plates.
1969. A Review of the Water Snakes of the Genus *Natrix* in Mexico. Bull. Amer. Mus. Nat. Hist., 142: 1–140, 22 plates.
1975. A Field Guide to Reptiles and Amphibians of Eastern and Central North America (second edition). Houghton Mifflin, Boston. xviii, 429 pages, 48 plates.
1990. Snakes of the *Agkistrodon* Complex: A Monographic Review. Soc. Study Amphib. Reptiles, Oxford (Ohio), Contributions to Herpetology, 6: vi, 1–614, 53 plates (with Howard K. Gloyd).
1991. A Field Guide to Reptiles and Amphibians of Eastern and Central North America (third edition). Houghton Mifflin, Boston. xx, 450 pages, 48 plates (with Joseph T. Collins).

•

Credits for photographs. Opposite page 17: courtesy of Roger Conant. Figure 1: Toledo Zoo (Peter Tolson). Figure 2: Roger Conant. Figure 3: Philadelphia Zoo (John D. Groves). Figure 4: M. Graham Netting. Figures 5-6: Roger Conant. Figure 7: Kraig Adler. Figure 8: James S. Jacob.

❦ Adler, K. 1994. The remarkable career of Roger Conant, p. 17–23. *In* J. B. Murphy, K. Adler, and J. T. Collins (eds.), Captive Management and Conservation of Amphibians and Reptiles. Society for the Study of Amphibians and Reptiles, Ithaca (New York). Contributions to Herpetology, volume 11.

Captive Management and Conservation of Amphibians and Reptiles: An Introduction to the Symposium

Robert O. Wagner*

Introduction

As I write these words, there are about 3,000 days remaining in the century, and all of us must re-dedicate ourselves if we are to stem the rapidly escalating tide of amphibian and reptilian species that are becoming endangered or seriously threatened. We have made great strides in recent years in calling the plight of a growing number of species of amphibians and reptiles to the attention of the general public and, more importantly, to local, county, state, and national regulatory agencies; much more must be done, however.

At the 1991 symposium, "Captive Management and Conservation of Amphibians and Reptiles," which formed the basis for this book, outstanding leaders from zoological parks, aquariums, academia, conservation organizations, museums, and research organizations shared their specific expertise as well as plans on how we might better position ourselves for the work ahead. The organizers for this symposium arranged for an open exchange on the latest developments in the management of amphibians and reptiles, and speakers included representatives from all the above-mentioned disciplines. The organizers recognized that the tasks before us cannot be accomplished by any one group, but must be a carefully coordinated effort if we are to accomplish our mission of saving as many species as possible. Those concerned with amphibians and reptiles in zoological parks and aquariums must work much more closely with their colleagues in museums, academia, and the private sector, and vice versa.

Declining Populations

We are all aware of the recently reported dramatic declines in the populations of many amphibian species. We are also aware that amphibians and reptiles do not ever seem to get their "fair share" of attention in the minds of the general public. Even various national agencies—when considering the continuation of scientific studies or the listing process required for advanced levels of protection—tend to overlook the needs of amphibians and reptiles. Several cases in point include the total or near decimation of several species of frogs. For example, Australia's unique Gastric Brooding Frog (*Rheobatrachus silus*) was doing very well just a few years ago. Its unique breeding habit was of special interest to scientists and was extensively studied. Then, in 1980, the species apparently became extinct. To date, there has not been a compelling argument as to the causes for this sudden extinction. This species may have suffered the same speedy decline in populations as other species of amphibians worldwide. In another classic example, the beautiful and widely known Golden Toad (*Bufo periglenes*) has either become extinct or nearly extinct in its native habitat of the Monteverde Cloud Forest of Costa Rica. Prior to 1980 these toads were abundant. Today the species may no longer exist.

Surely, the causes for these declines are very likely related to humans and our modification of the environment. Herpetologists have been concerned for more than two decades with respect to

*American Association of Zoological Parks and Aquariums[1]
Oglebay Park
Wheeling, West Virginia 26003-1698, USA

Acronyms used in this chapter:

AAZPA	American Association of Zoological Parks and Aquariums[1]
IUCN	International Union for the Conservation of Nature and Natural Resources
SSP	Species Survival Plan

[1]*Note*: The name of this organization was recently changed to "American Zoo and Aquarium Association" with the acronym "AZA."

these somewhat isolated, but distinct, declines in certain species of amphibians. Indeed, the United States National Academy of Sciences called together about 40 scientists, representing various disciplines from several countries, to wrestle with the problem and to attempt to focus on the reasons for such rapid declines. During that meeting and others on the same topic that followed, the widespread decimation of various populations and species became more widely known.

It is well known that there are identifiable factors working against the continuation of healthy populations of amphibians. These matters are evident when one considers habitat destruction, especially that occurring in developing countries. Guatemala is home to approximately 120 species of amphibians. During the last 15 years, between 50 and 75 percent of the rain forest in Guatemala has been destroyed. In such cases, the animals that are not eliminated directly, and that survive the initial destruction of the rain forest, are left with no natural habitat.

The drastic decline in populations of amphibians and reptiles is certainly not unique to developing countries. North America, especially the United States, records far more than its fair share of declining populations. In fact, one of the world's most dramatic examples of disregard for wildlife occurs in North America in the annual rattlesnake roundups. Moreover, until fairly recently, the unabated attempts at collecting Eastern Indigo Snakes (*Drymarchon corais*)—often by gassing them in their burrows—nearly caused their demise, as well as raising havoc with other burrowing species sharing their habitat, especially in the case of the Gopher Tortoise (*Gopherus polyphemus*).

I remember well the work done by Howard Lawler, and supported by AAZPA, when Lawler was Curator of Reptiles at Zoo Atlanta. Lawler called attention to the plight of the Eastern Indigo Snake. He informed the various state agencies throughout the snake's range of the impact of collecting on the species and others sharing its habitat, and was able to bring about some legislative relief. This is only one example of what can be done through perseverance and appropriate presentation of factual information.

Programs to Counter Population Declines

The purpose of the symposium on which this book is based was to focus on new and emerging methodologies to enhance the reproduction of amphibians and reptiles in captivity with the ultimate goal of many captive-propagation programs—reintroduction into natural habitats. The AAZPA and the Captive Breeding Specialist Group of the IUCN already have in place several programs to help accomplish this mission. AAZPA has established and is operating the SSP, an exciting program in which the majority of our member zoological parks and aquariums are participating.

As of July, 1992, the SSP included survival plans for 54 species—one for an invertebrate, six for reptiles and amphibians, 12 for birds, and 35 for mammals. On another level, the AAZPA has developed Taxon Advisory Groups; 20 such programs are currently active—one for an invertebrate, five for reptiles and amphibians, five for birds, and nine for mammals. (For details on these programs, see Wiese and Hutchins, this volume, page 37.)

❦

❦ Wagner, R. O. 1994. Captive management and conservation of amphibians and reptiles: an introduction to the symposium, p. 25–26. *In* J. B. Murphy, K. Adler, and J. T. Collins (eds.), Captive Management and Conservation of Amphibians and Reptiles. Society for the Study of Amphibians and Reptiles, Ithaca (New York). Contributions to Herpetology, volume 11.

CONSERVATION OF REPTILES AND AMPHIBIANS: A GLOBAL PERSPECTIVE

RUSSELL A. MITTERMEIER* AND JOHN L. CARR*

Introduction

THE MOST CRITICAL ISSUE FACED TODAY BY THE environmental movement is the conservation of biological diversity: the vast wealth of species, ecosystems, and ecological processes that make up our biosphere. The impending loss of this diversity over the next few decades through large-scale species extinctions is a very real concern. Since this crisis is of a global nature, those interested in the world's biota must look beyond local interests.

If conservationists hope to maintain the greatest possible portion of global biodiversity, then there must be a major focus on the tropical regions of the world, and especially on tropical forests and other high-diversity tropical ecosystems. The greatest portion of our planet's biological diversity resides in the tropics, and the worldwide destruction of tropical forests and other tropical ecosystems is our major conservation problem today. Efforts to conserve global biodiversity must include the conservation of amphibians and reptiles, because these animals account for about one-quarter of known vertebrate species, and the vast majority of amphibians and reptiles reside in tropical ecosystems (Mittermeier et al. 1992).

After briefly summarizing threats to amphibian and reptilian species in this chapter, we discuss the effort expended by international conservation organizations on behalf of amphibian and reptilian populations, examine approaches to setting conservation priorities, and review some of the actions needed to effect conservation of amphibians and reptiles and of biodiversity in general.

Threats to Amphibian and Reptilian Populations

Threats to amphibian and reptilian populations can be divided into three main categories: habitat destruction; hunting for both commercial and subsistence purposes; and indirect problems, such as introduced species, entrapment in fishing nets, and poorly planned tourism. Reviews of these threats and others have appeared in recent years and should be consulted for additional information (see, for example, Corbett 1989; Dodd 1987; Groombridge 1982; Honegger 1981; Mittermeier et al. 1992; National Research Council 1990; Swingland and Klemens 1989).

The major threat to natural populations of amphibians and reptiles is habitat loss and degradation, although historically, overexploitation by hunting has been a significant threat to many reptilian species (Prescott-Allen and Prescott-Allen *in* Reid and Miller 1989), particularly certain tortoises, sea turtles, and crocodilians (Fitzgerald 1989; Groombridge 1982; Redford and Robinson 1991; Swingland and Klemens 1989). Natural habitats, espe-

---

*Conservation International
1015 18th Street NW, Suite 1000
Washington, D.C. 20036, USA

Acronyms used in this chapter:

AID Agency for International Development, Washington, D.C., USA
CI Conservation International, Washington, D.C., USA
CITES Convention on International Trade in Endangered Species
FFPS Fauna and Flora Preservation Society, London, UK
IUCN International Union for the Conservation of Nature and Natural Resources
NGOs Non-governmental organizations
NYZS New York Zoological Society, Bronx, New York, USA
SG Specialist Group
SSC Species Survival Commission
WWF-US World Wildlife Fund–United States, Washington, D.C., USA
WCI Wildlife Conservation International, Bronx, New York, USA
WPTI Wildlife Preservation Trust International, Philadelphia, Pennsylvania, USA

cially those in the tropics, are under increasing pressure from rapidly growing human populations and concomitant economic and development activities.

Recently, it has been estimated that the average annual global deforestation during the 1980s was 20,000,000 ha, which is an area equal in size to that of Guyana (World Resources Institute 1990). Other estimates exist and there is disagreement over definitions, such as forest types and deforestation versus alteration, but it is generally agreed that the rate of tropical-forest loss is significantly high and is increasing (Sayer and Whitmore 1991). The implications this destruction holds for the extinction of species in these rich terrestrial ecosystems are also debated (Lugo 1988; Reid and Miller 1989; Sayer and Whitmore 1991), but there can be no doubt that extinctions will occur as a direct result of forest destruction. Additional species will be lost when remnant populations in isolated forest patches fall below minimum viable-population size and become extinct.

Currently, the number of amphibian and reptilian species considered threatened (for example, endangered or vulnerable on the CITES Appendices I and II, and in the IUCN "Red Data Books") is relatively small. These sources together list 590 species, which is only 5.5% of all known species of amphibians and reptiles (Groombridge 1988; Mittermeier et al. 1992). Rather than indicating a secure global herpetofauna, we suspect that this small figure is a reflection of the lack of attention to conservation issues within the herpetological community, and our ignorance of the biology of a majority of tropical species.

TABLE 1. Expenditures on amphibian and reptilian projects by a number of non-governmental organizations. Time periods are fiscal years. "Total" is the total project expenditures in 1,000s of United States dollars, rounded to the nearest 1,000 dollars unless otherwise specified (number of projects supported). "A&R Projects" is the amount spent on amphibian or reptilian projects (number of projects supported). "% of total" is the proportion of total expenditures that went to amphibian and reptilian projects (proportion of total projects related to amphibians and reptiles).

NGO	Period covered	Total	A&R projects	% of total
CI	1991	3,399	49	1.4
FFPS	1985–1990	687[1]	68[1]	9.8
NYZS[2]	1985–1989	182 (67)	– (8)	– (12)
WCI	1986–1990	8,895 (429)	210 (22)	2.4 (5.1)
WPTI	1990–1991	775	54	6.9
WWF-US	1990–1991	25,043 (863)	333 (21)	1.3 (2.4)

[1]Pounds sterling for "external" and "internal" projects.
[2]Nixon Griffis Fund for Zoological Research, New York Zoological Society, Bronx, New York, USA.

International Conservation Efforts

International efforts to conserve amphibians and reptiles appear as projects funded by conservation organizations. We have compiled new figures on project expenditures (Table 1) by sampling conservation NGOs, comparable to our earlier tabulation (Mittermeier et al. 1992).

As before, the figures show that the level of expenditures for species conservation is not proportional to the species diversity of amphibians and reptiles (that is, 25% of all vertebrates). For all four groups listed in Table 1, amphibian and reptilian projects accounted for less than 10% of species project expenditures. CI, in fiscal year 1991, spent a comparably low proportion of their budget for amphibian and reptilian projects—US$48,727 of $3,399,000 total project expenditure, or about 1.4%—but this represents 48.5% of the $100,493 expended on species-specific projects. Another group, the FFPS, has decided to focus on taxonomic groups that are overlooked by other conservation organizations, and this is reflected in the much higher spending level for amphibian and reptilian projects by that organization.

Conservation practices may be less expensive for amphibians and reptiles than for birds or mammals (for example, captive-propagation costs may be less per individual). This is revealed in the number of projects supported by WCI and WWF-US (Table 1), which constitute a greater proportion of the total number of projects than the expense figures alone might suggest (for example, grants for amphibian and reptilian projects are, on the average, smaller than for other taxa).

A taxonomic bias exists, however, among the amphibian and reptilian projects that are funded. FFPS has the broadest taxonomic coverage among its herpetofaunal projects, but the other conservation organizations focus mainly on two groups of reptiles: turtles and crocodilians. CI and WCI have limited their funding of reptilian projects to those dealing only with turtles and crocodiles, and only FFPS has supported amphibian projects at all. This form of bias is not restricted to conservation NGOs. Abramovitz (1991) recently compiled a list of projects that deal with biodiversity research and conservation. Of the 226 projects on vertebrates, 32 (14%) concern amphibians and reptiles, and of this number, 22 (69%) focus on turtles and crocodilians.

Priorities in the Conservation of Amphibians and Reptiles

Strategic planning is necessary to produce effective conservation. This is due to the immediate and worsening nature of the threats to amphibian and reptilian populations, and because the financial resources to support amphibian and reptilian conservation are limited. Conservation efforts need to be coordinated and priorities addressed. Available resources must be marshaled to maximize outputs, given time and financial constraints.

There are a number of issues to be addressed, which can be divided into research, taxonomic, and geographic priorities.

Research Priorities

Additional research is urgently needed in many areas. Basic to any efforts to conserve biodiversity is knowledge of the taxonomy and distribution of the taxa of interest. Herpetofaunal inventories are still needed throughout the tropics and other regions, and they are particularly important for protected areas (Sayer and Whitmore 1991). Systematic and taxonomic research are fundamental to our knowledge of biodiversity and ability to direct conservation efforts. Museum collections should be the first source of material for taxonomic studies, but it is clear that additional specimens need to be collected from little-known tropical areas to elucidate many taxonomic questions. For example, recent systematic study of tuatara populations has led to the conclusion that conservation efforts had failed to incorporate all of the taxonomic diversity of tuataras and thereby had allowed a distinctive subspecies to become extinct and an unacknowledged species to be reduced to a single population (Daugherty et al. 1990).

More ecological, demographic, and behavioral research is needed to develop strategies for conserving amphibians and reptiles. Behavioral and ecological studies can be applied to the design of captive-breeding facilities and reserves for endangered species (Zimmerman and Bierregaard 1986). Basic demographic research is needed in order to perform a population-viability analysis for any critically threatened taxon. Research efforts should be directed toward answering questions about the effects of various methods of deforestation and disturbance on species richness and relative abundance (Corn and Bury 1989).

An extensive review of priorities for conservation-biology research can be found in Soulé and Kohm (1989).

Taxonomic Priorities

With more than 10,000 described species of living amphibians and reptiles, we must consider which species are of greatest significance. Factors that may be important to consider include: ecological role, taxonomic uniqueness, or significance to humans. Species may be vital due to economic utility, degree of endangerment, or utility in promoting conservation issues in general, as is the case with flagship species. Flagship species are relatively large, especially attractive, or unusually interesting species that are more likely to draw attention to conserving the ecosystems in which they occur than are other less spectacular species in the same habitats.

Examples of various species that fit these criteria have been listed previously (Mittermeier et al. 1992). Additional species that merit mention include endangered species, such as the Golden Toad (*Bufo periglenes*) and the Geometric Tortoise (*Psammobates geometricus*), and taxonomically and phylogenetically unique species, such as the sole living species of the families Dermatemydidae (*Dermatemys mawii*) and the Shinisauridae (*Shinisaurus crocodilurus*). Examples of flagship species include Fijian iguanas (*Brachylophus*), Aldabra giant tortoises (*Geochelone*), West Indian ground iguanas (*Cyclura*), and Oriental giant salamanders (*Andrias*).

Geographic Priorities

We have already stated that the tropical regions of the world are of the most urgent priority. Biodiversity, however, is not evenly distributed in the tropics, not even within the forest biomes, and not from one landmass to another. Priority areas need to be identified on the basis of species richness and levels of endemism, which vary within biomes due to historical and ecological factors. One way of addressing amphibian and reptilian conservation priorities is by determining priority ecosystems or biogeographic regions, as well as priority political units (such as countries).

Myers (1988, 1990) has identified high-priority areas on the basis of species richness, level of endemism, and degree of present threat. He considers what he terms "threatened hotspots" as essential priorities for conservation of biological diversity during the next decade. He used plants as indicators in his analysis, but determination of the hotspots appears to be equally valid for most other groups of terrestrial organisms, including amphibians and reptiles, as we previously estimated (Mittermeier et al. 1992). If conservation action is not taken quickly in these hotspots, we risk a major extinction spasm for amphibians, reptiles, and many other organisms.

Another way of identifying priorities in the conservation of amphibians and reptiles is by country, using the concept of "megadiversity" countries (Mittermeier 1988; McNeely et al. 1990). This concept recognizes that conservation activities can only be conducted within the legal and social milieu of political entities, usually countries. This also is generally the level at which information on diversity is most readily available worldwide. Although there are more than 190 countries in the world, an inordinate proportion of the world's biological diversity dwells in about a dozen tropical countries.

A preliminary analysis of the top countries for amphibian and reptilian diversity and endemism (Mittermeier et al. 1992) pointed to the significance of Brazil, Indonesia, Mexico, Australia, Colombia, Madagascar, Ecuador, Peru, and Zaire. The first four of these countries together have more than a third of all amphibian and reptilian species; it is clear that we have to direct much conservation attention toward several of these countries that are rich in amphibian and reptilian species.

We do not mean to suggest de-emphasizing or ignoring other countries or regions of the world in setting geographic priorities. We are merely suggesting that much more attention be directed toward rich and diverse tropical countries and ecosystems. If we are unsuccessful in these countries, we will lose a major portion of our planet's herpetofaunal diversity, regardless of how successful we are in other less diverse countries. Investment in biodiversity research and conservation has thus far not reflected these sorts of geographic priorities, at least not that emanating from the United States (Abramovitz 1989, 1991).

Needed Actions

The approach to conservation and the activities undertaken on behalf of the world's herpetofauna need to be as multifaceted and adaptable as possible. We must employ that mix of conservation techniques most appropriate to the local circumstances. We present below a sampling of some conservation techniques, indicating instances in which they are or could be of use with reference to maintenance of stable amphibian and reptilian populations.

Species Survival Commission of IUCN—The World Conservation Union

The most longstanding group concerned with species conservation at the international level is the SSC of IUCN—The World Conservation Union. The SSC has over 100 specialist groups, with a membership of over 4,500 volunteer professionals working to conserve the taxa in which they have expertise.

TABLE 2. IUCN/SSC Specialist Groups concerned with amphibians and reptiles.

Longstanding Groups
Crocodile SG
Marine Turtle SG
Freshwater Turtle and Tortoise SG
New Groups in 1989
European Reptile and Amphibian SG
African Reptile and Amphibian SG
Indian Subcontinent Reptile and Amphibian SG
New Groups Post-1989
Australasian Reptile and Amphibian SG
China Reptile and Amphibian SG
Madagascar Reptile and Amphibian SG
Declining Amphibian Populations Task Force

Table 2 lists the currently active herpetofaunal specialist groups. There has been a rapid proliferation of groups in just the past few years, including a newly created task force to document and investigate the phenomenon of declines in amphibian populations. This is a very good avenue by which professional herpetologists can become actively involved with the conservation of the groups or areas of interest to them.

Action Plans

An important activity of SSC Specialist Groups is the preparation of action plans for the conservation of the taxa or region covered by the group. Action plans typically enumerate taxonomic and/or geographic priorities and outline the sorts of conservation projects required. The Freshwater Turtle and Tortoise Specialist Group has prepared an action plan (IUCN/SSC 1989), and the Crocodile Specialist Group has recently produced one as well (Thorbjarnarson 1992). The Freshwater Turtle and Tortoise Specialist Group has taken the step of arranging for the employment of a plan coordinator and implementor to ensure that action is taken on the projects identified in the action plan (Stevens 1990).

Status Surveys

The first step in conservation planning is often a status survey of a particular species, or a larger taxon in a particular ecosystem or political unit (Cott and Pooley 1972). Surveys are aimed at assessing the population status or geographic distribution of taxa otherwise poorly known, and therefore of uncertain, conservation status. Additional activities would be recommended on the basis of the survey results.

Endangered Species Recovery Projects

Recovery projects involve activities aimed at halting population decline and increasing population size by a variety of techniques in the natural habitat (in situ) and, where necessary, in captivity (ex situ). These activities often involve studies of the biology of the species to understand them better and to increase population size. Such studies have greatly assisted in understanding the decline of the Western Swamp Tortoise (*Pseudemydura umbrina*) in Western Australia and improving the sucess rates of captive breeding of these animals (Burbidge et al. 1990; Kuchling and DeJose 1989). In the case of the Atlantic Ridley (*Lepidochelys kempii*), a binational recovery project has failed to produce discernible progress with the wild population after more than a decade of effort, but this may be due to an inability to mitigate mortality factors, such as deaths due to shrimp trawling (National Research Council 1990). Recovery efforts may be costly and take years to produce results, but they invariably lead to advances in understanding of the biology of little-known species and provide valuable lessons that can be applied to other situations.

Protected Areas

It is imperative that existing parks and reserves be effectively managed for the benefit of all biodiversity, including amphibians and reptiles. Some protected areas may exist for the explicit purpose of preserving the habitat of a particular species, but more often they will have been created to conserve entire ecosystems, thereby protecting the amphibian, reptilian, and other plant and animal communities living in them. Gap analysis based on inventories of protected areas is important to determine which taxa are included within a system of protected areas (Sayer and Whitmore 1991).

There is still a great need for the creation of protected areas in the tropical regions of the world. It is very important that such protected areas be established with respect to geographic priorities as previously discussed, and with respect to taxonomic criteria if important taxa are not otherwise included in the protected-area system.

Sustainable Utilization

An excellent overview of the issues involved in utilization of wildlife species on a sustainable-yield basis can be found in Robinson and Redford (1991). There are both consumptive and nonconsumptive uses of wildlife, and thoughtful management for sustained yield may lead to continued use of certain species without depleting populations. In terms of consumptive use, certain species of reptiles have been heavily used commercially and it may be possible to continue harvesting wild populations of some species, such as tegus (*Tupinambis*) in Argentina (Fitzgerald et al. 1991), or the farming or ranching of species, such as Green Iguana (*Iguana*

iguana) in Costa Rica and Panama (Werner 1991), or the Spectacled Caiman (*Caiman crocodilus*) in Venezuela (Thorbjarnarson 1991). Ecotourism is a nonconsumptive use of wildlife, and may be feasible with certain amphibian or reptilian flagship species, or the herpetofauna may have broader wildlife appeal (for example, the giant tortoises and marine-adapted iguanas of the Galapagos); however, such activities must be carefully regulated to avoid negative consequences for the local fauna (Groom et al. 1991).

Conservation Education

Activities promoting the aesthetic, ecological, and natural-heritage values of amphibians and reptiles to local people are valuable techniques for creating public awareness of conservation issues. Simple conservation messages can be combined with attractive art work on shirts or posters (Figure 1) to help build awareness and a constituency that is receptive to conservation concerns. Other projects aimed primarily at school-age children might include distribution of imprinted pencils, comic books, coloring books and crayons, or activities such as mural painting or educational contests to celebrate holidays (for example, Earth Day) or new environmental laws. There is a tremendous need for conservation education around the globe, and amphibians and reptiles should be incorporated into those activities. At the same time, more educational components need to be incorporated into conservation projects.

FIGURE 1. (A, left) A poster highlighting some of the unique vertebrate species of the Solomon Islands (South Pacific), including amphibians (*Ceratobatrachus guentheri* and *Platymantis weberi*) and reptiles (*Corucia zebrata* and *Loveridgelaps elapoides*), with a message directed at forest conservation. (B, right) A poster created to commemorate the passage of new protective legislation for sea turtles in Belize (Central America), with brief text in all of the local languages.

Training

Opportunities need to be expanded for graduate-level training in the biological sciences and in natural-resources management for nationals from the tropical countries. Many programs focusing on tropical biology, conservation, and resource management have appeared on university campuses in the United States over the past decade, and some have included educational opportunities for foreign nationals. Another trend has been the establishment of cooperative educational ventures between universities in developed and developing countries, such as the graduate program in botany at the Pontificia Universidad Católica del Ecuador, which is run in conjunction with the University of Aarhaus in Denmark. In Madagascar, Conservation International, in collaboration with the Ministry of Higher Education and several other local groups, is presently designing an in-country, university-level training program that will provide government decision makers, collections managers, wildlands managers, and development specialists with the skills needed to accomplish desired conservation goals.

Workshops, short training courses, and symposia are means by which currently employed conservationists and biologists in developing countries can be exposed to new ideas and receive additional training to help them in their positions. Professional biologists in the developed countries can participate by teaching these sorts of courses, sponsoring attendees, or creating course materials.

Integration of Conservation Efforts

Conservation of amphibians and reptiles should be integrated with other conservation efforts, such as protected-area projects, multiple-use forest-management activities, and rural-development programs. Collaborating on projects that integrate the efforts of many scientists and conservationists—for example, those supported by institutions such as bilateral aid agencies (United States AID) and multilateral development banks (World Bank)—may be one of the more fruitful avenues for addressing herpetofaunal conservation objectives.

Summary

Amphibians and reptiles are of value to humans in many ways, among them scientific, cultural, ecological, economic, and aesthetic worth, and they play a critical role in the world's ecosystems. Threats to these resources demand that all herpetologists engage in conservation activities. The greatest threat to amphibians and reptiles is habitat loss, with the largest potential and current impact in tropical regions, where it is estimated that over 80% of all species of amphibians and reptiles reside. Currently, only 5.5% of amphibian and reptilian species are considered threatened or endangered, but this figure undoubtedly grossly underestimates the real threat to the global herpetofauna. Conservation organizations have invested little of their financial resources in amphibian and reptilian projects in proportion to the significance of these animals as part of the global vertebrate fauna.

Strategic planning is needed to attain conservation goals. Setting priorities is fundamental to the planning process, especially research, taxonomic, and geographic priorities. Action plans developed by collaborative efforts at an international level are recommended as a model to channel limited financial and human resources toward priority goals. A variety of conservation actions are called for to conserve amphibians and reptiles, including status surveys, species-recovery projects, establishment and maintenance of protected areas, sustainable-use projects, public awareness campaigns, and professional training activities.

The state of the environment has become a major global issue. Growing interest in the environment on the part of bilateral aid agencies, development banks, and legislative bodies, and the explosive growth of the non-governmental conservation movement are indicative of this trend. Preeminent among conservation concerns is the preservation of the world's biodiversity. The global herpetofauna constitutes a major component of this biodiversity, and success will require the dedication of many professionals. There is a large role for the herpetological community in contributing to international conservation efforts.

Acknowledgments

We thank those colleagues who provided information or commented on the manuscript: A. Gaski (WWF–US), J. Behler (NYZS), R. Wilson (FFPS), W. Konstant, T. Sullivan, and R. B. Mast.

Literature Cited

Abramovitz, J. N. 1989. A Survey of U.S.–based Efforts to Research and Conserve Biological Diversity in Developing Countries. World Resources Institute, Washington D.C. viii, 71 pages.

—. 1991. Investing in Biological Diversity: U.S. Research and Conservation Efforts in Developing Countries. World Resources Institute, Washington, D.C. vii, 94 pages.

Burbidge, A. A., G. Kuchling, P. J. Fuller, G. Graham, and D. Miller. 1990. The western swamp tortoise. Western Australian Manag. Prog., 6: 1–14.

Corbett, K. (ed.). 1989. The Conservation of European Reptiles and Amphibians. Christopher Helm, London. 274 pages.

Corn, P. S., and R. B. Bury. 1989. Logging in western Oregon: responses of headwater habitats and stream amphibians. Forest Ecol. Manag., 29: 39–57.

Cott, H. B., and A. C. Pooley. 1972. The status of crocodiles in Africa. Internatl. Union Cons. Nature Publ., new ser., Suppl. Pap., 33: 1–98.

Daugherty, C. H., A. Cree, J. M. Hay, and M. B. Thompson. 1990. Neglected taxonomy and continuing extinctions of tuatara (*Sphenodon*). Nature, 347: 177–179.

Dodd, C. K., Jr. 1987. Status, conservation, and management, p. 478–513. *In* R. A. Seigel, J. T. Collins, and S. S. Novak, (eds.), Snakes: Ecology and Evolutionary Biology. McGraw Hill, New York.

Fitzgerald, L. A., J. M. Chani, and O. E. Donadío. 1991. *Tupinambis* lizards in Argentina: implementing management of a traditionally exploited resource, p. 303–316. *In* J. G. Robinson and K. H. Redford (eds.), Neotropical Wildlife Use and Conservation. Univ. Chicago Press, Chicago.

Fitzgerald, S. 1989. International Wildlife Trade: Whose Business Is It? World Wildlife Fund, Washington, D.C. xix, 459 pages.

Groom, M. J., R. D. Podolsky, and C. A. Munn. 1991. Tourism as a sustained use of wildlife: a case study of Madre de Dios, southeastern Peru, p. 393–412. *In* J. G. Robinson and K. H. Redford (eds.), Neotropical Wildlife Use and Conservation. Univ. Chicago Press, Chicago.

Groombridge, B. (ed.) 1982. The IUCN Amphibia-Reptilia Red Data Book. Part 1. Testudines Crocodylia Rhynchocephalia. International Union for the Conservation of Nature and Natural Resources, Gland, Switzerland. xliii, 426 pages.

—. 1988. World Checklist of Threatened Amphibians and Reptiles. Nature Conservancy Council, London. viii, 117 pages.

Honegger, R. E. 1981. Threatened Amphibians and Reptiles in Europe. Akademische Verlagsgesellschaft, Wiesbaden. 158 pages.

IUCN/SSC Tortoise and Freshwater Turtle Specialist Group. 1989. Tortoises and Freshwater Turtles: An Action Plan for Their Conservation. International Union for the Conservation of Nature and Natural Resources, Gland, Switzerland. iv, 48 pages.

Kuchling, G., and J. P. DeJose. 1989. A captive breeding operation to rescue the critically endangered Western Swamp Turtle *Pseudemydura umbrina*. Internatl. Zoo Yearbook, 28: 103–109.

Lugo, A. E. 1988. Estimating reductions in the diversity of tropical forest species, p. 58–70. *In* E. O. Wilson (ed.), Biodiversity. National Academy Press, Washington, D.C.

McNeely, J. A., K. R. Miller, W. V. Reid, R. A. Mittermeier, and T. B. Werner. 1990. Conserving the World's Biological Diversity. International Union for the Conservation of Nature and Natural Resources, Gland, Switzerland. 193 pages.

Mittermeier, R. A. 1988. Primate diversity and the tropical forest: case studies from Brazil and Madagascar and the importance of the megadiversity countries, p. 145–154. *In* E. O. Wilson (ed.), Biodiversity. National Academy Press, Washington, D.C.

Mittermeier, R. A., J. L. Carr, I. R. Swingland, T. B. Werner, and R. B. Mast. 1992. Conservation of amphibians and reptiles, p. 59–80. *In* K. Adler (ed.), Herpetology: Current Research on the Biology of Amphibians and Reptiles. Proceedings of the First World Congress of Herpetology. Soc. Study Amphib. Reptiles, Oxford, Ohio. Contr. Herpetol., 9.

Myers, N. 1988. Threatened biotas: "hotspots" in tropical forests. Environmentalist, 8: 187–208.

—. 1990. The biodiversity challenge: expanded hot-spots analysis. Environmentalist, 10: 243–256.

National Research Council. 1990. Decline of the Sea Turtles: Causes and Prevention. National Academy Press, Washington, D.C. 259 pages.

Redford, K. H., and J. G. Robinson. 1991. Subsistence and commercial uses of wildlife in Latin America, p. 6–23. *In* J. G. Robinson and K. H. Redford (eds.), Neotropical Wildlife Use and Conservation. Univ. Chicago Press, Chicago.

Reid, W. V., and K. R. Miller. 1989. Keeping Options Alive: The Scientific Basis for Conserving Biodiversity. World Resources Institute, Washington, D.C. vii, 128 pages.

Robinson, J. G., and K. H. Redford (eds.). 1991. Neotropical Wildlife Use and Conservation. Univ. Chicago Press, Chicago. xvii, 520 pages.

Sayer, J. A., and T. C. Whitmore. 1991. Tropical moist forests: destruction and species extinction. Biol. Conserv., 55: 199–213.

Soulé, M. E., and K. A. Kohm (eds.). 1989. Research Priorities for Conservation Biology. Island Press, Washington, D.C. xii, 97 pages.

Stevens, W. K. 1990. Big effort is begun to reverse decline of turtles. New York Times, March 13: C4.

Swingland, I. R., and M. W. Klemens (eds.). 1989. The conservation biology of tortoises. Occas. Pap. Internatl. Union Cons. Nature Nat. Res., Spec. Surv. Comm., 5: 1–204.

Thorbjarnarson, J. B. 1991. An analysis of the spectacled caiman (*Caiman crocodilus*) harvest program in Venezuela, p. 217–235. *In* J. G. Robinson and K. H. Redford (eds.), Neotropical Wildlife Use and Conservation. Univ.

Chicago Press, Chicago.
—. (ed.). 1992. Crocodiles: An Action Plan for Their Conservation. International Union for the Conservation of Nature, Gland, Switzerland. vii, 136 pages.

Werner, D. I. 1991. The rational use of green iguanas, p. 181–201. *In* J. G. Robinson and K. H. Redford (eds.), Neotropical Wildlife Use and Conservation. Univ. Chicago Press, Chicago.

World Resources Institute. 1990. World Resources 1990–91. Oxford Univ. Press, New York. xiv, 383 pages.

Zimmerman, B. L., and R. O. Bierregaard. 1986. Relevance of the equilibrium theory of island biogeography and species-area relations to conservation with a case from Amazonia. Jour. Biogeog., 13: 133–143.

❦

❦ Mittermeier, R. A., and J. L. Carr. 1994. Conservation of reptiles and amphibians: a global perspective, p. 27–35. *In* J. B. Murphy, K. Adler, and J. T. Collins (eds.), Captive Management and Conservation of Amphibians and Reptiles. Society for the Study of Amphibians and Reptiles, Ithaca (New York). Contributions to Herpetology, volume 11.

The Role of Zoos and Aquariums in Amphibian and Reptilian Conservation

Robert J. Wiese* and Michael Hutchins*

Introduction

THE "IUCN RED LIST OF THREATENED ANIMALS" includes 93 reptilian and 63 amphibian species (IUCN 1990). Due to the combined effects of habitat alteration, pollution, and overexploitation, however, the actual number of endangered or threatened taxa may be considerably higher. Indeed, the preservation of biological diversity seems to be an overwhelming task, and success will only be possible through the cooperative efforts of numerous individuals and organizations (Prescott and Hutchins 1991). North America's zoos and aquariums are trying to do their part, and our intent is to summarize a number of the current efforts.

In 1980, the American Association of Zoological Parks and Aquariums—a nonprofit organization representing 160 of North America's finest zoological institutions—identified wildlife conservation as its highest priority. The role of professionally managed zoos and aquariums in conservation is multifaceted; however, they contribute in at least six ways by:

(1) Providing a refuge for threatened and endangered species by maintaining genetically and demographically healthy populations as reservoirs of genetic material and as an insurance policy against extinction;

(2) Propagating animals for reintroduction to areas where they have been extirpated, and developing successful reintroduction techniques;

(3) Conducting veterinary, nutritional, reproductive, behavioral, and other research, both basic and applied, which increases our ability to manage and conserve both captive and wild populations;

(4) Developing and testing technologies that can be applied to field conservation;

(5) Educating the general public in an attempt to change attitudes and lifestyles that affect wildlife and the environment; and

(6) Providing direct or indirect support for in situ conservation programs that may or may not involve a captive-breeding component.

Captive-Breeding Programs

Herpetology departments in zoological institutions throughout the world have long worked to develop effective and efficient husbandry protocols for the care and reproduction of reptiles and amphibians. This effort has led to an immense body of knowledge that can be applied to the development of successful breeding programs for endangered and threatened species. During 1988–1989, more than 69 amphibian and 575 reptilian taxa were bred in captivity, many of which are listed as endangered, threatened, or rare (Olney and Ellis 1991*a*, 1991*b*). The Captive Breeding Specialist Group of the International Union for the Conservation of Nature and Natural Resources's Species Survival Commission presently recognizes five regional captive breeding

---

*American Association of Zoological Parks and Aquariums
7970-D Old Georgetown Road
Bethesda, Maryland 20814, USA

Acronyms used in this chapter:

AAZPA	American Association of Zoological Parks and Aquariums
CAMPs	Conservation Assessment and Management Plans
CBSG	Captive Breeding Specialist Group
CPR	Captive Propagation Rescue
IUCN	International Union for the Conservation of Nature and Natural Resources
SSAR	Society for the Study of Amphibians and Reptiles
SSC	Species Survival Commission
SSP	Species Survival Plan
TAGs	Taxon Advisory Groups

TABLE 1. Reptilian and amphibian species with SSPs and the year that each program was established.

Common name	Scientific name	Year
Chinese Alligator	*Alligator sinensis*	1982
Radiated Tortoise	*Geochelone radiata*	1982
Aruba Island Rattlesnake	*Crotalus durissus unicolor*	1982
Dumeril's Ground Boa	*Acrantophis dumerili*	1983
Puerto Rican Crested Toad	*Peltophryne lemur*	1984
Mona Island Boa	*Epicrates monensis*	1990

programs, which cover Australasia, Europe, Japan, North America, and the United Kingdom. A number of other regions, such as Central America, Brazil, India, China, and Africa, are presently in the process of organization. While many of these programs share similar strategies and philosophies, considerable differences in their approaches exist. We will concentrate primarily on the strategies developed within the North American captive-breeding community, specifically the AAZPA Conservation Program. (Readers interested in the European Endangered Species Program and a similar program for the United Kingdom should consult Tudge [1992].)

The focal point of the AAZPA Conservation Program is the Species Survival Plan (Foose 1983; Hutchins and Wiese 1991). Through the Species Survival Plan program, member zoos and aquariums in North America work cooperatively to maintain genetically and demographically viable populations of endangered or threatened species as a hedge against extinction. Of course, captive-breeding programs are not a panacea for the endangered species problem and should only be implemented as part of a holistic effort to preserve species in their natural habitats (Hutchins and Wiese 1991). Thus, the ultimate goal of the SSP is to reinforce natural populations, not replace them (Foose 1983). As part of this holistic approach, it is also important that the original causes of decline in nature be addressed simultaneously with the development of captive-breeding programs (Gibbons, this volume, page 119).

With regard to amphibian and reptilian conservation, there are currently six species addressed by an SSP program and several others are likely to be added in the near future (Table 1). Each SSP program is overseen by a species coordinator with the assistance of a studbook keeper, a propagation group consisting of elected representatives of participating zoos and aquariums, and various scientific advisors. Without the dedication of these hardworking volunteers, the program would not be possible. The AAZPA Executive Office and Conservation Center in Bethesda, Maryland, and the AAZPA Wildlife Conservation and Management Committee oversee all SSP and related conservation and scientific programs and provide scientific, legal, public relations, and other services to species coordinators and propagation groups, as needed.

Basic population data on species of concern, including age, sex, and reproductive history are maintained in studbooks that allow analyses and specific management decisions to be based on populations of known pedigree (Glatston 1986). The AAZPA currently has 21 approved studbooks for various amphibian and reptilian taxa, including the SSP species listed in Table 1. A current list of all non-SSP species with approved studbooks is shown in Table 2.

The primary goal of the SSP is to preserve as much genetic variation as possible within the restrictions of the "captive carrying capacity" (Foose 1983). This translates into a balance between maximizing genetic diversity at the population level (equalizing relative founder lineage contribution)

TABLE 2. Non-SSP reptilian and amphibian species with AAZPA-approved studbooks.

Common name	Scientific name
Annulated Boa	*Corallus annulatus*
African Spurred Tortoise	*Geochelone sulcata*
Asian Brown Tortoise	*Manouria emys*
Galapagos Tortoise	*Geochelone elephantopus*
Pancake Tortoise	*Malacochersus tornieri*
Sideneck Turtles	*Podocnemis* sp.
Dwarf Caiman	*Paleosuchus palpebrosus*
Cuban Crocodile	*Crocodylus rhombifer*
Morelet's Crocodile	*Crocodylus moreletii*
Siamese Crocodile	*Crocodylus siamensis*
False Gharial	*Tomistoma schlegelii*
Gharial	*Gavialis gangeticus*
Madagascar Tomato Frog	*Dyscophus antongilii*
King Cobra	*Ophiophagus hannah*
Louisiana Pine Snake	*Pituophis melanoleucus ruthveni*
Black Pine Snake	*Pituophis melanoleucus lodingi*
Chinese Crocodile Lizard	*Shinisaurus crocodilurus*
Prehensile-tailed Skink	*Corucia zebrata*
Rock Iguanas	*Cyclura* sp.

and maximizing heterozygosity at the individual level (minimizing inbreeding).

Once studbook data have been analyzed, using the latest genetic and demographic software, recommendations are made concerning which animals should breed, with which individuals, and how many offspring should be produced (Foose 1983). Overrepresented lineages are identified so that breeding can be curtailed. For a captive population, it is as important to slow breeding in overrepresented lines as it is to stimulate breeding in underrepresented lines. These analyses and recommendations are then compiled and reported in a master plan. Master plans are updated regularly because the population structure changes as a result of management decisions.

Through responsible management and breeding, it is hoped that zoos and aquariums will be able to contribute significantly to the conservation of many species at risk. Captive populations act as reserves in the event that conditions change and wild populations decline or disappear. In addition to assisting endangered species, captive breeding also sustains populations of common species, thus minimizing the need to remove animals from the wild.

The threat to biological diversity is growing, and because of space limitations, captive-breeding programs will only be able to assist a small fraction of the species at risk (Soulé et al. 1986; McMahan 1991). Therefore, as responsible stewards, we must prioritize species and make our selections carefully, so that as much diversity as possible is ultimately preserved. This essentially amounts to a form of triage (Knowles 1986; Hutchins and Wiese 1991). For this purpose, specialized committees called Taxon Advisory Groups have been developed. In fact, the TAG concept had its beginnings within the North American zoo herpetology community with the establishment of the Crocodilian Advisory Group in 1986 (J. L. Behler, pers. comm.). The primary function of a TAG is to prioritize species for SSP and studbook designation and develop a regional strategic-collection plan (Hutchins and Wiese 1991). The TAGs also address more general issues, such as ethical concerns, husbandry protocols, research needs, and other topics that are common to an entire taxon. Working TAGs presently exist for amphibians, chelonians, crocodilians, snakes, and lizards.

Establishing priorities for future SSPs and studbooks is a complicated process and must include consideration of many different factors. Important resources include, when available, Action Plans produced by the IUCN/SSC and Conservation Assessment and Management Plans produced by the CBSG of the IUCN/SSC (Foose et al. 1992). Action Plans give the current conservation status of each species and information on their natural history, while CAMPs include general recommendations about which species are most in need of captive-breeding programs. CAMPs are formulated in consultation with the appropriate IUCN/SSC Taxonomic Specialist Groups, regional TAGs, and other relevant conservation organizations (Hutchins and Wiese 1991). Some of the factors considered include the degree of endangerment in the wild, availability of adequate founder stock, previous success with captive breeding, taxonomic uniqueness, probability of recovery, and ability to serve as a flagship species to help protect endangered ecosystems (Hutchins and Wemmer 1991).

While many SSP programs will need to manage populations in captivity for an extended period of time, this is not always the case. Short-term projects, often referred to as Captive Propagation Rescue, are designed to quickly reestablish natural populations, but they require that the original reasons for endangerment be eliminated (Conway 1989; Gibbons, this volume, page 119). CPR projects should receive more attention by zoos and aquariums than they do now. Members of the SSP for the Puerto Rican Crested Toad (*Peltophryne lemur*; Johnson 1990, and this volume, page 243) are currently trying to establish a CPR project for this species. With short-term CPR projects, species can be maintained and bred in captivity until sufficient habitat is acquired, preserved, or restored and the species is returned to a self-sustaining natural status. In these instances, zoos and aquariums act as temporary way stations for species on the road back to viable natural populations. With respect to many amphibians and reptiles, CPR projects may prove to be the most productive approach.

Captive-breeding and reintroduction programs for amphibians and reptiles have certain advantages relative to those for mammals and birds. First, many amphibians and reptiles have a relatively high reproductive potential allowing them to recover quickly from population bottlenecks. If a population can rebound quickly, there is a lower probability that allelic diversity will be lost due to genetic drift (Falconer 1981; Wiese 1990). Therefore, if adequate numbers of founders can be acquired and bred, it is possible to retain much of a population's natural evolutionary potential. This is especially true for species that experience high mortality during the egg or juvenile stage. In such cases, captive breeding may greatly increase survivability, thereby further increasing the population's growth potential. Of course, captive environments should duplicate natural conditions as closely as possible to minimize artificial selection in species maintained for conservation purposes (Frankham et al. 1986).

Second, the behavior of amphibians and reptiles is relatively "hard wired" when compared to mammals and birds (Warwick 1990; Chiszar et al., this volume, page 147). Thus, in many cases, it will be unnecessary to train the animals to identify appropriate foods or habitat or to interact appropriately with conspecifics. It is important to note, however, that this generalization may not always be true (Warwick 1990). Reintroduction efforts should therefore be monitored closely and techniques developed on a species-by-species basis (Dodd and Seigel 1991; Burke 1991). Because familiarity with the home range is important in some species, it may be beneficial to release individuals at a young age, perhaps soon after the egg or juvenile stage. It is also critical that the potential to spread pathogens from captive to free-ranging populations be carefully evaluated before any releases take place (Hutchins et al. 1991; Jacobson, this volume, page 109).

A third advantage comes from the relatively small area required to maintain a viable population of many amphibians and reptiles, both in captivity and in nature. Because the home ranges of many species are relatively small compared to those of mammals and birds, it is often feasible to set aside or purchase adequate habitat to maintain viable populations. Because such populations are small and fragmented, however, all are at risk from demographic catastrophes (Foose 1983). Thus, several wild populations will have to be established before a species can be considered out of danger. Furthermore, a healthy captive population may need to be maintained as a hedge against future catastrophic events.

Zoo and Aquarium Research

For captive breeding and reintroduction to be successful, managers must have accurate knowledge of a species' basic biology (Hutchins 1988; Murphy and Chiszar 1989; Warwick 1990). Information from a variety of disciplines including physiology, behavior, nutrition, reproduction, disease, and genetics are important to a program's success. In some instances, the knowledge gained and husbandry techniques developed are even more valuable than the captive populations themselves. This is especially true when common taxa are used as models to develop techniques for endangered or threatened species.

Collaboration between zoos, universities, and government wildlife agencies is not new to the field of herpetology (Murphy and Collins 1980). In fact, this cooperation has resulted in numerous research advances. The Society for the Study of Amphibians and Reptiles should be commended for recognizing this potential and being one of the first scientific societies to have and promote an official zoo liaison. The *Journal of Herpetology* and *Herpetological Review* contain numerous studies conducted by zoo and aquarium scientists or by university scientists in collaboration with zoo and aquarium personnel. SSAR has recently established a new series, *Herpetological Conservation*, dedicated to such issues.

Research on captive populations can assist conservation efforts and promote animal welfare in several ways. More specifically, it can aid in the:

(1) Development of successful husbandry protocols for a wide variety of species (documentation of normal physiological, nutritional, reproductive, and behavioral parameters is particularly useful in this regard);

(2) Clarification of pedigrees and resolution of taxonomic status (specific and subspecific) through detailed genetic analysis;

(3) Development of veterinary procedures that may help both wild and captive populations; and

(4) Development of capture, restraint, identification, monitoring, and other techniques for use in field conservation and in captive-breeding programs.

Development of Husbandry Protocols

When a species or population is threatened with extinction, immediate action needs to be taken. If captive-husbandry and propagation techniques have been previously established, a species' prospect for survival is often greatly enhanced. If zoo managers are faced with both a limited gene pool and a lack of knowledge concerning the species' basic biology, however, the chances of recovery are slim. This argues for the establishment of an experimental captive population well before a species becomes critically endangered. For example, the development of successful husbandry protocols for the Bog Turtle (*Clemmys muhlenbergii*) has been extremely valuable now that the species is threatened in nature (Tryon and Hulsey 1977; Herman and George 1986). Although more research is needed, husbandry protocols presently exist for a number of threatened or endangered reptiles and amphibians. A small sampling of these species include the Japanese Giant Salamander, *Andrias japonicus* (Kuwabara et al. 1989); Pancake Tortoise, *Malacochersus tornieri* (Darlington and Davis 1990); Morelet's Crocodile, *Crocodylus moreletii* (Hunt 1980); West Indian rock iguanas, *Cyclura* sp. (Noegel 1989; Duval and Christie 1990); Louisiana Pine Snake, *Pituophis melanoleucus ruthveni* (Reichling 1988); Puerto Rican Crested Toad, *Peltophryne lemur* (Miller 1985; Paine et al. 1989); San Francisco Garter Snake, *Thamnophis sirtalis tetrataenia* (Cover and Boyer 1988), and the Western Swamp Turtle, *Pseudemydura umbrina* (Kuchling and DeJose 1989). Breeding programs to assist the recovery of these species have a better chance of success because of the pioneering work that has already been accomplished.

Basic research on captive animals can complement field studies. For example, many amphibians and reptiles are secretive and their normal social behavior, feeding habits, and reproductive biology are often difficult to study under field conditions (Fitch 1987; Hutchins 1988; Warwick 1990). Captive populations allow for intensive physiological and behavioral data to be gathered in a more systematic manner. This may lead to new insights that would have been difficult or impossible to obtain in the field (Chiszar et al., this volume, page 147). Standard physiological values are also more easily obtained from captive animals in cases in which blood, tissues, venom, fecal, and other samples can be collected on a regular basis. Of course, data collected on captive populations should be verified with comparable data from wild populations when possible (Murphy and Chiszar 1989; Zimmermann 1989).

Resolution of Pedigree and Taxonomic Status

If captive-breeding programs are to assist in the long-term conservation of endangered and threatened species, they must retain as much of the original genetic variation available in the founding animals as possible (Allendorf 1986; Ralls and Ballou 1986). As mentioned previously, this requires careful management of a population and its reproduction, an essential component of which is the determination of the parentage of each individual in the population (Foose et al. 1986).

Establishing parentage is a fairly simple objective with species that form pair bonds and require only one pair of animals per enclosure. When several males are required for courtship or when sperm storage is possible, however, determining the exact parentage is not always simple. The Dumeril's Ground Boa (*Acrantophis dumerili*) SSP group has just recently completed a DNA study that targeted several animals of unknown parentage. As a result of this study, a number of holes in the pedigree were filled allowing for more efficient and accurate breeding recommendations to be made (R. D. Hudson et al., pers. comm.). Similar DNA fingerprint studies were used to illuminate the pedigree of Galapagos Tortoises, *Geochelone elephantopus* (Ryder et al. 1989).

Populations can possess co-adaptations to local environments and/or to other genes or chromosomes. Disruption of these co-adapted complexes may have devastating effects on reintroduction attempts (Templeton et al. 1986). DNA studies to determine the similarities or differences among species and subspecies, therefore, are potentially important to the success of reintroductions (Ryder et al. 1989).

Improving Veterinary Care

Veterinary advances have been an important result of zoo- and aquarium-based research. The ongoing efforts by members of the SSP for the Aruba Island Rattlesnake (*Crotalus durissus unicolor*) to develop a vaccine for reptilian *Paramyxovirus* is an excellent example (Odum and Goode, this volume, page 363). The knowledge gained from detailed necropsies is critical to the development of effective diagnostic and treatment protocols for both captive and free-ranging wildlife (Murphy and Shadduck 1979; Hutchins et al. 1991).

Innovative clinical techniques that were developed for human health care, such as endoscopy, have been used in the sexing of reptiles (Schildger and Wicker 1989). Artificial insemination is another important technique that provides a powerful management tool in captive-breeding programs in which specific individuals are designated to breed. Such techniques have been used for crocodilians (Larsen and Cardheilhac 1984) and snakes (Mengden et al. 1980; Quinn et al. 1989).

Development of New Technologies

Research on captive populations has led to the development of many technologies now commonly used in herpetological studies. The squeeze-box technique for safely obtaining accurate measurements of snakes was developed using captive specimens (Quinn and Jones 1974). Investigations of egg development and physiology require standardized, reliable, and simple artificial incubation protocols. Many laboratory incubation protocols in use today employ vermiculite—a substrate originally developed for use in captive propagation (Tryon 1975).

In addition to helping sustain captive populations, technologies developed and tested in zoos and aquariums can also benefit field conservation efforts. For example, biologists who employ radiotelemetry often test receivers or implantation and attachment procedures on captive animals before transferring them to field use (Asa 1991; Kingsmill 1991).

To reach their full potential, however, zoos and aquariums will need to increase their commitment to scientific research. Increased cooperation between scientists working for zoos, aquariums, and universities has the potential to further our present knowledge and to enhance our combined efforts to assist amphibians and reptiles threatened with extinction (Murphy and Chiszar 1989).

In Situ Conservation

In situ conservation efforts must also receive increased attention by the zoo and aquarium community. Zoos have been involved with several reintroduction efforts and these are important aspects of several SSPs. Members of the SSP for the Puerto Rican Crested Toad (Johnson 1990, and this volume, page 243) and that for the Virgin Islands Boa, *Epicrates monensis* (Tolson, this volume, page 353), have initiated reintroduction projects. The Jersey Wildlife Preservation Trust has also been a leader in the in situ conservation of threatened and endangered amphibians and reptiles (Bloxam and Tonge 1986; Reid et al. 1989).

Reintroduction may prove to be an important conservation tool. Captive programs must also expand their current scope, however, to include habitat protection (Hutchins and Wiese 1991). Many of these projects will likely be in conjunction with short-term CPR programs. In fact, a number of zoos and aquariums are already working with governmental agencies and other local, national, and international conservation organizations to protect critical habitat for endangered amphibians and reptiles. Current efforts to save the endangered Bog Turtle provide an excellent example. Several zoos, including the Knoxville Zoological Park, Zoo Atlanta, and the New York Zoological Park, are devoting considerable resources to the survival of this species, which has declined drastically due to habitat destruction and illegal collection for the pet trade (J. L. Behler et al., pers. comm.).

The Knoxville Zoological Park has recently entered into a renewable, eight-year agreement with the Tennessee Wildlife Resources Agency, The Nature Conservancy, and private landowners to protect some of the last remaining Bog Turtle habitat in Tennessee. Captive-breeding programs are also underway to provide a source of animals to establish new populations. This work is possible today because methods for captive breeding were established long before the threat became overwhelming (Tryon and Hulsey 1977; Herman and George 1986).

Similar programs are underway for many other species, including the Piebald Chuckwalla, *Sauromalus varius* (Lawler et al., this volume, page 333), Louisiana Pine Snake, *Pituophis melanoleucus ruthveni* (S. Hammack, pers. comm.), and Kirtland's Snake, *Clonophis kirtlandii* (W. McMahan, pers. comm.).

Public Education

The importance of conservation education cannot be overemphasized. Public education, both within North America and abroad, is extremely important to the success of various recovery efforts. While there are a number of advantages to working with amphibians and reptiles in zoos and aquariums, their public appeal is not as high as it is for mammals and birds (Hoff and Maple 1982; Steinhart 1984; Kellert 1989). Education programs are especially needed to change negative attitudes and to call attention to conservation issues surrounding reptiles and amphibians (Murphy and Mitchell 1989). The Dallas Zoo's graphics display of the rattlesnake roundup tragedy (Warwick et al. 1991) is an excellent example of what can be done to call the public's attention to specific conservation issues. Additional conservation topics about which institutions need to inform their constituents are the global decline of amphibians (Barinaga 1990; Borchelt 1990; Pechmann et al. 1991), the increased threat of micro- and macro-pollution (Hutchinson and Simmonds 1992), and the pet and animal products trade (International Union for the Conservation of Nature and Natural Resources 1989; Swingland and Klemens 1989; Das 1990; Hirth and Rohovit 1992).

Education programs are also extremely important to the success of reintroduction projects (Durrell and Mallinson 1987; Kleiman 1989). If attitudes of local people cannot be changed and an appreciation of wildlife fostered, then reintroduction efforts are unlikely to be successful. Therefore, local people must be educated concerning the ecological role and value of the species in question. Although not a zoo-based program, Dagmar Werner's captive-breeding program to save the Green Iguana (*Iguana iguana*) in Panama and Costa Rica provides an excellent model for other countries. Through intensive media and educational programs, local people now understand their natural heritage better and manage sustainable populations of this species. As a result, many acres of tropical forest have been preserved for Green Iguanas and other species (Cohn 1989; Vietmeyer 1989).

The SSP for the Puerto Rican Crested Toad (Johnson 1990, and this volume, page 243) has been highly successful with respect to education as well. Cooperation between the SSP and the Puerto Rican government has led to an intensive educational effort. Today, children of the Guánica region, where the toads are found, are well aware of this important part of their endemic fauna. Educational posters were distributed as part of a public relations campaign to inform Puerto Ricans about the importance and uniqueness of this species. Ownership of all captive toads has been retained by the government of Puerto Rico in order to ensure a sense of participation in and shared responsibility for the program. Members of the SSP for the Aruba Island Rattlesnake have adopted a similar strategy, that of educating the people of Aruba about the importance of their native wildlife. There is also a program to train medical doctors in the treatment of snake bites (Odum and Goode, this volume, page 363).

Summary

There is much work to be done if we are to assist even a fraction of the species currently at risk. Through the successful use of captive-breeding and reintroduction programs in conjunction with strategic collection planning, scientific research, in situ conservation efforts, and public education, professionally managed zoos and aquariums can play a significant role in amphibian and reptilian conservation.

Literature Cited

Allendorf, F. W. 1986. Genetic drift and loss of alleles versus heterozygosity. Zoo Biol., 5: 181–190.

Asa, C. (ed.). 1991. Biotelemetry Applications to Captive Animal Care and Research. Publ. American Assoc. Zool. Parks Aquar., Wheeling, West Virginia. x, 59 pages.

Barinaga, M. 1990. Where have all the froggies gone? Science, 247: 1033–1034.

Bloxam, Q. M. C., and S. J. Tonge. 1986. The Round Island boa *Casarea dussumieri* breeding programme at the Jersey Wildlife Preservation Trust. Dodo, Jour. Jersey Wildl. Preserv. Trust, 23: 101–107.

Borchelt, R. 1990. Scientists ponder the mysterious decline of amphibians. Atlantic Nat., 40: 20–25.

Burke, R. L. 1991. Relocation, repatriations, and translocations of amphibians and reptiles: taking a broader view. Herpetologica, 47: 350–357.

Cohn, J. P. 1989. Iguana conservation and economic development. BioScience, 39: 359–363.

Conway, W. G. 1989. The prospects for sustaining species and their evolution, p. 199–209. *In* D. Western and M. Pearl (eds.). Conservation for the Twenty-first Century. Oxford Univ. Press, New York, New York.

Cover, J. F., Jr., and D. M. Boyer. 1988. Captive reproduction of the San Francisco garter snake, *Thamnophis sirtalis tetrataenia*. Herpetol. Rev., 19: 29–33.

Darlington, A. F., and R. B. Davis. 1990. Reproduction in the pancake tortoise, *Melacochersus tornieri*, in captive collections. Herpetol. Rev., 21: 16–18.

Das, I. 1990. The trade in freshwater turtles from Bangladesh. Oryx, 24: 163–166.

Dodd, C. K., Jr., and R. A. Seigel. 1991. Relocation, repatriation, and translocation of amphibians and reptiles: are they conservation strategies that work? Herpetologica, 47: 336–350.

Durrell, L., and J. Mallinson. 1987. Reintroduction as a political and educational tool for conservation. Dodo, Jour. Jersey Wildl. Preserv. Trust, 24: 6–19.

Duval, J. J., and W. D. Christie. 1990. Husbandry of the Cuban ground iguana *Cyclura n. nubila* at the Indianapolis Zoo. Internatl. Zoo Yearbook, 29: 65–70.

Falconer, D. S. 1981. Introduction to Quantitative Genetics. 2nd ed. Longman Inc., New York, New York. ix, 340 pages.

Fitch, H. S. 1987. The sin of anecdotal writing. Herpetol. Rev., 18: 68.

Foose, T. 1983. The relevance of captive populations to the conservation of biotic diversity, p. 374–401. *In* C. M. Schonewald-Cox, S. M. Chambers, B. MacBryde, and W. L. Thomas (eds.), Genetics and Conservation. Benjamin Cummings Publishing, Menlo Park, California.

Foose, T. J., S. Ellis-Joseph, and U. S. Seal. 1992. Conservation assessment and management plans (CAMPs) progress report. Species, 18: 73–75.

Foose, T., R. Lande, N. R. Flesness, G. Rabb, and B. Read. 1986. Propagation plans. Zoo Biol., 5: 139–146.

Frankham, R., H. Hemmer, O. A. Ryder, E. G. Cothran, M. E. Soulé, N. D. Murray, and M. Snyder. 1986. Selection in captivity. Zoo Biol., 5: 127–138.

Glatston, A. R. 1986. Studbooks: the basis of breeding programmes. Internatl. Zoo Yearbook, 24/25: 162–167.

Herman, D. W., and G. A. George. 1986. Research, husbandry, and propagation of the bog turtle, *Clemmys muhlenbergi* (Schoepff) at Atlanta Zoo, p. 125–135. *In* S. McKeown, F. Caporaso, and K. Peterson (eds.), Proceedings of the 9th International Herpetological Symposium on Captive Propagation and Husbandry. Zool. Consortium, Thurmond, Maryland.

Hirth, H. F., and D. L. H. Rohovit. 1992. Marketing patterns of green and hawksbill turtles in Port Moresby, Papua New Guinea. Oryx, 26: 39–42.

Hoff, M. P., and T. L. Maple. 1982. Sex and age differences in the avoidance of reptile exhibits by zoo visitors. Zoo Biol., 1: 263–269.

Hunt, R. H. 1980. Propagation of Morelet's crocodile, p. 161–165. *In* J. B. Murphy and J. T. Collins (eds.), Reproductive Biology and Diseases of Captive Reptiles. Soc. Study Amphib. Reptiles, Oxford, Ohio. Contrib. Herpetol., 1.

Hutchins, M. 1988. On the design of zoo research programmes. Internatl. Zoo Yearbook, 27: 9–19.

Hutchins, M., T. Foose, and U. Seal. 1991. The role of veterinary medicine in endangered species conservation. Jour. Zoo Wildlife Med., 22: 277–281.

Hutchins, M., and C. Wemmer. 1991. In defense of captive breeding. Endangered Species Update, 8: 5–6.

Hutchins, M., and R. J. Wiese. 1991. Beyond genetic and demographic management: the future of the species survival plan and related AAZPA conservation efforts. Zoo Biol., 10: 285–292.

Hutchinson, J., and M. Simmonds. 1992. Escalation of threats to marine turtles. Oryx, 26(2): 95–102.

International Union for the Conservation of Nature and Natural Resources. 1989. Tortoises and freshwater turtles: an action plan for their conservation. Internatl. Union Conserv. Nat., Gland, Switzerland. iv , 48 pages.

—. 1990. 1990 IUCN Red List of Threatened Animals. Internatl. Union Conserv. Nat., Gland, Switzerland. xxiv, 192 pages.

Johnson, R. R. 1990. Release and translocation strategies for the Puerto Rican crested toad, *Peltophryne lemur*. Endangered Species Update, 8: 54–57.

Kellert, S. 1989. Perceptions of animals in America, p. 5–24. *In* R. J. Hoage (ed.) Perceptions of Animals in American Culture. Smithsonian Inst. Press, Washington, DC.

Kingsmill, S. 1991. How to track a toad. Internatl. Wildlife, 21: 29.

Kleiman, D. 1989. Reintroduction of captive mammals for conservation. BioScience, 39: 152–161.

Knowles, J. M. 1986. Wild and captive populations: triage, contraception and culling. Internatl. Zoo Yearbook, 24/25: 206–210.

Kuchling, G., and J. P. DeJose. 1989. A captive breeding operation to rescue the critically endangered Western swamp turtle *Pseudemydura umbrina* from extinction. Internatl. Zoo Yearbook, 28: 103–110.

Kuwabara, K., N. Suzuki, F. Wakabayashi, H. Ashikaga, T. Inoue, and J. Kobara. 1989. Breeding the Japanese giant salamander *Andrias japonicus* at Asa Zoological Park. Internatl. Zoo Yearbook, 28: 22–31.

Larsen, R. E., and P. T. Cardeilhac. 1984. Artificial insemination, semen handling and assessment of reproductive status in alligators. Ann. Proc. Amer. Assoc. Zoo Vets, 1984: 159.

McMahan, W. 1991. A declaration of interdependence. Internatl. Zoo News, 38: 9–10.

Mengden, G. A., C. Platz, R. Hubbard, and H. R. Quinn. 1980. Semen collection, freezing and artificial insemination in snakes, p. 71–78. *In* J. B. Murphy and J. T. Collins (eds.), Reproductive Biology and Diseases of Captive Reptiles. Soc. Study Amphib. Reptiles, Oxford, Ohio, Contrib. Herpetol., 1.

Miller, T. J. 1985. Husbandry and breeding of the Puerto Rican crested toad (*Peltophryne lemur*) with comments on its natural history. Zoo Biol., 4: 281–286.

Murphy, J. B., and D. Chiszar. 1989. Herpetological master planning for the 1990s. Internatl. Zoo Yearbook, 28: 1–7.

Murphy, J. B., and J. T. Collins (eds.). 1980. Reproductive Biology and Diseases of Captive Reptiles. Soc. Study Amphib. Reptiles, Oxford, Ohio. Contrib. Herpetol., 1.

Murphy, J. B., and L. A. Mitchell. 1989. 'The other side': an experiment in reptile appreciation at the Dallas Zoo. Internatl. Zoo Yearbook, 28: 205–207.

Murphy, J. B., and J. A. Shadduck. 1979. Suggestions for the post-mortem examination of reptiles. Herpetol. Rev., 10: 113–115.

Noegel, R. P. 1989. Husbandry of West Indian rock iguanas *Cyclura* at Life Fellowship Bird Sanctuary, Seffner. Internatl. Zoo Yearbook, 28: 131–136.

Olney, P. J. S., and P. Ellis. 1991*a*. Amphibians bred in captivity and multiple generation births 1988/1989. Internatl. Zoo Yearbook, 30: 323–325.

—. 1991*b*. Reptiles bred in captivity and multiple generation births 1988/1989. Internatl. Zoo Yearbook, 30: 326–342.

Paine, F. L., J. D. Miller, G. Crawshaw, B. Johnson, R. Lacy, C. F. Smith, III, and P. J. Tolson. 1989. Status of the Puerto Rican crested toad *Peltophryne lemur*. Internatl. Zoo Yearbook, 28: 53–58.

Pechmann, J. H. K., D. E. Scott, R. D. Semlitsch, J. P. Caldwell, L. J. Vitt, and J. W. Gibbons. 1991. Declining amphibian populations: the problem of separating human impacts from natural fluctuations. Science, 253: 892–895.

Prescott, J., and M. Hutchins. 1991. Joining efforts for the preservation of biodiversity, p. 227–232. *In* Transactions of the 56th North American Wildlife and Natural Resources Conference, Edmonton, Alberta, Canada.

Quinn, H., T. Blasedel, and C. Platz. 1989. Successful artificial insemination in the checkered garter snake *Thamnophis marcianus*. Internatl. Zoo Yearbook, 28: 177–183.

Quinn, H., and J. P. Jones. 1974. Squeeze box technique for measuring snakes. Herpetol. Rev., 5: 35.

Ralls, K., and J. D. Ballou. 1986. Preface to the proceedings of the workshop on genetic management of captive populations. Zoo Biol., 5: 81–86.

Reichling, S. B. 1988. Reproduction in captive Louisiana pine snakes, *Pituophis melanoleucus ruthveni*. Herpetol. Rev., 19: 77–78.

Reid, D., L. Durrell, and G. Rakotobearison. 1989. The captive breeding project for the angonoka *Geochelone yniphora* in Madagascar. Dodo, Jour. Jersey Wildl. Preserv. Trust, 26: 34–48.

Ryder, O. A., L. G. Chemnick, S. F. Schafer, and A. L. Shima. 1989. Individual DNA fingerprints from Galapagos tortoises *Geochelone elephantopus*. Internatl. Zoo Yearbook, 28: 84–87.

Schildger, B., and R. Wicker. 1989. Sex determination and clinical examination in reptiles using endoscopy. Herpetol. Rev., 20: 9–10.

Soulé, M., M. Gilpin, W. Conway, and T. Foose. 1986. The millennium ark: how long a voyage, how many staterooms, how many passengers? Zoo Biol., 5: 101–113.

Steinhart, P. 1984. Fear of snakes. Audubon, 86: 6–9.

Swingland, I. R., and M. W. Klemens (eds.). 1989. The Conservation Biology of Tortoises. Internatl. Union Conserv. Nat., Gland, Switzerland. iv, 204 pages.

Templeton, A. R., H. Hemmer, G. Mace, U. S. Seal, W. M. Shields, and D. S. Woodruff. 1986. Local adaptation, coadaptation, and population boundaries. Zoo Biol., 5: 115–126.

Tryon, B. W. 1975. How to incubate reptilian eggs: a proven technique. Bull. New York Herpetol. Soc., 11: 33–37.

Tryon, B. W., and T. G. Hulsey. 1977. Breeding and rearing the bog turtle, *Clemmys muhlenbergi*, at the Fort Worth Zoo. Internatl. Zoo Yearbook, 17: 125–130.

Tudge, C. 1992. Last Animals at the Zoo. Island Press, Washington, D.C. vi, 266 pages.

Vietmeyer, N. 1989. Iguana mama. Internatl. Wildlife, 19: 25–27.

Warwick, C. 1990. Reptilian ethology in captivity: observations of some problems and an evaluation of their aetiology. Appl. Anim. Behav. Sci., 26: 1–13.

Warwick, C., K. Steedman, and T. Holford. 1991. Rattlesnake collection drives—their implications for species and environmental conservation. Oryx, 25: 39–44.

Wiese, R. J. 1990. Genetic structure of native and introduced populations of the bullfrog, a successful colonist. Doctoral Dissertation, Colorado State University, Fort Collins, Colorado. ix, 113 pages.

Zimmermann, H. 1989. Conservation studies on the 'dart-poison' frogs Dendrobatidae in the field and in captivity. Internatl. Zoo Yearbook, 28: 31–45.

❦ Wiese, R. J., and M. Hutchins. 1994. The role of zoos and aquariums in amphibian and reptilian conservation, p. 37–45. *In* J. B. Murphy, K. Adler, and J. T. Collins (eds.), Captive Management and Conservation of Amphibians and Reptiles. Society for the Study of Amphibians and Reptiles, Ithaca (New York). Contributions to Herpetology, volume 11.

The Effects of Temperature on Captive Amphibians and Reptiles

Roger A. Avery*

Introduction

It is now almost universally accepted that the heat balances of reptiles, and hence their body temperatures, are key factors in understanding the biology of many species. Heat balances and body temperatures are also important for many amphibians, although the reasons are often slightly different. Many species—perhaps more than we realize—may thermoregulate by behavioral means, but environmental and body temperatures also have an immediate importance for amphibians, because they have a crucial effect on the rate of water loss from these animals.

A good knowledge of the temperature relations of a species is therefore one of the requirements for successful husbandry. Body temperatures (Tbs) and thermoregulation in reptiles and amphibians, because of their importance, are well studied and have been reviewed on many occasions (see, for example, Avery 1982; Duellman and Trueb 1986 [1985]; Lillywhite 1987; Meek and Avery 1988). The basic outlines of the subject are now well established. The thermal relations of a previously unstudied species can usually be predicted; often the exceptions are taxa whose geographical distributions are either remote from major centers of research or are too small for the animals to have received attention yet. Thermoregulation by reptiles and amphibians has also been studied more extensively in some biotopes than in others: diurnal lizards in deserts or Mediterranean climates are very well understood in this respect, for example, but fossorial lizards or those from the tropical rainforest canopy are not. An excellent recent example of a study that makes a major contribution to understanding behavioral thermoregulation in a previously little-known environment (garter snakes under rocks) has been described by Huey et al. (1989).

This essay attempts to identify cases in which further knowledge of thermal biology is required to significantly increase the effectiveness of efforts to keep and breed reptiles and amphibians in captive conditions. Such an approach must inevitably be speculative. It will also involve a synthesis of many subjects; it is not possible to discuss thermoregulation and body temperatures in a practical context without straying into many other areas of biology.

Sublety of Thermoregulatory Behavior

Many aspects of the lives of reptiles and amphibians are very subtle. This can be illustrated with some examples drawn from studies of thermoregulatory behavior in European lacertid lizards, especially *Lacerta vivipara* and *Podarcis muralis*. These lizards are typical "shuttling heliotherms." They raise Tbs in the morning by basking, and then maintain Tb within the activity temperature range (for definition, see Pough and Gans 1982) by alternating basking behavior, during which Tbs rise, with foraging and other movements, during which Tbs usually fall. This behavior can be reproduced in the laboratory by keeping lizards in open-topped arenas in which heat is provided by tungsten light bulbs suspended overhead. If the appropriate environmental variables have been measured—radiant heat intensity, surface temperature beneath the bulb, and air temperatures within the arena—the behavior of a lizard is highly predictable. The mean

*Department of Zoology
The University of Bristol
Bristol BS8 1UG, UK

Acronym used in this chapter:

Tbs Body temperatures

times spent basking and foraging, for example, together with their variances, remain relatively constant (Avery 1985).

This generalization must be qualified, however; it is only under fairly tightly specified conditions that the predictions hold. The alternating pattern of basking and foraging is disrupted if, for example, a lizard is fed a large meal; the animal then spends long periods basking (Avery, unpubl. data). The alternation tends not to occur at all if the lizards are in a very simple, wooden-floored cage or in a cage with a soil substrate, but without rocks, logs, or other "furniture." Under these conditions the lizards either do not emerge from the overnight retreat at all, or they spend very long periods basking. They seem to need some environmental diversification, which can be provided simply by using a number of 5 × 5 × 5 cm wooden blocks to induce foraging (Avery 1985). Whether such "spatial heterogeneity" provides a positive stimulus, or whether the reduction in foraging results from stress induced by its absence, is at present an open question.

Stress and the Endocrine System

Attempts have been made recently to measure stress in captive lizards. One method for doing this would be to measure levels of stress-related hormones (see below), but it is very difficult to remove adequate blood samples from small lizards and the procedure itself is stressful; thus non-invasive methods have been developed. One such method is to measure the frequency of respiration, which can be determined from the pumping movements of the anterior ribs. This can be quantified using the Doppler shift of an ultrasonic signal at 50 kHz (Avery and D'Eath 1986), but this technique is only effective if the lizard is otherwise immobile (for example, when it is basking); for non-basking lizards, a manually operated event recorder is used.

The frequency of respiration increases when a lizard is subjected to even relatively minor background events in the laboratory, such as a slammed door or someone moving nearby. Interest in this phenomenon was initiated by the need to find a means for recognizing and defining unstressed or undiverted subjects for studies of food capture, since stressed lizards frequently do not respond to a stimulus that would otherwise elicit feeding.

Seasonal Breeding and the Endocrine System

Seasonal breeding also illustrates the subtlety referred to above. It is well known that the factors that govern seasonal breeding in a wide range of vertebrates include the measurement of day length; animals have a "clock" and seasonal events such as courtship, spermatogenesis, or migration are induced by a comparison of the length of the day with some inbuilt standard (Reiter and Follett 1980). Much of the work on this phenomenon has been carried out with birds and mammals, but ectotherms have been studied too. The maintenance of breeding in *Anolis carolinensis*, for example, is mainly determined by day length, although unlike the situation in endotherms, the onset is induced by changes in temperature (for reviews relating to reptiles in general, see Crews 1980; Callard and Ho 1980; Underwood 1981; for amphibians, see Duellman and Trueb 1986 [1985]). The physiological mechanisms are clearly complex, and the sense organs involved include the lateral eyes, the parietal eye (in lizards), or parapineal organ (in many amphibians), the pineal gland, and in some species, other extraretinal photoreceptors (Underwood 1983, 1985; Underwood and Hyde 1989; Janik and Menaker 1990; Sievert and Hutchison 1991). Social interactions can also be involved (Crews 1980). Coordination of these responses is partly via the hormone melatonin (Gern et al. 1986), changes in levels of which can have other effects, for example, on temperature selection (Rismiller and Heldmaier 1987; Firth et al. 1988).

Transduction between the environmental events that proximately control the timing of seasonal behavior, such as breeding or migration, and the actual effector mechanisms is thus endocrinological (Reiter and Follett 1980). Although there have been some studies of the effects of temperature on these processes (Callard and Ho 1980), this aspect has not been given sufficient emphasis. There are many gaps in knowledge, some of which are important at a practical level. This can be illustrated by describing some preliminary work carried out a number of years ago on newts in the genus *Triturus* (Avery 1971).

All of the species of *Triturus* in Europe breed seasonally in spring. The males develop particularly striking secondary sexual characters—bright coloration, a dorsal crest, and pheromone secretion—at this time. If the animals are brought into captivity during the breeding season, the sexual characters are usually lost rather rapidly (although this can be avoided with appropriate care; see Halliday [1976]). The loss is undoubtedly an effect of stress that is mediated via the endocrine system; other consequences are seen too, for example, the animals tend to lose their intestinal worms (Avery, unpubl. data). The losses of both secondary sexual characters and parasitic worms are temperature-dependent; they occur more rapidly at high temperatures (Avery, unpubl. data).

Temperature can influence other rhythms and cycles too. There are diel cycles in physiology (Rismiller and Heldmaier 1985; Pati and Gupta 1991) and in the activity of lizards in an aktograph apparatus (Foà 1991), which can be important. Careful studies of wall lizards (*Podarcis muralis*) in artificial burrows show that the animals become increasingly active at about 0830 h during the summer, and often approach the entrance (but do not emerge) at this time. The duration and extent of these movements are temperature-dependent, but in quite subtle ways, because both the actual temperature and the rate of temperature change can influence the behavior (Avery, unpubl. data). These observations are preliminary; further study is needed. There is indirect evidence that the intrinsic diel rhythms of activity, and the ways in which they may respond to environmental factors, such as temperature, may vary even between closely related species (Cragg 1978).

Much of the work on thermoregulatory behavior in my laboratory is carried out during the winter months when the lizards would normally be hibernating. Hibernation is prevented by exposing the lizards to levels of radiant heat and light (from tungsten light bulbs), which enable them to thermoregulate each day and so remain active. This must give rise to some physiological stress. Infections by the bacterium *Aeromonas* (Cooper et al. 1980) sometimes create problems, and these are undoubtedly stress-related. The condition is difficult to treat, and the affected lizards often cease feeding and die. It has been discovered by trial and error that the risk can be minimized by reducing the amount of time during which the animals are allowed to thermoregulate (that is, the time the bulbs are switched on). The reasons for this are not known. This also is a temperature-related phenomenon that merits further study.

Growth Rates

A final example of a subtle, temperature-related aspect of biology involves the growth rates of captive lacertid lizards. Provided that a juvenile is well fed, its growth is determined by the amount of time during which it can thermoregulate. In the laboratory, this is the time for which the bulbs are switched on (Avery 1984; Perkins and Avery 1989). The optimum in the short term is about 12–14 hours per day (see Figure 1: note that these are not the conditions that minimize the risks of disease due to *Aeromonas* infection). If the bulbs are switched on for more than about 8 hours per day, however, the lizards usually die in the longer term. For any given period for which the bulbs are switched on, survival is better at lower ambient temperatures. These observations need to be more rigorously quantified.

Requirements for Further Research

Success in husbandry and captive breeding depends on attention to the sorts of details illustrated by these examples. Survival rates of *Lacerta vivipara* in my laboratory have progressively improved over the past 30 years (no attempt is made to breed these lizards, partly because of the complexity of the environmental programming of the reproductive cycle, especially in females [see Gavaud 1991*a*,

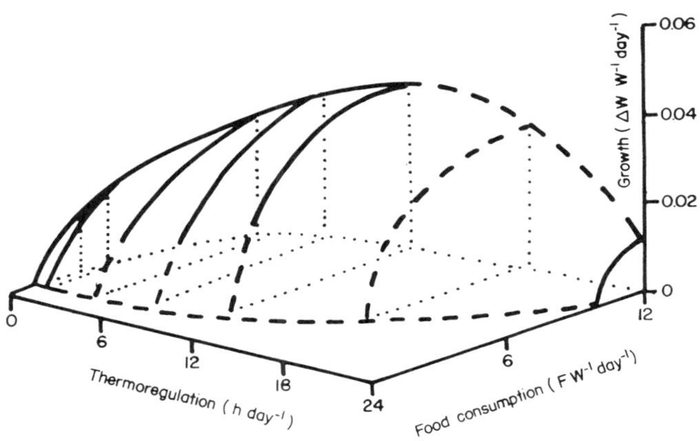

FIGURE 1. Three-dimensional graph showing the relationships between time for which lizards can thermoregulate, food consumption, and growth in juvenile *Lacerta vivipara*. Reprinted with permission from Avery (1984).

1991*b*]). Improvement has resulted from trial and error; it would be much better if improvements in the future could be based on a rational understanding of captive biology.

The development of this body of knowledge will require two important advances. The first is to find ways to determine which aspects of the overall environment are important for long-term survival and reproductive success, and how to mimic them artificially. This will probably be easier to achieve for some species than for others (see Avery 1985). For difficult species especially, it will require attention to subtleties in the biology of the animals, which I have discussed in this essay. One of the reasons why *Lacerta vivipara* may become progressively less healthy in the laboratory may be that seasonal changes to which the endocrine system responds are not reproduced with sufficient exactness. Various elements in the endocrine system therefore lose the essential cues, or they are presented with conflicting cues, which normally keep them programmed as an integrated whole; thus they begin to lose synchrony. This phenomenon has been called endocrinological collapse (Avery 1985), but this interpretation is almost entirely speculative. Individual components of the endocrine system have been studied, such as the effects on steroids of stress due to captivity (see Elsey et al. 1991 and Zerani et al. 1991 for recent examples). There have been no studies of captive reptiles or amphibians, however, in which the entire endocrine balance and its environmental control have been considered as an integrated interdependent system. This is a major priority for further research.

The second advance is more fundamental. There is currently no conceptual scheme on which to base thinking about the responses of animals to captivity. This problem has, to be sure, been addressed by ethologists; there is now an extensive literature on the behavior of captive animals, although too little of this relates to reptiles and amphibians. What is needed now is a similar approach to the environmental physiology of captive animals. We need a paradigm (Kuhn 1970); a system for organizing our thinking on the integration of environment, physiology, and behavior in maintaining the lives of reptiles and amphibians. The absence of such a scheme is hampering progress, and relegating the science of amphibian and reptilian husbandry to one of trial and error. This can produce some spectacular successes (see, for example, Tonge and Bloxam 1989), but progress will be more rapid if our efforts can be based on a more solid conceptual foundation.

Summary

Examples are given of husbandry problems whose understanding and ultimate solution may depend upon a knowledge of either the temperature relations of the animal concerned, or of the effects of body temperature, environmental temperature, or the interactions of temperature with other environmental "cues" on reproduction and long-term survival. Emphasis is placed on the complexity and apparent subtlety of many of these factors. It is concluded that there is a need for a conceptual paradigm; most husbandry programs are, at the present, conducted more on the basis of trial-and-error than on the application of rational principles derived from experimental science.

Literature Cited

Avery, R. A. 1971. Helminth parasite populations in newts and their tadpoles. Freshwater Biol., 1: 113–119.

—. 1982. Field studies of body temperatures and thermoregulation, p. 93–166. *In* C. Gans and F. H. Pough (eds.), Biology of the Reptilia, Vol. 12: Physiology C, Physiological Ecology. Academic Press, New York.

—. 1984. Physiological aspects of lizard growth. Symp. Zool. Soc. London, 52: 407–424.

—. 1985. Thermoregulatory behaviour of reptiles in the field and in captivity, p. 45–60. *In* S. Townson and K. Lawrence (eds.), Reptiles: Breeding, Behaviour and Veterinary Aspects. British Herpetological Society, London.

Avery, R. A., and F. M. D'Eath. 1986. Thermography, thermoregulation and animal behaviour, p. 71–75. *In* R. P. Clark and M. R. Goff (eds.), Recent Advances in Medical and Physiological Imaging. Taylor and Francis, London.

Callard, I. P., and S. M. Ho. 1980. Seasonal reproductive cycles in reptiles, p. 5–38. *In* R. J. Reiter and B. K. Follett (eds.), Progress in Reproductive Biology, Vol. 5: Seasonal Reproduction in Higher Vertebrates. S. Karger, Basel.

Cooper, J. E., M. H. McClelland, and J. R. Needham. 1980. An eye infection in laboratory lizards associated with an *Aeromonas* sp. Lab. Anim., 14: 149–151.

Cragg, P. A. 1978. Oxygen consumption in the lizard genus *Lacerta* in relation to diel variation, maximum activity and body weight. Jour. Exp. Biol., 77: 33–56.

Crews, D. 1980. Interrelationships among ecological, behavioral and neuroendocrine processes in the reproductive cycle of *Anolis carolinensis* and other reptiles. Adv. Stud. Behav., 11: 1–74.

Duellman, W. E. and L. Trueb. 1986 (1985). Biology of Amphibians. McGraw Hill, New York. i–xvii, 670 pages.

Elsey, R. M., V. A. Lance, T. Joanen, and L. McNease. 1991. Acute stress suppresses plasma estradiol levels in female alligators (*Alligator mississippiensis*). Comp. Biochem. Physiol., 100A: 649–651.

Firth, B. T., R. E. Mandlin, and C. L. Ralph. 1988. The role of the pineal complex in behavioral thermoregulation in the collared lizard *Crotaphytus collaris* under seminatural conditions. Physiol. Zool., 61: 176–185.

Foà, A. 1991. The role of the pineal and the retinae in the expression of circadian locomotor rhythmicity in the ruin lizard, *Podarcis sicula*. Jour. Comp. Physiol., 169A: 201–207.

Gavaud, J. 1991*a*. Role of cryophase temperature and thermophase duration in thermoperiodic regulation of the testicular cycle in the lizard *Lacerta vivipara*. Jour. Exp. Zool., 260: 239–246.

—. 1991b. Cold entrainment of the annual cycle of ovarian activity in the lizard *Lacerta vivipara*: thermoperiodic rhythm versus hibernation. Jour. Biol. Rhythms, 6: 201–215.

Gern, W. A., D. Duvall, and J. M. Nervina. 1986. Melatonin: a discussion of its evolution and actions in vertebrates. Amer. Zool., 26: 985–996.

Halliday, T. R. 1976. The libidinous newt. An analysis of variations in the sexual behaviour of the male smooth newt, *Triturus vulgaris*. Anim. Behav., 25: 39–45.

Huey, R. B., C. R. Peterson, and S. J. Arnold. 1989. Hot rocks and not-so-hot rocks: retreat-site selection by garter snakes and its thermal consequences. Ecology, 70: 931–944.

Janik, D. A., and M. Menaker. 1990. Circadian locomotor rhythms in the desert iguana. 1. The role of the eyes and the pineal. Jour. Comp. Physiol., 166A: 803–810.

Kuhn, T. S. 1970. The Structure of Scientific Revolutions. 2nd edition. Univ. Chicago Press, Chicago. 235 pages.

Lillywhite, H. B. 1987. Temperature, energetics and physiological ecology, p. 422–477. *In* R. A. Seigel, J. T. Collins, and S. S. Novak (eds.), Snakes: Ecology and Evolutionary Biology. McGraw Hill, New York.

Meek, R., and R. A. Avery. 1988. Mini review: thermoregulation in chelonians. Herpetol. Jour., 1: 253–259.

Pati, A. K., and S. Gupta. 1991. Circadian time dependence of erythropoietic and respiratory responses of the Indian garden lizard, *Calotes versicolor*, to mammalian urinary erythropoietin and thyroxine. Gen. Comp. Endocrinol., 82: 345–354.

Perkins, C. J., and R. A. Avery. 1989. Biology and conservation of the green lizard *Lacerta viridis* and the wall lizard *Podarcis muralis* in Jersey. Wildlife Preserv. Trust Spec. Sci. Report, 2: 1–55.

Pough, F. H., and C. Gans. 1982. The vocabulary of reptilian thermoregulation, p. 17–23. *In* C. Gans and F. H. Pough (eds.), Biology of the Reptilia, Vol. 12: Physiology C, Physiological Ecology. Academic Press, New York.

Reiter, R. J., and B. K. Follett (eds.). 1980. Progress in Reproductive Biology, Vol. 5. Seasonal Reproduction in Higher Vertebrates. S. Karger, Basel. 225 pages.

Rismiller, P. D., and G. Heldmaier. 1985. Thermal behavior as a function of time of day: heat exchange rates and oxygen consumption of the lizard *Lacerta viridis*. Physiol. Zool., 58: 71–79.

—. 1987. Melatonin and photoperiod affect body temperature selection in the lizard *Lacerta viridis*. Jour. Thermal Biol., 12: 131–134.

Sievert, L. M., and V. M. Hutchison. 1991. The influence of photoperiod and position of a light source on behavioral thermoregulation in *Crotaphytus collaris* (Squamata: Iguanidae). Copeia, 1991: 105–110.

Tonge, S., and Q. Bloxam. 1989. Breeding the Mallorcan midwife toad. Internatl. Zoo Yearbook, 28: 45–53.

Underwood, H. 1981. Circadian cycles in lizards: photoreception, physiology and photoperiodic time measurement, p. 137–152. *In* B. K. Follett and D. E. Follett (eds.), Biological Clocks in Seasonal Reproductive Cycles. Scientechnica, Bristol.

—. 1983. Circadian organization in the lizard *Anolis carolinensis*: a multioscillator system. Jour. Comp. Physiol., 152A: 265–274.

—. 1985. Pineal melatonin rhythms in the lizard *Anolis carolinensis*: effects of light and temperature cycles. Jour. Comp. Physiol., 157A: 57–65.

Underwood, H., and L. L. Hyde. 1989. The effects of day length on the pineal melatonin rhythm of the lizard *Anolis carolinenesis*. Comp. Biochem. Physiol., 94A: 53–56.

Zerani, M., F. Amabili, G. Mosconi, and A. Gobbetti. 1991. Effects of captivity stress on plasma steroid levels in the green frog, *Rana esculenta*, during the annual reproductive cycle. Comp. Biochem. Physiol., 98A: 491–496.

❦ Avery, R. A. 1994. The effects of temperature on captive amphibians and reptiles, p. 47–51. *In* J. B. Murphy, K. Adler, and J. T. Collins (eds.), Captive Management and Conservation of Amphibians and Reptiles. Society for the Study of Amphibians and Reptiles, Ithaca (New York). Contributions to Herpetology, volume 11.

LIGHT REQUIREMENTS OF CAPTIVE AMPHIBIANS AND REPTILES

WILLIAM H. GEHRMANN*

Introduction

RADIATION FROM LIGHT SOURCES CAN BE DIVIDED into several categories. Visible light is that part of the electromagnetic spectrum within the band of wavelengths from 400 nanometers (nm) to 700 nm. Ultraviolet radiation (UVR) is often included within the realm of "light" and is further subdivided into longwave, nearwave, blacklight, or ultraviolet A (UVA) from 320 to 400 nm, and middlewave, erythemal, or ultraviolet B (UVB) from 285 to 320 nm. Shortwave, farwave, germicidal, or ultraviolet C (UVC) radiation lies between 200 and 285 nm; it has few if any applications in amphibian and reptilian husbandry. Infrared radiation (IR) at wavelengths greater than 700 nm is primarily associated with heat, thermoregulation, and related behavioral or physiological states. Wavelengths differing from the boundary values given here are sometimes reported, indicating that some of the characteristics of a given bandwidth do not terminate abruptly but rather grade into adjacent regions (for further discussion and examples, see Parrish et al. 1978; Kaufman and Christensen 1985; Thorington 1985).

Three features of a light source may separately or conjointly influence biological systems: quality, intensity, and photoperiod. The biological effects of photoperiod on amphibians and reptiles have been the most investigated feature of light, but will not be treated in this article.

Light quality can be described by the spectral power distribution (SPD), which graphically denotes the actual or relative energy or power at various wavelengths. Lamps that have an SPD similar to that of natural light are referred to as full-spectrum lamps. SPD curves are readily available from manufacturers (see Cromer 1977 and General Electric [GE] Lighting Application Bulletin 905–61701R for a discussion of the correlated color-temperature and color-rendering index as indicators of light quality). Spectral curves for lamps commonly used in herpetoculture are given in Gehrmann (1994). Light intensity refers to the magnitude of energy associated with a light source. Intensity can be described by the irradiance (watts · cm^{-2}) or illuminance (lux). For some studies, particularly those involving UVR, the dose from a source can be important. Dose is the irradiance multiplied by the time of exposure.

Natural light differs from light emitted by artificial lamps in several ways. For example, natural light photoperiod varies systematically with season and latitude. Light quality and intensity vary unpredictably as a function of cloud cover and atmospheric turbidity. Sky-color temperature and light polarization change during the course of a day (McFarland and Munz 1975; Thorington 1985). Sunlight impinging on an ecosystem may be heterogeneously distributed among microhabitats within a system (see Evans 1966, for light distribution in a woodland ecosystem). In contrast, light from a lamp used in an enclosure housing amphibians or reptiles

*Department of Natural Sciences
Tarrant County Junior College
5301 Campus Drive
Fort Worth, Texas 76119, USA

Acronyms used in this chapter:

BLB	Blacklight blue
GE	General Electric Corporation
IR	Infrared radiation
nm	Nanometers
RSM	Reflector Sunlamp Mogul base
SPD	Spectral power distribution
UVA	Ultraviolet A
UVB	Ultraviolet B
UVC	Ultraviolet C
UVR	Ultraviolet radiation

will, in general, be less variable. These differences can be important when comparing the influence of natural light on some biological process with the effect of light from an artificial source.

Evaluating the influence of light on amphibians and reptiles calls for the specification of endpoints. In the broadest sense, the goals associated with the maintenance of captive collections at the organismal level are maturation of neonates, retention of specimens for educational, research, or other purposes, and propagation. Accordingly, criteria that can be used to evaluate these goals might be growth, longevity, fecundity, and various correlated morphological, physiological, and behavioral endpoints such as thermoregulation.

Light Quality

Experiments dealing with the influence of light quality on amphibians and reptiles are rare. Among the first is the work of Torelle (1903) who showed that frogs are more phototactically responsive to blue wavelengths in a choice situation than to other colors in the visible spectrum. In a monumental study, Hailman and Jaeger (1974) examined the phototactic responses of 127 species of anurans to different wavelengths (colors) of light. They demonstrated that some species have color vision, which can influence the nature of the phototactic response.

Mayhew (1965) was among the first to speculate that spectral characteristics of light might have an influence on growth. He found a greater growth rate in lizards (Desert Iguanas, *Dipsosaurus dorsalis*) lighted with 100-watt frosted-glass incandescent lamps compared to the rates of those illuminated with 250-watt IR heat lamps. Furthermore, body temperature differences could not reasonably account for the growth difference. Because frosted incandescent lamps emit more energy at the shorter wavelengths compared to IR lamps, he hypothesized that shorter wavelengths toward the blue might be more effective in stimulating growth. Licht (1969) showed that the effectiveness of red and green light in stimulating testicular recrudescence in Green Anoles (*Anolis carolinensis*) was comparable to that of white light, provided that the intensity was above a threshold value. Blue light, whether bright or dim, did not have a stimulatory effect.

Noting that some specimens of several species of snakes died after about eight weeks when illuminated with Sylvania Gro-Lux plant lamps, Mehrtens (1965) suggested that some feature of the light quality of these lamps might be fatal to reptiles. Logan (1969) reported that a variety of reptilian species had survived for years in apparent good health in enclosures illuminated at least in part with plant lamps. Roberts and Gehrmann (1990) raised hatchling Bearded Dragons (*Pogona vitticeps*) in enclosures illuminated with either a blacklight (Sylvania F2OT12/350) and a full-spectrum Vita-Lite (Duro-Test Corp.) or a blacklight and a Sylvania Gro-Lux plant lamp. Although their sample sizes were small and variance within groups was large, their results suggest that the "unbalanced" quality of a plant lamp is not fatal and furthermore may be capable of supporting growth rates comparable to those observed under full-spectrum lighting. Allen (1988) reported that body mass changes in juvenile Green Iguanas (*Iguana iguana*) illuminated with two GE Chroma 50 lamps were not significantly different from those lighted with a single GE Chroma 50 and a GE F40BL after a seven-month period. These studies indicate that balanced full-spectrum light may not be necessary for some processes (for example, growth and reproduction), even in some heliophilic species.

Light Intensity

The intensity of natural light that strikes ecosystems varies within a day, among days and seasons, and latitudinally. For example, illuminance may be about 113,000 lux at midday in June at 35°N latitude and about 59,000 lux at midday in December at the same latitude (Thorington 1985). In contrast, the illuminance of a 20 watt Vita-Lite lamp at 61 cm is 215 lux, while that of a 20 watt Sylvania cool white lamp at the same distance is 344 lux. The illuminance from a Sylvania 275 watt Reflector Sunlamp Mogul base (RSM) lamp at 61 cm below the bulb center is about 3443 lux (Gehrmann 1987). It is evident that for most reptiles in captivity, the intensity of light with which they are illuminated will be considerably less than natural light; exceptions are specimens maintained in outdoor enclosures or kept in transparent cages beneath a skylight.

Experiments dealing with the influence of light intensity on various processes in amphibians and reptiles are rare. Jaeger and Hailman (1973) examined 121 species of anurans in an effort to understand phototactic behaviors within an ecological-evolutionary context. Baker (1990) speculated that the clumped aggregation of Common Toads (*Bufo bufo*) observed under street lamps may reflect a positive phototaxis associated with the selection of an optimum light intensity. Licht (1969) reported that photosexual stimulation of the testes in Green Anoles by white light is independent of intensity above a threshold level lying between 5.4 and 129 lux. Spellerberg (1974) examined the effect of light intensity on selected body temperatures in a thermal gradient in two lizards, *Lacerta agilis* and *L. viridis*. The four levels of intensity used (13, 80, 450, and 1500 lux) did not affect the mean selected body temperatures, but an increase in the rate of body warming at the onset of the light phase was associated with the higher light intensities.

Ultraviolet Radiation

Both UVA and UVB radiation are an integral part of natural light. Atmospheric absorption of UVR, especially by the ozone layer, results in a lower limit at 290 nm reaching the biosphere. As is the case with visible light, there is considerable variation in the amount of UVR impinging on a surface within a day and among days and seasons. It is usual to describe the quantity of UVR as irradiance ($\mu W \cdot cm^{-2}$). The irradiance of UVA on 22 June 1979 at 1144 hours at 35°N latitude on a cloudless day was 5766 $\mu W \cdot cm^{-2}$, while that of UVB was 154 $\mu W \cdot cm^{-2}$. In contrast, the irradiance of UVA on 17 December 1979 at 1142 hours at the same latitude and with the same atmospheric conditions was 2641 $\mu W \cdot cm^{-2}$, while UVB was 43.5 $\mu W \cdot cm^{-2}$ (Thorington, 1985). See Gehrmann (1987) for UVR irradiances from various lamps used in herpetoculture.

Laszlo (1969) may be credited with being the first person to focus the attention of the herpetocultural community on the potential importance of ultraviolet and full-spectrum light from artificial sources for the maintenance and propagation of reptiles. Various reports such as those by Cole and Townsend (1977), Townsend (1979), McCrystal and Behler (1982), Phillips (1985), and Townsend and Cole (1985) appear to have been important in establishing the widespread practice of using a full-spectrum Vita-Lite lamp in conjunction with a fluorescent blacklight as the primary sources of visible and UV radiation, especially for lizards and turtles. An alternative combination that is used by some facilities is a GE Chroma 50 and a blacklight.

Most studies associated with assessing the biological effects of UVR involve either UVA or UVB. Moehn (1976) reported that a group of Desert Collared Lizards (*Crotaphytus insularis*) exposed to sunlight in an outdoor enclosure established a despotism as measured by the increased frequency of assertion and threat displays by the dominant male compared to relatively restricted activity of subdominant males. In addition, the dominant male showed an increase in the frequency of courtship and copulatory behaviors directed toward females. In contrast, when the group was maintained in an indoor enclosure with light supplied by three 250-watt reflector flood lamps and no measurable UVR, social interactions were almost nonexistent. Because sunlight contains both UVA and UVB, it cannot be established which type was of greater importance. In another paper, however, Moehn (1974) examined the influence of UVR on agonistic behaviors in several species of lizards (*Dipsosaurus dorsalis*, *Crotaphytus collaris*, and *Agama agama*). In this study, he used filters that allowed him to partition the light from a 275 watt sunlamp into either UVA (about 320–400 nm) or visible radiation above 400 nm. A significantly greater frequency of agonistic displays were observed when the lizards were exposed to UVA compared to the visible light. He further indicated that a similar enhancement of agonistic behaviors was observed when the lizards were exposed to two 15 watt blacklight (BLB) fluorescent lamps.

Alberts (1989) demonstrated that the lizard *D. dorsalis* was more likely to investigate femoral pore secretions from conspecifics by tongue touching when UVA was present in the light source. Although the neuroendocrine mechanisms underlying these UVA-elicited behaviors are unknown, the primary receptors are likely to be located in the lateral eyes or parietal eye or both in some lizards. Lateral eye sensitivity to UVA has been described in the Grass Frog, *Rana temporaria* (Govardovskii and Zueva 1974) and in the lizard *D. dorsalis* (Alberts 1989). UVA photoreceptors have also been identified in the parietal eye of *Iguana iguana* and *Anolis carolinensis* using electroretinographic techniques (Jenison and Nolte 1980).

While the mechanism whereby UVA exerts its effects remains obscure, at least one role of UVB on biological systems is better understood, especially in endothermal vertebrates. UVB penetrating the skin results in the photolysis of provitamin D_3 to previtamin D_3, which in turn undergoes a thermal isomerization to yield vitamin D_3. Vitamin D_3 is transferred to the circulatory system by binding to a vitamin D-binding protein. It can then be transported to the liver, where it may be hydroxylated at the carbon-25 position, followed by a 1a hydroxylation when it reaches the kidney. This results in the active form, 1,25 dihydroxyvitamin D_3, which exerts multiple effects on calcium-phosphorus metabolism and the immune system in bone and other tissues and organs in the body (Holick 1985, 1989).

The presence of provitamin D_3, previtamin D_3, and vitamin D_3 in the skin of the lizard *Anolis carolinensis* and the frogs *Rana pipiens* and *R. catesbeiana* after exposure to sunlight has been confirmed by St. Lezin (1983 as cited by Holick 1989). The subsequent hydroxylations resulting in 1,25 dihydroxyvitamin D_3 are presumed to occur in amphibians and reptiles, but experimental verification is lacking (Holick 1989). Although thermal isomerization to produce vitamin D_3 is relatively assured in endotherms with body temperatures of about 37°C, this step would be coupled with thermoregulatory behaviors in ectotherms. This could have important implications for captive husbandry with respect to establishing thermal gradients in enclosures (Allen 1989*a*; Moyle 1990).

Experimental studies that attempt to clarify the role of UVB on calcium-phosphorus metabolism in reptiles are almost nonexistent. Gehrmann et al. (1991) exposed juvenile Western Fence Lizards (*Sceloporus occidentalis*) to three different doses of UVB and used a zero-dose control group. The lizards received no dietary vitamin D_3, but adequate calcium in the form of $CaCO_3$ was available. They appeared healthy after ten weeks and there were no significant differences in growth rate, bone calcium, phosphorus, or magnesium concentrations or blood-calcium levels among the control and treatment groups. Blood-phosphorus concentrations were significantly lower in the two high-dose UVB groups, although the physiological significance of this remains obscure. One explanation for these results is to assume that the utilization of calcium and phosphorus for bone mineralization may be independent of UVB and dietary vitamin D_3 if adequate dietary calcium is available. Allen described a similar apparent independence from dietary vitamin D_3 in Leopard Geckos (*Eublepharis macularius*; Allen 1989*b*) and Green Iguanas (*Iguana iguana*; Allen 1988).

Although there are no reports of detrimental effects from exposure to UVA emitted by blacklights, prolonged exposure to UVB from sunlamps can lead to "burns." UVB toxicity in the Side-blotched Lizard (*Uta stansburiana*) was associated with anorexia, decreased motor activity, and diminished response to environmental stimuli (for example, handling). The skin assumed an initial "smoky" or milky appearance, which gradually darkened as thickening of the keratin layer occurred. These responses were reversible if exposure ceased at this stage. The outer epidermal layer of the cornea of the parietal eye showed marked hyperkeratosis, but the underlying cornea, lens, and retina appeared histologically undamaged (W. H. Gehrmann unpubl. data). The thickened keratin layer may have served a protective function by attenuating the penetration of UVB (Tercafs 1963; Porter 1967; Nietzke 1990).

Summary

Perusal of the reproductive-husbandry literature indicates a wide range of tolerance for variations in light quality, intensity, and photoperiod among taxa and within taxa. In general however, an insufficiency of experimentally derived data does not permit the specification of optimal values for various features of light. Studies addressing the following questions would be valuable in elucidating the role of light in captive husbandry:

(1) Will light from full-spectrum lamps have the same biological effectiveness as natural light in two otherwise identical environments?

(2) To what extent can light quality from different lamps influence growth, reproduction, or other end-points in various species?

(3) How important is UVA in initiating and maintaining agonistic and reproductive behaviors?

(4) Can UVB irradiation substitute for dietary vitamin D_3 by stimulating the cutaneous synthesis of this vitamin?

(5) Given a choice of various lights (for example, visible, UVA, UVB, and IR) in different positions in an enclosure, will amphibians and reptiles select different types to bask under during the day and will a selection pattern be discernible?

(6) How important are low intensity "dawn-dusk" lights presented before and after the primary light sources are turned on or off?

(7) Can the spatial or temporal separation of light and heat sources in enclosures have detrimental effects on growth or other endpoints (see Sievert and Hutchison 1988, 1991)?

(8) Will specimens reared in a relatively simple light environment exhibit lower survivorship or fertility when released into a complex natural ecosystem compared to specimens raised in an identical environment illuminated with natural light (see Murphy and Chiszar 1989)?

Acknowledgments

I express my appreciation to the following persons for their helpful comments and encouragement: Edmund D. Brodie, Jr., Gary W. Ferguson, and James B. Murphy. Histopathological evaluation of tissues in the UVB burn study was performed by Fredric L. Frye. Support for this work was supplied in part by special funds from Tarrant County Junior College. I thank Patsy A. Hemmings for her patience and perseverance in processing this manuscript.

Literature Cited

Alberts, A. C. 1989. Ultraviolet visual sensitivity in desert iguanas: implications for pheromone detection. Anim. Behav., 38: 129–137.

Allen, M. E. 1988. The effect of three light treatments on growth in the green iguana *Iguana iguana*, p. 64. *In* Proc. Joint Conf. American Assoc. Wildlife Veterinarians and American Assoc. Zoo Veterinarians, Toronto, Canada.

—. 1989*a*. The effects of dietary calcium and vitamin D on intake, growth and bone development in young geckos, *Eublepharis macularius* and *Phelsuma madagascariensis*, p. 85–128. *In* M. E. Allen (ed.), Nutritional Aspects of Insectivory. Doctoral Dissertation, Michigan State University, East Lansing, Michigan.

—. 1989*b*. Dietary induction and prevention of osteodystrophy in an insectivorous reptile *Eublepharis macularius*: characterization by radiography and histopathology, p. 83. *In* Third Internationl Colloquium on the Pathology of Reptiles and Amphibians.

Baker J. 1990. Toad aggregations under street lamps. British Herpetol. Soc. Bull., 31: 26–27.

Blaustein, A. R., P. D. Hoffman, D. G. Hokit, J. M. Kiesecker, S. C. Walls, and J. B. Hays. 1994. UV repair and resistance to solar UV-B in amphibian eggs: a link to population declines? Proc. Natl. Acad. Sci. USA, 91: 1791–1795.

Cole, C. J., and C. R. Townsend. 1977. Parthenogenetic reptiles: new subjects for laboratory research. Experientia, 33: 285–289.

Cromer, A. H. 1977. Physics for the Life Sciences. McGraw-Hill, New York. xiv, 530 pages.

Evans, G. C. 1966. Model and measurement in the study of woodland light climates, p. 53–76. *In* R. Bainbridge, G. G. C. Evans, and O. Rackham (eds.), Light as an Ecological Factor. Blackwell Scientific Publ., Oxford.

Fleishman, L. J., E. R. Loew, and M. Leal. 1993. Ultraviolet vision in lizards. Nature, 365: 397.

Gehrmann, W. H. 1987. Ultraviolet irradiances of various lamps used in animal husbandry. Zoo Biol., 6: 117–127.

—. 1994. Spectral characteristics of lamps commonly used in herpetoculture. Vivarium, 5(5): 16–21, 29.

Gehrmann, W. H., G. W. Ferguson, T. W. Odom, D. T. Roberts, and W. J. Barcellona. 1991. Early growth and bone mineralization of the iquanid lizard *Sceloporus occidentalis* in captivity: is vitamin D_3 supplementation or ultraviolet B irradiation necessary? Zoo Biol., 10: 409–416.

Govardovskii, V. I., and L. V. Zueva. 1974. Spectral sensitivity of the frog eye in the ultraviolet and visible region. Vision Res., 14: 1317–1321.

Hailman, J. P., and R. G. Jaeger. 1974. Phototactic responses to spectrally dominant stimuli and use of colour vision by adult anuran amphibians. Anim. Behav., 22: 757–795.

Holick, M. F. 1985. The photobiology of vitamin D and its consequences for humans, p. 1–13. *In* R. J. Wurtman, M. J. Baum, and J. T. Potts (eds.), The Medical and Biological Effects of Light. Vol. 453. New York Acad. Sci., New York.

—. 1989. Phylogenetic and evolutionary aspects of vitamin D from phyto-plankton to humans, p. 7–43. *In* P. K. T. Pang, and M. P. Schreibman (eds.), Vertebrate Endocrinology: Fundamentals and Biomedical Implications. Vol. 3. Academic Press, New York.

Jaeger, R. G., and J. P. Hailman. 1973. Effects of intensity on the phototactic responses of adult anuran amphibians: a comparative survey. Zeitschr. Tierpsychol., 33: 352–407.

Jenison, G., and J. Nolte. 1980. An ultraviolet-sensitive mechanism in the reptilian parietal eye. Brain Res., 194: 506–510.

Kaufman, J. E., and J. F. Christensen (eds.). 1985. IES Lighting Ready Reference. Illum. Engineer. Soc. North America, New York. 168 pages.

Laszlo, J. 1969. Observations on two new artificial lights for reptile displays. Internatl. Zoo Yearb., 9: 12–13.

Licht, P. 1969. Illuminance threshold and spectral sensitivity of photo-sexual responses in the male lizard, *Anolis carolinensis*. Comp. Biochem. Physiol., 30: 233–246.

Logan, T. 1969. Experiments with gro-lux light and its effect on reptiles. Internatl. Zoo Yearb., 9: 9–11.

Mayhew, W. W. 1965. Growth response to photoperiodic stimulation in the lizard *Dipsosaurus dorsalis*. Comp. Biochem. Physiol., 14: 209–216.

McCrystal, M., and J. L. Behler. 1982. Husbandry and reproduction of captive giant *Ameiva* lizards. Internatl. Zoo Yearb., 22: 159–163.

McFarland, W. N., and F. W. Munz. 1975. The visible spectrum during twilight and its implications to vision, p. 249–270. *In* G. C. Evans, R. Bainbridge, and O. Rackham (eds.), Light as an Ecological Factor II. Blackwell Sci. Publ., Oxford.

Mehrtens, J. 1965. Leuchtstofflampen Gro Lux in der Terrarienkunde. Salamandra, 1: 26–27.

Moehn, L. D. 1974. The effect of quality of light on agonistic behavior of iquanid and agamid lizards. Jour. Herpetol., 8: 175–183.

—. 1976. The effect of sunlight on a despotism in the desert collared lizard, Crotaphytus insularis. Jour. Herpetol., 10: 259–261.

Moyle, M. 1990. Vitamin D and UV radiation: guidelines for the herpetoculturist, p. 61–70. *In* M. J. Uricheck (ed.), Proc. 13th Internatl. Herpetol. Sympos. Captive Propagation and Husbandry, Stanford, California.

Murphy, J. B., and D. Chiszar. 1989. Herpetological master planning for the 1990s. Internatl. Zoo Yearb., 28: 1–7.

Nietzke, G. 1990. Zur Durchlässigkeit von UV-Strahlen der Reptilien-Hornhaut (Ordnung Squamata). Salamandra, 26: 50–57.

Parrish, J. A., R. R. Anderson, F. Urbach, and D. Pitts. 1978. UVA. Plenum Press, New York. ix, 262 pages.

Phillips, J. A. 1985. A holistic view of reptile physiology, p. 25–38. *In* R. L. Gray (ed.), Captive Propagation and Husbandry of Reptiles and Amphibians. Northern California Herpetol. Soc./Bay Area Amphib. Reptile Soc., Davis, California.

Porter, W. P. 1967. Solar radiation through the living body walls of vertebrates with emphasis on desert reptiles. Ecol. Monogr., 37: 273–296.

Roberts, D. T., and W. H. Gehrmann. 1990. Light quality and growth in the bearded lizard *Amphibolurus*: a preliminary study. Bull. Chicago Herpetol. Soc., 25: 101–103.

Sievert, L. M., and V. H. Hutchison. 1988. Light versus heat: thermoregulatory behavior in a nocturnal lizard (*Gekko gecko*). Herpetologica, 44: 266–273.

—. 1991. The influence of photoperiod and position of a light source on behavioral thermoregulation in *Crotaphytus collaris* (Squamata: Iguanidae). Copeia, 1991: 105–110.

Spellerberg, I. F. 1974. Influence of photoperiod and light intensity on lizard voluntary temperatures. British Jour. Herpetol., 5: 412–420.

Tercafs, R. R. 1963. Transmission of ultra-violet, visible and infrared radiation through the keratinous layer of reptile skin. Ecology, 44: 214–218.

Thorington, L. 1985. Spectral irradiance, and temporal aspects of natural and artificial light, p. 28–54. *In* R. J. Wurtman, M. J. Baum, and J. T. Potts (eds.), The Medical and Biological Effects of Light. Vol. 453. New York Acad. Sci., New York.

Torelle, E. 1903. The response of the frog to light. Amer. Jour. Physiol., 9: 466–488.

Townsend, C. R. 1979. Establishment and maintenance of colonies of parthenogenetic whiptail lizards. Internatl. Zoo Yearb., 19: 80–84.

Townsend, C. R., and C. J. Cole. 1985. Additional notes on requirements of captive whiptail lizards (*Cnemidophorus*) with emphasis on ultraviolet radiation. Zoo Biol., 4: 49–55.

Note Added in Proof

While this paper was in press, two reports were published that further illuminate the importance of UVR to amphibians and reptiles. Fleishman et al. (1993) demonstrated UVA sensitivity of lateral eyes in several species of the lizard *Anolis*, and showed that UVA reflectance from dewlaps, used for communication in this genus, is correlated with UVA irradiance in the environment. Blaustein et al. (1994) reported that the differential resistance to detrimental UVB effects on hatching success of embryos in a number of amphibian species is correlated with the activity of an ultraviolet repair enzyme, photolyase.

Appendix

The following manufacturers can furnish lamp catalogs, spectral power distributions, and other technical information. In addition, general suppliers of light bulbs and tubes can often provide information for lamps produced by smaller companies.

Duro-Test Corporation
Customer Service
9 Law Drive
Fairfield, New Jersey 07004, USA
Telephone (800) 289–3876

General Electric Company
Lighting Information Center #4165
Nela Park
Cleveland, Ohio 44112, USA
Telephone (800) 327–7105

National Biological Corporation (UV lamps)
1532 Enterprise Parkway
Twinsburg, Ohio 44087, USA
Telephone (800) 338–5045

Philips Lighting Company
Technical Information Services
P. O. Box 6800
Somerset, New Jersey 08875–6800, USA
Telephone (800) 752–2852

Sylvania Lighting
Technical Information Services
GTE Products Corp., 100 Endicott Street
Danvers, Massachusetts 01923, USA
Telephone (800) 343–1807

❦

❦ Gehrmann, W. H. 1994. Light requirements of captive amphibians and reptiles, p. 53–59. *In* J. B. Murphy, K. Adler, and J. T. Collins (eds.), Captive Management and Conservation of Amphibians and Reptiles. Society for the Study of Amphibians and Reptiles, Ithaca (New York). Contributions to Herpetology, volume 11.

Chemoreception in the Feeding Behavior of Reptiles: Considerations for Maintenance and Management

Paul J. Weldon,*,** Béla J. Demeter,* Trooper Walsh,* and J. S. E. Kleister**

Introduction

A formidable body of literature has been built over the past few decades on the responses of reptiles to chemicals from prey, predators, and conspecifics (Halpern 1992). The importance of chemical cues demonstrated in these behavioral and ecological studies indicates the potential for applications from chemoreception research to the maintenance and management of reptiles.

In this chapter, we relate the results of studies on food-chemical perception in reptiles to methods of maintenance and management. In the following section, we describe for each major taxonomic group of reptiles the taxon-typical, experiential, and other factors that contribute to food-chemical responses—parameters of potential relevance to feeding captive animals. Next, we discuss how food chemicals have been used to monitor and manipulate captive and free-ranging reptiles. Finally, we provide a prospectus on reptilian chemoreception that outlines avenues of research from which practical benefits may be derived.

The extensive investigation of stimuli that elicit feeding behaviors in reptiles and the importance of captive diets in successful maintenance programs render food-chemical perception a propitious topic on which to focus when considering applied aspects of chemoreception research. We acknowledge, however, that vision, thermoreception, and other sensory modalities may also mediate feeding responses, depending upon the species, an individual's experience, and other factors (see Murphy and Campbell [1987] on feeding cues used by different snakes).

Responses to Food Chemicals

Crocodylia

Crocodilians typically submerge and wave their head from side to side with their mouth open when meat or meat drippings are introduced into their aquaria (Weldon et al. 1990). When juvenile American Alligators (*Alligator mississippiensis*) raised primarily on the meat of Nutria (*Myocastor coypus*) were presented with extracts from a variety of vertebrates and invertebrates, Nutria extract was most effective in eliciting foraging responses (Banta et al. 1992). These results are consistent with the hypothesis that American Alligators imprint to food chemicals, although further studies are needed to confirm this interpretation.

American Alligators presented with meat scents exhibit high rates of gular pumping, a form of "sniffing" in which the floor of the pharynx is lowered and raised to pulse air through the nasal cavity (Weldon et al. 1992). The scents of putrified meats elicited numerically more gular pumps than did fresh meats in several experiments, although no significant effects were detected.

Free-ranging crocodilians occasionally consume carrion and are known to locate it from considerable distances (Weldon and Ferguson 1993). Farm-reared Nile Crocodiles (*Crocodylus niloticus*), however, preferred fresh rather than thawed fish when presented with a choice of these foods (Morpurgo et al. 1991), indicating that even mild decomposition may render food less acceptable to them.

Observations of Saltwater Crocodiles (*C. porosus*) suggest that clutch-specific food preferences

---

*Department of Herpetology
National Zoological Park
Smithsonian Institution
Washington, D.C. 20008, USA

**Department of Biology
Texas A&M University
College Station, Texas 77843, USA

are displayed within the first month of life (Webb et al. 1990). Quantitative behavioral studies of neonatal subjects are needed to further investigate this phenomenon.

Rhyncocephalia

Tuatara (*Sphenodon* spp.), which consume a variety of vertebrates and invertebrates, have been shown to rely primarily on visual cues in hunting (Meyer-Rochow and Teh 1991). It has been hypothesized, however, that tuatara use chemoreception to avoid unpalatable prey, such as some beetles (Walls 1981).

Tuatara can use their tongue to secure prey, but they do not routinely tongue-flick to investigate their environment, as do squamates (J. C. Gillingham, pers. comm.). Thus, other behavioral measures may have to be scored to assess their interest in food chemicals.

Squamata

Food-chemical responses have been studied most extensively in squamates, in which tongue-flicking, a behavior that facilitates the delivery of odorants to the vomeronasal organ, and biting at cotton swabs laden with prey extracts (Figure 1) have been scored in behavioral tests (Cooper and Burghardt 1990). Snakes and lizards generally tongue-flick and attack more in response to extracts from prey that are typically consumed in nature rather than to extracts from non-prey items (Burghardt 1970; von Achen and Rakestraw 1984; Cooper 1990), although some exceptions do occur. Butler's Garter Snakes (*Thamnophis butleri*), for example, eat worms and leeches in nature, but in the laboratory they also eat fish and tongue-flick and attack extracts of amphibians and fishes (Burghardt 1969; Lyman 1990).

FIGURE 1. A young Common Kingsnake (*Lampropeltis getula*) bites the tip of a swab treated with a shed skin extract from a garter snake (*Thamnophis* sp.)(from Weldon and Schell 1984).

Some squamates exhibit high rates of tongue-flicking and side-to-side head movements after predatory strikes, a response called "strike-induced chemosensory searching" (Chiszar, Lee, et al. 1992; Burghardt and Chmura 1993). Rattlesnakes (*Crotalus* spp.) typically exhibit this behavior while trailing rodents, and have been shown to distinguish between the trails of envenomated versus non-envenomated prey (Chiszar, Lee, et al. 1992).

Species differences in the responses of unfed neonatal snakes to prey extracts are generally thought to reflect genetic differences in prey-chemical preferences. Inter- and intra-litter variation in prey-chemical responses, including behavioral polymorphism, also have been indicated (Burghardt 1975). Breeding experiments on the Wandering Garter Snake (*T. elegans vagrans)* suggest that some aspects of the prey-chemical response may be heritable (Arnold 1981), but much work remains to elucidate the genetic underpinnings of snake food preferences (Burghardt 1993).

Geographic variation in diet and chemosensory responses to prey has been documented in Garter Snakes (*Thamnophis* spp.; Burghardt 1970; Arnold 1980; Schwartz 1989). In California, for example, coastal populations of *T. elegans* eat mostly slugs, while inland snakes subsist on anurans and fishes (Arnold 1980). Unfed neonates prefer prey from their respective habitats and they exhibit higher tongue-flick/attack scores to extracts of prey from the appropriate habitat. In laboratory tests, inland snakes spent more time hunting for fish and were more successful at capturing them than were snakes from the coast (Drummond and Burghardt 1983); however, coastal snakes that had failed to forage for fish were induced to do so by extreme food deprivation and greater accessibility to cues from live prey (for example, by removing fish hiding shelters).

Ontogenetic variation in prey-chemical responses has been reported in the Plainbelly Water Snake (*Nerodia erythrogaster*; Mushinsky and Lotz 1980). Two-month-old subjects from groups reared on fish or frogs tongue-flicked more to fish extract, but snakes eight to nine months old responded most to frog chemicals. This shift in interest from fish to frog chemicals parallels a shift in the prey consumed by these snakes in nature.

The maternal diet of snakes has no apparent effect on the prey-chemical preferences of offspring (Burghardt 1971, 1977), and, in some cases at least, food-chemical preferences persist in subjects maintained on non-preferred diets. Force-feeding various subspecies of the Common Garter Snake (*T. sirtalis*) strained liver baby food for six months, for example, did not alter their relative interest in extracts from a variety of natural prey organisms (Burghardt and Hess 1968). Similarly, *T. sirtalis* that had been reared on fish attacked frog extract as readily as did frog-fed subjects (Arnold 1978). Tests of other colubrid snakes also suggest that maintenance on one food item does not alter prey-chemical preferences (Dunbar 1979) or impair the ability to identify alternative prey items (Williams and Brisbin 1978).

In other cases, feeding experience apparently does affect prey-chemical preferences. Neonatal *T. sirtalis*, for example, were screened for their initial tendencies to tongue-flick or attack several prey extracts (Fuchs and Burghardt 1971). Subjects were then fed either redworms or minnows for eight feedings before being switched to the alternate prey item. Snakes at the end of the first feeding period responded strongly to extracts of whichever prey they had first been fed, but their responses to the initially ingested items decreased after eating a different food. Similarly, Rat Snakes (*Elaphe obsoleta*) fed mice over an eight-month period showed enhanced responses to rat odors and diminished responses to those of domestic chickens (Loop 1970; see also Stimac et al. 1982 on cobras).

Even a single encounter with prey has been suggested to influence the feeding responses of snakes. *T. sirtalis* initially fed a live fish showed a greater tendency to accept dead, thawed fish than did subjects previously offered only thawed prey (Arnold 1978). Subjects were thought to have acquired from their first feeding experience a learned association between chemical cues and (visually perceived) prey movement that later disposed them to attack thawed prey in response to chemicals alone.

In addition to the effects of ingested foods, the chemosensory responses of snakes may be influenced by exposure to ambient food odors. Unfed neonates of the "prey generalist" *T. sirtalis* were exposed for a week to the odors of live fish or earthworms (Burghardt 1992, 1993). When tested later, subjects were less responsive to extracts from the items to which they had been exposed. The preferences of several "prey specialists"—*T. brachystoma, T. melanogaster,* and *T. sauritus*—however, appeared unaffected by exposure to these scents. Neutral odors repeatedly paired with food reward may also influence behavior, as reflected by the tendencies of some garter snakes (*T. radix* and *T. sirtalis*) to enter lemon- or amyl acetate–scented chambers after routinely receiving food in them (Begun et al. 1988).

Negative experiences may cause snakes to avoid certain prey. Adult *T. sirtalis* accustomed to eating fish were fed earthworms and were then injected with saline or lithium chloride, a toxic compound often used to induce food aversions (Burghardt et al. 1973). Lithium chloride–injected subjects exhibited longer attack-latencies and accepted fewer earthworms than did saline-injected subjects. Saline-treated subjects, on the other hand, continued to accept earthworms, indicating that stress associated with injection had no negative effects (G. M. Burghardt, pers. comm.).

Many of the studies cited above involve tests with extracts of thawed prey. Studies on the Mexican Garter Snake (*T. melanogaster*) indicate that thawed food is less attractive than fresh food (Marcias Garcia and Drummond 1988). This species prefers to eat fish freshly killed by freezing rather than fish frozen and thawed. These results suggest that decomposition may render fish less acceptable to snakes.

Testudines

Turtles use olfaction in both aquatic and aerial environments (Manton 1979). Several accounts suggest that turtles use chemoreception to locate food underwater and that they employ gular pumping to enhance olfaction.

Hatchling turtles of several species have been examined for their acquisition and retention of food preferences. Snapping Turtles (*Chelydra serpentina*) fed horsemeat, guppies, or redworms once a day for 12 days were offered a different food on each of 12 subsequent days (Burghardt and Hess 1966). Subjects preferred the food on which they initially had fed, even after eating a different food item. One feeding was sufficient to establish a preference (Burghardt 1967), but since not all foods were consumed with the same alacrity, it was concluded that the first feeding experience interacts with natural preferences to influence feeding behavior. Loggerheads (*Caretta caretta*) in a similar experiment exhibited less fidelity to their initial food (Grassman and Owens 1984). Hatchlings fed shrimp, flounder, or commercial pellets for 14 days were switched to a different diet for 14 more days. Subjects exhibited strong preferences for their initial foods after their first feeding period, but not at the end of the second period.

An experiment on Sliders (*Trachemys scripta*) provides results that suggest a reconciliation of the apparently discrepant trends in the studies outlined above (Mahmoud and Lavenda 1969). Subjects were offered three items and were tested after a period of feeding on each. A significant preference was exhibited for the initial foods after the first two feedings, but it was not detected after the third feeding. These results indicate the transient nature of food preferences in *T. scripta*, and they suggest, more generally, that longer monitoring periods are needed to assess the effects of early feeding experiences in turtles.

Behavioral Monitoring and Manipulation

Screening Potential Captives

Individual differences often occur in the willingness of reptiles to feed in captivity. Behavioral studies also indicate variability in their chemoinvestigatory responses to food. Sibling snakes, for example, may differ in their propensity to tongue-flick to prey chemicals, as described above. We also have observed individual variability in the exhibition of gular pumping by juvenile American Alligators in response to distilled water and various meat scents (Figure 2).

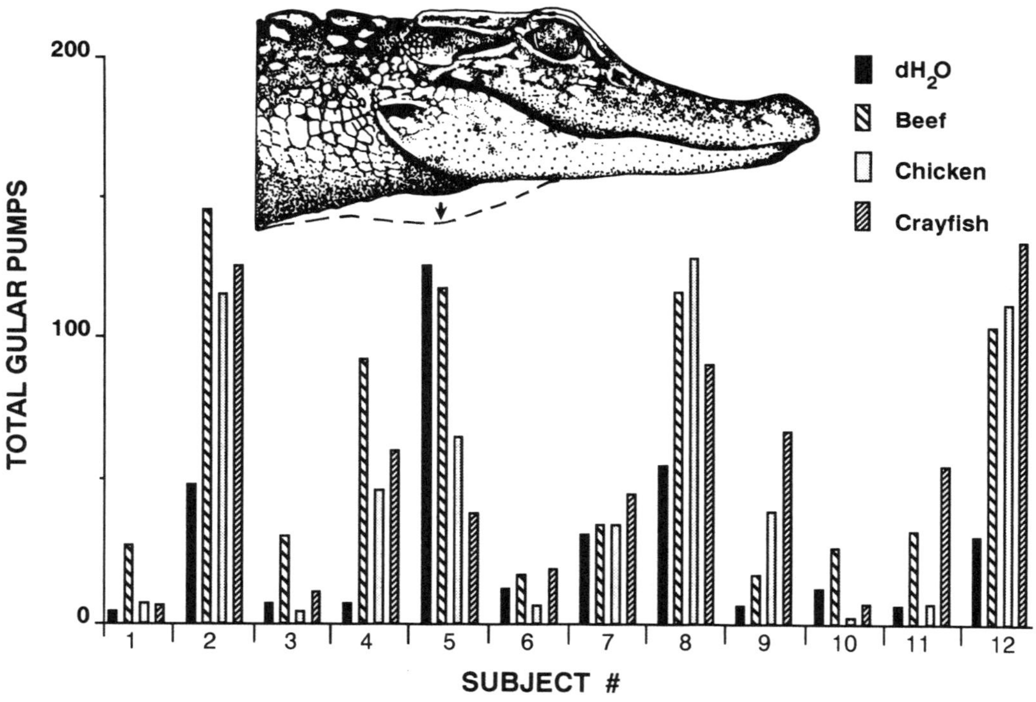

FIGURE 2. Total number of gular pumps in a sample of twelve juvenile American Alligators (*Alligator mississippiensis*) in an olfactometer during 10 minutes of exposure to distilled water (dH_2O) and the scents of beef, chicken, and crayfish, showing individual variation in the display of this behavior. Subjects were allowed to acclimate to an airstream passed over distilled water before scoring was begun. Detailed methods given in Weldon et al. (1992).

The uncertainty confronting collectors of reptiles faced with selecting viable captives may be mitigated by screening prospective specimens for their willingness to feed or initiate foraging behaviors to prey or prey extracts. Although the reliability of behavioral screening may vary, since it depends upon a subject's vulnerability to captive stress, skin-shedding condition, and other factors, it may be useful in some cases.

In one case, freshly collected Yellowbelly Sea Snakes (*Pelamis platurus*) were selected for zoological display on the basis of their

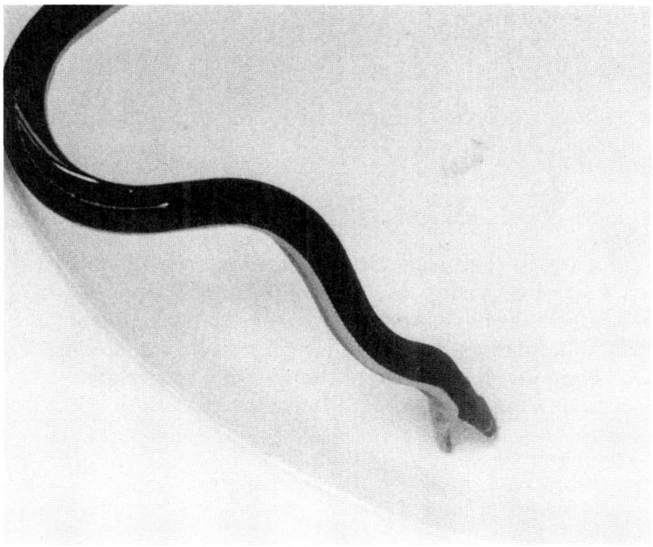

FIGURE 3. A Yellowbelly Sea Snake (*Pelamis platurus*) submerges and bites the floor of the bucket filled with seawater after an aqueous rinse of thawed fish was poured into it.

responses to food extracts (P. Freed and P. J. Weldon, unpubl. observ.). This snake captures small fishes near the water surface by rapidly swimming backwards and snapping laterally at them. Strips of thawed fish dropped into an aquarium, on the other hand, are seized when snakes submerge and wave their head from side to side with their mouth open (Figure 3). Open-mouth underwater foraging apparently is elicited by fish chemicals since snakes typically exhibit this behavior after aqueous rinses of thawed minced fish have been poured into aquaria with them, but not when plain seawater is introduced.

More than 30 immature Yellowbelly Sea Snakes (total lengths ranging from 295 to 360 mm) were netted during late November on the water surface in the Gulf of Chiriquí, Panama, and were held for several days in an aquarium at the Smithsonian Tropical Research Institute. An aqueous rinse of thawed fish was filtered through a paper towel and poured into the aquarium with the snakes. Eight individuals of those exhibiting open-mouth underwater foraging were transported to the Houston Zoological Gardens, Texas. All snakes readily fed on live goldfish and did so for years. Some of these snakes were maintained for more than five years, setting a longevity record for this species in captivity.

The successful maintenance of Yellowbelly Sea Snakes in this case, we suspect, was facilitated by selecting captives on the basis of their response to fish chemicals. Controlled studies comparing the captive success of subjects screened for food chemical responses are needed.

Feeding on Novel Foods

In nature, snakes and some other reptiles often restrict their diets to one or a few food items. These natural foods are not always available for captive specimens, thus prompting caretakers to seek alternative staple.

A variety of methods have been used to induce reptiles to eat new and even unnatural foods. King Cobras (*Ophiophagus hannah*), for example, which eat snakes in the wild, were coerced into eating skinned *Anguilla anguilla* by tying the eels onto the ends of prey snakes and allowing the snakes to be consumed first (Petzold 1976). After several such feedings, cobras accepted skinned eels alone. We have observed that King Cobras also eat rodents that have been stuffed into the shed skins of other snakes.

Another method of inducing captive subjects to feed involves adding small quantities of the new food item to standard rations. Snedigar (1963), for example, stated that garter snakes will accept raw beef if it is mixed with earthworms, which are then gradually eliminated over a number of meals. Likewise, farm-reared American Alligators may be induced to accept novel food by mixing approximately 15% of the new food with standard rations (T. Joanen, pers. comm.). The proportion of new to old food is increased in successive feedings over seven to ten days, thus feeding (and growth) is not interrupted during the transition from one food item to another.

Herpetologists have long known that captive subjects may be enticed to eat novel foods treated with substances from routine prey, a procedure referred to as "scenting" (Mills 1990). Scenting has been used most routinely in feeding snakes, but it may also be used with other taxa. Cuban Crocodiles (*Crocodylus rhombifer*), for example, were induced to eat rats soaked in canned chicken soup (J. Marlin and R. A. Odum, pers. comm.). Possible scenting sources for various snake species, based on recommendations of zoo herpetologists, are listed in Table

1. The reported use of integumental and internal tissues (Chiszar, Fox, and Smith 1992; Chiszar, Dunn, and Smith 1993; Chiszar, Hobika, and Smith 1993) and the efficacy of routine as well as atypical prey, should prompt future investigators to consider a wide range of materials, including compounds identified in food chemistry studies of fish, chicken, and other meats, in campaigns to identify new scenting materials. Experimentation with different methods of food preparation—boiling, freezing and

TABLE 1. Snakes (listed alphabetically) and scenting materials from which chemicals eliciting feeding responses may be obtained. Adult or newborn laboratory mice, often after having been washed with surgical soap, are the prey to which scenting materials have routinely been applied. The scenting materials indicated here have not necessarily been tested experimentally, thus we suspend judgment on their efficacy. Individuals providing personal communications here (indicated by the superscript numbers in the legend below) do not in all cases claim originality for the use of the scenting materials.

Snake species or feeding type	Scenting materials
Atheris chloroechis and *Bothriechis schlegelii*[1]	Chirping Frog (*Syrrhophus cystignathoides*) skin
Atheris superciliaris[2], *Bitis cornuta*, *Bothriechis schlegelii*, and other frog-eating viperids[3]	Treefrog (*Hyla*) skin
Bitis spp.[1] and *Scaphiodontophis annulatus*[4]	Skink (*Scincella* and *Eumeces*) blood
Boiga cynodon, *B. dendrophila*[5], and *Candoia carinata*[2,4]	Frog (*Hyla* and *Rana*) skin or eviscerated geckos (*Hemidactylus* or *Gehyra*) or their brain tissue
Causus maculatus[1]	Toad (*Bufo*) skin
Causus resimus[6]	Boiled, blended Gulf Coast Toad (*Bufo valliceps*)
Chondropython viridis[3]	Gecko (*Hemidactylus*) skin
Chondropython viridis[7], *Epicrates* spp.[8], *Liopholdophis lateralis*, *Mimophis mahfalensis*, and *Tropidophis feicki*[6]	Anole (*Anolis*) skin
Crotalus pricei[1]	Fence lizard (*Sceloporus*) blood
Farancia abacura[5]	Amphiuma (*Amphiuma*) skin
Heterodon platirhinos[2]	Boiled, blended toads (*Bufo*)
Lampropeltis getula[9]	Blended spiny lizards (*Sceloporus*)
Lampropeltis mexicana, *L. triangulum*, and *Trimorphodon* spp.[2,3]	Lizard (*Sceloporus* or *Uta*) skin or feces
Lampropeltis mexicana, *L. triangulum*, and other rodent-eating colubrids[4]; *Liasis childreni*[9]	Mouse (*Mus*) brain tissue
Lioheterodon madagascariensis[5]	Northern Leopard Frog (*Rana pipiens*) skin
Micrurus fulvius[1,2]	Skink (*Scincella*) or thamnophine snake feces or blood
Micrurus surinamensis[1]	Red Salamander (*Pseudotriton ruber*) skin
Naja haje and *Ophiophagus hannah*[3,8]	Boiled, blended snakes
Porthidium godmani[2]	House Cricket (*Acheta domestica*) integument
Python boeleni[7,8]	Boiled, canned chicken soup
Python regius[8]	Domestic Chicken (*Gallus gallus*) skin
Thamnophis sirtalis tetrataenia[1]	Goldfish (*Carassius auratus*) skin

[1]P. Freed (Houston Zoological Gardens, Texas)
[2]C. Garrett, A. Mitchell, J. B. Murphy, and D. Roberts (Dallas Zoo, Texas)
[3]D. A. Blody and R. Hudson (Fort Worth Zoological Park, Texas)
[4]L. Porras (Zooherp, Sandy, Utah)
[5]M. Goode (Columbus Zoological Gardens, Ohio)
[6]A. Kardon and E. Holmback (San Antonio Zoological Gardens and Aquarium, Texas)
[7]D. Barker and T. Miller (Vida Preciosa, Inc., Boerne, Texas)
[8]J. Marlin and R. A. Odum (Toledo Zoological Gardens, Ohio)
[9]W. F. Holmstrom and R. Zerilli (New York Zoological Park, Bronx, New York)

thawing, and allowing putrification—also is needed. The identification of potent scenting sources could provide additives to enhance the acceptability of artificial diets.

Chemical Attractants in the Field

Traps baited with food have traditionally been used to capture game and pests. Trapping campaigns directed at free-ranging reptiles have been used to collect specimens (Plummer 1979), estimate population sizes (Lagler 1943*a*, 1943*b*), and capture nuisance animals (Walsh 1987).

In field studies of the Komodo Monitor (*Varanus komodoensis*), carrion was used to attract free-ranging subjects for observation and capture (Auffenberg 1981). These lizards reportedly traveled distances of up to 11 km to decomposed mammalian carcasses. Komodo Monitors correctly followed the trails of putrified goat carcasses that were dragged along the ground, but they failed to orient to directional cues from freshly killed goats.

Intensive trapping efforts for population monitoring and control have been directed at two nuisance snakes, the Habu (*Trimeresurus flavoviridis*) and the Brown Tree Snake (*Boiga irregularis*). The Habu is a large pit viper known to linger near and enter human dwellings on the Amami Islands of southern Japan. The Brown Tree Snake is an arboreal, rear-fanged colubrid accidentally introduced from islands near New Guinea onto the island of Guam where it has eliminated bird populations and threatens other native and domestic animals, causes power outages (by entering and short-circuiting electrical transformers), and inflicting venomous bites on humans, especially infants.

In field tests to capture Habu, traps were baited with live rodents or rat feces (Hayashi et al. 1979). When using live bait, the Black Rat (*Rattus rattus*), which is eaten by free-ranging snakes, was most effective, followed by the laboratory rat and mouse. Traps containing rat feces failed to attract free-ranging Habu (Hayashi et al. 1979), but those baited with rat urine lured snakes that were confined in a semi-natural enclosure (Kihara, Yamashita, and Tanaka 1979; Kihara, Hayashi, et al. 1979). Measurements of heart rates, on the other hand, failed to indicate that snakes respond to whole mice or their urine (Fukada et al. 1979); these negative results underscore the importance of using behavioral tests to assess the efficacy of chemical lures.

Initial field experiments on the Brown Tree Snake indicated that it is attracted to traps baited with the bedding materials (containing feces, feathers, and cloacal secretions) of domestic quail and chicken (Fritts et al. 1989). In a subsequent study, live geckos (*Hemidactylus frenatus* or *Lepidodactylus lugubris*) or a mixture of chicken feces and feathers were used as bait (Rodda et al. 1992). Half of the traps were equipped with a 5-m long rope soaked in chicken feces that served as a potential guide to the trap entrance. Geckos were more effective at luring snakes than were chicken-derived materials, suggesting that visual stimuli from live prey are more effective than chemicals alone. Odiferous guide ropes appeared ineffective. More recent studies suggest that the scent of live mice may attract Brown Tree Snakes (G. H. Rodda, pers. comm.).

Further studies are needed on the use of chemical lures to trap reptiles. Since different species may be attracted to different foods or foods in different states of decomposition (Lagler 1943*b*; Ernst 1965; Walsh 1987), a variety of materials should be screened for activity. Even unorthodox materials may be effective, as with Komodo Monitors being attracted to shoe polish (Auffenberg 1981). The identification of particularly attractive materials may lead to the development of potent synthetic lures.

Summary and Prospectus

Experimental studies demonstrate the importance of chemical cues in food recognition by reptiles, primarily snakes. Quantitative investigations are needed into the role of chemoreception in the feeding behavior of other taxa, including amphisbaenians, tuatara, tortoises, and herbivorous reptiles in general (Cooper and Alberts 1991). This research should be directed at elucidating congenital food preferences; the capacities for imprinting and learning in food recognition; and inter-litter, ontogenetic, and other sources of behavioral variation to food chemicals. In addition to measuring chemoinvestigatory responses, such as tongue-flicking and gular pumping, the propensity of subjects to consume foods should be assessed.

A number of factors governing the feeding responses of reptiles have been demonstrated in experimental studies, some of which provide results that bear on maintenance and management practices. For example, demonstrations of the possible effects of early feeding experiences on food-chemical responses should be borne in mind before captive neonates are offered foods other than those intended for their long-term maintenance. The expression of heightened interest in chemicals from locally abundant prey by wild-caught snakes (Gove and Burghardt 1975) suggests that familiar food items could be preferred and should be proffered as a captive staple. Conversely, reptiles propagated and reared for release may ultimately fare best if offered foods in captivity that they are likely to encounter in nature.

We have described here several ways in which food chemicals have been used to monitor or manipulate captive or free-ranging reptiles. Research is needed to refine these applied techniques and define the limitations of their use. Which behavioral responses to food chemicals should be examined to screen hopeful captives of different taxa? What prey species and tissues bear palatable or attractive chemicals? How can these substances be obtained and stored? What baits, trap designs, and strategies of trap placement will be most effective to lure free-ranging reptiles? Zoo, academic, and conservation-oriented herpetologists may benefit by addressing these questions.

Acknowledgments

D. Barker, D. A. Blody, G. M. Burghardt, W. Card, D. Chiszar, W. E. Cooper, Jr., A. Cree, D. Duvall, P. Freed, C. Garrett, J. C. Gillingham, M. Goode, S. Gotte, E. Holmback, W. F. Holmstrom, R. Hudson, T. Joanen, A. Kardon, J. Marlin, T. Miller, A. Mitchell, B. Morpurgo, J. B. Murphy, R. A. Odum, D. W. Owens, L. Porras, F. H. Pough, D. Roberts, G. H. Rodda, G. J. W. Webb, and R. Zerilli provided comments on the manuscript or valuable discussions. G. Brandy, J. Christy, P. Freed, I. Rubinoff, O. Vallarino, A. Velarde, and D. West permitted access to or provided information on Yellowbelly Sea Snakes. M. Allen and A. Wynn helped prepare the manuscript. T. Leto and J. Westhoff prepared Figure 2. R. Kuhse translated some important references. This paper was written while Paul Weldon was supported by the National Geographic Society and the Smithsonian Institution.

References

Arnold, S. J. 1978. Some effects of early feeding experience on feeding responses in the common garter snake, *Thamnophis sirtalis*. Anim. Behav., 26: 455–462.

—. 1980. The microevolution of feeding behavior, p. 409–453. *In* A. C. Kamil and T. D. Sargent (eds.), Foraging Behavior: Ecological, Ethological and Psychological Approaches. Garland STPM Press, New York.

—. 1981. Behavioral variation in natural populations. II. The inheritance of a feeding response in crosses between geographic races of the garter snake, *Thamnophis elegans*. Evolution, 35: 510–515.

Auffenberg, W. 1981. The Behavioral Ecology of the Komodo Monitor. Univ. Florida Press, Gainesville. 406 pages.

Banta, M. R., T. Joanen, and P. J. Weldon. 1992. Foraging responses by the American alligator to meat extracts, p. 413–417. *In* R. L. Doty and D. Müller-Schwarze (eds.), Chemical Signals in Vertebrates, volume 6. Plenum Press, New York.

Begun, D., J. L. Kubie, M. P. O'Keefe, and M. Halpern. 1988. Conditioned discrimination of airborne odorants by garter snakes (*Thamnophis radix* and *T. sirtalis sirtalis*). Jour. Comp. Psych., 102: 35–43.

Burghardt, G. M. 1967. The primacy effect of the first feeding experience in the snapping turtle. Psychon. Sci., 7: 383–384.

—. 1969. Comparative prey-attack studies in newborn snakes of the genus *Thamnophis*. Behaviour, 33: 77–114.

—. 1970. Chemical perception in reptiles, p. 241–308. *In* J. W. Johnston, Jr., D. G. Moulton, and A. Turk (eds.), Communication by Chemical Signals. Appleton-Century-Crofts, New York.

—. 1971. Chemical-cue preferences of newborn snakes: influence of prenatal maternal experience. Science, 171: 921–923.

—. 1975. Chemical prey preference polymorphism in newborn garter snakes *Thamnophis sirtalis*. Behaviour, 52: 202–225.

—. 1977. The ontogeny, evolution, and stimulus control of feeding in humans and reptiles, p. 253–275. *In* M. Kare and O. Moller (eds.), The Chemical Senses and Nutrition. Academic Press, New York.

—. 1992. Prior exposure to prey cues influences chemical prey preference and prey choice in neonatal garter snakes. Anim. Behav., 44: 787–789.

—. 1993. The comparative imperative: genetics and ontogeny of chemoreceptive prey responses in natricine snakes. Brain, Behav. Evol., 41: 138–146.

Burghardt, G. M., and P. Chmura. 1993. Strike-induced chemosensory searching by ingestively naive garter snakes, *Thamnophis sirtalis*. Jour. Comp. Psych., 107: 116–121.

Burghardt, G. M., and E. H. Hess. 1966. Food imprinting in the snapping turtle, *Chelydra serpentina*. Science, 151: 108–109.

—. 1968. Factors influencing the chemical release of prey attack in newborn snakes. Jour. Comp. Physiol. Psychol., 66: 289–295.

Burghardt, G. M., H. C. Wilcoxon, and J. A. Czaplicki. 1973. Conditioning in garter snakes: aversion to palatable prey induced by delayed illness. Anim. Learn. Behav., 1: 317–320.

Chiszar, D., T. M. Dunn, and H. M. Smith. 1993. Response of brown tree snakes (*Boiga irregularis*) to human blood. Jour. Chem. Ecol., 19: 91–96.

Chiszar, D., K. Fox, and H. M. Smith. 1992. Stimulus control of predatory behavior in the brown tree snake (*Boiga irregularis*) IV. Effect of mammalian blood. Behav. Neural Biol., 57: 167–169.

Chiszar, D., G. Hobika, and H. M. Smith. 1993. Prairie rattlesnakes (*Crotalus viridis*) respond to rodent blood with chemosensory searching. Brain, Behav., Evol. 41: 229–233.

Chiszar, D., R. K. Lee, C. W. Radcliffe, and H. M. Smith. 1992. Searching behaviors by rattlesnakes following predatory strikes, p. 369–382. *In* J. A. Campbell and E. D. Brodie, Jr. (eds.), Biology of the Pitvipers. Selva Press, Tyler, Texas.

Cooper, W. E., Jr. 1990. Prey odour discrimination by lizards and snakes, p. 533–538. *In* D. W. Macdonald, D. Müller-Schwarze, and S. Natynczuk (eds.), Chemical Signals in Vertebrates, volume 5. Oxford Univ. Press, Oxford.

Cooper, W. E., Jr., and A. C. Alberts. 1991. Tongue-flicking and biting in response to chemical food stimuli by an iguanid lizard (*Dipsosaurus dorsalis*) having sealed vomeronasal ducts: vomerolfaction may mediate these responses. Jour. Chem. Ecol., 17: 135–146.

Cooper, W. E., Jr., and G. M. Burghardt. 1990. A comparative analysis of scoring methods for chemical discrimination of prey by squamate reptiles. Jour. Chem. Ecol., 16: 45–65.

Drummond, H., and G. M. Burghardt. 1983. Geographic variation in the foraging behavior of the garter snake, *Thamnophis elegans*. Behav. Ecol. Sociobiol., 12: 43–48.

Dunbar, G. L. 1979. Effects of early feeding experience on chemical preference of the northern water snake, *Natrix s. sipedon* (Reptilia, Serpentes, Colubridae). Jour. Herpetol., 13: 165–169.

Ernst, C. H. 1965. Bait preferences of some freshwater turtles. Jour. Ohio Herpetol. Soc., 5: 53.

Fritts, T. H., N. J. Scott, Jr., and B. E. Smith. 1989. Trapping *Boiga irregularis* on Guam using bird odors. Jour. Herpetol., 23: 189–192.

Fuchs, J. L., and G. M. Burghardt. 1971. Effects of early feeding experience on the responses of garter snakes to food chemicals. Learn. Motiv., 2: 271–279.

Fukada, H., H. Kihara, and Y. Hayashi. 1979. Studies on attractants and repellents to habu using electrocardiogram. The Snake, 11: 16–19.

Gove, D., and G. M. Burghardt. 1975. Responses of ecologically dissimilar populations of the water snake *Natrix s. sipedon* to chemical cues from prey. Jour. Chem. Ecol., 1: 25–40.

Grassman, M. A., and D. W. Owens. 1984. Development and extinction of food preferences in the loggerhead sea turtle, *Caretta caretta*. Copeia, 1984: 965–969.

Halpern, M. 1992. Nasal chemical senses in reptiles: structure and function, p. 423–523 *In* C. Gans and D. Crews (eds.), Biology of the Reptilia, Vol. 18. Univ. Chicago Press, Chicago and London.

Hayashi, Y., H. Kihara, H. Tanaka, Y. Noboru, H. Yamashita, and T. Minami. 1979. Studies on attractancy of habu (*Trimeresurus flavoviridis*) in the field of Tokunoshima Islands. The Snake, 11: 45–53.

Kihara, H., Y. Hayashi, Y. Wada, H. Yamashita, and Y. Noboru. 1979. Studies on assay methods of attractants to habu. 2. Assay methods in the enclosure for habu. The Snake, 11: 54–58.

Kihara, H., H. Yamashita, and H. Tanaka. 1979. The development of assay methods of attractants to habu. 1. The assay method in a laboratory. The Snake, 11: 11–15.

Lagler, K. F. 1943*a*. Food habits and economic relations of the turtles of Michigan with special reference to fish management. Amer. Midl. Nat., 29: 257–312.

—. 1943*b*. Methods of collecting freshwater turtles. Copeia, 1943: 21–25.

Loop, M. S. 1970. The effects of feeding experience on the response to prey-object extracts in rat snakes. Psychon. Sci., 21: 189–190.

Lyman, L. P. 1990. The Effects of Dietary and Social Experience on the Development of Behavior in Butler's Garter Snake, *Thamnophis butleri*. Master's Thesis, Univ. Tennessee, Knoxville. 178 pages.

Mahmoud, I. Y., and N. Lavenda. 1969. Establishment and eradication of food preferences in red-eared turtles. Copeia, 1969: 298–300.

Manton, M. L. 1979. Olfaction and behavior, p. 289–301. *In* M. Harless and H. Morlock (eds.), Turtles: Perspectives and Research. John Wiley and Sons, New York.

Marcias Garcia, C., and H. Drummond. 1988. The use of frozen fish to test chemoreceptive preferences of garter snakes. Copeia, 1988: 785–787.

Meyer-Rochow, V. B., and K. L. Teh. 1991. Visual predation by tuatara (*Sphenodon punctatus*) on the beach beetle (*Chaerodes trachyscelides*) as a selective force in the production of distinct colour morphs. Tuatara, 13: 1–8.

Mills, T. 1990. To scent or not to scent (techniques for feeding baby snakes). The Vivarium, 2: 8–10.

Morpurgo, B., G. Gvaryahu, and B. Robinzon. 1991. Food preference, fish attractability and behavior manifested toward new feed in young Nile crocodiles, *Crocodylus niloticus*. Physiol. Behav., 50: 1–4.

Murphy, J. B., and J. A. Campbell. 1987. Captive maintenance, p. 165–181. *In* R. A. Seigel, J. T. Collins, and S. S. Novak (eds.), Snakes: Ecology and Evolutionary Biology. McGraw-Hill, New York.

Mushinsky, H. R., and K. H. Lotz. 1980. Chemoreceptive responses of two sympatric water snakes to extracts of commonly ingested prey species: ontogenetic and ecological considerations. Jour. Chem. Ecol., 6: 523–535.

Petzold, H.-G. 1976. Bemerkungen zur Fütterungstechnik bei nahrungsspezialisierten Giftnattern und einige Angaben zur Haltungsdauer von Elapiden im Tierpark Berlin. Zool. Garten, new ser., 46: 9–23.

Plummer, M. V. 1979. Collecting and marking, p. 45–60. *In* M. Harless and H. Morlock (eds.), Turtles: Perspectives and Research. John Wiley and Sons, New York.

Rodda, G. H., R. J. Rondeau, T. H. Fritts, and O. E. Maughan. 1992. Trapping the arboreal snake *Boiga irregularis*. Amphibia-Reptilia, 13: 47–56.

Schwartz, J. M. 1989. Multiple Paternity and Offspring Variability in Wild Populations of the Garter Snake *Thamnophis sirtalis*. Doctoral Dissertation, Univ. Tennessee, Knoxville. 188 pages.

Snedigar, R. 1963. Our Small Native Animals: Their Habits and Care. Dover, New York. 248 pages.

Stimac, K., C. W. Radcliffe, and D. Chiszar. 1982. Prey recognition learning by red spitting cobras, *Naja mossambica pallida*. Bull. Psychon. Soc., 19: 187–188.

von Achen, P. H., and J. L. Rakestraw. 1984. The role of chemoreception in the prey selection of neonate reptiles, p. 163–172. *In* R. A. Seigel, L. E. Hunt, J. L. Knight, L. Malaret, and N. L. Zuschlag (eds.), Vertebrate Ecology and Systematics—A Tribute to Henry S. Fitch. Univ. Kansas Mus. Nat. Hist., Spec. Publ. 10: 1–278.

Walls, G. Y. 1981. Feeding ecology of the tuatara (*Sphenodon punctatus*) on Stephens Island, Cook Strait. New Zealand Jour. Ecol., 4: 89–97.

Walsh, B. 1987. Crocodile capture methods used in the Northern Territory of Australia, p. 249–252. *In* G. J. W. Webb, S. C. Manolis, and P. J. Whitehead (eds.), Wildlife Management: Crocodiles and Alligators. Surrey Beatty and Sons Pty. Limited, Chipping Norton, New South Wales, Australia.

Webb, G. J. W., S. C. Manolis, and H. Cooper–Preston. 1990. Crocodile management and research in the Northern Territory: 1988–90, p. 254–273. *In* 10th Working Meeting of the International Union for the Conservation of Nature and Natural Resources Species, Survival Commission, Crocodile Specialist Group. IUCN, Gland, Switzerland.

Weldon, P. J., W. G. Brinkmeier, and H. Fortunato. 1992. Gular pumping responses by immature American alligators (*Alligator mississippiensis*) to meat scents. Chem. Senses, 17: 79–83.

Weldon, P. J., and M. W. J. Ferguson. 1993. Chemoreception in crocodilians: anatomy, natural history, and empirical results. Brain, Behav. Evol., 41: 239–245.

Weldon, P. J., and F. M. Schell. 1984. Responses by king snakes (*Lampropeltis getulus*) to chemicals from colubrid and crotaline snakes. Jour. Chem. Ecol., 10: 1509–1520.

Weldon, P. J., D. J. Swenson, J. K. Olson, and W. G. Brinkmeier. 1990. The American alligator detects food chemicals in aquatic and terrestrial environments. Ethology, 85: 191–198.

Williams, P. R., Jr., and I. L. Brisbin, Jr. 1978. Responses of captive-reared eastern kingsnakes (*Lampropeltis getulus*) to several prey odor stimuli. Herpetologica, 34: 79–83.

❦ Weldon, P. J., B. J. Demeter, T. Walsh, and J. S. E. Kleister. 1994. Chemoreception in the feeding behavior of reptiles: considerations for maintenance and management, p. 61–70. *In* J. B. Murphy, K. Adler, and J. T. Collins (eds.), Captive Management and Conservation of Amphibians and Reptiles. Society for the Study of Amphibians and Reptiles, Ithaca (New York). Contributions to Herpetology, volume 11.

THE NUTRITION OF CARNIVOROUS REPTILES

MARY E. ALLEN* AND OLAV T. OFTEDAL*

Introduction

IN NATURE, ANIMALS HAVE EVOLVED FEEDING habits that presumably allow energy and nutrient requirements to be met, given adequate food supplies. Choice of individual foods will depend both upon their availability and the presence of physical, chemical, and other cues that trigger feeding responses (see Weldon et al., this volume, page 61, for discussion of chemical cues). Animals consuming a diversity of foods may be able to obtain a balance of nutrients even if the individual food items are deficient in a particular amino acid, mineral, or vitamin. In contrast, captive animals are usually offered fixed diets consisting of few individual foods. If these foods are nutritionally incomplete, nutrient deficiencies or toxicities may result, compromising animal health and reproduction.

Our understanding of nutritionally balanced diets is based primarily on research on the dietary requirements of a variety of domestic and laboratory mammals, birds, and fish. At the cellular level, nutrient needs appear to be fairly similar across diverse taxa and diets. This is a vital concept, because it allows extrapolation of general principles of nutrition from one species or taxonomic group to another. At the whole-animal level, however, there may be large interspecific differences in nutrient requirements due to differences in digestive anatomy, enzymatic machinery, intermediary metabolism, excretory pathways, patterns of tissue growth, reproductive investment, and other factors. Given the limited amount of research on the nutrition of reptiles, it is not possible to define their requirements with much accuracy. Thus, in the present paper we refer to research results on other taxa to provide practical estimates of reptilian requirements and to identify areas in which nutritional problems may arise due to management practices in zoos or private collections.

In the final analysis, the goal of any feeding program is optimal long-term performance, as measured by growth, reproduction, morbidity, and mortality. In domestic animal agriculture, nutrition has been shown to be an important factor affecting animal performance, and, as a consequence, much effort has been devoted to elucidating nutritional needs. A similar awareness is growing among professionals dedicated to the care and breeding of exotic species, including reptiles. We seek to promote greater awareness of the importance of the nutritional requirements of reptiles and to encourage further research in this area.

We also hope that herpetologists will recognize that studies conducted with animals that are nutritionally compromised may yield misleading results. For example, studies in which turtles have predominantly been fed fish, or in which lizards have predominantly been fed crickets, should be considered suspect unless it can be demonstrated that supplements provided adequate vitamin or mineral levels to avoid deficiencies (or, indeed, toxicities). Thus, it is incumbent upon scientific reviewers and journal editors to require that adequate dietary information be presented in scientific studies on captive reptiles, and that potentially inadequate diets be identified as such. Unfortunately, this is rarely done in either zoological, physiological, or veterinary publications.

---

*National Zoological Park
Smithsonian Institution
Washington, D.C. 20008, USA

Acronyms used in this chapter:

DHA Docosahexaenoic acid
EPA Eicosapentaenoic acid
IU International unit
UV Ultraviolet

Nutritional Adaptations and Requirements of Carnivorous Reptiles

Omnivory versus Carnivory

Many aquatic turtles that are highly carnivorous in nature also consume some plant materials, probably on an opportunistic basis (Ernst and Barbour 1989). Although plants are typically a minor source of nutrients, the turtles presumably possess digestive, enzymatic, and metabolic abilities that permit them to digest plants, when available. At the extreme, some species of *Chrysemys*, *Pseudemys*, *Trachemys*, and *Terrapene* shift from carnivory as juveniles to a predominance of herbivory as adults, even though they do not exhibit many of the digestive adaptations that are typical of herbivores (Guard 1980; Ernst and Barbour 1989; Bjorndal and Bolton 1990). Thus, most aquatic turtles cannot be considered strict or obligate carnivores, in that they retain the flexibility to utilize at least some plant material.

The distinction between obligate carnivory and facultative (opportunistic) carnivory may be important. Studies on the metabolic adaptations and nutrient needs of domestic cats and dogs reveal many differences that are thought to reflect the long evolutionary dependence of felids on a strictly carnivorous diet. Felids appear to have lost the ability to adapt to diets that are low in nitrogen, certain amino acids, preformed vitamin A, niacin, and certain fatty acids, all of which are abundant in vertebrate prey (Morris and Rogers 1983; National Research Council 1986; Allen et al., in press). In contrast, canids retain digestive, enzymatic, metabolic, and excretory characteristics that enable them to subsist on omnivorous diets when necessary. The cat is, therefore, an obligate carnivore, but the dog is not.

It is not known whether any reptile is an obligate carnivore, in the sense of having nutritional dependencies similar to those of the cat. It seems probable, however, that the long evolutionary history devoted to carnivory by snakes, crocodilians, and some families of lizards (for example, anguids, chamaeleonids, and gekkonids) indicates that these taxa are now obligate carnivores. It is also possible that the nutritional adaptations of obligate carnivores that specialize on fish and other aquatic prey, or on insects and other invertebrates, differ from those of species that specialize on terrestrial vertebrates, given that these food types differ in nutrient composition (for example, nitrogenous constituents, fatty acid profiles, fat-soluble vitamins, calcium, and phosphorus). Unfortunately, relatively little is known about the nutrient requirements of any specialized fish- or insect-eating tetrapod, because these dietary specializations are not found among domestic animals.

Digestive Tract Characteristics

In establishing the appropriate form and nutrient levels for a diet, it is important to consider details of oral and digestive anatomy and function that may constrain the ability of an animal to cope with particular dietary constituents. In most respects the biting/chewing parts of the mouth (dentition or horny beak) and the digestive tract are anatomically simple in carnivorous reptiles (Guard 1980). Of course, snakes exhibit specialized features of cranial morphology, dentition, and glandular tissues associated with the capture, immobilization, and ingestion of various types of large prey (Cundall 1983; Pough and Groves 1983; Savitzky 1983). Snake venoms contain potent proteolytic enzymes that contribute to the digestion of prey (Thomas and Pough 1979). Among lizards, the grooved teeth of venomous Gila Monsters (*Heloderma suspectum*) and Mexican Beaded Lizards (*H. horridum*) and the projectile tongue of chameleons are important in the capture and immobilization of prey.

The anatomy and physiology of the reptilian digestive tract are described by Parsons and Cameron (1977) and Skoczylas (1978), and Reese (1915) devotes a chapter to the anatomy of the alligator digestive system. Carnivorous reptiles, like their mammalian and avian counterparts, tend to have relatively simple gastrointestinal tracts, without compartmentalization or extensive outpocketings of either the stomach or hindgut (Guard 1980; Stevens 1988). The esophagus of some snakes may serve a storage function, since feeding in snakes is episodic, and prey may be quite large relative to the size of the digestive tract of the predator (Skoczylas 1978). The stomach may be tubular, as in the Eastern Diamondback Rattlesnake (*Crotalus adamanteus*) and Blanding's Turtle (*Emydoidea blandingii*), or somewhat outpocketed as in the Spectacled Caiman (*Caiman crocodilus*). Carnivorous reptiles possess longer small intestines than do herbivorous reptiles, while their large intestines are shorter (Guard 1980; Skoczylas 1978). The small intestines of fish-eating snakes tend to be especially convoluted (Savitzky 1983). The large intestine of carnivorous reptiles is not partitioned, in contrast to herbivorous lizards in the families Agamidae, Iguanidae, and Scincidae (Iverson 1980). In mammals and birds, enlarged caeca are found in herbivorous species, but this does not seem to be the case in lizards, since some insectivorous species possess an especially large caecum (Skoczylas 1978).

Because diets of carnivores are usually highly digestible and do not require prolonged retention in the digestive tract for the purpose of microbial fermentation (as in some herbivorous species; McBee and McBee 1982), the simplicity of digestive-tract anatomy of carnivorous reptiles is expected. Even among carnivores, however, differences in digestive-tract structure may relate to diet. Pianka (1986) suggested that the large stomach (13% of body weight) of the Desert Horned Lizard (*Phrynosoma platyrhinos*) is an important adaptation to a specialized diet of low-energy, high-chitin ants; comparable insectivorous lizards that consume a more universal diet have stomachs that average about 6% of body weight (Pianka 1986).

Estimation of Nutrient Requirements

Snakes, crocodilians, many lizards (including anguids, chamaeleonids, gekkonids, pygopodids, varanids, and numerous species in other families), and many aquatic turtles (including many pelomedusids, chelids, kinosternids, and trionychids) are carnivorous, but it is not clear to what extent these are obligate rather than facultative (opportunistic) carnivores. From a practical point of view, it is safer to assume that carnivorous reptiles have the restrictive nutrient requirements characteristic of obligate carnivores rather than the more generalized needs of facultative (omnivorous) carnivores. Erring in the direction of higher nitrogen, amino acid, fatty acid, or vitamin requirements involves little risk (but some cost), as compared to the possibility of nutrient deficiency if requirement levels are underestimated. For present purposes, we will use the domestic cat as a model of an obligate carnivore, and assume that the nutrient requirements of carnivorous reptiles can be extrapolated from this model.

Cats have a number of specific nutritional and metabolic features, many of which appear to be associated with carnivory (see Morris and Rogers 1983; National Research Council 1986; Allen et al., in press):

(1) a limited ability to conserve nitrogen via regulation of transaminases and urea-cycle enzymes, which results in relatively high dietary nitrogen (protein) requirements;

(2) sensitivity to a dietary deficiency of the amino acid arginine, as indicated by rapid elevation of blood ammonia levels;

(3) an elevated requirement for the sulfur amino acids, methionine and cystine, which are abundant in animal tissues;

(4) need for a dietary source of the free amino acid taurine, which is not found in plants;

(5) the lack of the hepatic glycolytic enzyme glucokinase, which functions in carbohydrate metabolism in omnivores;

(6) the lack of ability to utilize carotenes (vitamin A precursors in plant material) to meet vitamin A requirements;

(7) the negligible conversion of tryptophan to niacin (a B vitamin found in high concentration in animal tissues); and

(8) the low rate of conversion of the essential fatty acid linoleic acid to arachidonic acid, resulting in a dietary requirement for arachidonic acid (a fatty acid usually found in animal tissues).

The above features suggest that obligate carnivores are best fed on foods high in nitrogen, amino acids, taurine, vitamin A, niacin, and both linoleic and arachidonic acid. The available information indicates that most vertebrate prey would fill these requirements; invertebrate prey are typically high in nitrogen and amino acids, but little data are available on their taurine, vitamin, or fatty acid composition.

Artificial Diets

It has been demonstrated that American Alligators (*Alligator mississippiensis*) can be reared on artificial diets containing plant by-products (Brisbin et al. 1990; Kercheval and Little 1990), just as cats can. Earlier reports that alligators and Red-eared Sliders (*Trachemys scripta elegans*) are unable to digest most plant proteins and complex carbohydrates (Coulson and Hernandez 1983; Coulson et al.

1987) were based on short-term experiments rather than long-term studies. By using protein and carbohydrate sources that were processed and refined, Staton et al. (1990*a*) were able to achieve relatively high digestibility, but concluded that the carbohydrate should not exceed 20% of the diet.

Essential Amino Acids

Considerable research has been conducted on amino acid metabolism in American Alligators (Coulson and Hernandez 1983), but less is known about amino acid requirements. Coulson and Hernandez (1970) reported that the Red-eared Slider and the Green Anole (*Anolis carolinensis*) do not have an elevated requirement for arginine. The addition of taurine to a diet based on plant proteins did not improve growth of hatchling and juvenile alligators (Kercheval and Little 1990), but no other measures of taurine status were made.

Essential Fatty Acids

Although arachidonic acid (carbon chain length of 20, with 4 double bonds) has not been conclusively shown to be an essential fatty acid for the American Alligator (as it has for the cat), a recent study by Staton et al. (1990*b*) indicates that growth in alligators was improved by inclusion of arachidonic acid in the diet. It appears, however, that alligators convert linoleic acid to arachidonic acid, at least to some extent (Staton et al. 1990*b*). It is not clear whether crocodilians require long-chain, polyunsaturated fatty acids, such as eicosapentaenoic acid (EPA; carbon chain length 20, with 5 double bonds) and docosahexaenoic acid (DHA; carbon chain length 22, with 6 double bonds), as suggested by Garnett (1985); some carnivorous marine fish appear to require EPA and DHA (Watanabe 1982). Because animal tissues are a good source of arachidonic acid, and because fish and other marine oils are a source of EPA and DHA, crocodilians maintained on a mixed diet, including meat and fish, are not apt to develop fatty acid deficiencies.

Diet and Gout

Although carnivorous reptiles such as American Alligators may respond positively to high protein levels (up to 50% of the diet) during periods of rapid growth (Staton et al. 1990*b*), at other stages of life the very high protein levels consumed when eating prey may lead to deamination and excretion of large amounts of nitrogen. Although most reptiles excrete nitrogen predominantly as uric acid, reptiles that dwell in an aqueous medium tend to excrete excess nitrogen predominantly as urea (for example, aquatic turtles) or as ammonia (for example, crocodilians and sea turtles) (Rogers 1966; Coulson and Hernandez 1970; Minnich 1972). Within a species, the relative proportions of various nitrogenous wastes may depend on the amount and composition of food, frequency of feeding, and hydration state (Rogers 1966; Coulson and Hernandez 1983).

Gout is the excessive precipitation of urate crystals in the joints, or in kidneys and other organs. This is a relatively common and usually fatal disease of captive reptiles. The etiology of gout is unclear, but it is commonly thought that diets high in protein may predispose reptiles to gout by increasing the concentration of uric acid in blood. Impaired renal function and dehydration have also been suggested as etiogenic factors. Although Maixner et al. (1987) demonstrated a transient rise in serum uric acid levels in three species of carnivorous reptiles (Rat Snakes, *Elaphe obsoleta*; Savanna Monitors, *Varanus exanthematicus*; and Gila Monsters, *Heloderma suspectum*) following the feeding of a high-protein meal (mice), this is apparently a normal phenomenon that may have little bearing on why abnormal deposits of uric acid occur. During their study, however, one monitor died due to gout and, just prior to death, had markedly elevated concentrations of serum uric acid, post-feeding, as compared to those of the other monitors. Coulson and Hernandez (1964, 1983) noted that visceral gout was especially prevalent in American Alligators that fed well, but grew slowly, during warm winter months. They suggest that gout does not occur as frequently during summer months because of the regularity of feeding and the fact that much of the ingested nitrogen is incorporated into protein during rapid growth. In the absence of data linking gout to dietary protein concentration, we do not recommend the feeding of low-protein diets to carnivorous reptiles.

Minerals and Vitamins

Relatively little is known about the mineral or vitamin requirements of reptiles, so target levels for captive diets (Table 1) are determined largely by referring to studies on mammals and birds. In an experiment with young Leopard Geckos, *Eublepharis macularius*, Allen (1989*a*, 1989*b*) demonstrated greater weight gain and improved bone condition (as measured by radiography, histology and chemical analysis) when the lizards were fed crickets containing 0.85% calcium than when fed crickets containing 0.20% calcium. In a second study of calcium retention in these geckos, which had been previously depleted of calcium, Allen (1989*a*) found that 0.85% dietary calcium met the requirements for growth and calcium repletion, but 0.61% calcium or less did not. Thus, the calcium requirements of growing Leopard Geckos appear to be about 0.8%, which is the same as the minimum requirement estimated for growing kittens (National Research Council 1986). Terrestrial vertebrates are fairly similar in mineral composition (see below); thus it should not be surprising that mineral requirements for growth should be quite similar even among species of very different phylogenetic origin.

TABLE 1. Suggested minimum nutrient levels[1] in diets of captive carnivorous reptiles.

Nutrient	Recommended minimum level (dry basis)	Nutrient	Recommended minimum level (dry basis)
Crude protein[2]	30-50%	Copper (Cu)	5-8 ppm
Ether extract	10-15%	Manganese (Mn)	5 ppm
Linoleic acid[3]	1.0%	Selenium (Se)	0.1-0.3 ppm
Lysine (Lys)	0.8%	Zinc (Zn)	50 ppm
Methionine (Met) + Cystine (Cys)	0.75%	Thiamin[4]	1-5 ppm
		Riboflavin	2-4 ppm
Isoleucine (Ile)	0.50%	Vitamin B6	1-4 ppm
Threonine (Thr)	0.70%	Vitamin B12	20 ppb
Tryptophan (Trp)	0.15%	Niacin	10-40 ppm
Arginine (Arg)	1.00%	Folate	200-800 ppb
Calcium (Ca)	0.8-1.0%	Biotin	70-100 ppb
Phosphorus (P)	0.5-0.9%	Choline	1250-2400 ppm
Sodium (Na)	0.2%	Pantothenate	10 ppm
Potassium (K)	0.4-0.6%	Vitamin A[5]	5000-10000 IU/kg
Magnesium (Mg)	0.04%	Vitamin E[6]	100 IU/kg
Iron (Fe)	60-80 ppm	Vitamin D[7]	500-1000 IU/kg
Iodine (I)	0.3-0.6 ppm		

[1]Nutrient levels are expressed on a dry-matter basis.
[2]Taurine requirements have not been determined for reptiles (the requirement for cats is 400–500 mg taurine/kg dry diet).
[3]A dietary source of arachidonic acid at 200 mg/kg dry diet.
[4]Thiamin concentrations should be increased to 10-20 mg/kg if fish constitute more than 25% of the diet offered.
[5]A source of preformed dietary vitamin A may be required, because it is not known if reptiles can convert carotenes to retinol (vitamin A).
[6]300 IU/kg dry matter is advisable if the diet is high in fat, especially unsaturated fat.
[7]Requirements for vitamin D may be partially or totally satisfied by exposure to sunlight or artificial UV.

Requirements for most vitamins may also prove to be similar among various carnivores. For example, many of the B-vitamins are intimately involved in the biochemistry of metabolic pathways and requirements may be more closely related to rates of metabolism than to type of diet. Requirements for ascorbic acid (vitamin C), however, are known to differ greatly among vertebrate species; although ascorbic acid can be synthesized in the liver and/or kidney in many mammals, some species, such as bats, anthropoid primates (including humans), and the Guinea Pig (*Cavia porcellus*), are incapable of synthesizing this compound and hence require a dietary source (Oftedal and Allen, in press). Although relatively few reptiles have been studied, at least 11 species have the enzymatic pathways for renal synthesis of ascorbic acid, including such carnivores as a gecko (*Hemidactylus flaviviridis*), a varanid (*Varanus bengalensis*), a water snake (*Xenochrophis piscator*), and two garter snakes (*Thamnophis radix* and *T. sirtalis*) (Chatterjee et al. 1975; Birney et al. 1980; Vosburgh et al. 1982). Vosburgh et al. (1982) found that inclusion of vitamin C in the diets of garter snakes led to a reduction in vitamin C synthesis, but tissue levels and body stores did not change. The suggestion that ulcerative stomatitis in snakes and lizards is associated with a dietary deficiency of vitamin C (Frye 1981) may not be correct (Vosburgh et al. 1982).

Another dietary requirement that warrants further research is that for vitamin D. Vitamin D is involved in the regulation of calcium metabolism (including calcium absorption from the diet) at a systemic level, and in its activated form functions as a steroid hormone (Collins and Norman 1991). Most vertebrates can either absorb vitamin D from the diet, or synthesize it in the skin from 7-dehydrocholesterol using energy from UV light of certain wavelengths (285–315 nanometers) in a temperature-dependent reaction. Thus, vitamin D is required in the diet only when endogenous synthesis is inadequate, as occurs when animals are not exposed to

UV light of appropriate wavelengths. In a study of growing Leopard Geckos kept without UV exposure, Allen (1989*a*) demonstrated a significant effect of dietary vitamin D on bone calcium concentration. In growing animals, vitamin D deficiency typically results in formation of abnormal (demineralized) bone, and is exacerbated by low dietary calcium.

Although it has been recognized for some years that UV light is beneficial to reptiles, and especially insectivorous species (Demeter 1976; Townsend and Cole 1985; Gehrmann 1987; Allen 1989*a*, 1989*b*), zoo animal nutritionists have assumed that reptiles, like birds and mammals, could utilize a dietary source of vitamin D if appropriate UV light was not provided. There is now compelling evidence, however, that suggests this may not always be so. A large number of Green Iguanas (*Iguana iguana*) being used in nutritional studies at the National Zoological Park developed severe bone demineralization and had very low levels of circulating 25-hydroxy vitamin D, despite being fed formulated diets containing high (>1.2%) levels of calcium and 2000 IU vitamin D_3 per kg (Allen and Oftedal, unpubl. data). These same animals responded rapidly to artificial sources of UV light (Bernard et al. 1991). Bone demineralization also occurred in Madagascar Day Geckos (*Phelsuma madagascariensis*) when they were maintained without UV light on a diet of crickets that had been enriched with both calcium and vitamin D, even though this diet promoted normal bone development in nocturnal Leopard Geckos (Allen 1989*a*). We hypothesize that some basking lizards (and possibly other reptiles), poorly utilize, or are not able to utilize, a dietary source of vitamin D, and hence must be exposed to UV light of appropriate wavelengths to sustain normal levels of active vitamin-D metabolites. Further research is urgently needed in this area, since the implications for captive management of basking reptiles are obviously profound.

Considerations in the Selection of Foods

Rodents and Other Terrestrial Vertebrates as Prey

Large snakes, varanid lizards, and many other large carnivorous reptiles feed predominantly on rodents, birds, lizards, and other vertebrate prey that are swallowed whole. Thus, the diet includes all tissues, including viscera, bones, fat and integument, not just muscle meat. Muscle by itself is not nutritionally balanced. Although the muscle of various species is a good source of amino acids, some minerals (for example, sodium, potassium, iron, selenium, and zinc), and some B vitamins (for example, niacin, B_6, and B_{12}), it is very low in calcium (calcium-to-phosphorus ratios are about 1:15 to 1:30), manganese, and fat-soluble vitamins (vitamin D, vitamin E, and in most cases vitamin A) (Bodwell and Anderson 1986; National Research Council 1986; Ullrey and Bernard 1989). Severe and often fatal nutritional bone disease has been produced in a variety of mammals, birds, and reptiles by feeding a diet of muscle meats without adequate calcium or vitamin D supplementation (Slusher et al. 1965; Gorham et al. 1970; Fowler 1986). For example, caiman and other crocodilians fed unsupplemented diets of muscle meats such as beef heart and fish fillets may develop severe bone demineralization and fibrous osteodystrophy (Frye 1981). Pathological bone disease manifests itself most readily in growing, egg-laying, or lactating animals due to the high calcium demands associated with these processes. Thus, hatchling turtles fed hamburger rapidly develop soft shells due to bone demineralization. The low vitamin A content of unsupplemented muscle meat may also lead to vitamin A deficiency.

Calcium deficiency is not likely to occur when entire prey are fed. Although the relative proportions of fat, protein, and water differ among such prey as laboratory mice, rats, and chicks depending on age, sex, and condition, all contain relatively high levels of calcium (>1.5%) and calcium-to-phosphorus ratios of 1.2 : 1.0 or greater (Table 2; Spray and Widdowson 1950). The high calcium concentration of vertebrate prey is attributable to calcium in the skeleton. The bones of neonatal rodents and chicks are somewhat less calcified than those of adults, but the effect is not sufficient to reduce total body calcium when expressed on a dry-matter basis (Table 2).

Nutritionists usually regard live rodents and chicks as nutritionally complete foods that do not require supplementation. A caveat must be made, however, with regard to fat-soluble vitamins, such as vitamins A and D. These vitamins are stored in liver and other tissues in direct response to dietary intake. Thus, vertebrate prey maintained on vitamin-deficient diets may contain negligible stores of vitamins A and D.

Fish as Food

Fish is often used as food for some snakes, turtles, and crocodilians. As with terrestrial prey, particular tissues (such as fillets of muscle meat) may be nutritionally unbalanced, but whole fish (including heads, viscera, and scales) are comparable in many respects to whole terrestrial vertebrates (Table 2). Fish contain substantial amounts of both protein and fat, but the latter may vary greatly depending on the species of fish and season of catch (Table 2; Oftedal and Boness 1983; Bernard and Ullrey 1989). Some species of fish are also high in the fat-soluble vitamins A and D (Allen and Baer 1989). Vitamin E is probably also abundant in fresh fish, but the oxidation of fish lipids that occurs during storage may deplete vitamin E content.

The relative instability of the long-chain polyunsaturated fatty acids in fish oils and the hospitable environment for bacterial growth provided by fish tissues can result in a rapid decline in the quality of harvested fish if the fish is not properly caught, iced, frozen, and stored (Syme 1966). Time from catch to freezing, rate of freezing, freezer temperature, duration of frozen storage, and type of packing may all influence nutrient losses, bacterial proliferation, and generation of potentially toxic or unpalatable compounds. Fish should be stored at about –20°F or lower, and stock should be rotated so that fish are stored no longer than 4–6 months (Geraci 1981, 1986). Proper thawing of frozen fish can be accomplished by thawing fish under refrigeration; thawing at room temperature may promote bacterial growth due to unequal thawing and exposure of surfaces to warm temperature.

Given the susceptibility of fish oils to oxidation, it is prudent to use supplemental vitamin E to compensate for potential losses. Polyunsaturated lipids in the diet also tend to increase the vitamin E requirements of the consumer (Machlin 1980). Crocodilians fed fish diets are prone to steatitis (pathologic changes in body fat) that is probably due to vitamin E deficiency (Larsen et al. 1983; Wallach

TABLE 2. Proximate, energy, calcium, and phosphorus analyses of vertebrate prey.[1, 2]

Prey[3]	Weight g	Dry matter %	Crude protein %	Ether extract (fat) %	Ash %	Gross energy kcal/g	Calcium %	Phosphorus %
House mice	40	34.5	54.3	22.8	10.3	5.6	2.7	1.8
	20	32.9	60.2	22.6	9.8	5.5	2.9	2.0
	6	25.2	58.7	23.7	9.5	5.8	2.3	1.8
Laboratory rats	340	32.9	58.5	23.9	10.8	5.8	3.5	1.9
	250	32.9	59.2	24.8	10.3	5.7	3.2	2.0
	64	28.2	63.0	21.1	10.9	5.4	3.0	2.0
Chicks	30	22.4	64.7	13.9	8.9	5.4	1.9	1.3
Capelin	40	15.6	72.9	10.6	9.6	5.4	2.1	1.7
Herring	190	28.3	9.1	34.9	8.3	6.3	1.7	1.7
Atlantic mackerel	190	26.5	72.7	11.9	10.4	5.4	1.9	2.0
Smelt (fresh water)	12	16.0	67.6	18.2	9.1	5.9	2.2	1.9
Smelt (ocean)	19	25.9	66.4	16.7	9.2	5.5	1.8	1.7

[1]Dry matter is expressed as a percentage of fresh (live) weight; all other nutrients are expressed on a dry-matter basis.
[2]Data represent composite samples of between 5 and 25 individual prey items, analyzed in duplicate, and do not reflect seasonal or other sources of variation; M. E. Allen, D. J. Baer, D. E. Ullrey, unpubl. data.
[3]House mice (*Mus musculus*), laboratory rats (*Rattus norvegicus*), Chicks (*Gallus domesticus*), Capelin (*Mallotus villosus*), Herring (*Clupea harengus*), Atlantic mackerel (*Scomber scombrus*), Smelt (freshwater) (*Allosmerus elongatus*), Smelt (ocean) (*Osmerus mordax*).

and Hoessle 1968). It has also been suggested that the type of diet fed (fish versus nutria) influences circulating vitamin E levels as well as reproductive performance; however, the type and level of supplemental vitamin E was not reported (Lance et al. 1983). Supplementation can be provided by placing gel capsules containing vitamin E into the mouths or gills of feed fish. Dosage rates of 50–100 IU vitamin E per kg of fish appear to be reasonable (Geraci 1981, 1986; Oftedal and Boness 1983).

Some species of fish contain enzymes (thiaminases) that are active after the death of the fish, and that act to destroy thiamin, one of the B vitamins (Fujita 1954). Thiaminases have been found in carp, catfish, goldfish, herring, rainbow smelt, Pacific mackerel, whitefish, and other fishes; for a listing of tested species, see Table 15 in "The Nutrient Requirements of Mink and Foxes" (National Research Council 1982). Juvenile Snapping Turtles (*Chelydra serpentina*) fed a diet of thawed Rainbow Smelt (*Osmerus mordax*) without thiamin supplements developed persistent tremors, weakness, and anorexia, which are signs characteristic of thiamin deficiency (Oftedal, pers. observ.). Shrunken eyes in turtles appear to be another sign of thiamin deficiency (Frye 1981). Thiamin deficiency also occurs in aquatic and semi-aquatic mammals fed unsupplemented fish (Rigdon and Drager 1955; White 1970; Geraci 1972; National Research Council 1982). Given the problems associated with fish quality and vitamin losses, it is often preferable to use other types of foods for carnivorous reptiles, but if dead fish are provided as food, thiamin supplements should be included at a level of 25–30 mg per kg of fish (Geraci 1986).

Insects and Other Invertebrates

In contrast to vertebrate prey, which are relatively similar to each other in chemical composition and are nutritionally well-balanced (other than post-mortem vitamin losses), invertebrate prey can be extremely varied in composition and nutritionally unbalanced (Allen 1989*a*). Invertebrate prey commonly consumed by various reptiles in the wild include earthworms and other oligochaetes; ants, flies, beetles, and other insects (both larval and adult); snails, slugs, clams, and other mollusks; and crayfish, crabs, and other crustaceans. The proximate composition and calcium and phosphorus values for some examples of these types of prey are included in Table 3. While it is not possible to describe here all the factors that may affect nutrient composition of invertebrates, it should be obvious that the presence of a calcareous shell or exoskeleton (for example, in some mollusks and crustaceans) will influence calcium content; that a volumi-

TABLE 3. Proximate, energy, calcium, and phosphorus analyses of some invertebrates.[1,2]

Common name	Dry matter %	Ether extract (fat) %	Total nitrogen %	Ash %	Gross energy kcal/g	Calcium %	Phosphorus %
Insects							
Mealworm larvae	36.1	41.7	7.74	4.6	7.49	0.07	0.60
American cockroach	33.3	—	10.16	5.6	5.52	0.57	0.74
Fruitfly	29.6	12.6	11.22	4.5	5.12	0.10	1.05
Corn borer larvae	27.3	17.2	9.66	2.9	5.69	0.23	0.64
Wax moth larvae	43.9	61.5	4.92	1.8	—	0.03	0.39
House cricket	29.9	17.3	10.58	6.1	5.34	0.18	0.86
Oligochaetes							
Common earthworm	17.4	7.2	10.39	10.3	4.71	1.18	0.90
Tubifex worms	—	15.1	7.38	6.9	—	0.19	0.73

[1]Dry matter is expressed as a percentage of fresh (live) weight; all other nutrients are expressed on a dry-matter basis.
[2]Data from Allen (1989*a*): Mealworm larvae (*Tenebrio molitor*); American cockroach (*Periplaneta americana*); Fruitfly (*Drosophila melanogaster*); Corn borer larvae (*Ostrinia nubilalis*); Wax moth larvae (*Galleria mellonella*); House cricket (*Acheta domestica*); Earthworm (*Lumbricus terrestris*); Tubifex worm (*Tubifex* sp.).

nous digestive tract full of soil, wood, or leaves (as is the case with earthworms, termites, and caterpillars) may affect ash, mineral, and digestible-energy content; and that lipid storage in larval insects prior to pupation (such as waxmoth larvae, mealworm larvae, and beetle grubs) may alter fat content (Allen 1989*a*).

The low calcium content of most insects that have been analyzed can be attributed to the fact that structural support (the exoskeleton) and rigidity (for example, mouth parts) are provided by chitin-protein complexes that are not calcified (Richards 1951; Chapman 1982), rather than a calcified skeleton and teeth (which together account for 98% of the calcium in tetrapods). In the wild, reptiles that feed on earthworms, or on insects that are geophagous (for example, some beetle grubs and termites) or herbivorous (for example, caterpillars) may benefit from the calcium contained in gut contents of these insects (see Bilby and Widdowson 1971; Allen 1989*a*).

Insectivorous reptiles in captivity may not be so fortunate. Insect prey commonly used by zoos and hobbyists (for example, mealworms, crickets, waxmoth larvae, and fruitflies) are low in calcium (0.03–0.3% on a dry-matter basis) and have an inverse calcium-to-phosphorus ratio (0.08–0.4) (Table 3). The feeding of these insects, without calcium supplementation, will produce frank calcium deficiency that is characterized by cortical thinning and demineralization of bone, spontaneous fractures of long bones, and ultimately death (Modzelewski and Culley 1974; Fowler 1986; Allen 1989*a*, 1989*b*).

Two methods have commonly been used to supplement the live insects used in feeding programs: (1) placing the insects on a high calcium diet before use or (2) coating ("dusting") the insects with a supplement in powder form. For example, when crickets were fed diets ranging from 2 to 12% calcium, the calcium concentration in the whole cricket (including gut contents) varied in direct proportion to dietary calcium (Allen and Oftedal 1989). We concluded that cricket diets should contain at least 8% calcium and that this diet should be fed for at least 48 hours before the crickets are used if they are to provide the desired 1:1 calcium-to-phosphorus ratio. Radiographs revealed that most if not all of the supplemental calcium was resident in the gastrointestinal tract (Allen and Oftedal 1989). Preliminary studies indicate that the calcium content of mealworm larvae may also be manipulated by feeding a high-calcium diet (Allen, unpubl. data; Zwart and Rulkens 1979).

This method of supplementing crickets may be preferable to the alternative "dusting" method widely practiced in zoos. Dusted crickets appear to groom the calcium dust from their bodies within a short time. If the crickets are not immediately eaten by the predator, the effect of dusting with a calcium source may be lost. If crickets remain in the reptile's cage for any period of time, it is also possible to place the high-calcium feed in the cage so that the digestive tracts of the crickets do not become empty. In all cases in which crickets are fed a high-calcium food, other more palatable foods (for example, fruits and vegetables, and fresh vegetation) should be eliminated from the enclosure so that the crickets are forced to eat the calcium-enriched diet.

Summary

It is increasingly evident that reptiles, like mammals, birds, and fish, are sensitive to nutrient imbalances, especially during periods of maximal nutrient needs, such as early growth and egg production. In captivity, reptiles are often fed simplified diets containing just a few items, increasing the risk of nutrient deficiency or excess. Unfortunately, supplementation with vitamin or mineral mixes may not solve the problem. Vitamin and mineral supplements are of very diverse composition, and some (especially those marketed for pets or exotic animals) contain inappropriate proportions of nutrients. Thus, if careful attention is not paid both to the composition and amount of the supplement used, the nutrient levels in the supplemented diet may be dangerous to animal health.

The increased involvement of nutritionists in establishing diets for reptiles has led to the development of a number of artificial diets, and this trend will undoubtedly continue into the future. For example, artificial (manufactured) diets are currently being used in large-scale rearing of Green Iguanas, American Alligators, and Desert Tortoises (*Gopherus agassizii*), as well as in captive propagation of Land Iguanas (*Conolophus subcristatus*) in the Galapagos Islands. A commercial "cricket diet" is also available for feeding to the insects that are to be fed to reptiles. Artificial diets have the advantage that the levels of specific nutrients can be designed to meet the expected requirements of reptiles, a task that is not easily achieved when an array of food items are fed. The nutrient levels of manufactured diets are also easily manipulated in order to study nutrient requirements.

Reptilian husbandry has long been an art, rather than a science. Even less is known about the nutrient needs of amphibians. There is clearly an urgent need for sound nutritional research that addresses the practical problems of feeding captive reptiles and amphibians.

Acknowledgments

We thank Paul Weldon for comments on a draft of this paper. We gratefully acknowledge the financial support of the Friends of the National Zoo and the Office of Fellowships and Grants, Smithsonian Institution, for research on reptilian nutrition.

Literature Cited

Allen, M. E. 1989*a*. Nutritional aspects of insectivory. Doctoral Dissertation, Michigan State Univ., East Lansing. 205 pages.

—. 1989*b*. Dietary induction and prevention of osteodystrophy in an insectivorous reptile *Eublepharis macularius*: characterization by radiography and histopathology, p. 83. *In* Third International Colloquium on the Pathology of Reptiles and Amphibians. Eastern States Veterinary Association, Gainesville, Florida.

Allen, M. E., and D. J. Baer. 1989. Fat soluble vitamin concentrations in fish commonly fed to zoo animals, p. 104. *In* Proceedings of the 1989 Annual Meeting, American Association of Zoo Veterinarins, Philadelphia, Pennsylvania

Allen, M. E., and O. T. Oftedal. 1989. Dietary manipulation of the calcium concentration of feed crickets. Jour. Zoo Wildl. Med., 20: 26–33.

Allen, M. E., O. T. Oftedal and D. J. Baer. In press. The feeding and nutrition of carnivores. *In* D. G. Kleiman, S. Lumpkin, and M. E. Allen (eds.), Wild Mammals in Captivity. Univ. Chicago Press, Chicago.

Bernard, J. B., O. T. Oftedal, P. S. Barboza, C. E. Mathias, M. E. Allen, S. B. Citino, D. E. Ullrey, and R. J. Montali. 1991. The response of vitamin-D deficient green iguanas (*Iguana iguana*) to artificial ultraviolet light, p. 147–150. *In* Proceedings of the 1991 Annual Meeting, American Association of Zoo Veterinarians, Philadelphia, Pennsylvania.

Bernard, J. B., and D. E. Ullrey. 1989. Evaluation of dietary husbandry of marine mammals at two major zoological parks. Jour. Zoo Wildl. Med., 20: 45–52.

Bilby, L. W., and E. M. Widdowson. 1971. Chemical composition of growth in nestling blackbirds and thrushes. British Jour. Nutr., 25: 127–134.

Birney, E. C., R. Jenness, and I. D. Hume. 1980. Evolution of an enzyme system: ascorbic acid biosynthesis in monotremes and marsupials. Evolution, 34: 230–239.

Bjorndal, K. A., and A. B. Bolton. 1990. Digestive processing in a herbivorous freshwater turtle: consequences of small intestine fermentation. Physiol. Zool., 63: 1232–1247.

Bodwell, C. E., and B. A. Anderson. 1986. Nutritional composition and value of meat and meat products, p. 321–369. *In* P. J. Bechtel (ed.), Muscle as Food. Academic Press, New York.

Brisbin, L. I., C. D. McCreedy, H. S. Zippler, and M. A. Staton. 1990. Extended maintenance of American alligators on a dry formulated ration, p. 16–31. *In* Crocodiles. Proceedings of the 10th Working Meeting of the Crocodile Specialist Group of the Species Survival Commission of IUCN. IUCN—The World Conservation Union, Gland, Switzerland.

Chapman, R. F. 1982. The insects, structure and function. Third ed. Harvard Univ. Press, Cambridge, Massachusetts. 919 pages.

Chatterjee, I. B., A. K. Majumder, B. K. Nandi, and N. Subramanian. 1975. Synthesis and some major functions of vitamin C in animals. Ann. New York Acad. Sci., 258: 24–47.

Collins, E. D., and A. W. Norman. 1991. Vitamin D, p. 59–98. *In* L. J. Machlin (ed.), Handbook of Vitamins. Second ed. Marcel Dekker, New York.

Coulson, R. A., T. D. Coulson, J. D. Herbert, and M. A. Staton. 1987. Protein nutrition in the alligator. Comp. Biochem. Physiol., [A] 87: 449–459.

Coulson, R. A., and T. Hernandez. 1964. Biochemistry of the alligator. A study of metabolism in slow motion. Louisiana State Univ. Press, Baton Rouge. 138 pages.

—. 1970. Nitrogen metabolism and excretion in the living reptile, p. 639–710. *In* J. W. Campbell (ed.), Comparative Biochemistry of Nitrogen Metabolism. Volume 2. The Vertebrates. Academic Press, New York.

—. 1983. Alligator metabolism. Studies on chemical reactions in vivo. Comp. Biochem. Physiol., [B] 74: 1–182.

Cundall, D. 1983. Activity of head muscles during feeding by snakes: a comparative study. Amer. Zool., 23: 383–396.

Demeter, B. J. 1976. Observations on the care, breeding and behaviour of the Giant day gecko *Phelsuma madagascariensis* at the National Zoological Park, Washington. Internatl. Zoo Yearbook, 16: 130–133.

Ernst, C. H. and R. W. Barbour. 1989. Turtles of the World. Smithsonian Inst. Press, Washington, D.C. 313 pages.

Fowler, M. E. 1986. Metabolic bone disease, p. 69–90. *In* M. E. Fowler (ed.), Zoo and Wildlife Medicine. Second ed. W. B. Saunders, Philadelphia.

Frye, F. L. 1981. Biomedical and Surgical Aspects of Captive Reptile Husbandry. Veterinary Medicine Publishing Co., Edwardsville, Kansas. 456 pages.

Fujita, A. 1954. Thiaminase, p. 389–421. *In* F. F. Nord (ed.), Advances in Enzymology. Interscience Publishers, New York.

Garnett, S. 1985. Fatty acid nutrition of the estuarine crocodile *Crocodylus porosus*. Comp. Biochem. Physiol.,

[B] 81: 1033–1035.

Gehrmann, W. H. 1987. Ultraviolet irradiances of various lamps used in animal husbandry. Zoo Biol., 6: 117–127.

Geraci, J. R. 1972. Experimental thiamine deficiency in captive harp seals (*Phoca groenlandica*) induced by eating herring (*Clupea harengus*) and smelts (*Osmerus mordax*). Canadian Jour. Zool., 50: 179–195.

—. 1981. Dietary disorders in marine mammals: synthesis and new findings. Jour. Amer. Vet. Med. Assoc., 179: 1183–1191.

—. 1986. Marine mammals: nutrition and nutritional disorders, p. 760–764. *In* M. E. Fowler (ed.), Zoo and Wildlife Medicine. Second ed. W.B. Saunders, Philadelphia.

Gorham, J. R., J. C. Peckham, and J. Alexander. 1970. Rickets and osteodystrophia fibrosa in foxes fed a high horsemeat ration. Jour. Amer. Vet. Med. Assoc., 156: 1331–1333.

Guard, C. L. 1980. The reptilian digestive system: general characteristics, p. 43–51. *In* K. Schmidt-Nielsen, L. Bolis, and C. R. Taylor (eds.), Comparative Physiology: Primitive Mammals. Cambridge Univ. Press, New York.

Iverson, J. B. 1980. Colic modifications in iguanine lizards. Jour. Morphol., 163: 79–93.

Kercheval, D. R., and P. Little. 1990. Comparative growth rates of young alligators utilizing rations of plant and/or animal origins, p. 286–312. *In* Crocodiles. Proceedings of the 10th Working Meeting of the Crocodile Specialist Group of the Species Survival Commission of IUCN. IUCN—The World Conservation Union, Gland, Switzerland.

Lance, V., T. Joanen, and L. McNease. 1983. Selenium, vitamin E, and trace elements in the plasma of wild and farm-reared alligators during the reproductive cycle. Canadian Jour. Zool., 61: 1744–1751.

Larsen, R. E., C. Buergelt, P. T. Cardeilhac, and E. R. Jacobson. 1983. Steatitis and fat necrosis in captive alligators. Jour. Amer. Vet. Med. Assoc., 183: 1202–1204.

Machlin, L. J. 1980. Vitamin E: A Comprehensive Treatise. Marcel Dekker, New York. 660 pages.

Maixner, J. M., E. C. Ramsay, and L. H. Arp. 1987. Effects of feeding on serum uric acid in captive reptiles. Jour. Zoo Anim. Med., 18: 62–65.

McBee, R. H., and V. H. McBee. 1982. The hindgut fermentation in the green iguana, *Iguana iguana*, p. 77–83. *In* G. M. Burghardt and A. S. Rand (eds.), Iguanas of the World: Their Behavior, Ecology and Conservation. Noyes Publishers, Park Ridge, New Jersey.

Minnich, J. E. 1972. Excretion of urate salts by reptiles. Comp. Biochem. Physiol., [A] 41: 535–549.

Modzelewski, E. H., and D. D. Culley. 1974. Growth responses of the bullfrog *Rana catesbeiana* fed various live foods. Herpetologica, 30: 396–405.

Morris, J. G., and Q. R. Rogers. 1983. Nutritionally related metabolic adaptations of carnivores and ruminants, p. 165–180. *In* N. S. Margaris, M. Arianoutsou-Faraggitaki, and R. J. Reiter (eds.), Plant, Animal, and Microbial Adaptations to Terrestrial Environments. Plenum, New York.

National Research Council. 1982. Nutrient Requirements of Mink and Foxes. Second revised ed. National Acad. Press, Washington, D.C. 72 pages.

—. 1986. Nutrient Requirements of Cats. Revised ed. National Acad. Press, Washington, D.C. 78 pages.

Oftedal, O. T., and M. E. Allen. In press. The feeding and nutrition of omnivores, with emphasis on primates. *In* D. G. Kleiman, S. Lumpkin, and M. E. Allen (eds.), Wild Mammals in Captivity. Univ. Chicago Press, Chicago.

Oftedal, O. T., and D. J. Boness. 1983. Considerations in the use of fish as food, p. 149–161. *In* T. P. Meehan, and M. E. Allen (eds.), Proceedings of the Third Annual Dr. Scholl Conference on the Nutrition of Captive Wild Animals. Lincoln Park Zoological Gardens, Chicago, Illinois.

Parsons, T. S., and J. E. Cameron. 1977. Internal relief of the digestive tract, p. 159–224. *In* C. Gans, and T. S. Parsons (eds.), Biology of the Reptilia. Vol. 6. Academic Press, New York.

Pianka, E. R. 1986. Ecology and Natural History of Desert Lizards. Princeton Univ. Press, Princeton, New Jersey. 208 pages.

Pough, F. H., and J. D. Groves. 1983. Specializations of the body form and food habits of snakes. Amer. Zool., 23: 443–454.

Reese, A. M. 1915. The Alligator and its Allies. Putnam's Sons, New York. 358 pages.

Richards, A. G. 1951. The Integument of Arthropods. Univ. Minnesota Press, Minneapolis. 411 pages.

Rigdon, R. H., and G. A. Drager. 1955. Thiamine deficiency in sea lions fed only frozen fish. Jour. Amer. Vet. Med. Assoc., 127: 453– 455.

Rogers, L. J. 1966. The nitrogen excretion of *Chelodina longicollis* under conditions of hydration and dehydration. Comp. Biochem. Physiol., 18: 249–260.

Savitzky, A. H. 1983. Coadapted character complexes among snakes: fossoriality, piscivory and durophagy. Amer. Zool., 23: 397–409.

Skoczylas, R. 1978. Physiology of the digestive tract, p. 589–717. *In* C. Gans and K. A. Gans (eds.), Biology of the Reptilia. Vol. 8. Academic Press, New York.

Slusher, R., S. I. Bistner, and C. Kircher. 1965. Nutritional secondary hyperparathyroidism in a tiger. Jour. Amer. Vet. Med. Assoc., 147: 1109–1115.

Spray, C. M., and E. M. Widdowson. 1950. The effect of growth and development on the composition of mammals. British Jour. Nutr., 4: 332– 353.

Staton, M. A., H. M. Edwards, I. L. Brisbin, T. Joanen, and L. McNease. 1990*a*. Protein and energy relationships in the diet of the American alligator (*Alligator mississippiensis*). Jour. Nutr., 120: 775–785.

—. 1990*b*. Essential fatty acid nutriton of the American alligator (*Alligator mississippiensis*). Jour. Nutr., 120: 674–685.

Stevens, C. E. 1988. Comparative Physiology of the Vertebrate Digestive System. Cambridge Univ. Press, New York. 300 pages.

Syme, J. D. 1966. Fish and Fish Inspection. Lewis and Co., London. 209 pages.

Thomas, R. G., and F. H. Pough. 1979. The effect of rattlesnake venom on digestion of prey. Toxicon, 17: 221–228.

Townsend, C. R., and C. J. Cole. 1985. Additional notes on requirements of captive whiptail lizards (*Cnemidophorus*) with emphasis on ultraviolet radiation. Zoo Biol., 4: 49–55.

Ullrey, D. E., and J. B. Bernard. 1989. Meat diets for performing exotic cats. Jour. Zoo Wildl. Med., 20: 20–25.

Vosburgh, K. M., P. S. Brady, and D. E. Ullrey. 1982. Ascorbic acid requirements of garter snakes: plains (*Thamnophis radix*) and eastern (*T. sirtalis sirtalis*). Jour. Zoo Anim. Med., 13: 38–42.

Wallach, J. D. and C. Hoessle. 1968. Steatitis in captive crocodilians. Jour. Amer. Vet. Med. Assoc., 153: 845–847.

Watanabe, T. 1982. Lipid nutrition in fish. Comp. Biochem. Physiol., [B] 73: 3–15.

White, J. R. 1970. Thiamine deficiency in an Atlantic bottlenosed dolphin (*Tursiops truncatus*) on a diet of raw fish. Jour. Amer. Vet. Med. Assoc., 157: 559–562.

Zwart, P., and R. J. Rulkens. 1979. Improving the calcium content of mealworms. Internatl. Zoo Yearbook, 19: 254–255.

❦

❦ Allen, M. E., and O. T. Oftedal. 1994. The nutrition of carnivorous reptiles, p. 71–82. *In* J. B. Murphy, K. Adler, and J. T. Collins (eds.), Captive Management and Conservation of Amphibians and Reptiles. Society for the Study of Amphibians and Reptiles, Ithaca (New York). Contributions to Herpetology, volume 11.

THE NUTRITION OF HERBIVOROUS REPTILES

DAVID J. BAER*

Introduction

SUCCESSFUL PROPAGATION OF CAPTIVE ANIMALS requires the interaction of many disciplines. The formulation of nutritionally balanced and palatable diets for herbivorous reptiles should incorporate data derived from field studies, controlled experimentation, trial and error, and casual observation. Unfortunately, our understanding of quantitative nutrient requirements of herbivorous reptiles is limited and must be extrapolated from many sources. If these extrapolations are made rationally, however, it is not difficult to formulate a captive diet that is successful for long term management. Too often irrational, subjective, or emotional arguments are used in developing diets, and these claims often have no scientific basis.

An integral step in developing a diet for any captive species is a basic understanding of nutrients, feeding strategy, anatomy, and digestive physiology. Proper nutritional management is important for all captive species, including herbivorous reptiles. Inappropriate feeding can result in a variety of problems that can interfere with reproduction and may ultimately result in increased morbidity or mortality. Some of the same problems that affect carnivorous reptiles (see Allen and Oftedal, this volume, page 71) can affect herbivorous reptiles. Adaptations and constraints of the herbivorous feeding strategy must be considered when developing captive diets for optimum performance or longevity. This chapter reviews some of the basic concepts of plant fiber, anaerobic fermentation, and digestion in herbivorous reptiles.

Herbivory in Reptiles

Herbivory is a general term describing animals that consume plant material. Specialized herbivores may include animals with feeding strategies such as frugivores, which consume primarily fruit, or folivores which consume primarily leaves. The evolution of herbivory in reptiles is limited generally to the families Cheloniidae, Testudinidae, Agamidae, and "Iguanidae" (Zimmerman and Tracy 1989). Herbivorous species do occur in other families, and some species may be herbivorous as adults, but are carnivorous or omnivorous as hatchlings or juveniles. Herbivory in reptiles occurs in species with small and large body mass. Many species are generalist herbivores and will consume fruits, buds or flowers when available. These animals alter their feeding habits based on food availability, whereas other species consume a monotypic diet, such as the seagrass diet of *Chelonia mydas* (Bjorndal 1980). The limited evolution of herbivory has been the subject of several reports (Szarski 1962; Ostrum 1963; Sokol 1967; Pough 1973). Many proposed hypotheses have been questioned, and there remains no underlying reason for the limited evolution of herbivory in reptiles.

Nutritional Characteristics of Plant Material

Plant fiber is a heterogeneous matrix consisting of many different components. Nutrients and energy from plants can be derived from cellular contents or from the cell wall. The cell wall surrounds the cellular contents and provides structural support for the plant. Primary constituents of the cell wall are the fiber components of plants, and include

*Allen and Baer Associates, Inc.
713 Hillsboro Drive
Silver Spring, Maryland 20902, USA

Acronyms used in this chapter:

ADF	Acid detergent fiber
IU/kg	International units per kilogram
NDF	Neutral detergent fiber
TDF	Total dietary fiber
VFAs	Volatile fatty acids

cellulose, hemicellulose, lignin, cutin, silica, and pectin (Van Soest 1982). Cellulose is a relatively homogeneous compound, whereas hemicellulose is much more heterogeneous. Digestibility of cellulose and hemicellulose depends on many factors, but microbial fermentation of these components contributes significantly to the energy requirement of the herbivore. Lignin, also a heterogeneous compound of the cell wall, is composed of polyphenolic compounds. Lignin is not readily digestible, and its primary function appears to be structural support of the plant. The chemical and physical composition of the plant cell wall is species-specific and can be affected by age of the plant and environmental conditions (Van Soest 1982). Plants also produce a variety of non-nutritional compounds that function as important chemical defense mechanisms. These secondary plant compounds can affect palatability, and thus forage choice. Some of these compounds may act as mild feeding deterrents, while others may be toxic or deadly. Secondary plant compounds include, but are not limited to, alkaloids, soluble phenolics, and terpenoids.

Analysis of Plant Fiber

The complexity of fiber has been the impetus for the development of different methods of analyses (Van Soest 1982). Historically, the crude fiber method has been used as the legal entity for food labelling in declarations of the fiber content of human and animal foods. Theoretically, this method mimics the digestive process; however, its use in understanding physiological responses has been limited. Newer methods of analysis include the total dietary fiber method (TDF) commonly used for analyzing human foods.

Animal feeds are now analyzed by the "Van Soest Detergent Analytical Method." Through a series of chemical treatments, the plant cell is divided into the cell wall constituents or neutral detergent fiber (NDF), lignocellulose or acid detergent fiber (ADF), and lignin (Van Soest 1982). The NDF fraction represents cellulose, hemicellulose, lignin, and cutin. The ADF represents cellulose, lignin, and some pectin. Thus, the difference between NDF and ADF is the hemicellulose, and the difference between ADF and lignin is cellulose. Analyses of these components can be accomplished successfully in diets and feces, and thus, the digestibility of different fiber fractions can be calculated. This method of analysis is useful in elucidating physiological effects of dietary fiber on food intake and digestive processes.

Anaerobic Fermentation

Vertebrate herbivores lack digestive enzymes necessary to break down and extract the nutrients and energy bound in plant fiber. Microbial organisms produce suitable enzymes, however, and in a symbiotic relationship with their vertebrate host, these microbes provide the host with nutrients and energy derived from the plant fiber. Symbiotic microbes include bacteria, protozoa, and fungi which process plant fiber through anaerobic fermentation. Many of these microbes are ubiquitous in the environment, and it is suggested that behavioral interactions between hatchlings and their parents may be important in acquisition of these microbes (Troyer 1982, 1984). Geophagy may also play a role in microbial acquisition by the hatchling (Sokol 1971).

End products of fermentation can include microbially synthesized proteins, vitamins, and volatile fatty acids (VFAs). Production of VFAs has been measured in digesta from herbivorous lizards (McBee and McBee 1982; Foley et al. 1987) and in turtles (Bjorndal, 1979). All microbially derived nutrients potentially can be used by the vertebrate host. Volatile fatty acids are especially important because they can be used directly as a source of energy or as precursors for the synthesis of glucose, protein and fats by the host. McBee and McBee (1982) estimate that VFAs may contribute as much as 30–40% of the daily energy requirement of *Iguana iguana*. Bjorndal (1979) reports that VFAs provide 15% of the daily energy requirement of *Chelonia mydas*. Contribution of VFAs to daily energy requirement can be as high as 80% for some mammalian herbivores, such as ruminants. It is not clear why the potential contribution of VFAs to the daily energy requirement of herbivorous reptiles is low compared to that of mammalian herbivores. This may be a consequence of difficulties in the precise measurement of VFA production rate in reptiles or actual differences in production or absorption rate of VFAs in herbivorous reptiles.

Typically, herbivorous species possess a capacious organ used to house the microbial population (Stevens 1988). This organ provides an environment suitable for microbial growth and reproduction. The fermentation chamber can be either anterior to the stomach ("foregut fermenters" as in ruminants) or posterior to the stomach ("hindgut fermenters" such as *I. iguana*). Many reptilian herbivores are hindgut fermenters with an enlarged cecum or colon for microbial fermentation. In general, the small intestine is shorter, and the long intestine is longer and more highly developed in herbivores than it is in carnivores (Stevens 1988). Bjorndal and Bolton (1990) report a significant degree of fermentation in the small intestine of *Pseudemys nelsoni*. Fermentation in the small intestine is not common and has not been described in birds, mammals, or other reptiles.

Digestion and Fiber Fermentation

Many factors influence plant fiber digestibility. These include diet quality and composition, length of exposure of the microbes to the diet, and particle size of the diet. Rate of digestion and rate of transit are two competing processes. The net effect of these two competing processes determines diet digestibility. Different strategies, ranging from behavioral to physiological, operate to optimize diet digestibility and the rate of nutrient and energy acquisition.

In the wild, diet quality and fiber content can change as a function of season, environment, and age of the plant. Lignification (increase in the amount of lignin relative to fiber content) increases with increasing age of the plant (Van Soest 1982). As lignification increases, digestibility of the plant can decrease because the presence of lignin can physically inhibit the microbial attack. Environmental conditions such as daylength, temperature, or water availability can alter the proportion of cellulose, hemicellulose, and lignin in plants. Hemicellulose is generally more digestible than cellulose. As the plants produce flowers or fruits, energy can be mobilized from one botanical part to another. Presumably feed selection in free-ranging herbivores has co-evolved with these seasonal changes. Seasonal changes in the plant part consumed or seasonal changes in plant choice may be related to availability of energy that potentially can be derived from fiber.

Residence time, rate of digesta passage, and time of first appearance of a marker are all measures of the time that digesta may be exposed to digestive enzymes and the microbes. Length of exposure may be an important determinant of the extent to which fiber can be digested. Increasing retention time may increase the extent of fermentation.

Morphological adaptations, coprophagy, and retrograde flux of digesta are some the mechanisms that have evolved to control rate of digesta flow. Morphological adaptations of the gastrointestinal tract can include valves, sphincters or mucosal folds. "Iguanidae" and Agamidae have several valves in the cecum and colon to increase compartmentalization (Guard 1980); however, the digestive tract of *Geochelone carbonaria* (Guard 1980) and *Xerobates agassizii* (Meienberger et al. 1993) are relatively simple. Typical transit time of herbivorous reptiles may be as long as 300 hours (Bjorndal, Bolton, and Moore 1990; Guard 1980). Transit times of herbivorous reptiles are longer than for many mammalian herbivores (Warner 1981).

Particle size not only affects rate of digesta flow, but also determines the surface of the plant accessible to microbial attack relative to the particle volume. Smaller particles have a larger surface area to volume ratio, and can, theoretically, have a higher digestibility than larger pieces (Bjorndal, Bolton, Moore 1990). Herbivorous mammals have developed elaborate jaw structures, efficient tooth grinding surfaces, and physiological mechanisms (e.g., rumination) that help reduce particle size. These mechanisms have apparently not evolved in reptilian herbivores. Unlike the simple teeth of carnivorous lizards, herbivorous lizards have cusp-like teeth that may aid in the cutting of plant material (Hotton 1955). Cropping is accomplished by the movement of the jaw around the atlantooccipital and mandibular joints (Throckmorton 1976). Herbivorous reptiles do not masticate food, and swallow relatively large pieces (Throckmorton 1976; Norman and Weishampel 1985). Gastroliths have been reported in the stomachs of some herbivorous reptiles, and these stones may assist in reducing particle size of ingested plant material. Given the limited ability to physically reduce particle size, it appears that reptilian herbivores rely on longer transit times to maximize plant fiber digestibility (Bjorndal, Bolton, and Moore 1990).

Digestion and Environment

Ambient temperature can affect many physiological processes, including digestive processes. Digestive processes of ectotherms may be more sensitive to changes in temperature than those of endotherms. Ambient temperature is an important aspect of management of captive reptiles. In previous reports, it was suggested that herbivorous species need to increase their body temperature to digest their diet more efficiently (see Zimmerman and Tracy 1989 for review). Recent data suggest, however, that dry matter, energy, and fiber digestibility is thermally stable, at least in *Iguana iguana* (van Marken Lichtenbelt 1992; Baer 1993). In iguanas, temperature does affect other digestive processes. At higher temperatures (35°C), iguanas consume more food, have faster transit times and growth rates than at lower temperatures (28°C). Similar data have been reported for omnivorous turtles (Avery et al. 1993) but the effect of temperature on digestive physiology of herbivorous turtles or tortoises has not been published, and requires further investigation.

Diets Consumed by Free-Ranging Herbivorous Reptiles

There are few comprehensive reports on nutrient intakes of free-ranging herbivorous reptiles. Neutral detergent fiber and crude protein content of plants known to be consumed by free ranging herbivorous reptiles are presented in Table 1. Limited information on nutrient intake is a consequence of many factors, including the infrequent feeding bouts of many reptilian species. For example, of 378 hours of observation of *Iguana iguana*, only 145 minutes were spent feeding (Rand et al. 1990). Furthermore, it often is difficult to determine quantitatively the amount of food, or the nutrient content of the feed consumed compared to the uneaten portion. This can be particularly problematic in species that are highly selective in foraging strategy.

Diets for Captive Herbivorous Reptiles

Limited availability of food items, and lack of information on the nutrient content of diets consumed by free-ranging herbivorous reptiles make it difficult to mimic diets fed to captive reptiles. Historically,

TABLE 1. Fiber and protein compositions of some feeds known to be consumed by free-ranging herbivorous reptiles (expressed on a dry matter basis).

Species	Diet type	Neutral detergent fiber (%)	Crude protein (%)	Reference
Chelonia mydas	leaves	43.6	16.8	Bjorndal 1980
Gopherus polyphemus	leaves	43.0	33.1	Bjorndal 1987
Xerobates agassizii	leaves	25.7	15.6	Meienberger et al. 1993
	leaves	72.4	5.0	Meienberger et al. 1993
Pseudemys nelsoni	leaves	38.5	31.9	Bjorndal and Bolten 1990
	leaves	36.7	19.4	Bjorndal and Bolton 1990
Geochelone carbonaria	fruit	56.0	7.2	Moskovits and Bjorndal 1990
and	fruit	41.6	4.8	Bjorndal 1989
Geochelone denticulata	leaves	48.9	17.2	Bjorndal 1989
Iguana iguana	fruit	42.2	11.1	van Marken Lichtenbelt 1993
	leaves	38.6	20.6	van Marken Lichtenbelt 1993
	leaves	50.7	25.0	Troyer 1984
Sauromalus obesus	mixed	not reported	14.0	Nagy and Shoemaker 1975

zoos have taken the approach of feeding the animals items which are readily available, and somewhat similar, at least in terms of botanical classification, to what they consume in the wild. For instance, folivorous species may be offered lettuce, kale, or other leafy greens. Frugivores may be offered a diet containing cultivated fruits such as apples, oranges, or bananas, even though these items have little in common with the foods the animals consume in the wild. Many zoos offer "salads" to captive herbivorous reptiles. Since cultivated fruits and vegetables do not constitute a nutritionally balanced diet; however, pelleted feeds formulated for rabbits or other herbivorous animals may be used to help provide necessary nutrients. Nutrient composition of commonly used cultivated leafy greens and fruits are presented in Table 2.

Free-ranging *Geochelone carbonaria* and *G. denticulata* are reported to consume fruits containing (mean value on a dry matter basis) 7.2% crude protein, 56% NDF, 0.35% calcium, and 0.11% phosphorus (Moskovits and Bjorndal 1990). By contrast, the nutrient composition of typical cultivated fruits these tortoises may be offered in captivity is lower (Table 2). Thus, diets prepared from cultivated fruits cannot provide similar nutrient intakes to diets that tortoises select in the wild. A similar comparison can be made between the leaves that *Iguana iguana* consume in the wild and leafy greens that they might be offered in captivity (Tables 1 and 2).

Supplements

In order to overcome some potential nutritional deficiencies, the use of supplements for captive animals has become popular, especially when only fruits and vegetables are used. Unfortunately, inappropriate use of supplements can be detrimental to animal health. A comparison of five supplements is presented in Table 3. There can be large differences in nutrient ratios and concentrations among supplements. The ratio between vitamin A and vitamin D in Reptical is approximately 7:1 but the ratio of these two nutrients in Nekton-Rep is 660:1. A ratio of 10:1 is typical in animals that have established requirements for vitamin A and vitamin D. In some cases a nutrient may be provided by the supplement, but the concentration of the nutrient in the supplement is not reported on the label. These factors make it difficult to use supplements intelligently. Care must be given in selecting the appropriate supplement and controlling the amount provided. More often than not, these two steps in selecting and using a supplement are overlooked with potentially dire consequences. It is important to know the specific nutrients lacking in a particular diet, and the amounts of a specific supplement that is needed to correct a deficiency. Label directions from a supplement may not be appropriate since these recommendations do not take into account the nutrient composition of other components of the diet.

TABLE 2. Nutrient composition of some cultivated vegetables and fruits (expressed on a dry matter basis, except water).[1]

	Produce item					
Nutrient	Lettuce	Kale	Celery	Apple	Banana	Orange
Water (%)	95.9	84.5	94.7	83.9	74.3	86.8
Crude protein (%)	24.6	21.3	12.5	1.2	4.0	7.1
Crude fat (%)	4.6	4.5	2.3	2.2	1.9	0.9
Neutral detergent fiber (%)	22.0	Not available	17.0	12.6	5.4	Not available
Calcium (%)	0.46	0.87	0.68	0.04	0.02	0.30
Phosphorus (%)	0.49	0.36	0.49	0.04	0.08	0.11

[1]From United States Department of Agriculture, "Composition of Foods" Agriculture Handbook 8–9 (1982) and 8–11 (1984).

TABLE 3. Comparison of common dietary vitamin and mineral supplements used in feeding captive reptiles.

	Nutrient			
Product	Calcium (%)	Phosphorus (%)	Vitamin A (IU/kg)	Vitamin D (IU/kg)
Nekton-Rep[1]	6.24	0.0	6,600,000.00	10,000.00
Vionate[2]	10.82	5.44	220,000.00	22,000.00
Chaparral Zoo Vitamins[3]	2.22	1.61	642,437.00	636.00
Reptical[4]	32.10	20.00	270,315.00	40,526.00
Reptovit[4]	9.1	8.3	500,000.00	12,500.00

[1]Nekton USA Inc., 1917 Tyrone Blvd., St. Petersburg, Florida 33710, USA
[2]Rich Health, Inc., P.O. Box 18258, Irvine, California 92713, USA
[3]Chaparral Sales Co., 6810 Edith NE, Albuquerque, New Mexico 87113, USA
[4]TetraWerke, Dr. rer. nat. Ulrich Baensch GmbH, D-4520, Melle 1, Germany

Nutritionally Complete Feeds

Development of nutritionally complete feeds (feeds that contain all of the known nutrients in appropriate concentrations and ratios) are better suited for long-term captive management of herbivorous lizards. Pelleted and extruded feeds have long been used for many species of captive mammals and birds. Diets have been developed and tested for herbivorous lizards (*Iguana iguana*) and for tortoises (*Xerobates agassizii*) (Baer 1993; O. T. Oftedal, pers. comm.). Studies with these species and others have helped determine the effect of different levels of dietary fiber, minerals, and protein on several physiological responses. Feed manufacturers have used the information from research studies to produce nutritionally balanced, complete feeds. The composition of these diets is loosely based on the nutrient content of plants known to be eaten by these species, and on the known nutrient requirements for mammalian herbivores. These diets con-

TABLE 4. Comparison of some commercially available, nutritionally complete feeds used in feeding captive herbivorous reptiles (expressed on a dry matter basis, assuming 10% moisture and available information from company literature).

	Diet			
Nutrient	Mazuri Turtle Breeder 35[1,2]	Zeigler Starter/Grower Tortoise Diet[3]	Zeigler Maintenance Tortoise Diet[3]	Zeigler Iguana Diet[3]
Crude protein (%)	38.9	20.0	13.9	22.2
Crude fat (%)	3.9	6.3	4.4	3.3
Neutral detergent fiber (%)	Not available	13.9	20.0	24.0
Calcium (%)	1.4	1.8	1.1	1.7
Phosphorus (%)	0.8	0.8	0.6	0.8

[1]PMI Feeds, St. Louis, Missouri 63166, USA
[2]Based on company literature, this diet was designed for green sea turtles and may be useful for other large herbivorous turtles.
[3]Zeigler Bros. Inc., Gardners, Pennsylvania 17324, USA

tain all of the required nutrients in amounts and ratios appropriate for herbivores. In commercial preparations, some nutrients may be increased to account for the stress in captivity or storage. A comparison of selected commercial diets for herbivorous reptiles is presented in Table 4. One important advantage of commercial diets is the ease with which they can be modified as new data become available. In addition to the use of nutritionally complete feeds, small amounts of leafy green vegetables may be added. Small amounts of fresh greens can improve acceptance of dry diets and also provide water. Clean, fresh water should be available at all times whenever dry diets are fed.

Protein requirement and dietary protein concentrations often generate much interest. Animals do not have requirements for specific proteins but require the constituent amino acids. Proteins are composed of different combinations, varying in length and sequence, of approximately 22 different amino acids. During digestion, dietary proteins are hydrolyzed to these constituent amino acids. Amino acids are then absorbed, and can be metabolized, oxidized, or resynthesized into other proteins. Proteins are the major component of muscle and are important for synthesis of all tissues. Thus, protein requirements are usually greater for growing animals. Low concentrations of dietary protein can impair growth and immunological function. On the other hand, there are few data which suggest that detrimental effects occur due to excessive protein, if the protein contains the proper ratio of amino acids. In one study with 300 *Chelonia mydas* (Wood and Wood 1981), 14-month and 44-month old turtles were fed 25%, 30%, and 35% protein diets for 16 weeks. When fed the diet of 35% protein, younger turtles grew faster, and exhibited lower mortality, than those fed the two other diets. Older turtles, as well, grew faster when fed the 30% and 35% protein diets than those fed the 25% protein diet. Only one older turtle (out of 150) died during the study (this turtle was fed the 25% crude protein diet). In a similar study with hatchling and one year old *I. iguana*, iguanas fed 25% crude protein grew faster than those fed 15% or 20% crude protein (Allen et al. 1991). These types of controlled studies are crucial to improving our understanding of the nutritional requirements of herbivorous reptiles, and greatly help in establishing a scientific basis for dietary formulation.

Summary

It is difficult to replicate natural diets in captivity. Attempts to use nutritional supplements to improve diet quality are well-intentioned, yet may be inappropriate or inadequate. Oversupplementation and undersupplementation of some nutrients can lead to nutrient toxicities or deficiencies. A more appropriate approach to feeding captive animals is to develop and use nutritionally complete feeds that have been tested in feeding trials. These diets should form the foundation of a rational diet, with small amounts of leafy greens used judiciously. Supplements should not be needed. In addition, development of nutritionally complete diets will facilitate nutritional research that can help define nutrient requirements of herbivorous reptiles. Proper diet and environment are important management tools useful in controlling growth rate and maximizing reproductive capacity. Ultimately, a successful breeding program is dependent on a successful nutrition program.

Literature Cited

Allen, M. E., O. T. Oftedal, D. J. Baer, and D. Werner. 1991. Nutritional studies with the green iguana, p. 73–81. *In* T. P. Meehan, S. D. Thompson, and M. E. Allen (eds.). Proceedings of the Eighth Dr. Scholl Conference on the Nutrition of Captive Wild Animals. Lincoln Park Zoological Society, Chicago, Illinois. 163 pages.

Avery, H. W., J. R. Spotila, J. D. Congdon, R. U. Fischer, E. A. Standora, and S. B. Avery. 1993. Roles of diet protein and temperature in the growth and nutritional energetics of juvenile slider turtles, *Trachemys scripta*. Physiol. Zool., 66: 902–925.

Baer, D. J. 1993. Effects of diet composition and ambient temperature on digestive function and bioenergetics of the green iguana (*Iguana iguana*). Doctoral Dissertation, Michigan State University, East Lansing, Michigan. v, 150 pages.

Bjorndal, K. A. 1979. Cellulose digestion and volatile fatty acid production in the green turtle, *Chelonia mydas*. Comp. Biochem. Physiol., 63A: 127–133.

——. 1980. Nutrition and grazing behavior of the green turtle *Chelonia mydas*. Marine Biol., 56: 147–154.

——. 1987. Digestive efficiency in a temperate herbivorous reptile, *Gopherus polyphemus*. Copeia, 1987: 714–720.

Bjorndal, K. A., and A. B. Bolton. 1990. Digestive processing in a herbivorous freshwater turtle: consequences of small-intestine fermentation. Physiol. Zool., 63: 1232–1247.

Bjorndal, K. A., A. B. Bolton, and J. E. Moore. 1990. Digestive fermentation in herbivores: effect of food particle size. Physiol. Zool., 63: 710–721.

Foley, W. J., A. Bouskila, A. Sholnik, and I. Choshniak. 1987. Microbial digestion in the herbivorous lizard *Uromastyx aegyptius*, p. 117–118. *In* M. Rose (ed.), Herbivore Nutrition Research – Second International Symposium on the Nutrition of Herbivores. Australian Society of Animal Production (occasional publication), University of Queensland, St. Lucia.

Guard, C. L. 1980. The reptilian digestive system: general characteristics, p. 43–51. *In* K. Schmidt-Nielsen, L. Bolis, and C. R. Taylor (eds.), Comparative Physiology: Primitive Mammals. Cambridge Univ. Press, Cambridge, UK.

Hotton, N. 1955. A survey of adaptive relationships of dentition to the diet in the North American Iguanidae. Amer. Midl. Nat., 53: 88–114.

McBee, R. H., and V. H. McBee. 1982. The hindgut fermentation in the green iguana, *Iguana iguana*, p. 77–83. *In* G. M. Burghardt, and A. S. Rand (eds.), Iguanas of the World. Noyes Publications, Park Ridge, New Jersey. xix, 472 pages.

Meienberger, C., I. R. Wallis, and K. A. Nagy. 1993. Food intake rate and body mass influence transit time and digestibility in the desert tortoise (*Xerobates agassizii*). Physiol. Zool., 66: 847–862.

Moskovits, D. K., and K. A. Bjorndal. 1990. Diet and food preferences of the tortoises *Geochelone carbonaria* and *G. denticulata* in northwestern Brazil. Herpetologica, 46: 207–218.

Nagy, K. A., and V. H. Shoemaker. 1975. Energy and nitrogen budgets of the free-living desert lizard *Sauromalus obesus*. Physiol. Zool., 48: 252–262.

Norman, D. B., and D. B. Weishampel. 1985. Ornithopod feeding mechanisms: their bearing on the evolution of herbivory. Amer. Nat., 126: 151–164.

Ostrum, J. H. 1963. Further comments on herbivorous lizards. Evolution, 17: 368–369.

Pough, F. H. 1973. Lizard energetics and diet. Ecology, 54: 837–844.

Rand, S. A., B. A. Dugan, H. Monteza, and D. Vianda. 1990. The diet of a generalized folivore: *Iguana iguana* in Panama. Jour. Herpetol., 24: 211–214.

Sokol, O. M. 1967. Herbivory in lizards. Evolution, 21: 192–194.

——. 1971. Lithophagy and geophagy in reptiles. Jour. Herpetol., 5: 69–71.

Stevens, C. E. 1988. Comparative Physiology of the Vertebrate Digestive System. Cambridge University Press, Cambridge, UK. xi, 300 pages.

Szarski, H. 1962. Some remarks on herbivorous lizards. Evolution, 16: 529.

Throckmorton, G. S. 1976. Oral food processing in two herbivorous lizards, *Iguana iguana* (Iguanidae) and *Uromastix aegyptius* (Agamidae). Jour. Morphol., 148: 363–390.

Troyer, K. 1982. Transfer of fermentative microbes between generations in a herbivorous lizard. Science, 216: 540–542.

——. 1984. Behavioral acquisition of the hindgut fermentation system by hatchling *Iguana iguana*. Behav. Ecol. Sociobiol., 14: 189–193.

van Marken Lichtenbelt, W. 1992. Digestion in an ectothermic herbivore, the green iguana (*Iguana iguana*): effect of food composition and body temperature. Physiol. Zool., 65: 649–673.

Van Soest, P. J. 1982. Nutritional Ecology of the Ruminant. O & B Books, Inc., Corvallis, Oregon. v, 374 pages.

Warner, A. C. I. 1981. Rate of passage of digesta through the gut of mammals and birds. Nutrit. Abst. Rev., 51: 789–820.

Wood, J. R., and F. E. Wood. 1981. Growth and digestibility for the green turtle (*Chelonia mydas*) fed diets containing varying protein levels. Aquaculture, 25: 269–274.

Zimmerman, L. C., and C. R. Tracy. 1989. Interactions between the environment and ectothermy and herbivory in reptiles. Physiol. Zool., 62: 374–409.

❦

❦ Baer, D. J. 1994. The nutrition of herbivorous reptiles, p. 83–90. *In* J. B. Murphy, K. Adler, and J. T. Collins (eds.), Captive Management and Conservation of Amphibians and Reptiles. Society for the Study of Amphibians and Reptiles, Ithaca (New York). Contributions to Herpetology, volume 11.

Captive Maintenance and Lineage Senescence in Parthenogenetic Lizards (Family Teiidae)

Warren P. Porter,* Charles J. Cole,** and Carol R. Townsend**

Introduction

For the past 20 years, Charles J. Cole and Carol R. Townsend have maintained colonies of parthenogenetic Whiptail Lizards (*Cnemidophorus*) and Shiny Lizards (*Gymnophthalmus*) for research on reproduction, genetics, evolution, and systematics (Cole and Townsend 1990). We have worked with several species and often several population samples of a species, and we have had varying degrees of success in developing lineages. The longest lineage, for *Cnemidophorus exsanguis*, extended from the P_1 to the F_7 generation over a period of twelve years. The shortest lineages are represented by *C. tesselatus*, for which we have yet to obtain viable eggs from an F_1 female.

Prior to 1972, we were unable to raise captive hatchlings of any species of *Cnemidophorus* to adulthood. Since then we have learned that these lizards are particularly susceptible to metabolic bone disease (MBD) in captivity. Initially, ultraviolet radiation (UVR) prevented MBD and allowed production of viable eggs by some laboratory-reared females (Cole and Townsend 1977; Townsend 1979). Next we learned that a regular replacement schedule is necessary for certain light bulbs that produce UVR (UVR output decreases with age of the bulb, although general illumination remains strong), and different species of lizards require different doses of UVR (Townsend and Cole 1985). Even so, we have noticed that successful lineages show decreasing production of healthy offspring (lineage senescence), and they may fail altogether after several generations in captivity (Hardy et al. 1989).

Inbreeding depression often is hypothesized as the cause of lineage senescence in captive animals. This is ruled out in the case of these parthenogenetic lizards, because genetic data from karyotypic and electrophoretic analyses demonstrate that normally a lineage is a clone—all individuals within a lineage are genetically identical (Dessauer and Cole 1986; Cole et al. 1990). Consequently, each individual should have the same traits as its sisters, mother, grandmother, and other female relatives, including the ability to reproduce.

Perhaps parthenogenetic lineages last for only a few generations in nature and they are renewed by continuing hybridization (for reviews of hybrid origins, see Darevsky et al. 1985; Dessauer and Cole 1989). This explanation is rejected also, as certain populations of unisexual species (including ones in which we have observed captive lineage senescence) occur in nature hundreds of kilometers away from the nearest extant populations of their bisexual ancestors and/or in isolation on islands, yet these populations remain healthy after dozens or hundreds of generations, at least.

We hypothesize that the problem is in the captive environment. As such, it could be unique to our colonies or it could be a broad problem that affects

* Department of Zoology
University of Wisconsin
Madison, Wisconsin 53706, USA

** American Museum of Natural History
Central Park West at 79th Street
New York, New York 10024, USA

Acronyms used in this chapter:

AOAC	Association of Official Analytical Chemists, Washington, DC
F	Filial (offspring) generation
FAD	Flavin adenine dinucleotide
FDA	Food and Drug Administration, Washington, DC
MBD	Metabolic bone disease
P	Parental generation
ppb	Parts per billion
ppm	Parts per million
QA	Quality assurance
UVR	Ultraviolet radiation

other captive vertebrates that have similar requirements, including endangered species in captive-breeding programs. In organisms with long generation times (for example, ten years or more), such a problem could take decades to recognize, and then it could be too late to salvage the lineage after identifying the cause.

For the present, three possible causes appear most likely to explain the lineage senescence observed: (1) an accumulating deficiency of a critical component of the diet, such as a necessary trace element; (2) chronic low-level exposure to or accumulation of a toxin that poisons the lizards (this includes possible overdose of an essential dietary element, as in hypervitaminosis); or (3) a combination of these factors. As it is very difficult to document dietary problems involving trace elements, particularly among small organisms whose nutritional requirements are so poorly known, we initiated a search for toxins in the captive environment.

In the last few years, "nonstandard" effects of pesticides (insecticides and herbicides) have been discovered. These include immune suppression by carbamate insecticides, such as aldicarb, at levels as low as 1 part per billion (ppb)(Olson et al. 1987; Selvan et al. 1989; Dean et al. 1990). Triazene herbicides, such as atrazine and metribuzin, have been implicated in thyroxine, testosterone, and luteinizing hormone changes and changes in learning behavior (Boyd et al. 1990; Babic-Gojmerac et al. 1989; Ghinea et al. 1979). Neuroendocrine-immune connections and interactions have been the subject of two recent books (Cotman et al. 1987; Bockman and Kirby 1990). We hypothesized that effects on the nervous system by insecticides would have ramifications for the immune and endocrine system, too. Similarly, herbicides that have endocrine effects might also affect immune and nervous-system functions, because of the feedbacks among these three systems. Reproduction is very sensitive to endocrine levels that could conceivably be modulated by pesticides.

Prior work (Boyd et al. 1990; Olson et al. 1987; Porter et al. 1984) and recently published data (Porter et al. 1993) on three mammalian species indicate that pesticide effects can be induced by 1 to 10 ppb exposure in drinking water and often are caused by interactions of pesticides that commonly occur in drinking water. Some of the carbamates, such as thiram, are also used as fungicides for grain storage and have been shown to halt egg laying in poultry (Waibel et al. 1955).

Carbamate insecticides mimic the structure of acetylcholine. They are designed to attach to acetylcholinesterase, which leads to prolonged opening of the postsynaptic sodium-ion channel, thereby promoting nerve dysfunction (Amdur et al. 1991). Carbamate insecticides also chelate copper and zinc in humans and poultry, which is typically countered with massive doses of these elements (Wu et al. 1990). Zinc is a key element in the binding of DNA polymerase to DNA and is implicated in the binding of hormones to cell-surface receptors (Cummingham et al. 1990). Copper is essential in the structure of superoxide dismutase, an important detoxifying enzyme in the liver.

In this paper we present reproductive data that document lineage senescence in captive parthenogenetic lizards and results of an initial screening for toxins in the food and water provided both to the lizards and to the insects that constitute the bulk of their diet.

Methods

Procedures for maintaining colonies of *Cnemidophorus* and *Gymnophthalmus* have been detailed elsewhere (Townsend 1979; Townsend and Cole 1985; Hardy et al. 1989). Since 1985, we have made two modifications. Instead of giving the lizards milk, we gave them tribasic calcium phosphate powder, both in their water dish (saturated solution) and mixed in equal volume with Avia (a powdered vitamin mixture for birds, produced by Nutra-Vet Research Corp., Poughkeepsie, New York), which was dusted onto the insects (primarily crickets and mealworms) twice weekly while feeding the lizards, until September 1991. And in an effort to improve the nutritive value of the insects and gut-load them with balanced calcium and phosphorus, we fed the mealworms and crickets a chicken mash (Agway Country Egg Layer) that has a mineral content suitable for laying hens. We now question whether the chicken mash has been detrimental (see below), and we have stopped using it.

Most recently (September 1991, after observations in Table 1 were recorded), we replaced the tribasic calcium phosphate used in the lizard water dishes with OsteoForm (a calcium-phosphorus powder with vitamins, manufactured by Vet-A-Mix, Inc., Shenandoah, Iowa). OsteoForm is more soluble in water than is tribasic calcium phosphate. As OsteoForm contains vitamins, the vitamin-mineral supplement dusted onto the food items is now applied only once weekly. These new changes did not affect the present study, but we mention them in case readers are unaware of OsteoForm.

Samples of the following items were screened for carbamates, dithiocarbamates, chlorinated hydrocarbons, organophosphates, atrazine, and thiram: the wheat bran and chicken mash fed to the mealworms and crickets; the mealworms and crickets fed to the lizards; and the water provided to the lizards. Analyses were performed by the State of Wisconsin Department of Agriculture, Trade and Consumer Protection, Bureau of Laboratory Services. Dithiocarbamates, which include thiram, were assayed by the evolution of decomposition products that were measured by a Cary 219 spectrophotometer and by a Perkin Elmer LC55 spectrophotometer. This method is described in "Analytical Methods for Pesticides" (Anonymous 1964). Thiram was used as the quality-assurance (QA) control. Method sensitivity is 1.0 ppm for most dithiocarbamates, including thiram. N-methyl carbamates were assayed by a post-column fluorescence-derivative method. The liquid chromatography was done using a Spectra Physics 8800, followed by a Kratos PCRS 520 post-column unit, followed by a Kratos Spectroflow 980 fluorescence unit using a 230 nm excitation wavelength and measuring at an emission wavelength of 418 nm. The extraction protocol is described in the "FDA Pesticide Analytical Manual" (Anonymous 1982). The clean-up and determination followed the Association of Official Analytical Chemists (AOAC) methods (Anonymous 1991). The QA control used was carbaryl. Method sensitivity is 0.1 ppm. Organophosphates were measured following AOAC methods (Anonymous 1990). Chlorpyrifos was used as the QA control. Method sensitivity is 0.1 ppm.

TABLE 1. Reproduction and survival in laboratory-reared lineages of parthenogenetic lizards (*Cnemidophorus* and *Gymnophthalmus*).

Species	Generation	Number in colony	Number that laid eggs (%)	Number of eggs laid	Number of eggs hatched (%)	Survival (%)[1]
Cnemidophorus opatae	P_1	4	4 (100)	71	37 (52)	–
	F_1	37	17 (46)	112	59 (53)	(81)
	F_2	59	3 (5)[2]	21[2]	10 (48)	(32)
	F_3	10[2]	–	–	–	(20)[2]
Cnemidophorus sonorae	P_1	4	4 (100)	20	18 (90)	–
	F_1	18	7 (39)	42	9 (21)	(83)
	F_2	9[3]	0 (0)	0	0 (0)	(0)
Gymnophthalmus underwoodi	P_1	2	2 (100)	21	21 (100)	–
	F_1	21	8 (38)	32	17 (53)	–
	F_2	17	8 (47)	52	26 (50)	–
	F_3	26	2 (8)	66	9 (14)	–
	F_4	9	3 (33)	17	5 (29)	–
	F_5	5	3 (60)	7[4]	0 (0)[4]	–

[1]Lizards of the generation specified that lived at least three months after hatching.
[2]Some F_2-generation *C. opatae* are still alive, so more eggs and F_3 offspring could be produced, but most of the F_2s have died, the survivors have laid very few eggs even though they are adults, and mortality has increased in F_3 hatchlings.
[3]The nine F_2 *C. sonorae* are all dead. Some F_1 adults remain alive, but they are not reproducing.
[4]The secretive *Gymnophthalmus* are not monitored as intensively as the *Cnemidophorus*, so their data are less complete (see Hardy et al. 1989). The F_5 *G. underwoodi* are known to have produced a total of ten eggs to date, three of which were frozen for experiments and the remaining seven of which died.

TABLE 2. Results of testing for specific substances in items used in maintaining the colonies of parthenogenetic lizards.

Item analyzed	Substances tested for (sensitivity of test)[1]	Results (amount)[1]
Wheat bran	Atrazine (0.10)	None detected
	Carbamates (0.15)	None detected
	Thiram (1.00)	None detected
Chicken mash	Atrazine (0.10)	None detected
	Carbamates (0.15)	None detected
	Thiram	Present (1.4)
Water	Carbamates (0.50)	None detected
	Organophosphate (0.25)	None detected
	Chlorinated hydrocarbons (0.25)	None detected
Mealworms	Carbamates (0.10)	None detected
	Organophosphate (0.10)	None detected
	Dithiocarbamate (1.0)	None detected
	Thiram (1.0)	None detected
Crickets	Carbamates (0.10)	None detected
	Organophosphate (0.10)	None detected
	Dithiocarbamate (1.0)	None detected
	Thiram (1.0)	None detected

[1]Sensitivity of test means presence above this amount would have been detected (parts per million).

Results

Lineage Senescence. The data in Table 1 and Figure 1 document lineage senescence in laboratory lineages (clones) of *Cnemidophorus opatae*, *C. sonorae*, and *Gymnophthalmus underwoodi*. All of the *Cnemidophorus* that had been in the laboratory during recent years had been fed throughout their lives on prey which ate the chicken mash and these lineages have not survived as well as some others of *Cnemidophorus* that we maintained previously. The earlier generations (about half) of the *Gymnophthalmus* were not exposed to possible effects of the chicken mash in our laboratory (although the mail-ordered crickets fed to them might have been), but the last ones definitely were.

Chemical Screening. The data in Table 2 record the discovery of thiram in the batch of chicken mash used for a year to feed the insects that were fed to the lizards discussed above; and we used the same brand of mash for six years. Thiram (tetramethylthiuram disulfide) is manufactured by Sigma Chemical Company, which states, among other things, the following about this product (excerpted from the "Material Safety Data Sheets" from Sigma, dated July 1, 1991 and April 1, 1988): "Harmful if swallowed, inhaled, or absorbed through skin. Overexposure may cause reproductive disorder(s) based on tests with laboratory animals. Laboratory experiments have shown mutagenic effects. Avoid prolonged or repeated exposure."

Discussion

Carbamates can affect reproduction and growth as well as immune function. Thiram has been shown to inhibit egg-laying in poultry at 30 ppm concentration in feed (Waibel et al. 1955). It also induces abnormal cartilage formation, suppresses primary humoral immunity, and reduces bone strength in poultry at 30 ppm (Wu et al. 1990).

We have not yet conducted toxicity experiments with lizards to determine whether they are affected by thiram and related compounds in the same way as are the organisms discussed above. Therefore, we cannot demonstrate that the thiram caused or contributed to the lineage senescence (Table 1, Figure 1). Such research is warranted, however, as thiram is known to have direct toxic effects on vertebrates, including detrimental effects on development, growth, and reproduction (Wailbel et al. 1955; Wu et al. 1990). In addition, by binding copper and zinc, it has the added effect of causing a deficiency in their availability for essential metabolic functions. Therefore, it is possible that a combination of poisoning and nutritional deficiency can compound problems of lineage senescence.

The absence of thiram at detectable levels from the mealworms and crickets tested (Table 2) is not necessarily good news. The mealworms tested were purchased from a supplier, fed the chicken mash containing thiram for a week, removed from the

→

FIGURE 1 (opposite page). Lineage senescence in captive lizards (data in Table 1). (A) Absolute number of lizards (*Cnemidophorus opatae*) and number of eggs laid by them, in four generations in captivity. (B) Percentages of lizards (*C. opatae*) that laid eggs, of eggs that hatched, and of hatchlings that lived more than three months, in three generations in captivity. (C) Percentages of lizards (*C. sonorae*) that laid eggs, of eggs that hatched, and of hatchlings that lived more than three months, in two generations in captivity. (D) Percentage of *Gymnophthalmus underwoodi* eggs that hatched in five generations in captivity (line fitted by eye).

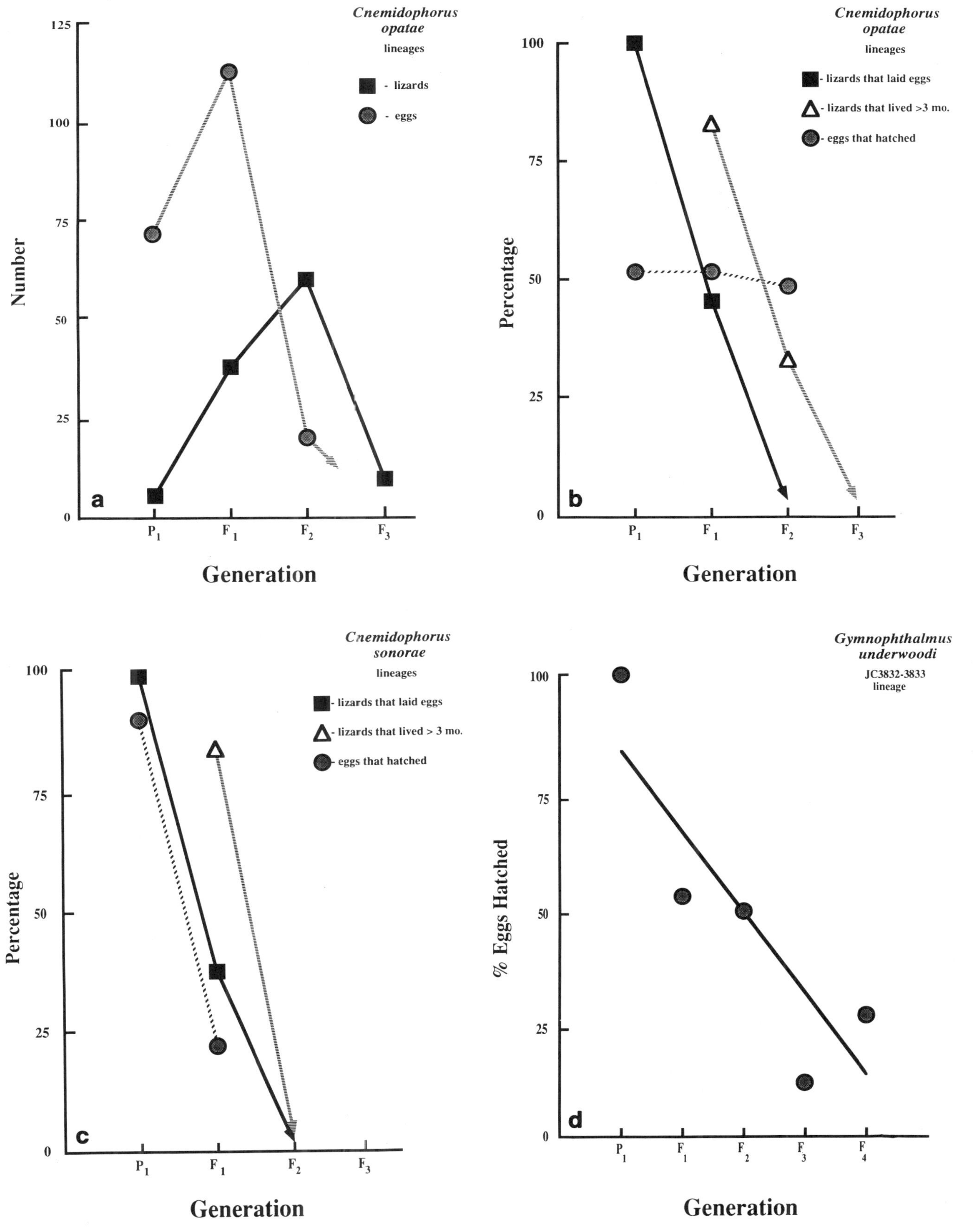
Cnemidophorus opatae lineages
- lizards
- eggs
Number
125
100
75
50
25
0
a
P1 F1 F2 F3
Generation
Cnemidophorus opatae lineages
- lizards that laid eggs
- lizards that lived >3 mo.
- eggs that hatched
Percentage
100
75
50
25
0
b
P1 F1 F2 F3
Generation
Cnemidophorus sonorae lineages
- lizards that laid eggs
- lizards that lived > 3 mo.
- eggs that hatched
Percentage
100
75
50
25
0
c
P1 F1 F2 F3
Generation
Gymnophthalmus underwoodi
JC3832-3833 lineage
% Eggs Hatched
100
75
50
25
0
d
P1 F1 F2 F3 F4
Generation

mash and frozen, then thawed and analyzed. We know these mealworms ingested thiram in the feed. It is comforting to suggest that thiram is not accumulating in the tissues of the mealworms, but we know nothing about the physiology of the metabolites of thiram that may be present.

Metabolites of pesticides can be more toxic than the substances from which they are derived (Amdur et al. 1991). This is particularly true for "less toxic" compounds, because detoxification of many of these compounds in the liver, kidney, lungs, or other tissues may produce highly reactive epoxides or other electrophilic intermediate molecules by cytochrome P450 isozymes, FAD-containing mono-oxygenase, epoxide hydratase, monoamine oxidase, and/or xanthine oxidase. These more water-soluble versions of toxicants may then be conjugated by glucuronidation, sulfation, or glutathione-S-transferases to facilitate excretion. Conjugation rates may be inadequate to accommodate all reactive compounds that may conjugate with DNA or with various proteins, such as enzymes, or structural proteins, such as tubulin, actin or myosin, leading to toxic effects that may be acute or chronic with subtle or obvious symptoms (Amdur et al. 1991).

Similarly, the apparent absence of thiram from the crickets (Table 2) may or may not be good news. We had the crickets sent directly to Wisconsin from a commercial cricket supplier, which took several days. If thiram had been present in the cricket food, they may have lost their gut-load or converted it to metabolites prior to testing. Because some commercial insect suppliers use commercially obtained feeds, including chicken mash, it is possible (or even likely?) that commercial crickets eat thiram (and other additives) on occasion as well.

Finally, it should be noted that the state of the art in detection of carbamates in solids is such that the absolute sensitivity is still two orders of magnitude too high to detect levels that in water cause immune suppression (Olson et al. 1987).

After discovering thiram in the chicken mash tested, we telephoned the supplier and asked why they put it in the mixture, and whether it is a preservative. The response was that the company does not put it in, and it might have appeared during storage of grain in a Midwest grain elevator or elsewhere in the process of obtaining the grains used.

Commercial animal feeds usually are a mixture of many grains and animal components, the various ingredients of which are obtained from diverse and scattered sources. Different growers, transporters, storage agents, and local feed manufacturers may use different compounds as pesticides, herbicides, fungicides, and other spoilage inhibitors. Consequently, the potential exists for each batch of feed that is prepared to contain different additives or combinations thereof (or maybe even none?), and such chemical analyses as we had performed reveal only those compounds specifically sought, if present at the levels of detection used. Therefore, if we bought another batch of the "same" chicken mash from the same commercial supplier, it might not contain thiram; but it might contain aldicarb. And if we bought another batch of the "same" wheat bran that contained no thiram when last tested (Table 2), it might contain thiram, aldicarb, and/or something else.

If such compounds are detrimental to development, growth, and reproduction of captive animals, they could cause similar problems for animals in nature. Be that as it may, for now we ask how might we reduce the exposure of captive animals to such compounds in commercial feeds. One solution is to ask suppliers what preservatives they use, and buy only feeds without such additives. Thiram was not put into the chicken mash by the supplier from which we bought it; it came as an accidental contaminant, as far as they were concerned. Thus, it would appear as if the only solution would be to feed the prey insects expensive commercial laboratory feeds that are sold as being certified free of any and all of the compounds we wish to avoid. Such feeds probably would have to be purchased frequently, for they may not have a very long shelf-life. Once we know specifically which compounds to avoid, new ones about which we know nothing will probably be on the market. In essence, this could be a rerun of the DDT story, with the effects of modern replacement compounds being more difficult to demonstrate.

Summary

Our ignorance of the nutritional requirements of captive reptiles and amphibians is vast, particularly concerning trace elements and effects of increasing dietary deficiencies over several generations.

We know even less about the sensitivity of these organisms to various food additives, ingested directly or as metabolites obtained in prey, and possible toxic effects accumulating over several generations. Detailed research should be directed toward solving these problems, although researchers must be aware that as the toxicity of compounds becomes proven, those compounds become eliminated from use, and new and unproven compounds may then come in vogue, and the research will have to be repeated with the new compounds.

Biologists who are breeding captive reptiles, particularly species with a long generation time (10 years or more), cannot rest easy if they have a good population going in the F_1 generation; the population may crash dramatically in subsequent generations, and this may have nothing to do with inbreeding depression (Figure 1). Even extensive, well-intended efforts of "tender loving care" may doom a lineage to extinction from poisoning and/or nutritional deficiency. Captive breeding and rearing may be, in some cases, detrimental to endangered species. Populations of endangered species may survive best if protected in natural preserves.

Acknowledgments

We are grateful to B. Patricia Escalante-Pliego for assistance in the field and Margaret G. Arnold, Philip Damiani, and Anthony E. Zammit for attentive care of the lizards in recent years. Research with these colonies was supported in part by the United States National Science Foundation (BSR 8105454 to C. J. Cole).

Literature Cited

Amdur, M. O., J. Doull, and C. D. Klaassen. 1991. Casarett and Doull's Toxicology: The Science of Poisons. Fourth edition. Pergamon Press, New York. 1033 pages.

Anonymous. 1964. Analytical methods for pesticides, plant growth regulators, and food additives, p. 69–77. *In* Fungicides, Nematocides and Soil Fumigants, Rodenticides, and Food and Feed Additives, Vol. 3. Academic Press, New York.

—. 1982. Food and Drug Administration Pesticide Analytical Manual. Vol. 1, Section 232.42. Federal Drug Administration, Washington, DC.

—. 1990. Chapter 10. Pesticide and industrial chemical residues, p. 282–283. *In* AOAC Method, Organochlorine and Organophosphorus Pesticide Residues, Gas Chromatographic Method, Section 985.22. Assoc. Official Analyt. Chemists, Washington, D. C.

—. 1991. Chapter 10. Pesticide and industrial chemical residues, p. 293–294. *In* Official Methods of Analysis of the Association of Official Analytical Chemists (AOAC), N-Methylcarbamate Insecticide and Metabolite Residues, Liquid Chromatographic Method, Section 985.23. Assoc. Official Analyt. Chemists, Washington, DC.

Babic-Gojmerac, T., Z. Kniewald, and J. Kniewald. 1989. Testosterone metabolism in neuroendocrine organs in male rats under atrazine and deethylatrazine influence. Jour. Steroid. Biochem., 33: 141–146.

Bockman, D. E., and M. L. Kirby. 1990. Neuroendocrine Immune Network. CRC Press, Boca Raton, Florida. 266 pages.

Boyd, C. A., M. H. Weiler, and W. P. Porter. 1990. Behavioral and neurochemical changes associated with chronic exposure to low-level concentration of pesticide mixtures. Jour. Tox. Environ. Health, 30: 209–221.

Cole, C. J., H. C. Dessauer, C. R. Townsend, and M. G. Arnold. 1990. Unisexual lizards of the genus *Gymnophthalmus* (Reptilia: Teiidae) in the Neotropics: genetics, origin, and systematics. Amer. Mus. Novit., 2994: 1–29.

Cole, C. J., and C. R. Townsend. 1977. Parthenogenetic reptiles: new subjects for laboratory research. Experientia, 33: 285–289.

—. 1990. Parthenogenetic lizards as vertebrate systems. Jour. Exper. Zool., suppl. 4: 174–176.

Cotman, C. W., R. E. Brinton, A. Galaburda, B. McEwen, and D. N. Schneider. 1987. The Neuro-Immune-Endocrine Connection. Raven Press, New York. 150 pages.

Cummingham, B. C., S. Bass, G. Fuh, and J. A. Wells. 1990. Zinc mediation of the binding of human growth hormone to the human prolactin receptor. Science, 250: 1709–1712.

Darevsky, I. S., L. A. Kupriyanova, and T. Uzzell. 1985. Parthenogenesis in reptiles, p. 411–526. *In* C. Gans and F. Billett (eds.), Biology of the Reptilia, Vol. 15 (Development B). John Wiley and Sons, New York. x, 731 pages.

Dean, T. N., V. N. Kakkanaiah, M. Nagarkatti, and P. S. Magarkatti. 1990. Immunosuppression by aldicarb of T cell responses to antigen-specific and polyclonal stimuli results from defective IL-1 production by the macrophages. Tox. Appl. Pharm., 106: 408–417.

Dessauer, H. C., and C. J. Cole. 1986. Clonal inheritance in parthenogenetic whiptail lizards: biochemical evidence. Jour. Hered., 77: 8–12.

—. 1989. Diversity between and within nominal forms of unisexual teiid lizards, p. 49–71. *In* R. M. Dawley and J. P. Bogart (eds.), Evolution and Ecology of Unisexual Vertebrates. Bull. 466 New York State Mus., Albany. v, 302 pages.

Ghinea, E., L. Simionescu, and M. Oprescu. 1979. Studies on the action of pesticides upon the endocrines using in vitro human thyroid cells culture and in vivo animal models. I. Rev. Romaine Med. Endocrinol., 17: 185–190.

Hardy, L. M., C. J. Cole, and C. R. Townsend. 1989. Parthenogenetic reproduction in the Neotropical unisexual lizard, *Gymnophthalmus underwoodi* (Reptilia: Teiidae). Jour. Morphol., 201: 215–234.

Olson, L. J., B. J. Erickson, R. D. Hinsdill, J. A. Wyman, W. P. Porter, L. K. Binning, R. C. Bidgood, and E. V. Nordheim. 1987. Aldicarb immunomodulation in mice: an inverse dose-response to parts per billion levels in drinking water. Arch. Environ. Contam. Toxicol., 16: 433–439.

Porter, W. P., S. M. Green, N. L. Debbink, and I. Carlson. 1993. Groundwater pesticides: interactive effects of low concentrations of carbamates aldicarb and methomyl and the triazine metribuzin on thyroxine and somatotropin levels in white rats. Jour. Tox. Environ. Health, 40: 15–34.

Porter, W. P., R. D. Hinsdill, A. Fairbrother, L. J. Olson, J. Jaeger, T. Yuill, S. Bisgaard, W. G. Hunter, and K. Nolan. 1984. Toxicant-disease-environment interactions associated with suppression of immune system, growth, and reproduction. Science, 224: 1014–1017.

Selvan, R. S., T. N. Dean, P. M. Hara, P. S. Nagarkatti, and M. Nagarkatti. 1989. Aldicarb suppresses macrophage but not natural killer (NK) cell-mediated cytotoxicity of tumor cells. Bull. Environ. Contam. Toxicol., 43: 676–682.

Townsend, C. R. 1979. Establishment and maintenance of colonies of parthenogenetic whiptail lizards. Internatl. Zoo Yearb., 19: 80–86.

Townsend, C. R., and C. J. Cole. 1985. Additional notes on requirements of captive whiptail lizards (*Cnemidophorus*), with emphasis on ultraviolet radiation. Zoo Biol., 4: 49–55.

Waibel, P. E., B. S. Pomeroy, and E. L. Johnson. 1955. Effect of arasan-treated corn on laying hens. Science, 121: 411–412.

Wu, W., M. E. Cook, and E. B. Smalley. 1990. Prevention of thiram-induced dyschondroplasia by copper. Nutr. Res., 10: 555–566.

❦

❦ Porter, W. P., C. J. Cole, and C. R. Townsend. 1994. Captive maintenance and lineage senescence in parthenogenetic lizards (family Teiidae), p. 91–98. *In* J. B. Murphy, K. Adler, and J. T. Collins (eds.), Captive Management and Conservation of Amphibians and Reptiles. Society for the Study of Amphibians and Reptiles, Ithaca (New York). Contributions to Herpetology, volume 11.

International Conservation and Captive Management of Tortoises

Ian R. Swingland*

Introduction

With the current pressure on land and natural resources—and the necessity for governments to reconcile the conflict between use and conservation (Swingland 1984, 1987)—captive breeding in modern species-recovery programs has become a vital means of preserving species in breeding groups. Our ignorance of the basic ecology of most species and the pace at which such management practices have had to be mounted leave doubts as to the long-term conservation value of these expensive and lengthy projects, and the viability of the end-product—the reintroduction of a self-perpetuating population (Swingland and Klemens 1989).

There are 40 species of tortoises in the world, of which about one-quarter are endangered, vulnerable, or rare (see Table 1). Most of these species are being captive bred by hobbyists and in small, private facilities for commercial purposes, but rarely in public institutions for conservation. The need for captive stock, and the simultaneous depredations in the wild to supply these captive groups, together with the worldwide bulk trade for pets (which is estimated by the International Union for the Conservation of Nature and Natural Resources [IUCN] Tortoise and Freshwater Turtle Specialist Group at well over 200,000 animals per year, and includes about twelve species) is a significant factor threatening wild species.

Current evidence points to an increase in captive-breeding activities, which can exacerbate the decline of the world's tortoise populations through over-zealous collecting. The lack of any long-term, successful reintroduction program (with the possible exception of the Galapagos Islands tortoise program, which still lacks concrete evidence of second-generation [F_2] breeding in the wild without constant and substantial human support) diminishes the justification of such practices without exceptional reasons. It is clear, however, that in a few species (for example, *Geochelone yniphora, G. elephantopus*, *Testudo kleinmanni*, and *Gopherus flavomarginatus*) such programs are fully justified and indeed are vital, given that there is clear scientific evidence of their possible extinction within specific criteria (Mace and Lande 1991).

Species mentioned in Table 1 are either in commercial trade or under threat from a wide variety of factors, such as feral mammals, collecting, fires, development, gassing, dune buggies and other off-road vehicles, military activity, roadkill, competition with grazing stock, or as material for musical instruments and for human food (even when the normal staple foods are present). With the exception of the three European species (including *T. marginata*, which is not ranked by IUCN in Table 1), the bulk trade of which has been banned by the European Parliament since January 1984, and the species in southern Namibia (*Homopus bergeri*), all of these species are available on the market and the herpetofaunal trade researchers at the Durrell Insti-

*The Durrell Institute of Conservation and Ecology
University of Kent
Canterbury, Kent CT2 7PD, UK

Acronyms used in this chapter:

CITES	Convention on International Trade in Endangered Species
IUCN	International Union for the Conservation of Nature and Natural Resources
JWPT	Jersey Wildlife Preservation Trust
RSPCA	Royal Society for the Prevention of Cruelty to Animals
SOPTOM	Société d'Observation et Protection des Tortues des Maures

TABLE 1. Status of tortoise species of the world. (From IUCN Tortoise Specialist Group meeting 1980 [unpubl.] and Groombridge 1982.)

Tortoises—Family Testudinidae (40 species worldwide)
Endangered species
Madagascar Tortoise (*Geochelone yniphora*)[1, 2]
Galapagos Tortoise (*Geochelone elephantopus*)[1, 2]
Bolson Tortoise (*Gopherus flavomarginatus*)[1, 2]
Flat-shelled Tortoise (*Acinixys planicauda*)[3]
Vulnerable species
Radiated Tortoise (*Geochelone radiata*)[1, 2]
Gopher Tortoise (*Gopherus polyphemus*)[2]
Geometric Tortoise (*Psammobates geometricus*)[2]
Spur-thighed Tortoise (*Testudo graeca*)[2]
Hermann's Tortoise (*Testudo hermanni*)[1, 2]
Egyptian Tortoise (*Testudo kleinmanni*)[3]
Pancake Tortoise (*Malacochersus tornieri*)[3]
Rare species
Aldabra Tortoise (*Geochelone gigantea*)[1, 2]

[1]Species being bred in captivity in 1992 with an explicit conservation objective.
[2]Protected species, as listed in IUCN Tortoise and Freshwater Turtle Specialist Group, Action Plan 1989.
[3]Species that could be added with reasonable justification (heavy trade, very small populations) but not on proven scientific criteria.

tute have gained access in the commercial market to specimens (A. Smart and I. Bride, unpubl. report).

In this chapter I will concentrate on some aspects of tortoise ecology and behavior pertinent to their management and conservation; review the scientific data necessary to plan pragmatic efforts to prevent extinction, concentrating on captive breeding and translocation; and describe existing projects and problems in tortoise conservation projects.

Conservation Management

In the management of wild tortoise populations and captive groups, basic information is necessary in five areas: systematics, populations, behavior, ecology and management (Table 2). Although the acquisition of such information is important, however, in situ conservation must move forward even if the data are incomplete. The reconciliation of incomplete ecological data with responsible, on-ground action can only be achieved by a transdisciplinary approach that involves socio-economics, education, local interests, restoration ecology, species ecology and behavior, and a minimalist approach to biological interference until more advanced scientific insights are gained through the continuing research that is necessary within any project. There is little justifiable argument for delay when a species and its habitat is under threat, even if the data are not sufficiently reliable and relevant.

A considerable danger exists, however. An increasing number of so-called captive-breeding projects—in Europe and elsewhere—are receiving public funds; these projects are purely money-making initiatives for private gain, and have garnered support through the fallacious use and misappropriation of scientific data. Without appropriate, impartial, and objective criteria for the licensing and support of captive-breeding projects, it is difficult to prevent the spread of such enterprises. Reliable data are the only means of judging or curtailing this damaging activity, which adversely affects responsible and professional projects (such as Société d'Observation et Protection des Tortues des Maures [SOPTOM] and Projêt Angonoka/Kapi-

TABLE 2. Data and calculations needed before sustainable conservation can be assured in wild populations and captive groups of tortoise species.

Aspect	Data
Systematics	individual/population genetics parsimony analysis
Populations	distribution, provenance structure dynamics, life table population viability analysis individual/population genetics
Behavior	movement/migration reproduction
Ecology	breeding sites life history characteristics environmental sex determination
Management	maximum sustainable yield socio-economic infrastructure

dolo) and the wild populations, and also creates further work for conservation biologists.

Systematics

Many species-recovery programs are executed before the taxonomy and phylogenetics of the target species are understood. There are instances of elaborate programs that have been conducted for vertebrate species that have subsequently proven to be common or genetically indistinct from what were thought to be separate species; this redundancy emphasizes the need for clarification of the classification of a species before any program is mounted. Of the 40 living species of tortoises (Swingland and Klemens 1989), the status, distribution, and ecology of only about eight clearly defined species are well known. Work on those in North America and Mexico is highly advanced, although the species classification is still obscured in *Gopherus agassizii* and proposed species or subspecies, such as *Geochelone donosobarrosi* (from Argentina).

Information regarding tortoises in Central America, South America, and Africa is sparse and inadequate, except perhaps for what is known about *Geochelone elephantopus, G. gigantea,* and the eleven South African species that are well documented. Systematics of the tortoises of the Indian subcontinent and Southeast Asia are confused with respect to the taxonomic status of the various morphotypes of *Geochelone elegans* and *G. platynota*. Much confusion also exists concerning the European species, because some amateur herpetologists have described new subspecies, species, and even genera in recent years without undertaking a comprehensive study of large samples and this has unnecessarily clouded the situation. Future classifications should not be based entirely on morphology, but also on additional information from genetic and cladistic analysis.

Population Ecology

The natural distribution and provenance of individuals frequently are either not known or are wrongly ascribed, which hampers both the estimation of the degree of threat to the wild populations and any proposed future reintroduction or restocking. Fear of gross genetic pollution or, in emergency seizures of contraband consignments (which are becoming more frequent), translocation to the wrong sites are current concerns.

Knowledge of tortoise-population structure is vital data, and is generally inadequate because of the difficulty of finding young tortoises and correctly estimating the age of older individuals from scute rings (Swingland 1978; Zug 1991). We can, however, produce sensible approximations by using certain iterative statistical techniques and by using data derived from knowledge of the population dynamics. No robust life table exists for any tortoise species and without one for the species population under consideration, sustainable management plans cannot be drawn up. As governments become more aware of the value of their indigenous species, and as their responsibilities to these species are now being enforced internationally, governmental agencies increasingly need such analyses to plan management of species, especially in areas in which there are conflicts of interest.

Some societies have traditional practices of tortoise-keeping and breeding that work well, such as in the Seychelles Islands in the Indian Ocean, but these cultural practices have fallen into disuse in recent times. Governments, as political entities, sometimes obtain an income from indigenous tortoises and if this income is not derived from tourism, then governments are prepared to sell their tortoises either locally or for export. This is not generally sustainable, unless captive-breeding facilities are established on the basis of the best ecological and behavioral information on wild populations and individuals, and operated with sound, compatible husbandry techniques.

This dilemma may improve with better techniques being developed to measure population structure and census population size. One proven technique, which allows for individual identity and approximate age to be determined from an animal's feces, is being developed by the Durrell Institute and relies on the gut epithelial cells that are sloughed off in the feces. Such a technique, together with a hormone assay of the feces to determine sex, gives a unique genetic fingerprint of each individual that is invaluable for structuring captive groups to reduce inbreeding and outbreeding depression, thus maintaining the appropriate coefficient of relatedness commensurate with the coefficient in wild populations. Blood-isozyme analyses as well as other modern techniques are also useful in discriminating different populations.

Behavioral Ecology

Genetic information can verify observations on movement and migration patterns in wild populations (Swingland and Lessells 1979). Such information is fundamental to maintain healthy captive groups, especially when translocation is planned. The possibility of introducing an alien genome or race, with different behavioral characteristics, is always present. Individuals are highly philopatric and can navigate back to exactly the same locale (home range) they habitually used, even in the case of the removal of all habitat features (*Testudo graeca* and *T. hermanni*, Swingland and Stubbs 1986; *Geochelone gigantea*, Swingland et al. 1989; *Gopherus polyphemus*, Diemer, 1989; *Malacochersus tornieri*, M. W. Klemens, pers. comm.). For this reason translocation programs are often unsuccessful.

Zoo curators who lead the field in captive breeding—in which the maximum number of viable offspring is the objective—are concerned with questions of mate selection, assortative and disassortative mating, and which individuals are successful parents (Swingland and Stubbs 1985). The appropriate husbandry protocols have often been worked out by trial and error, rather than by the application of field observations (Reid et al. 1989). Groups of tortoises often will not breed or will be highly variable in their success. Matings will be observed, but few progeny are produced.

The behavior of individuals in the wild invariably produces clues for better captive-management practices, although the danger of permanent behavioral modification after generations in captivity are always present. The requirements of a species for a suitable nesting site are very particular and constrained (Swingland and Coe 1978; Stubbs and Swingland 1985); the general nesting area that females use is determined by proximity to food, temperature characteristics, and the depth and consistency of earth. Individual females frequently nest in the same site each year, often in exactly the same position, and in some species, even in the very place where they were hatched (Swingland et al. 1990).

Species Recovery Programs Using Captive Breeding

Mediterranean. For years tortoises have been traded in Europe as pets. In the decade 1968–1978 over 2,000,000 tortoises were imported into the United Kingdom (about 200,000 a year), and even in 1938, some 250,000 were brought in. There is now substantial evidence that the majority died within a few years (Lawrence 1988), although some people have been successful in keeping them for a considerable time (P. Evans, pers. comm.; Lawrence 1988). Some have even bred them, and one person in the United Kingdom (Patricia Evans) has produced young from parents bred in Britain. There is no doubt, however, that the combination of variable (sometimes warm) temperatures in winter (which keeps bringing them out of hibernation) and the generally low temperatures throughout the rest of the year (which means that their eggs will not incubate and their digestion will not be working as efficiently as necessary to support the energetic demands of the year; Swingland and Frazier 1980) ensures that they do not fare well ex situ.

One of the last substantial natural populations of *Testudo hermanni* exists in southern France. Using a population-dynamics analysis, it is clear that the population is inexorably declining due to human neglect of the few open areas (olive groves and vegetable gardens) in this forest habitat where shrub encroachment has prevented their use as nesting areas (Stubbs and Swingland 1985). Our understanding of individual movement patterns has enabled us to define the limits of the conservation area (Swingland and Stubbs 1986). This knowledge prompted the establishment of a locally based organization, SOPTOM, to conserve the forest and its tortoise population that has attracted international funding and recognition. SOPTOM has also provided for local, multiple land-use concepts that involve tourists, forestry, and conservation interests, and which fit well with the interests of the local villagers and commune. Their self-funding initiative has been planned scientifically and the "Village des Tortues" allows the paying public to see the work on captive breeding and re-introduction. The body of expertise that has developed is being transferred to other countries that are setting up similar facilities.

Bans on the importation of some species expand commercial trade in other species and increase private captive breeding and the "black market" between fanciers. Since January 1, 1984, there has been a ban throughout Europe on the bulk importation of tortoises under the Convention on the International Trade in Endangered Species (CITES).

The history of this ban goes back twelve years to the time when the Royal Society for the Prevention of Cruelty to Animals (RSPCA), in the United Kingdom, published a booklet on the tortoise trade and an international group of specialists was formed to advise on the conservation of these reptiles under the IUCN Tortoise Specialist Group Species Survival Commission. This group recommended to the European Community a total ban on the bulk trade in tortoises. In 1982, using existing legislation, an attempt was made to limit the imports. It proved impractical, but at least the methods of shipping were improved. By the end of that year, however, the European Community had acted, and now the bulk exportation and importation of Hermann's Tortoises (*Testudo hermanni*), Spur-thighed Tortoises (*T. graeca*), and Marginated Tortoises (*T. marginata*) are banned throughout Europe. The trade in Asian *T. horsfieldi* increased, as did the transatlantic trade in North American Box Turtles (*Terrapene* spp.), and the increase in price made captive breeding in private commercial operations very lucrative.

The absence of the control and resources to support a monitoring system generally results in local extirpation. The tortoises that were once imported to Europe came from Turkey and Yugoslavia. They also used to come from Morocco, until supplies there apparently "dried up"; that is, wild populations had become exhausted. Although there is no unequivocal evidence, because few populations were properly censused before or during exploitation, it appears that commercial interests in populations quickly resulted in decimation. Most of the collecting was done by village children, who received about US$0.30 for each animal. These animals were then collected by the company truck and taken to a packing center, where they were kept without food and water for some time (to prevent defecation in transit), before being put into crates and transported to northern Europe. The transporters were refrigerated to reduce the activity of the animals; nevertheless, some were damaged by badly built crates or died within weeks of arrival, probably from the stress of the journey.

Legislative development and enforcement are lacking in most countries. In the northeastern corner of Greece close to Thessaloniki, at a tiny place called Alyki, there is a coastal sandy heath where a very substantial population of Hermann's Tortoises has existed quite happily alongside an ancient, but still working, saltworks. The villagers, who own the heath and want to put up villas there to create much-needed work, unfortunately have simply burned, plowed, and harrowed the area in the hope that it would consign all the animals and plants to oblivion and remove any barriers to construction (Stubbs et al. 1985). The wildlife has persisted, however, even though 40% of the tortoises were killed. The Greek Government has apparently offered to give the villagers another nearby area that is similar, but without tortoises, if they relinquish the heath. A recent decree by the President of Greece has provided for the protection of the heath, over the objection of local graziers and other vested interests, but the decree has been ignored.

Indian Ocean (Seychelles). Europe is not the only area where the future of tortoises is in jeopardy. Aldabra Atoll, which is 400 km northwest of the northern tip of Madagascar and is one of the most remote places on earth, is protected from any significant exploitation in that it has little soil for agriculture and limited freshwater, and is extremely rugged and inhospitable to people. Nevertheless, in the early 1960s, the British Government considered building an airbase there for the United States, which would have involved bulldozing the Aldabra Tortoises (*Geochelone gigantea*) out of the way, dynamiting breeding colonies of Frigate Birds and Boobies (because these birds are involved in collisions with aircraft), and setting off a controlled atomic explosion within the internal lagoon to provide an instant harbor for tankers to refuel the aircraft. An island off Diego Garcia elsewhere in the Indian Ocean was eventually bought for the American airbase, and consequently most of that island's wildlife has been exterminated—but Aldabra was saved.

Aldabra had faced threats in previous centuries when sailors removed so many of the giant tortoises for meat that even Charles Darwin complained about it to the governor responsible for Aldabra. Nothing was done, and it was the low numbers of animals (as it also was in the Galapagos Islands) that eventually turned the pirates and traders away from their traditional detours to such a remote place, because they yielded such little profit, and thus the tortoise population was able to recover. It is possible, for instance, to look at the age structure of the current population and determine when tortoise collection temporarily ceased; for example, tortoises born (or which were quite small) during

World War II are over-represented in the population. Small ones are easy to put in a person's pocket and remove to be sold, or perhaps given to newborn Seychelles girls who, when marrying, would eat the by-then fully grown tortoise at the wedding feast. This custom was supported by a steady supply of home-bred tortoises from the family herd, now a thing of the past.

From 1970 to 1980 the Royal Society ran a research station at the western end of Aldabra. In 1980 the Seychelles Islands Foundation took over responsibility for Aldabra, and today the island is a World Heritage Site. Because the atoll is composed of three separated islands, it was possible to make comparative investigations of the population ecology of tortoises as if they were in an open-air laboratory. More importantly, it was possible to show that a behavioral polymorphism existed in one island population in which some individuals migrated to the coast prior to the rainy season each year while the majority stayed inland, and that it was the same individuals that either migrated or stayed. These behavioral differences cannot be ascribed to differences in sex or age, but it was later discovered that migrants had a differently shaped shell, which helped discard one of the possible explanatory models (Swingland and Lessells 1979; Swingland et al. 1989). Another major discovery was that females took great care in selecting nest sites and that each nest produced hatchings predominantly of a single sex (Swingland et al. 1990).

Although an introduction program from Aldabra to Curieuse Island, which is close to the main Seychelles tourist center, was initiated in the 1970s to provide access to Aldabra Tortoise herds for tourists, a natural increase in the tortoise population has been hindered by poaching and illicit trade in hatchlings. The new Seychelles Department of Conservation, however, intends to mount a plan to encourage captive breeding by families and hotels to meet the tourist demands and to provide a supply of animals for export, thereby producing an income for the country and its people. Seychellois people have hundreds of years of experience in breeding these animals and this proposed program will reduce the market for poachers, but the organizational problems and methods of control have yet to be established.

Indian Ocean (Madagascar). In November 1984, the IUCN Species Survival Commission named *Geochelone yniphora*, the Madagascar Tortoise, as one of the top twelve animal species for conservation (Juvik et al. 1980). The Species Recovery Program was started by the IUCN Tortoise and Freshwater Turtle Group in 1985 with the support of numerous agencies, including the Jersey Wildlife Preservation Trust (JWPT), the New York Zoological Society, and especially the World Wildlife Fund–US and World Wildlife Fund International. A captive-breeding program was proposed and on-ground reviews of the current status were made (Curl et al. 1985). The first field officer arrived in Madagascar in March 1986 (Curl 1986) to begin the Species Recovery Program and, under JWPT management, the second field officer arrived in January, 1987 (Reid et al. 1989). Such species-recovery programs involving captive breeding are necessary when the species is in extreme danger of extinction; captive-breeding programs, however, are not a first choice, because they are fraught with difficulties and often do not address habitat maintenance for eventual reintroduction.

This project has been successful in producing hatchlings and, although the long-term objective is to restock the known range of this species, the range is currently infested with pigs and would require fencing. Moreover, although the project management will be handed over to Malagasy control, it is necessary for the captive-breeding program to be consolidated and the requirements of the IUCN policies on reintroduction and translocation to be met. Future work will include surveys of possible habitats, populations censuses, and work on the genetics of the species.

The Malagasy Tortoise Species Survival Program will also address the other three species of terrestrial chelonians: *Acinixys planicauda*, Flat-shelled Tortoise; *Pyxis arachnoides*, Spider Tortoise; and *Geochelone radiata*, Radiated Tortoise. Although a massive commercial captive-breeding initiative using *G. radiata* has started on Mauritius Island, current political difficulties are hindering most conservation projects in Madagascar.

Africa. Conservation projects in South Africa are being conducted by the Natal and Western Cape Parks boards. One-quarter of the world's species of tortoises live in this area and there has been some confusion over the precise status of these species. Moreover, it has been confirmed that one species thought to be extinct—*Homopus bergeri*—is still alive in small populations. The Geometric Tortoise (*Psammobates geometricus*) has a declining distribution (Baard 1992) and is vulnerable, although there are no plans for captive breeding. In Kenya, the Pancake Tortoise (*Malacochersus tornieri*) is collected in large numbers for the commercial trade and many consignments are being confiscated in Europe. Little is known of the ecology of either species and and it is not clear if captive breeding will be necessary. No major captive-breeding or conservation project on tortoises currently exists on the mainland of Africa.

North America. In the United States and Mexico, all species of *Gopherus* are facing considerable problems that require attention if their populations are not to be decimated and extinguished. The current status of *Gopherus agassizii* (Desert Tortoise), *G. polyphemus* (Gopher Tortoise), *G. berlandieri* (Texas Tortoise), and *G. flavomarginatus* (Bolson Tortoise) gives rise for concern. Turner (1986), Morafka et al. (1989), Diemer (1989), and Berry (1989) have reviewed the available information and have shown that various problems exist with differing degrees of seriousness.

All species are faced with competition from the effects of overgrazing and agricultural encroachment on their range, roadkill, urbanization, habitat damage from off-road vehicles, and the depredations of pet collecting. A wealth of information shows that in many areas repeated sampling has tracked the decline in tortoise densities, and the health of those individuals remaining and my own analysis of population structure indicates that within 20 years most known populations of *G. agassizi* will be extinct unless dramatic strides are made to improve their management.

In long-lived species, when the problem becomes acute and the evidence of threat is overwhelming, conservation action and legislation are invariably too late, because by then the population is biased in age structure and is too small to recover. In the case of *G. agassizii*, the Mojave and Sonoran desert populations, together with the population in Nevada, are threatened and the Arizona population may be vulnerable. The Beaver Dam Mountains population in southwestern Utah is apparently in serious trouble.

Captive Breeding and Future Directions

Justification. The formal position of the IUCN Tortoise and Freshwater Turtle Specialist Group is that captive breeding is an option of dire necessity and that it is justified when the only chance of survival for a species or subspecies is removal from the wild (for example, in the case of *Geochelone elephantopus hoodensis*). Most existing projects, however, were started not because of impending extinction, but because of other factors, such as politics, fund-raising, the profit motive, and convenience.

Science. Should a population be left until it is reduced to very few individuals, by which time genetic bottlenecks and other related factors may extinguish the population regardless of any species-recovery actions? The decision to start a major captive-breeding exercise of any terrestrial chelonian, however, must be planned in detail and there should be rigorous scientific reason to begin such a project. Once started, financial and political support must be long-term, reliable, and the objective of reintroduction and the benefit to the local people must be clearly stated. Too often there is little or no ecological information on a species and those executing the project are not trained biologists or experienced in chelonian biology. Habitat maintenance during the captive-breeding phase should be a major part of the program. Education is not as important as is the benefit to the local people from the project, although it is an inexpensive option.

Methods. The IUCN Reintroduction Specialist Group is developing guidelines for reptilian captive breeding and translocation that will embrace the need for data on population structure and dynamics, genetics (such as taxonomy, phylogenetics, population genetics, and individual relatedness), health, behavior (and the problems of modification), immunological-response modification (for example, loss of natural immunity), socio-economics, politics, project feasibility, infrastructure, management structure, and developing a future support base through self-sufficiency.

The conflict between ex situ and in situ captive breeding is of little consequence, because it is clear that in situ projects are more legitimate in every sense, so long as they provide the technical expertise and long-term prospects are equal to anything supported ex situ. In some instances, such as politics, resources, expertise, or simply the existence of more than one captive breeding group, ex situ programs are sensible. Ex situ programs infrequently result in successful reintroductions, and because they are located in "foreign" climes and are challenged by alien infections and other forms of selection, they are less attractive than in situ initiatives, which are less expensive and have a higher probability of success.

Realistic management plans must take into consideration other wildlife, the habitat, and local human factors and uses; thus a high degree of liaison with other projects should be involved, which normally includes joint work with senior personnel and collaborating researchers from many countries and different agencies. Occasionally, the support of researchers who are in the field to collect specific data will be needed. Field work on population dynamics ought to be carried out in the same manner at each site visited, to whatever extent possible. A controlled sampling program in well-defined areas (in which all tortoises are found are uniquely marked and measured and their activity is noted) is standard procedure as a preliminary and post hoc monitoring exercise. All data should be recorded in a standard format that is directly comparable among sites and with existing data sets for other species.

Summary

In the last 20 years, interest in the 40 species of tortoises has become very widespread. Their value to nations and communities has been recognized. This has brought increased and unwanted attention to a defenseless and vulnerable group of reptiles. Their market value has increased enormously and their rate of removal or eradication from the wild has, if anything, accelerated. The role of captive breeding is now vital but can only be of long-term use with proper scientific knowledge and management, and with professional, achievable objectives to put viable populations back in the wild.

Literature Cited

Baard, E. 1992. Distribution and status of the geometric tortoise *Psammobates geometricus* in South Africa. Biol. Conserv., 63: 235–239.

Berry, K. 1989. *Gopherus agassizi*, p. 5–7. *In* I. R. Swingland and M. W. Klemens (eds.), The Conservation Biology of Tortoises. Occas. Pap. Internatl. Union Cons. Nature Nat. Res., Spec. Surv. Comm., 5.

Curl, D. A. 1986. A recovery program for the Madagascan plowshare tortoise. Dodo, 23: 68–79.

Curl, D. A., I. C. Scoones, M. K. Guy, and G. Rakotoarisoa. 1985. The Madagascar tortoise *Geochelone yniphora*: current status and distribution. Biol. Conserv., 34: 35–54.

Diemer, J. E. 1989. *Gopherus polyphemus*, p. 14–16. *In* I. R. Swingland and M. W. Klemens (eds.), The Conservation Biology of Tortoises. Occas. Pap. Internatl. Union Cons. Nature Nat. Res., Spec. Surv. Comm., 5.

Groombridge B. 1982 The IUCN Amphibia Reptilia Red Data Book. Part 1: Testudinidae, Crocodylia, Rhyncocephalia. Internatl. Union Cons. Nature Nat. Res., Gland, Switzerland. xiii, 426 pages.

Juvik, J. O., A. J. Andrianarivo, and C. P. Blanc. 1980. The ecology and status of *Geochelone yniphora*: a critically endangered tortoise of northwestern Madagascar. Biol. Conserv., 19: 297–316.

Lawrence, K. 1988. Some Aspects of the Biology of Captive Mediterranean Tortoises. Doctoral Dissertation. Univ. of Kent, Canterbury, UK. 477 pages.

Mace, G. M., and R. Lande. 1991. Assessing extinction threats: toward a reevaluation of IUCN threatened species categories. Conserv. Biol., 5: 148–157.

Morafka, D. J., G. Aguirre, and G. A. Adest. 1989. *Gopherus flavomarginatus*, p. 10–13. *In* I. R. Swingland and M. W. Klemens (eds.), The Conservation Biology of Tortoises. Occas. Pap. Internatl. Union Cons. Nature Nat. Res., Spec. Surv. Comm., 5.

Reid, D., L. Durrell, and G. Rakotobearison. 1989. The captive breeding project for the angonoka *Geochelone yniphora* in Madagascar. Dodo, 26: 34–48.

Stubbs D., and I. R. Swingland. 1985. The ecology of a Mediterranean tortoise (*Testudo hermanni*): a declining population. Canadian Jour. Zool., 63: 169–180.

Stubbs, D., I. R. Swingland, A. Hailey, and E. Pulford. 1985. The ecology of the Mediterranean tortoise *Testudo hermanni* in northern Greece: the effects of a catastrophe on population structure and density. Biol. Conserv., 31: 125–152.

Swingland I. R. 1978. Marking reptiles, p. 119–132. *In* B. Stonehouse (ed.), Animal Marking. Macmillan, London.

—. (ed.) 1984. International symposium on tortoises. Amphibia-Reptilia, 5: 1–80.

—. 1987. The ecology and conservation of Aldabran giant tortoises. Proc. Biol. Soc. Washington, 8: 108–115.

Swingland, I. R., J. Adams, and P. J. Greenwood. 1990. Sex determination and sex ratios in patchy environments, p. 219–240. *In* I. R. Swingland and B. Shorrocks (eds.), Living in a Patchy Environment. Oxford Univ. Press, Oxford, UK.

Swingland, I. R., and M. Coe. 1978. The natural regulation of giant tortoise populations on Aldabra Atoll: reproduction. Jour. Zool., London, 186: 285–310.

Swingland, I. R., and J. G. Frazier. 1980. The conflict between feeding and overheating in the Aldabran giant tortoises, p. 611–615. *In* C. J. Amlaner and D. W. Macdonald (eds.), A Handbook of Biotelemetry and Radio

Tracking. Pergamon Press, New York.

Swingland, I. R., and M. W. Klemens (eds.) 1989. The conservation biology of tortoises. Occas. Pap. Internatl. Union Cons. Nature Nat. Res., Spec. Surv. Comm., 5: iv, 1–204.

Swingland, I. R., and C. M. Lessells. 1979. The natural regulation of giant tortoise populations on Aldabra Atoll. Movement polymorphism, reproductive success and mortality. Jour. Anim. Ecol., 48: 639–654.

Swingland, I. R., P. M. North, A. Dennis, and M. J. Parker. 1989. Movement patterns and morphometrics of giant tortoises. Jour. Anim. Ecol., 58: 971–985.

Swingland, I. R., and D. Stubbs. 1985. The ecology of a Mediterranean tortoise *Testudo hermanni*: reproduction. Jour. Zool., London, 205: 595–610.

—. 1986. Movement patterns in *Testudo hermanni* and implications for management, p. 573–578. *In* Z. Roček (ed.), Studies in Herpetology. Charles Univ., Prague.

Turner, F. B. (ed.). 1986. Management of the desert tortoise in California. Herpetologica, 42: 56–138.

Zug, G. R. 1991. Age determination in turtles. Soc. Study Amphib. Reptiles, Herpetol. Circ., 20: 1–29.

❦

❦ Swingland, I. R. 1994. International conservation and captive management of tortoises, p. 99–107. *In* J. B. Murphy, K. Adler, and J. T. Collins (eds.), Captive Management and Conservation of Amphibians and Reptiles. Society for the Study of Amphibians and Reptiles, Ithaca (New York). Contributions to Herpetology, volume 11.

Veterinary Procedures for the Acquisition and Release of Captive-Bred Herpetofauna

Elliott R. Jacobson*

Introduction

Amphibians and reptiles are susceptible to infection with a range of pathogens, including viruses, bacteria, fungi, and parasites (Anver and Pond 1984; Migaki et al. 1984; Jacobson 1980, 1986*a*, 1986*b*). While many of the reports of illness and disease in herpetofauna involve individual cases, there are a number of well-documented epizootic diseases that have involved a substantial number of animals. In the African Clawed Frog (*Xenopus laevis*), deaths resulting from infection with *Chlamydia psittaci* have been reported (Newcomer at al. 1982). An iridovirus has been incriminated as the cause of mortality in tadpoles (Wolf et al. 1968). In reptiles, a number of pathogens have been reported as major causes of mortality in research, private, and zoo collections, and include *Entamoeba invadens* (Jacobson 1986*a*), *Cryptosporidium* (Brownstein et al. 1977), a variety of herpesviruses (Jacobson 1986*b*), various strains of an ophidian *Paramyxovirus* (OPMV) (Jacobson et al. 1992), and a recently identified retro-like virus (Schumacher et al. 1990). The release of captive Desert Tortoises (*Gopherus agassizii*) that were ill with an upper respiratory-tract disease (URTD) may have been responsible for an epizootic outbreak in populations of wild Desert Tortoises in the western Mojave Desert of California (Jacobson et al. 1991).

It is becoming abundantly clear that if conservation programs that involve captive-bred herpetofauna are to be successful, animals entering these programs must be scrutinized more intensely and guidelines developed for both selecting and determining which animals should be bred and which captive-reared animals should be returned to the wild. This problem has come to the forefront of conservation efforts with captive-breeding and reintroduction programs of endangered mammals. For instance, if Golden Lion Tamarins (*Leontopithecus rosalia*) infected with the callitrichid hepatitis virus (Ramsay et al. 1989) are returned to the wild, the effect on the naïve population could be disastrous. The source of this virus remains a mystery. The same scenario could be written with respect to *Paramyxovirus* and the Aruba Island Rattlesnake (*Crotalus durissus unicolor*) breeding program. OPMV has been isolated from this species (Jacobson et al. 1992) and breeding collections will have to be screened for exposure to this virus. In a recent serologic survey of snakes on Aruba, there was no evidence for exposure to this agent (R. A. Odum, pers. comm.; Odum and Goode, this volume, page 363).

In this chapter I will review the most significant causes of infectious diseases of herpetofauna, discuss problems regarding health assessment, and present recommendations for establishing a preventive medicine program for controlling the spread of pathogens from infected to naïve animals.

Infectious Diseases

Amphibians

Compared to reptiles, there is a paucity of information on infectious diseases and pathogens in amphibians. Much of the information in the literature

* College of Veterinary Medicine
University of Florida
Gainesville, Florida 32610, USA

Acronyms used in this chapter:

CNS	Central nervous system
FEV	Frog erythrocytic virus
FV	Frog virus
HI	Hemagglutination-inhibition assay
OPMV	Ophidian *Paramyxovirus*
PCDV	Polyhedral cytoplasmic deoxyribovirus
TEV	Tadpole edema virus
URTD	Upper respiratory-tract disease

is based on animals housed in the amphibian facilities of universities. For instance, while it was in existence, the Amphibian Facility at the University of Michigan was a tremendous resource, not only for providing animals for research, but also for documenting disease problems in laboratory-housed and -reared animals. Given the global decline in amphibian populations, disease needs to be considered as a potential problem.

Polyhedral Cytoplasmic Viruses. These viruses were originally identified in several laboratories in monolayers of Northern Leopard Frog (*Rana pipiens*) kidney cells (Granoff et al. 1965). Isolates of this virus were obtained from the kidney cells of normal adult frogs, liver homogenates of normal frogs or frogs with Lucké tumors, and homogenates of Lucké tumors (Granoff et al. 1965, 1966). This virus was designated as frog virus (FV) and was given a sequential number for the isolates obtained. These viruses have also been named polyhedral cytoplasmic deoxyribovirus (PCDV). Clark et al. (1969) obtained 15 isolates from normal tissues of the Eastern Newt (*Notophthalmus viridescens*). Subsequently, PCDV was isolated from visceral homogenates of normal adult frogs and both normal and edematous tadpoles of the Bullfrog (*Rana catesbeiana*; Wolf et al. 1968, 1969). This agent was designated tadpole edema virus (TEV). Metamorphosing Bullfrogs are highly susceptible to infection with, and death from, TEV (Wolf et al. 1969). Adult Bullfrogs do not develop signs of disease, but are thought to transmit the infection to tadpoles. With each new crop of tadpoles, some infected animals will survive into adulthood, becoming reservoirs of infection for future generations.

In vivo studies of infection in the Western Spadefoot (*Scaphiopus hammondii*), American Toad (*Bufo americanus*), and Fowler's Toad (*Bufo woodhousii fowleri*) demonstrated that anurans injected with TEV will develop a fatal disease characterized by hemorrhagic necrosis of visceral organs (Wolf et al. 1968). Clinical signs in tadpoles include subcutaneous edema of the limbs and diffuse hemorrhage on the ventral surface (Wolf et al. 1968). When first seen, these tadpoles were suspected of having red-leg, but the bacterium *Aeromonas liquefaciens* was isolated from affected tadpoles. While the virus alone was able to cause disease in stressed toads, a participation of *Aeromonas* in natural outbreaks could not be discounted.

Icosahedral viruses, presumptively included in the family Iridoviridae (based on size, morphology, and DNA content), have been seen in the erythrocytes of a variety of frogs, including the Bullfrog, Mink Frog (*Rana septentrionalis*), and Green Frog (*R. clamitans*)(Gruia-Gray et al. 1989). Collectively, these viruses are referred to as frog erythrocytic virus (FEV). Beyond their ultrastructure, biochemical, and biophysical properties, little is known about this group of viruses. The relationship of this virus to TEV is unknown.

A five-year survey in Canada revealed that the prevalence of FEV was significantly higher in juveniles than in adult Bullfrogs (Gruia-Gray and Desser 1992). Tadpoles were not found to be infected naturally. While anemia was reported in infected frogs, no other pathological problems were noted.

Chlamydiosis. Of the three species within the genus *Chlamydia*, *C. psittaci* has the broadest range of hosts. It is the etiologic agent of psittacosis/ornithosis, infecting numerous species of birds, mammals, and humans. *Chlamydia* is also known to cause illness and mortality in snakes and lizards (Jacobson et al. 1989; Jacobson and Telford 1990). An epizootic outbreak of chlamydiosis, with high morbidity and mortality rates, has been reported in a commercial African Clawed Frog rearing operation (Newcomer et al. 1982). Clinical signs of illness seen in adult frogs prior to death were lethargy, disequilibrium, patchy cutaneous depigmentation and petechiation, and a bloated, edematous appearance. The disease was characterized by a pyogranulomatous inflammation in a variety of visceral structures, including the heart, liver, spleen, and kidney. Basophilic intracytoplasmic inclusion bodies were seen in these tissues. Using electron microscopy, inclusions were found to be composed of organisms with developmental stages compatible with chlamydia. Ultimately, this organism was determined to be *C. psittaci.* The source of the infection could not be determined, but it was thought that condemned beef liver, which was fed to the frogs, was potentially the source. Since the frogs were kept outdoors for a period of time prior to the epizootic, the infection could have resulted from contact with wild animals.

"Red Leg." A bacterial disease called "red leg," named because of associated petechial and ecchymotic lesions of the skin on the hind legs, is associated with a variety of gram-negative bacteria. The

major bacteria, isolated either alone or in combination, include *Aeromonas hydrophila*, *Pseudomonas* spp., *Providencia* spp., *Citrobacter*, and *Flavobacterium* (Glorioso et al. 1974). This disease is a major problem in anurans and urodeles that are purchased from scientific supply houses. Outbreaks often follow shipment of amphibians during the warm months of the year. Amphibians that are in poor condition or shipped in filthy circumstances are particularly prone to red leg. This disease has also been reported in wild populations of frogs (Hird et al. 1981).

A range of clinical presentations can be seen with red leg. In peracute infections, amphibians may be found without any prior clinical signs for illness. In those amphibians manifesting illness, clinical signs include lethargy, anorexia, subcutaneous edema, cutaneous ulcers, and coelomic effusion. Affected animals may also develop cutaneous hemorrhage, which is particularly prominent on the ventral aspect of the hindlimbs and abdomen. It is these lesions that are responsible for the name red leg.

Ideally, new arrivals should be housed individually in clean cages under optimum husbandry conditions. A variety of antibiotics have been used for ill animals including tetracycline, chloramphenicol, and gentamicin (Anver and Pond 1984).

Chromomycosis. Amphibians, particularly anurans, appear to be susceptible to infection with a variety of fungi. In a study of fungi in wild amphibians in Brazil, 33 (18%) were culture-positive for fungi from viscera (Mok et al. 1983). Of the various fungi identified in amphibians, the brown-pigmented septate fungi of the genera *Fonsecaea*, *Phialophora*, *Cladosporium*, and *Scolecosbasidium* are a particular problem. These organisms can produce cutaneous ulcers and visceral nodules. It is thought that they enter the animal's body through traumatic lesions to the skin. To date, beyond surgical excision of a localized lesion, there is no effective treatment for this disease. It is recommended that infected animals with extensive lesions be euthanatized.

Reptiles

A wider variety of infectious diseases have been reported in reptiles than in amphibians. A reason for this may be that ill reptiles are evaluated more thoroughly and that dead reptiles are necropsied more often than are amphibians. This may also be attributable to the smaller size of many amphibians compared to reptiles. The smaller the animal, the more limited the diagnostic repertoire. Several viruses and protozoans are known to be responsible for significant mortality in collections of captive reptiles. Until recently, little was known about disease problems in wild populations of reptiles. An URTD has been identified in wild populations of Desert Tortoises in the Mojave Desert of California; released captive tortoises that have this disease may be involved in these epizootic outbreaks (Jacobson et al. 1991).

Ophidian Paramyxovirus *Infections*. In 1976 a respiratory epizootic spread through a collection of Fer-de-lance (*Bothrops moojeni*) at a snake farm in Switzerland (Foelsch and Leloup 1983). Although *Pseudomonas* and *Aeromonas* were isolated from the respiratory tracts of dead snakes, a virus (Fer-de-Lance virus) with ultrastructural properties similar to the myxoviruses was identified (Clark and Lunger 1981). In the case of the first reported deaths in the United States from which OPMV was recovered, eight of nine Rock Rattlesnakes (*Crotalus lepidus*) died with clinical signs of central nervous system (CNS) disease (Jacobson et al. 1980). In a subsequent report, 8% of the total viperid collection in a Louisiana zoo died during a two-to-three-month period; the affected genera were *Bitis*, *Bothrops*, *Crotalus*, *Trimeresurus*, and *Vipera* (Jacobson et al. 1981). In 1987, OPMV was recovered from the lungs of two dead Ottoman Vipers (*Vipera x. xanthina*) from a zoological collection in Tennessee (Potgieter et al. 1987).

Over the last seven years, OPMV-associated deaths have been identified in a variety of private and zoo collections in the United States and Europe. In some collections, only one or two species per collection were severely affected, although multiple species of viperid snakes were maintained. In 1988, OPMV was isolated from a Black Mamba (*Dendroaspis polylepis*) in a serpentarium that was experiencing an epizootic outbreak among viperids, elapids, boids, and colubrids. In 1988, OPMV was also isolated from clinically ill Corn Snake (*Elaphe guttata*), Beauty Snake (*E. taeniurus*), and Möllendorff's Rat Snake (*E. moellendorffi*)(Jacobson and Gaskin 1989). In Germany, a myxovirus-like agent was recovered from a Red-tailed Rat Snake (*Elaphe oxycephala*), Gaboon Viper (*Bitis gabonica*), and Carpet Python (*Morelia spilotes*)(Ahne et al. 1987; Ahne and Neubert 1989).

Clinical signs of illness are variable. In some cases, no signs are exhibited; the snake is found dead in its cage without suspicion of a problem. In other cases, snakes may simply stop feeding, regurgitate, or be polyuric. Foelsch and Leloup (1983) described a series of stages in affected Fer-de-lance. In stage 1, snakes had a loss of muscle tone with affected snakes exhibiting a "stretched out" linear posture with the head slightly elevated. During stage 2, which lasted one to two days, snakes showed abnormal activity. Affected snakes crawled about restlessly and kept their mouths partially opened. Their tongues were incompletely withdrawn into the sheaths and their pupils were extremely dilated. Stage 3 was seen from several hours to one day before death. The mouth was kept completely open and the snakes expelled a purulent material from the glottis. Stage 4 was seen from several minutes to one hour preceding death. The mouth was kept maximally opened, the pupils were dilated, and snakes were excessively active.

In an epizootic disease involving Rock Rattlesnakes, a new breeder male was introduced into an established collection without being quarantined (Jacobson et al. 1980). Ultimately this snake was in contact with eight other Rock Rattlesnakes, seven of which died. On day 3 following introduction, the new snake developed head tremors and loss of equilibrium; it died on day 14. Over the next 2.5 months, four females and three males died after manifesting clinical signs. Only one rattlesnake remained healthy and survived.

In an epizootic outbreak at a zoological park in Louisiana, clinical signs included a sudden gaping of the mouth followed within one day by violent convulsions, causing the entire body to spiral (Jacobson et al. 1981). Frequently, there would be an expulsion of brownish fluid from the glottis. Several snakes regurgitated ingested mice or passed greenish mucoid feces from one to three weeks prior to death. Presumptive diagnosis of OPMV infection can be made upon finding characteristic light microscopic changes in the lung. The most significant of these lung changes is proliferation of epithelial cells lining the air passageways, with or without interstitial inflammation. In some affected rattlesnakes, an enlarged pancreas has been seen (Jacobson et al. 1992).

OPMV has been isolated in a wide variety of cell types of reptilian and mammalian origin, including gecko embryo, rattlesnake fibroma, rattlesnake spleen, viper heart, and baby hamster kidney cells (Clark and Lunger 1981; Jacobson et al. 1981). Application of serological methods has been useful with regard to exposure of snakes to OPMV. The hemagglutination-inhibition (HI) assay has been most useful, because of its relative simplicity and rapid turn-around time (Gaskin et al. 1989).

It is unknown if snakes infected with OPMV ever become clear of the virus or if they remain carriers for life. Thus, until more work is done, all seropositive snakes need to be considered a potential source of infection of naïve animals.

Inclusion Body Disease of Boid Snakes. This disease has been seen in a variety snakes in the family Boidae (Schumacher et al. 1990), including Boa Constrictor (*Boa constrictor*), Anaconda (*Eunectes murinus*), Haitian Boa (*Epicrates striatus*), Burmese Python (*Python molurus bivittatus*), Indian Python (*P. m. molurus*), Reticulated Python (*P. reticulatus*), and Ball Python (*P. regius*). In Boa Constrictors, the first clinical sign manifested is regurgitation of a prey item within several days of feeding. While some snakes die within several weeks of the first sign of this illness, others may survive for months. Some of the snakes may eventually show signs of central nervous system disease by exhibiting disorientation, head tilting, and opisthotonos. In Burmese Pythons, the disease is more chronic, with primary signs of CNS disease; several snakes with flaccid paralysis have been seen. Regurgitation is seldom seen in Burmese Pythons.

The major histologic finding characteristic of this disease is the presence of eosinophilic intracytoplasmic inclusions within hematoxylin- and eosin-stained tissue sections. In Boa Constrictors the inclusions are most prominent in the kidney, pancreas, liver, and brain. In Burmese Pythons the inclusions are mostly found within neurons in the CNS. The inclusions are generally associated with an encephalitis, which is generally more severe in Burmese Pythons than it is in Boa Constrictors. An RNA virus, which morphologically resembles members of the family Retroviridae, has been identified in tissues of affected snakes and also in cultured kidney cells. Although the route of transmission is unknown, affected snakes are often from collections with severe mite infestations. It is possible that the

Snake Mite (*Ophionyssus natricis*) is involved in the transmission.

Amebiasis. The protozoan, *Entamoeba invadens*, represents one of the most clinically significant parasites that infect reptiles. Epizootics have been seen in squamates and chelonians, including captive Loggerheads (*Caretta caretta*). The author has seen amebiasis in a wild Eastern Kingsnake (*Lampropeltis getula*), which was found clinically ill in the field.

The infective stage, the quadrinucleate cyst, is shed in the feces. Cysts are very resistant to desiccation and may persist in the environment for considerable periods of time. Control measures for preventing an epizootic should include isolation of ill animals and disinfection of contaminated cages. Crocodilians and chelonians should not be kept in the same enclosures with snakes and lizards. Contaminated cages should be steam-cleaned and disinfected with a 3% sodium hypochlorite solution before the introduction of new animals.

There are no clinical signs of illness pathognomonic for amebiasis. Affected animals may be listless and anorexic and may pass a mucoid, bloody feces. Snakes may appear clinically normal up to 24 hours before death or may slowly decline in condition over a period lasting several weeks. In clinically affected animals, trophozoites can be found in sedimentation or by a direct smear of fecal material. Trophozoites will not be found in a flotation specimen (that is, a specimen which is added to a hypertonic salt solution, allowing certain helminth ova to float to the surface).

Cryptosporidiosis. This is an extremely subtle disease in reptiles. The causative agent, *Cryptosporidium* sp., was first documented as a pathogen in reptiles by Brownstein et al. (1977), who reported infections in four species of captive snakes. Clinical signs included regurgitation of ingested food and enlarged stomachs. Histologically, there was dilatation of gastric tubules, increased interstitial connective tissue, and eventual glandular atrophy.

Since this first report, other cases of cryptosporidiosis have been seen in a variety of colubrid, viperid, and elapid snakes. While most affected snakes are adults, a juvenile wild-caught Corn Snake was found by the author to have typical signs and lesions associated with the disease. The author has also seen the disease in a juvenile scaleless Texas Rat Snake (*Elaphe obsoleta lindheimerii*). Cryptosporidiosis has also been identified in lizards (Dillehay et al. 1986; Upton and Barnard 1987) and tortoises (Heuschele et al. 1986).

Cryptosporidium is insidious, because the disease often goes undetected until clinical signs are dramatic. Snakes manifesting clinical signs of the illness may live with the disease for months or even over one year before dying. As in other animals, there is no effective chemotherapeuticy for treating reptiles ill with cryptosporidiosis.

Recent studies in a variety of wild and captive reptiles indicated that more than one species of *Cryptosporidium* probably exists in reptiles (Upton et al. 1989). In that study, prolonged shedding of oocysts was found. The exact route of transmission is unknown and predisposing factors are yet to be determined. For instance, adenovirus has been seen by the author in the gastric mucosal epithelial cells of snakes with concurrent cryptosporidiosis. Possibly a virus may be present first, immuno-compromising the host and allowing the disease to commence.

Health Assessment

Acquisition

With regard to the pet trade, amphibians and reptiles are an extremely mobile group of vertebrates. The international trade in herpetofauna is big business and large numbers of animals are shipped around the world. Sources of amphibians and reptiles include those from the wild and those captive-bred either in private collections or in zoo collections. Although there is no information on differential disease and mortality in amphibians and reptiles originating from these three sources, it is fair to assume that herpetofauna from the wild will be parasitized to a greater degree than those bred in captivity. Still, captive-bred animals may acquire pathogens both horizontally (that is, through the spread of an infectious agent from one individual to another, usually through contact with excreta or respiratory secretions) and vertically (by the transmission of an infectious agent from one generation to another) and never should be considered totally free of infectious agents.

Amphibians and reptiles are often transported under harsh and stressful conditions; this is especially true for wild-caught animals. Transport-related immunosuppression may allow latent pathogens to become active. Cowan (1968) described a maladaptation syndrome in the herpetological collection of a major zoological park. In a review of necropsy reports for 1,249 reptiles dying over a 66-year period at the Philadelphia Zoological Garden, the major cause of death was inability to adapt to the zoo environment. Most animals included in this diagnostic category died within two years of acquisition. Reptiles dying of this syndrome had a highly stereotyped pattern that was unmistakable at necropsy. Specimens were wasted, all fat depots were metabolized, and various tissues (especially the skin) would easily tear.

Animals collected for the pet trade and for display in zoological collections are often intermixed with other species with little concern for interspecific transmission of pathogens. Stressed animals, with a compromised immune system, are at the greatest risk for developing infectious diseases. When animals are purchased from importers or from private breeders, there is usually only limited information given on the health status of the animal being purchased, except for general mention of feeding behavior and major injuries. Animals that are exchanged between zoological parks would, it is hoped, be evaluated more intensely prior to transport.

The key for reducing the risk of occurrence of an epizootic disease in any collection is a sound preventive-medicine program. Although the value of preventive medicine should be obvious to everyone, often it is the most simple precautions that are neglected. It may be an old cliché, but it is true that bad habits are difficult to break. In this case, it takes a major epizootic outbreak for most persons to realize that improvement is needed. Unfortunately, the value of a sound preventive-medicine program is only appreciated after many animals in a population have died of a disease.

A sound preventive-medicine program begins with the quarantine of all new animals. This should include both wild and captive-bred animals. Based on the author's experience with a variety of pathogens, it is recommended that all new animals entering a collection should be quarantined for 90 days. The quarantine room should be at a distance from the main collection. A minimum requirement is the prevention of any air exchange between the quarantine room and the main collection.

The larger and more valuable a collection, the more important it becomes to quarantine all new acquisitions. New animals should be weighed upon arrival and monitored throughout the quarantine period. Ideally, fecal examinations should be performed on all new animals and appropriate parasiticides administered as needed. It must be realized that all animals in the wild have parasites and determining whether or not an animal with parasites should be administered a parasiticide is a matter partly of experience and partly of guesswork. Certain endoparasites, such as *Entamoeba invadens*, should always be considered a potential pathogen and infected animals should be medicated. Others, such as oxyurid nematodes of tortoises and iguanas, are generally considered commensals, with few reports linking mortality with presence of these parasites. The role that most parasites of amphibians and reptiles play in disease is poorly documented.

Ectoparasites should be considered significant whenever encountered. While tick infestations are for the most part relatively easy to control, mite infestations are more problematical. The Snake Mite continues to be a significant pest in reptilian collections. Control of this parasite has been made difficult by what appears to be resistance to various mitacides. Once established in a large collection of reptiles, this parasite may be impossible to eradicate. It certainly is far easier to eliminate this parasite from individuals in quarantine than from affected animals and their environment in the main collection. For every mite on the snake there may be a dozen within the cage.

When possible, new animals entering the quarantine room should be given a physical examination (Jacobson 1988). This may not be practical with small amphibians and reptiles or for those species that are easily stressed by manipulation. For the larval stages of amphibians this would be unrealistic, unless the clinician wants to examine each one under a dissecting microscope. At times, it is wise to let the animal acclimate for a period of time before a physical examination is conducted. In zoo collections, protocols should be worked out between the herpetological department and the animal health department for evaluating new acquisitions. Weights should be obtained on all new acquisitions and the animal given a cursory visual inspection, at the very least.

Amphibians and reptiles should be monitored throughout the quarantine period. This includes noting both anatomical and behavioral abnormalities. Behavioral problems are often noted prior to the development of clinical signs of illness. While some diseases, such as inclusion body disease of boid snakes, result in rather dramatic signs and have a protracted course, other diseases may go unnoticed for long periods of time. As already mentioned, some diseases, such as cryptosporidiosis, are very subtle and go unnoticed until pathologic changes are extremely severe. With many diseases, it is not uncommon to find an animal dead in its cage in the morning, although it appeared clinically normal the day before. It is extremely important to be a keen observer to identify disease problems while the animal is still treatable. With some species, such as tortoises, it may be advisable to keep biweekly weight records, because loss of weight may be the only clinical signs observed.

As with higher vertebrates, complete blood counts and plasma and serum biochemical determinations may provide invaluable information on the health status of the animal being evaluated. While blood samples can be obtained rapidly and safely in some species, for many others, however, this is not practical. Because normal blood data are available for only a few of the more than 10,000 species of amphibians and reptiles (Anver and Pond 1984; Jacobson 1988), each collection needs to establish its own data base. Additionally, plasma and serum banks need to be established for all major collections, because these samples are invaluable in retrospective seroepidemiologic studies. For instance, exposure to OPMV can be determined by a hemagglutination-inhibition serologic assay. As more assays for exposure to various pathogens are developed for herpetofauna, the value of plasma and serum banks becomes more apparent.

Assessment of the health of animals prior to their release from the quarantine room to the main collection is extremely important. It is at this point that the animals must be most closely scrutinized. Animals that are doing poorly (for example, those not feeding or those that have lost a moderate amount of weight) should not be released into the main collection. It goes without saying that an ill animal should never make it out of quarantine.

All animals that die while in quarantine should be necropsied. Necropsy is the key in determining causes of mortality. Dead animals should be refrigerated if the necropsy cannot be performed immediately, but do not freeze them—freezing results in artifactual change in tissues—and should be avoided. Tissues from all major organ systems should be collected and fixed in neutral-buffered 10% formalin, not just those tissues with gross lesions. Zoo collections should use either commercial, state, or university diagnostic laboratories for histopathological evaluation of collected tissues. A complete history and description of gross findings should go along with the tissues to the laboratory. When possible, depending upon the size of the necropsied animal, samples of liver, heart, lung, kidney, and spleen should be collected and frozen for microbiology, ideally in an ultrafreezer at –70°C. All major zoological parks should either have on site or have access to a ultrafreezer for long-term storage of frozen tissues as well as plasma and serum.

Establishing Captive-Breeding Programs and Release of Captive-Bred Herpetofauna

Many species of reptiles, and to a lesser extent amphibians, are being bred in captivity. For those species being bred for release into the wild, there are tremendous responsibilities to insure that only healthy animals will be released. It is only recently that the impact of infectious disease on captive-breeding programs began to be appreciated. Twenty years ago we knew little about pathogens in amphibians and reptiles. Today we realize that these animals can potentially harbor an array of pathogens. More than likely, the infectious diseases thus far listed in the literature represent just a small part of the total. For instance, while an URTD has been seen in captive tortoises for many years, only recently has work with a similar disease in free-ranging Desert Tortoises shed some light on the etiology of this disease (Jacobson et al. 1991). *Mycoplasma*, which is now implicated as a possible cause of this disease, was for the most part unknown in reptiles. Further, URTD may have been introduced to wild populations in the Mojave Desert through illegal releases of ill, captive Desert Tortoises. Wild tortoises with signs of URTD are more commonly found near cities and towns that have concentrations of captive tortoises with this disease, as well as in localities where illegal releases of captive are known to occur. The herpetological community that is involved in captive-breeding programs must realize that similar events could occur if apparently healthy captive-bred animals with subclinical disease are released into a naïve population.

The Aruba Island Rattlesnake breeding program is an example of this problem. These snakes are known to be susceptible to OPMV, and if captive-bred animals are ever released to the wild, screening of snakes to determine exposure to this virus is imperative. The introduction of pathogenic organisms could be devastating, especially to small, insular populations. Such is the case with the Black-footed Ferret (*Mustela nigripes*) and canine distemper virus.

Amphibians and reptiles being bred in captivity for release to the wild need to be quarantined in a facility isolated from other quarantined herpetological specimens. Also, the breeding facility must be isolated from the main collection. This is the only way to ensure that pathogens from a reservoir species will not infiltrate the breeding program. Pathogens that can be latent or silent in one species may have dramatic effects in another species. For example, with an outbreak of herpesvirus infection in Argentine Tortoises (*Geochelone chilensis*), in which Red-footed Tortoises (*G. carbonaria*) were in the same shipment, only the Argentine Tortoises were affected (Jacobson et al. 1985). The Red-footed Tortoises may have served as a reservoir of the pathogen for the Argentine Tortoises. For the most part, we do not have any idea of the variety or range of pathogens that can cross-infect different species of amphibians and reptiles.

Health status is one of a number of items that need to be considered in selecting animals for a breeding program and in determining which animals are going to be released to the wild. Animals entering the breeding program should be given as thorough an examination as possible and practical. Animals with an infectious disease should never be allowed into the program. Even those with metabolic and congenital diseases should be excluded. There should be no exchange of equipment or containers between animals in the breeding program and in the main collection. Caretakers involved with the breeding program should not have immediate contact with the main collection, because fomites (that is, objects that are not in themselves harmful, but may harbor pathogenic microorganisms) containing pathogens can be carried on clothing and may be transferred from site to site. Ideally, a dressing room should be adjacent to the breeding-program site so that caretakers can clean themselves before and after entering the premises.

It is essential that all animals that die in the breeding program be given a complete necropsy. For some species, such as larval amphibians, this may not be practical, especially if large numbers have died. In such cases, animals representative of those that have died should be examined. Even with larval amphibians, significant information can be discerned through histopathology.

Exchange of information among breeding programs is essential. This will necessitate standardizing the methods of collecting and storing information. Data should be computerized in a way that allows ease of access and distribution. Further, formal networks need to be established to facilitate this exchange of information. This is far superior to reliance on rumor, which, up to now, has been one of the major paths for the distribution of information in the herpetological community.

Summary

It is well documented that the evolution of human and other animal populations has centered around mechanisms for protection against a wide range of potentially lethal pathogens. Numerous pathogenic organisms are known to cause illness and death in captive amphibians and reptiles, and it is only recently that the effects of disease are being appreciated in wild populations of herpetofauna. Captivity tends to exacerbate certain infectious diseases by bringing together diverse species under stressful conditions. For the most part, the factors responsible for epizootics are poorly understood. With regard to acquisition and exchange between zoological and private collections, amphibians and reptiles are an extremely mobile group of animals. With them come, however, an assortment of viruses, bacteria, fungi, and parasites. Relatively few zoological or private collections have adopted the strict quarantine programs that are necessary to prevent the introduction of potential pathogens into collections of naïve animals. Furthermore, while in captivity, amphibians and reptiles are often exposed to foreign species that are carrying foreign pathogens. This may have disastrous implications for release of captive-bred amphibians and reptiles back into the wild. We must begin evaluating more carefully the amphibians and reptiles that are selected for captive-breeding programs so that efforts that are intended to conserve a species do not contribute to its demise.

Literature Cited

Ahne, W., and W. Neubert. 1989. Isolation of pleomorphic syncytial viruses from four different species of reptiles, p. 20. *In* Third International Colloquium on the Pathology of Reptiles and Amphibians—Abstracts. Orlando, Florida.

Ahne, W., W. Neubert, and I. Thomsen. 1987. Reptilian viruses: isolation of myxovirus-like particles from the snake *Elaphe oxycephala*. Jour. Vet. Med., 34: 607–612.

Anver, M. R., and C. L. Pond. 1984. Biology and diseases of amphibians, p. 427–447. *In* J. G. Fox, B. J. Cohen, and F. M. Loew. Laboratory Animal Medicine. Academic Press, New York.

Brownstein, D. G., J. D. Strandberg, R. J. Montali, M. Bush, and J. Fortner. 1977. *Cryptosporidium* in snakes with hypertrophic gastritis. Vet. Pathol., 14: 606–617.

Clark, H. F., C. Gray, F. Fabian, R. Zeigel, and D. T. Karzon. 1969. Comparative studies of amphibian cytoplasmic virus strains isolated from the leopard frog, bullfrog, and newt, p. 310–326. *In* M. Mizell (ed.), Recent Results in Cancer Research. Special Supplement. Biology of Amphibian Tumors. Springer-Verlag, New York.

Clark, H. F., and P. D. Lunger. 1981. Viruses, p. 135–164. *In* J. E. Cooper and O. F. Jackson (eds.), Diseases of the Reptilia, Vol. I. Academic Press, London.

Cowan, D. F. 1968. Diseases of captive reptiles. Jour. Amer. Vet. Med. Assoc., 153: 848–859.

Dillehay, D. L., T. R. Boosinger, and S. MacKenzie. 1986. Gastric cryptosporidiosis in a chameleon. Jour. Amer. Vet. Med. Assoc., 189: 1139–1140.

Foelsch, D. W., and P. Leloup. 1983. Infection enzootique grave dans un serpentarium, p. 25–31. *In* C. Vago and G. Matz (eds.), Proceedings of the First International Colloquium on Pathology of Reptiles and Amphibians, Angers, France.

Gaskin, J. M., M. Haskell, N. Keller, and E. R. Jacobson. 1989. Serodiagnosis of ophidian *Paramyxovirus* infections, p. 21–23. *In* Third International Colloquium on the Pathology of Reptiles and Amphibians. Abstracts. Orlando, Florida.

Glorioso, J. C., R. L. Amborski, J. M. Larkin, G. F. Amborski, and D. C. Culley. 1974. Microbiological studies on septicemic bullfrogs. Amer. Jour. Vet. Res., 35: 1241–1245.

Granoff, A., P. E. Came, and D. C. Breeze. 1966. Viruses and renal carcinoma of *Rana pipiens*. I. The isolation and properties of virus from normal and tumor tissue. Virology, 29: 133–148.

Granoff, A., P. E. Came, and K. A. Raferty. 1965. The isolation and properties of viruses from *Rana pipiens:* their possible relationship to the renal adenocarcinoma of the leopard frog. Ann. New York Acad. Sci., 126: 237–255.

Gruia-Gray, J., and S. S. Desser. 1992. Cytopathological observations and epizootiology of frog erythrocyte virus in bullfrogs (*Rana catesbeiana*). Jour. Wildlife Dis., 28: 34–41.

Gruia-Gray, J., M. Petric, and S. Desser. 1989. Ultrastructural, biochemical and biophysical properties of an erythrocytic virus of frogs from Ontario, Canada. Jour. Wildlife Dis. 25: 497–506.

Heuschele, W. P., J. Oosterhuis, D. Janssen, T. Robinson, P. K. Ensley, J. E. Meier, T. Olson, M. P. Anderson, and K. Bernirschke. 1986. Cryptosporidial infections in captive wild animals. Jour. Wildlife Dis., 22: 493–496.

Hird, D. W., S. L. Diesch, R. G. McKinnell, E. Gorham, F. B. Martin, W. Kurtz, and C. Durbrovolny. 1981. *Aeromonas hydrophila* in wild caught frogs and tadpoles (*Rana pipiens*) in Minnesota. Lab. Anim. Sci., 31: 166–169.

Jacobson, E. R. 1980. Infectious diseases of reptiles, p. 625–633. *In* R. W. Kirk (ed.), Current Veterinary Therapy, volume VII. Small Animal Practice. W. B. Saunders Co., New York.

—. 1986*a*. Parasitic diseases of reptiles, p. 162–186. *In* M. E. Fowler (ed.), Zoo and Wild Animal Medicine. Second ed. W. B. Saunders Co., Philadelphia.

—. 1986*b*. Viruses and viral associated diseases of reptiles, p. 73–89. *In* V. L. Bels and A. P. Van Den Sande (eds.), Maintenance and Reproduction of Reptiles in Captivity. Vol. II Diseases. Acta Zoologica et Pathologica Antverpiensia. Bulletins de la Société Royale de Zoologie d'Anvers.

—. 1988. Evaluation of the reptile patient, p. 1–18. *In* E. R. Jacobson and G. V. Kollias (eds.), Exotic Animals. Churchill Livingstone, New York.

Jacobson, E. R., S. L. Clubb, J. M. Gaskin, and C. Gardiner. 1985. Herpesvirus-like infection in Argentine tortoises. Jour. Amer. Vet. Med. Assoc., 187: 1227–1229.

Jacobson, E. R., and J. M. Gaskin. 1989. Paramyxoviral infections of snakes: an historical review, p. 15–16. *In* Third International Colloquium on the Pathology of Reptiles and Amphibians. Abstracts. Orlando, Florida.

Jacobson, E. R., J. M. Gaskin, M. B. Brown, R. K. Harris, C. H. Gardiner, J. L. LaPointe, H. P. Adams, and C. Reggiardo. 1991. Chronic upper respiratory tract disease of free-ranging desert tortoises (*Xerobates agassizii*). Jour. Wildlife Dis., 27: 296–316.

Jacobson, E. R., J. M. Gaskin, and J. Mansell. 1989. Chlamydial infection in puff adders (*Bitis arietans*). Jour. Zoo Wildlife Med., 20: 364–369.

Jacobson, E. R., J. M. Gaskin, D. Page, W. O. Iverson, and J. W. Johnson. 1981. Paramyxo-like virus associated illness in a zoological collection of snakes. Jour. Amer. Vet. Med. Assoc., 179: 1227–1230.

Jacobson, E. R., J. M. Gaskin, C. F. Simpson, and T. G. Terrell. 1980. Paramyxo-like virus infection in a rock rattlesnake. Jour. Amer. Vet. Med. Assoc., 177: 796–799.

Jacobson, E. R., J. M. Gaskin, S. Wells, K. Bowler, and J. Schumacher. 1992. Epizootic of ophidian paramyxovirus in a zoological collection: pathological, microbiological and serological findings. Jour. Zoo Wildlife Med., 23: 318–327.

Jacobson, E. R., and S. R. Telford. 1990. Chlamydial and poxvirus infections of circulating monocytes of a flap-necked chameleon (*Chamaeleo dilepis*). Jour. Wildlife Dis., 26: 572–577.

Migaki, G., E. R. Jacobson, and H. W. Casey. 1984. Fungal diseases in reptiles, p. 183–204. *In* G. L. Hoff, F. L. Frye, and E. R. Jacobson (eds.), Diseases of Amphibians and Reptiles. Plenum Press, New York.

Mok, W. Y., C. Morato de Carvalho, L. C. Ferreira, and J. W. S. Meirelles. 1983. Natural mycotic infections in Amazonian anurans, p. 59–65. *In* C. Vago and G. Matz (eds.), Comptes Rendus Premier Colloque International de Pathologie des Reptiles et des Amphibians. Presse de Université de Angers, Angers, France.

Newcomer, C. E., M. R. Anver, J. L. Simmons, B. W. Wilcke, and G. W. Nace. 1982. Spontaneous and experimental infections of *Xenopus laevis* with *Chlamydia psittaci*. Lab. Anim. Sci., 32: 680–686.

Potgieter, L. N. D., R. E. Sigler, R. G. Russell. 1987. Pneumonia in Ottoman vipers (*Vipera xanthina xanthina*) associated with a parainfluenza 2-like virus. Jour. Wildlife Dis., 23: 355–360.

Ramsay, E. C., R. J. Montali, M. Worley, C. B. Stephensen, and K. V. Holmes. 1989. Callitrichid hepatitis: epizootiology of a fatal hepatitis in zoo tamarins and marmosets. Jour. Zoo Wildlife Med., 20: 178–183.

Schumacher, J., E. R. Jacobson, and J. M. Gaskin. 1990. Inclusion-body disease in boid snakes: a retrospective and prospective study, p. 289. *In* Proceedings of the American Association of Zoo Veterinarians, South Padre Island, Texas.

Upton, S. J., and S. M. Barnard. 1987. Two new species of coccidia (*Apicomplexa:* Eimeriidae) from Madagascar gekkonids. Jour. Protozool., 34: 452–454.

Upton, S. J., C. T. McAllister, P. S. Freed, and S. M. Barnard. 1989. *Cryptosporidium* spp. in wild and captive reptiles. Jour. Wildlife Dis., 25: 20–30.

Wolf, K., G. L. Bullock, C. E. Dunbar, and M. C. Quimby. 1968. Tadpole edema virus: a viscerotropic pathogen for anuran amphibians. Jour. Infect. Dis., 118: 253–262.

—. 1969. Tadpole edema virus: pathogenesis and growth studies and additional sites of virus infected bullfrog tadpoles, p. 326–336. *In* M. Mizell (ed.), The Biology of Amphibian Tumors. Springer-Verlag, New York.

❦

❦ Jacobson, E. R. 1994. Veterinary procedures for the acquisition and release of captive-bred herpetofauna, p. 109–118. *In* J. B. Murphy, K. Adler, and J. T. Collins (eds.), Captive Management and Conservation of Amphibians and Reptiles. Society for the Study of Amphibians and Reptiles, Ithaca (New York). Contributions to Herpetology, volume 11.

Reproductive Patterns of Reptiles and Amphibians: Considerations for Captive Breeding and Conservation

J. Whitfield Gibbons*

Introduction

Alteration or destruction of the reproductive link in the life cycle of a species can cause dramatic declines in population sizes and lead to the imminent disappearance of the species from a region. Thus, reproductive patterns are vital in the captive management and conservation of amphibians and reptiles.

The topic of reproductive patterns of particular groups of reptiles and amphibians has been addressed thoroughly. Amphibian reproduction has been bountifully covered by Duellman and Trueb (1986 [1985]). A variety of publications have satisfactorily covered reptilian reproductive strategies, such as Ford and Seigel (1989) for snakes; Moll (1979), Wilbur and Morin (1988), and Iverson (1991) for turtles; and Tinkle et al. (1970), Dunham et al. (1988), and others for lizards. The emphasis of this chapter is on the connection between reproductive patterns and conservation efforts.

The Importance of Reproductive Cycles in Conservation Efforts

Knowledge of reptilian and amphibian reproductive patterns is critical to species conservation efforts. Obviously, if individuals are saved, but do not reproduce in the wild, the natural population is doomed. Although some reproductive phases represent a small proportion of the life cycle, each is critical. My objective is to identify the potential of the effects of humans, including conservation efforts themselves, on vital reproductive links and to emphasize the continuing need for knowledge of the basic sequence of reproductive events. The way in which each link in the chain of reproductive events can be key to the success of natural populations is demonstrated, for example, in that sea turtles need to nest on beaches; amphibians require wetland habitats, both for breeding and for larval development; and some snakes must congregate to mate at denning sites before dispersal.

Development of a management plan for a species requires knowing its reproductive patterns and the significance of the sequence of reproductive events. To properly manage wild herpetofaunal populations, conservationists need to concentrate on field research that is designed to increase understanding of the reproductive processes of reptiles and amphibians. We cannot meet the management challenges in a satisfactory manner without this information.

Human-induced impacts on the critical parts of the life cycles of the species in the examples given above could eliminate populations. Coastal development can permanently destroy nesting habitats for sea turtles. Direct destruction of wetlands or the placement of barriers (such as highways) between the terrestrial habitat and wetlands can reduce or eliminate amphibian breeding. Overzealous collecting, intentional killing of individual snakes, or destruction of denning sites can eliminate snake populations.

Artificial Protection of the Reproductive Cycle

Assuring completion of the reproductive cycle by artificially safeguarding populations is one conservation approach for protecting a species. Thus, numerous sea turtle hatcheries artificially incubate eggs (Mrosovsky 1983). More effective ways to illuminate developed coastal areas have been identi-

* Savannah River Ecology Laboratory
University of Georgia
Drawer E
Aiken, South Carolina 29802, USA

fied, following research on the responses of sea turtles to various types of beach lighting (Witherington and Bjorndal 1991*a*, 1991*b*; Witherington 1992).

Many experiments using cattle tanks for amphibian breeding, successfully conducted on both anurans and salamanders (Wilbur and Travis 1984; Morin 1983; Semlitsch 1987), have demonstrated that amphibian eggs can be hatched and the larvae raised in artificial aquatic habitats. Some conservationists are optimistic about the creation of artificial refuge ponds to replace natural aquatic habitats and the use of "toad tunnels" to reinstate destroyed migration routes (Tyning 1989).

Captive breeding with the potential for reintroduction into the wild is a conservation approach used or proposed for use for endangered species of snakes (Speake et al. 1992). In addition, captive breeding can create a source and supply of specimens that some view as a way to reduce the removal of animals from the wild for the pet trade, as evidenced in the international bird trade (Graham 1988; Bergman 1991).

Potential Problems Arising from Artificial Protection

Each of the above approaches has been used successfully or has the potential for success. Each also has, however, a potential for failure. In most instances, information verifying the long-term success of the target species is unavailable.

With sea turtles, one obvious concern during the past decade has been the influence of artificial incubation programs on hatchling sex ratios (Morreale et al. 1982). Vast numbers of a single sex can be produced due to variations in incubation temperatures (Bull and Vogt 1979), a phenomenon now recognized by most programs. Research on the effects of light wavelengths and intensities on sea turtles has revealed differential responses among species and between hatchlings and adults (Witherington and Bjorndal 1991*a*, 1991*b*; Witherington 1992). Therefore, cautious interpretations will be necessary in considering the impact of beach lighting on the life cycle of sea turtles.

For amphibians, cattle tanks can be used to raise eggs and larvae, but extensive understanding of the complex life cycles of the manipulated species is essential. For example, the timing of metamorphosis can be regulated to some degree (Semlitsch and Wilbur 1988; Alford and Harris 1988), but it is not clear what is the most appropriate time for release of recent metamorphs. Before a release program can be established with assurance of success, the issue of how far the "wetland habitat" extends must be resolved. It is important to know how much terrestrial "buffer zone" habitat is required to maintain a population of a given species, even if the aquatic portion of the wetland is intact, and how close a clearcut area can be to a wetland before it affects the disposition of populations. In considering the use of artificial refuge ponds, two points are apparent from studies at Sun Bay, a natural freshwater wetland on the Savannah River Site in South Carolina (Gibbons and Semlitsch 1991). This Carolina bay was destroyed during the building of the United States Department of Energy Defense Waste Processing Facility and parking lot, and four artificial refuge ponds were constructed near the former wetland. During more than a decade of daily surveys at the artificial ponds, it became clear that not all amphibian species from Sun Bay successfully colonized the artificial ponds, and that great variability in success of individual species occurred among and within the refuge ponds themselves.

How would conservation managers interpret and act on these facts? Clearly, extensive research is needed before reliable predictions can be made on the success of refuge ponds or of captive-rearing and reintroduction programs for amphibians.

When captive breeding is used as a conservation measure for snakes, individuals bred and raised in captivity will not experience natural selection and will be more likely to retain abnormal traits as a consequence of inbreeding. Obviously, an albino of any species is unsuitable for reintroduction into a natural habitat, because its color will lower its chance for survival; the danger is that it might live to pass on this color to its offspring, thereby lowering their fitness.

Finally, when captive breeding and reintroduction programs fail to correct the initial problem in the environment, reintroduction is then a gratuitous exercise (Griffith et al. 1989). Research may be necessary to reveal and understand the problem, including identification of the life-cycle component of a species that is being adversely affected. Often, disruption of the reproductive cycle will be identified as the primary problem.

Reproductive traits that are sensitive to human disturbance can be subtle and difficult to study. For example, in the Painted Turtle (*Chrysemys picta*), energy for current reproduction comes from energy that has been stored as lipids as much as a year prior to egg laying (Congdon and Tinkle 1982). The separation of energy acquisition and allocation in the reproductive cycle is critical for many populations of turtles. Although egg-laying species are known to be vulnerable to egg predation and nest failure as a result of human activities, it is not yet clear how our activities affect these species prior to egg laying. The effects on preovulatory lipid storage that have been caused by human alteration of the environment, which are perhaps subtle to humans, may be devastating to animals. A vital part of the reproductive cycle of some reptiles, and probably some amphibians, too, is the acquisition of energy stores for future reproduction. If a species is dependent on a particular season, site, or resource for this energy, its reproductive output and effectiveness could be disrupted unwittingly, even while its breeding area is being protected.

The potential impact of preovulatory stresses on reproductive success may be apparent on some alligator farms. Care is given to the breeding, nesting, and incubation periods, but during autumn, females are sequestered with minimum care while facilities are repaired. Reproductive output reportedly declines when this is done (L. J. Guillette, pers. comm.), perhaps because of stress (Lance 1989) or due to an inadequate buildup of energy stores (Congdon and Tinkle 1982).

Factors affecting migration to breeding sites and breeding success in amphibians must be understood to mitigate disruptions caused by humans. At Rainbow Bay, a freshwater wetland on the Savannah River Site (Gibbons and Semlitsch 1991), the numbers of breeding adult and juvenile frogs and salamanders were dramatically affected by natural changes, especially in annual hydrological cycles (Pechmann et al. 1991). In four amphibian species, normal variation resulted in annual differences of more than five orders of magnitude in the numbers of animals that successfully metamorphosed over a 12-year period (Pechmann et al. 1991). Conservation management programs must take into account this tremendous variability in natural populations. Extensive research programs are needed to reveal the patterns of population responses to natural environmental variability.

Occasional undetected long-range migration of female Diamondback Terrapins (*Malaclemys terrapin*) to oviposition sites is another example of subtle factors that affect reproductive success. An eight-year mark-release-recapture study on the *Malaclemys* population in the Kiawah River near Charleston, South Carolina, resulted in 779 original captures and 451 recaptures (J. W. Gibbons, pers. observ.). Most terrapins showed long-term fidelity to 100–200 m stretches of one of three tidal creeks separated from one another by approximately 0.5 km of salt marsh. Only ten individuals shifted locations from the site of original capture to another creek. Although the terrapins are relatively sedentary within the salt marsh ecosystem, in 1991, we discovered nesting individuals more than one km from their home creek. Obviously, human activity that affects the nesting habitat or creates a barrier between the home creek and the nesting area can seriously disrupt the population.

Similar examples exist for other species or groups shown to be susceptible to specific human activities. Sensitivities of the reproductive cycle to human disturbance are still poorly known. We must not become complacent about how much we think we know about the basic ecology and reproductive patterns of reptilian and amphibian species. Instead, we must accept that we still have a lot to learn and not be reticent about conducting basic studies and reporting the findings. This point has been reinforced by Dodd and Seigel (1991).

The above examples identify ways that disruption of reproductive cycles can result in the demise of populations. The primary emphasis of this volume is on captive breeding as a means of conservation. Captive breeding and reintroducing species to the wild is a disservice, however, unless at the same time we solve the environmental problems that resulted in the need for these programs in the first place.

To solve real environmental problems in a meaningful manner will require in-depth, long-term research. For example, headstarting* Atlantic Ridley sea turtles (*Lepidochelys kempii*) without curbing the effect of the shrimp-harvesting industry and other impacts on adults in the open seas appears futile, yet too little is known about the basic open-

*Programs in which hatchling turtles are retained in captivity to a body size at which they are believed to be no longer susceptible to most predators they might encounter in the wild.

sea biology of most sea turtles for ecologists to make persuasive recommendations (Frazer et al. 1990; Mangan et al. 1990). Captive raising of snakes to reduce the effect of wild captures without placing strict, enforced controls on the removal of wild specimens is ineffective. The State of Virginia has recently put some very strict laws into place regarding the capture of wild specimens and the sale of any native wildlife (J. C. Mitchell, pers. comm.). We should also be conducting the research necessary to demonstrate what the impact of removal of wild-caught snakes or other animals really is.

The Problem of "Halfway Technology"

The late Lewis Thomas (1974) used the term "halfway technology" in his essay on the technology of medicine in "The Lives of a Cell." Thomas defined halfway technology as "the kinds of things that must be done after the fact, in efforts to compensate for the incapacitating effects of certain diseases whose course one is unable to do very much about. It is a technology designed to make up for disease, or to postpone death." In short, halfway technology does not address the cause or the cure of disease. It is simply a mechanism to treat a disease in cases in which we really do not understand it.

Nat B. Frazer, in his keynote address, "Sea Turtle Conservation and Halfway Technology," delivered at the Tenth Annual Workshop on Sea Turtle Conservation and Biology (1990), stated that, "How we define a problem often will determine what we are willing to consider as a solution. When we define the impending extinction of a sea turtle species solely in terms of there being too few turtles, we are tempted to think of solutions solely in terms of increasing the numbers of turtles. Hence, some of what we are doing in our attempts to conserve sea turtles involves 'halfway technology,' which does not address the causes of or provide amelioration for the actual threats turtles face."

Frazer went on to state that "Programs such as headstarting, captive breeding, and hatcheries may serve only to release more turtles into a degraded environment in which their parents have already demonstrated that they cannot flourish. Furthermore, captive programs may keep turtles from serving important ecological functions in the natural environment, or place them at some disadvantage relative to their natural counterparts once released."

Frazer's final analysis is that what we need for sea turtles are clean and productive marine and coastal environments. He emphasizes that without a commitment to long-term goals of cleanup and repair of degraded environments, efforts to protect sea turtles will be futile. Although his message was for sea turtles biologists, the generality of the message for all of us who work with and are concerned about the environmental health of any group of reptiles and amphibians is obvious.

Summary

We must be concerned with the specter of conservation "welfare" programs, in which we assume responsibility for a disadvantaged species by caring for individuals instead of correcting the environmental situation so that the population can survive by itself. We must not become complacent about the environmental health and prosperity of reptiles and amphibians simply because we have discovered ways to breed or raise them in captivity for release into the wild. If populations face the same problems in the wild as they did before we captive-raised and reintroduced individuals, and the "disease" is still rampant, then this is not a remedy. In many—perhaps most—instances, we know the cause of the disease, but do not take the necessary measures for its eradication. We need to put as much or more effort into wiping out the disease as we do into curing the patient. We need preventive medicine, not simply better treatments of the symptoms.

Captive breeding and maintenance can be worthwhile practices for reintroduction programs, but they are not ends unto themselves. All programs should carefully consider the criteria by which they can be considered successful. The truly successful captive-breeding program, for purposes of conservation and preservation, is one that can be terminated—because the species is healthy in its native habitat. Let us not develop a permanent "welfare" program for these animals. Instead let us be sure we put our efforts into curing the problems at the source, in their natural environments.

Acknowledgments

I thank Nat B. Frazer of Mercer University for discussions of the topic and thank Tracy Lynch, David E. Scott, and Barbara Dietsch for reading the final manuscript. Parts of the manuscript were also read by Judy Greene and Justin D. Congdon. Research and manuscript preparation were supported by United States Department of Energy contract DE-AC09-76SR00819 with the University of Georgia.

Literature Cited

Alford, R. A., and R. N. Harris. 1988. Effects of larval growth history on anuran metamorphosis. Amer. Nat., 131: 91–106.

Bergman, C. A. 1991. The bust. Audubon, 93: 66–76.

Bull, J. J., and R. C. Vogt. 1979. Temperature-dependent sex determination in turtles. Science, 206: 1186–1188.

Congdon, J. D., and D. W. Tinkle. 1982. Reproductive energetics of the painted turtle (*Chrysemys picta*). Herpetologica, 38: 228–237.

Dodd, C. K., Jr., and R. A. Seigel. 1991. Relocation, repatriation and translocation of amphibians and reptiles: are they conservation strategies that work? Herpetologica, 47: 336–350.

Duellman, W. E., and L. Trueb. 1986 (1985). Biology of Amphibians. McGraw Hill, New York. xvii, 670 pages.

Dunham, A. E., D. M. Miles, and D. Reznick. 1988. Life history patterns in squamate reptiles, p. 443–511. *In* C. Gans and R. B. Huey (eds.), Biology of the Reptilia, Vol. 16. Alan R. Liss, New York.

Ford, N. B., and R. A. Seigel. 1989. Relationships among body size, clutch size, and egg size in three species of oviparous snakes. Herpetologica, 45: 75–83.

Frazer, N. B. 1992. Sea turtle conservation and halfway technology. Conserv. Biol., 6: 179–184.

Frazer, N. B., J. I. Richardson, C. Crouse, E. Possardt, and J. Woody. 1990. Population dynamics and life history of sea turtles, p. 89–100. *In* Tucker and Associates, Inc. (compilers), Sea Turtles and Marine Mammals of the Gulf of Mexico. OCS Study MMS 90-0009, United States Dept. Interior, Minerals Management Serv., Gulf of Mexico OCS Regional Office, New Orleans, Louisiana.

Gibbons, J. W., and R. D. Semlitsch. 1991. Guide to the Reptiles and Amphibians of the Savannah River Site. Univ. Georgia Press, Athens. 131 pages.

Graham, F., Jr. 1988. A bird in the hand is worth . . . plenty! Audubon, 90: 96–98.

Griffith, B., J. M. Scott, J. W. Carpenter, and C. Reed. 1989. Translocation as a species conservation tool: status and strategy. Science, 245: 477–480.

Iverson, J. B. 1991. Patterns of survivorship in turtles (Order Testudines). Canadian Jour. Zool., 69: 385–391.

Lance, V. 1989. Reproductive cycle of the American alligator. Amer. Zool., 29: 999–1018.

Mangan, P., K. Bjorndal, and A. Bolten. 1990. Principal findings and conclusions, p. 77–81. *In* Tucker and Associates, Inc. (compilers), Sea Turtles and Marine Mammals of the Gulf of Mexico. OCS Study MMS 90-0009, United States Dept. Interior, Minerals Management Serv., Gulf of Mexico OCS Regional Office, New Orleans, Louisiana.

Moll, E. O. 1979. Reproductive cycles and adaptations, p. 305–331. *In* M. Harless and H. Morlock (eds.), Turtles: Perspectives and Research. John Wiley and Sons, New York.

Morin, P. J. 1983. Predation, competition, and the composition of larval anuran guilds. Ecol. Monogr., 53: 119–138.

Morreale, S. J., G. J. Ruiz, J. R. Spotila, and E. A. Standora. 1982. Temperature-dependent sex determination: current practices threaten conservation of sea turtles. Science, 216: 1245–1247.

Mrosovsky, N. 1983. Conserving Sea Turtles. Publ. British Herpetol. Soc., London. 174 pages.

Pechmann, J. H. K., D. E. Scott, R. D. Semlitsch, J. P. Caldwell, L. J. Vitt, and J. W. Gibbons. 1991. Declining amphibian populations: the problem of separating human impacts from natural fluctuations. Science, 253: 892–895.

Semlitsch, R. D. 1987. Interactions between fish and salamander larvae. Oecologia (Berlin), 72: 481–486.

Semlitsch, R. D., and H. M. Wilbur. 1988. Effects of pond drying time on metamorphosis and survival in the salamander *Ambystoma talpoideum*. Copeia, 1988: 978–983.

Speake, D., D. McGlincy, and C. Smith. 1992. Captive breeding and experimental reintroduction of the eastern indigo snake, p. 84–89. *In* R. R. Odom, K. A. Riddleberger and J. C. Ozier (eds.), Proc. 3rd Southeastern Nongame and Endangered Wildlife Symposium, Athens, Georgia.

Thomas, L. 1974. The Lives of a Cell. Viking Press, New York. viii, 180 pages.

Tinkle, D. W., H. M. Wilbur, and S. G. Tilley. 1970. Evolutionary strategies in lizard reproduction. Evolution, 24: 55–74.

Tyning, T. 1989. Amherst's tunneling amphibians. Defenders, September/October 1989: 20–23.

Wilbur, H. M., and P. J. Morin. 1988. Life history evolution of turtles, p. 387–439. *In* C. Gans and R. Huey (eds.), Biology of the Reptilia Vol. 16. Alan R. Liss, New York.

Wilbur, H. M., and J. Travis. 1984. An experimental approach to understanding pattern in natural communities, p. 113–122. *In* D. R. Strong, Jr., D. S. Simberloff, L. G. Abele, and A. B. Thistle (eds.), Ecological Communities: Conceptual Issues and the Evidence. Princeton Univ. Press, New Jersey.

Witherington, B. E. 1992. Behavioral responses of nesting sea turtles to artificial lighting. Herpetologica, 48: 31–39.

Witherington, B. E., and K. A. Bjorndal. 1991*a*. Influences of artificial lighting on the seaward orientation of hatchling loggerhead turtles (*Caretta caretta*). Biol. Conserv., 55: 139–149.

—. 1991*b*. Influences of wavelength and intensity on hatchling sea turtle phototaxis: implications for sea-finding behavior. Copeia, 1991: 1060–1069.

❦

❦ Gibbons, J. W. 1994. Reproductive patterns of reptiles and amphibians: considerations for captive breeding and conservation, p. 119–123. *In* J. B. Murphy, K. Adler, and J. T. Collins (eds.), Captive Management and Conservation of Amphibians and Reptiles. Society for the Study of Amphibians and Reptiles, Ithaca (New York). Contributions to Herpetology, volume 11.

Complexity in the Control of Amphibian Reproduction: Reproductive Behavior and Physiology of a Salamander

Frank L. Moore*

Introduction

Amphibians use a complex array of external and internal signals to control reproductive events, such as sex determination and sexual differentiation; seasonal cycles in reproduction, migration, courtship and mating behaviors; and egg-laying. External signals that influence reproduction include many types of environmental cues, from photoperiod to sex pheromones. Internal signals include the neurotransmitters and hormones that mediate responses to environmental cues and activate or inhibit reproduction. These signals serve many functions (for example, structural, physiological, and behavioral) that relate to successful reproduction.

This chapter illustrates the complexity in the control of amphibian reproduction by describing what is known about the reproductive biology and physiology of the Roughskin Newt (*Taricha granulosa*), a species that has been studied extensively. Information about the reproductive biology of these newts is related to what is known about the neuroendocrine control mechanisms of this species. Readers interested in learning more about neuroendocrine control mechanisms and methodologies should look to other recent publications (Moore 1983, 1987*a*, 1987*b*, 1990; Moore et al. 1987; Moore and Orchinik 1991).

Although we focus here on *Taricha granulosa*, our overall goal extends beyond that to argue, by analogy for other species, that there are many external and internal factors interacting with each other to regulate reproduction—in other words, that there is complexity in the control of amphibian reproduction.

Some of the external and internal factors that are used to regulate reproduction in *Taricha granulosa* undoubtedly will be similar to those used by other amphibians. Considering the diversity in amphibian reproductive patterns, however, it is almost axiomatic that other factors will be peculiar to certain taxa. Currently, not enough information is available to make claims about which external or internal regulatory factors are species-specific and which ones are universal among amphibians. Nevertheless, the primary conclusion of this chapter—that amphibian reproduction is controlled by an array of external and internal factors—has implications for the captive management and conservation of amphibians. The complexity of amphibian reproduction leads us to three conclusions: management and conservation problems will probably not be solved by finding a "golden bullet" (a simple drug or hormone treatment that solves reproductive problems in captive amphibians); success in rearing amphibians in captivity will most likely relate to the ability to simulate the natural environmental conditions of that species; and there are many unanswered questions about the control of amphibian reproduction that need to be studied.

* Department of Zoology
Oregon State University
Corvallis, Oregon 97331-2914, USA

Acronyms used in this chapter:

ACTH	Adrenocorticotrophic hormone
αMSH	Alpha melanophore-stimulating hormone
CRH	Corticotropin-releasing hormone
FSH	Follicle-stimulating hormone
GABA	Gamma-aminobutyric acid
GnRH	Gonadotropin-releasing hormone
LH	Luteinizing hormone
PGE_2	Prostaglandin E_2
$PGF_{2\alpha}$	Prostaglandin $F_{2\alpha}$
PRL	Prolactin

The Reproductive Biology of Taricha granulosa

Annual cycles of reproduction for males and females reflect a continuum of changes, with variations that prepare the animals for reproduction, sustain reproductive functions and behaviors, and then allow the animals to recuperate from the reproductive costs.

Although Roughskin Newts (*T. granulosa*) reproduce in environments that cover a wide range of latitudes and altitudes in the Pacific Northwest of North America, this chapter describes the reproductive biology of populations that live at lower elevations, where the winters are cool and rainy and the summers are warm and dry. Additional details about the reproductive cycles of this salamander are explained in Pimentel (1960), Efford and Mathias (1969), Oliver and McCurdy (1974), Specker and Moore (1980), Moore and Zoeller (1985), and Deviche et al. (1990).

Seasonal Cycles in Reproduction

Like other amphibians from higher latitudes, males and females of *Taricha granulosa* exhibit predictable seasonal cycles in reproduction. The seasonal reproductive cycles form a continuous year-long sequence of events, as certain seasons are used for mating and egg laying and others for preparing for the next episode of reproduction.

The reproductive cycles of male Roughskin Newts begin with spermatogenesis in late spring and summer (Specker and Moore 1980). Sexual structures and behaviors develop from late summer through the fall, a process that is completed by late fall or early winter. These sexual structures and behaviors regress in late spring, at which point the male cycle starts over again.

In early June, males exhibit a drop in sexual libido, regression of secondary sex characteristics, and recrudescence of spermatogenesis (Deviche et al. 1990). The most conspicuous changes in secondary sex characteristics in post-breeding males are a decrease in tail-fin height, disappearance of smooth and puffy skin, decrease in body mass, regression of cloacal glands, and regression of nuptial pads.

Concurrent with these changes, males of *T. granulosa* also begin to undergo testicular recrudescence. Spermatogenesis commences during the last weeks of spring, when male sexual activity is waning. With germ-cell proliferation, testes increase in weight throughout the summer. By the end of August, the testes are near maximal size and contain a large complement of spermatids and spermatozoa (Specker and Moore 1980). In autumn, the spermatozoa continue to mature (spermiogenesis) and start to move from the seminiferous lobules into the sperm ducts. With spermiation, the testes decrease in size and reach their minimum masses by late autumn. Although small, the testes actively secrete reproductive hormones. Plasma androgen concentrations rise when spermiation begins, remain elevated during the winter, and then decrease in late spring when the steroidogenic tissues are resorbed (Specker and Moore 1980; Zoeller and Moore 1985).

Elevated plasma androgen concentrations prepare male salamanders for reproduction by stimulating the development of primary and secondary sex structures (Norris 1985; Moore 1987*b*, 1987*c*). Androgen-sensitive structures in Roughskin Newts include the brain, vas deferens, sex accessory glands, caudal fin, nuptial pads, and skeletal muscles. Nuptial pads in this species include dark keratinized skin on the femoral region and keratinized skin on the tips of the toes. All of these structures exhibit annual cycles of development and regression, in concert with the annual cycles in plasma androgen concentrations (Specker and Moore 1980; Zoeller and Moore 1985; Deviche et al. 1990).

Female salamanders exhibit annual reproductive cycles similar to those of males (Miller and Robbins 1954; Reimer 1954; Oliver and McCurdy 1974). About two weeks after being inseminated, usually in early to middle spring, female Roughskin Newts begin to ovulate and oviposit (Moore et al. 1979). Oogonia and oocytes proliferate during the summer, and the ovarian follicles increase in size and accumulate yolk during the period from late autumn into early spring. Annual changes in ovarian mass reflect cycles of ovulation and yolk deposition. In many amphibians, ovarian cycles are linked to seasonal changes in ovarian hormones (mainly testosterone, 17β-estradiol, and progesterone), which cause seasonal changes in the oviducts, sex accessory structures, and behaviors (Licht et al. 1983; Polzonetti-Magni et al. 1984; Cayrol et al. 1985; Pierantoni et al. 1984; Gobbetti et al. 1990). Thus, in females as in males, annual cycles in the gonads are matched with cycles in sex-steroid hormones to prepare steroid-sensitive structures for the breeding season.

Seasonal Migrations

A significant event in the reproductive cycle of many amphibians is the migration to and from breeding sites. Amphibians can migrate several kilometers with surprising accuracy using a variety of environmental cues and mechanisms, such as magnetoreception (Pimentel 1960; Phillips 1986).

Females of *Taricha granulosa* migrate into the ponds in the spring, stay there throughout the dry summer, and then exit the ponds and retreat into the forests in the fall. Like other amphibians, these newts migrate during periods of rain and mild temperature, but many of these salamanders continue to migrate during daylight hours, most likely because of the significant toxicity of these animals to predators (Brodie and Brodie 1991). Males in the larger and deeper ponds tend to remain in the water throughout the year (Oliver and McCurdy 1974). Sexually active males exhibit local migrations within the ponds; during periods of rain and mild temperature, they move into shallow water along the shore, where incoming females are likely to be intercepted. During periods of dry or cold weather, males migrate into deeper water and away from the shore.

Thus, reproductive activities in *T. granulosa,* particularly courtship and insemination, are modulated by those environmental cues that trigger migratory movements in females; migration to and from breeding ponds depends somewhat on the size and depth of the pond (Reimer 1954; Pimentel 1960; Oliver and McCurdy 1974).

Courtship and Mating Behaviors

The mating sequence of *Taricha granulosa* involves a complex series of signals, which involve reciprocal actions between partners. Three main stages of reproductive behaviors are described in recent work by Propper (1991): courtship behaviors (pre-insemination behaviors), mating behaviors (behaviors associated with insemination), and post-insemination behaviors.

It typically takes Roughskin Newts from one to five days to complete the entire reproductive sequence, which begins when the male first moves toward a prospective mate and ends when he disengages from post-insemination amplexus. Males appear to recognize females as conspecifics and potential mates by using visual information, such as shape, color, and behaviors (Twitty 1966; Propper et al. 1986; Roth 1987; Hedlund 1990). Although not proven, males also appear to use olfactory information (pheromones) to discriminate between uninseminated and inseminated females.

Courtship is initiated when a male salamander approaches a female and grasps her in dorsal amplexus (Propper 1991). Males in amplexus exhibit periodic bouts of vigorous hind-limb contractions and chin-rubbing behaviors. Males contract muscles in their hind limbs, stroking or striking the female's pelvic region. As courtship progresses, contraction rates increase. In chin-rubbing behavior, the male presses his chin against the female's nares and, although not proven in *T. granulosa,* is suspected of transferring sex pheromones.

Initially, females respond to chin rubbing by flexing their head ventrally, away from the male's chin, and vigorously swimming forward. This response apparently communicates to the male that the female is sexually unreceptive. Early in courtship females invariably are sexually unreceptive, and males disengage from courtship when females remain unreceptive. When females become sexually receptive, they respond to chin-rubbing behaviors by holding still and raising their heads. These behavioral changes during amplexus indicate that reciprocal behavioral interactions between male and female cause internal changes in each, bringing them both to the next stage.

In Roughskin Newts, amplectic clasping behaviors are followed by mating (insemination) behaviors. An insemination attempt is accomplished when the male disengages from amplectic clasping and swim-walks forward over the female. The male then produces a spermatophore (combining spermatozoa with mucopolysaccharide secretions from his cloacal glands) and attaches it to the substrate. The female, in stereotyped coordination with the male, positions her cloaca over the spermatophore and picks up the sperm cap (Propper 1991). Following each sperm-transfer attempt, the male re-clasps the female.

Post-insemination, clasping behaviors in *T. granulosa* appear to give the pair an opportunity to assess whether insemination was successful. Uninseminated females remain sexually receptive and the pair may initiate another sperm-transfer attempt. Females that have been inseminated and exposed to the post-insemination behavior, on the other hand, become sexually unreceptive. When that occurs, the male remains in amplexus for one to three days before disengaging from the post-insemination clasping and swimming away. Although not proven, this post-insemination clasping behavior appears to be a form of mate-guarding behavior.

This description of the courtship and mating sequence in *T. granulosa* illustrates the complexity of the external signals. Males must use sensory information to locate a breeding pond, find a likely position in the pond to intercept entering females, recognize that the female is a prospective mate, detect that she has not yet been inseminated, and use reciprocal behavioral interactions with females to accomplish the mating sequence. These behavioral and pheromonal responses must be temporally associated with changes in internal physiological signals to accomplish internal fertilization.

Ovulation and Oviposition

Some amphibians are induced ovulators. Females of *Taricha granulosa* ovulate only when exposed to male courtship and insemination (Moore et al. 1979); interestingly, they do not ovulate when paired with vasectomized males (S.P. Spielvogel and F. L. Moore, unpubl. data). Female Roughskin Newts normally start to ovulate about two weeks after being courted and inseminated. They then continue to deposit eggs during the months from April into August. Eggs are attached singly to submerged vegetation and other structures (Oliver and McCurdy 1974; Moore et al. 1979). Females of *T. granulosa* retain eggs in their oviducts when stressed, as may happen when in captivity, or when appropriate substrates for the eggs are absent. Thus it appears that control mechanisms for mating behaviors, ovulation, and egg-laying behaviors are different; these are temporally separate events with different environmental and physiological constraints.

Control of Amphibian Reproduction

Environmental Control of Seasonal Cycles

In some amphibians, photoperiod and temperature have profound effects on seasonal reproductive development (reviewed in Salthe and Mecham 1974; Moore and Deviche 1988). These environmental factors appear to accelerate or retard reproductive functions, rather than to switch them on or off. Annual reproductive cycles in some amphibians appear to be controlled by endogenous circannual rhythms, with photoperiod and temperature influencing the timing of the cycle. The net result is that photoperiod and temperature tend to synchronize breeding in local populations of species with broad ranges in latitude or altitude.

Amphibians held in captivity often fail to become sexually active, not because of inappropriate photoperiod or temperature regimes, but because captivity triggers physiological stress responses (Moore and Miller 1984; Orchinik et al. 1991). Although what is stressful to amphibians may vary with the species, examples of potential stressors include harsh environment (too dry or wet, too hot or cold), intense social interaction, inadequate nutrition, or perhaps too many potential "predators" (large, moving objects elicit predator-avoidance responses in amphibian species; Ingle and Hoff 1990). This list is speculative, because little is known about amphibian stress responses. Nevertheless, physiological stress responses can inhibit amphibian reproduction (Moore and Miller 1984; Moore and Zoeller 1985; Deviche and Moore 1987; Boyd and Moore 1990; Orchinik et al. 1991).

Hormonal Control of Seasonal Cycles

Annual cycles in sex-steroid hormones prepare males and females for reproduction by stimulating both the development of primary and secondary sex structures and the development of neural pathways associated with reproductive behaviors. The sex hormones involved include those of the hypothalamus-pituitary-gonad axis (gonadotropin-releasing hormone [GnRH], luteinizing hormone [LH], follicle-stimulating hormone [FSH], prolactin [PRL], and inhibin-like peptides), as well as β-endorphin and prostaglandins. In males of *Taricha granulosa*, plasma concentrations of testosterone and 5α-dihydrotestosterone increase markedly in autumn and remain elevated into early spring (Specker and Moore 1980; Zoeller and Moore 1985), stimulating the development and differentiation of the brain, vas deferens, cloacal glands, nuptial pads, and the caudal tail fin. In female amphibians generally, the principal sex-steroid hormones are testosterone, estrone, 17β-estradiol, and progesterone (Polzonetti-Magni et al. 1984; Pierantoni et al. 1984; Gobbetti et al. 1990); in addition, neuropeptides, such as

GnRH and vasotocin, also appear to control female reproductive behaviors (Diakow 1978; Propper 1989; Propper and Moore 1991).

When sex-steroid hormones act through intracellular receptors, rather than through the recently discovered membrane receptors for steroid hormones (Orchinik et al. 1991; Moore and Orchinik 1991), the activated intracellular receptors function as transcription factors to direct the synthesis of specific proteins. Genomic mechanisms of action for steroid hormones are slow, taking weeks or months. Thus seasonal reproductive development in males and females usually requires an extended exposure to high concentrations of steroids to develop full reproductive function.

Androgens are not the only hormones involved in the control of male sexual development; other hormones are also involved. First, there are those hormones that directly and indirectly control the synthesis of testosterone and 5α-dihydrotestosterone. These include GnRH, the gonadotropins (LH and FSH), inhibin-like peptides, β-endorphin, and prostaglandins. Second, there are those hormones that act in conjunction with androgens on target tissues to facilitate sexual development. Examples of these include prolactin, 17β-estradiol, thyroid hormones, and glucocorticoids. Prolactin, for example, acts synergistically with androgens to promote the development of nuptial pads and caudal tail fins in males (Norris 1985; Moore et al. 1978). Third, insofar as stress inhibits reproduction in amphibians, there are stress hormones that act as regulators of sexual development. The main stress hormones in amphibians are corticotropin-releasing hormone (CRH), adrenocorticotrophic hormone (ACTH), glucocorticoids, epinephrine, and opioid peptides (Moore and Miller 1984; Moore and Zoeller 1985; Boyd and Moore 1990; Lowry and Moore 1991; Orchinik et al. 1991). Many of the problems with rearing amphibians in captivity can be attributed to physiological stress responses involving these hormones.

Hormonal Control of Migration

In *Taricha granulosa*, overland migrations are most frequent during periods of rain and mild temperature. Although migration in this species varies with sex and season, it seems likely that rainfall causes hormonal changes that activate migrations to or from the ponds. Injections of prolactin can stimulate migrations to the ponds; in fact, the "newt water drive" was an important bioassay for early work on prolactin (Chadwick 1941; Grant and Grant 1956). Likewise, injections of thyroxine can stimulate migrations out of the pond and onto land (Duvall and Norris 1980). So it is possible that, in female Roughskin Newts, rains stimulate prolactin secretions in the spring and thyroxine secretions in the fall. This, in turn, would enhance migrations and result in reproductive activities in this species.

Hormonal Control of Courtship and Mating Behaviors

Once males and females of *Taricha granulosa* are in full reproductive condition, and when the courtship and mating sequence progresses, numerous external signals are used to enhance successful reproduction.

Given the complexity of sensory inputs associated with reproductive behaviors, it is not surprising that the underlying neuroendocrine control mechanisms are also complex. In *T. granulosa* and in other amphibians, the list of endogenous chemical messengers that appear to be involved in the control of reproductive behaviors is long and includes neurotransmitters (gamma-aminobutyric acid [GABA], epinephrine, serotonin, and dopamine), neuropeptides (vasotocin, GnRH, corticotropin-releasing hormone [CRH], ACTH, alpha melanophore-stimulating hormone [αMSH], prolactin, dynorphin, and β-endorphin), prostaglandins (PGE_2 and $PGF_{2\alpha}$), and steroid hormones (testosterone, 5α-dihydrotestosterone, 17β-estradiol, progesterone, and corticosterone). Detailed discussions about the neuroendocrine control of reproductive behaviors in *T. granulosa* are available in Moore (1983, 1987*a*, 1987*b*) and Moore et al. (1987).

It is far too simple a generalization to say that androgens control male behaviors and estrogens control female behaviors. Not only do both sexes use androgenic and estrogenic steroids (Deviche and Moore 1988), but there is a variety of ways in which those hormones control behaviors.

Some of the control mechanisms are analogous to the hormonal control of the development of the oviducts, vas deferens, and other morphological structures. Sex-steroid hormones can cause the development, differentiation, and maintenance of specific somatic systems and neural pathways. For example, testosterone controls reproductive behaviors in many amphibians by stimulating the development of muscles used in amplectic clasping and male vocalizations (Sassoon et al. 1987; Tobias and Kelley 1987). Sex-steroid hormones also can influence neural systems and modify neuroanatomical structures and neurochemical systems. In *T. granulosa*, for example, sex-steroid hormones appear to stimulate structural changes in the brain to activate the synthesis of vasotocin and vasotocin receptors (Boyd and Moore 1991). These molecular changes may modify an animal's sensitivity to specific sensory stimuli and change neural processing in the brain and motor pathways.

Summary

Amphibians have very complex control mechanisms underlying their reproductive functions and behaviors. Exogenous factors (that is, environmental stimuli) of many types contribute to an animal's reproductive success. Some of these factors, such as ambient temperature, influence the timing of the seasonal reproductive cycles. Other factors—such as rainfall that triggers amphibian migrations to breeding sites—influence the day-to-day reproductive activities. Still other factors, for example, sex pheromones that elicit courtship behaviors, exert more rapid reproductive responses. Consistent with the complexity in the exogenous factors that influence amphibian reproduction, the endogenous neuroendocrine mechanisms controlling reproduction are likewise complex. The number of chemical messengers that control amphibian reproduction extends far beyond the sex-steroid hormones. While some of these neuroendocrine regulators excite, others inhibit reproductive functions and behaviors.

Literature Cited

Boyd, S. K., and F. L. Moore. 1990. Evidence for GABA involvement in stress-induced inhibition of male amphibian sexual behaviors. Horm. Behav., 24: 128–138.

—. 1991. Gonadectomy reduces the concentration of putative receptors for arginine vasotocin in the brain of an amphibian. Brain Res., 541: 193–197.

Brodie, E. D., III, and E. D. Brodie, Jr. 1991. Evolutionary response of predators to dangerous prey: reduction of toxicity of newts and resistance of garter snakes in island populations. Evolution, 45: 221–224.

Cayrol, C., D. H. Garnier, and P. Deparis. 1985. Comparative plasma levels of androgens and 17β-estradiol in the diploid and triploid newt, *Pleurodeles waltl*. Gen. Comp. Endocrinol., 58: 342–346.

Chadwick, C. S. 1941. Further observations on the water drive in *Triturus viridescens*. II. Induction of the water drive with the lactogenic hormone. Jour. Exp. Zool., 86: 175–187.

Deviche, P., and F. L. Moore. 1987. Opioid kappa-receptor agonists suppress sexual behaviors in male rough-skinned newts. Horm. Behav., 21: 371–383.

—. 1988. Steroidal control of sexual behavior in the rough-skinned newt (*Taricha granulosa*): effect of testosterone, estradiol, and dihydrotestosterone. Horm. Behav., 22: 26–34.

Deviche, P., C. R. Propper, and F. L. Moore. 1990. Neuroendocrine, behavioral, and morphological changes associated with the termination of the reproductive period in a natural population of male rough-skinned newts (*Taricha granulosa*). Horm. Behav., 24: 284–300.

Diakow, C. 1978. Hormonal basis for breeding behavior in female frogs: vasotocin inhibits the release call of *Rana pipiens*. Science, 199: 1456–1457.

Duvall, D., and D. O. Norris. 1980. Stimulation of dry-substrate preference and locomotor activity in newly transformed tiger salamanders (*Ambystoma tigrinum*) by exogenous or endogenous thyroxine. Anim. Behav., 28: 116–123.

Efford, I. E., and J. A. Mathias. 1969. A comparison of two salamander populations in Marion Lake, British Columbia. Copeia, 1969: 723–736.

Gobbetti, A., M. Zerani, O. Carnevali, and V. Botte. 1990. Prostaglandin $F_{2\alpha}$ in female water frog, *Rana esculenta*: plasma levels during the annual cycle and effects of exogenous $PGF2_{2\alpha}$ on circulating sex hormones. Gen. Comp. Endocrinol., 80: 175–180.

Grant, W. C., Jr., and J. A. Grant. 1956. The induction of water drive in the land stage of *Triturus viridescens* following hypophysectomy. Anat. Rec., 125: 604.

Hedlund, L. 1990. Factors affecting differential mating success in male crested newts, *Triturus cristatus*. Jour. Zool., 220: 33–40.

Ingle, D. J., and K. Hoff. 1990. Visually elicited evasive behavior in frogs (giving memory research an ethological context). BioScience, 40: 284–291.

Licht, P., B. R. McCreery, R. Barnes, and R. Pang. 1983. Seasonal and stress related changes in plasma gonadotropins, sex steroids, and corticosterone in the bullfrog, *Rana catesbeiana*. Gen. Comp. Endocrinol., 50: 124–145.

Lowry, C. A., and F. L. Moore. 1991. Corticotropin-releasing factor (CRF) antagonist suppresses stress-induced locomotor activity in an amphibian. Horm. Behav., 25: 84–96.

Miller, M. R., and R. E. Robbins. 1954. The reproductive cycle in *Taricha torosa* (*Triturus torosus*). Jour. Exp. Zool., 125: 415–446.

Moore, F. L. 1983. Behavioral endocrinology of amphibian reproduction. BioScience, 33: 557–561.

—. 1987*a*. Behavioral actions of neurohypophysial peptides, p. 61–87. *In* D. Crews (ed.), Psychobiology of Reproductive Behavior: An Evolutionary Perspective. Prentice-Hall, Englewood Cliff, New Jersey.

—. 1987*b*. Regulation of reproductive behaviors, p. 505–522. *In* D. O. Norris and R. E. Jones (eds.), Hormones and Reproduction in Fishes, Amphibians, and Reptiles. Plenum Press, New York.

—. 1987*c*. Reproductive endocrinology of amphibians, p. 207–221. *In* I. Chester Jones, P. M. Ingleton, and J. G. Phillips (eds.), Fundamentals of Comparative Vertebrate Endocrinology. Plenum Press, New York.

—. 1990. An amphibian model system for problems in behavioral neuroendocrinology. Jour. Exp. Zool., Suppl. 4: 157–158.

Moore, F. L., and P. Deviche. 1988. Neuroendocrine processing of environmental information in amphibians, p. 19–45. *In* M. Stetson (ed.), Processing of Environmental Information in Vertebrates. Springer Verlag, New York.

Moore, F. L., C. McCormack, and L. Swanson. 1979. Induced ovulation: effects of sexual behavior and insemination on ovulation and progesterone levels in *Taricha granulosa*. Gen. Comp. Endocrinol., 39: 262–269.

Moore, F. L., and L. J. Miller. 1984. Stress-induced inhibition of sexual behavior: corticosterone inhibits courtship behaviors of a male amphibian (*Taricha granulosa*). Horm. Behav., 18: 400–410.

Moore, F. L., L. Muske, and C. R. Propper. 1987. Regulation of reproductive behaviors in amphibians by LHRH. Ann. New York Acad. Sci., 519: 108–116.

Moore, F. L., and M. Orchinik. 1991. Multiple molecular actions for steroids in the regulation of reproductive behaviors. Semin. Neurosci., 3: 489–496.

Moore, F. L., R. L. Seide, and J. L. Specker. 1978. Effects of prolactin and methallibure on second metamorphosis and plasma androgens in male newts, *Taricha granulosa*. Comp. Biochem. Physiol., 61: 419–422.

Moore, F. L., and R. T. Zoeller. 1985. Stress-induced inhibition of reproduction: evidence of suppressed secretion of LHRH in an amphibian. Gen. Comp. Endocrinol., 60: 252–258.

Norris, D. O. 1985. Vertebrate Endocrinology. Second ed. Lea and Febiger, Philadelphia. xii, 505 pages.

Oliver, M. G., and H. M. McCurdy. 1974. Migration, overwintering, and reproductive patterns of *Taricha granulosa* on southern Vancouver Island. Canadian Jour. Zool., 52: 541–545.

Orchinik, M., T. F. Murray, and F. L. Moore. 1991. A corticosteroid receptor in neuronal membranes. Science, 252: 1848–1851.

Phillips, J. B. 1986. Two magnetoreception pathways in a migratory salamander. Science, 233: 765–767.

Pierantoni, R., L. Iela, G. Delrio, and R. Rastogi. 1984. Seasonal plasma sex steroid levels in the female *Rana esculenta*. Gen. Comp. Endocrinol., 53: 126–134.

Pimentel, R. A. 1960. Inter- and intrahabitat movements of the rough-skinned newt, *Taricha torosa granulosa* (Skilton). Amer. Midl. Natl., 63: 470–496.

Polzonetti-Magni, A., V. Botte, L. Bellini-Cardellini, A. Gobbetti, and A. Crasto. 1984. Plasma sex hormones and post-reproductive period in the green frog, *Rana esculenta* complex. Gen. Comp. Endocrinol., 54: 372–377.

Propper, C. R. 1989. Courtship-induced Changes in Female Sexual Receptivity: a Neuroendocrine Study in an Amphibian. Doctoral Dissertation, Oregon State University, Corvallis, Oregon. 181 pages.

—. 1991. Courtship in the rough-skinned newt *Taricha granulosa*. Anim. Behav., 41: 547–554.

Propper, C. R., P. Deviche, and F. L. Moore. 1986. Male-male interactions in an amphibian: cues for sex recognition. Amer. Zool., 26: 97A (Abstract 505).

Propper, L. E., and F. L. Moore. 1991. Effects of courtship on brain gonadotropin hormone-releasing hormone and plasma steroid concentrations in a female amphibian (*Taricha granulosa)*. Gen. Comp. Endocrinol., 81: 304–312.

Riemer, W. J. 1954. Variation and systematic relationships within the salamander genus *Taricha*. Univ. California Publ. Zool., 56: 301–390.

Roth, G. 1987. Studies of Brain Function. Vol. 14. Visual Behavior in Salamanders. Springer Verlag, Berlin. vii, 301 pages.

Salthe, S. N., and Mecham, J. S. 1974. Reproductive and courtship patterns, p. 309–521. *In* B. Lofts (ed.), Physiology of the Amphibia. Vol. II. Academic Press, New York.

Sassoon, D. A., G. E. Gray, and D. B. Kelley. 1987. Androgen regulation of muscle fiber type in the sexually dimorphic larynx of *Xenopus laevis*. Jour. Neurosci., 7: 3198–3206.

Specker, J., and F. L. Moore. 1980. Annual cycle of plasma androgens and testicular composition in the rough-skinned newt, *Taricha granulosa*. Gen. Comp. Endocrinol., 42: 297–303.

Tobias, M. L., and D. B. Kelley. 1987. Vocalizations by a sexually dimorphic isolated larynx: peripheral constraints on behavioral expression. Jour. Neurosci., 7: 3191–3197.

Twitty, V. C. 1966. Of Scientists and Salamanders. W. H. Freeman, San Francisco. ix, 178 pages.

Zoeller, R. T., and F. L. Moore. 1985. Seasonal changes in LHRH concentrations in microdissected brain regions of male rough-skinned newts (*Taricha granulosa)*. Gen. Comp. Endocrinol., 58: 222–230.

❦ Moore, F. L. 1994. Complexity in the control of amphibian reproduction: reproductive behavior and physiology of a salamander, p. 125–131. *In* J. B. Murphy, K. Adler, and J. T. Collins (eds.), Captive Management and Conservation of Amphibians and Reptiles. Society for the Study of Amphibians and Reptiles, Ithaca (New York). Contributions to Herpetology, volume 11.

Considerations for Inducing Reproduction in Captive Reptiles

David Crews,* Alan Tousignant,* and Thane Wibbels*

Introduction

Reproduction is the most energetically expensive event in the life of a female and is timed to occur when stress to the mother is minimized, yet when the probability of the young living long enough to reproduce is maximized. For the male, energetics is no less of a concern, but for them, the important elements tend to revolve around somatic, behavioral, and environmental requirements for mating. For both sexes, the importance of coordinating events at *every* level of biological organization (that is, environment, population, organism, physiology, tissue, cell, and molecule) is paramount. Thus, anyone hoping to induce reproduction in captive populations of reptiles must have a basic understanding of the reproductive process and the factors that govern it.

Reproductive seasons can be viewed as adaptations that have been shaped by selection. Classically, the seasonal reproduction characteristic of natural populations has been viewed as the result of both ultimate and proximate factors (Baker 1938). Ultimate factors may include the quantity and quality of food, the availability of adequate nesting conditions, and the presence of predators. Proximate factors, on the other hand, are those events in the individual's environment that best predict optimal conditions for reproduction. In many temperate environments, the daily change in day length is the most reliable and regular physical factor. As such, many species have co-opted the photoperiod as the means to time the onset and offset of reproductive periods. In many reptiles, temperature or rainfall may be equally important cues.

Wingfield (1980; Wingfield et al. 1992) recently divided the factors regulating reproduction somewhat differently, classifying the types of environmental signals that influence reproductive function as either initial predictive information or supplementary information. Initial predictive information would include those factors that in the long term control the initiation, maintenance, and cessation of the reproductive process; for example, photoperiod, temperature, and endogenous rhythms in sensitivity to environmental cues. Supplementary information includes those factors that are predictive in the short term and serve to synchronize and coordinate the reproductive activity of individuals with the immediate changing physical and biotic environments; examples include the changing nutritional content of food, inclement weather, and specific behaviors of conspecifics. Supplementary cues may either accelerate or inhibit the reproductive process. Figure 1 illustrates how the predictability of the environment relates to the types of factors that are used by a species to regulate reproduction.

In this chapter we do not reconsider the information contained in recent reviews of the physical and biotic control of reproduction in reptiles (Crews 1979; Crews and Garrick 1980; Duvall et al. 1982; Licht 1984; Whittier and Crews 1987). Instead, we focus on three factors that influence reproduction, but which have not received the attention they deserve. These are: (1) the importance of specific behaviors of conspecifics, (2) how experience as an embryo can influence the adult phenotype, includ-

*Institute of Reproductive Biology
Department of Zoology
University of Texas at Austin
Austin, Texas 78712, USA

Acronyms used in this chapter:

TSD Temperature-dependent sex determination
Tb Body temperature
GSD Genotypic sex determination

ing reproductive competence, and (3) how these and other recent discoveries in reptilian reproduction can be used to manipulate sex ratios in captive and perhaps wild populations. Indeed, disregard of even one of these factors may account for why some captive-breeding programs are unsuccessful despite the presence of the obvious environmental necessities.

Behavioral Modulation of Reproduction

An important source of cues that regulate reproduction is an animal's social environment. Courtship displays evolved to assist in the identification of individuals of the same species, the appropriate sex, and to assess their competence to reproduce. The complementary interactions between individuals during breeding can, like physical and biotic stimuli, regulate the onset, maintenance, and offset of reproduction. They do so by synchronizing and coordinating the intricate physiological processes that underlie both male and female reproduction.

It has only been relatively recently that this aspect of reproduction has been subjected to rigorous scientific study. Daniel S. Lehrman and Robert A. Hinde were pioneers in behavioral endocrinology with their description of how courtship exchanges between the male and female modulate the phases and nature of the reproductive cycle of the ring dove and the canary, respectively. Subsequent research on species of other vertebrate classes established that social cues include not only visual signals, but signals mediated by every known sensory modality. There have been five such demonstrations with reptiles, three with lizards (each representing a distinct clade), and two with snakes. Taken together, this evidence clearly indicates that behavior is a potent regulator of reproductive performance in captive reptiles.

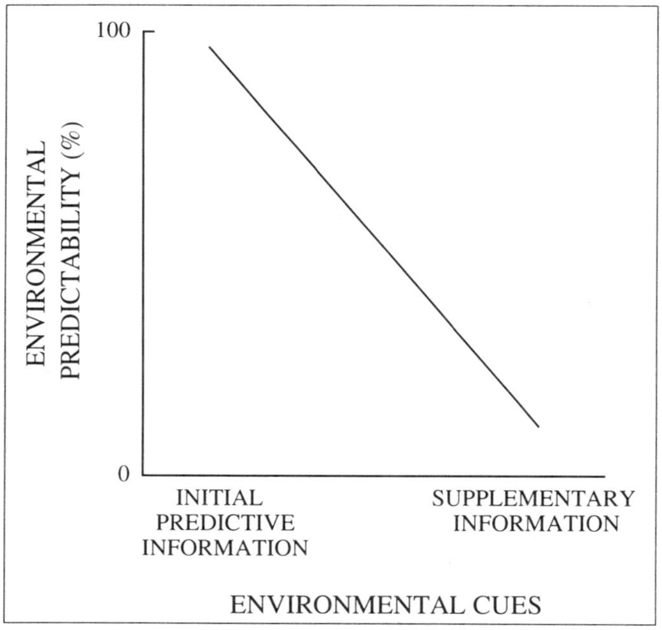

FIGURE 1. Relation between the types of environmental cues that regulate reproduction and the predictability of the environment that the species inhabits (adapted from Wingfield et al. 1991).

The first demonstration of behavioral facilitation of reproduction in any reptile was with the Green Anole (*Anolis carolinensis*). In these studies, winter-dormant female Green Anoles were exposed to a stimulatory photo-thermal regimen while being housed under different social conditions (Crews 1974*a*; Crews et al. 1974). Females housed as isolates or in all-female groups underwent ovarian growth in response to this unseasonal environmental regimen. Although many of these females eventually ovulated and laid eggs, the eggs were always lightly shelled or completely lacking an eggshell. This is an indication of subnormal pituitary gonadotropin secretion. If females were housed with sexually active males, the rate of ovarian growth was facilitated significantly (Figure 2).

The mere presence of a male is not sufficient, however. Studies using castration-and-hormone-replacement therapy have established that in many vertebrates sexual activity is dependent on gonadal sex hormones. Thus, female Green Anoles housed with a castrated male, which is not sexually active, show a pattern of ovarian growth that is not different from that of females that are housed in all-female groups or as isolates (Crews 1974*b*). On the other hand, if females are exposed to castrated males that have received androgen replacement therapy (which reinstates sexual activity), the pattern of ovarian response is similar to that of females housed with intact, sexually active males.

This behavioral facilitation of reproduction is due specifically to the courtship display of the male (Crews et al. 1974). Indeed, the more frequently a male displays, which in this species consists of bobbing movements associated with extensions of the dewlap, the more rapid the rate of ovarian growth (Crews 1974*a*). Taken together, these studies suggest that failure in a captive-breeding program requires assessment of the behavior and level of activity of males in the breeding population.

It is important to keep in mind that specific behaviors can also inhibit reproduction. Female Green Anoles exposed to male-male aggression, rather than to male courtship, never initiate ovarian growth, even if they are exposed to a stimulatory environmental regimen (Crews 1974*a*)(Figure 2). Indeed, this aggressive behavior, which is not directed towards the female, but rather to other males, is so potent a stimulus that reproductive females will cease all further reproductive activity and any yolking follicle(s) that are present will undergo atresia. Obviously, a captive-breeding program should be designed to minimize agonistic interactions among males.

It also is important to understand that this behavioral modulation of reproduction operates in a reciprocal manner. That is, not only does male behavior influence female ovarian growth, but so does female behavior influence male reproductive activity. This can be seen in male Green Anoles (Crews and Garrick 1980). Using the same conditions as in the above experiments, males housed in all-male groups or in isolation show a diminished pattern of testicular activity compared to males housed with intact females.

Behavioral facilitation of reproduction has also been documented in teiid lizards, such as whiptails (*Cnemidophorus* spp.). As for the Green Anole, with the Little Striped Whiptail (*C. inornatus*), the presence, and more specifically, the reproductive status, of the male is an important feature of the female's housing environment. Females housed as isolates or housed with castrated, sexually inactive males, fail to ovulate (Crews et al. 1986)(Figure 3). Only those females exposed to intact, sexually active males undergo complete ovarian growth and lay eggs. It is not known what aspect of the male is important for facilitating the stimulatory effects of the environment, although the behavior of the animals suggest that chemical signals are likely to be important.

The fundamental importance of complementary behavioral interactions (for example, mounting and receptive behaviors) is seen particularly clearly in studies with the parthenogenetic Desert Grassland Whiptail (*Cnemidophorus uniparens*). In this spe-

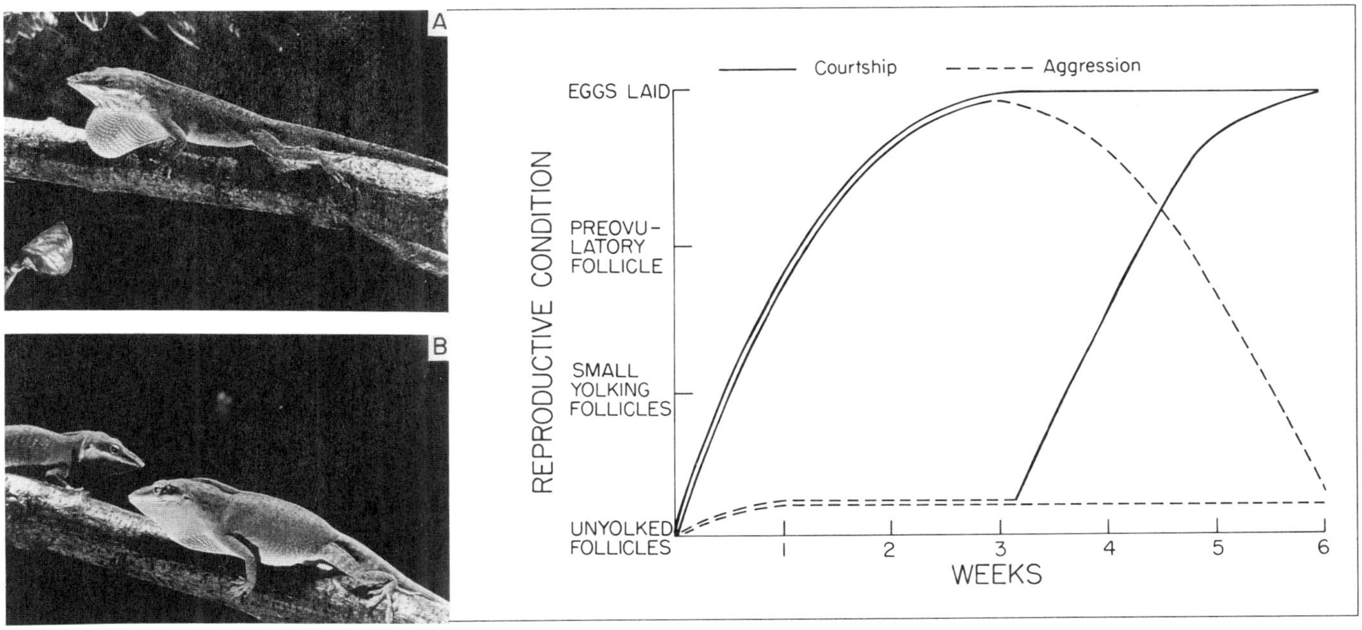

FIGURE 2. Conspecific behavioral displays modulate reproduction. In the left panel are pictures of male Green Anoles (*Anolis carolinensis*) performing a courtship display (A) and an aggressive display (B). Note the differences in body posture. In the right panel, the courtship display facilitates ovarian growth in females, whereas the aggressive posture inhibits ovarian growth. In this experiment, females were exposed to the courtship or aggression stimulus for a six-week period, or for three weeks followed by a three-week period in which the stimuli were switched.

cies there are no males and reproduction is via obligate parthenogenesis. In other words, the species consists entirely of females and sperm are not required for ovarian development. Interestingly, these parthenogens exhibit both male- and female-like behaviors during specific stages of their reproductive cycle (Crews 1989; Crews and Fitzgerald 1980); these behaviors are seen both in the laboratory as well as in nature (Crews and Young 1991). Experiments indicate that although males are not

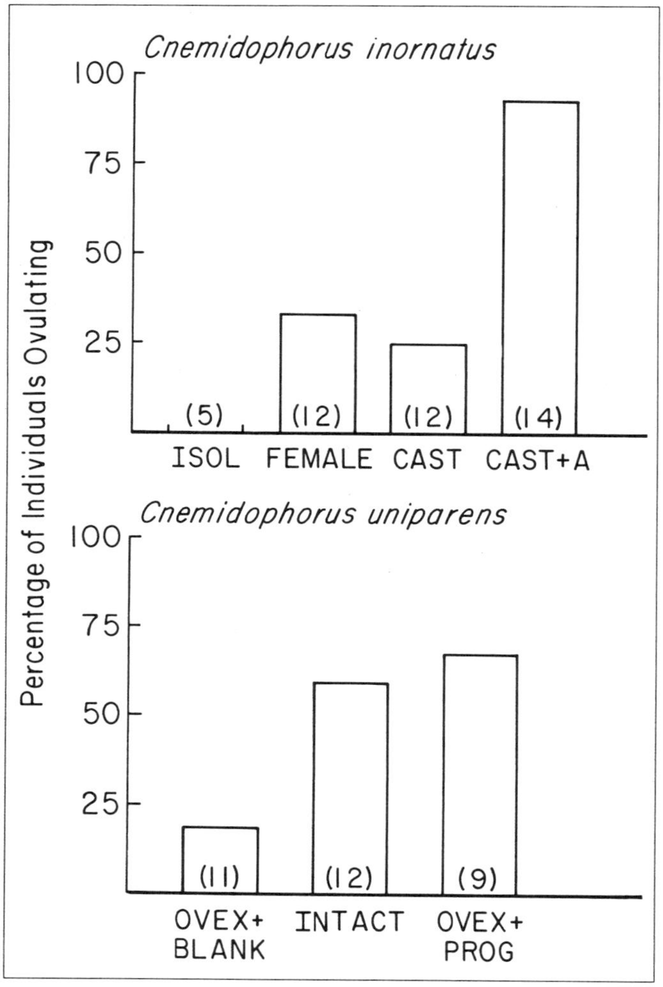

FIGURE 3. Behavioral facilitation of reproduction in gonochoristic and parthenogenetic species of whiptails (*Cnemidophorus*). Shown is the percentage of individual lizards ovulating when housed under different social conditions. ISOL isolation; FEMALE female cagemate; CAST castrated male cagemate; CAST + A androgen-treated castrated male cagemate; OVEX + BLANK sham-treated ovariectomized cagemate; INTACT intact cagemate; OVEX + PROG progesterone-treated ovariectomized cagemate (from Crews et al. 1986).

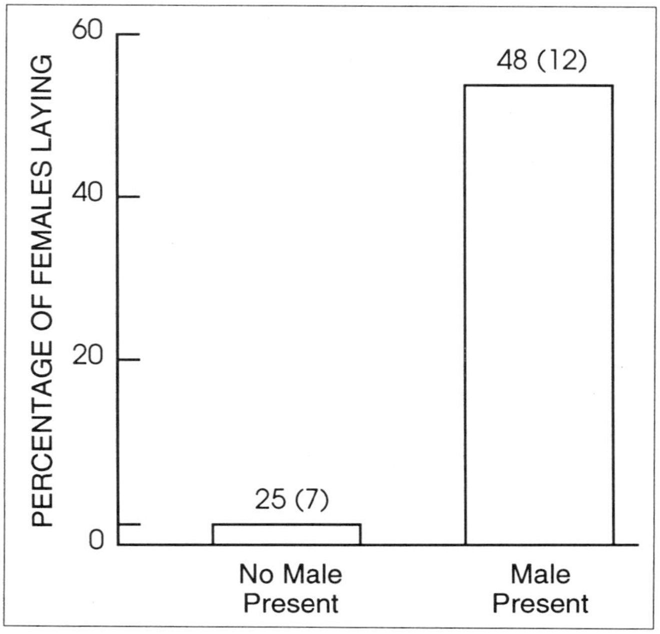

FIGURE 4. Behavioral facilitation of reproduction in the Leopard Gecko (*Eublepharis macularius*). Sample size is given outside the parentheses; the number within the parentheses represents the number of group cages.

essential for ovarian growth in the parthenogen, participation in pseudosexual interactions greatly facilitates the rate of ovarian growth (Crews et al. 1986) (Figure 3), as well as the total number of eggs produced during a breeding season (Crews and Moore 1993; Crews et al. 1983). As with the Little Striped Whiptail, one of the sexual ancestral species of *C. uniparens*, the specific stimuli responsible for this facilitation are not known, but the question is amenable to experimentation.

In a gekkonid lizard, the Leopard Gecko (*Eublepharis macularius*), females will lay eggs only if sexually active males are present (Figure 4). The fertility of the male is also important. That is, females housed with sexually active, but vasectomized, males will lay eggs, but the eggs often lack a shell coating (J. J. Bull, unpubl. data). This suggests that not only is the behavior of the male important, but that at least in some species there must exist within the female's reproductive tract sensory receptors that are activated by sperm deposition. Specialized sperm-storage ducts are known to occur in many reptiles. This may be why in many reptiles the female can continue to lay fertile eggs for years in captivity in the absence of males. These data also suggest that while it is advisable in a captive-breeding program to establish that each male is depositing sperm during mating, a fertile male is not an absolute requirement, so long as the females mate successfully, at least occasionally.

The importance of behavioral facilitation of reproduction is evident in snakes as well. The Red-sided Garter Snake (*Thamnophis sirtalis parietalis*) has the northern-most range in North America of any snake. As a consequence, it has developed adaptations that defy many of the "rules" in reproductive biology that have been derived from research with domesticated mammals and birds. For example, females emerge at a time when their ovaries are completely regressed (Figure 5). This means that ovarian development follows mating, rather than preceding mating. Indeed, the act of mating initiates a neuroendocrine reflex characterized by an immediate rise in circulating prostaglandins (Whittier and Crews 1986*a*, 1989), followed by a rapid increase in circulating concentrations of estrogens that peak for 24 to 48 hours and then decline over the next two weeks (Mendonça and Crews 1989; Garstka et al. 1982; Whittier et al. 1987). Ovarian growth does not begin until approximately three weeks after mating and ovulation does not occur for six weeks.

If the female garter snake is prevented from sensing the mating stimulus, she will not undergo these predictable and reliable neuroendocrine events (Mendonça and Crews 1990)(Figure 5). Further, she often will not exhibit ovarian growth or will fail to ovulate (Bona Gallo and Licht 1983; Mendonça and Crews 1990). This latter occurrence appears to be ameliorated if the female is in good nutritional condition (Whittier and Crews 1986*b*, 1990).

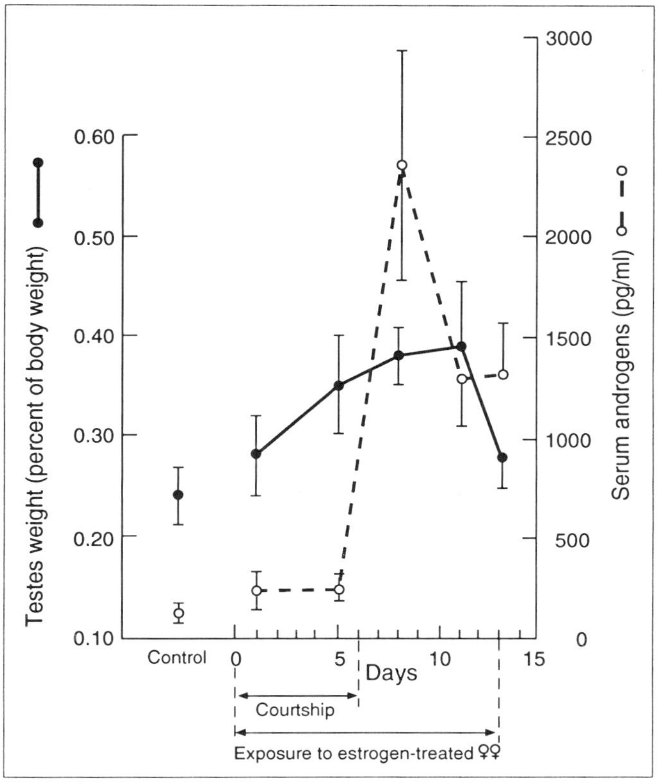

FIGURE 6. Behavioral facilitation of reproduction in the Mexican Garter Snake (*Thamnophis melanogaster*). Exposing males in the laboratory to estrogen-treated and hence attractive females induces a complete reproductive cycle in males (from Garstka and Crews 1982).

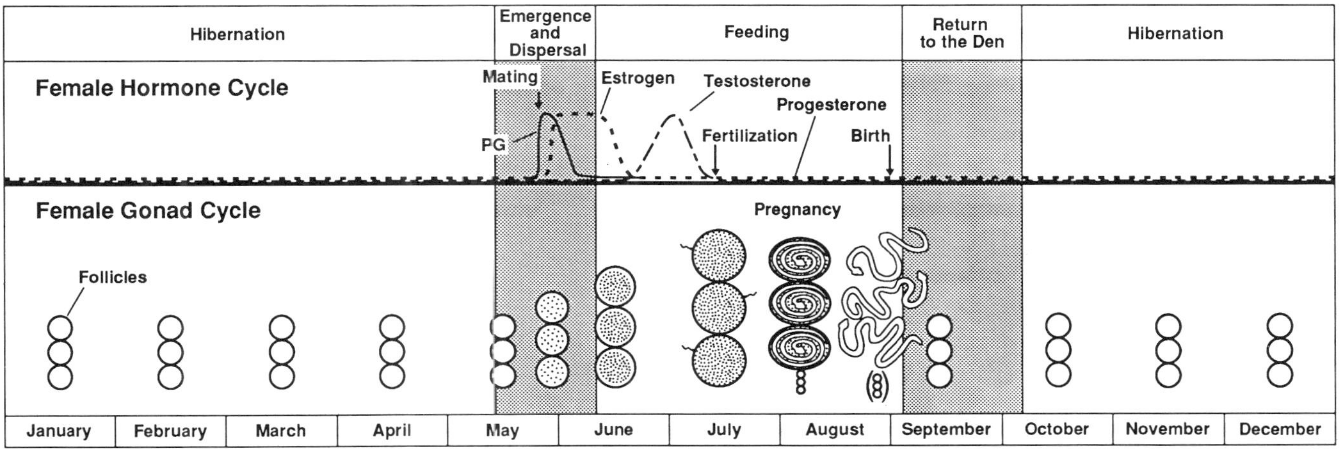

FIGURE 5. The major hormonal events in the female Red-sided Garter Snake (*Thamnophis sirtalis parietalis*) that are initiated by mating. The corresponding major life-history events and months of the year are indicated at the top and bottom, respectively. See text for details.

The reciprocal relationship whereby the female affects male reproductive physiology is seen in the Mexican Garter Snake (*Thamnophis melanogaster*) (Garstka and Crews 1982). In Lago de Cuitzeo, Michoacan, Mexico, this species exhibits several brief, synchronous breeding periods in the course of the year. The timing of these periods varies both within and among years and appears to depend upon a specific social cue. Like all garter snakes, this species exhibits a dissociated reproductive cycle in which gonadal growth occurs after, rather than before, sexual activity; the sperm used to inseminate the females are produced during a prior spermatogenic cycle and stored in the vasa deferentia (Garstka et al. 1982; Halpert et al. 1982).

Experiments conducted in the field and in the laboratory show that the cue that initiates breeding is an attractiveness pheromone associated with reproductively competent females (Garstka and Crews 1982). The production of this pheromone can be induced by estrogen treatment (Garstka and Crews 1981); by releasing estrogen-treated females into the field, a complete reproductive cycle can be induced in males (Figure 6). Indeed, observations indicate that previously sexually inactive males immediately begin courtship activity when exposed to such females. In this species the entire breeding period lasts only a few days. Coincident with the cessation of sexual activity is testicular growth; the mature sperm produced are deposited in the vas deferens and epididymides. In garter snakes, female attractiveness is based on the individual female's nutritional condition (Garstka and Crews 1986; Whittier and Crews 1990). Thus, the health of the female is communicated by a pheromone that acts as the proximate factor that drives the reproductive cycle in this species. The variability and timing of breeding periods of other tropical and subtropical reptiles may be explained by similar phenomena.

TABLE 1. Factors that influence morphology, physiology, behavior, and reproductive fitness in reptiles. Although only oviparous species are listed, similar categories apply to viviparous and ovoviviparous species. Some of the types of control manipulations that can be used to uncover the degree of involvement are noted.

Source	Control
Temperature	
During incubation	Various but specific temperatures
After incubation	Constant (intermediate) temperature
Social experience or hierarchy	Rear in isolation
Hormones	
During incubation	Hormone manipulation
After incubation	Removal of gonads at birth or as adult
Food	Standard diet with regular weighing
Genetics	
Maternal	Split clutches with treatment
Paternal	Compare lineages

Embryonic Determinants of Adult Phenotype

The importance of understanding early development in relation to captive-breeding and conservation-management programs cannot be overstated. The embryo experiences a host of physical and biological stimuli independent of maternal control that can affect their development. For example, yolk is a significant repository of circulating hormones and as such reflects the hormonal profile of the mother at the time of yolk deposition (Bern 1990). This means that the hormone levels in the laying female will be imposed on their offspring. Steroid hormones have traditionally been thought to have organizational effects during embryonic development, but they can affect the animal after birth and even into adulthood. Thus, it is important to keep in mind for captive-breeding programs that factors that can adversely affect the hormonal profile of a female could also have long-term consequences on the resulting young.

It is becoming evident that careful regulation and manipulation of the embryonic environment will aid in our efforts to maintain present species diversity and conservation efforts. In this section we consider how events and factors experienced by the embryo influence the growth, physiology, and behavior of the adult (Table 1).

In oviparous reptiles, embryonic development is exquisitely sensitive to the temperature(s) experienced during incubation of the egg. Besides the obvious lethal temperatures (too hot or too cold), Fox (1948) was the first to demonstrate that temperature during gestation affected scutellation in developing embryos of snakes (in the Santa Cruz

Garter Snake, *Thamnophis atratus*). The idea that factors, such as temperature, could have more important and far-reaching effects was slow to develop, however. Charnier (1966) was the first to observe that incubation temperature may be involved in the determination of sex. It was only when Pieau (1971) and Yntema (1976) reported temperature-dependent sex determination (TSD) in the European Pond Turtle (*Emys orbicularis*) and in the Snapping Turtle (*Chelydra serpentina*), respectively, that TSD was accepted as a genuine mechanism that operates in oviparous reptiles. Subsequent studies have revealed ranges of temperatures which determine sex in a number of reptilian species (see reviews by Bull 1980, 1983; Raynaud and Pieau 1985; Deeming and Ferguson 1988; Ewert and Nelson 1991).

There are three general patterns of TSD in oviparous reptiles (Figure 7): (1) in some species, a range of higher temperatures produce males, whereas a lower range of temperatures produce females; (2) other species show an opposite pattern in which higher temperatures produce females and lower temperature produce males; and (3) still others show a pattern in which intermediate temperatures produce males and higher and lower temperatures produce females. It is important to note that in every instance the effect of temperature is all-or-none, the transition from male-determining to female-determining temperatures is narrow, and morphological intersexes are rare, even at intermediate temperatures.

Temperature, hydric conditions, and exposure to hormones during incubation can influence embryonic growth, hatching success, neonatal viability and morphology, sex determination, and even adult physiology and behavior. In the American Alligator (*Alligator mississippiensis*), relatively low incubation temperatures result in the production of females, intermediate incubation temperatures result in both males and females, and high incubation temperatures produce males. Joanen et al. (1987) examined the effect of incubation temperature on the post-hatching growth rate. Comparisons of individuals from intermediate male-biased incubation temperatures show that males grow significantly faster than do females in both total length and body weight; at the intermediate female-biased incubation temperature, the females are heavier. This relationship between incubation temperature and growth is seen also within the female sex, with individuals from 30.6°C-incubation conditions growing faster than those incubated at 31.7°C. Overall, the effect of temperature on growth was such that, within a limited range, individuals from higher incubation temperatures grow faster than do individuals from cooler incubation temperatures. This interpretation is complicated, however, by a differential "runt" effect between temperatures; that is, the temperature that resulted in the largest animals also had the lowest percentage of runts (delineated as the bottom 10% of the best growing group), while the two extreme temperatures (29.4° and 32.8°C) had the highest incidence of runts.

Incubation temperature can also affect thermoregulatory behaviors that have consequences for growth. Lang (1987) studied the effect of incubation temperature on body-

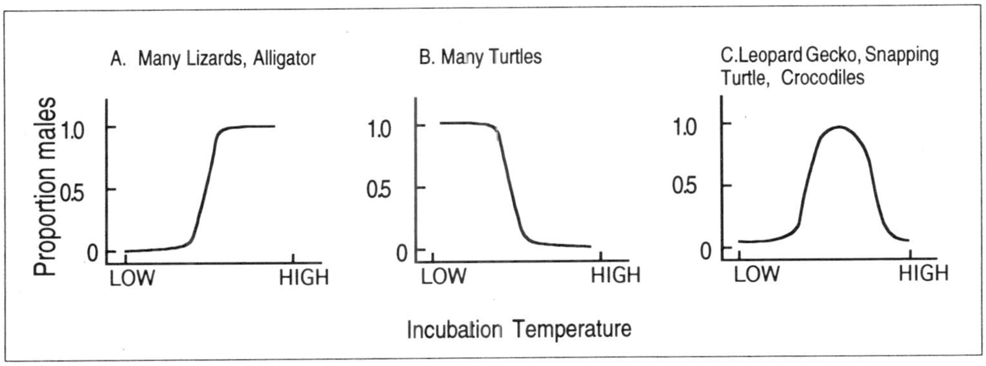

FIGURE 7. Response of sex ratio to incubation temperature in oviparous reptiles. In temperature-dependent sex determination, temperatures that vary by a few degrees can result in either all-male or all-female hatchlings being produced. Three patterns are recognized at present: (A) females develop at low temperatures and males at high temperatures, as in some lizards and in alligators; (B) the reverse of A, in that males develop at low temperatures and females at high temperatures, as in most turtles; and (C) females develop at low and high temperatures, and males at intermediate temperatures. The latter pattern may be widespread; it occurs in the Leopard Gecko (*Eublepharis macularius*), Snapping Turtle (*Chelydra serpentina*), and some crocodilians (adapted from Bull 1980).

temperature (Tb) selection in the Siamese Crocodile (*Crocodylus siamensis*). Eggs were incubated at 28°C, a temperature that produces all females, or at 32.5°–33.5°C, which produces all males. Individuals from the higher incubation temperature not only grew faster, but selected a higher Tb.

In all of these studies, animals were housed in social groups and hence social interactions, such as dominance and subordination, may translate into access to food, thereby influencing the results. Similarly, the temperature at which animals are raised (versus the temperature at which they were incubated as eggs) or possible sex differences in thermoregulatory behavior could have an effect. To avoid these problems, reasonable controls would be to raise subjects at a constant temperature prior to tests for thermoregulation and to rear each individual in isolation.

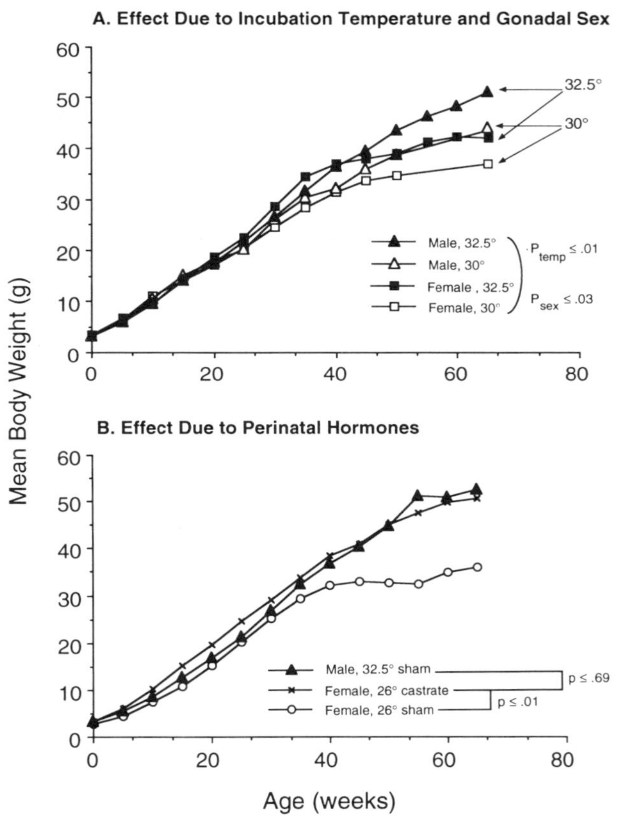

FIGURE 8. Change in body weight of Leopard Geckos (*Eublepharis macularius*) from different incubation temperatures and post-hatching manipulation. Each individual was measured every five weeks from hatching until adulthood. All animals are raised in isolation under the same environmental conditions. (A) Males and females incubated at either 30° or 32.5°C. (B) Animals incubated at either 26° or 32.5°C, which then received either a sham operation or surgical castration on the day of hatching.

Incubation temperature can also influence development and later behavior of species that possess sex chromosomes. All snakes have genotypic sex determination (GSD). Burger (1989, 1990) tested hatchlings of three species of snake incubated at a variety of temperatures and then evaluated their ability to survive in the wild. All tests were conducted at a constant temperature. The general pattern that emerges is that, within limits, higher incubation temperatures correlate with increased performance. At extreme temperatures, either warmer or colder, performance drops off quickly.

It is common knowledge among breeders of captive reptiles that incubation temperature can influence adult behavior. Recent studies with the Leopard Gecko provide an excellent example of how temperature during embryogenesis affects subsequent development. In this species, mostly males are produced at intermediate temperatures (30.5°–32.5°C), whereas only females are produced at relatively low (26°–28°C) and at near-lethal incubation temperatures (34°–35°C). In our studies we have raised Leopard Geckos in isolation at a temperature intermediate to the incubation temperatures.

As adults, Leopard Geckos have marked sexual dimorphisms in morphology. For example, one secondary sex character is the specialized secretory pores located anterior to the cloaca. In males, as well as in females from high-incubation temperatures, these pores are open, while in females from low-incubation temperatures, they are closed. Head size also is sexually dimorphic, with males having wider heads than females. Within each sex, however, the higher the incubation temperature, the wider the head of the adult (Crews 1988).

It must be appreciated that in species with TSD, incubation temperature and sex co-vary. That is, the TSD differences between individuals could be due to the incubation temperature of the egg, the gonadal sex of the individuals, or both factors combined. If the contribution of each is to be assessed, they must be dissociated. Our studies with the Leopard Gecko have entailed removing the gonads of individuals upon hatching (to determine the role of gonadal hormones in postnatal development), administering hormone to incubating eggs (to override the normal effects of temperature), and comparing the growth and behavior of individuals of the same sex, but produced at different temperatures. Figure 8 indicates that in the Leopard Gecko, both incubation temperature and the sex of the animal have significant effects on body growth. Further, the presence of the ovaries, but not the testes, attenuates body growth. It should be noted that the opposite pattern is found in the Red-Sided Garter Snake; in this species males are smaller than females and the presence of the testes attenuates growth.

The endocrine physiology of the adult also appears to be influenced by the temperature experienced during incubation (Gutzke and Crews 1988). Overall, circulating concentrations of androgens are significantly higher in adult males compared to adult females. Within females, however, androgen levels are significantly higher and estrogen levels significantly lower in females from high-incubation temperatures compared to females from low-incubation temperatures. In this study, most females from high temperatures failed to lay eggs, suggesting that the primary alteration is at the neuroendocrine level, as it is in androgenized female rodents.

The sexual behaviors of individual Leopard Geckos from different incubation temperatures varies in a systematic manner, with the responses of females to male courtship showing the greatest difference (Gutzke and Crews 1988). Females from low-incubation temperatures readily exhibit receptivity when courted by a male. On the other hand, females from high-incubation temperatures respond more like males than like females from low-incubation temperatures. They often will aggressively reject the male or attack him as would occur in a male-male encounter. This effect of a male-producing temperature on the female phenotype is reminiscent of the well-known masculinizing effects of androgen treatment in neonatal female mammals. In other words, high-incubation temperature may be acting in a fashion analogous to androgen during development in mammals.

Proper hydric conditions are another potentially important factor in development. Two studies have suggested that the hydric environment during incubation can also affect sex determination (Gutzke and Paukstis 1983; Paukstis et al. 1984), although recent studies on the same species (Miller et al. 1987; Packard et al. 1991; Packard and Phillips, this volume, page 195) fail to show these effects. It is clear, though, that soil moisture influences other fundamental processes. Turtle eggs incubated on comparatively dry substrates have higher mortality relative to those incubated on moist substrates (Packard et al. 1989, 1991). Further, hatchlings that emerge from relatively moist incubations appear later and are larger. These results are consistent with recent results obtained for the Green Iguana (*Iguana iguana*)(Phillips et al. 1990). Hatchling Snapping Turtles from moist incubations are larger and they exhibit better locomotor performance both on land and in the water (Miller et al. 1987). Interestingly, experiments reveal that a physiological factor is largely responsible for this difference; the larger turtles from moist incubation conditions accumulate lactate more slowly than their counterparts from dry incubation conditions. These results suggest that the hydric environment during incubation can affect such physiological factors as aerobic capacity, which is a limiting factor in sustained activity in reptiles (Lang 1987).

Captive Management of Reptiles with TSD

The occurrence of TSD in many reptiles affords the unique opportunity to artificially control sex determination within a captive population. Several basic questions must be addressed, however, to optimize the captive management of reptiles with TSD. These questions include: (1) Which temperatures produce a particular sex? (2) Do all temperatures producing a particular sex result in individuals of equal sexual competence? and (3) Which sex ratios are best for a captive population?

The first question is beginning to be answered in a number of species. It is becoming clear that species that show similar patterns of TSD can have different "pivotal temperatures"; that is, an incubation temperature that produces a 1:1 sex ratio (Bull et al. 1982; Mrosovsky et al. 1984*a*; Wibbels et al. 1991*a*). Because of this variability in the patterns and pivotal temperatures of TSD, manipulating the sex ratio of a given species would require that a variety of incubation temperatures be studied simultaneously to determine which specific temperature ranges produce a given sex ratio.

Are there certain optimal temperatures for producing sexually competent individuals? In the Leopard Gecko, the occasional females resulting from relatively high male-producing incubation temperatures may have reduced reproductive competence (see above). Further, the "sexual potency" of an incubation temperature can vary (Bull et al. 1990; Wibbels, Bull, and Crews 1991). For example, in the Slider (*Trachemys scripta*), shifting eggs to a higher (female-producing) or a lower (male-producing) temperature will result in more skewed sex ratios (Figure 9). Such studies could prove difficult for turtles because of the length of time separating incubation and adult reproductive success. A lizard, such as the Leopard Gecko, which matures rapidly and adapts well to captivity, could, however, prove to be a model species for such studies.

The ability to manipulate sex determination by temperature necessitates the choice of an appropriate sex ratio for a given captive-rearing program.

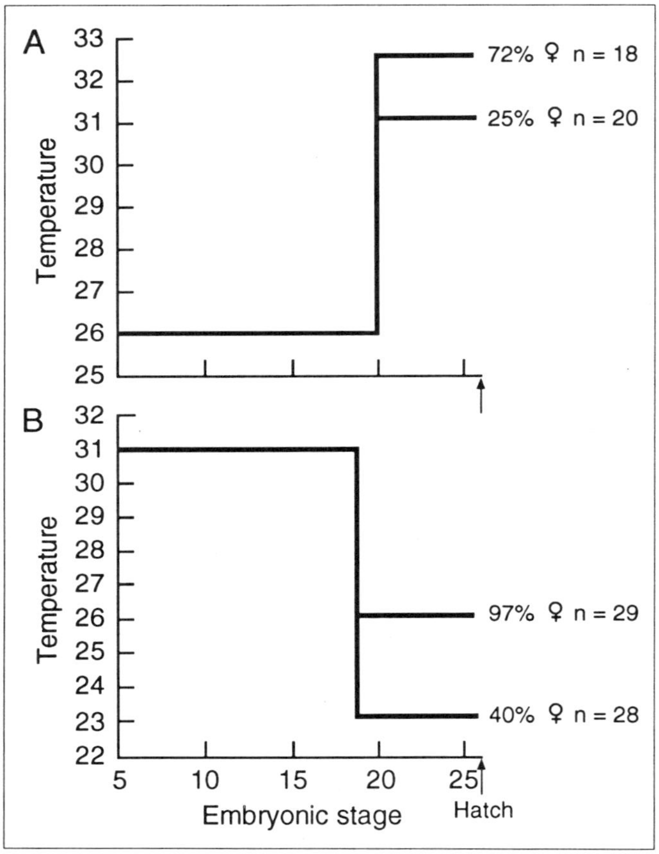

FIGURE 9. Temperature potency in the Slider (*Trachemys scripta*), a turtle with temperature-dependent sex determination. (A) Eggs initially incubated at a male-producing temperature until stage 20 and then shifted to one of two female-producing temperatures (31° or 32.5°C). (B) Eggs initially incubated at a female-producing temperature until stage 19 and then shifted to one of two male-producing temperatures (23° or 26°C) (from Wibbels et al. 1991*b*).

This issue can be approached using two distinctly different strategies. In the first approach, one could attempt to duplicate the sex ratio of naturally occurring populations. The sex ratios in natural populations of reptiles with TSD do not always conform to the 1:1 ratio suggested by sex-allocation theory (reviewed by Bull and Charnov 1988; see also Limpus 1985; Mrosovsky and Provancha 1989; Wibbels et al. 1991*a*). In fact, many female-biased sex ratios have been detected as well as at least one male-biased sex ratio (Limpus 1985). The evolutionary basis of skewed sex ratios is unknown, although Bull and Charnov (1989) have proposed that factors, such as thermal environment preferences and/or posthatchling growth rates, could affect the fitness of a particular sex and thus select for biased sex ratios. Regardless, our present knowledge of TSD and the resulting sex ratios prevent us from assigning an evolutionarily stable sex ratio to a given population of reptiles with TSD.

While the effects of sex ratio on the reproductive output of a population of reptiles with TSD has not been empirically addressed, it seems somewhat intuitive that in situations in which reproduction is female-limited, an increased production of female offspring could significantly increase the reproductive output of a captive population. Thus, an alternative strategy would simply be to disregard sex ratios that occur in the wild and manipulate the sex ratio of the captive population in order to maximize reproductive success.

If one decides to generate a biased sex ratio, what incubation temperatures should be used? That is, should an incubation temperature that produces the desired sex ratio be utilized or should a proportion of the eggs be incubated at a male-producing temperature and the remainder incubated at a female-producing temperature? These questions can be addressed by studies investigating the effects of incubation temperature on sexual competence (as discussed above for the Leopard Gecko).

If a female-biased sex ratio is desired, an alternative method would be the treatment of eggs with estrogen. A variety of past studies have shown that injecting estrogen into developing eggs results in ovarian differentiation regardless of incubation temperature (reviewed by Raynaud and Pieau 1985; see also Gutzke and Bull 1986; Bull et al. 1988; Crews et al. 1989). This method, however, suffers from a low survivorship. A recent study has shown that topical application of estrogen to the egg shell acts in similar fashion and has negligible mortality (Crews et al. 1991)(Figure 10). Studies with the Leopard Gecko indicate that such estrogen-induced females lay fertile eggs and exhibit normal nest-building behavior.

We presently are investigating the mechanism by which estrogen induces ovarian differentiation (Figure 11). Experiments indicate that estrogen and temperature act synergistically on sex determination, suggesting that they may act in a common pathway (Wibbels et al. 1991*b*). Furthermore, incubation at 26°C and 32°C induce different patterns of steroidogenic enzyme activity.

Summary

We have described how the social environment can determine the level of reproduction in captive populations. It is also clear that environmental variables have effects on the development of embryos which can last into adulthood. Thus, maintenance of captive populations of endangered (or even extinct in the wild) reptiles should be mindful of these factors.

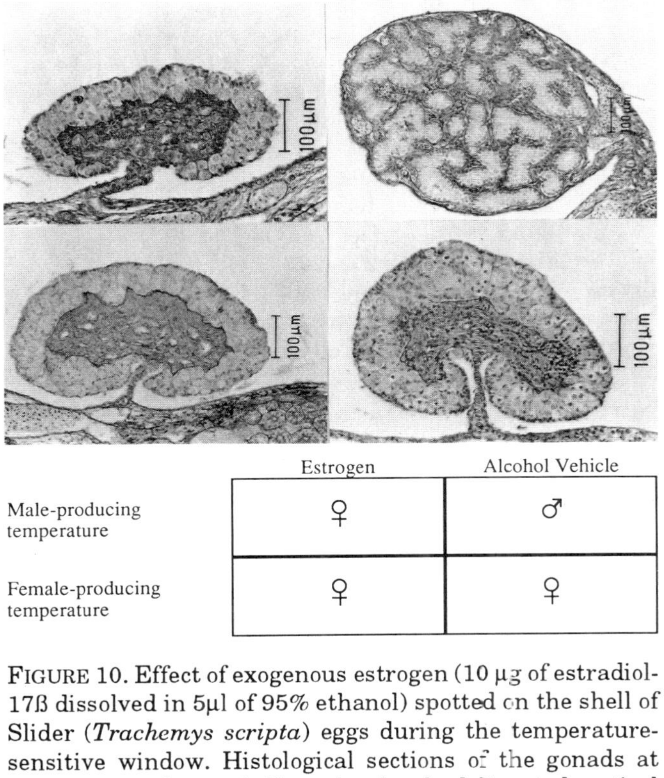

FIGURE 10. Effect of exogenous estrogen (10 µg of estradiol-17ß dissolved in 5µl of 95% ethanol) spotted on the shell of Slider (*Trachemys scripta*) eggs during the temperature-sensitive window. Histological sections of the gonads at hatching are depicted. Note the clearly delineated cortical and medullary regions (from Crews 1992).

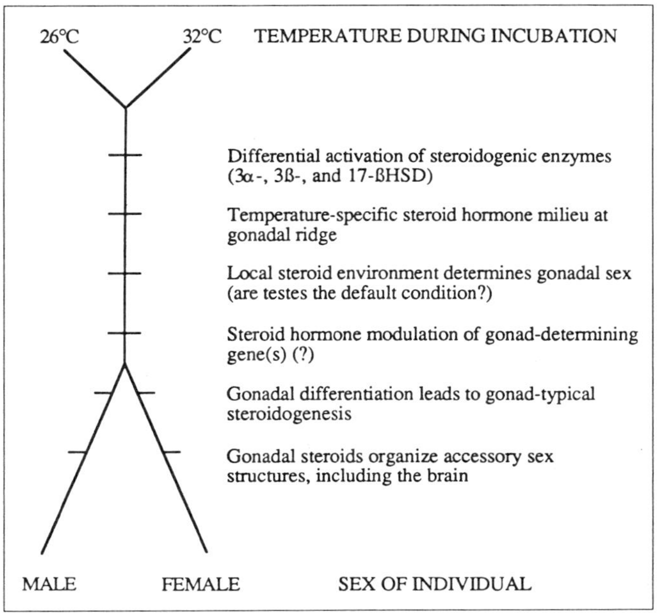

FIGURE 11. Hypothetical sequence of events that underlie temperature-dependent sex determination (from Crews 1992).

The information presented here only scratches the surface of the problem. More studies are needed on the physiology of TSD and the physiological basis by which embryonic temperatures affect adult reproductive competence. Also needed are more studies of the effects of sex ratio on the reproductive potential of captive, as well as naturally occurring populations of reptiles, and manipulation of sex ratio in the field by either physical manipulation (for example, erecting or removing shade) or hormonal manipulation (such as hormonal spotting of eggs in the nest).

Acknowledgments

The research described in this chapter has been supported by NSF 9205207 and NIMH Research Scientist Award 00135 (David Crews), NIMH NRSA MH 0991 (Alan Tousignant), and NIH NRSA HD 07319 (Thane Wibbels).

Literature Cited

Baker, J. R. 1938. The evolution of breeding seasons, p. 161–177. *In* G. R. DeBeer (ed.), Evolution. Essays on Aspects of Evolutionary Biology. Clarendon Press, Oxford.

Bern, H. A. 1990. The "new" endocrinology: its scope and its impact. Amer. Zool., 30: 877–885.

Bona Gallo, A., and P. Licht. 1983. Effects of temperature on sexual receptivity and ovarian recrudescence in the garter snake, *Thamnophis sirtalis parietalis*. Herpetologica, 39: 173–182.

Bull, J. J. 1980. Sex determination in reptiles. Quart. Rev. Biol., 55: 3–41.

—. 1983. Evolution of Sex Determining Mechanisms. Benjamin/Cummings, Menlo Park, California. 316 pages.

Bull, J. J., and E. L. Charnov. 1988. How fundamental are Fisherian Sex Ratios. Oxford Surv. Evol. Biol., 5: 96–135.

—. 1989. Enigmatic reptilian sex ratios. Evolution, 43: 1561–1566.

Bull, J. J., W. H. N. Gutzke, and D. Crews. 1988. Sex reversal by estradiol in three reptilian orders. Gen. Comp. Endocrinol., 70: 425–428.

Bull, J. J., R. C. Vogt, and C. J. McCoy. 1982. Sex determining temperatures in turtles: a geographic comparison. Evolution, 36: 326–332.

Bull, J. J., T. Wibbels, and D. Crews. 1990. Sex potencies vary among female incubation temperatures in a turtle. Jour. Exp. Zool., 256: 339–341.

Burger, J. 1989. Incubation temperature has long-term effects on behaviour of young pine snakes (*Pituophis melanoleucus*). Behav. Ecol. Sociobiol., 24: 201–207.

—. 1990. Effects of incubation temperature on behavior of young black racers (*Coluber constrictor*) and kingsnakes (*Lampropeltis getulus*). Jour. Herpetol., 24: 158–163.

Charnier, M. 1966. Action de la temperature sur la sex-ratio chez l'embryon d'*Agama agama* (Agamidae, Lacertilien). Soc. Biol. Ouest Africa, 160: 620–622.

Crews, D. 1974*a*. Effects of group stability and male aggressive and sexual behavior on environmentally-induced ovarian recrudescence in the lizard, *Anolis carolinensis*. Jour. Zool., London, 172: 419–441.

—. 1974*b*. Effects of castration and subsequent androgen replacement therapy on male courtship behavior and environmentally-induced ovarian recrudescence in the lizard, *Anolis carolinensis*. Jour. Comp. Physiol. Psychol., 87: 963–969.

—. 1979. Endocrine control of reptilian reproductive behavior, p. 167–222. *In* C. Beyer (ed.), Endocrine Control of Sexual Behavior. Raven Press, New York.

—. 1988. The problem with gender. Psychobiology, 16: 321–334.

—. 1989. Unisexual organisms as model systems for research in the behavioral neurosciences, p. 132–143. *In* R. M. Dawley and J. P. Bogart (eds.), Evolution and Ecology of Unisexual Vertebrates. New York State Museum, Albany, New York.

—. 1992. Behavioral endocrinology and reproduction: an evolutionary perspective, p. 303–370. *In* S. Milligan (ed.), Oxford Reviews in Reproductive Biology. Oxford Univ. Press, Oxford.

Crews, D., J. J. Bull, and T. Wibbels. 1991. Estrogen and sex reversal in turtles: a dose-dependent phenomenon. Gen. Comp. Endocrinol., 81: 357–364.

Crews, D., and K. Fitzgerald. 1980. "Sexual" behavior in parthenogenetic lizards (*Cnemidophorus*). Proc. Natl. Acad. Sci. USA, 77: 499–502.

Crews, D., and L. D. Garrick. 1980. Methods of inducing reproduction in captive reptiles, p. 49–70. *In* J. B. Murphy and J. T. Collins (eds.), Reproductive Biology of Captive Reptiles. Soc. Study Amphib. Reptiles, Oxford (Ohio), Contrib. Herpetol. 1.

Crews, D., M. Grassman, and J. Lindzey. 1986. Behavioral facilitation of reproduction in sexual and parthenogentic whiptail (*Cnemidophorus*) lizards. Proc. Natl. Acad. Sci. USA, 83: 9547–9550.

Crews, D., J. E. Gustafson, and R. R. Tokarz. 1983. Psychobiology of parthenogenesis in reptiles, p. 205–231. *In* R. Huey, T. Schoener, and E. Pianka (eds.), Lizard Ecology. Harvard Univ. Press, Cambridge.

Crews, D., and M. C. Moore. 1993. Psychobiology of reproduction of unisexual whiptail lizards, p. 257–282. *In* J. W. Wright and L. J. Vitt (eds.), Biology of Whiptail Lizards. Oklahoma Mus. Nat. Hist., Norman.

Crews, D., J. S. Rosenblatt, and D. S. Lehrman. 1974. Effects of unseasonal environmental regimen, group presence, group composition and male's physiological state on ovarian recrudescence in the lizard, *Anolis carolinensis*. Endocrinology, 94: 541–547.

Crews, D., T. Wibbels, and W. H. N. Gutzke. 1989. Action of sex steroid hormones on temperature-induced sex determination in the snapping turtle (*Chelydra serpentina*). Gen. Comp. Endocrinol., 76: 159–166.

Crews, D., and L. J. Young. 1991. Pseudocopulation in nature in a unisexual whiptail lizard. Anim. Behav., 42: 512–514.

Deeming, D. C., and M. W. Ferguson. 1988. Environmental regulation of sex determination in reptiles. Philos. Trans. Royal Soc. London, B, 322: 19–39.

Duvall, D., L. J. Guillette, and R. E. Jones. 1982. Environmental control of reptilian reproductive cycles, p. 201–231. *In* C. Gans and F. H. Pough (eds.), Biology of the Reptilia, Vol. 13. Academic Press, London.

Ewert, M. A., and C. E. Nelson. 1991. Sex determination in turtles: diverse patterns and some possible adaptive values. Copeia, 1991: 50–69.

Fox, W. 1948. Effect of temperature on development of scutellation in the garter snake, *Thamnophis elegans atratus*. Copeia, 1948: 252–262.

Garstka, W. R., B. Camazine, and D. Crews. 1982. Interactions of behavior and physiology during the annual reproductive cycle of the red-sided garter snake, *Thamnophis sirtalis parietalis*. Herpetologica, 38: 104–123.

Garstka, W. R., and D. Crews. 1981. Female sex pheromone in the skin and circulation of a garter snake. Science, 214: 681–683.

—. 1982. Female control of male reproductive function in a Mexican snake. Science, 217: 1159–1160.

—. 1986. Phermones and reproduction in garter snakes, p. 243–260. *In* D. Duvall, D. Müller-Schwarze, and R. M. Silverstein (eds.), Chemical Signals in Vertebrates. Volume 4. Plenum Publ. Corp., New York.

Gutzke, W. H. N., and J. J. Bull. 1986. Steroid hormones reverse sex in turtles. Gen. Comp. Endocrinol., 64: 368–372.

Gutzke, W. H. N., and D. Crews. 1988. Incubation temperature determines adult sexuality in a reptile. Nature, 332: 832–834.

Gutzke, W. H. N., and G. L. Paukstis. 1983. Influence of the hydric environment on sexual differentiation of turtles. Jour. Exp. Zool., 226: 467–469.

Halpert, A., W. R. Garstka, and D. Crews. 1982. Sperm transport and storage and its relation to the annual sexual cycle of the female red-sided garter snake, *Thamnophis sirtalis parietalis*. Jour. Morphol., 174: 149–159.

Joanen, T., L. McNease, and M. W. J. Ferguson. 1987. The effects of egg incubation temperature on post-hatching growth of American alligators, p. 533–537. *In* G. J. W. Webb, S. C. Manolis, and P. J. Whitehead (eds.), Wildlife Management: Crocodiles and Alligators. Surrey Beatty and Sons, Chipping Norton, New South Wales, Australia.

Lang, J. W. 1987. Crocodilian thermal selection, p. 301–317. *In* G. J. W. Webb, S. C. Manolis, and P. J. Whitehead (eds.), Wildlife Management: Crocodiles and Alligators. Surrey Beatty and Sons, Chipping Norton, New South Wales, Australia.

Licht, P. 1984. Reptiles, p. 206–282. *In* G. E. Lamming (ed.), Marshall's Physiology of Reproduction. Vol. 1, Reproductive Cycles of Vertebrates. Churchill Livingston, Edinburgh.

Limpus, C. 1985. A Study of the Loggerhead Sea Turtle, *Caretta caretta*, in Eastern Australia. Dissertation, Univ. Queensland, Brisbane, Australia. Volume 1, 269 pages; volume 2, 242 pages.

Mendonça, M. T., and D. Crews. 1989. Effect of fall mating on ovarian development in the red-sided garter snake. Amer. Jour. Physiol., 26: R1548–R1550.

—. 1990. Mating-induced ovarian recrudescence in the red-sided garter snake. Jour. Comp. Physiol., A, 166: 629–632.

Miller, K., G. C. Packard, and M. J. Packard. 1987. Hydric conditions during incubation influence locomotor performance of hatchling snapping turtles. Jour. Exp. Biol., 127: 401–412.

Mrosovsky, N., P. H. Dutton, and C. P. Whitmore. 1984*a*. Sex ratios of two species of sea turtles nesting in Suriname. Canadian Jour. Zool., 62: 2227–2239.

Mrosovsky, N., and J. Provancha. 1989. Sex ratio of loggerhead sea turtles hatching on a Florida beach. Canadian Jour. Zool., 67: 2533–2539.

Packard, G. C., M. J. Packard, and L. Benigan. 1991. Sexual differentiation, growth, and hatching success by embryonic painted turtles incubated in wet and dry environments at fluctuating temperatures. Herpetologica, 47: 125–132.

Packard, G. C., M. J. Packard, and G. F. Birchard. 1989. Sexual differentiation and hatching success by painted turtles incubating in different thermal and hydric environments. Herpetologica, 45: 385–392.

Paukstis, G. L., W. H. N. Gutzke, and G. C. Packard. 1984. Effects of substrate water potential and fluctuating temperatures on sex ratios of hatchling painted turtles (*Chrysemys picta*). Canadian Jour. Zool., 62: 1491–1494.

Phillips, J. A., A. Garel, G. C. Packard, and M. J. Packard. 1990. Influence of moisture and temperature on eggs and embryos of green iguanas (*Iguana iguana*). Herpetologica, 46: 238–245.

Pieau, C. 1971. Sur la proportion sexuelle chez les embryons de deux cheloniens (*Testudo graca* L. et *Emys orbicularis* L.) issus d'oeufs incubes artifciellement. Comp. Rend. Acad. Sci., 272: 3071–3074.

Raynaud, A. and C. Pieau. 1985. Embryonic development of the genital system, p. 149–300. *In* G. Gans and F. Billet (eds.), Biology of the Reptilia, Vol. 15. John Wiley and Sons, New York.

Whittier, J. M., and D. Crews. 1986*a*. Effects of prostaglandin F2a on sexual behavior and ovarian function in female garter snakes (*Thamnophis sirtalis parietalis*). Endocrinology, 119: 787–792.

—. 1986*b*. Ovarian development in red-sided garter snakes, *Thamnophis sirtalis parietalis*: relationship to mating. Gen. Comp. Endocrinol., 61: 5–12.

—. 1987. Seasonal reproduction: patterns and control, p. 385–409. *In* D. O. Norris and R. E. Jones (eds.), Hormones and Reproduction in Fishes, Amphibians, and Reptiles. Plenum Press, New York.

—. 1989. Mating increases plasma levels of prostaglandin F2a in female garter snakes. Prostaglandins, 37: 359–366.

—. 1990. Body mass and reproduction in female red-sided garter snakes (*Thamnophis sirtalis parietalis*). Herpetologica, 46: 219–226.

Whittier, J. M., R. T. Mason, and D. Crews. 1987. Plasma steroid hormone levels of female red-sided garter snakes, *Thamnophis sirtalis parietalis*: relationship to mating and gestation. Gen. Comp. Endocrinol., 67: 33–43.

Wibbels, T., J. J. Bull, and D. Crews. 1991*a*. Chronology and morphology of temperature-dependent sex determination. Jour. Exp. Zool., 260: 371–381.

—. 1991*b*. Synergism between temperature and estradiol: a common pathway in turtle sex determination? Jour. Exp. Zool., 260: 130–134.

Wibbels, T., F. C. Killebrew, and D. Crews. 1991. Sex determination in Cagle's map turtle: evolutionary, developmental, and conservational implications. Canadian Jour. Zool., 69: 2693–2696.

Wibbels, T., R. E. Martin, D. W. Owens, and J. Max S. Amoss. 1991. Female-biased sex ratio of immature loggerhead sea turtles inhabiting the Atlantic coastal waters of Florida. Canadian Jour. Zool., 69: 2973–2977.

Wingfield, J. C. 1980. Fine temporal adjustment of reproductive functions, p. 367–389. *In* A. Epple and M. H. Stetson (eds.), Avian Endocrinology. Academic Press, New York.

Wingfield, J. C., T. P. Hahn, R. Levin, and P. Honey. 1992. Environmental predictability and control of gonadal cycles in birds. Jour. Exp. Zool., 261: 214–231.

Yntema, C. L. 1976. Effects of incubation temperature on sexual differentiation in the turtle, *Chelydra serpentina*. Jour. Morph., 150: 453–462.

❦ Crews, D., A. Tousignant, and T. Wibbels. 1994. Considerations for inducing reproduction in captive reptiles, p. 133–145. *In* J. B. Murphy, K. Adler, and J. T. Collins (eds.), Captive Management and Conservation of Amphibians and Reptiles. Society for the Study of Amphibians and Reptiles, Ithaca (New York). Contributions to Herpetology, volume 11.

An Ethological Approach to Reproductive Success in Reptiles

David Chiszar,* Hobart M. Smith,** and Charles C. Carpenter***

Introduction

The earliest reference known to us on the subject of herpetoculture demonstrates how far we have come in the last 250 years. Charles Owen (1742) was aware of the natural diets of many reptiles and amphibians, yet his statements about captive maintenance were remarkably unsophisticated. For example, in discussing European vipers he said, "These vipers are usually kept in a box with bran or moss, not that these ingredients serve to feed upon, as some may fancy, because 'tis said, they never eat after they are taken and confin'd, but live on the air, and will live so, many months..." (p. 53). Later he described a "salamander" from the Indies that was kept 11 months "without any other food but what it took by licking the earth... on which it had been brought out of the Indies..." (p. 94). It is, perhaps, not surprising that Owen had very little to say about captive propagation of amphibians and reptiles. (Compare Owen's book with any state-of-the-art tome on herpetoculture [for example, Frye 1991, but see Bels and Gans 1986] for a succinct statement of problems yet to be solved.)

*Department of Psychology
Campus Box 345
University of Colorado
Boulder, Colorado 80309, USA

**Department of Environmental, Population, and Organismic Biology
Campus Box 334
University of Colorado
Boulder, Colorado 80309, USA

***Department of Zoology
University of Oklahoma
Norman, Oklahoma 73069, USA

Acronyms used in this chapter:

MAP Modal action pattern
TSCA Tail-search copulatory attempt

In 1980, Carpenter published a paper bearing the same title as does this chapter, and our initial purpose in writing this report was simply to update that paper by surveying the subsequent literature (Carpenter 1980). Carpenter concentrated mainly on sequences of modal action patterns (MAPs) involved in reptilian courtship and on the sensory channels involved in the activation of these patterns, as well as the channels (in recipients) that are affected by them (see also Duvall 1979; Duvall et al. 1987). Accordingly, we set the goal of discovering how much new material along these lines had accumulated in the last decade. Two realizations grew as the literature review progressed: (1) much new data have appeared regarding MAPs, indicating that classical ethology continues to play a productive role in herpetology (see Table 1), and (2) the literature on reptilian reproduction during the last decade is voluminous and multifaceted, indicating that many theoretical concerns have been motivating herpetologists (for list, see appendix to this chapter).

TABLE 1. Number of papers on reptilian reproduction in three herpetological journals (1980–1990). The number of these papers using classical ethological approaches (for example, descriptive ethology, quantitative analyses of topography, analyses of stimulus effects, behavior sequences, or sensory mechanisms [categories of Carpenter 1980]) is given. For original data set, see appendix to this chapter.

	Copeia	*Journal of Herpetology*	*Herpetologica*
Papers on reptilian reproduction	207	209	187
Ethological papers on reptilian reproduction	19	32	33

Herpetological studies of reproduction fall into relatively discrete categories: (1) anatomy-endocrinology, (2) ecology, (3) ethology, and (4) conservation and captive propagation. While some studies certainly fit into more than one category, many do not. Following Bronson (1989), we believe that an integrative approach is long overdue and is likely to be superior to these "separatist" approaches. Saying that we are interested in behavior, for example, should not be taken to mean that autecological, anatomical, and other aspects of reproduction are of no consequence. Also, an integrative perspective is likely to help us identify principles that would be hard to see from some specialized research areas.

Our approach, therefore, is integrative, and includes a conceptual framework that appears to be guiding many researchers; a series of general principles that exist in the literature (although they have been more or less the province of different subsets of researchers): an analysis of the problems of captive propagation; relevant reproductive phenomena; and a few (rather speculative) hypotheses, which reflect the potential value of the conceptual framework used here.

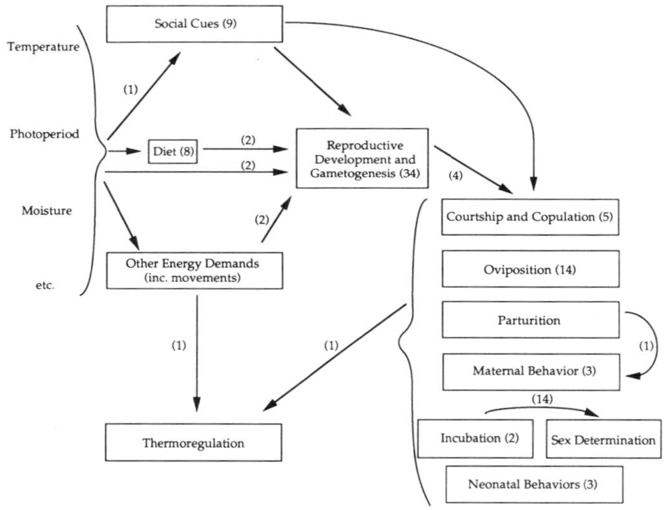

FIGURE 1. Influences (levels of analysis) contributing to reproductive events. Numbers refer to the frequency of papers published in *Copeia* (1980–1990). Numbers within boxes represent descriptive-ecological studies, whereas numbers next to arrows represent experimental studies that establish causal links. The descriptive foundations of herpetology are clearly reflected by the relatively large number of such papers. Yet an emphasis on proximate causation is also clear. (Not all papers indicated in Table 1 are included here. We have omitted papers that deal with topics other than those shown in the figure, mainly to keep the figure to manageable size.) This illustration is representative of similar analyses for papers in *Herpetologica* and the *Journal of Herpetology*.

Figure 1 is the sort of illustration commonly used in textbooks to represent the various levels of analysis that can occur during the study of reproduction. Consider, for example, the physical parameters on the left. While it is clear that animals respond to them, it is not clear how these factors are detected or assessed. Herein are the linkages between stimulus events and eventual reproductive responses that must be understood. This issue can be drawn into sharper focus by considering diet, which is unquestionably vital for reproduction. How do reptiles assess the quantity and quality of their diets? Food availability can be assessed indirectly through somatic growth and energy sequestered in fat bodies; it can also be assessed directly through sensory modalities, such as vision and chemosensation (Stamps and Tanaka 1981). Yet we know little about how these monitoring systems interact, especially in an animal that is in lean condition yet is exposed to abundant resources.

Consider also a female responding to courtship advances by a male. Her current state of sexual readiness is likely to influence her behavior, but the male's condition, behavior, and his social status are also influential (Gillingham et al. 1983; Schuett and Gillingham 1988). Should such factors be conceptualized as minor events, contributing only little variance to reproductive processes, or can we expect to observe more complex (for example, compensatory) interactions in which particularly attractive males might be able to stimulate receptivity in females that would otherwise be unreceptive?

These questions can be answered by appropriate experimentation, but notice that we are stepping beyond the boundaries of classical ethology. We are not focusing exclusively on display action patterns or other MAPs, although these continue to be very important. Rather, we are embracing areas ranging from sensory physiology to behavioral endocrinology and energetics. Crews (1987) speaks of the "psychobiology of reptilian reproduction" in his attempt to draw together this same diversity of factors, and we agree with him and with Bronson (1989) that this broad approach is necessary not only for integrating the material now available in the research literature, but also for conceiving of new research questions that have the potential to advance our understanding. The ethology of the 1990s must combine its classical legacy with interdisciplinary theory and methods to quantify the assessment and decision processes that are now only beginning to be conceptualized.

One goal of herpetological research on reproduction is to explain variability that may be seasonal, situational, geographic, or phylogenetic in origin. Variability in reproduction can be conceptualized as resulting from variation in organismic processes that represent linkages between upstream physical and environmental parameters, on the one hand, and downstream reproductive events, on the other. The advantage of the present framework is that it focuses attention on these linkages and on the manner in which they contribute to variation. As behaviorists, we are most interested in assessment processes that involve specialized behaviors (for example, searching, trail following, combat, courtship, persuasion, and rejection), but we recognize that numerous other assessments exist. The psychobiological approach we envision must quantify the linkages between assessments and reproductive processes in terms of the variance they explain, in terms of their compensatory interactions, and, eventually, in terms of their contributions to fitness and to captive propagation.

Behavioral Implications of Latitude and Seasonality

It is useful to recognize that gametogenesis and reproductive behaviors are products of a chain of interacting events, anchored (proximately and ultimately) to annual climatic phenomena. Without doubt, genetic regulation of reproduction occurs within a physical-organic context that contains numerous cues. Data, for example Figure 2, which is redrawn from Fitch (1970), indicates that latitude has a profound effect on length of the reproductive season within the Side-blotched Lizard (*Uta stansburiana*). Such findings are well known in mammals, and not particularly rare for reptiles (although cross-species comparisons are usually needed to show the effect). It is, of course, impossible to specify which of the many climatic correlates of latitude is responsible for this effect, and it is likely that several factors are involved. Temperature cycles, for example, have multiple effects, one of which is to influence food availability. In mammals the literature clearly reveals a profound connection between temperature and diet, and between diet and reproductive success, and there is good reason to believe the same is true in reptiles (Ballinger and Congdon 1980; Kennett and Georges 1990; Turner et al. 1986).

Consideration of the behavioral implications of environmental factors has led us to a speculative idea that cuts across several subdisciplinary boundaries, such as foraging theory, physiological ecology, and reproduction. The typical husbandry situation for small mammals involves provision of ad libitum and inexhaustible quantities of food. Laboratory rats and mice, for example, always have a large quantity of chow stacked in a readily accessible hopper. By comparison, the typical husbandry situation for many captive reptiles (especially snakes) never incorporates the presence of food, except on feeding days when prey items are introduced by keepers. Yet, it is well established that reptiles in nature seek areas with abundant prey populations (Duvall et al. 1985; Reinert et al. 1984). Perhaps these assessments, quite apart from actual captures and ingestions of prey, contribute to reproductive investment. If such effects occur in nature, then our captive husbandry situations can be understood as depriving reptiles of sensory cues that influence reproductive events, even though adequate food is provided. We are not aware of any

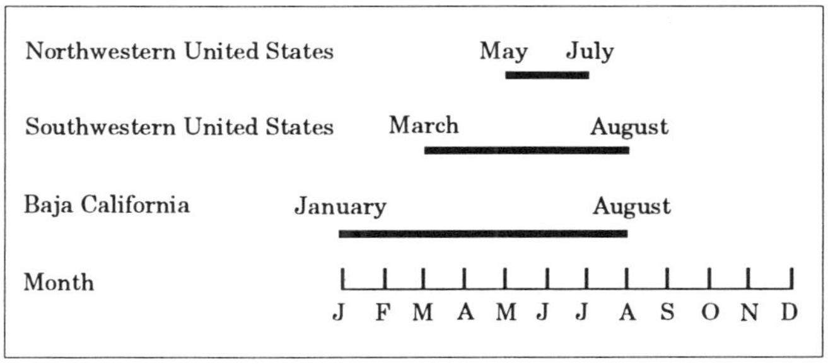

FIGURE 2. Temperate-zone reptiles have sharply delimited reproductive seasons and many tropical species have longer seasons, some breeding continuously throughout the year. In the case of Side-blotched Lizards (*Uta stansburiana*), sufficient data were presented by Fitch (1970) to exhibit this effect of latitude within a single species (illustrated above). It is not possible to identify the critical aspect of latitude (for example, temperature, photoperiod, or diet). Also, it is not possible to say that specimens from the Northwest United States would experience a lengthier reproductive season if they were exposed to conditions in Baja California, Mexico. Both problems appear worthy of pursuit.

study that has assessed the effects of prey sign on reproductive indices, such as gonadal recrudescence, onset of puberty, willingness of males to search for females, or of females to respond to courtship. Research in this area is needed; if such effects exist, they will have profound implications for husbandry procedures.

We are not talking about MAPs or what ethologists would call key or releasing stimuli. Instead, we are concerned with relatively subtle stimulus conditions that might influence the development or the maintenance of reproductive motivation. We regard this kind of information to be as important as the data deriving from classical studies of courtship sequences in highly motivated animals. With progress having been made in this latter domain (see Carpenter 1980, and Table 1), it is becoming increasingly important to take the next logical steps toward an analysis of the antecedents of motivation.

Bronson (1989) showed that female lagomorphs are sharply seasonal at high latitudes, have increasingly broader seasons at middle latitudes, and become continuous breeders in the neotropics and tropics (see Fitch 1970, and Figure 2). Of course, there are many exceptions to continuous breeding in the tropics (see below). For the moment, it is important to recognize that lagomorphs from high latitudes will breed continuously under utopian laboratory conditions, suggesting that inhibitory cues are satisfactorily removed by a 12:12 light:dark photoperiod, 25°C, and ad libitum food and water. Whether or not an expanded breeding season can occur in a comparably treated temperate reptile is unclear. Such an organism, if one exists, would be a valuable model for the identification of inhibitory and excitatory cues.

The shift to continuous breeding at low latitudes is strongly influenced by life span in mammals—the shorter the life span, the higher the latitude at which the shift occurs (for example, white-footed mice become continuous breeders at 40°, lagomorphs at 30°, and deer at 10°). We are aware of no taxon of reptile (of any body size) living anywhere in the temperate zones that is as short-lived as small rodents. Hence, the pressure to start reproduction as early as possible and to continue across the year may simply not be as strong in relatively long-lived temperate reptiles as it is in some small mammals. Several ideas follow from this. First is the suggestion that life span is not only a major determinant of reproductive strategy, but also that it may be a determinant of a fundamental difference between mammals and reptiles. Second, there may well be an association between relatively long life span and sensitivity to environmental cues that inhibit reproduction. Hence, the "window" of reproductive flexibility in reptiles is unlikely to be as wide as the one for mammals. Yet the dimensions of this window ought to be explored through experiments aimed at identifying and manipulating the stimulus factors that prime or inhibit reproductive phenomena.

Tropical environments, although relatively constant in temperature and photoperiod, can be quite variable in other properties, such as rainfall and plant growth (Jenssen 1970; see Duvall et al. 1982 for a review). Consequently, animals in the tropics can be subjected to quite variable energetic conditions, depending on their diet and other features of their microniche. Those species that depend upon variable resources can be expected to exhibit seasonal reproduction in the tropics, whereas those that have constantly available resources can be expected to exhibit continuous reproduction. This holds for mammals and the accumulated evidence suggests that the same is true for reptiles. Nevertheless, even seasonal breeders in the tropics may be induced to have broader or continuous seasons in captivity if inhibitory stimuli can be identified and removed.

Although it is unquestionably true that a permissive ambient temperature is necessary for reproduction, numerous organisms are stimulated to begin physiological preparation for reproduction by other environmental cues that reliably predict the coming of appropriate climatic and nutritional conditions. The best understood predictor is photoperiod, at least for mammals and birds; a light period of 12.5 hours is critical for some species (see Bronson 1989, for a review). For reptiles, by contrast, little evidence exists for photoperiodic cueing (Fischer 1974); rather, the literature suggests that temperature is most often the critical factor (Duvall et al. 1982; Licht 1972; Marion 1982). On the other hand, many other climatic variables have been hypothesized to make contributions (for example, ultraviolet light, rainfall, and humidity). Measuring the relative effects of these stimulus conditions remains to be accomplished.

The literature appears to be consistent with the following conclusions: (1) many reptiles do not use increasing photophase to trigger gonadal events, (2) temperature increase may be a trigger following a period of hibernation, and (3) low temperatures may inhibit gonadal and behavioral events that, otherwise, will develop completely under more permissive conditions. The difference between conclusions 2 and 3 is subtle, but important. We tend to think of reproductive processes as being stimulated and as requiring excitatory cues, but it is possible that endogenously organized events are programmed to unfold according to more-or-less cyclical patterns, subject only to temporary inhibition arising from external cues. In such cases, it is the removal of inhibition, rather than the onset of excitation, that governs reproductive events. Current evidence suggests that all three conclusions apply to reptilian reproductive processes (see Licht 1972, 1973; Marion 1982).

However this matter turns out, we urge that a broad psychobiological approach continue to be taken in future studies of climatic cueing. Such an approach would measure many dependent variables, including behavioral ones (for example, activity level, foraging, and basking and other thermoregulatory movements) that are distally related to reproduction, but that are part of a cascade of events that are causal antecedents of reproduction. Different dependent variables may respond in different ways to photothermal regimens. If this is so, then focusing on only a few terminal measures of reproductive condition is bound to produce a myopic view. Also, complex interactions are likely to occur among stages and within them (Angelini et al. 1976, 1980; Licht 1971). An investigative approach that is correspondingly multistaged and multivariate is likely to capture these complexities, and this is precisely the hope we have for the ethology of the 1990s. Similar points of view have been expressed by endocrinologists working on the synchronization of reproductive processes with environmental conditions (Duvall et al. 1982; Garstka et al. 1982; Jones and Guillette 1982; Marion 1982).

Puberty

The timing of fertility onset is also an event related to diet and to other environmental variables. As a general rule, we can recognize a positive relationship across species among adult body size, life span, and age of puberty. Within this context, however, age of puberty can vary among populations of a species and among individuals of a population. This variation is important in that it reveals flexibility in the genetic plan and the importance of environmental variables (see, for example, the extensive literature on pheromonal control of puberty in mice; see also a review of variation in fertility onset in amphibians by Jorgensen 1992). Deceleratory and inhibitory effects must be common in nature, leading to relatively long delays before puberty and to reduced investment in reproduction (presumably to be compensated by higher investments later, when conditions are favorable). Understanding these effects is of paramount importance for captive propagation. If the conditions of captive maintenance inadvertently simulate these inhibitory effects, then difficulties are bound to arise for breeding programs. Whereas the timing of puberty has primarily been of interest to population ecologists, an ethological approach must also be taken with this matter, because this is the pathway to understanding the factors that inhibit reproduction, and removing them from captive environments.

Food-Supplementation Studies

Because mammals experience the high costs of endothermy and lactation, it is not surprising that a host of energy-saving adaptations characterize these animals (for example, hibernation, daily torpor, food hoarding, seasonal moulting, seasonal metabolic adjustments, brown fat, and enforced seasonal breeding). Furthermore, daily fat-body cycles have been observed in mice and recent studies have reported risk-sensitive foraging tactics in endotherms (Stephens and Krebs 1986). Although reptiles are liberated from the energy demands of endothermy and lactation, it does not follow that energy-saving adaptations are unimportant in reptiles. Yet we have so far developed only a partial view of the connection between energetics and reproduction in reptiles. For example, we are not aware of any studies of risk-sensitive foraging in reptiles.

Mammalogists have conducted food-supplementation studies, partly because of the strong connections perceived to exist between energetics and reproduction in mammals, and also because such studies are needed to document whether or not food is a limiting resource. These projects usually have produced positive results, revealing at least marginally increased reproduction and, by implication, that food was a limiting resource. Incidentally, similar projects have added supplemental water to xeric habitats and have obtained positive results on rodent reproduction. We are aware of few comparable field experiments with reptiles (Ferguson et al. 1982; Mayhew 1966; Rose 1982; Simon 1975; Stamps and Tanaka 1981). Such work is crucial if we are to identify limiting resources, and if we are to develop testable hypotheses about how these stimulus conditions inhibit or otherwise influence reproductive events.

"Stimulation" and Several Hypotheses

We are not concerned here with the conditions necessary to produce gonadal recrudescence or puberty. Instead, we are interested in reptiles that are in reproductive condition, but that nevertheless refuse to mate. This antilibidinal situation has been reported often enough to have received a name, "captive stagnation" (Huff 1980).

Our thoughts on captive stagnation are admittedly incomplete, so the following comments should be viewed as a beginning rather than as a finished product. First, so many libidinal therapies have been reported that we are convinced there is something important in this area. Second, we propose that captive stagnation is based upon profound inhibitory processes, and that the therapies are successful because they somehow remove inhibition.

A very large literature exists on the effects of controllability versus uncontrollability of important stimuli, such as food, water, or various aversive events. Most of this work has been done with rats and dogs. When stimuli (appetitive or aversive) are presented or withdrawn independently of the animal's behavior, the animal is said to have no control over them. By contrast, the same stimuli can be presented or withdrawn in ways that are dependent on the animal's foraging or defensive behaviors. In this case, the animal is said to have at least some degree of control. The uncontrollable condition leads to a set of drastic behavioral and physiological deteriorations, including serious immunological deficits. We mention this situation for two reasons: (1) standard conditions of captivity often resemble the uncontrollable condition, so we might expect some of the same results, and (2) loss of libido is among the deficits known to occur in mammals subjected to uncontrollable environments (S. Maier, pers. comm.). Accordingly, we propose that captive stagnation might very well be a manifestation of this same process. Psychobiologists have developed various drug and behavioral therapies that are effective for rats and dogs, and perhaps the same techniques might be effective for treating captive stagnation in zoo animals (Maier and Seligman 1976; Maier et al. 1990; Rodgers 1989).

In addition to stimulus uncontrollability, social domination is also known to induce lethargy and reduced libido, and the effects are well documented in mammals, birds, reptiles, amphibians, and fish. Victims of domination frequently do not court or mate (see Bronson 1989, for a review). Although there is nothing new about these effects of stress and domination—and they are indeed well known to herpetoculturists (Callard and Callard 1978; Greenberg 1985, 1990; Lance and Elsey 1984)—we should consider the manner in which animals are handled during routine husbandry and how some herpetologists "tame" their animals so that they can be carried (Wiley 1930). These procedures may not be innocuous; many breeders, for example, caution against handling animals, especially males (Ross 1980; Ross and Marzec 1990). Perhaps handling, even that which is required during cage cleaning, represents a sort of domination of reptiles by humans. We suggest that some libidinal deficits in males may be responses of subordinated creatures to the environment that subordinates them. This hypothesis, which might explain some instances of captive stagnation, can be tested; if valid, it would be easy to alter husbandry routines and cage design to reduce these unwanted effects of inadvertent human domination (see also Warwick 1990).

If a male refuses to court a female because he is suffering from some libidinal obstruction, what can we conclude about the female's state of receptivity? Unless she mates with another male directly after the first test, it is difficult to conclude anything about her. She may or may not have been receptive. It would be useful to have a behavioral bioassay of female sexuality that could be applied independently of copulatory trials with males. Such assays exist for female rats, in that lordosis can be elicited by touching an estrus female at the base of her tail. With this in mind, David Chiszar used a snake hook to rub the back of a female prairie rattlesnake while simulating a tail-search copulatory attempt (TSCA). That female raised her tail and gaped her cloaca, even though a male rattlesnake had refused to court her moments earlier. Chiszar did not mention this episode in previous papers, mainly because it is based on a single observation, but also due to concern that interest in cloacal gaping might be seen as arcane. James Gillingham, an authority on the copulatory pattern of many snakes, however, recently told Chiszar that he has been able to induce cloacal gaping in female *Elaphe* by simulating TSCAs. Perhaps this is the pathway to developing a behavioral bioassay of ophidian female receptivity (see Garstka et al. 1982).

Offspring Competence

Successful breeding is only one part of successful propagation. The second part is raising competent offspring. We define competent offspring as those possessing the behavioral, anatomical, and physiological characteristics necessary for survival in natural habitats. Accordingly, wild conspecifics constitute the baseline or standard against which captive-born propagules should be compared. At present there is no systematic program for making such comparisons, and we tend to regard captive propagation efforts as successful if offspring survive to reproductive maturity in captivity. This is a good beginning, but is short sighted and incomplete in the long term (Chiszar et al. 1990; Murphy and Chiszar 1989).

If one purpose of captive propagation is the production of offspring for eventual release into suitable natural habitat, then it becomes obvious that offspring competence is a necessary concern. Long-term follow-up work will be needed to study this matter (Burke 1991; Dodd and Seigel 1991; Griffith et. al. 1990; Reinert 1991).

Summary

Ethology can make a major contribution to this vital aspect of propagation. This discipline must become all-encompassing, incorporating psychobiology, comparative psychology, behavioral ecology, and other disciplines that possess relevant methods and theories. To put matters bluntly, the task before us has always been there. It is the old job of understanding development and all of the factors that contribute to it. Yet we see an important new aspect of the job, an aspect that comes into focus because we have the reasonable goal of producing animals that can survive in natural habitats.

It becomes necessary for us to use wild conspecifics as a comparison group whenever possible, and it is necessary for us to measure all relevant traits, not merely those of interest to particular theoretical systems. We must be concerned with locomotion, migration, food getting, mate finding, predator avoidance, and all the rest. We must develop techniques for quantifying these factors and for analyzing their development. This will, in turn, require that we identify the experiences critical for ontogeny and that we learn how to provide them (or effective surrogates) in captive environments.

If work along these lines is introduced into every captive propagation program, we will—in short order—learn a vast amount about reptilian developmental psychobiology. Not only will the herpetological ethology of the 1990s take on an expanded nature, but zoos will take on collegial relationships with a wider variety of supportive personnel than has been true in the past. Numerous developmentally oriented scientists exist, and they all have contributions to make to this new enterprise. We see the immediate future as a time of great excitement and of great potential progress for ethology as a discipline and for captive propagation as both a goal and a golden opportunity. Carpenter ended his 1980 paper on a similar optimistic note. Several lines of research have been proposed here and several others were proposed by Carpenter (1980). Since most of these questions have practical applications, with a direct bearing on conservation, we close with a quotation from Robert Oppenheimer that underscores our call for interdisciplinary effort:

"When we work alone, trying to get something straight, it is right that we be lonely; and I think in the really decisive thoughts that advance a science loneliness is an essential part. When we are trying to do something practical it is nice to have an excess of talent, to have more sailors than are needed to sail the ship and more cooks than are needed to cook the meal; the reason is that in this way a certain elegance, a certain proper weighing of alternatives, guides the execution of the practical task" (Oppenheimer 1956, p. 135).

Acknowledgments

Ideas contained in this paper have been discussed with numerous persons and we are indebted to all of them. Of particular importance have been David Duvall, James Gillingham, Richard Jones, James Murphy, Matthew Rand, Gordon Schuett, and Albert Petkus. Bronson's (1989) book served as an organizational framework for this paper, and we are much in his debt.

An earlier version of this paper contained tables listing all behaviorally oriented references discovered during our literature review; space limitations on the present paper do not permit anything more than the numerical summary contained in Table 1. Interested readers can request copies of the original tables from David Chiszar.

Literature Cited

Angelini, F., V. Botte, and R. Boschi. 1980. The regulation of the reproductive cycle of *Podarcis s. sicula* Raf. (Reptilia, Lacertidae): influence of the refractory period on the springtime testicular activity. Monit. Zool. Ital., new ser., 14: 27–39.

Angelini, F., O. Picariello, and V. Botte. 1976. Influence of photoperiod and temperature on the testicular activity of the lizard *Lacerta s. sicula* Raf. Bull. Zool., 43: 111–123.

Ballinger, R. W. and J. D. Congdon. 1980. Food resource limitations of body growth rate in *Sceloporus scalaris* (Sauria: Iguanidae). Copeia, 1980: 921–923.

Bels, V. L., and C. Gans. 1986. Conclusions: perspectives on breeding reptiles in captivity. Acta Zool. Pathol. Antverpiensia, 79: 110–112.

Bronson, F. H. 1989. Mammalian Reproductive Biology. Univ. Chicago Press, Chicago. ix, 325 pages.

Burke, R. L. 1991. Relocations, repatriations, and translocations of amphibians and reptiles: taking a broader view. Herpetologica, 47: 350–357.

Callard, I. P., and G. V. Callard. 1978. The adrenal gland in Reptilia. Part 2. Physiology, p. 370–418. *In* I. Chester-Jones and I. W. Hendersdon (eds.), Comparative and Clinical Endocrinology of the Adrenal Cortex. Academic Press, New York.

Carpenter, C. C. 1980. An ethological approach to reproductive success in reptiles, p. 33–48. *In* J. B. Murphy and J. T. Collins (eds.), Reproductive Biology and Diseases of Captive Reptiles. Soc. Study Amphib. Reptiles, Oxford (Ohio), Contrib. Herpetol., 1.

Chiszar, D., J. B. Murphy, and W. Iliff. 1990. For zoos. Psychol. Rec., 40: 3–13.

Crews, D. (ed.). 1987. Psychobiology of Reproductive Behavior: An Evolutionary Perspective. Prentice-Hall, Englewood Cliffs, New Jersey. xiii, 350 pages.

Dodd, C. K., Jr., and R. A. Seigel. 1991. Relocation, repatriation and translocation of amphibians and reptiles: are they conservation strategies that work? Herpetologica, 47: 336–350.

Duvall, D. 1979. Western fence lizard (*Sceloporus occidentalis*) chemical signals 1. Conspecific discriminations and release of a species-typical visual display. Jour. Exp. Zool., 210: 321–325.

Duvall, D., B. M. Graves, and G. C. Carpenter. 1987. Visual and chemical composite signaling effects of *Sceloporus* lizard fecal boli. Copeia, 1987: 1028–1031.

Duvall, D., L. J. Guillette, Jr., and R. E. Jones. 1982. Environmental control of reptilian reproductive cycles, p. 201–231. *In* C. Gans and F. H. Pough (eds.), Biology of the Reptilia, Vol. 13, Physiology D, Physiological Ecology. Academic Press, New York.

Duvall, D., M. B. King, and K. J. Gutzwiller. 1985. Prairie rattlesnake (*Crotalus viridis viridis*) behavioral ecology: preliminary analyses of migration, predation, interspecific defense, and communal birthing, rookeries and neonate den location. Nat. Geogr. Res., 1: 80–111.

Ferguson, G. W., K. L. Brown, and V. C. DeMarco. 1982. Selective basis for the evaluation of variable egg and hatchling size in some iguanid lizards. Herpetologica, 38: 178–188.

Fischer, K. 1974. Die Steuerung der Fortflanzungszyklen bei männlichen Reptilien. Fortschr. Zool., 22: 362–390.

Fitch, H. S. 1970. Reproductive cycles of lizards and snakes. Univ. Kansas Mus. Nat. Hist. Misc. Publ., 52: 1–247.

Frye, F. L. 1991. Biomedical and Surgical Aspects of Captive Reptile Husbandry. 2 Vols. Krieger Publishing Co., Malabar, Florida. xv, 325, 16 pages; xxi, 326–637, 16 pages.

Garstka, W. R., B. Camazine, and D. Crews. 1982. Interactions of behavior and physiology during the annual reproductive cycle of the red-sided garter snake (*Thamnophis sirtalis parietalis*). Herpetologica, 38: 104–123.

Gillingham, J. C., C. C. Carpenter, and J. B. Murphy. 1983. Courtship, male combat and dominance in the western diamondback rattlesnake, *Crotalus atrox*. Jour. Herpetol., 17: 265–270.

Greenberg, N. 1985. Exploratory behavior and stress in the lizard, *Anolis carolinensis*. Zeitschr. Tierpsychol., 70: 89–102.

—. 1990. Behavioral endocrinology of physiological stress in a lizard. Jour. Exp. Zool., suppl., 4: 170–173.

Griffith, B., J. M. Scott, J. W. Carpenter, and C. Reed. 1990. Translocations of captive-reared terrestrial vertebrates, 1973–1986. Endang. Spec. Update, 8: 10–14.

Huff, T. A. 1980. Captive propagation of the subfamily Boinae with emphasis on the genus *Epicrates*, p. 125–134. *In* J. B. Murphy and J. T. Collins (eds.), Reproductive Biology and Diseases of Captive Reptiles. Soc. Study Amphib. Reptiles, Oxford (Ohio), Contrib. Herpetol., 1.

Jenssen, T. A. 1970. The ethoecology of *Anolis nebulosus* (Sauria, Iguanidae). Jour. Herpetol., 4: 1–38.

Jones, R. E., and L. J. Guillette, Jr. 1982. Hormonal control of oviposition and parturition in lizards. Herpetologica, 38: 80–93.

Jorgensen, C. B. 1992. Growth and reproduction, p. 439–466. *In* M. E. Feder and W. W. Burggren (eds.), Environmental Physiology of the Amphibians. Univ. Chicago Press, Chicago.

Kennett, R. M., and A. Georges. 1990. Habitat utilization and its relationship to growth and reproduction of the eastern long-necked turtle, *Chelodina longicollis* (Testudinata: Chelidae), from Australia. Herpetologica, 46: 22–33.

Lance, V., and R. M. Elsey. 1984. Stress-induced suppression of testosterone secretion in male alligators. Jour. Exp. Zool., 239: 241–246.

Licht, P. 1971. Regulation of the annual testes cycle by photoperiod and temperature in the lizard *Anolis carolinensis*. Ecology, 52: 240–252.

—. 1972. Environmental physiology of reptilian breeding cycles: role of temperature. Gen. Comp. Endocrinol., suppl., 3: 477–488.

—. 1973. Influence of temperature and photoperiod and the annual ovarian cycle in the lizard *Anolis carolinensis*. Copeia, 1973: 465–472.

Maier, S. F., and M. E. P. Seligman. 1976. Learned helplessness: theory and evidence. Jour. Exp. Psychol. Gen., 105: 3–46.

Maier, S. F., L. H. Silbert, W. W. Woodmansee, and P. H. Desan. 1990. Adinazolam both prevents and reverses the long-term reduction of daily activity produced by inescapable shock. Pharm. Biochem. Behav., 36: 767–773.

Marion, K. R. 1982. Reproductive cues for gonadal development in temperate reptiles: temperature and photoperiod effects on the testicular cycle of the lizard *Sceloporus undulatus*. Herpetologica, 38: 26–39.

Mayhew, W. W. 1966. Reproduction in the arenicolous lizard *Uma notata*. Ecology, 47: 9–18.

Murphy, J. B., and D. Chiszar. 1989. Herpetological master planning for the 1990s. Internatl. Zoo Yearb., 28: 1–7.

Oppenheimer, R. 1956. Analogy in science. Amer. Psychol., 11: 127–135.

Owen, C. 1742. An Essay Towards a Natural History of Serpents. Privately printed, London. xiii, 240, (12) pages.

Reinert, H. K. 1991. Translocations as a conservation strategy for amphibians and reptiles: some comments, concerns and observations. Herpetologica, 47: 357–363.

Reinert, H. K., D. Cundall, and L. M. Busher. 1984. Foraging behavior of the timber rattlesnake, *Crotalus horridus*. Copeia, 1984: 976–981.

Rodgers, R. J. 1989. Ethoexperimental analysis of "stress" analgesia, p. 214–228. *In* R. J. Blanchard, P. F. Brain, D. C. Blanchard, and S. Parmigiani (eds.), Ethoexperimental Approaches to the Study of Behavior. Martinus Nijhoff, Dordrecht, The Netherlands.

Rose, B. 1982. Food intake and reproduction in *Anolis acutus*. Copeia, 1982: 322–330.

Ross, R. A. 1980. The breeding of pythons (subfamily Pythoninae) in captivity, p. 135–139. *In* J. B. Murphy and J. T. Collins (eds.), Reproductive Biology and Diseases of Captive Reptiles. Soc. Study Amphib. Reptiles, Oxford (Ohio), Contrib. Herpetol., 1.

Ross, R. A., and G. Marzec. 1990. The Reproductive Husbandry of Pythons and Boas. Inst. Herpetol. Res., Stanford, California. 270 pages.

Schuett, G. W., and J. C. Gillingham. 1988. Courtship and mating of the copperhead, *Agkistrodon contortrix*. Copeia, 1988: 374–381.

Simon, C. A. 1975. The influence of food abundance on territory size in the iguanid lizard *Sceloporus jarrovi*. Ecology, 56: 993–998.

Stamps, J. A., and S. Tanaka. 1981. The relationship between food and social behavior in juvenile lizards (*Anolis aeneus*). Copeia, 1981: 422–434.

Stephens, D. W., and J. R. Krebs. 1986. Foraging Theory. Princeton Univ. Press, Princeton, New Jersey. 256 pages.

Turner, F. B., P. Hayden, B. L. Burge, and J. B. Roberson. 1986. Egg production by the desert tortoise (*Gopherus agassizii*) in California. Herpetologica, 42: 93–104.

Warwick, C. 1990. Reptilian ethology in captivity: observations on some problems and an evaluation of their aetiology. Appl. Anim. Behav. Sci., 26: 1–13.

Wiley, G. O. 1930. Notes on the Neotropical rattlesnake (*Crotalus terrificus basiliscus*) in captivity. Bull. Antivenin Inst. Amer., 3: 100–103.

Appendix

During the preparation of this chapter, we surveyed four herpetological journals over the period 1980–1990, tabulating all reports that dealt directly or indirectly with reproduction in reptiles. The journals were: *Bulletin of the Chicago Herpetological Society*, *Copeia*, *Herpetologica*, and *Journal of Herpetology*. We present here the entire bibliography, exclusive of those papers already cited in our chapter. The enormous diversity of approaches taken to the study of reptilian reproduction is clearly illustrated by these references, as is the explosive quantity of relevant publications during the past decade. We hope this bibliography will facilitate the efforts of colleagues who are working in this general area.

Abts, M. L. 1988. Reproduction in the saxicolous desert lizard, *Sauromalus obesus*: the female reproductive cycle. Copeia, 1988: 382–393.

—. 1988. Reproduction in the saxicolous desert lizard, *Sauromalus obesus*: the male reproductive cycle. Herpetologica, 44: 404–415.

Ackerman, R. A. 1981. Growth and gas exchange of embryonic sea turtles (*Chelonia*, *Caretta*). Copeia, 1981: 757–765.

Ackerman, R. A., R. C. Seagrave, R. Dmi'el, and A. Ar. 1985. Water and heat exchange between parchment-shelled reptile eggs and their surroundings. Copeia, 1985: 703–711.

Adams, C. S., and W. E. Cooper, Jr. 1988. Oviductal morphology and sperm storage in the keeled earless lizard, *Holbrookia propinqua*. Herpetologica, 44: 190–197.

Aldridge, R. D. 1982. The ovarian cycle of the watersnake *Nerodia sipedon*, and effects of hypophysectomy and gonadotropin administration. Herpetologica, 38: 71–79.

Allen, R. F., and J. F. Lhotka, Jr. 1982. *Crotalus atrox*: notes on the gastric wall. Copeia, 1982: 198–200.

Andrén, C. 1982. The role of the vomeronasal organs in the reproductive behavior of the adder *Vipera berus*. Copeia, 1982: 148–157.

Andrews, R. M. 1982. Spatial variation in egg mortality of the lizard *Anolis limifrons*. Herpetologica, 38: 165–171.

—. 1985. Mate choice by females of the lizard, *Anolis carolinensis*. Jour. Herpetol., 19: 284–289.

—. 1985. Oviposition frequency of *Anolis carolinensis*. Copeia, 1985: 259–262.

Andrews, R. M., S. J. Stahl, and P. F. Nicoletto. 1989. Intrapopulational variation in age of sexual maturity of the tropical lizard *Anolis limifrons* in Panama. Copeia, 1989: 751–753.

Antonio, F. B. 1980. Mating behavior and reproduction of the eyelash viper (*Bothrops schlegeli*) in captivity. Herpetologica, 36: 231–233.

Astheimer, L. B., S. C. Manolis, and C. R. Grau. 1989. Egg formation in crocodiles: avian affinities in yolk deposition. Copeia, 1981: 221–224.

Baker, R. E., and J. C. Gillingham. 1983. An analysis of courtship behavior in Blanding's turtle, *Emydoidea blandingi*. Herpetologica, 39: 166–173.

Bakhuis, W. L. 1982. Size and sexual differentiation in the lizard *Iguana iguana* on a semi-arid island. Jour. Herpetol., 16: 322–325.

Ballinger, R. E., and T. G. Hipp. 1985. Hematological variations in the collared lizard, *Crotaphytus collaris* (Sauria: Iguanidae). Copeia, 1985: 782–784.

—. 1985. Reproduction in the collared lizard, *Crotaphytus collaris*, in west central Texas. Copeia, 1985: 976–980.

Ballinger, R. E., and D. J. Ketels. 1983. Male reproductive cycle of the lizard *Sceloporus virgatus*. Jour. Herpetol., 17: 99–102.

Ballinger, R. E., and J. W. Nietfeldt. 1989. Ontogenetic stages of reproductive maturity in the viviparous lizard, *Sceloporus jarrovi* (Iguanidae). Jour. Herpetol., 23: 282–292.

Barbault, R., and Y.-P. Mou. 1988. Population dynamics of the common wall lizard, *Podarcis muralis*, in southwestern France. Herpetologica, 44: 38–47.

Barrett, S. L. 1990. Home range and habitat of the desert tortoise (*Xerobates agassizi*) in the Picacho Mountains of Arizona. Herpetologica, 46: 202–206.

Barten, S. L. 1980. The consumption of turtle eggs by a western hognose snake, *Heterodon nasicus*: a field observation. Bull. Chicago Herpetol. Soc., 15: 97–98.

—. 1986. Egg retention in captive snakes. Bull. Chicago Herpetol. Soc., 21: 65–71.

Bartlett, R. D. 1981. Notes on the captive reproduction of Storr's monitor, *Varanus storri*. Bull. Chicago Herpetol. Soc., 16: 65–66.

—. 1984. Notes on the captive propagation of the Australian lizard *Tiliqua s. scincoides*. Bull. Chicago Herpetol. Soc., 19: 33–34.

Bauer, A. M. 1989. Extracranial endolymphatic sacs in *Eurydactylodes* (Reptilia: Gekkonidae), with comments on endolymphatic function in lizards. Jour. Herpetol., 23: 172–175.

Bauwens, D. 1981. Survivorship during hibernation in the European common lizard, *Lacerta vivipara*. Copeia, 1981: 741–744.

Bauwens, D., R. V. Damme, and R. F. Verheyen. 1989. Synchronization of spring molting with the onset of mating behavior in male lizards, *Lacerta vivipara*. Jour. Herpetol., 23: 89–91.

Bauwens, D., and R. F. Verheyen. 1985. The timing of reproduction in the lizard *Lacerta vivipara*: differences between individual females. Jour. Herpetol., 19: 353–364.

Beal, A. M., and G. J. W. Webb. 1989. Effect of incubation temperature on tooth eruption in embryos of *Crocodylus johnstoni*. Copeia, 1989: 325–331.

Beardsley, H., and S. Barten. 1983. A note on reproduction in a captive born indigo snake, *Drymarchon corais couperi*. Bull. Chicago Herpetol. Soc., 18: 15–18.

Beck, D. D. 1990. Ecology and behavior of the Gila monster in southwestern Utah. Jour. Herpetol., 24: 54–68.

Bels, V. L. 1986. Analysis of the display-action-pattern of *Anolis chlorocyanus* (Sauria: Iguanidae). Copeia, 1986: 963–970.

—. 1987. Observation of the courtship and mating behavior in the snake *Hydrodynastes gigas*. Jour. Herpetol., 21: 350–352.

Berry, K. H. 1986. Desert tortoise (*Gopherus agassizii*) relocation: implications of social behavior and movements. Herpetologica, 42: 113–125.

Best, T. L., and A. L. Gennaro. 1984. Feeding ecology of the lizard, *Uta stansburiana*, in southeastern New Mexico. Jour. Herpetol., 18: 291–301.

Beuchat, C. A. 1986. Reproductive influences on the thermoregulatory behavior of a live-bearing lizard. Copeia, 1986: 971–979.

Bickler, P. E., and K. A. Nagy. 1980. Effects of parietalectomy on energy expenditure in free ranging lizards. Copeia, 1980: 923–925.

Bissinger, B. E., and C. A. Simon. 1981. The chemical detection of conspecifics by juvenile Yarrow's spring lizard, *Sceloporus jarrovi*. Jour. Herpetol., 15: 77–81.

Bjorndal, K. A. 1980. Demography of the breeding population of the green turtle, *Chelonia mydas*, at Tortuguero, Costa Rica. Copeia, 1980: 525–530.

—. 1985. Nutritional ecology of sea turtles. Copeia, 1985: 736–751.

Bjorndal, K. A., and A. Carr. 1989. Variation in clutch size and egg size in the green turtle nesting population at Tortuguero, Costa Rica. Herpetologica, 45: 181–189.

Blair, K. D. 1987. Sex determination in snakes. Bull. Chicago Herpetol. Soc., 22: 150.

Blem, C. R. 1982. Biennial reproduction in snakes: an alternative hypothesis. Copeia, 1982: 961–963.

—. 1987. Development of combat rituals in captive cottonmouths. Jour. Herpetol., 21: 64–65.

Bock, B. C., and G. F. McCracken. 1988. Genetic structure and variability in the green iguana (*Iguana iguana*). Jour. Herpetol., 22: 316–322.

Bock, B. C., and A. S. Rand. 1989. Factors influencing nesting synchrony and hatching success at a green iguana nesting aggregation in Panama. Copeia, 1989: 978–986.

Bock, B. C., A. S. Rand, and G. M. Burghardt. 1989. Nesting season movements of female green iguanas (*Iguana iguana*) in Panama. Copeia, 1989: 214–216.

Bona-Gallo, A., and P. Licht. 1983. Effects of temperature on sexual receptivity and ovarian recrudescence in the garter snake, *Thamnophis sirtalis parietalis*. Herpetologica, 39: 173–182.

Breitenbach, G. L., J. D. Congdon, and R. C. van Loben Sels. 1984. Winter temperatures of *Chrysemys picta* nests in Michigan: effects on hatchling survival. Herpetologica, 40: 76–81.

Brewster, C. M. 1985. Wood turtle, *Clemmys insculpta*, research in northern Wisconsin. Bull. Chicago Herpetol. Soc., 20: 13–20.

Brewster, K. N. 1981. Observing the courtship of the American alligator, *Alligator mississippiensis*. Bull. Chicago Herpetol. Soc., 16: 53–58.

Brewster, K. N. 1983. Behavioral notes on *Alligator mississippiensis* and *Caiman crocodilus*. Bull. Chicago Herpetol. Soc., 18: 7–11.

—., and C. M. Brewster. 1988. Notes on aggression and courtship in the wood turtle, *Clemmys insculpta*. Bull. Chicago Herpetol. Soc., 23: 144.

Brown, C. W. 1990. The significance of the south Atlantic equatorial counter current to the ecology of the green turtle breeding population of Ascension Island. Jour. Herpetol., 24: 81–84.

Brown, W. S. 1984. Background information for the protection of the timber rattlesnake in New York state. Bull. Chicago Herpetol. Soc., 19: 94–97.

Brown, W. S., and F. M. MacLean. 1983. Conspecific scent-trailing by newborn timber rattlesnakes, *Crotalus horridus*. Herpetologica, 39: 430–436.

Brown, W. S., D. W. Pyle, K. R. Greene, and J. B. Friedlaender. 1982. Movements and temperature relationships of timber rattlesnakes (*Crotalus horridus*) in northeastern New York. Jour. Herpetol., 16: 151–161.

Bull, C. M. 1987. A population study of the viviparous Australian lizard, *Trachydosaurus rugosus* (Scincidae). Copeia, 1987: 749–757.

Bull, J. J., J. M. Legler, and R. C. Vogt. 1985. Non-temperature dependent sex determination in two suborders of turtles. Copeia, 1985: 784–786.

Burchfield, P. M. 1982. Additions to the natural history of the crotaline snake *Agkistrodon bilineatus taylori*. Jour. Herpetol., 16: 376–382.

Burchfield, P. M., T. F. Beimler, and C. S. Doucette. 1982. An unusual precoital head-biting behavior in the Texas patch-nosed snake, *Salvadora grahamiae lineata* (Reptilia: Serpentes: Colubridae). Copeia, 1982: 192–193.

Burger, J. 1990. Effects of incubation temperature on behavior of young black racers (*Coluber constrictor*) and king snakes (*Lampropeltis getulus*). Jour. Herpetol., 24: 158–163.

Burger, J., and R. T. Zappalorti. 1986. Nest site selection by pine snakes, *Pituophis melanoleucus*, in the New Jersey Pine Barrens. Copeia, 1986: 116–121.

—. 1988. Habitat use in free-ranging pine snakes, *Pituophis melanoleucus*, in New Jersey Pine Barrens. Herpetologica, 44: 48–55.

—. 1989. Habitat use by pine snakes (*Pituophis melanoleucus*) in the New Jersey Pine Barrens: individual and sexual variations. Jour. Herpetol., 23: 68–73.

Camazini, B., W. Garstka, and D. Crews. 1981. Techniques for gonadectomizing snakes (*Thamnophis*). Copeia, 1981: 884–886.

Camilleri, C., and R. Shine. 1990. Sexual dimorphism and dietary divergence: differences in trophic morphology between male and female snakes. Copeia, 1990: 649–658.

Campbell, J. A., E. D. Brodie, Jr., D. G. Barker, and A. H. Price. 1989. An apparent natural hybrid rattlesnake and *Crotalus willardi* (Viperidae) from the Peloncillo Mountains of southwestern New Mexico. Herpetologica, 45: 344–349.

Case, S. M., and E. E. Williams. 1984. Study of a contact zone in the *Anolis distichus* complex in the central Dominican Republic. Herpetologica, 40: 118–137.

Castanet, J., D. G. Newman, and H. Saint-Girons. 1988. Skeletochronological data on the growth, age, and population structure of the tuatara, *Sphenodon punctatus*, on Stephens and Lady Alice Islands, New Zealand. Herpetologica, 44: 25–37.

Castilla, A. M., and D. Bauwens. 1990. Reproductive and fat body cycles of the lizard, *Lacerta lepida*, in central Spain. Jour. Herpetol., 24: 261–266.

Cebula, J. J., and M. Redmer. 1988. Observations on the reproduction of *Storeria dekayi* in DuPage County, Illinois. Bull. Chicago Herpetol. Soc., 23: 29.

Chan, E. 1989. White spot development, incubation and hatching success of leatherback turtle (*Dermochelys coriacea*) eggs from Rantau Abang, Malaysia. Copeia, 1989: 42–47.

Charland, M. B., and P. T. Gregory. 1990. The influence of female reproductive status on thermoregulation in a viviparous snake, *Crotalus viridis*. Copeia, 1990: 1089–1098.

Chase, J. D., K. R. Dixon, J. E. Gates, D. Jacobs, and G. J. Taylor. 1989. Habitat characteristics, population size, and home range of the bog turtle, *Clemmys muhlenbergii*, in Maryland. Jour. Herpetol., 23: 356–362.

Chondropoulos, B. P., and J. J. Lykakis. 1983. Ecology of the Balkan wall lizard, *Podarcis taurica ionica* (Sauria: Lacertidae) from Greece. Copeia, 1983: 991–1001.

Choo, B. L., and L. M. Chou. 1987. Effect of temperature on the incubation period and hatchability of *Trionyx sinensis* Wiegmann eggs. Jour. Herpetol., 21: 230–232.

Christens, E. 1990. Nest emergence lag in loggerhead sea turtles. Jour. Herpetol., 24: 400–402.

Christens, E., and J. R. Bider. 1987. Nesting activity and hatching success of the painted turtle (*Chrysemys picta marginata*) in southwestern Quebec. Herpetologica, 43: 55–65.

Christian, K. A., C. R. Tracy, and W. P. Porter. 1986. The effect of cold exposure during incubation of *Sceloporus undulatus* eggs. Copeia, 1986: 1012–1014.

Christian, K. A., and S. Waldschmidt. 1984. The relationship between lizard home range and body size: a reanalysis of the data. Herpetologica, 40: 68–75.

Chua, T. H. 1988. Nesting population and frequency of visits in *Dermochelys coriacea* in Malaysia. Jour. Herpetol., 22: 192–207.

Chua, T. H., and J. I. Furtado. 1988. Nesting frequency and clutch size in *Dermochelys coriacea* in Malaysia. Jour. Herpetol., 22: 208–218.

Cinquini-Janeiro, T. R. F., and E. C. Farias. 1988. The occurrence of twins in *Bothrops jacaraca* (Serpentes, Viperidae, Crotalinae). Bull. Chicago Herpetol. Soc., 23: 106.

Cintra, R. 1988. Nesting ecology of the Paraguayan caiman (*Caiman yacare*) in the Brazilian Pantanal. Jour. Herpetol., 22: 219–222.

—. 1989. Maternal care and daily pattern of behavior in a family of caimans, *Caiman yacare* in the Brazilian Pantanal. Jour. Herpetol., 23: 320–322.

Congdon, J. D., G. L. Breitenbach, R. C. van Loben Sels, and D. W. Tinkle. 1987. Reproduction and nesting ecology of snapping turtles (*Chelydra serpentina*) in southeastern Michigan. Herpetologica, 43: 39–54.

Congdon, J. D., and R. E. Gatten, Jr. 1989. Movements and energetics of nesting *Chrysemys picta*. Herpetologica, 45: 94–100.

Congdon, J. D., and J. W. Gibbons. 1983. Relationships of reproductive characteristics to body size in *Pseudemys scripta*. Herpetologica, 39: 147–151.

—. 1985. Egg components and reproductive characteristics of turtles: relationships to body size. Herpetologica, 41: 194–205.

—. 1989. Posthatching yolk reserves in hatchling American alligators. Herpetologica, 45: 305–309.

Congdon, J. D., and D. W. Tinkle. 1982. Reproductive energetics of the painted turtle (*Chrysemys picta*). Herpetologica, 38: 228–237.

Congdon, J. D., D. W. Tinkle, G. L. Breitenbach, R. C. Van Loben Sels. 1983. Nesting ecology and hatching success in the turtle *Emydoidea blandingi*. Herpetologica, 39: 417–429.

Congdon, J. D., D. W. Tinkle, and P. C. Rosen. 1983. Egg components and utilization during development in aquatic turtles. Copeia, 1983: 264–268.

Cooper, W. E., Jr. 1986. Chromatic components of female secondary sexual coloration: influence on social behavior of male keeled earless lizards (*Holbrookia propinqua*). Copeia, 1986: 980–986.

Cooper, W. E., Jr., C. Caffrey, and L. J. Vitt. 1985. Aggregation in the banded gecko, *Coleonyx variegatus*. Herpetologica, 41: 342–350.

—. 1985. Diel activity patterns in the banded gecko, *Coleonyx variegatus*. Jour. Herpetol., 19: 308–311.

Cooper, W. E., Jr., and R. F. Clarke. 1982. Steroidal induction of female reproductive coloration in the keeled earless lizard, *Holbrookia propinqua*. Herpetologica, 38: 425–429.

Cooper, W. E., Jr., W. R. Garstka, and L. J. Vitt. 1986. Female sex pheromone in the lizard *Eumeces laticeps*. Herpetologica, 42: 361–366.

Cooper, W. E., Jr., M. T. Mendonça, and L. J. Vitt. 1987. Induction of orange head coloration and activation of courtship and aggression by testosterone in the male broad-headed skink (*Eumeces laticeps*). Jour. Herpetol., 21: 96–101.

Cooper, W. E., Jr., and L. J. Vitt. 1985. Responses of the skinks, *Eumeces fasciatus* and *E. laticeps*, to airborne conspecific odors: further appraisal. Jour. Herpetol., 19: 481–486.

—. 1987. Intraspecific and interspecific aggression in lizards of the scincid genus *Eumeces*: chemical detection of conspecific sexual competitors. Herpetologica, 43: 7–14.

—. 1988. Orange head coloration of the male broad-headed skink (*Eumeces laticeps*), a sexually selected social cue. Copeia, 1988: 1–6.

Corn, P. S., and R. B. Bury. 1986. Morphological variation and zoogeography of racers (*Coluber constrictor*) in the central Rocky Mountains. Herpetologica, 42: 258-264.

Cox, M. J. 1989. Notes on the natural history (breeding) of *Naja kaouthia* and *Python molurus bivittatus* in Thailand. Bull. Chicago Herpetol. Soc., 24: 127–128.

Cox, W. A., M. C. Nowak, and K. R. Marion. 1980. Observations on courtship and mating behavior in the musk turtle, *Sternotherus minor*. Jour. Herpetol., 14: 200–204.

Crabtree, C. B., and R. W. Murphy. 1984. Analysis of maternal-offspring allozymes in *Crotalus viridis*. Jour. Herpetol., 18: 75–80.

Crowell-Comuzzie, D. K., and D. W. Owens. 1990. A quantitative analysis of courtship behavior in captive green sea turtles (*Chelonia mydas*). Herpetologica, 46: 195–202.

Czechura, G. V. 1981. The rare scincid lizard, *Nannoscincus graciloides*: a reappraisal. Jour. Herpetol., 15: 315–320.

Dalrymple, G. H., J. C. Hampp, and D. J. Wellins. 1985. Male-biased sex ratio in a cold nest of a hawksbill sea turtle (*Eretmochelys imbricata*). Jour. Herpetol., 19: 158–159.

Davis, J. 1980. The times of mating and oviposition of the western fence lizard, *Sceloporus occidentalis occidentalis*. Jour. Herpetol., 14: 102.

Davis, J., and R. G. Ford. 1983. Home range in the western fence lizard (*Sceloporus occidentalis occidentalis*). Copeia, 1983: 933–940.

Deitz, D. C., and T. C. Hines. 1980. Alligator nesting in north-central Florida. Copeia, 1980: 249–258.

Dellinger, T., and G. von Hegel. 1990. Sex identification through cloacal probing in juvenile marine iguanas (*Amblyrhynchus cristatus*). Jour. Herpetol., 24: 424–426.

Demeter, B. J., and D. L. Marcellini. 1981. Courtship and agressive behavior of the streak lizard (*Gonatodes vittatus*) in captivity. Herpetologica, 37: 250–256.

Deslippe, R. J., R. M'Closkey, S. P. Dajczak, and C. P. Szpak. 1990. A quantitative study of the social behavior of tree lizards, *Urosaurus ornatus*. Jour. Herpetol., 24: 337–341.

—. 1990. Female tree lizards: oviposition and activity patterns during the breeding season. Copeia, 1990: 877–880.

Dial, B. E. 1987. Energetics and performance during nest emergence and the hatchling frenzy in loggerhead sea turtles (*Caretta caretta*). Herpetologica, 43: 307–315.

Diemer, J. E. 1986. The ecology and management of the

gopher tortoise in the southeastern United States. Herpetologica, 42: 125–133.

Diller, L. V., and R. L. Wallace. 1984. Reproductive biology of the northern Pacific rattlesnake (*Crotalus viridis oreganus*) in northern Idaho. Herpetologica, 40: 182–193.

Dloogatch, M. A., and T. A. Zaremba. 1981. Captive propagation of the scarlet king snake, *Lampropeltis triangulum elapsoides*. Bull. Chicago Herpetol. Soc., 16: 81–85.

Dodd, C. K. 1989. Secondary sex ratio variation among populations of the flattened musk turtle, *Sternotherus depressus*. Copeia, 1989: 1041–1045.

—. 1985. Conserving sea turtles: constructive criticism is still needed. Herpetologica, 41: 103–111.

Doroff, A. M., and L. B. Keith. 1990. Demography and ecology of an ornate box turtle (*Terrapene ornata*) population in south-central Wisconsin. Copeia, 1990: 387–399.

Drajeske, P. W. 1983. Husbandry and captive reproduction of the mata mata, *Chelus fimbriatus* (Schneider). Bull. Chicago Herpetol. Soc., 18: 73–81.

Droge, D. L., S. M. Jones, and R. E. Ballinger. 1982. Reproduction of *Holbrookia maculata* in western Nebraska. Copeia, 1982: 356–362.

Drummond, H. 1983. Adaptiveness of island nest-sites of green iguanas and slider turtles. Copeia, 1983: 529–530.

Drummond, H., and G. M. Burghardt. 1983. Nocturnal and diurnal nest emergence in green iguanas. Jour. Herpetol., 17: 290–292.

Duda, P. L., and V. K. Gupta. 1981. Studies on the yolk nucleus of some freshwater turtles. Bull. Chicago Herpetol. Soc., 16: 12–17.

Dugan, B. A., A. S. Rand, G. M. Burghardt, and B. C. Bock. 1981. Interactions between nesting crocodiles and iguanas. Jour. Herpetol., 15: 409–414.

Dunham, A. E. 1982. Demographic and life-history variation among populations of the iguanid lizard *Urosaurus ornatus*: implications for the study of life-history phenomena in lizards. Herpetologica, 38: 208–221.

Dunlap, K. D., and J. W. Lang. 1990. Offspring sex ratio varies with maternal size in the common garter snake, *Thamnophis sirtalis*. Copeia, 1990: 568–570.

Dunson, W. A., and E. O. Moll. 1980. Osmoregulation in sea water of hatchling emydid turtles, *Callagur borneoensis*, from a Malaysian sea beach. Jour. Herpetol., 14: 31–36.

Duvall, D., R. Herskowitz, and J. Trupiano-Duvall. 1980. Responses of five-lined skinks (*Eumeces fasciatus*) and ground skinks (*Scincella lateralis*) to conspecific and interspecific chemical cues. Jour. Herpetol., 14: 121–127.

Eckert, K. L. 1987. Environmental unpredictability and leatherback sea turtle (*Dermochelys coriacea*) nest loss. Herpetologica, 43: 315–323.

—. 1990. Twinning in leatherback sea turtle (*Dermochelys coriacea*) embryos. Jour. Herpetol., 24: 317–320.

Eckert, K. L., and S. A. Eckert. 1988. Pre-reproductive movements of leatherback sea turtles (*Dermochelys coriacea*) nesting in the Carribean. Copeia, 1988: 400–406.

Eckert, K. L., S. A. Eckert, T. W. Adams, and A. D. Tucker. 1989. Inter-nesting migrations by leatherback sea turtles (*Dermochelys coriacea*) in the West Indies. Herpetologica, 45: 190–194.

Eckert, S. A., D. W. Nellis, K. L. Eckert, and G. L. Kooyman. 1986. Diving patterns of two leatherback sea turtles (*Dermochelys coriacea*) during internesting intervals at Sandy Point, St. Croix, U. S. Virgin Islands. Herpetologica, 42: 381-388.

Ellis, T. M. 1980. *Caiman crocodilus*: an established exotic in south Florida. Copeia, 1980: 152–154.

Erasmus, H., and W. R. Branch. 1983. Egg retention in the South African blind snake *Typhlops bibronii*. Jour. Herpetol., 17: 97–99.

Erdelen, W. 1988. Population dynamics and dispersal in three species of agamid lizards in Sri Lanka: *Calotes calotes*, *C. versicolor* and *C. nigrilabris*. Jour. Herpetol., 22: 42–52.

Ernst, C. H. 1982. Environmental temperature and activities in wild spotted turtles, *Clemmys guttata*. Jour. Herpetol., 16: 112–120.

—. 1986. Ecology of the turtle, *Sternotherus odoratus*, in southeastern Pennsylvania. Jour. Herpetol., 20: 341–352.

—. 1986. Environmental temperatures and activities in the wood turtle, *Clemmys insculpta*. Jour. Herpetol., 20: 222–229.

Estrada-Flores, E., M. Villagrán-Santa Cruz, F. R. Méndez-de la Cruz, and G. Casas-Andreu. 1990. Gonadal changes throughout the reproductive cycle of the viviparous lizard *Sceloporus mucronatus* (Sauria: Iguanidae). Herpetologica, 46: 43–50.

Etchberger, C. R., and L. M. Ehrhart. 1987. The reproductive biology of the female loggerhead musk turtle, *Sternotherus minor minor*, from the southern part of its range in central Florida. Herpetologica, 43: 66–73.

Etheridge, K., L. C. Wit, and J. C. Sellers. 1983. Hibernation in the lizard *Cnemidophorus sexlineatus* (Lacertilia: Teiidae). Copeia, 1983: 206–214.

Etheridge, K., L. C. Wit, J. C. Sellers, and S. E. Trauth. 1986. Seasonal changes in reproductive condition and energy stores in *Cnemidophorus sexlineatus*. Jour. Herpetol., 20: 554–559.

Ferguson, G. W., and H. L. Snell. 1986. Endogenous control of seasonal change of egg, hatchling, and clutch size of the lizard *Sceloporus undulatus garmani*. Herpetologica, 42: 185–191.

Ferguson, G. W., H. L. Snell, and A. J. Landwer. 1990. Proximate control of variation of clutch, egg, and body size in a west-Texas population of *Uta stansburiana stejnegeri* (Sauria: Iguanidae). Herpetologica, 46: 227–238.

Fitch, H. S., and D. M. Hillis. 1984. The *Anolis* dewlap: interspecific variability and morphological associations with habitat. Copeia, 1984: 315–323.

Fleishman, L. J. 1988. The social behavior of *Anolis auratus*, a grass anole from Panama. Jour. Herpetol., 22: 13–23.

Fogleman, B., W. Byrd, and E. Hanebrink. 1986. Observations of the male combat dance in the cottonmouth (*Agkistrodon piscivorous*). Bull. Chicago Herpetol. Soc., 21: 26–28.

Ford, N. B. 1982. Species specificity of sex pheromone trails of sympatric and allopatric garter snakes (*Thamnophis*). Copeia, 1982: 10–13.

Ford, N. B., and D. W. Killebrew. 1983. Reproductive tactics and female body size in Butler's garter snake, *Thamnophis butleri*. Jour. Herpetol., 17: 271–275.

Ford, N. B., and M. L. O'Bleness. 1986. Species and sexual specificity of pheromone trails of the garter snake, *Thamnophis marcianus*. Jour. Herpetol., 20: 259–262.

Ford, N. B., and C. W. Schofield. 1984. Species specificity of sex pheromone trails in the plains garter snake, *Thamnophis radix*. Herpetologica, 40: 51–55.

Ford, N. B., and R. A. Seigel. 1989. Relationships among body size, clutch size, and egg size in three species of oviparous snakes. Herpetologica, 45: 75–83.

Fowler, M. E. 1984. Husbandry, stress and disease as limiting factors in the captive propagation of reptiles: an overview. Bull. Chicago Herpetol. Soc., 19: 3–6.

Fowler de Neira, L. E., and J. H. Roe. 1984. Emergence success of tortoise nests and the effect of feral burros on nest success on Volcan Alcedo, Galapagos. Copeia, 1984: 702–707.

Frankenberg, E. 1984. Interactions between two species of colonizing house geckos, *Hemidactylus turcicus* and *Hemidactylus garnotii*. Jour. Herpetol., 18: 1–7.

Franz, R., and D. F. Gicca. 1982. Observations on the Haitian snake *Antillophis parvifrons alleni*. Jour. Herpetol., 16: 419–421.

Frazer, N. B. 1983. Effect of tidal cycles on loggerhead sea turtles (*Caretta caretta*) emerging from the sea. Copeia, 1983: 516–519.

—. 1983. Survivorship of adult female loggerhead sea turtles, *Caretta caretta*, nesting on Little Cumberland Island, Georgia, U.S.A. Herpetologica, 39: 436–447.

—. 1984. A model for assessing mean age-specific fecundity in sea turtle populations. Herpetologica, 40: 281–291.

—. 1986. Survival from egg to adulthood in a declining population of loggerhead turtles, *Caretta caretta*. Herpetologica, 42: 47–55.

Frazer, N. B., and L. M. Ehrhart. 1985. Preliminary growth models for green, *Chelonia mydas*, and loggerhead, *Caretta caretta*, turtles in the wild. Copeia, 1985: 73–79.

Frazer, N. B., J. W. Gibbons, and T. J. Owens. 1990. Turtle trapping: preliminary tests of conventional wisdom. Copeia, 1990: 1150–1152.

Frazer, N. B., and J. I. Richardson. 1985. Annual variation in clutch size and frequency for loggerhead turtles, *Caretta caretta*, nesting at Little Cumberland Island, Georgia, U.S.A. Herpetologica, 41: 246–251.

—. 1985. Seasonal variation in clutch size for loggerhead sea turtles, *Caretta caretta*, nesting on Little Cumberland Island, Georgia, USA. Copeia, 1985: 1083–1085.

—. 1986. The relationship of clutch size and frequency to body size in loggerhead turtles, *Caretta caretta*. Jour. Herpetol., 20: 81–84.

Frazier, J. 1985. A review of *in vivo* labels for studies of age determination and growth in amphibians and reptiles. Herpetologica, 41: 222–227.

—. 1985. Tetracycline as an *in vivo* label in bones of green turtles, *Chelonia mydas* (L.). Herpetologica, 41: 228–234.

Freed, P. 1989. Delayed fertilization in the African egg eating snake, *Dasypeltis scabra*, including a brief bibliography of delayed fertilization in other species of snakes. Bull. Chicago Herpetol. Soc., 24: 239–240.

Fritts, T. H. 1981. Marine turtles of the Galapagos Islands and adjacent areas of the eastern Pacific on the basis of observations made by J. R. Slevin, 1905–1906. Jour. Herpetol., 15: 293–301.

Fritts, T. H., and W. Hoffman. 1982. Diurnal nesting of marine turtles in southern Brevard County, Florida. Jour. Herpetol., 16: 84–86.

Frye, F. L. 1984. Psex and the psingle *Pseudemys*. Bull. Chicago Herpetol. Soc., 19: 7–19.

Galbraith, D. A., R. J. Brooks, and M. E. Obbard. 1989. The influence of growth rate on age and body size at maturity in female snapping turtles (*Chelydra serpentina*). Copeia, 1989: 896–904.

Gannon, V. P., and D. M. Secoy. 1984. Growth and reproductive rates of a northern population of the prairie rattlesnake, *Crotalus v. viridis*. Jour. Herpetol., 18: 13–19.

Gans, C., J. C. Gillingham, and D. L. Clark. 1984. Courtship, mating and male combat in tuatara, *Sphenodon punctatus*. Jour. Herpetol., 18: 194–197.

Ganzhorn, D., and P. Licht. 1983. Regulation of seasonal gonadal cycles by temperature in the painted turtle, *Chrysemys picta*. Copeia, 1983: 347–358.

Garnett, S. T., G. M. Crowley, and N. Goudberg. 1985. Observations of non-nesting emergence by green turtles in the Gulf of Carpentaria. Copeia, 1985: 262–264.

Garstka, W. R., and D. Crews. 1985. Mate preferences in garter snakes. Herpetologica, 41: 9–19.

Gasith, A., and I. Sidis. 1982. Lung disorder as a possible explanation for the non-swimming behavior observed in aquatic turtles. Copeia, 1982: 200–201.

—. 1985. Sexual activity in the terrapin, *Mauremys caspica rivulata*, in Israel, in relation to the testicular cycle and climatic factors. Jour. Herpetol., 19: 254–260.

Geffen, E., and H. Mendelssohn. 1988. Home range use and seasonal movements of the Egyptian tortoise (*Testudo kleinmanni*) in the northwestern Negev, Israel. Herpetologica, 44: 354–359.

Georges, A. 1982. Diet of the Australian freshwater turtle *Emydura krefftii* (Chelonia: Chelidae), in an unproductive lentic environment. Copeia, 1982: 331–336.

—. 1988. Sex determination is independent of incubation temperature in another chelid turtle, *Chelodina longicollis*. Copeia, 1988: 248–254.

Gibbons, J. R. H. 1981. The biogeography of *Brachylophus* (Iguanidae) including the description of a new species, *B. vitiensis*, from Fiji. Jour. Herpetol., 15: 255–273.

Gibbons, J. W. 1982. Reproductive patterns in freshwater turtles. Herpetologica, 38: 222–227.

—. 1983. Reproductive characteristics and ecology of the mud turtle, *Kinosternon subrubrum* (Lacépède). Herpetologica, 39: 254–271.

—. 1986. Movement patterns among turtle populations: applicability to management of the desert tortoise. Herpetologica, 42: 104–113.

Gibbons, J. W., J. L. Greene, and J. D. Congdon. 1983.

Drought-related responses of aquatic turtle populations. Jour. Herpetol., 17: 242–246.

Gibbons, J. W., J. L. Greene, and K. K. Patterson. 1982. Variation in reproductive characteristics of aquatic turtles. Copeia, 1982: 776–784.

Gillingham, J. C. 1980. Communication and combat behavior of the black rat snake (*Elaphe obsoleta*). Herpetologica, 36: 120–127.

Gillingham, J. C., and J. A. Chambers. 1982. Courtship and pelvic spur use in the Burmese python, *Python molurus bivittatus*. Copeia, 1982: 193–196.

Gist, D. H., J. A. Michaelson, and J. M. Jones. 1990. Autumn mating in the painted turtle, *Chrysemys picta*. Herpetologica, 46: 331–336.

Glinski, T. H., and C. O. Krekorian. 1985. Individual recognition in free-living adult male desert iguanas, *Dipsosaurus dorsalis*. Jour. Herpetol., 19: 541–544.

Goldberg, S. R. 1989. A hermaphroditic western fence lizard, *Sceloporus occidentalis* (Iguanidae). Copeia, 1989: 486–488.

Gorman, G. C., P. Licht, and F. McCollum. 1981. Annual reproductive patterns in three species of marine snakes from the central Philippines. Jour. Herpetol., 15: 335–354.

Grassman, M. A., and D. W. Owens. 1982. Development and extinction of food preferences in the loggerhead sea turtle, *Caretta caretta*. Copeia, 1982: 965–969.

Gravelle, K., and C. A. Simon. 1980. Field observations on the use of the tongue-Jacobson's organ system in two iguanid lizards, *Sceloporus jarrovi* and *Anolis trinitatis*. Copeia, 1980: 356–359.

Graves, B. M. 1989. Defensive behavior of female prairie rattlesnakes (*Crotalus viridis*) changes after parturation. Copeia, 1989: 791–794.

Graves, B. M., and D. Duvall. 1987. An experimental study of aggregation and thermo-regulation in prairie rattlesnakes (*Crotalus viridis viridis*). Herpetologica, 43: 259–264.

—. 1990. Spring emergence patterns of wandering garter snakes and prairie rattlesnakes in Wyoming. Jour. Herpetol., 24: 351–356.

Green, D. 1984. Long-distance movements of Galapagos green turtles. Jour. Herpetol., 18: 121–130.

Greenberg, N., and L. Hake. 1990. Hatching and neonatal behavior of the lizard, *Anolis carolinensis*. Jour. Herpetol., 24: 402–405.

Greer, A. E. 1985. The relationships of the lizard genera *Anelytropsis* and *Dibamus*. Jour. Herpetol., 19: 116–156.

—. 1986. On the absence of visceral fat bodies within a major lineage of scincid lizards. Jour. Herpetol., 20: 267–269.

Griffith, H. 1990. Miniaturization and elongation in *Eumeces* (Sauria: Scincidae). Copeia, 1990: 751–758.

Groves, J. D. 1982. Egg-eating behavior of brooding fine-lined skinks, *Eumeces fasciatus*. Copeia, 1982: 969–971.

Guillette, L. J., Jr. 1981. On the occurrence of oviparous and viviparous forms of the Mexican lizard *Sceloporus aeneus*. Herpetologica, 37: 11–15.

—. 1982. The evolution of viviparity and placentation in the high elevation, Mexican lizard *Sceloporus aeneus*. Herpetologica, 38: 94–103.

—. 1983. Notes concerning reproduction of the montane skink, *Eumeces copei*. Jour. Herpetol., 17: 144–148.

Guillette, L. J., Jr., and G. Casas-Andreu. 1980. Fall reproductive activity in the high altitude Mexican lizard, *Sceloporus grammicus microlepidotus*. Jour. Herpetol., 14: 143–147.

—. 1981. Seasonal variation in fat body weights of the Mexican high elevation lizard *Sceloporus grammicus microlepidotus*. Jour. Herpetol., 15: 366.

—. 1987. The reproductive biology of the high elevation Mexican lizard, *Barisia imbricata*. Herpetologica, 43: 29–38.

Guillette, L. J., Jr., and G. L. Gongora. 1986. Notes on oviposition and nesting in the high elevation lizard, *Sceloporus aeneus*. Copeia, 1986: 232–233.

Guillette, L. J., Jr., C. A. Herman, and D. A. Dickey. 1988. Synthesis of prostaglandins by tissues of the viviparous lizard, *Sceloporus jarrovi*. Jour. Herpetol., 22: 180–185.

Guillette, L. J., Jr., and R. E. Jones. 1982. Further observations on arginine vasotocin-induced oviposition and parturition in lizards. Jour. Herpetol., 16: 140–144.

Guillette, L. J., Jr., R. E. Jones, K. T. Fitzgerald, and H. M. Smith. 1980. Evolution of viviparity in the lizard genus *Sceloporus*. Herpetologica, 36: 201–215.

Guillette, L. J., Jr., M. S. Rand, V. DeMarco, and K. Etheridge. 1988. Fixative and alcohol-induced weight change in eggs from the lizard, *Sceloporus undulatus*. Jour. Herpetol., 22: 115–118.

Guillette, L. J., Jr., and W. P. Sullivan. 1985. The reproductive and fat body cycles of the lizard, *Sceloporus formosus*. Jour. Herpetol., 19: 474–480.

Guillette, L. J. Jr., J. Weigel, and G. Flater. 1983. Unilateral testicular pigmentation in the Mexican lizard *Sceloporus variabilis*. Copeia, 1983: 155–161.

Gupta, V. K., and P. L. Duda. 1981. Deviant oogonia and oocytes in the ovaries of immature turtles. Bull. Chicago Herpetol. Soc., 16: 70–71.

Gutzke, W. H. N., and G. C. Packard. 1987. The influence of temperature on eggs and hatchlings of Blanding's turtles, *Emydoidea blandingii*. Jour. Herpetol., 21: 161–163.

Gutzke, W. H. N., G. C. Packard, M. J. Packard, and T. J. Boardman. 1987. Influence of the hydric and thermal environments on eggs and hatchlings of painted turtles (*Chrysemys picta*). Herpetologica, 43: 393–404.

Gutzke, W. H. N., and G. L. Paukstis. 1984. A low threshold temperature for sexual differentiation in the painted turtle, *Chrysemys picta*. Copeia, 1984: 546–547.

Gutzke, W. H. N., G. L. Paukstis, and L. L. McDaniel. 1985. Skewed sex ratios for adult and hatchling bullsnakes, *Pituophis melanoleucus*, in Nebraska. Copeia, 1985: 649–652.

Gutzke, W. H. N., G. L. Paukstis, and G. C. Packard. 1984. Pipping versus hatching as indices of time of incubation in reptiles. Jour. Herpetol., 18: 494–496.

Hall, P. M. 1985. Embryo growth curves as a method of determining the age of clutches of New Guinea crocodiles (*Crocodylus novaeguineae*). Jour. Herpetol., 19: 538–541.

Hall, P. M., and D. R. Johnson. 1987. Nesting biology of

Crocodylus novaeguineae in Lake Murray District, Papua, New Guinea. Herpetologica, 43: 249–258.

Halliday, T. R., and P. A. Verrell. 1988. Body size and age in amphibians and reptiles. Jour. Herpetol., 22: 253–265.

Hammock, M. W. 1984. Reproduction and breeding behavior in captive black pine snakes. Bull. Chicago Herpetol. Soc., 19: 125–130.

Harding, J. H. 1981. Observations on the African helmeted turtle, *Pelomedusa subrufa*, in captivity, with comments on breeding behavior. Bull. Chicago Herpetol. Soc., 16: 86–89.

Harding, J. H., and M. A. Ewert. 1989. Notes on reproductive behavior in captive *Phrynops gibbus*. Bull. Chicago Herpetol. Soc., 24: 48–49.

Harlow, P., and G. Grigg. 1984. Shivering thermogenesis in a brooding diamond python, *Python spilotes spilotes*. Copeia, 1984: 959–965.

Hasegawa, M. 1984. Biennial reproduction in the lizard *Eumeces okadae* on Miyake-Jima, Japan. Herpetologica, 40: 194–199.

—. 1985. Effect of brooding on egg mortality in the lizard *Eumeces okadae* on Miyake-Jima, Izu Islands, Japan. Copeia, 1985: 497–500.

Hayes, F. E., K. R. Beaman, W. K. Hayes, and L. E. Harris, Jr. 1988. Defensive behavior in the Galapagos tortoise (*Geochelone elephantopus*), with comments on the evolution of insular gigantism. Herpetologica, 44: 11–17.

Hayes, W. K. 1986. Observations of courtship in the rattlesnake, *Crotalus viridis oreganus*. Jour. Herpetol., 20: 246–249.

Hazlett, B. A. 1980. Temporal patterns of the assertion display of the lizard *Iguana iguana*. Herpetologica, 36: 221–224.

Henle, K. 1990. Population ecology and life history of three terrestrial geckos in arid Australia. Copeia, 1990: 759–781.

Herron, J. C., L. H. Emmons, and J. E. Cadle. 1990. Observations on reproduction in the black caiman, *Melanosuchus niger*. Jour. Herpetol., 24: 314–316.

Ho, S. M., S. Kleis, R. McPherson, G. J. Heisermann, and I. P. Callard. 1982. Regulation of vitellogenesis in reptiles. Herpetologica, 38: 40–50.

Hotaling, E. C., D. C. Wilhoft, and S. B. McDowell. 1985. Egg position and weight of hatchling snapping turtles, *Chelydra serpentina*, in natural nests. Jour. Herpetol., 19: 534–536.

Hover, E. L. 1985. Differences in aggressive behavior between two throat color morphs in a lizard, *Urosaurus ornatus*. Copeia, 1985: 933–940.

How, R. A., J. Dell, and B. D. Wellington. 1986. Comparative biology of eight species of *Diplodactylus* gecko in Western Australia. Herpetologica, 42: 471–482.

Hunt, R. H. 1987. Nest excavation and neonate transport in wild *Alligator mississippiensis*. Jour. Herpetol., 21: 348–350.

Hunt, R. H., and M. E. Watanabe. 1982. Observations on maternal behavior of the American alligator, *Alligator mississippiensis*. Jour. Herpetol., 16: 235–239.

Ineich, I., and A. S. Gardner. 1989. Qualitative analysis of the development of endolymphatic sacs by a gecko (*Lepidodactylus lugubris*) in French Polynesia. Jour. Herpetol., 23: 414–418.

Iverson, J. B. 1985. Geographic variation in sexual dimorphism in the mud turtle *Kinosternon hirtipes*. Copeia, 1985: 388–393.

—. 1986. Notes on the natural history of the Oaxaca mud turtle, *Kinosternon oaxacae*. Jour. Herpetol., 20: 119–123.

—. 1990. Sex ratios in snakes: a cautionary note. Copeia, 1990: 571–573.

Jackson, D. R., and R. Franz. 1981. Ecology of the eastern coral snake (*Micrurus fulvius*) in northern peninsular Florida. Herpetologica, 37: 213–228.

Jacob, J. S., and C. W. Painter. 1980. Overwinter thermal ecology of *Crotalus viridis* in the north-central plains of New Mexico. Copeia, 1980: 799–805.

Jaksic, F. M., and K. Schwenk. 1983. Natural history observations on *Liolaemus magellanicus*, the southernmost lizard in the world. Herpetologica, 39: 457–461.

Jameson, E. W., Jr., A. A. Heusner, and D. Lem. 1980. Seasonal, sexual, and altitudinal variations in stomach content and ingested fat in *Sceloporus occidentalis*. Jour. Herpetol., 14: 255–261.

Janeiro-Cinquini, T. R. F., F. F. Leinz, and M. M. Ishizuka. 1990. Body size-litter size relationships and some characteristics of litters in *Bothrops jararaca*. Bull. Chicago Herpetol. Soc., 25: 84–85.

Janzen, F. J., and S. O'Steen. 1989. An instance of male combat in the common snapping turtle (*Chelydra serpentina*). Bull. Chicago Herpetol. Soc., 25: 11.

Jenssen, T. A. 1981. Unusual display behavior by *Anolis grahami* from western Jamaica. Copeia, 1981: 728–733.

Jenssen, T. A., and R. M. Andrews. 1984. Seasonal growth rates in the Jamaican lizard, *Anolis opalinus*. Jour. Herpetol., 18: 338–341.

Jenssen, T. A., and N. L. Gladson. 1984. A comparative display analysis of the *Anolis brevirostris* complex in Haiti. Jour. Herpetol., 18: 217–230.

Jenssen, T. A., D. L. Marcellini, and E. P. Smith. 1988. Seasonal micro-distribution of sympatric *Anolis* lizards in Haiti. Jour. Herpetol., 22: 266–274.

Johnsen, P. B., and J. L. Wellington. 1982. Detection of glandular secretions by yearling alligators. Copeia, 1982: 705–708.

Johnson, K. A. 1983. The decline of the spotted turtle, *Clemmys guttata*, in northeastern Illinois. Bull. Chicago Herpetol. Soc., 18: 37–41.

Johnson, L. F., and J. S. Jacob. 1984. Pituitary activity and reproductive cycle of male *Cnemidophorus sexlineatus* in west Tennessee. Jour. Herpetol., 18: 396–405.

Johnson, L. F., J. S. Jacob, and P. Torrance. 1982. Annual testicular and androgenic cycles of the cottonmouth (*Agkistrodon piscivorus*) in Alabama. Herpetologica, 38: 16–25.

Jones, K. B. 1983. Movement patterns and foraging ecology of Gila monsters (*Heloderma suspectum* Cope) in northwestern Arizona. Herpetologica, 39: 247–253.

Jones, R. E., T. Swain, L. J. Guillette, Jr., and K. T. Fitzgerald. 1982. The comparative anatomy of lizard ovaries, with emphasis on the number of germinal beds. Jour. Herpetol., 16: 240–252.

Jones, S. M., and D. L. Droge. 1980. Home range size and spatial distributions of two sympatric lizard species (*Sceloporus undulatus, Holbrookia maculata*) in the sand hills of Nebraska. Herpetologica, 36: 127–132.

Judd, F. W., and J. C. McQueen. 1980. Incubation, hatching, and growth of the tortoise, *Gopherus berlandieri*. Jour. Herpetol., 14: 377–380.

Judd, F. W., and F. L. Rose. 1989. Egg production by the Texas tortoise, *Gopherus berlandieri*, in southern Texas. Copeia, 1989: 588–596.

Khan, M. S. 1989. Rediscovery and redescription of the highland ground gecko, *Tenuidactylus montiumsalsorum* (Annandale, 1913). Herpetologica, 45: 46–54.

Khan, M. S., and R. Tasnim. 1990. A new gecko of the genus *Tenuidactylus* from northeastern Punjab, Pakistan, and southwestern Azad Kashmir. Herpetologica, 46: 142–148.

King, D., and L. Rhodes. 1982. Sex ratio and breeding season of *Varanus acanthurus*. Copeia, 1982: 784–787.

King, R. B. 1986. Population ecology of the Lake Erie water snake, *Nerodia sipedon insularum*. Copeia, 1986: 757–772.

Kingsbury, B. A. 1989. Factors influencing activity in *Coleonyx variegatus*. Jour. Herpetol., 23: 399–404.

Kitchener, D. J., R. A. How, and J. Dell. 1988. Biology of *Oedura reticulata* and *Gehyra variegata* (Gekkonidae) in an isolated woodland of western Australia. Jour. Herpetol., 22: 401–402.

Kofron, C. P. 1983. Female reproductive cycle of the neotropical snail-eating snake *Sibon sanniola* in northern Yucatan, Mexico. Copeia, 1983: 963–969.

Kraemer, J. E., and R. Bell. 1980. Rain-induced mortality of eggs and hatchlings of loggerhead sea turtles (*Caretta caretta*) on the Georgia coast. Herpetologica, 36: 72–77.

Kraemer, J. E., and S. H. Bennett. 1981. Utilization of posthatching yolk in loggerhead sea turtles, *Caretta caretta*. Copeia, 1981: 406–411.

Kramer, M., and U. Fritz. 1989. Courtship of the turtle, *Pseudemys nelsoni*. Jour. Herpetol., 23: 84–86.

Krekorian, C. O'N. 1984. Life history of the desert iguana, *Dipsosaurus dorsalis*. Herpetologica, 40: 415–424.

Krohmer, R. W. 1989. Reproductive physiology and behavior of a gynandromorph red-sided garter snake, *Thamnophis sirtalis parietalis*, from central Manitoba, Canada. Copeia, 1989: 1064–1068.

Krohmer, R. W., and R. D. Aldridge. 1985. Female reproductive cycle of the lined snake (*Tropidoclonion lineatum*). Herpetologica, 41: 39–44.

—. 1985. Male reproductive cycle of the lined snake (*Tropidoclonion lineatum*). Herpetologica, 41: 33–38.

Kronen, D. 1980. Notes on the eggs and hatchlings of the longnose snake, *Rhinocheilus lecontei*, including the occurrence of a semi-striped pattern. Bull. Chicago Herpetol. Soc., 15: 54–56.

Kuchling, G. 1989. Assessment of ovarian follicles and oviductal eggs by ultra-sound scanning in live freshwater turtles, *Chelodina oblonga*. Herpetologica, 45: 89–94.

Kushlan, J. A. 1981. Egg cache of a Galapagos gecko. Jour. Herpetol., 15: 121–122.

Kushlan, J. A., and T. Jacobsen. 1990. Environmental variability and the reproductive success of Everglades alligators. Jour. Herpetol., 24: 176–184.

Kushlan, J. A., and M. S. Kushlan. 1980. Everglades alligator nests: nesting sites for marsh reptiles. Copeia, 1980: 930–932.

—. 1980. Function of nest attendance in the American alligator. Herpetologica, 36: 27–32.

Kushlan, J. A., and F. J. Mazzotti. 1989. Population biology of the American crocodile. Jour. Herpetol., 23: 7–21.

Kushlan, J. A., and J. C. Simon. 1981. Egg manipulation by the American alligator. Jour. Herpetol., 15: 451–454.

Kwiat, G. A., and D. H. Gist. 1987. Annual reproductive cycle of an introduced population of European wall lizards (*Podarcis muralis*) in Ohio. Jour. Herpetol., 21: 205–209.

Lamb, T., and J. Congdon. 1985. Ash content: relationships to flexible and rigid eggshell types of turtles. Jour. Herpetol., 19: 527–530.

Landers, J. L., J. A. Garner, and W. A. McRae. 1980. Reproduction of gopher tortoises (*Gopherus polyphemus*) in southwestern Georgia. Herpetologica, 36: 353–361.

Langerwerf, B. A. W. A. 1984. Captive maintenance and breeding of the Oman lizard *Lacerta jayakari* Boulenger. Bull. Chicago Herpetol. Soc., 19: 35–39.

Lazell, J. D., Jr. 1980. New England waters: critical habitat for marine turtles. Copeia, 1980: 290–295.

—. 1981. Predation on diamondback terrapin (*Malaclemys terrapin*) eggs by dunegrass (*Ammophila breviligulata*). Copeia, 1981: 723–724.

Lederer, G. 1987. An additional contribution to the ethology of the sail lizard (*Hydrosaurus amboinensis* Schloss.). Bull. Chicago Herpetol. Soc., 22: 152.

Lee, J. C., D. Clayton, S. Eisenstein, and I. Perez. 1989. The reproductive cycle of *Anolis sagrei* in southern Florida. Copeia, 1989: 930–937.

Leuck, B. E. 1982. Comparative burrow use and activity patterns of parthenogenetic and bisexual whiptail lizards (*Cnemidophorus*: Teiidae). Copeia, 1982: 416–424.

—. 1985. Comparative social behavior of bisexual and unisexual whiptail lizards (*Cnemidophorus*). Jour. Herpetol., 19: 492–506.

Leuck, B. E., K. W. Hughes, and H. Y. Cheng. 1990. Social displays of experimentally paired dwarf geckos (*Sphaerodactylus clenchi*). Jour. Herpetol., 24: 416–418.

Levell, J. P. 1985. Some observations on the mating behavior of *Terrapene carolina triunguis* in captivity. Bull. Chicago Herpetol. Soc., 20: 40–41.

Lewis, A. R. 1986. Body size and growth in two populations of the Puerto Rican ground lizard (Teiidae). Jour. Herpetol., 20: 190–195.

Lewis, A. R., and J. E. Saliva. 1987. Effects of sex and size on home range, dominance, and activity budgets in *Ameiva exsul* (Lacertilia: Teiidae). Herpetologica, 43: 374–383.

Licht, P. 1982. Endocrine patterns in the reproductive cycle of turtles. Herpetologica, 38: 51–61.

Lieberman, A. 1980. Nesting of the basilisk lizard (*Basiliscus basiliscus*). Jour. Herpetol., 14: 103–105.

Lilley, T. 1984. Captive care and breeding of Jackson's chameleons *Chamaeleo jacksonii*. Bull. Chicago Herpetol. Soc., 19: 65–68.

Lillywhite, H. B. 1985. Trailing movements and sexual behavior in *Coluber constrictor*. Jour. Herpetol., 19: 306–308.

Limpus, C. J. 1980. Observations on the hawksbill turtle (*Eretmochelys imbricata*) nesting along the Great Barrier Reef. Herpetologica, 36: 265–271.

Limpus, C. J., and D. G. Walker. 1980. The growth of immature green turtles (*Chelonia mydas*) under natural conditions. Herpetologica, 36: 162–165.

Lin, J.-Y. 1982. Sperm retention in the lizard *Chamaeleo hoehnelii*. Copeia, 1982: 488–489.

Lin, J.-Y., and K.-H. Lu. 1982. Population ecology of the lizard *Japalura swinhonis formosensis* (Sauria: Agamidae) in Taiwan. Copeia, 1982: 425–434.

Linck, M. H., J. A. De Pari, B. O. Butler, and T. E. Graham. 1989. Nesting behavior of the turtle, *Emydoidea blandingi*, in Massachusetts. Jour. Herpetol., 23: 442–444.

Long, D. R. 1985. Lipid utilization during reproduction in female *Kinosternon flavescens*. Herpetologica, 41: 58–65.

Losos, J. B. 1985. An experimental demonstration of the species-recognition role of *Anolis* dewlap color. Copeia, 1985: 905–910.

Loumbourdis, N. S. 1987. Lipid storage and utilization in the lizard *Agama stellio stellio*. Jour. Herpetol., 21: 237–239.

Lovich, J. 1988. Aggressive basking behavior in eastern painted turtles (*Chrysemys picta picta*). Herpetologica, 44: 197–202.

Lovich, J. E., W. R. Garstka, and W. E. Cooper, Jr. 1990. Female participation in courtship behavior of the turtle *Trachemys s. scripta*. Jour. Herpetol., 24: 422–424.

Lund, P. F. 1985. Hawksbill turtle (*Eretmochelys imbricata*) nesting on the east coast of Florida. Jour. Herpetol., 19: 164–166.

Lutz, P. L., and A. Dunbar-Cooper. 1984. The nest environment of the American crocodile (*Crocodylus acutus*). Copeia, 1984: 153–161.

Macartney, J. M. 1989. Diet of the Northern Pacific rattlesnake, *Crotalus viridis oreganus*, in British Columbia. Herpetologica, 45: 299–304.

Macartney, J. M., and P. T. Gregory. 1988. Reproductive biology of female rattlesnakes (*Crotalus viridis*) in British Columbia. Copeia, 1988: 47–57.

Macartney, J. M., P. T. Gregory, and M. B. Charland. 1990. Growth and sexual maturity of the western rattlesnake, *Crotalus viridis*, in British Columbia. Copeia, 1990: 528–542.

Macartney, J. M., P. T. Gregory, and K. W. Larsen. 1988. A tabular survey of data on movements and home ranges of snakes. Jour. Herpetol., 22: 61–73.

Madsen, T. 1984. Movements, home range size and habitat use of radio-tracked grass snakes (*Natrix natrix*) in southern Sweden. Copeia, 1984: 707–713.

Madsen, T., and M. Osterkamp. 1982. Notes on the biology of the fish-eating snake *Lycodonomorphus bicolor* in Lake Tanganyika. Jour. Herpetol., 16: 185–188.

Magnusson, W. E. 1980. Hatching and creche formation by *Crocodylus porosus*. Copeia, 1980: 359–362.

—. 1982. Mortality of eggs of the crocodile *Crocodylus porosus* in northern Australia. Jour. Herpetol., 16: 121–130.

—. 1987. Reproductive cycles of teiid lizards in Amazonian Savanna. Jour. Herpetol., 21: 307–316.

Magnusson, W. E., L. J. De Paiva, R. M. Da Rocha, C. R. Franke, L. A. Kasper, and A. P. Lima. 1985. The correlates of foraging mode in a community of Brazilian lizards. Herpetologica, 41: 324–332.

Magnusson, W. E., and A. P. Lima. 1984. Perennial communal nesting by *Kentropyx calcaratus*. Jour. Herpetol., 18: 73–75.

Magnusson, W. E., A. P. Lima, J. M. Hero, T. M. Sanaiotti, and M. Yamakoshi. 1990. *Paleosuchus trigonatus* nests: sources of heat and embryo sex ratios. Jour. Herpetol., 24: 397–400.

Magnusson, W. E., A. P. Lima, and R. M. Sampaio. 1985. Sources of heat for nests of *Paleosuchus trigonatus* and a review of crocodilian nest temperatures. Jour. Herpetol., 19: 199–207.

Magnusson, W. E., and J. A. Taylor. 1981. Growth of juvenile *Crocodylus porosus* as effected by season of hatching. Jour. Herpetol., 15: 242–245.

—. 1982. Wallows of *Crocodylus porosus* as dry season refuges in swamps. Copeia, 1982: 478–480.

Malone, D. R. 1982. Captive care and breeding of the ball python. Bull. Chicago Herpetol. Soc., 17: 96–98.

Maloney, J. E., C. Darian-Smith, Y. Takahashi, and C. J. Limpus. 1990. The environment for development of the embryonic loggerhead turtle (*Caretta caretta*) in Queensland. Copeia, 1990: 378–387.

Marquet, P. A., F. Bozinovic, R. G. Medel, Y. L. Werner, and F. M. Jaksic. 1990. Ecology of *Garthia gaudichaudi*, a gecko endemic to the semiarid region of Chile. Jour. Herpetol., 24: 431–434.

Martin, D. L. 1984. An instance of sexual defense in the cottonmouth, *Agkistrodon piscivorus*. Copeia, 1984: 772–774.

Matz, G. 1985. *Tupinambis* Daudin (Teiidae). Bull. Chicago Herpetol. Soc., 20: 105–106.

Mautz, W. J. 1982. Observations on an oviposition site of the side blotched lizard, *Uta stansburiana*. Jour. Herpetol., 16: 331–332.

Mazzotti, F. J., B. Bohnsack, M. P. McMahon, and J. R. Wilcox. 1986. Field and laboratory observations on the effects of high temperature and salinity on hatchling *Crocodylus acutus*. Herpetologica, 42: 191–196.

McAllister, C. T. 1989. Eggs and hatchlings of the Texas spring lizard, *Sceloporus olivaceus* (Sauria: Iguanidae) from north-central Texas. Bull. Chicago Herpetol. Soc., 24: 79.

McBee, K., J. W. Sites, Jr., M. D. Engstrom, C. Rivero-

Blanco, and J. W. Bickham. 1984. Karyotypes of four species of neotropical gekkos. Jour. Herpetol., 18: 83–84.

McCoy, C. J., R. C. Vogt, and E. J. Censky. 1983. Temperature-controlled sex determination in the sea turtle *Lepidochelys olivacea*. Jour. Herpetol., 17: 404–406.

McGehee, M. A. 1990. Effects of moisture on eggs and hatchlings of loggerhead sea turtles (*Caretta caretta*). Herpetologica, 46: 251–258.

McKeown, S. 1984. Captive maintenance and propagation of Indian Ocean day geckos (genus *Phelsuma*). Bull. Chicago Herpetol. Soc., 19: 55–63.

McKinney, R. B., and K. R. Marion. 1985. Reproductive and fat body cycles in the male lizard, *Sceloporus undulatus*, from Alabama, with comparisons of geographic variation. Jour. Herpetol., 19: 208–217.

McPherson, R. J., and K. R. Marion. 1981. Seasonal testicular cycle of the stinkpot turtle (*Sternotherus odoratus*) in central Alabama. Herpetologica, 37: 33–40.

—. 1981. The reproductive biology of female *Sternotherus odoratus* in an Alabama population. Jour. Herpetol., 15: 389–396.

—. 1983. Reproductive variation between two populations of *Sternotherus odoratus* in the same geographic area. Jour. Herpetol., 17: 181–184.

McRae, W. A., T. L. Landers, and G. D. Cleveland. 1980. Sexual dimorphism in the gopher tortoise (*Gopherus polyphemus*). Herpetologica, 37: 46–52.

Méndez de la Cruz, F. R., L. J. Guillette, Jr., M. V. Santa Cruz, and G. Casas-Andreu. 1988. Reproductive and fat body cycles of the viviparous lizard, *Sceloporus mucronatus* (Sauria: Iguanidae). Jour. Herpetol., 22: 1–12.

Mendonça, M. T. 1987. Photothermal effects on the ovarian cycle of the musk turtle, *Sternotherus odoratus*. Herpetologica, 43: 82–90.

Mendonça, M. T., and L. M. Ehrhart. 1982. Activity, population size and structure of immature *Chelonia mydas* and *Caretta caretta* in Mosquito Lagoon, Florida. Copeia, 1982: 161–167.

Mendonça, M. T., and P. C. H. Pritchard. 1986. Offshore movements of post-nesting Kemp's ridley sea turtles (*Lepidochelys kempi*). Herpetologica, 42: 373–381.

Merritt, D. A., Jr. 1980. The wood turtle, *Clemmys insculpta* (LeConte): natural history, behavior, and food habits. Bull. Chicago Herpetol. Soc., 15: 6–9.

Meshaka, W. E., S. E. Trauth, and B. P. Butterfield. 1988. Natural nests, eggs, and hatchlings of the broad-headed skink, *Eumeces laticeps*, from northeastern Arkansas. Bull. Chicago Herpetol. Soc., 23: 104–105.

Meylan, A., and P. Meylan. 1985. Nesting of *Dermochelys coriacea* in Carribbean Panama. Jour. Herpetol., 19: 293–297.

Michaels, S. J. 1986. Husbandry and captive propagation of the light-phase Indian python, *Python molurus molurus*, with a report of a predominantly male clutch of offspring. Bull. Chicago Herpetol. Soc., 21: 53–64.

—. 1989. Some observations on multiple egg clutches and a case of delayed fertilization in a colony of captive Pueblan milk snakes, *Lampropeltis triangulum campbelli*. Bull. Chicago Herpetol. Soc., 24: 109–111.

Miller, M. J. 1980. The leopard gecko, *Eublepharis macularis* (Gray). Bull. Chicago Herpetol. Soc., 15: 10–15.

—. 1982. The South African ground gecko, *Chondrodactylus angulifer angulifer*, Peters 1870. Bull. Chicago Herpetol. Soc., 17: 46–50.

—. 1982. The Turkestan plate-tailed gecko, *Teratoscincus scincus* (Schlegel 1858). Bull. Chicago Herpetol. Soc., 17: 77–81.

—. 1984. Captive husbandry and propagation of geckos. Bull. Chicago Herpetol. Soc., 19: 41–54.

Mitchell, J. C. 1985. Female reproductive cycle and life history attributes in a Virginia population of painted turtles, *Chrysemys picta*. Jour. Herpetol., 19: 218–226.

—. 1985. Female reproductive cycle and life history attributes in a Virginia population of stinkpot turtles, *Sternotherus odoratus*. Copeia, 1985: 941–949.

—. 1985. Variation in the male reproductive cycle in a population of painted turtles, *Chrysemys picta*, from Virginia. Herpetologica, 41: 45–51.

—. 1985. Variation in the male reproductive cycle in a population of stinkpot turtles, *Sternotherus odoratus*, from Virginia. Copeia, 1985: 50–56.

Mitchell, J. C., and G. R. Zug. 1984. Spermatogenic cycle of *Nerodia taxispilota* (Serpentes: Colubridae) in southcentral Virginia. Herpetologica, 40: 200–204.

Mitchell, L. A. 1990. Reproduction of Gould's monitors (*Varanus gouldii*) at the Dallas Zoo. Bull. Chicago Herpetol. Soc., 25: 8–9.

Moehn, L. D. 1980. Microhabitat preference in the broad-headed skink. Bull. Chicago Herpetol. Soc., 15: 49–53.

Moll, D. 1983. A proposed origin of nesting location divergence and a shared feeding range in Brazilian green turtle populations. Copeia, 1983: 121–125.

Moll, E. O., K. E. Matson, and E. B. Krehbiel. 1981. Sexual and seasonal dichromatism in the Asian river turtle *Callagur borneoensis*. Herpetologica, 37: 181–194.

Montanucci, R. R. 1981. Habitat separation between *Phrynosoma douglassi* and *P. orbiculare* (Lacertilia: Iguanidae) in Mexico. Copeia, 1981: 147–153.

—. 1983. Natural hybridization between two species of collared lizards (*Crotaphytus*). Copeia, 1983: 1–11.

—. 1989. Maintenance and propagation of horned lizards (*Phrynosoma*) in captivity. Bull. Chicago Herpetol. Soc., 24: 229–238.

Montanucci, R. R., and B. E. Baur. 1982. Mating and courtship-related behaviors of the short-horned lizard, *Phrynosoma douglassi*. Copeia, 1982: 971–974.

Montgomery, W. B., and G. W. Schuett. 1989. Autumnal mating with subsequent production of offspring in the rattlesnake *Sistrurus miliarius streckeri*. Bull. Chicago Herpetol. Soc., 24: 205–207.

Mora B., J. M. 1987. Predation by *Loxocemus bicolor* on the eggs of *Ctenosaura similis* and *Iguana iguana*. Jour. Herpetol., 21: 334–335.

—. 1989. Eco-behavioral aspects of two communally nesting iguanines and the structure of their shared nesting burrows. Herpetologica, 45: 293–298.

Moritz, C., M. Adams, S. Donnellan, and P. Baverstock. 1990. The origin and evolution of parthenogenesis in *Heteronotia binoei* (Gekkonidae): genetic diversity among bisexual populations. Copeia, 1990: 333–348.

Morris, K. A., G. C. Packard, T. J. Boardman, G. L. Paukstis, and M. J. Packard. 1983. Effect of the hydric environment on growth of embryonic snapping turtles (*Chelydra serpentina*). Herpetologica, 39: 272–285.

Mortimer, J. A. 1990. The influence of beach sand characteristics on the nesting behavior and clutch survival of green turtles (*Chelonia mydas*). Copeia, 1990: 802–817.

Mortimer, J. A., and A. Carr. 1987. Reproduction and migrations of the Ascension Island green turtle (*Chelonia mydas*). Copeia, 1987: 103–113.

Mortimer, J. A., and K. M. Portier. 1989. Reproductive homing and internesting behavior of the green turtle (*Chelonia mydas*) at Ascension Island, South Atlantic Ocean. Copeia, 1989: 962–977.

Moskovits, D. K. 1988. Sexual dimorphism and population estimates of the two Amazonian tortoises (*Geochelone carbonaria* and *G. denticulata*) in northwestern Brazil. Herpetologica, 44: 209–217.

Mrosovsky, N. 1985. Conserving sea turtles: hatchet fails to crack carapace. Herpetologica, 41: 112–115.

Muddle, P. M. 1986. Flying geckos (*Ptychozoon* sp.) in the terrarium and in the greenhouse. Bull. Chicago Herpetol. Soc., 21: 47–48.

Muir, J. H. 1981. Two unusually large egg clutches from a corn snake, *Elaphe guttata guttata*. Bull. Chicago Herpetol. Soc., 16: 42–43.

—. 1984. Captive reproduction of the Uracoan rattlesnake, *Crotalus vegrandis*. Bull. Chicago Herpetol. Soc., 19: 131–133.

—. 1987. Notes on the husbandry and breeding of the mangrove snake, *Boiga dendrophila*. Bull. Chicago Herpetol. Soc., 22: 49–52.

Murphy, J. B., and D. G. Barker. 1980. Courtship and copulation of the Ottoman viper (*Vipera xanthina*) with special reference to use of the hemipenes. Herpetologica, 36: 165–170.

Murphy, J. B., J. E. Rehg, P. F. A. Maderson, and W. B. McCrady. 1987. Scutellation and pigmentation defects in a laboratory colony of western diamondback rattlesnakes (*Crotalus atrox*): mode of inheritance. Herpetologica, 43: 292–300.

Murphy, J. C. 1980. The lyre snakes. Bull. Chicago Herpetol. Soc., 15: 24–28.

—. 1986. Babiche: the crocodilian with many names. Bull. Chicago Herpetol. Soc., 21: 4–13.

—. 1988. An overview of the Asian file snakes, family Acrochordidae. Bull. Chicago Herpetol. Soc., 23: 1–4.

Murphy, R. W., and C. B. Crabtree. 1988. Genetic identification of a natural hybrid rattlesnake: *Crotalus scutulatus scutulatus* × *C. viridis viridis*. Herpetologica, 44: 119–123.

Muth, A., and J. J. Bull. 1981. Sex determination in desert iguanas: does incubation termperature make a difference? Copeia, 1981: 869–870.

Newman, D. G. 1987. Burrow use and population densities of tuatara (*Sphenodon punctatus*) and how they are influenced by fairy prions (*Pachyptila turtur*) on Stephens Island, New Zealand. Herpetologica, 43: 336–344.

Nicol, E. 1985. Breeding of *Chelodina novaeguineae* and *Chelodina longicollis*. Bull. Chicago Herpetol. Soc., 20: 29–34.

—. 1989. Twinning in three turtle species. Bull. Chicago Herpetol. Soc., 24: 129–130.

Nijs, J., and C. Navez. 1990. Delayed fertilization in the striped mud turtle, *Kinosternon baurii*. Bull. Chicago Herpetol. Soc., 25: 146.

Nilson, G. 1980. Male reproductive cycle of the European adder, *Vipera berus*, and its relation to annual activity periods. Copeia, 1980: 729–737.

Nuitja, I. N. S., and J. D. Lazell, Jr. 1982. Marine turtle nesting in Indonesia. Copeia, 1982: 708–710.

Nussbaum, R. A. 1980. The Brahminy blind snake (*Ramphotyphlops braminus*) in the Seychelles Archipelago: distribution, variation, and further evidence for parthenogenesis. Herpetologica, 36: 215–221.

Obbard, M. E., and R. J. Brooks. 1980. Nesting migrations of the snapping turtle (*Chelydra serpentina*). Herpetologica, 36: 158–162.

—. 1981. A radio-telemetry and mark-recapture study of activity in the common snapping turtle, *Chelydra serpentina*. Copeia, 1981: 630–637.

—. 1987. Prediction of the onset of the annual nesting season of the common snapping turtle, *Chelydra serpentina*. Herpetologica, 43: 324–328.

Olmo, E. 1984. Genomic composition of reptiles: evolutionary perspectives. Jour. Herpetol., 18: 20–32.

Ortega, A. 1986. Fat body cycles in a montane population of *Sceloporus grammicus*. Jour. Herpetol., 20: 104–108.

Ortega, A., S. Álvarez, P. Galina, and G. Arnaud. 1987. Mating of the San Lucan alligator lizard, *Gerrhonotus paucicarinatus*: an endemic Baja California lizard. Bull. Chicago Herpetol. Soc., 22: 71–72.

Ortega, A., and R. Barbault. 1984. Reproductive cycles in the mesquite lizard, *Sceloporus grammicus*. Jour. Herpetol., 18: 168–175.

—. 1986. Reproduction in the high elevation Mexican lizard *Sceloporus scalaris*. Jour. Herpetol., 20: 111–114.

Ortega, A., and A. Gutiérrez. 1986. Parturition of the Mexican lizard, *Sceloporus grammicus*: behavior of the gravid female and the newborn. Bull. Chicago Herpetol. Soc., 21: 23–25.

Ouboter, P. E., and L. M. R. Nanhoe. 1988. Habitat selection and migration of *Caiman crocodilus crocodilus* in a swamp and swamp-forest habitat in northern Suriname. Jour. Herpetol., 22: 283–294.

Owens, D. W., M. A. Grassman, and J. R. Hendrickson. 1982. The imprinting hypothesis and sea turtle reproduction. Herpetologica, 38: 124–135.

Owens, D. W., and Y. A. Morris. 1985. The comparative endocrinology of sea turtles. Copeia, 1985: 723–735.

Packard, G. C., and M. J. Packard. 1984. Effects of the hydric environment on metabolism of embryonic snapping turtles do not result from altered patterns of sexual differentiation. Copeia, 1984: 547–550.

—. 1987. Water relations and nitrogen excretion in embryos of the oviparous snake *Coluber constrictor*. Copeia, 1987: 395–406.

Packard, G. C., M. J. Packard, and G. F. Birchard. 1989. Sexual differentiation and hatching success by painted turtles incubating in different thermal and hydric environments. Herpetologica, 45: 385–392.

Packard, M. J., G. C. Packard, and T. J. Boardman. 1982. Structure of eggshells and water relations of reptilian eggs. Herpetologica, 38: 136–155.

Papiernik, M. W. 1988. Temperature-dependent sex determination in reptiles. Bull. Chicago Herpetol. Soc., 23: 137–144.

Parker, E. D., Jr., and R. K. Selander. 1984. Low clonal diversity in the parthenogenetic lizard *Cnemidophorus neomexicanus* (Sauria: Teiidae). Herpetologica, 40: 245-252.

Parmenter, C. J. 1983. Reproductive migration in the hawksbill turtle (*Eretmochelys imbricata*). Copeia, 1983: 271–273.

Patchell, F. C., and R. Shine. 1986. Food habits and reproductive biology of the Australian legless lizards (Pygopodidae). Copeia, 1986: 30–39.

Patterson, J. W. 1988. Liver glycogen levels in the tropical lizard *Mabuya striata*. Copeia, 1988: 1066–1067.

Paulissen, M. R., J. M. Walker, and J. E. Cordes. 1988. Ecology of syntopic clones of the parthenogenetic whiptail lizard, *Cnemidophorus 'laredoensis.'* Jour. Herpetol., 22: 331–342,

Pence, D. B., and K. W. Selcer. 1988. Effects of pentastome infection on reproduction in a southern Texas population of the Mediterranean gecko, *Hemidactylus turcicus*. Copeia, 1988: 565–572.

Pérez-Higareda, G., A. Rangel-Rangel, and H. M. Smith. 1989. The courtship and mating behavior of Morelet's crocodile (*Crocodylus moreleti*) in southern Veracruz, Mexico. Bull. Chicago Herpetol. Soc., 24: 131–132.

Perrill, S. A. 1980. Social communication in *Eumeces inexpectatus*. Jour. Herpetol., 14: 129–135.

Perry-Richardson, J. J., C. W. Schofield, and N. B. Ford. 1990. Courtship of the garter snake, *Thamnophis marcianus*, with a description of a female behavior for coitus interruption. Jour. Herpetol., 24: 76–78.

Peterson, K. H. 1989. Further comments on anecdotal data. Bull. Chicago Herpetol. Soc., 24: 190–191.

Petokas, P. J., and M. M. Alexander. 1980. The nesting of *Chelydra serpentina* in northern New York. Jour. Herpetol., 14: 239–244.

Phillips, J. A., A. Garel, G. C. Packard, and M. J. Packard. 1990. Influence of moisture and temperature on eggs and embryos of green iguanas (*Iguana iguana*). Herpetologica, 46: 238–245.

Pilorye, T. 1987. Density, size, structure, and reproductive characteristics of three populations of *Lacerta vivipara* (Sauria: Lacertidae). Herpetologica, 43: 345–356.

Plummer, M. V. 1981. Communal nesting of *Opheodrys aestivus* in the laboratory. Copeia, 1981: 243–246.

—. 1983. Annual variation in stored lipids and reproduction in green snakes (*Opheodrys aestivus*). Copeia, 1983: 741–745.

—. 1985. Demography of green snakes (*Opheodrys aestivus*). Herpetologica, 41: 373–381.

—. 1985. Growth and maturity in green snakes (*Opheodrys aestivus*). Herpetologica, 41: 28–33.

—. 1990. Nesting movements, nesting behavior, and nest sites of green snakes (*Opheodrys aestivus*) revealed by radiotelemetry. Herpetologica, 46: 190–195.

Plummer, M. V., and D. B. Farrar. 1981. Sexual dietary differences in a population of *Trionyx muticus*. Jour. Herpetol., 15: 175–179.

Plummer, M. V., and H. L. Snell. 1988. Nest site selection and water relations of eggs in the snake, *Opheodrys aestivus*. Copeia, 1988: 58–64.

Pluto, T. G., and E. D. Bellis. 1988. Seasonal and annual movements of riverine map turtles, *Graptemys geographica*. Jour. Herpetol., 22: 152–158.

Polis, G. A., and C. A. Myers. 1985. A survey of intraspecific predation among reptiles and amphibians. Jour. Herpetol., 19: 99–107.

Price, A. H., and J. L. La Pointe. 1981. Structure-functional aspects of the scent gland in *Lampropeltis getulus splendida*. Copeia, 1981: 138–146.

Pritchard, P. C. H. 1982. Nesting of the leatherback turtle, *Dermochelys coriacea*, in Pacific Mexico, with a new estimate of the world population status. Copeia, 1982: 741–747.

Punzo, F. 1982. Clutch and egg size in several species of lizards from the desert southwest. Jour. Herpetol., 16: 414–417.

Rand, A. S. 1982. Clutch and egg size in Brazilian iguanid lizards. Herpetologica, 38: 171–178.

Rand, A. S., and B. Dugan. 1980. Iguana egg mortality within the nest. Copeia, 1980: 531–534.

—. 1983. Structure of complex iguana nests. Copeia, 1983: 705–711.

Rao, R. J. 1986. Notes on the sexual cycle of female *Trionyx gangeticus* in central India. Jour. Herpetol., 20: 455–457.

Rao, R. J., and F. U. Shaad. 1985. Sexual cycle of the male freshwater turtle *Trionyx gangeticus* (Cuvier). Herpetologica, 41: 433–437.

Redmer, M. 1987. Notes on the courtship and mating behavior of the Central American wood turtle, *Rhinoclemmys pulcherrima incisa*. Bull. Chicago Herpetol. Soc., 22: 117–118.

—. 1987. Notes on the eggs and hatchlings of the smooth green snake, *Opheodrys vernalis*, in Dupage County, Illinois. Bull. Chicago Herpetol. Soc., 22: 149.

Reichenbach, N. G. 1983. An aggregation of female garter snakes under corrugated metal sheets. Jour. Herpetol., 17: 412–413.

Reichenbach, N. G., and G. H. Dalrymple. 1986. Energy use, life histories, and the evaluation of potential competition in two species of garter snake. Jour. Herpetol., 20: 133–153.

Reinert, H. K., and W. R. Kodrich. 1982. Movements and habitat utilization by the massasauga *Sistrurus catenatus catenatus*. Jour. Herpetol., 16: 162–171.

Reinert, H. K., and R. T. Zappalorti. 1988. Timber rattlesnakes (*Crotalus horridus*) of the Pine Barrens: their movement patterns and habitat preference. Copeia, 1988: 964–978.

Reznick, D., and O. Sexton. 1986. Annual variation of fecundity in *Sceloporus malachiticus*. Jour. Herpetol., 20: 457–459.

Reznick, D., O. J. Sexton, and C. Mantis. 1981. Initial prey preferences in the lizard *Sceloporus malachiticus*. Copeia, 1981: 681–686.

Rhodin, A. G. J., R. A. Mittermeier, and J. R. McMorris. 1984. *Platemys macrocephala*, a new species of chelid turtle from central Bolivia and the Pantanal region of Brazil. Herpetologica, 40: 38–46.

Rhodin, A. G. J., and R. C. Schoelkopf. 1982. Reproductive data on a female leatherback turtle, *Dermochelys coriacea*, stranded in New Jersey. Copeia, 1982: 181–183.

Robinson, C., and J. R. Bider. 1988. Nesting synchrony—a strategy to decrease predation of snapping turtle (*Chelydra serpentina*) nests. Jour. Herpetol., 22: 470–473.

Rodda, G. H. 1990. Highway madness revisited: roadkilled *Iguana iguana* in the Llanos of Venezuela. Jour. Herpetol., 24: 209–211.

Rose, B. 1982. Lizard home ranges: methodology and functions. Jour. Herpetol., 16: 253–269.

Ross, D. A., and R. K. Anderson. 1990. Habitat use, movements, and nesting of *Emydoidea blandingi* in central Wisconsin. Jour. Herpetol., 24: 6–12.

Ross, J. P. 1984. Adult sex ratio in the green sea turtle. Copeia, 1984: 774–776.

Ross, R. 1984. The husbandry of python egg incubation. Bull. Chicago Herpetol. Soc., 19: 25–26.

Ross, R. K., and F. W. Judd. 1982. Comparison of lipid cycles of *Holbrookia propinqua* from Padre Island and mainland Texas. Jour. Herpetol., 16: 53–60.

Rosskopf, W. J., R. W. Woerpel, and T. Lyndon. 1981. Egg yolk peritonitis in a Jackson's chameleon. Bull. Chicago Herpetol. Soc., 16: 100–101.

Routman, E. J., and A. C. Hulse. 1984. Ecology and reproduction of a parthenogenetic lizard, *Cnemidophorus sonorae*. Jour. Herpetol., 18: 381–386.

Ruby, D. E. 1984. Male breeding success and differential access to females in *Anolis carolinensis*. Herpetologica, 40: 272–280.

—. 1986. Selection of home range site by females of the lizard, *Sceloporus jarrovi*. Jour. Herpetol., 20: 466–469.

Ruby, D. E., and A. E. Dunham. 1984. A population analysis of the ovoviviparous lizard *Sceloporus jarrovi* in the Pinaleño Mountains of southeastern Arizona. Herpetologica, 40: 425–436.

Sabath, M. D. 1981. Gekkonid lizards of Guam, Mariana Islands: reproduction and habitat preference. Jour. Herpetol., 15: 71–75.

Sahl, D. N., and P. L. Duda. 1986. Morphological and ecological notes on *Scincella himalayanum* and *Mabuya dissimilis* from Kashmir, India. Bull. Chicago Herpetol. Soc., 21: 89–91.

Saint-Girons, H. 1982. Reproductive cycles of male snakes and their relationships with climate and female reproductive cycles. Herpetologica, 38: 5–16.

—. 1985. The *Sphenodon*: ecological features and some hypotheses concerning its evolution. Bull. Chicago Herpetol. Soc., 20: 48–51.

—. 1987. Diet and prey items of snakes. Bull. Chicago Herpetol. Soc., 22: 162–165.

—. 1990. Notes on ecology and population structure of the Laticaudinae (Serpents, Hydrophidae) in New Caledonia. Bull. Chicago Herpetol. Soc., 25: 197–209.

Sanders, J. S., and J. S. Jacob. 1981. Thermal ecology of the copperhead (*Agkistrodon contortrix*). Herpetologica, 37: 264–270.

Schafer, S. F., and C. O. Krekorian. 1983. Agonistic behavior of the Galapagos tortoise, *Geochelone elephantopus*, with emphasis on its relationship to saddle-backed shell shape. Herpetologica, 39: 448–456.

Schall, J. J. 1983. Small clutch size in a tropical whiptail lizard (*Cnemidophorus arubensis*). Jour. Herpetol., 17: 406–408.

Schall, J. J., and G. A. Sarni. 1987. Malarial parasitism and the behavior of the lizard, *Sceloporus occidentalis*. Copeia, 1987: 84–93.

Schamberger, M. L., and F. B. Turner, 1986. The application of habitat modeling to the desert tortoise (*Gopherus agassizii*). Herpetologica, 42: 134–138.

Scheidt, V. N. 1989. Basic colubrid breeding techniques. Bull. Chicago Herpetol. Soc., 19: 27–31.

Schivre, M. 1985. Observations on reproduction in *Python regius* (Shaw). Bull. Chicago Herpetol. Soc., 20: 58.

Schuett, G. W. 1982. A copperhead (*Agkistrodon contortrix*) brood produced from autumn copulations. Copeia, 1982: 700–702.

Schuett, G. W., and J. C. Gillingham. 1986. Sperm storage and multiple paternity in the copperhead, *Agkistrodon contortrix*. Copeia, 1986: 807–811.

Schwaner, T. D. 1989. A field study of thermoregulation in black tiger snakes (*Notechis ater niger*: Elapidae) on the Franklin Islands, South Australia. Herpetologica, 45: 393–401.

Schwaner, T. D., and S. D. Sarre. 1988. Body size of tiger snakes in southern Australia, with particular inference to *Notechis ater serventyi* (Elapidae) on Chappell Island. Jour. Herpetol., 22: 24–33.

Schwarzkopf, L., and R. J. Brooks. 1987. Nest-site selection and offspring sex ratio in painted turtles, *Chrysemys picta*. Copeia, 1987: 53–61.

Secor, S. M. 1987. Courtship and mating behavior of the speckled kingsnake, *Lampropeltis getulus holbrooki*. Herpetologica, 43: 15–28.

—. 1990. Reproductive and combat behavior of the Mexican king snake, *Lampropeltis mexicana*. Jour. Herpetol., 24: 217–221.

Seidel, M. E., and R. V. Lucchino. 1981. Allozymic and morphological variation among the musk turtles *Ster-*

notherus carinatus, *S. depressus* and *S. minor* (Kinosternidae). Copeia, 1981: 119–128.

Seigel, R. A. 1980. Courtship and mating behavior of the diamondback terrapin, *Malaclemys terrapin tequesta*. Jour. Herpetol., 14: 420–421.

Seigel, R. A., H. S. Fitch, and N. B. Ford. 1986. Variation in relative clutch mass in snakes among and within species. Herpetologica, 42: 179–185.

Selcer, K. W. 1986. Life history of a successful colonizer: the Mediterranean gecko, *Hemidactylus turcicus*, in southern Texas. Copeia, 1986: 956–962.

—. 1987. Season variation in fatbody and liver mass of the introduced Mediterranean gecko, *Hemidactylus turcicus*, in Texas. Jour. Herpetol., 21: 74–78.

—. 1990. Egg-size relationships in a lizard with fixed clutch size: variation in a population of the Mediterranean Gecko. Herpetologica, 46: 15-21.

Semlitsch, R. D., K. L. Brown, and J. P. Caldwell. 1981. Habitat utilization, seasonal activity, and population size structure of the southeastern crowned snake *Tantilla coronata*. Herpetologica, 37: 40–46.

Semlitsch, R. D., and J. W. Gibbons. 1982. Body size dimorphism and sexual selection in two species of water snakes. Copeia, 1982: 974–976.

Semlitsch, R. D., J. H. K. Pechmann, and J. W. Gibbons. 1988. Annual emergence of juvenile mud snakes (*Farancia abacura*) at aquatic habitats. Copeia, 1988: 243–245.

Serena, M. 1984. Distribution and habitats of parthenogenetic and sexual *Cnemidophorus lemniscatus* (Sauria: Teiidae) in Surinam. Copeia, 1984: 713–719.

Shen, L.-T., and H.-H. Li. 1987. Notes on the distribution and habits of the lizard *Shinisaurus crocodilurus* Ahl. Bull. Chicago Herpetol. Soc., 22: 4–5.

Shine, R. 1980. Comparative ecology of three Australian snake species of the genus *Cacophis* (Serpentes: Elapidae). Copeia, 1980: 831–838.

—. 1980. Ecology of eastern Australian whipsnakes of the genus *Demansia*. Jour. Herpetol., 14: 381–389.

—. 1980. Ecology of the Australian death adder *Acanthophis antarcticus* (Elapidae): evidence for convergence with the Viperidae. Herpetologica, 36: 281–289.

—. 1980. Reproduction, feeding, and growth in the Australian burrowing snake *Vermicella annulata*. Jour. Herpetol., 14: 71–77.

—. 1981. Ecology of Australian elapid snakes of the genera *Furina* and *Glyphodon*. Jour. Herpetol., 15: 219–224.

—. 1981. Venomous snakes in cold climates: ecology of the Australian genus *Drydalia* (Serpentes: Elapidae). Copeia, 1981: 14–25.

—. 1982. Ecology of the Australian elapid snake *Echiopsis curta*. Jour. Herpetol., 16: 388–393.

—. 1983. Arboreality in snakes: ecology of the Australian elapid genus *Hoplocephalus*. Copeia, 1983: 198–205.

—. 1983. Food habits and reproductive biology of Australian elapid snakes of the genus *Denisonia*. Jour. Herpetol., 17: 171–175.

—. 1983. Reptilian reproductive modes: the oviparity-viviparity continuum. Herpetologica, 39: 1–8.

—. 1984. Reproductive biology and food habits of the Australian elapid snakes of the genus *Cryptophis*. Jour. Herpetol., 18: 33–39.

—. 1986. Ecology of a low-energy specialist: food habits and reproductive biology of the Arafura filesnake (Acrochordidae). Copeia, 1986: 424–437.

—. 1986. Food habits, habitats and reproductive biology of four sympatric species of varanid lizards in tropical Australia. Herpetologica, 42: 346–360.

—. 1986. Natural history of two monotypic snake genera of southwestern Australia, *Elapognathus* and *Rhinoplocephalus* (Elapidae). Jour. Herpetol., 20: 436–439.

—. 1986. Predation upon filesnakes (*Acrochordus arafurae*) by aboriginal hunters: selectivity with respect to body size, sex and reproductive condition. Copeia, 1986: 238–239.

—. 1987. Ecological comparisons of island and mainland populations of Australian tigersnakes (*Notechis*: Elapidae). Herpetologica, 43: 233–240.

—. 1987. Ecological ramifications of prey size: food habits and reproductive biology of Australian copperhead snakes (*Austrelaps*, Elapidae). Jour. Herpetol., 21: 21–28.

—. 1987. Food habits and reproductive biology of Australian snakes of the genus *Hemiaspis* (Elapidae). Jour. Herpetol., 21: 71–74.

—. 1987. The evolution of viviparity: ecological correlates of reproductive mode within a genus of Australian snakes (Pseudechis: Elapidae). Copeia, 1987: 551–563.

—. 1988. Food habits and reproductive biology of small Australian snakes of the genera *Unechis* and *Suta* (Elapidae). Jour. Herpetol., 22: 307–315.

—. 1989. Constraints, allometry, and adaptation: food habits and reproductive biology of Australian brownsnakes (*Pseudonaja*: Elapidae). Herpetologica, 45: 195–207.

Shine, R., and N. Charles. 1982. Ecology of the Australian elapid snake *Tropidechis carinatus*. Jour. Herpetol., 16: 383–387.

Shine, R., and J. Covacevich. 1983. Ecology of the highly venomous snakes: the Australian genus *Oxyuranus* (Elapidae). Jour. Herpetol., 17: 60–69.

Shine, R., G. C. Grigg, T. G. Shine, and P. Harlow. 1981. Mating and male combat in Australian blacksnakes, *Pseudechis porphyriacus*. Jour. Herpetol., 15: 101–107.

Shine, R., and D. J. Slip. 1990. Biological aspects of the adaptive radiation of Australian pythons (Serpentes: Boidae). Herpetologica, 46: 283–290.

Shine, R., and J. K. Webb. 1990. Natural history of Australian typhlopid snakes. Jour. Herpetol., 24: 357–363.

Shoop, C. R., C. A. Ruckdeschel, and N. B. Thompson. 1985. Sea turtles in the southeast United States: nesting activity as derived from aerial and ground surveys, 1982. Herpetologica, 41: 252–259.

Sigmund, W. R. 1983. Female preference for *Anolis carolinensis* males as a function of dewlap color and background coloration. Jour. Herpetol., 17: 137–143.

Simbotwe, M. P. 1980. Reproductive biology of the skinks *Mabuya striata* and *Mabuya quinquetaeniata* in Zambia. Herpetologica, 36: 99–104.

Simon, C. A., and G. A. Middendorf. 1980. Spacing in juvenile lizards (*Sceloporus jarrovi*). Copeia, 1980: 141–146.

Slip, D. J., and R. Shine. 1988. The reproductive biology and mating system of diamond pythons, *Morelia spilota* (Serpentes: Boidae). Herpetologica, 44: 396–404.

—. 1988. Thermoregulation of free-ranging diamond pythons, *Morelia spilota* (Serpentes, Boidae). Copeia, 1988: 984–995.

Smith, C. R., E. Cartee, J. T. Hathcock, and D. W. Speake. 1989. Radiographic and ultrasonographic scanning of gravid eastern indigo snakes. Jour. Herpetol., 23: 426–429.

Smits, A. W. 1985. Behavioral and dietary responses to aridity in the chuckwalla, *Sauromalus hispidus*. Jour. Herpetol., 19: 441–449.

Snell, H. L., and K. A. Christian. 1985. Energetics of Galapagos land iguanas: a comparison of two island populations. Herpetologica, 41: 437–442.

Snow, J. E. 1980. Second clutch laying by painted turtles. Copeia, 1980: 534–536.

Solórzano, A. 1990. Reproduction in the pit viper *Porthidium picadoi* Dunn (Serpentes: Viperidae) in Costa Rica. Copeia, 1990: 1154–1157.

Solórzano, A., and L. Cerdas. 1989. Reproductive biology and distribution of the terciopelo, *Bothrops asper* Garman (Serpentes: Viperidae), in Costa Rica. Herpetologica, 45: 444–450.

Somma, L. A. 1990. Observations on the nesting ecology of the prairie skink (*Eumeces septentrionalis*) in Nebraska. Bull. Chicago Herpetol. Soc., 25: 77–80.

Spencer, B. 1988. The elongated tortoise and its management at the Minnesota Zoo. Bull. Chicago Herpetol. Soc., 23: 37–40.

Spotila, J. R., and E. A. Standora. 1986. Sex determination in the desert tortoise: a conservative management strategy is needed. Herpetologica, 42: 67–72.

Spotila, J. R., E. A. Standora, S. J. Morreale, and G. J. Ruiz. 1987. Temperature dependent sex determination in the green turtle (*Chelonia mydas*): effects on the sex ratio on a natural nesting beach. Herpetologica, 43: 74–81.

Stamps, J. A. 1988. The effect of body size on habitat and territory choice in juvenile lizards. Herpetologica, 44: 369–376.

Standora, E. A., and J. R. Spotila. 1985. Temperature dependent sex determination in sea turtles. Copeia, 1985: 711–722.

Stearns, B. C. 1989. Captive management of turtles and tortoises—an overview. Bull. Chicago Herpetol. Soc., 19: 71–74.

Stevens, T. P. 1980. Notes on thermoregulation and reproduction in *Cnemidophorus flagellicaudus*. Jour. Herpetol., 14: 418–420.

Stewart, J. R. 1984. Thermal biology of the live bearing lizard *Gerrhonotus coeruleus*. Herpetologica, 40: 349–355.

Stewart, J. R., and D. G. Blackburn. 1988. Reptilian placentation: structural diversity and terminology. Copeia, 1988: 839–852.

Stewart, J. R., and D. Duvall. 1985. Ovariectomy fails to block egg-brooding behavior in nesting, female five-lined skinks (*Eumeces fasciatus*). Copeia, 1985: 777–779.

Stickel, L. F. 1989. Home range behavior among box turtles (*Terrapene c. carolina*) of a bottomland forest in Maryland. Jour. Herpetol., 23: 40–44.

Stickel, L. F., and C. M. Bunck. 1989. Growth and morphometrics of the box turtle, *Terrapene c. carolina*. Jour. Herpetol., 23: 216–223.

Stoneburner, D. L. 1982. Satellite telemetry of loggerhead sea turtle movement in the Georgia Bight. Copeia, 1982: 400–408.

Stoneburner, D. L., and J. A. Kushlan. 1984. Heavy metal burdens in American crocodile eggs from Florida Bay, Florida, USA. Jour. Herpetol., 18: 192–193.

Stoneburner, D. L., and J. I. Richardsen. 1981. Observations on the role of temperature in loggerhead turtle nest site selection. Copeia, 1981: 238–241.

Stoneburner, D. L., J. I. Richardson, and G. K. Williamson. 1982. Observations on the movement of hatchling sea turtles. Copeia, 1982: 963–965.

Storment, D. 1990. Field observations of sexual dimorphism in head pattern (markings) in timber rattlesnakes (*Crotalus horridus*). Bull. Chicago Herpetol. Soc., 25: 160–162.

Sullivan, B. K. 1986. Intra-populational variation in the intensity of sexual selection in breeding aggregations of Woodhouse's toad (*Bufo woodhousii*). Jour. Herpetol., 20: 88–90.

Swain, T. A., F. Arp, and R. D. Younkin. 1980. A preliminary report on the ecology of a tropical, high altitude lizard, *Anadia brevifrontalis*. Jour. Herpetol., 14: 321–326.

Takenaka, S. 1980. Growth of the Japanese grass lizard *Takydromus tachydromoides* in relation to reproduction. Herpetologica, 36: 305–310.

Talbert, O. R., Jr., S. E. Stancyk, J. M. Dean, and J. M. Will. 1980. Nesting activity of the loggerhead turtle (*Caretta caretta*) in South Carolina I: a rookery in transition. Copeia, 1980: 709–718.

Tanaka, S., and M. Nishihira. 1987. A field study of seasonal, daily, and diel activity patterns of *Eublepharis kuroiwae kuroiwae*. Herpetologica, 43: 482–489.

Taylor, H. L. 1988. A morphological analysis of intergradation between the teiid lizards *Cnemidophorus tigris tigris* and *C. tigris septentrionalis*. Herpetologica, 44: 176–185.

—. 1990. A morphological analysis of the teiid lizards *Cnemidophorus tigris tigris* and *C. tigris gracilis* from a contact zone in northwestern Arizona. Herpetologica, 46: 447–456.

Taylor, H. L., C. Currie, and J. J. Baker. 1989. The mode of origin for males collected from natural clones of parthenogenetic lizards (*Cnemidophorus*): cytological evidence. Jour. Herpetol., 23: 202–205.

Taylor, J. A. 1985. Reproductive biology of the Australian lizard *Ctenotus taeniolatus*. Herpetologica, 41: 408–418.

—. 1986. Seasonal energy storage in the Australian lizard, *Ctenotus taeniolatus*. Copeia, 1986: 445–453.

Telford, S. R., III. 1980. Notes on *Agkistrodon himalayanus* from Pakistan's Kaghan Valley. Copeia, 1980: 154–155.

Temple, S. A. 1987. Predation on turtle nests increases near ecological edges. Copeia, 1987: 250–252.

Thompson, M. B. 1988. Influence of incubation temperature and water potential on sex determination in *Emydura macquarii* (Testudines: Pleurodira). Herpetologica, 44: 86–90.

—. 1988. Nest temperatures in the pleurodiran turtle, *Emydura macquarii*. Copeia, 1988: 996–1000.

Thornhill, G. M. 1982. Comparative reproduction of the turtle, *Chrysemys scripta elegans*, in heated and natural lakes. Jour. Herpetol., 16: 347–353.

Thorpe, R. S. 1989. Pattern and function of sexual dimorphism: a biometric study of character variation in the grass snake (*Natrix natrix*, Colubridae) due to sex and its interactions with geography. Copeia, 1989: 53–63.

Tinkle, D. W., and A. E. Dunham. 1983. Demography of the tree lizard, *Urosaurus ornatus*, in central Arizona. Copeia, 1983: 585–598.

—. 1986. Comparative life histories of two syntopic sceloporine lizards. Copeia, 1986: 1–18.

Tollestrup, K. 1981. The social behavior and displays of two species of horned lizards, *Phrynosoma platyrhinos* and *Phrynosoma coronatum*. Herpetologica, 37: 130–131.

Trauth, S. E., W. E. Cooper, Jr., L. J. Vitt, and S. A. Perrill. 1987. Cloacal anatomy of the broad-headed skink, *Eumeces laticeps*, with a description of a female pheromonal gland. Herpetologica, 43: 458–466.

Tremper, R. L., and G. R. Barnes. 1984. An overview of the Center for Reptile and Amphibian Propagation. Bull. Chicago Herpetol. Soc., 19: 69–70.

Troyer, K. 1983. The biology of iguanine lizards: present status and future directions. Herpetologica, 39: 317–328.

—. 1987. Posthatching yolk in a lizard: internalization and contribution to growth. Jour. Herpetol., 21: 102–106.

Tu, M. C., S. C. Fong, and K. Y. Lue. 1990. Reproductive biology of the sea snake, *Laticauda semifasciata*, in Taiwan. Jour. Herpetol., 24: 119–126.

Turner, F. B., and P. A. Medica. 1982. The distribution and abundance of the flat-tailed horned lizard (*Phrynosoma mcallii*). Copeia, 1982: 815–823.

Turner, F. B., P. A. Medica, and C. L. Lyons. 1984. Reproduction and survival of the desert tortoise (*Scaptochelys agassizii*) in Ivanpah Valley, California. Copeia, 1984: 811–820.

Turner, J. S. 1984. Raymond B. Cowles and the biology of temperature in reptiles. Jour. Herpetol., 18: 421–436.

Uribe, M. C. A., S. R. Velasco, L. J. Guillette, Jr., and E. F. Estrada. 1988. Oviduct histology of the lizard, *Ctenosaura pectinata*. Copeia, 1988: 1035–1042.

Vaeth, R. H. 1983. A note on courtship and copulatory behavior in *Micrurus fulvius*. Bull. Chicago Herpetol. Soc., 18: 86–88.

VanDamme, R., D. Bauwens, and R. F. Verheyen. 1987. Thermoregulatory responses to environmental seasonality by the lizard *Lacerta vivipara*. Herpetologica, 43: 405–415.

—. 1989. Effect of relative clutch mass on sprint speed in the lizard *Lacerta vivipara*. Jour. Herpetol., 23: 459–461.

Vanderhaege, M. 1985. Reproduction in captivity of *Dracaena guianensis* Daudin 1802. Bull. Chicago Herpetol. Soc., 20: 56–57.

van der Heiden, A. M., R. Briseno-Duenas, and D. Rios-Olmeda. 1985. A simplified method for determining sex in hatchling sea turtles. Copeia, 1985: 779–782.

Van Devender, R. W. 1982. Comparative demography of the lizard *Basiliscus basiliscus*. Herpetologica, 38: 189–208.

vanWyk, J. H. 1990. Seasonal testicular activity and morphometric variation in the femoral glands of the lizard *Cordylus polyzonus polyzonus* (Sauria: Cordylidae). Jour. Herpetol., 24: 405–409.

Vial, J. L., and J. R. Stewart. 1985. The reproductive cycle of *Barisia monticola*: a unique variation among viviparous lizards. Herpetologica, 41: 51–57.

Vitt, L. J. 1982. Sexual dimorphism and reproduction in the microteiid lizard, *Gymnophthalmus multiscutatus*. Jour. Herpetol., 16: 325–329.

—. 1983. Ecology of an anuran-eating guild of terrestrial tropical snakes. Herpetologica, 39: 52–66.

—. 1983. Reproduction and sexual dimorphism in the tropical teiid lizard *Cnemidophorus ocellifer*. Copeia, 1983: 359–366.

—. 1986. Reproductive tactics of sympatric gekkonid lizards with a comment on the evolutionary and ecological consequences of invariant clutch size. Copeia, 1986: 773–786.

Vitt, L. J., and W. E. Cooper, Jr. 1985. The relationship between reproduction and lipid cycling in the skink *Eumeces laticeps* with comments on brooding ecology. Herpetologica, 41: 419–432.

—. 1986. Skink reproduction and sexual dimorphism: *Eumeces fasciatus* in the southeastern United States, with notes on *Eumeces inexpectatus*. Jour. Herpetol., 20: 65–76.

—. 1989. Maternal care in skinks (*Eumeces*). Jour. Herpetol., 23: 29–34.

Vitt, L. J., and S. R. Goldberg. 1983. Reproductive ecology of the tropical iguanid lizards: *Tropidurus torquatus* and *Platynotus semitaeniatus*. Copeia, 1983: 131–141.

Vitt, L. J., J. M. Howland, and A. E. Dunham. 1985. The effect of formalin fixation on weight of lizard eggs. Jour. Herpetol., 19: 298–299.

Vitt, L. J., and T. E. Lacher, Jr. 1981. Behavior, habitat, diet, and reproduction of the iguanid lizard *Polychrus acutirostris* in the Caatinga of northeastern Brazil. Herpetologica, 37: 53–63.

Vitt, L. J., and H. J. Price. 1982. Ecological and evolutionary determinants of relative clutch mass in lizards. Herpetologica, 38: 237–255.

Vogel, P. 1984. Seasonal hatchling recruitment and juvenile growth of the lizard *Anolis lineatopus*. Copeia, 1984: 747–757.

Vogel, P., W. Hettrich, and K. Ricono. 1986. Weight growth of juvenile lizards, *Anolis lineatopus*, maintained on different diets. Jour. Herpetol., 20: 50–58.

Vogt, R. C. 1981. Turtle egg (Graptemys: Emydidae) infestation by fly larvae. Copeia, 1981: 457–459.

Vogt, R. C., and J. J. Bull. 1982. Genetic sex determination in the spiny softshell *Trionyx spiniferus* (Testudines: Trionychidae) (?). Copeia, 1982: 699–700.

—. 1982. Temperature controlled sex-determination in turtles: ecological and behavioral aspects. Herpetologica, 38: 156–164.

Vogt, R. C., J. J. Bull, C. J. McCoy, and T. W. Houseal. 1982. Incubation temperature influences sex determination in kinosternid turtles. Copeia, 1982: 480–482.

Voris, H. K., and G. S. Glodek. 1980. Habitat, diet, and reproduction of the file snake, *Acrochordus granulatus*, in the Straits of Malacca. Jour. Herpetol., 14: 108–111.

Walker, J. 1981. Systematics of *Cnemidophorus gularis*. II. Specific and subspecific identity of the Zacatecas whiptail (*Cnemidophorus gularis semiannulatus*). Copeia, 1981: 850–868.

—. 1980. Reproductive characteristics of the San Pedro Martin whiptail, *Cnemidophorus martyris*. Jour. Herpetol., 14: 431–432.

—. 1981. Reproductive characteristics of sympatric whiptail lizards (genus *Cnemidophorus*) in southern Mexico. Jour. Herpetol., 15: 321–328.

Walker, J. M., J. E. Cordes, and M. A. Paulissen. 1989. Hybrids of two parthenogenetic clonal complexes and a gonochoristic species of *Cnemidophorus*, and the relationship of hybridization to habitat characteristics. Jour. Herpetol., 23: 119–130.

Walker, J. M., W. C. Guest, J. E. Cordes, and M. A. Paulissen. 1989. Morphological and chromosomal evidence of hybridization between all-female *Cnemidophorus laredoensis* and gonochoristic *Cnemidophorus gularis*. Copeia, 1989: 1059–1064.

Walker, J. M., E. D. Parker, H. L. Taylor, J. E. Cordes, and R. M. Abuhteba. 1990. Hybridization between all-female *Cnemidophorus tesselatus* and gonochoristic *Cnemidophorus sexlineatus*. Jour. Herpetol., 24: 388–396.

Webb, G. J. W., S. C. Manolis, P. J. Whitehead, and K. Dempsey. 1987. The possible relationship between embryo orientation, opaque banding and the dehydration of albumen in crocodile eggs. Copeia, 1987: 252–257.

Weldon, P. J., and H. W. Sampson. 1988. The gular glands of *Alligator mississippiensis*: histology and preliminary analysis of lipoidal secretions. Copeia, 1988: 80–86.

Wellins, D. J. 1987. Use of an H-Y antigen assay of sex determination in sea turtles. Copeia, 1987: 46–52.

Wenzel, D. E. 1990. Observations of captive breeding behavior, matings, and oviposition in the eastern hognose snake (*Heterodon platirhinos*). Bull. Chicago Herpetol. Soc., 25: 86.

Werman, S. D. 1982. Notes on the ecology of the chuckwalla, *Sauromalus obesus* near Baker, California. Jour. Herpetol., 16: 417–418.

Werner, D. I. 1988. The effect of varying water potential on body weight, yolk and fat bodies in neonate green iguanas. Copeia, 1988: 406–411.

White, D. R., J. C. Mitchell, and W. S. Woolcott. 1982. Reproduction cycle and embryonic development of *Nerodia taxispilota* (Serpentes: Colubridae) at the northeastern edge of its range. Copeia, 1982: 646–652.

Whitehead, P. J. 1990. Yolk depletion and metabolic rate of hatchling *Crocodylus johnstoni*. Copeia, 1990: 871–875.

Whitmore, C., P. Dutton, and N. Mrosovsky. 1985. Sexing of hatchling sea turtles: gross appearance versus histology. Jour. Herpetol., 19: 430–431.

Whittier, J. M., and D. Crews. 1990. Body mass and reproduction in female red-sided garter snakes (*Thamnophis sirtalis parietalis*). Herpetologica, 46: 219–226.

Wikramanayake, E. D., and G. L. Dryden. 1988. The reproductive ecology of *Varanus indicus* on Guam. Herpetologica, 44: 338–344.

Wilbern, S. E., and D. A. Ingold. 1983. Sexual dimorphism in *Terrapene* shells. Bull. Chicago Herpetol. Soc., 18: 34–36.

Wilhoft, D. C., E. Hotaling, and P. Franks. 1983. Effects of temperature on sex determination in embryos of the snapping turtle, *Chelydra serpentina*. Jour. Herpetol., 17: 38-42.

Williams, E. C., Jr., and W. S. Parker. 1987. A long-term study of a box turtle (*Terrapene carolina*) population at Allen Memorial Woods, Indiana, with emphasis on survivorship. Herpetologica, 43: 328–335.

Williams, E. E., and S. M. Case. 1986. Interactions among members of the *Anolis distichus* complex in and near the Sierra de Baoruco, Dominican Republic. Jour. Herpetol., 20: 535–546.

Willis, L., S. T. Threlkeld, and C. C. Carpenter. 1982. Tail loss patterns in *Thamnophis* (Reptilia: Colubridae) and the probable fate of injured individuals. Copeia, 1982: 98–101.

Witherington. B. E., K. A. Bjorndal, and C. M. McCabe. 1990. Temporal pattern of nocturnal emergence of loggerhead turtle hatchlings from natural nests. Copeia, 1990: 1165–1168.

Witzell, W. N. 1982. Observations on the green sea turtle (*Chelonia mydas*) in western Samoa. Copeia, 1982: 183–185.

Wood, F. E., and J. R. Wood. 1982. Sex ratios in captive-reared green turtles, *Chelonia mydas*. Copeia, 1982: 482–485.

Woodward, A., T. Hines, C. Abercrombie, and C. Hope. 1984. Spacing patterns in alligator nests. Jour. Herpetol., 18: 8–12.

Worthington, R. D. 1982. Dry and wet year comparisons of clutch and adult body sizes of *Uta stansburiana stejnegeri*. Jour. Herpetol., 16: 332–334.

Wright, J. W., C. Spolsky, and W. M. Brown. 1983. The origin of the parthenogenetic lizard *Cnemidophorus laredoensis* inferred from mitochondrial DNA analysis. Herpetologica, 39: 410–416.

Wyneken, J., T. J. Burke, M. Salmon, and D. K. Pedersen. 1988. Egg failure in natural and relocated sea turtle nests. Jour. Herpetol., 22: 88–96.

Xavier, F. 1982. Progesterone in the viviparous lizard *Lacerta vivipara*: ovarian biosynthesis, plasma levels, and binding to transcortin-type protein during the sexual cycle. Herpetologica, 38: 62–70.

Yntema, C. L., and N. Mrosovsky. 1980. Sexual differentiation in hatchling loggerheads (*Caretta caretta*) incubated at different controlled temperatures. Herpetologica, 36: 33–36.

York, D. S. 1984. The combat ritual of the Malayan pit viper (*Calloselasma rhodostoma*). Copeia, 1984: 770–772.

Zappalorti, R. T., E. W. Johnson, and Z. Leszczynski. 1983. The ecology of the northern pine snake *Pituophis melanoleucus melanoleucus* (Daudin) (Reptilia, Serpentes, Colubridae), in southern New Jersey, with special notes on habitat and nesting behavior. Bull. Chicago Herpetol. Soc., 18: 57–72.

Zaworski, J. P. 1987. A note on calcium supplementation in geckos. Bull. Chicago Herpetol. Soc., 22: 131.

—. 1987. Egg guarding behavior by a male *Gekko gecko*. Bull. Chicago Herpetol. Soc., 22: 193.

—. 1987. Egg molding behavior by male *Gekko gecko* and *Gekko petricolus*. Bull. Chicago Herpetol. Soc., 22: 77.

—. 1987. Observations on unusual behavior in the parthenogenetic gecko, *Lepidodactylus lugubris* Fitzinger. Bull. Chicago Herpetol. Soc., 22: 76.

—. 1987. The captive maintenance and propagation of *Gekko petricolus* Taylor. Bull. Chicago Herpetol. Soc., 22: 129–130.

—. 1988. A note on sex recognition in the tokay gecko, *Gekko gecko*. Bull. Chicago Herpetol. Soc., 23: 42.

—. 1988. Captive husbandry and breeding of the tokay, *Gekko gecko* Linnaeus. Bull. Chicago Herpetol. Soc., 23: 101–103.

Zucker, N. 1986. Perch height preferences of male and female tree lizards, *Urosaurus ornatus*: a matter of food competition or social role. Jour. Herpetol., 20: 547–553.

—. 1989. Dorsal darkening and territoriality in a wild population of the tree lizard, *Urosaurus ornatus*. Jour. Herpetol., 23: 389–398.

Zucker, N., and W. Boecklen. 1990. Variations in female throat colorations in the tree lizard (*Urosaurus ornatus*): relation to reproductive cycle and fecundity. Herpetologica, 46: 387–394.

Zug, G. R., M. M. Barber, and J. C. Dudley. 1982. Gonadal histology and reproduction in *Carlia bicarinata* (Scincidae, Sauria, Reptilia) of the Port Moresby area, Papua, New Guinea. Herpetologica, 38: 418–425.

Chiszar, D., H. M. Smith, and C. C. Carpenter. 1994. An ethological approach to reproductive success in reptiles, p. 147–173. *In* J. B. Murphy, K. Adler, and J. T. Collins (eds.), Captive Management and Conservation of Amphibians and Reptiles. Society for the Study of Amphibians and Reptiles, Ithaca (New York). Contributions to Herpetology, volume 11.

Phenotypic Plasticity: Implications for Captive-Breeding and Conservation Programs

Neil B. Ford* and Richard A. Seigel**

Introduction

Phenotypic plasticity is defined as variation in life-history characteristics resulting from proximal environmental factors, such as prey availability (Bull 1987; Stearns 1976). Although considered to be extremely important from an evolutionary perspective (Ballinger 1983; Bradshaw 1965; Bull 1987; Stearns 1989), little attention has been given to the implications of phenotypic plasticity for captive-breeding programs of endangered or threatened species. The ultimate goal of captive-breeding and release programs is the establishment of self-sustaining natural populations (Griffith et al. 1989). Clearly, the success of any such program is dependent on the number and quality of offspring released in the wild. Consequently, any mechanism that increases the number and quality of offspring will enhance the likelihood of success. In this chapter we provide an overview of phenotypic plasticity, using snakes as model organisms, and argue that a detailed understanding of this phenomenon may be important for the success of captive-breeding programs of amphibians and reptiles.

*Department of Biology
University of Texas at Tyler
3900 University Boulevard
Tyler, Texas 75701, USA

**Department of Biological Sciences
Southeastern Louisiana University
P.O. Box 814
Hammond, Louisiana 70402, USA

Acronyms used in this chapter:

LD_{50}	Lethal dose for 50% of litter or population
RCM	Relative clutch mass
SVL	Snout-to-vent length

Methods of Studying Phenotypic Plasticity

The most common method for studying phenotypic plasticity among amphibians and reptiles is the examination of temporal variation of life-history traits in naturally occurring populations. Studies on turtles, lizards, and snakes in the wild have documented considerable temporal variation in growth rates and fecundity (Andrén and Nilson 1983; Ballinger 1977; Berven 1988; Dunham 1978; Gibbons et al. 1982; Jones et al. 1987; Plummer 1983; Seigel and Fitch 1985). Although these field studies have demonstrated convincingly that some life-history traits are highly correlated with environmental factors, such as prey availability, interpretation of these results is difficult due to the number of uncontrolled (or uncontrollable) variables.

Because studies of animals in captivity can easily control individual environmental conditions, experimental manipulation of variables (such as temperature and diet) can give more precise insights into the influence of environmental factors on variation of life-history traits. For example, laboratory experiments conducted with frogs have shown that both diet and temperature can have important effects on clutch size and egg size (Kaplan 1987), effects that would be difficult to interpret under natural conditions. Hence, as is true for many areas of ecological research, observational studies alone are probably not sufficient to determine the causes and implications of phenotypic plasticity (see Hom and Cochran [1991] for a discussion of ecological experiments on reptiles and amphibians).

A Model of Phenotypic Plasticity for Adult Female Snakes

The general energy budget of an organism is subdivided between the energy required for maintenance and the energy that is used in its production budget (Congdon et al. 1982). The maintenance budget includes all the energy needed for the individual to survive (for activities such as resting metabolism, locomotion, foraging, and defense). In general, snakes are characterized by a low maintenance metabolism (Lillywhite 1987). Any energy intake above that required for maintenance goes into the production budget and is available for growth, energy storage, and reproduction (Congdon et al. 1982). Because of their low energy requirement for maintenance and the occurrence of wide variability in foraging success (Mushinsky 1987; Shine 1986), the production budget for snakes may exhibit substantial short-term variability. For example, when prey items are concentrated or are large, snakes are known to eat a substantial percentage of their body mass in a single foraging bout (Greene 1983; Pough and Groves 1983).

For an adult female snake, short-term fluctuations in energy intake (for example, high or low foraging success in the weeks prior to vitellogenesis and ovulation), would cause a change in the body-mass-to-length ratio. Because adult snakes grow slowly in length (Parker and Plummer 1987), a female with high foraging success in a short period would have an increase in body mass relative to her length, whereas a female with low foraging success would have a decrease in her body mass. Therefore, short-term variation in foraging success will cause changes in a female's body condition, and this, in turn, may be reflected in the reproductive event. The effect of variation in foraging success has been documented in snakes under field conditions (Andrén 1982).

Under conditions of varying foraging success, females of the same length have several options in terms of reproductive tactics (Figure 1). According to the first option, a female could produce a fixed total clutch mass (that is, total mass of reproductive material). The body mass of a female following this option would then vary relative to energy intake (that is, females would add somatic mass when foraging success was high and potentially lose somatic mass when foraging success was low). Because body mass varies with foraging success, the

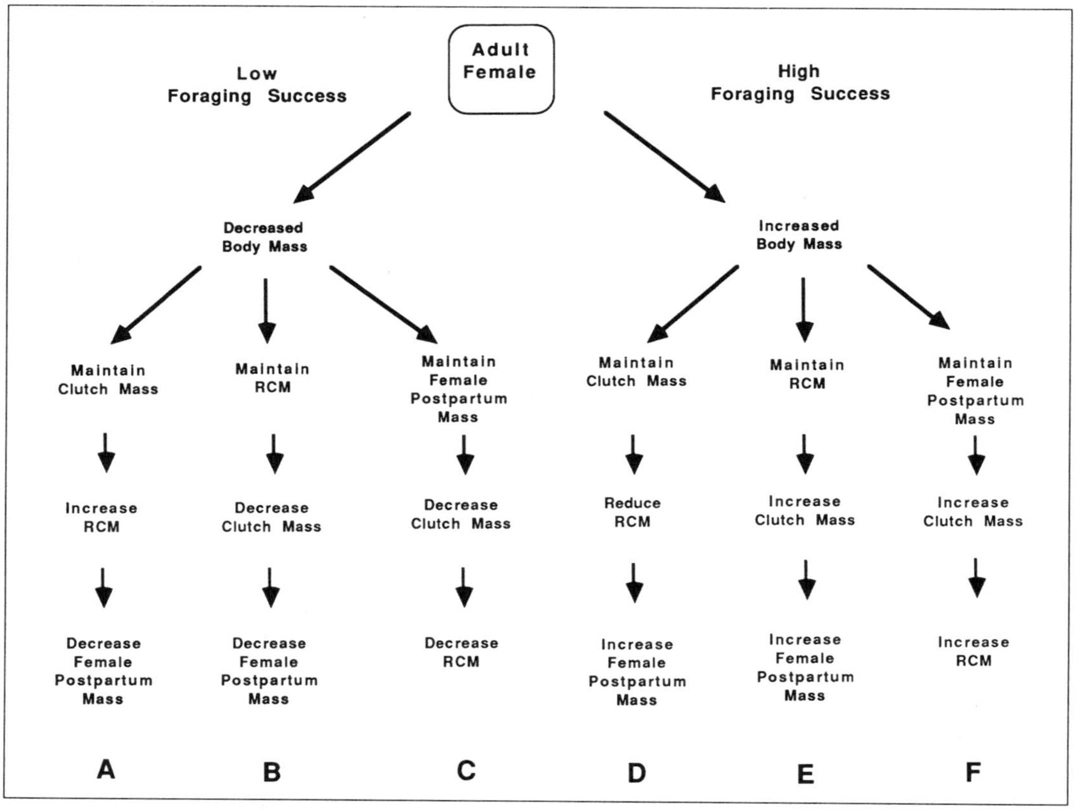

FIGURE 1. Flow chart of the options available to female snakes encountering variation in food intake prior to reproduction.

ratio of clutch mass to female postpartum body mass (known as relative clutch mass [RCM]) would also have to vary. Under conditions of high energy intake, RCM would go down, whereas RCM would increase when energy intake was low (Figure 1A, 1D).

A second option for females would be to have an invariant RCM. RCM is a life-history trait that is related to locomotor performance, reproductive mode, and foraging behavior (Seigel and Fitch 1984; Seigel et al. 1987; Shine 1980; Vitt and Congdon 1978; but see Brodie 1989). Under most hypotheses, RCM is constrained by natural selection relative to the foraging and by the ability of pregnant females to escape predators. To maintain a fixed RCM, a female experiencing high foraging success (and hence higher body mass) would have to increase clutch mass to compensate for the change in body mass. The opposite would be true for females with decreased foraging success and body mass (Figure 1B, 1E). The change in clutch mass could be achieved either by adjusting clutch size, offspring size, or both. Because RCM is fixed, postpartum mass would still vary among females.

A third option for females would be to maintain an invariant postpartum body mass (for example, a case in which a female would have the same body mass after reproduction as before; Figure 1C, 1F). This situation might be expected to evolve in situations in which postpartum mass is critical to survival, such as when females enter hibernation soon after parturition and hence have little time to recover lost body mass. To maintain a fixed body mass, a female with low foraging success would have to sharply reduce her clutch mass, which, in turn, would result in a decreased RCM (Figure 1C). A female with increased foraging success would have to increase her clutch mass at a level that would increase her RCM (Figure 1F). Again, these adjustments could be made by either changing clutch size, offspring size, or both.

Field and Experimental Tests of the Model

Field data are very limited in evaluation of whether these models reflect actual reproductive tactics of snakes. Seigel and Fitch (1984, 1985) studied temporal variation in RCM in five populations of snakes from northeastern Kansas during years with significant differences in environmental conditions and (presumably) foraging success. The fact that RCM did not differ among years for any of the populations suggests that these snakes exhibited option 2 (for example, they maintained RCM at some specific level; Figure 1B, 1E). Other studies have reported similar results; Andrén and Nilson (1983) found that the European Adder, *Vipera berus*, when exposed to a fluctuating food resource in the wild, responded by adjusting clutch mass at a level that produced an invariant RCM, and Brodie and Ducey (1989) found no yearly variation in RCM in the Redbelly Snake (*Storeria occipitomaculata*).

Although these field studies suggest that an invariant RCM may be the predominant tactic for snakes, the number of uncontrolled environmental variables that might be influencing females in the field make such a statement premature. Recently, we began a number of experiments in a controlled laboratory environment to evaluate precisely the influence of energy intake on the reproductive characteristics of female snakes.

To date, we have examined phenotypic plasticity in the reproductive traits of two species of North Temperate zone colubrid snakes, the viviparous Checkered Garter Snake (*Thamnophis marcianus*; Ford and Seigel 1989) and the oviparous Corn Snake (*Elaphe guttata*; Seigel and Ford 1991). The exact design of our experiments is outlined in the papers cited above, but our general procedure was as follows: a laboratory colony of adult snakes was established and maintained on an intermediate diet for at least four months prior to artificial hibernation. We used regimens adequate for normal growth and maintenance for both species and all individuals were in a uniform body condition by fall. Immediately following hibernation, female snakes were sorted by length and then randomly placed on either a high- or low-energy diet. We chose diets that approximated the maximum amount of food females would accept consistently and the minimum necessary for normal health and reproduction. Females were given multiple opportunities to mate, then isolated in individual cages until parturition or egg-laying. Females were weighed just prior to parturition, snout-to-vent length (SVL) was measured, and they were re-weighed after parturition. Eggs and neonates were measured and weighed, and clutch mass consisted of all shelled eggs or all full-term young.

In general, the responses of female snakes to variation in energy intake were similar for both species; females on the high-energy diet produced higher clutch masses and larger clutches than did females on low-energy diets. Offspring size was not plastic in either species. Females of *Thamnophis marcianus* adjusted clutch mass at a level that maintained a fixed RCM, however, whereas female *Elaphe guttata* showed significant plasticity in RCM. This difference in plasticity in RCM between species suggests that *Thamnophis* used option 2, but that *Elaphe* used option 3.

The postpartum masses of Checkered Garter Snakes on the high-energy diet were significantly higher than those on the low-energy diet, whereas the postpartum masses of female Corn Snakes did not differ between diets. Figure 2 illustrates the reasons why this may have occurred. In female *Thamnophis marcianus*, as energy is allocated to reproductive mass, a percentage is also devoted to somatic mass. Therefore, a high-energy diet produces gains in both somatic and reproductive mass. When reproduction occurs on a low-energy diet, however, it may be at the sacrifice of somatic mass (Figure 2A). For female *Elaphe guttata*, intake of energy after emergence from hibernation is apparently devoted primarily to reproduction and is not invested in somatic tissue. Therefore, any variation in foraging success is reflected in changes in clutch mass, not somatic mass. The ratio of those two factors (RCM) would then vary with diet, but the postpartum masses of the females would not necessarily be different (Figure 2B).

In our laboratory experiments, the changes in the somatic masses of females support this explanation. For example, *Thamnophis marcianus*, when fed a high-energy diet, not only increased clutch mass, but also gained significant amounts of body mass as well, whereas females on a low-energy diet had a postpartum mass equivalent to their post-

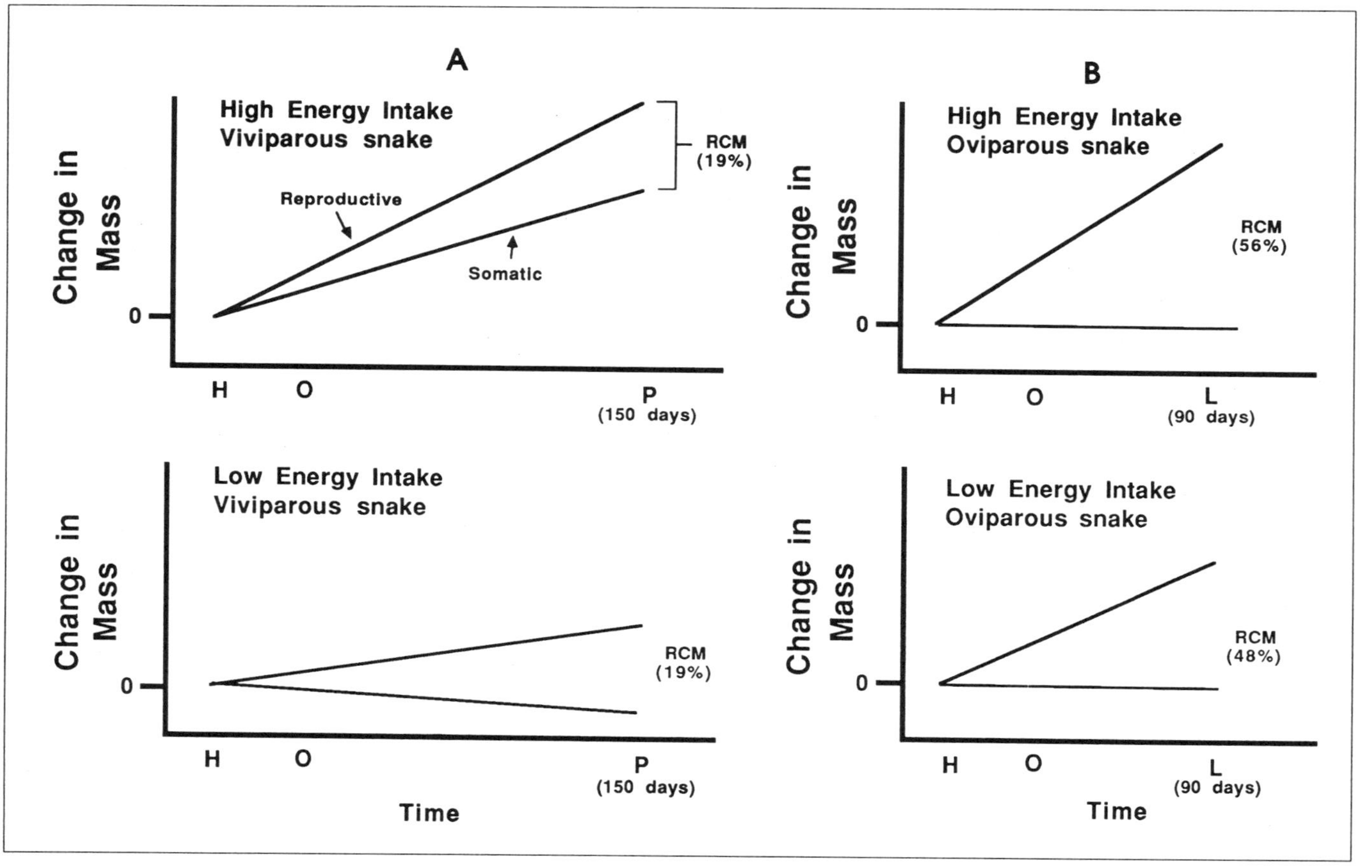

FIGURE 2. Theoretical comparison of the changes in body mass following reproduction in viviparous (A) and oviparous (B) snakes under conditions of high and low food intake. H emergence from hibernation; O ovulation; P parturition; L egg-laying. Gestation times for each group are approximate.

hibernation mass (Figure 3). Conversely, the clutch masses of *Elaphe guttata* were produced with a sacrifice in body mass, even on a high-energy diet (Figure 3). Admittedly, these values would change relative to the caloric differences in the two diets: mice for *Elaphe* and tadpoles for *Thamnophis*. Because the changes in body mass from post-hibernation to preparturition were comparable (at least on low-energy diets), it seems valid to compare the two species in this way. It is possible that the reason that both groups of Corn Snakes lost body mass between emergence and parturition (whereas the Checkered Garter Snakes either maintained or gained body mass) is related to reproductive mode. As an egg-layer, *Elaphe* females are gravid for a relatively short time (Figure 2B); consequently, individuals have more time to recoup energy losses before the onset of hibernation. Because females of viviparous species, such as *Thamnophis*, are gravid for a much longer interval, only a limited time is available for foraging before hibernation. Consequently, sacrifices in somatic mass cannot be as easily recouped in viviparous species.

Although susceptibility to predation during pregnancy has been suggested as the reason viviparous snakes have a lower RCM than do oviparous forms (Seigel and Fitch 1984), another explanation is possible. The difference in RCMs between reproductive modes may reflect the fact that oviparous snakes lose somatic mass during pregnancy (and consequently have a high RCM), whereas viviparous snakes increase or maintain somatic mass during pregnancy (and hence have a low RCM). According to this hypothesis, RCM may not be a target of selection, but rather is a byproduct of differential allocation of energy to somatic and reproductive tissues in each reproductive mode. Discriminating between these hypotheses (which are not necessarily mutually exclusive) would require further experimental data on reproductive allocation in egg-laying and viviparous squamates, and intensive field studies on the survival of gravid females.

Assessing Plasticity in Reproductive Traits Among Years

Although females of both *Elaphe guttata* and *Thamnophis marcianus* exhibited changes in reproductive traits within the same season in which the energy intake was manipulated, post-hibernation body mass was standardized for all animals by placing them on intermediate diets the previous autumn. In natural situations and in our model for garter snakes, pre-hibernation masses of females would probably show considerable yearly variation related to individual foraging success. Consequently, some females will enter hibernation with higher energy stores than others, and some response to this variation in energy reserves would be expected to occur in the next reproductive event.

Our experimental manipulations with *Thamnophis marcianus* produced two very different groups of females at the end of the first year; females with the same or slightly lower postpartum mass as compared with mass at first emergence (reflecting low foraging success; Figure 1B), or females with increased postpartum mass (reflecting high foraging success; Figure 1E). If the foraging success that created this variation continues for a second season, we should see some effect on the next reproductive event. The simplest prediction is that females will utilize the same tactics as they did in the first year

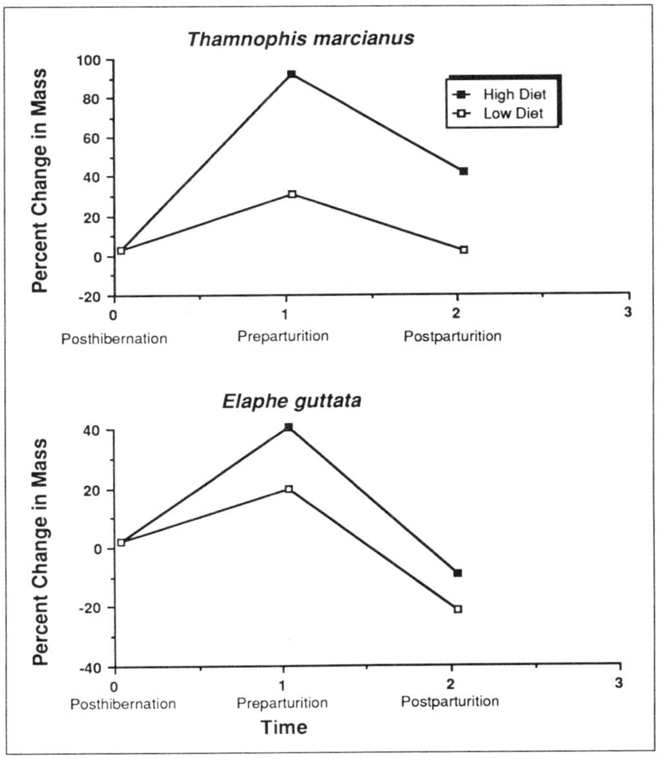

Figure 3. Comparison of actual changes in body mass in female *Thamnophis marcianus* (upper panel) and *Elaphe guttata* (lower panel) on different diets.

(for example, maintain RCM by increasing clutch mass under high-energy conditions or decreasing clutch mass under low-energy conditions). By the time females enter hibernation in year 2, this hypothesis predicts that females on the high-energy diet would have a still higher postpartum body mass than they did at the original emergence, whereas females on the low-energy diet would continue to maintain the same body mass as they had at emergence or they might suffer some loss in mass.

To examine this hypothesis we maintained a number of female *Thamnophis marcianus* on their dietary regimens for a second year. In all other respects they were kept under the same conditions in the second season as they were in the first. In general, these results verified the simple prediction—females in both groups showed the same RCM as they did in year 1 by increasing clutch mass in the high-energy group and decreasing clutch mass in the low-energy group. After parturition, females on the high-energy diet had again increased in body mass, whereas females on the low-energy diet had actually lost mass (Table 1). To some degree, these results are counter-intuitive. We might have predicted that females on the high-energy diet would actually increase RCM (that is, take advantage of high foraging success and body mass), whereas females on the low-energy diet would preserve body mass by reducing RCM or by skipping reproduction entirely. The fact that the tactics used by both groups did not change between years may indicate that these individuals are "locked in" to a particular strategy. The absence of changes in tactics between years was especially surprising for a group of individuals maintained on the low-energy diet for a third year; these snakes continued to reproduce even though body mass continued to decrease, and clutch size was reduced to about three offspring per female. Such individuals may be subject to increased mortality with several years of low foraging success (Andrén 1982).

Effects of Energy Intake on Offspring Survival

Our experiments with garter snakes showed that although clutch size and clutch mass were plastic relative to energy intake, neonate size was not affected. Because offspring size and survival are often thought to be correlated (Brockelman 1975; Smith and Fretwell 1974), the initial implication of our findings that energy intake does not influence offspring SVL or mass would seem to suggest that energy intake is unrelated to offspring fitness. It is possible, however, that our measures of neonate size (SVL and mass) are not adequate indicators of offspring quality.

An obvious correlate of fitness for a neonate snake would be the ability to survive for long periods without food, a factor that influences survival rates in North Temperate zone snakes (Fitch 1965; Gregory 1977; Parker and Brown 1973). To determine whether neonate garter snakes from the two dietary regimens differed in their ability to survive without food, we isolated four individuals (two males and two females) from five litters from each diet in gallon jars with water only. Animals were maintained at 28°C with a light:dark cycle of 14:10 until 50% of the individuals from a litter had died (LD_{50}). At that time the remainder of the litter was killed. Results are summarized in Table 2. Mean time to LD_{50} was over 40% longer in the high-energy group, and the differences were statistically significant (Mann-Whitney U-test, $z = 2.19$, $P = 0.028$).

TABLE 1. Reproductive characteristics of Checkered Garter Snakes, *Thamnophis marcianus*, maintained on different energy intake diets over two years. Means and standard deviations are given.

Diet	Year	Number	Snout–vent length (cm)	Prepar-turition mass (g)	Postpar-turition mass (g)	Clutch size	Clutch mass (g)	Relative clutch mass (%)	Neonate SVL (cm)	Neonate mass (g)
High	1	9	56 ± 6.6	195 ± 72.9	140 ± 52.4	16.0 ± 8.03	33.3 ± 15.47	16.7 ± 2.98	15.6 ± 0.83	2.1 ± 0.31
	2	9	59 ± 5.5	228 ± 93.2	158 ± 59.4	20.0 ± 9.95	41.5 ± 18.30	18.2 ± 2.68	14.8 ± 0.93	2.2 ± 0.40
Low	1	6	53 ± 7.7	123 ± 52.7	93 ± 42.4	9.0 ± 1.26	19.3 ± 4.54	16.9 ± 4.16	5.6 ± 1.17	2.1 ± 0.33
	2	6	53 ± 7.4	100 ± 46.6	82 ± 37.9	7.0 ± 2.76	14.1 ± 6.97	13.9 ± 3.82	14.8 ± 0.95	1.9 ± 0.35

TABLE 2. Survival rates of neonate *Thamnophis marcianus* born to mothers on different diets. Days to death was determined as the time when half of the sample from each litter died. See text for experimental design. Means are followed by one standard deviation and range in parentheses. Sample sizes were five litters from each diet.

Diet	Days to death	
Low energy	76.0 ± 13.4	(57–91)
High energy	108.4 ± 23.3	(84–146)

These data strongly suggest that, although neonates from the two dietary regimens did not differ in either size or mass (Ford and Seigel 1989), there are significant differences in their ability to survive without food. Presumably, these differences reflect changes in the composition of body tissues, and we are currently examining whole-body lipid levels in these offspring. Thus, although neonate size is not plastic relative to maternal foraging success, at least one measure of neonate fitness apparently is. Assessing offspring quality by simply measuring body size may thus be misleading.

Summary

We are not suggesting that reproductive traits of snakes are simply a function of energy intake. Obviously, the demographic environment plays a major role in shaping reproductive strategies. Both field and experimental data clearly show, however, that life-history characteristics of reptiles and amphibians are subject to a high degree of phenotypic plasticity, especially relative to prey availability. We suggest that the implications of such plasticity have been largely overlooked by most captive-breeding programs. The probability of success of such programs is clearly dependent on the number and quality of the offspring produced. Our data indicate that both fecundity and offspring survival can be modified by changes in energy input.

It has also been documented that incubation temperature of snake eggs can have important effects on neonate behavior (Burger 1990). Consequently, an understanding of how diet and other environmental factors affect reproductive traits may be essential in developing a successful captive-breeding program. We recommend especially that levels of energy input not be chosen arbitrarily. What appears to be an adequate level of food for growth and reproduction may, in fact, produce litter sizes lower than the maximum possible, or offspring of lower fitness, or both. To illustrate, consider that a group of 25 female *Thamnophis marcianus* on a high-energy diet would produce 325 offspring in one year, whereas the same females on a low-energy diet would produce only 220 offspring. An "extra" 100 offspring (with higher survival potential) would be of obvious value in a captive-breeding program.

We realize that our experimental results are based on only two species and recognize the need for additional studies on a diversity of species. This is an area of research in which individuals and institutions with large colonies of captive reptiles may make important contributions.

Acknowledgments

For assistance in the field and the laboratory, we thank D. Holland, M. M. Huggins, J. Perry-Richardson, and L. Sanders. We are grateful to J. W. Gibbons for supporting this research during our stay at Savannah River Ecology Laboratory. We thank J. Murphy, R. Shine, J. Congdon, and an anonymous reviewer for comments on an earlier version of the manuscript. This research was supported by grant LEQSF-RD-A-16 (1987–1989) from the Louisiana Education Quality Support Fund to R. A. Seigel, University of Texas at Tyler Faculty research grants to N. B. Ford, the Visiting Faculty Program of the Oak Ridge National Laboratory (to N. B. Ford), and by contract DE-AC09-7SROO-819 between the Department of Energy and the University of Georgia's Savannah River Ecology Laboratory.

Literature Cited

Andrén, C. 1982. Effect of prey density on reproduction, foraging and other activities in the adder, *Vipera berus*. Amphibia-Reptilia, 3: 81–96.

Andrén, C., and G. Nilson. 1983. Reproductive tactics in an island population of adders, *Vipera berus* (L.), with a fluctuating food resource. Amphibia-Reptilia, 4: 63–79.

Ballinger, R. E. 1977. Reproductive strategies: food availability as a source of proximal variation in a lizard. Ecology, 58: 628–635.

—. 1983. Life-history variations, p. 301–330. *In* R. B. Huey, E. R. Pianka, and T. W. Schoener (eds.), Lizard Ecology: Studies on a Model Organism. Harvard Univ. Press, Cambridge, Massachusetts.

Berven, K. A. 1988. Factors affecting variation in reproductive traits within a population of wood frogs (*Rana sylvatica*). Copeia, 1988: 606–615.

Bradshaw, A. D. 1965. Evolutionary significance of phenotypic plasticity in plants. Adv. Genet., 13: 115–155.

Brockelman, W. Y. 1975. Competition, the fitness of offspring, and optimal clutch size. Amer. Nat., 109: 677–699.

Brodie, E. D., III. 1989. Behavioral modification as a means of reducing the cost of reproduction. Amer. Nat., 134: 225–238.

Brodie, E. D., III, and P. K. Ducey. 1989. Allocation of reproductive investment in the redbelly snake *Storeria occipitomaculata*. Amer. Midl. Nat., 122: 51–58.

Bull, J. J. 1987. Evolution of phenotypic variance. Evolution, 41: 303–315.

Burger, J. 1990. Effects of incubation temperature on behavior of young black racers (*Coluber constrictor*) and kingsnakes (*Lampropeltis getulus*). Jour. Herpetol., 24: 158–163.

Congdon, J. D., A. E. Dunham, and D. W. Tinkle. 1982. Energy budgets and life histories of reptiles, p. 233–271. *In* C. Gans, and F. H. Pough (eds.), Biology of the Reptilia, Vol. 13: Physiology D. Academic Press, New York.

Dunham, A. E. 1978. Food availability as a proximate factor influencing individual growth rates in the iguanid lizard *Sceloporus merriami*. Ecology, 59: 770–778.

Fitch, H. S. 1965. An ecological study of the garter snake, *Thamnophis sirtalis*. Univ. Kansas Publ. Mus. Nat. Hist., 15: 493–564.

Ford, N. B., and R. A. Seigel. 1989. Phenotypic plasticity in reproductive traits: evidence from a viviparous snake. Ecology, 70: 1768–1774.

Gibbons, J. W., J. L. Greene, and K. K. Patterson. 1982. Variation in reproductive patterns of aquatic turtles. Copeia, 1982: 776–784.

Greene, H. W. 1983. Dietary correlates of the origin and radiation of snakes. Amer. Zool., 23: 431–441.

Gregory, P. T. 1977. Life-history parameters of the red-sided garter snake (*Thamnophis sirtalis parietalis*) in an extreme environment, the Interlake Region of Manitoba. Natl. Mus. Canada Publ. Zool., 13: 1–44.

Griffith, B., J. M. Scott, J. W. Carpenter, and C. Reed. 1989. Translocation as a species conservation tool: status and strategy. Science, 245: 477–480.

Hom, C. L., and M. E. Cochran. 1991. Ecological experiments: assumptions, approaches, and prospects. Herpetologica, 47: 460–473.

Jones, S. M., R. E. Ballinger, and W. P. Porter. 1987. Physiological and environmental sources of variation in reproduction: prairie lizards in a food-rich environment. Oikos, 48: 325–335.

Kaplan, R. H. 1987. Developmental plasticity and maternal effects of reproductive characteristics in the frog *Bombina orientalis*. Oecologia (Berlin), 71: 273–279.

Lillywhite, H. B. 1987. Temperature, energetics, and physiological ecology, p. 422–477. *In* R. A. Seigel, J. T. Collins, and S. S. Novak (eds.), Snakes: Ecology and Evolutionary Biology. McGraw Hill, New York.

Mushinsky, H. R. 1987. Foraging ecology, p. 302–334. *In* R. A. Seigel, J. T. Collins, and S. S. Novak (eds.), Snakes: Ecology and Evolutionary Biology. McGraw Hill, New York.

Parker, W. S., and W. S. Brown. 1973. Species composition and population changes in two complexes of snake hibernacula in northern Utah. Herpetologica, 29: 319–326.

Parker, W. S., and M. V. Plummer. 1987. Population ecology, p. 253–302. *In* R. A. Seigel, J. T. Collins, and S. S. Novak (eds.), Snakes: Ecology and Evolutionary Biology. McGraw Hill, New York.

Plummer, M. V. 1983. Annual variation in stored lipids and reproduction in green snakes (*Opheodrys aestivus*). Copeia, 1983: 741–745.

Pough, F. H., and J. D. Groves. 1983. Specialization of the body form and food habits of snakes. Amer. Zool., 23: 443–454.

Seigel, R. A., and H. S. Fitch. 1984. Ecological patterns of relative clutch mass in snakes. Oecologia (Berlin), 61: 293–301.

—. 1985. Annual variation in reproduction in snakes in a fluctuating environment. Jour. Animal Ecol., 54: 497–505.

Seigel, R. A., and N. B. Ford. 1991. Phenotypic plasticity in the reproductive characteristics of an oviparous snake, *Elaphe guttata*: implications for life-history studies. Herpetologica, 301–307.

Seigel, R. A., M. M. Huggins, and N. B. Ford. 1987. Reduction in locomotor ability as a cost of reproduction in gravid snakes. Oecologia (Berlin), 73: 481–485.

Shine, R. 1980. "Costs" of reproduction in reptiles. Oecologia (Berlin), 46: 92–100.

—. 1986. Ecology of a low-food specialist: food habits and reproductive biology of the Arafura file snake (Acrochordidae). Copeia, 1986: 424–437.

Smith, C. C., and S. D. Fretwell. 1974. The optimal balance between size and number of offspring. Amer. Nat., 108: 499–506.

Stearns, S. C. 1976. Life-history tactics: a review of the ideas. Quart. Rev. Biol., 51: 3–47.

—. 1989. The evolutionary significance of phenotypic plasticity. BioScience, 39: 436–445.

Vitt, L. J., and J. D. Congdon. 1978. Body shape, reproductive effort, and relative clutch mass in lizards: resolution of a paradox. Amer. Nat., 112: 595–608.

Ford, N. B., and R. A. Seigel. 1994. Phenotypic plasticity: implications for captive-breeding and conservation programs, p. 175–182. *In* J. B. Murphy, K. Adler, and J. T. Collins (eds.), Captive Management and Conservation of Amphibians and Reptiles. Society for the Study of Amphibians and Reptiles, Ithaca (New York). Contributions to Herpetology, volume 11.

Manipulations of Clutch and Offspring Size in Lizards: Mechanistic, Evolutionary, and Conservation Considerations

Barry Sinervo*

Introduction

The trade-off between the number and the size of individual offspring that a female can produce is a fundamental tenet of life-history theory (Lack 1954; Wilbur 1977; Williams 1966) and is a general feature of reptilian reproduction. Given functional limitations on total clutch mass (Bauwens and Thoen 1981; Reznick 1985; Shine 1980; Sinervo et al. 1991; Van Damme et al. 1989; Vitt and Congdon 1978; Vitt and Price 1982), a female producing large offspring clearly must produce fewer offspring than a female producing small offspring. In this chapter, I describe new techniques (Sinervo and Licht 1991*a*, 1991*b*) for altering clutch size and offspring size in lizards, as well as several applications of these techniques.

The benefits accrued to a captive-rearing program from increasing the number of eggs in a clutch are straightforward. Increasing the clutch size can potentially result in a greater intrinsic rate of increase (r_m), both in captive populations or in restocking programs in the wild. Although the advantage in fecundity of increased clutch size is obvious, the consequences of the correlated decreases in offspring size are not as well characterized, and offspring size may have critical effects on offspring growth and survival. For example, very small hatchlings may have difficulty in finding food items of the right size in natural populations, and they may not be able to defend suitable territories (Fox 1978). Moreover, within the context of natural populations, increasing offspring size is generally thought to enhance offspring quality as indexed by offspring survival (Smith and Fretwell 1974; Stearns 1976; Wilbur 1977; Williams 1966; and studies that support these theoretical expectations: Ferguson and Fox 1984; Jayne and Bennett 1990). If so, experimentally increasing hatchling size might, in fact, enhance offspring survival sufficiently to compensate for the associated decline in clutch size. Nevertheless, natural selection on some populations might conceivably be relaxed in some environments, such that the most efficient restocking program might entail releasing as small an offspring as feasible, because this has the benefit of an increased clutch size. Moreover, in studies on natural selection on offspring size, we have found that large size does not always result in high survival in the wild (Sinervo et al. 1992). This might be true generally in situations in which local extinction of the species has occurred and thus there is reduced competition from conspecifics. Within a laboratory setting, competition among hatchlings can be eliminated by housing individuals separately. Under such conditions, growth may be similar despite large differences in initial size at hatching (Sinervo 1990). By simultaneously increasing clutch size at the expense of reduced offspring size, the efficiency of a restocking program might be greatly enhanced and accelerated.

I will present a review of the experimental and comparative data illustrating the mechanistic basis of the trade-off between egg size and egg number, as well as the relationship between these two traits and other important life-history attributes, such as

* Department of Biology
Indiana University
Bloomington, Indiana 47405, USA

Acronyms used in this chapter:

FSH	Follicle-stimulating hormone
GnRH	Gonadotropin releasing hormone
RCM	Relative clutch mass
r_m	Intrinsic rate of increase
SE	Standard error
SVL	Snout-to-vent length

total clutch mass. By referencing such experiments to comparative patterns, one can infer potential constraints on the evolution of reproductive patterns. In general, if traits covary in a consistent way among related taxa, evolutionary biologists become more certain that such patterns reflect some underlying constraints (Sinervo 1993). "Allometric engineering" of offspring size in reptiles—via the mechanisms governing the determination of clutch size (Sinervo and Licht 1991*a*, 1991*b*) or the manipulation of the developmental mechanisms involving the growth of the embryo (Sinervo 1990; Sinervo and Huey 1990; Sinervo and McEdward 1988)—can provide direct experimental evidence concerning the causal proximate mechanisms that underlie presumed "phylogenetic constraints" (Sinervo 1993). Such issues are not strictly in the esoteric realm of life-history theory (Pease and Bull 1988). By uncovering such constraints, we delimit those potential clutch sizes and egg sizes that are readily achieved by experimental manipulations—information that is useful when applying these methods to captive-rearing programs. Moreover, by referencing these offspring size manipulations to survival of offspring in the wild (Sinervo et al. 1992), we provide direct experimental evidence concerning the adaptive value of these life-history traits. Such information is useful for designing suitable strategies for restocking efforts in natural populations.

Use of Physiological and Hormonal Mechanisms to Manipulate Clutch Size and Offspring Size

The trade-off between egg size and egg number is typified by patterns found among populations of the Side-blotched Lizard (*Uta stansburiana*) located in the inner Coast Range of California. Females from populations that produce relatively large clutches usually produce relatively small eggs (Figure 1B). This is only one hierarchical level of intraspecific covariation involved in the trade-off. Similarly, the trade-off is found among females within populations (Figures 1A and 1B) (Nussbaum 1981; Sinervo and Licht 1991*a*). Moreover, as female *U. stansburiana* produce successive clutches during the reproductive season, clutch size decreases and offspring size increases. Thus, the trade-off exists within individual females among the clutches they lay during the reproductive season (Figure 1A) (Ferguson and Snell 1986; Nussbaum 1981; Sinervo and Licht 1991*a*).

In a complementary set of experiments, we have found that all of these hierarchies of covariation involving the trade-off between egg size and egg number appear to be regulated by a simple hormonal and physiological interaction (Sinervo and Licht 1991*a*, 1991*b*). The first experiment involves administration of exogenous gonadotropin. We injected early vitellogenic female *U. stansburiana* (2–3 mm follicles) with 10 μg of ovine follicle-stimulating hormone (FSH) every other day over a six-day period. Thereafter and until ovulating, females received 2 μg in 100 μl saline every other day. The lizards that received FSH typically produced larger clutches of viable (but smaller) eggs (Figure 1B), indicating that additional follicles were recruited into the clutch. Moreover, when vitellogenic females from Corral Hollow Road and Del Puerto Canyon Road, California, populations that produce relatively large eggs and small clutches, were given exogenous gonadotropin (FSH), the average number of eggs increased from 4.3 to 6.5 eggs, and the average egg size dropped from 0.43 g to 0.35 g (Figure 1B)—values that are similar to those in a population near Los Baños Grandes, California, which naturally produces relatively small eggs and large clutches (Figure 1B).

These experimental manipulations were calibrated to explore the range of clutch sizes and egg sizes potentially available to a population. For example, the comparative data indicate that females in the northern populations (Corral Hollow and Del Puerto Canyon) rarely lay clutches larger than six eggs, but females from Los Baños routinely do so. Experimentally increasing levels of FSH resulted in some females from northern populations which naturally produce small clutches to produce a large clutch of up to seven eggs. While there are problems with interpreting results of an exogenous, heterologous hormone treatment, the increases in clutch size and egg size were within the range of phenotypes observed in other geographic areas (e.g. Los Baños) and, for the most part, we obtained viable, hatchable eggs from these females.

Other studies on *Anolis carolinensis*, a lizard of comparable mass (about 4.0 g), have demonstrated that administration of a daily 10 μg dose of FSH increases the number of yolking follicles, but that daily doses of 1 μg are not sufficient to illicit a response (Jones et al. 1976). Larger doses of FSH are apparently pharmacological and can result in a dramatic proliferation of vitellogenic and previtellogenic follicles (Licht 1970; Jones et al. 1976) and can block ovulation (Licht 1970).

The reciprocal effects of clutch size on offspring size can be further illustrated by a second technique for changing clutch size—surgically decreasing the number of yolking follicles and thus decreasing the number of eggs in a clutch (Sinervo and Licht 1991*a*, 1991*b*). When follicles are relatively small, that is, about 3–5 mm (follicles in *U. stansburiana* are ovulated when they are about 8 mm in diameter), they can be surgically exposed by making a small incision in the abdomen (female is anesthetized with metafane). A small hole is made with a syringe needle in a few of the follicles in one or both ovaries, yolk is gently squeezed from the follicle in a "yolkectomy," and the female's abdomen is sutured closed. Females undergoing this surgery typically produce a smaller clutch of eggs that consists of much larger offspring (Figures 1B and 1C). Yolk is reallocated to the remaining intact follicles, because the follicle yolkectomy selectively terminates the growth of a subset of follicles. Clutch size is reduced from an average of 4.3 eggs to 2.3 eggs, and average egg size is increased from 0.42 to 0.50 g. The size of eggs from females that undergo a yolkectomy are very similar to the size of eggs from females that lay naturally small clutches (Figure 1B). Thus, the surgical re-

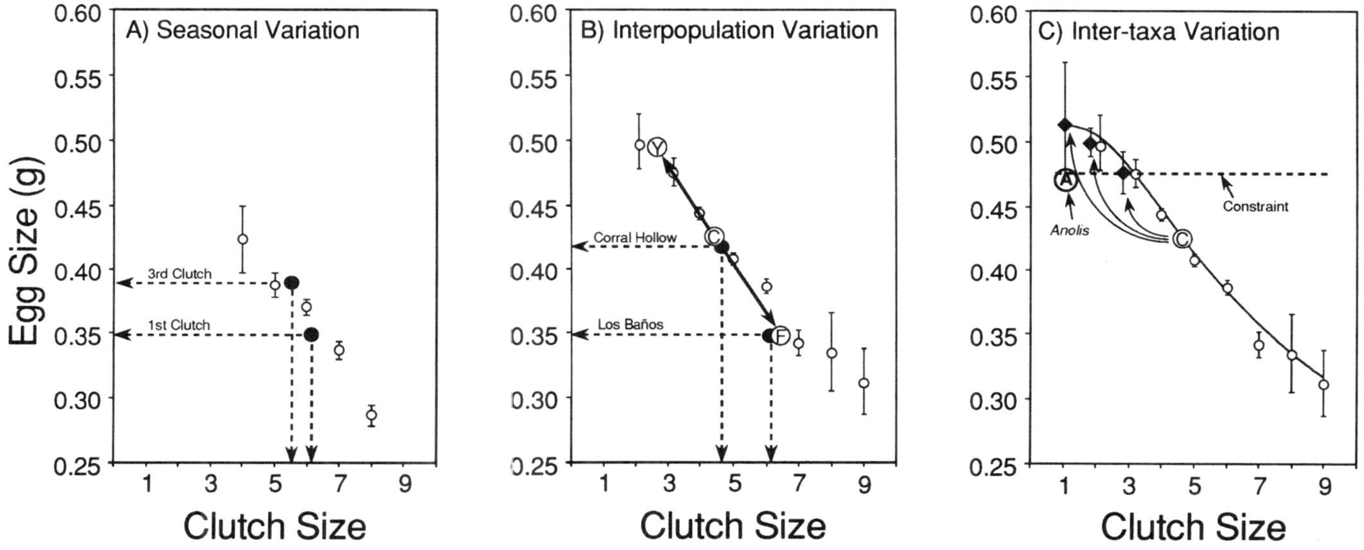

FIGURE 1. (A) Seasonal trade-off between clutch size and egg size. Variation in mean (± SE) egg size (in g) of female *Uta stansburiana* with different number of eggs (clutch size) (o) from a population near Los Baños Grandes, California. Also plotted are the mean egg and clutch size for the first and third clutches laid during the reproductive season (•). (B) Geographic variation in the trade-off relative to experimentally-induced trade-off. Variation in mean (± SE) egg size (g) and clutch size among female *U. stansburiana* from populations from the Inner Coast Range (o). Also plotted are the mean egg and clutch size for two populations (•) near Los Baños Grandes and Corral Hollow Road that lay different-sized eggs and clutches on the first clutch of the reproductive season. The results from two complementary experimental manipulations of clutch size are also plotted. Females receiving exogenous gonadotropin (ovine FSH) Ⓕ produce larger clutches of small eggs relative to either sham or control females Ⓒ. Females with surgically reduced clutch size achieved by follicle "yolkectomy" Ⓨ produce a smaller clutch of large eggs. Note the concordance between the experimentally induced trade-off between egg size and clutch size (for example, arrows between treatments groups C → F or C → Y) and the trade-off as it is expressed at the various hierarchies of population variation: (1) among females, (2) among clutches laid during the reproductive season, and (3) among population averages. (C) Inter-taxa comparison of a multi-egged *Uta* with a single-egged *Anolis*. Average clutch size and egg size for female *U. stansburiana* in the Inner Coast Range (o) and the overall average egg size and clutch size Ⓒ. Note the non-linear relationship between clutch size and egg size for *U. stansburiana* that levels off for females laying either naturally small clutches (o) or experimentally induced clutches (◆) of one, two, and three eggs. The dashed line reflects the egg size (0.48 g) for which *Uta* females experience a noticeable increase in the frequency of burst eggs at oviposition or oviducally bound eggs (see also Figure 2). Owing to significant effects of the covariate body size on both traits, all data have been adjusted to the average post-laying female mass of 4.0 g. The average egg size for a comparable-sized 4.0 g female *Anolis* Ⓐ is effectively below functional constraints delimited for *U. stansburiana*. Redrawn from Sinervo and Licht (1991*a*, 1991*b*).

duction of clutch size makes eggs larger in a fashion that reflects the trade-off between intrapopulation egg size and egg number.

The yolkectomy surgery only affects the current clutch and females lay subsequent clutches on the same schedule—that is, on a one-month schedule—as sham-manipulated females (females that have been subjected to surgery, but have not had yolk removed from their follicles). Subsequent clutches revert back to the unmanipulated clutch size and egg size that is characteristic of controls or sham-manipulated females. Sham-manipulated females have the same average clutch and egg size as unmanipulated females, that is, 4.3 eggs that weigh 0.42 g (Sinervo and Licht 1991*a*, 1991*b*).

These complementary experiments suggest that egg size is largely a function of the number of eggs recruited into the developing clutch, which is regulated by gonadotropin levels or female sensitivity to gonadotropin (FSH). Moreover, our complementary experimental manipulations explain the patterns of covariation between egg size and clutch size at the various hierarchical levels of covariation found in *U. stansburiana*: within females during the reproductive season (Figure 1A), among females within a population (Figure 1B), and among population averages (Figure 1B). The trade-off, as it is expressed at each of these levels of variation, tracks very closely the experimentally induced trade-off that is achieved by manipulating clutch size (Figure 1B).

Constraints on the Evolution of Clutch Size and Egg Size

It has been suggested that adaptive evolution of egg size is constrained among turtles (Congdon and Gibbons 1987) and among lizard taxa that are phylogenetically conservative in their production of one or two eggs (for example, anoles and geckos [Andrews and Rand 1974; Shine and Greer 1991; Vitt 1986]). Due to the trade-off between egg size and egg number, lizard taxa that produce one or two eggs per clutch might be expected to have much larger eggs than more typical multi-egged lizards, such as *Uta*. A comparison of experimentally induced one-egg clutches from *Uta stansburiana*, which normally does not lay one-egg clutches (Figures 1C and 2), with lizards of the genus *Anolis*, which exclusively lay one-egg clutches, provides a direct experimental comparison of these reproductive strategies (Sinervo and Licht 1991*b*).

The curve relating egg size and egg number in *U. stansburiana* is markedly nonlinear with a sigmoidal shape (Figure 1C), which suggests that a functional ceiling in egg size has been reached in one-, two- and three-egg clutches. Indeed, the number of eggs that became oviducally bound or eggs that burst at oviposition increases with decreased clutch size in *U. stansburiana* and this effect becomes most pronounced in clutches of three and fewer eggs (Figure 2) or at egg sizes greater than 0.48 g (Figure 1C)(Sinervo and Licht 1991*b*). Noteworthy in light

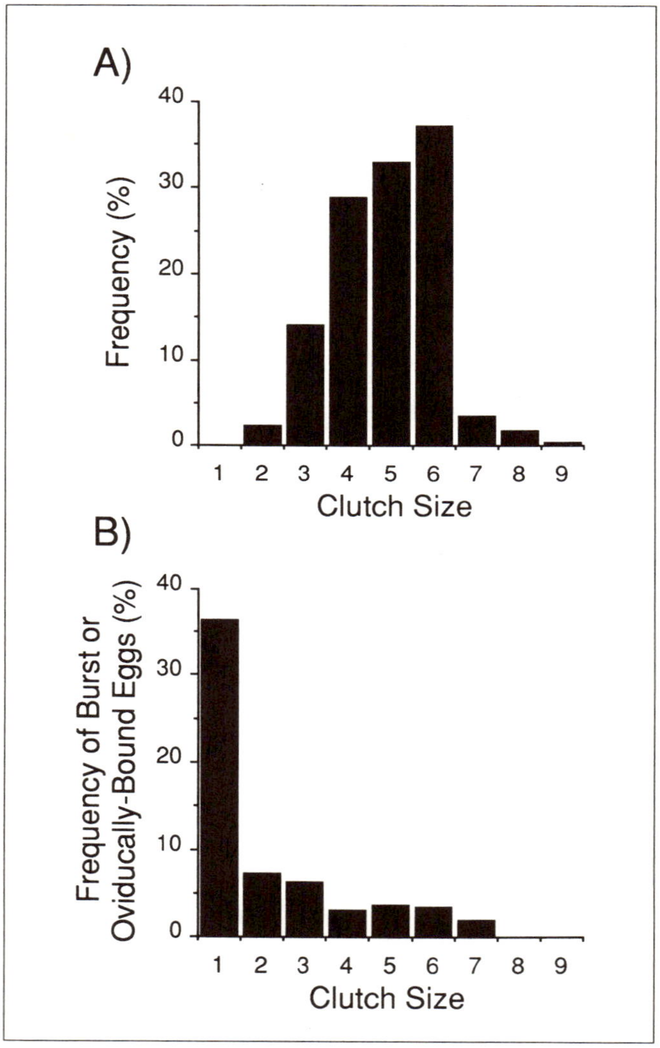

FIGURE 2. (A) Frequency histogram of clutch size for *Uta stansburiana* in the Coast Range of California. Note the low frequency of two-egged clutches and the absence of one-egged clutches. (B) Increase in probability of burst eggs or oviducally bound eggs in *U. stansburiana* with decreased clutch size. Data from Sinervo and Licht (1991*b*).

of these experimental observations is the average egg size of a lizard of the genus *Anolis* as compared with that of a *U. stansburiana* of similar body size. Lizards of the genus *Anolis*, which exclusively lay one-egg clutches, lay eggs that are slightly smaller (0.48 g) than the egg size of *U. stansburiana* from experimentally induced clutches of one, two, and three eggs—which are those clutch sizes and egg sizes with which *U. stansburiana* experienced the greatest increase in burst or oviducally bound eggs (Figure 3).

These structural constraints on the evolution of maximum offspring size also limit the evolution of total clutch mass or relative clutch mass (RCM) of *U. stansburiana* (Sinervo and Licht 1991*b*). In small clutches, particularly in clutches with three and fewer eggs (Figure 1B), egg size in *U. stansburiana* is not as large as one would predict from a simple yolk-allocation model (Sinervo and Licht 1991*b*) and for very good reasons. Eggs that are too large either burst at oviposition, resulting in the death of the embryo, or become oviducally bound, which inevitably results in the death of the female (Figure 3) if the egg is not surgically removed. These limitations on maximum egg size in small clutches dramatically reduces total clutch mass, in addition to the drop in clutch mass that is expected from a simple decrease in the number of offspring (for example, clutch size). Thus, egg size, egg number, total clutch mass, and RCM are physiologically linked life-history traits due to the proximate constraints on egg size and the mechanisms by which this group of traits is regulated.

Mechanisms of Regulation of Clutch and Egg Size

The correlations between egg size, egg number, and total clutch mass are explicable in terms of the known mechanisms that govern reptilian reproduction, and these mechanisms suggest a mechanistic model whereby this group of life-history traits could

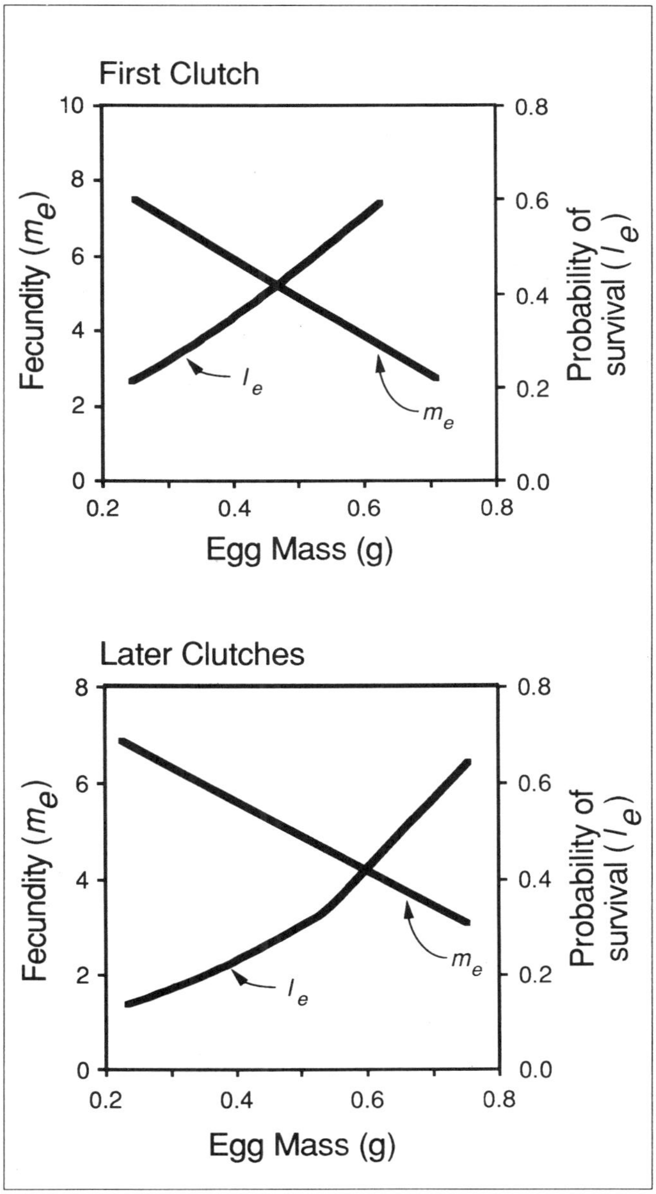

FIGURE 3. In natural populations of *Uta stansburiana* in the Coast Range of California, fecundity selection (m_e) results from the trade-off between egg size and egg number. Females that produce small eggs produce more offspring. Fecundity selection is balanced, however, by the effects of selection on offspring survival (l_e). In this case the survival of female offspring is higher if the female parent provisioned the eggs with more yolk. The curves describing the probability of survival to maturity as a function of egg size (l_e) are based on results from 493 female neonates that were released into a population located near Los Baños Grandes, during the summers of 1989 and 1990. Survival data are based on control, experimentally miniaturized, and experimentally gigantized hatchlings that were released into nature. Survival selection acting on offspring produced on the first clutch was significantly different from survival selection acting on offspring produced on later clutches. The survival curve for later clutches is shifted to larger egg sizes relative to the survival curve for the first clutch. The net effect of this seasonal change in offspring survival is a shift in the optimum to larger egg sizes (see also Figures 4 and 5)(redrawn from Sinervo et al. 1992).

be linked physiologically. Jones (1978) has proposed that clutch size in lizards is dependent on a process termed "follicular selection." An assumption of this model is that follicles compete for FSH, such that follicles that do not receive enough FSH undergo atresia. Those follicles ahead in the competition for FSH have greater vascularization, perhaps resulting from higher rates of estrogen production (Gavaud 1986; Gerstle and Callard 1972; Hahn 1967; Yaron and Widzer 1978) and thus their uptake of FSH and yolk is further enhanced (Jones et al. 1976; Jones 1978). Their more rapid growth further depletes the available pool of FSH, which further limits the growth of smaller follicles.

Our experimental observations on *Uta stansburiana* are consistent with this hypothesis (Sinervo and Licht 1991*a*, 1991*b*). The administration of exogenous gonadotropin in *U. stansburiana* may have prevented some follicles from going atretic by making FSH less limiting. It is important to note that the FSH treatment was only effective if initiated very early during the reproductive cycle, for example when follicles are about 3–4 mm or less in diameter. A typical cycle between clutches for *U. stansburiana* is 24 days; the 3 mm follicle size is reached within the first half week. If treatment was initiated after this point, clutch size or egg size were unaffected (Sinervo and Licht 1991*a*). Presumably follicular selection can only take place during this early period of vitellogenesis. Once the maximum number of follicles is set, they compete for the available pool of FSH to maintain growth rate. If a follicle does not receive sufficient FSH to maintain growth after it reaches 3 mm in size, it could potentially undergo follicular atresia even up to a size of about 5 mm (Sinervo and Licht 1991*a* and unpubl. data). Additionally, the model provides a mechanistic framework for interpreting seasonal changes in clutch size and egg size that appear to be prevalent in lizards (DeMarco 1989; Ferguson and Snell 1986; Nussbaum 1981; Sinervo 1990; Sinervo and Licht 1991*a*). For example, other hormones that are correlated with reproductive condition, such as corticosterone levels (Wilson and Wingfield 1992), might potentially modulate circulating levels of gonadotropin and as such would have proximate effects on clutch size and egg size through a process of follicular recruitment or through atresia. Nevertheless, the modulating effects of such hormones would be restricted to the earlier time points of vitellogenesis, because recruitment and atresia are apparently limited to earlier stages of the reproductive cycle (Sinervo and Licht 1991*a*).

Thus, clutch size in lizards is presumably determined by the levels of gonadotropin or perhaps the timing of a surge in plasma levels of gonadotropin during the earliest stages of vitellogenesis (Sinervo and Licht 1991*b*). Once clutch size is determined through a process of follicular selection (Jones 1978; Jones et al. 1976), the egg size of the resultant clutch is also determined (Sinervo and Licht 1991*a*, 1991*b*). We hypothesize (Sinervo and Licht 1991*b*) that the additional linking between egg and clutch size and total clutch mass would arise if the level of vitellogenin produced by the liver in response to estrogen (Gavaud 1986; Gerstle and Callard 1972; Hahn 1967; Ho et al. 1982; Yaron and Widzer 1978) is also quantitatively related to the number of yolking follicles and their estrogen production. Increased numbers of follicles would increase the total surface area of follicles, which is the site of estrogen production. Presumably, elevated levels of estrogen associated with a large clutch would enhance total clutch volume through its potential effects on production of vitellogenin by the liver, circulating levels of vitellogenin in the bloodstream, and subsequent uptake by follicles.

Effects of Egg Size on Offspring Survival in the Wild

We have used the techniques of offspring-size manipulation and allometric engineering, in combination with studies of natural selection, to determine causal relationships between egg size and offspring survival in two populations of *Uta stansburiana* (Sinervo et al. 1992). Our results experimentally validate the basic premises that underly theories of optimal egg size—fecundity selection that favors the production of large clutches of small eggs is balanced by survival selection that favors the production of large offspring (Figure 3). The balance between fecundity and survival selection results in an "optimum egg size"—the reproductive strategy that produces the most surviving offspring at maturity (Figure 4). Despite these general trends, large hatchlings did not always have the highest survival rate, contrary to most theoretical expectations (Smith and Fretwell 1974; Stearns 1976; Wilbur

1977; Williams 1966); survival depended on size, season, and even the sex of the offspring. Natural selection consistently favored large female hatchlings, as theory predicted (Figure 3). Size selection on male hatchlings was more complex than selection on female hatchlings, however, and the largest male hatchlings did not have the highest survival rate (Sinervo et al. 1992). Survival selection on males from birth to one month of age typically included a significant optimizing component that favored intermediate-sized hatchlings. In one case, survival selection was directional, but favored small male hatchlings.

Average egg size in *U. stansburiana* also increases during the reproductive season (Figure 1A) and if this reflects an adaptive reproductive strategy, these shifts in egg size of adult females should coincide with a shift in optimal egg size of their offspring. The prediction always holds qualitatively in that both observed average egg size and optimal egg size shift during the reproductive season. Quantitatively, however, average egg size did not shift nearly as much (about 9% increase in the average) as did optimal egg size (about 66% increase in the optimum). Moreover, average egg size did not track optimum egg size precisely.

These detailed observations on natural selection on egg size in *U. stansburiana* could potentially be applied to restocking programs of threatened or endangered species in the wild. Certainly, *U. stansburiana* is not endangered or threatened, but our results on natural selection provide a useful model for any future restocking programs. For simplicity, I have only considered fitness effects on female offspring, because they contribute directly to the r_m

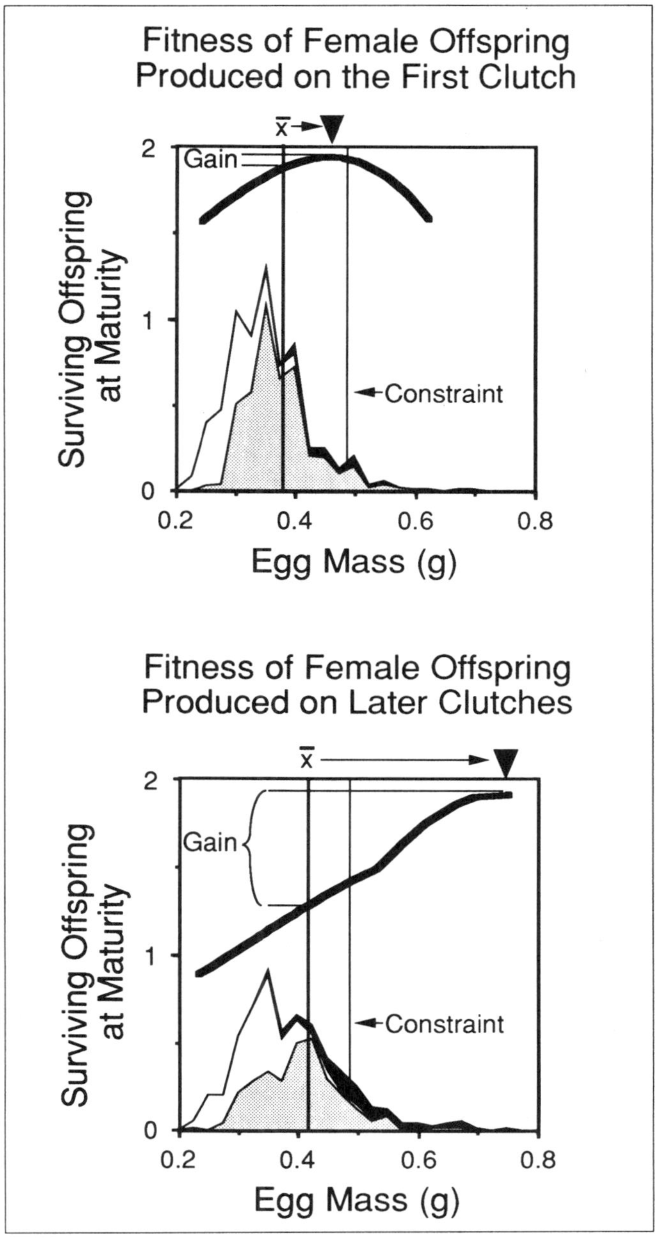

FIGURE 4. Fitness of female offspring as a function of egg size (thick line). Fitness is equivalent to number of surviving female offspring at maturity and was calculated by multiplying $m_e \cdot l_e$ (number of offspring for each egg size multiplied by the probability of survival for each egg size; see also Figure 3). The optimum egg size (▼) is the reproductive strategy that leaves the most surviving offspring at maturity. Also plotted are the frequency histograms (shaded portion) for natural variation in egg size along with the observed average egg size ($\bar{x}$). Data are partitioned by first versus later clutches because of a seasonal shift in the intensity of natural selection on offspring size (see also Figure 3). The detection of selection on offspring size was facilitated by experimentally decreasing egg size (open portion of graph) and increasing egg size (solid portion of graph) relative to the distribution of unmanipulated offspring (shaded graph)(see also Figure 5). There is a significant shift in observed average egg size on first versus later clutches. There is also a shift in optimum egg size (▼). The observed average egg size of females does not, however, match the optimum. An increase in the number of surviving offspring or a "gain" in fitness could be achieved over the average fitness resulting from natural variation in egg size by experimentally increasing offspring size to the optimum egg size (for example, $\bar{x} \rightarrow$ ▼). The gain in fitness on later clutches (50%) is much larger than the gain that could be achieved on the first clutch (8%). Constraints on the production of excessively large eggs (increased probability of reproductive difficulties) may, however, limit such gains in practice (see discussion in the text)(redrawn from Sinervo et al. 1992).

of a population (that is, through egg production). For example, the most efficient restocking program with *U. stansburiana* would entail experimentally increasing the size of female offspring throughout the reproductive season. That is, reproductive females are not producing an egg size as large as the optimal egg, and production of even larger offspring that have enhanced survival would more than offset the fecundity advantage arising from producing large clutches of small eggs. Whereas increasing egg size would result in a "fitness gain" (increase in the number of offspring that survive to maturity) of only 8% on the first clutch, it would result in a fitness gain of 50% on later clutches (Figure 4). Clearly, survival of offspring as a function of egg size should be closely monitored in any restocking program, because this important parameter may be experimentally adjusted to increase efficiency.

An important caveat to these increases in efficiency relates to the constraints described earlier regarding maximum offspring size in *U. stansburiana*. These constraints may explain why females do not primarily track the optimum egg size with their later clutches. Females with experimentally decreased clutch size and thus enlarged eggs (as described above) often become egg-bound or produce eggs that burst at oviposition (Sinervo and Licht 1991*b*). A pronounced increase in the probability of such problems occurs at about 0.48 g (Sinervo and Licht 1991*b*), well below many of the later-clutch optima detected in our field studies (Figure 4). Females that become egg-bound would ultimately die in natural populations, and thus the production of excessively large eggs required to match the optimum egg size in later clutches would result in a cost of reproduction that could potentially decrease future reproductive success of free-ranging lizards (Reznick 1985; Sinervo et al. 1992). Such considerations may or may not apply to captive reproductive stock, because oviducally bound eggs can be readily removed by surgery.

Summary

The two manipulations discussed above—that increase and decrease clutch size—demonstrate that clutch size is involved in the regulation of offspring size. It is relatively easy to alter clutch size and egg size. The biology of the animal dictates which direction of clutch-size manipulation would be most beneficial. Moreover, changes in clutch size simultaneously affect egg size in a fashion that reflects the trade-off between these two traits (Figure 1).

Although the techniques for increasing offspring size by ablating follicles require surgery, it is relatively straightforward. In fact it is a much simpler surgery than removing necrotic eggs from egg-bound lizards and snakes. The benefits to a captive-rearing program are measured in terms of offspring health. Larger offspring have higher sprint performance and stamina (Sinervo 1990; Sinervo and Huey 1990) and thus, are often (though not always) more vigorous in nature (Sinervo et al. 1992). Increasing offspring size would also be quite useful for some snakes that produce very small offspring that are very difficult to rear (for example, some of the Central American dwarf boas, *Ungaliophis* spp., or in Pacific Ground Boa, *Candoia carinata*, which produce 10–64 very small offspring that mature at less than 30 cm snout-to-vent length [SVL]). As mentioned earlier, enhanced offspring size might enhance survival in the wild, thereby increasing the success of a restocking program.

The techniques for increasing clutch size are even more straightforward. They only require injections of FSH every other day and the results on clutch size can be quite dramatic. (Other methods that might be used to provide a continuous delivery of gonadotropin over a defined time course include the implantation of an Alzet® pump in larger reptiles or perhaps implantation of subcutaneous FSH pellets in small reptiles [both are available from Innovative Research, Inc].) For example, in *Uta stansburiana*, we augmented clutch size from an average of 4.3 to 6.0 eggs—almost a 50% increase. Although injection of FSH does increase clutch size, it does so by reducing the size of the offspring. This may or may not be much of problem if the offspring are easy to rear. Increasing clutch size and reducing offspring size has an additional benefit—it may reduce the risk of female lizards becoming egg bound or eggs bursting when they are laid (Sinervo and Licht 1991*b*). If this is generally true, it might be quite important for lowering the risk of reproductive mortality of breeding stock.

Gonadotropin may also be an effective hormone that primes the reproduction of animals that are difficult to breed. FSH alone is sufficient to elicit growth of ovaries and follicles, even without overwintering, in a sceloporine lizard, *U. stansburiana*

(Licht 1970; B. Sinervo and D. DeNardo, unpubl. data). Additionally, in a gekkonid lizard (*Teratoscincus przewalskii*), we have successfully obtained follicle growth by only using FSH stimulation with no overwintering (D. DeNardo and B. Sinervo, unpubl. data). Despite our success in initiating follicle growth in *U. stansburiana* and *T. przewalskii*, ovulation did not occur. FSH treatment alone at the doses used (about 2.5 μl/1.0 g of body mass) may not be sufficient to complete the reproductive cycle. Noteworthy in this regard is that a single high dose (about 25 μl/1.0 g body mass) results in successful ovulation (Licht and Crews 1975; Jones et al. 1988).

Perhaps gonadotropin releasing hormone (GnRH) might stimulate a complete reproductive cycle without overwintering that apparently primes the reproductive cycle of many temperate reptiles. Recent success in stimulating reproduction in the Green Iguana, *Iguana iguana*, using Chicken I-GnRH (Phillips et al. 1985, 1987), suggests that GnRH stimulation might be possible in at least some lizards. Nevertheless, the endocrine systems of many reptiles, including snakes (D. DeNardo, pers. comm.) and turtles (P. Licht, pers. comm.), are apparently unresponsive to mammalian or avian GnRH.

The techniques of clutch enlargement via FSH stimulation or of offspring enlargement by surgical reduction of clutch size have not been tested on other reptiles, such as snakes and turtles. Limited success in stimulating the ovaries of gravid Northern Water Snakes (*Nerodia sipedon*) with FSH (Aldridge 1982) suggest that it might have wider applicability. Increased clutch size could indeed prove useful in reptiles that produce small clutches of relatively large offspring: snakes, such as Madagascan Boa, *Acrantophis madagascariensis* (1–8 offspring); Burrowing Python, *Calabaria reinhardtii* (2–4 eggs); and Ball Python, *Python regius* (2–8 eggs)(Ross and Marzec 1990); or turtles, such as the African Pancake Tortoise, *Malacochersus tornieri* (1 egg), Common Mud turtle, *Kinosternon subrubrum* (2–5 eggs); and Desert Tortoise, *Gopherus agassizii* (5 eggs)(Ballinger 1978).

Due to the similarity of the hormonal regulation of reproduction among reptiles (Licht et al. 1977; Licht 1982), comparable methods could likely be found for altering clutch size (and offspring size) in many reptilian groups. The usefulness of the hormonal approaches is limited, however, by the specificity of action that has been found for certain preparations (Licht et al. 1977). Clearly, there is considerable scope for future research to test the efficacy of these experimental approaches on a wide range of reptilian species.

Our measurements of natural selection using manipulations of clutch size and offspring size (Figure 5) indicate that these life-history parameters are potentially important in the maintenance of captive-breeding colonies or in restocking programs in the wild. In restocking programs of wild populations, every effort should be made to collect vital statistics on the female (such as clutch size, offspring size, and age, as well as reproductive difficulties as a function of these variables), their offspring (for example, hatchling mass and snout-vent length), and the survival of individually marked neonates in the wild. Clutch size and offspring size can be readily "adjusted" in laboratory stock to increase the efficiency of the restocking effort as assessed by the number of surviving offspring at maturity.

Because of the importance of these life-history parameters in the wild (Figure 4), captive breeders should also maintain careful records of these reproductive attributes. In a captive setting, the magnitude of attrition necessary to maintain captive-breeding programs at a stable population size dictates that some offspring will not contribute to the next generation's breeding pool. Many more offspring are produced than can be reared to matu-

FIGURE 5. Detecting natural selection on offspring size in *Uta stansburiana* was facilitated by using miniaturized, gigantized, and control hatchlings. Hatchling size variation of experimentally altered offspring ranged from the 0.22 g miniaturized hatchling up to the 0.92 g gigantized hatchling. An average-sized control hatchling (0.48 g) is shown in the center. Photograph by B. Sinervo.

rity, due to the space limitations in any facility. Given this attrition, breeders may be inadvertently causing dramatic "artificial selection" of breeding stock for life-history traits like egg size and clutch size, that would ultimately result in genetic changes that render the genetic constitution of a species unsuitable for restocking efforts in the wild. Such artificial selection may arise from using the fastest growing or fastest maturing individuals as stock for the next generation. Maintaining the genetic diversity of life-history attributes or the original "wild-type" life-history characteristics (for example, clutch size, egg size, and body size) should be just as important as the efforts that now go into maintaining baseline genetic diversity (such as prevention of inbreeding), particularly if the ultimate aim of the reproductive surplus of a captive population is a restocking program in the wild.

In this regard, experimentally increasing offspring size produces higher quality offspring (as measured by survival in the wild, for example; see Figure 4) without a genetic alteration of the original life-history attributes. For example, if captive stock has poor neonate survival, perhaps due to small offspring size, rather than selecting for the largest offspring to contribute to the next generation of captive stock (artificial selection), the breeder could experimentally enhance offspring size (and thus offspring survival to maturity) without the undesirable effects that artificial selection has on the "wild-type" life history.

Literature Cited

Aldridge, R. D. 1982. The ovarian cycle of the watersnake *Nerodia sipedon*, and effects of hypophysectomy and gonadotropin administration. Herpetologica, 38: 71–79.

Andrews, R., and A. S. Rand. 1974. Reproductive effort in anoline lizards. Ecology, 55: 1317–1327.

Ballinger, R. E. 1978. Variation in and evolution of clutch and litter size, p. 789–825. *In* R. E. Jones (ed.), The Vertebrate Ovary. Plenum Press, New York.

Bauwens, D., and C. Thoen. 1981. Escape tactics and vulnerability to predation associated with reproduction in the lizard *Lacerta vivipara*. Jour. Anim. Ecol., 50: 733–743.

Congdon, J. D., and J. W. Gibbons. 1987. Morphological constraint on egg size: a challenge to optimal egg size theory? Proc. Natl. Acad. Sci. USA, 84: 4145–4147.

DeMarco, V. G. 1989. Annual variation in the seasonal shift in egg size and clutch size in *Sceloporus woodi*. Oecologia, 80: 525–532.

Ferguson, G. W., and S. F. Fox. 1984. Annual variation of survival advantage of large juvenile side-blotched lizards, *Uta stansburiana*: its causes and evolutionary significance. Evolution, 38: 342–349.

Ferguson, G. W., and H. L. Snell. 1986. Endogenous control of seasonal change of egg, hatchling, and clutch size of the lizard *Sceloporus undulatus garmani*. Herpetologica, 42: 185–191.

Fox, S. F. 1978. Natural selection on behavioral phenotypes of the lizard *Uta stansburiana*. Ecology, 59: 834–847.

Gavaud, J. 1986. Vitellogenesis in the lizard *Lacerta vivipara* Jacquin. II. Vitellogenin synthesis during the reproductive cycle and its control by ovarian steroids. Gen. Comp. Endocrinol., 63: 11–23.

Gerstle, J. F., and I. P. Callard. 1972. Reproduction and estrogen-induced vitellogenesis in *Dipsosaurus dorsalis*. Comp. Biochem. Physiol., 42A: 791–801.

Hahn, W. E. 1967. Estradiol-induced vitellogenesis and concomitant fat mobilization in the lizard *Uta stansburiana*. Comp. Biochem. Physiol., 23A: 83–93.

Ho, S.-M., S. Kleis, R. McPherson, G. J. Heisermann, and I. P. Callard. 1982. Regulation of vitellogenesis in reptiles. Herpetologica, 38: 40–50.

Jayne, B. C., and A. F. Bennett. 1990. Selection on locomotor performance capacity in natural populations of garter snakes. Evolution, 44: 1204–1229.

Jones, R. E. 1978. Control of follicular selection, p. 763–788. *In* R. E. Jones (ed.), The Vertebrate Ovary. Plenum Press, New York.

Jones, R. E., J. B. Austin, K. H. Lopez, M S. Rand, and C. H. Summers. 1988. Gonadotropin-induced ovulation in a reptile (*Anolis carolinensis*): histological observations. Gen. Comp. Endocrinol., 72: 312–322.

Jones, R. E., R. R. Tokarz, F. T. LaGreek, and K. T. Fitzgerald. 1976. Endocrine control of clutch size in reptiles. VI. Patterns of FSH-induced ovarian stimulation in adult *Anolis carolinensis*. Gen. Comp. Endocrinol., 30: 101–116.

Lack, D. 1954. The Natural Regulation of Animal Numbers. Clarendon Press, Oxford. viii, 343 pages.

Licht, P. 1970. Effects of mammalian gonadotropins (ovine FSH and LH) in female lizards. Gen. Comp. Endocrinol., 22: 463–469.

—. 1982. Endocrine patterns in the reproductive cycle of turtles. Herpetologica, 38: 51–61.

Licht, P., and D. Crews. 1975. Stimulation of ovarian and oviductal growth and ovulation in female lizards by reptilian (turtle) gonadotropins. Gen. Comp. Endocrinol., 25: 466–471.

Licht, P., H. Papkoff, S. W. Farmer, C. H. Muller, H. W. Tsui, and D. Crews. 1977. Evolution of gonadotropin structure and function. Recent Progress Hormone Res., 33: 169–248.

Nussbaum, R. A. 1981. Seasonal shifts in clutch size and egg size in the side-blotched lizard, *Uta stansburiana* Baird and Girard. Oecologia, 49: 8–13.

Pease, C. M., and J. J. Bull. 1988. A critique of methods for measuring life history trade-offs. Jour. Evol. Biol., 1: 293–303.

Phillips, J. A., N. Alexander, W. B. Karesh, R. Millar, and B.

L. Lasley. 1985. Stimulating male sexual behavior with repetitive pulses of GnRH in female green iguanas, *Iguana iguana*. Jour. Exp. Zool., 234: 481–484.

Phillips, J. A., F. Frye, A. Berkovitz, P. Calle, R. Millar, J. Rivier, and B. E. Lasley. 1987. Exogenous GnRH overrides the endogenous annual reproductive rhythm in green iguanas, *Iguana iguana*. Jour. Exp. Zool., 241: 227–236.

Reznick, D. 1985. Costs of reproduction: an evaluation of the empirical evidence. Oikos, 44: 257–267.

Ross, R. A., and G. Marzec. 1990. The Reproductive Husbandry of Pythons and Boas. Inst. Herpetol. Research, Stanford, California. 270 pages.

Shine, R. 1980. 'Costs' of reproduction in reptiles. Oecologia, 46: 92–100.

Shine, R., and A. E. Greer. 1991. Why are clutch sizes more variable in some species than in others? Evolution, 45: 1696–1706.

Sinervo, B. 1990. The evolution of maternal investment in lizards: an experimental and comparative analysis of egg size and its effects on offspring performance. Evolution, 44: 279–294.

—. 1993. The effect of offspring size on physiology and life history: manipulation of size using allometric engineering. BioScience, 43: 210–218.

Sinervo, B., P. Doughty, R. B. Huey, and K. Zamudio. 1992. Allometric engineering: a causal analysis of natural selection on offspring size. Science, 258: 1927–1930.

Sinervo, B., R. Hedges, and S. C. Adolph. 1991. Decreased sprint speed as a cost of reproduction in the lizard *Sceloporus occidentalis*: variation among populations. Jour. Exp. Biol., 155: 323–336.

Sinervo, B., and R. B. Huey. 1990. Allometric engineering: an experimental test of the causes of interpopulational differences in locomotor performance. Science, 248: 1106–1109.

Sinervo, B., and P. Licht. 1991*a*. The physiological and hormonal control of clutch size, egg size, and egg shape in *Uta stansburiana*: constraints on the evolution of lizard life histories. Jour. Exp. Zool., 257: 252–264.

—. 1991*b*. Proximate constraints on the evolution of egg size, egg number, and total clutch mass in lizards. Science, 252: 1300–1302.

Sinervo, B., and L. R. McEdward. 1988. Developmental consequences of an evolutionary change in egg size: an experimental test. Evolution, 42: 885–899.

Smith, C. C., and S. D. Fretwell. 1974. The optimal balance between size and number of offspring. Amer. Nat., 108: 499–506.

Stearns, S. C. 1976. Life-history tactics: a review of the ideas. Quart. Rev. Biol., 51: 3–47.

Van Damme, R., D. Bauwens, and R. F. Verheyen. 1989. Effect of relative clutch mass on sprint speed in the lizard *Lacerta vivipara*. Jour. Herpetol., 23: 459–461.

Vitt, L. J. 1986. Reproductive tactics of sympatric gekkonid lizards with a comment on the evolutionary and ecological consequences of invariant clutch size. Copeia, 1986: 773–786.

Vitt, L. J., and J. D. Congdon. 1978. Body shape, reproductive effort, and relative clutch mass in lizards: resolution of a paradox. Amer. Nat., 112: 595–608.

Vitt, L. J., and H. J. Price. 1982. Ecological and evolutionary determinants of relative clutch mass in lizards. Herpetologica, 38: 237–255.

Wilbur, H. M. 1977. Propagule size, number, and dispersion patterns in *Ambystoma* and *Asclepias*. Amer. Nat., 111: 43–68.

Williams, G. C. 1966. Natural selection, the costs of reproduction, and a refinement of Lack's principle. Amer. Nat., 100: 687–690.

Wilson, B., and J. C. Wingfield. 1992. Correlation between female reproductive condition and plasma corticosterone in the lizard *Uta stansburiana*. Copeia, 1992: 691–697.

Yaron, Z., and L. Widzer. 1978. The control of vitellogenesis by ovarian hormones in the lizard *Xantusia vigilis*. Comp. Biochem. Physiol., 60: 279–284.

Sinervo, B. 1994. Manipulations of clutch and offspring size in lizards: mechanistic, evolutionary, and conservation considerations, p. 183–193. *In* J. B. Murphy, K. Adler, and J. T. Collins (eds.), Captive Management and Conservation of Amphibians and Reptiles. Society for the Study of Amphibians and Reptiles, Ithaca (New York). Contributions to Herpetology, volume 11.

The Importance of the Physical Environment for the Incubation of Reptilian Eggs

Gary C. Packard* and John A. Phillips **

Introduction

Several conservation programs for rare or endangered species of reptiles entail incubating their eggs under controlled conditions in the laboratory (Burbidge et al. 1990; Cree and Daugherty 1990). Many investigators consequently have sought to establish the limits of tolerance of embryos to variables—such as temperature, moisture, and oxygen tension—because the primary criterion for success or failure in these programs has been hatching success. Every embryo has a range of tolerance for each of these environmental factors (Figure 1) and can develop to the point of hatching if the limits of tolerance are not exceeded or are exceeded only briefly (Ackerman 1981; Fitch and Fitch 1967; Leshem et al. 1991; Muth 1980; Packard et al. 1987). Nonetheless, recent research reveals that different combinations of temperature, moisture, and oxygen tension may interact in complex ways with the physiology of developing embryos and that the resultant modulation of physiology may produce hatchlings with different probabilities for surviving the neonatal period. Such differences in the probability for survival by neonates have important bearing on all conservation-oriented programs, regardless of whether hatchlings are to be maintained in captivity or to be released into the wild.

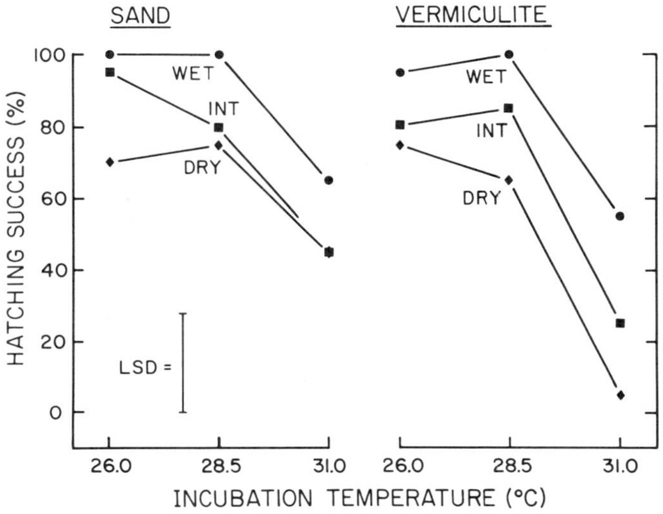

Figure 1. Hatching success for Snapping Turtles (*Chelydra serpentina*) incubated at different temperatures and water potentials on substrates of sand and vermiculite (from Packard et al. 1987). Each of the treatments contained 20 eggs. Values separated by the LSD (least significant difference) are significantly different ($P = 0.05$). "WET" substrates were at –150 kPa at the beginning of the experiment; "INT" (= intermediate) substrates were at –550 kPa; "DRY" media were at –950 kPa.

We shall first summarize evidence for non-lethal effects of temperature, moisture, and oxygen tension on developing embryos of oviparous reptiles, and then shall consider the possible ecological importance of these effects. Lastly, we shall draw on the preceding body of information and try to formulate a simple, yet reliable, protocol for incubating eggs in management programs.

* Department of Biology
Colorado State University
Fort Collins, Colorado 80523, USA

** Center for Reproduction of Endangered Species
Zoological Society of San Diego
P.O. Box 551
San Diego, California 92112, USA

Acronyms used in this chapter:

ESD Environmental sex determination
kPa Kilopascal
LSD Least significant difference
Q_{10} Metabolic quotient

Ecological Physiology of Reptilian Embryos

Temperature

Sexual Differentiation. Most of the attention given in recent years to effects of temperature on reptilian embryos has focused on the process of sexual differentiation (see Janzen and Paukstis 1991 for a recent review). Temperature affects this process in some lizards (such as members of the families Agamidae, Anguidae, Gekkonidae, and Lacertidae), numerous turtles (including Carettochelyidae, Cheloniidae, Chelydridae, Dermatemydidae, Dermochelyidae, Emydidae, Kinosternidae, Pelomedusidae, and Testudinidae), and all crocodilians (see Janzen and Paukstis 1991; Paukstis and Janzen 1990). No snake, however, is known to be subject to environmental sex determination (ESD)(Janzen and Paukstis 1991; Paukstis and Janzen 1990) and sexual differentiation by the Tuatara (*Sphenodon punctatus*) also is unaffected by incubation temperature (M. B. Thompson, pers. comm.). Earlier reports that sexual differentiation in a turtle is affected by moisture regime (Gutzke and Paukstis 1983; Paukstis et al. 1984) have not been confirmed (Packard et al. 1989, 1991). Additionally, hypoxia has no influence on sexual differentiation of crocodilians (Deeming and Ferguson 1991) or turtles (Etchberger et al. 1991). Thus, temperature apparently intervenes directly in the physiology of developing embryos to affect their differentiation as males or females.

Embryos of many of the turtles that exhibit ESD develop as females at high incubation temperatures and as males at low incubation temperatures (Table 1). In other species, however, females develop at all viable temperatures and usually only females emerge from eggs that are incubated at the higher and lower ends of the temperature range (Table 2). Differentiation of males in this second group of species occurs mainly (or exclusively) in the middle range of temperatures.

Embryos of crocodiles (Crocodylinae) and of one lizard (*Gekko japonicus*) have a pattern of sexual differentiation similar to that described for the second group of turtles, in that females are formed primarily at high and low temperatures and males are formed only at intermediate temperatures (Lang et al. 1989; Tokunaga 1985; Webb and Cooper-Preston 1989; Webb and Smith 1984; Webb et al. 1987). Embryos of alligators (Alligatorinae) and of other lizards, however, seem to have only a single transitional temperature; development above it leads to the differentiation of males and incubation below this temperature elicits the formation of females (Charnier 1966; Gutzke and Crews 1988; Joanen et al. 1987; Lang et al. 1989).

The means by which temperature directs the differentiation of reptilian embryos into males or females is unknown (Deeming and Ferguson 1989; Janzen and Paukstis 1991; Standora and Spotila 1985; Webb et al. 1987). According to one plausible hypothesis, however, temperature-labile enzymes act on steroids transmitted via the yolk from the female parent to her offspring (Crews et al. 1989). When the enzymes are activated by temperature, the steroids are converted to estrogens, which cause the gonads of the embryo to differentiate into ovaries. Conversely, when the enzymes are inactivated by temperature, the gonads of the embryo differentiate into testes in response to a background of androgens. Further differentiation of secondary sexual characters then occurs in response to hormones produced by the differentiated gonads.

Temperatures generally are held constant in laboratory experiments (Janzen and Paukstis 1991), whereas temperatures fluctuate daily and seasonally in natural nests (Packard and Packard 1988). This raises a question about the ecological relevance of laboratory-based research, because patterns of sexual differentiation by embryos are influenced by the timing of exposure to high or low temperatures (Bull 1987; Bull and Vogt 1981; Ynte-

TABLE 1. Species of turtles in which females differentiate at high temperatures and males differentiate at low temperatures (type Ia of Ewert and Nelson 1991). The only species listed in this and the following table are those for which data on sexual differentiation have been gathered over a broad range of temperatures.

Cheloniidae	*Caretta caretta*
	Chelonia mydas
Emydidae	*Chrysemys picta*
	Emydoidea blandingii
	Emys orbicularis
	Graptemys geographica
	Graptemys pseudogeographica
	Pseudemys concinna
	Pseudemys (=Trachemys) scripta
	Terrapene ornata

TABLE 2. Species of turtles in which females differentiate at both high and low temperatures and males differentiate at intermediate temperatures (type II of Ewert and Nelson 1991).

Chelydridae	*Chelydra serpentina*
	Macroclemys temminckii
Emydidae	*Melanochelys trijuga*
Kinosternidae	*Kinosternon flavescens*
	Kinosternon leucostomum
	Kinosternon scorpioides
	Sternotherus carinatus
	Sternotherus minor
	Sternotherus odoratus
Pelomedusidae	*Pelomedusa subrufa*
	Pelusios castaneus

ma 1979; Yntema and Mrosovsky 1982). Moreover, temperatures differ in their potency for eliciting differentiation of a particular sex (Bull et al. 1990).

Nonetheless, findings from the field generally are in accord with predictions based on results from laboratory studies. For example, turtle eggs incubating in relatively warm nests generally give rise to female hatchlings, whereas those in cooler nests usually produce males (Alho et al. 1985; Bull 1985; Bull and Vogt 1979; Morreale et al. 1982; Mrosovsky et al. 1984; Pieau 1982; Schwarzkopf and Brooks 1985, 1987; Vogt and Bull 1984; Wilhoft et al. 1983). Moreover, when a nest is not so warm or so cool as to cause all embryos to differentiate as the same sex, thermal stratification within the nest cavity commonly results in formation of females in eggs in warmer strata at the top and of males in eggs in cooler strata at the bottom (Wilhoft et al. 1983).

The pattern of sexual differentiation manifested by crocodilian embryos that develop in nature is also consistent with predictions based on laboratory studies. Warm nests of American Alligators (*Alligator mississippiensis*) produce primarily male hatchlings, whereas cool nests produce mainly females (Ferguson and Joanen 1982, 1983; Lang et al. 1989), and the stratification of temperature in nests that produce both males and females commonly causes hatchlings near the top to be males and those near the bottom to be females (Ferguson and Joanen 1982, 1983). In contrast, extremely warm nests of crocodiles (*Crocodylus porosus*, *C. johnstoni*) tend to yield female offspring, and so too do extremely cool nests (Webb and Cooper-Preston 1989; Webb and Smith 1984). Crocodile nests at intermediate temperatures produce primarily males.

Metabolism and Growth. Changes in temperature of a reptilian embryo elicit changes in rates of chemical reaction which, in turn, affect the rate of metabolism. Other potential effects of temperature are more subtle but no less important. For example, the fluidity of cell membranes is sensitive to temperature, and so too is the structure of enzymes and other proteins (Hochachka and Somero 1984). If thermally induced changes in membranes and proteins are not compensated, major—and potentially deleterious—changes may occur in rates of diffusion (or transport) of metabolic substrates across cell membranes and in the activity of metabolic pathways (Hochachka and Somero 1984). Overall metabolism of the embryo may thereby be affected. Additionally, different cellular functions have different sensitivities to temperature (for example, they differ in terms of metabolic quotient, or Q_{10}), so a change in temperature may also cause some disruption in the integration of these functions.

Two related questions are of particular concern in any examination of the effects of temperature on metabolism and growth of reptilian embryos. First, how does a single embryo respond metabolically when it is exposed sequentially (and briefly) to a series of temperatures similar to those that would be encountered in natural nests at different times of day? And second, how do different embryos respond metabolically when they are exposed to temperatures that are higher or lower than normal and that are held constant for all or part of incubation? The time frame for exposure is critical in distinguishing these questions, because the metabolism of an embryo immediately after its transfer to a new temperature may be quite different from its metabolism after it has been exposed to that temperature for a longer period (Grainger 1956).

Unfortunately, only two studies have examined the first question. In these two studies, rapid increases in temperature elicited increases in oxygen consumption by embryonic Smooth Green Snakes (*Opheodrys vernalis*) and Nile Crocodiles (*Crocodylus niloticus*), but the pattern of response was itself sensitive to temperature (Aulie et al. 1989; Zarrow and Pomerat 1937). The Q_{10} for metabolism was higher at lower temperatures than at higher ones (Aulie et al. 1989; Zarrow and Pomerat 1937), so an equivalent change in temperature had a greater influence on metabolism over the lower range of temperatures than over the higher range. We do not know how other facets of physiology are affected by acute exposure to different temperatures, nor do we know what control mechanisms may be used to integrate physiological processes at the different temperatures.

Numerous studies have addressed the second question by incubating different embryos at a variety of constant temperatures. When comparisons are made among embryos that have attained comparable stages of development, those that developed at high temperatures have higher rates of oxygen consumption than do those that developed at low temperatures (Leshem et al. 1991; Whitehead 1987; Whitehead and Seymour 1990; Whitehead et al. 1990). This does not mean, however, that more oxygen is consumed over the full course of incubation in warm settings than in cool ones. Indeed, integration of oxygen consumption over time reveals that embryos in some studies consume the same amount of oxygen at low temperatures as they do at high temperatures (Leshem et al. 1991) and that embryos in other studies actually consume more oxygen at low temperatures than they do in warm conditions (Whitehead 1987).

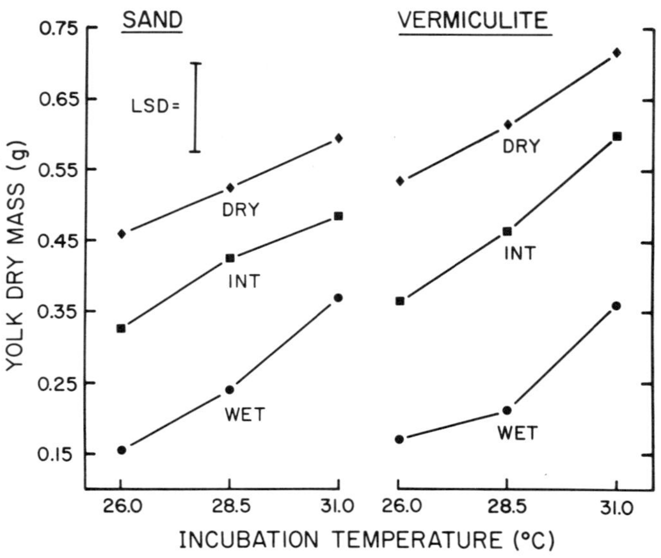

FIGURE 3. Mean values for dry masses of residual yolks dissected from the carcasses of Snapping Turtles (*Chelydra serpentina*) hatching at different temperatures and water potentials on substrates of sand and vermiculite (from Packard et al. 1987). For other labeling, see the caption to Figure 1.

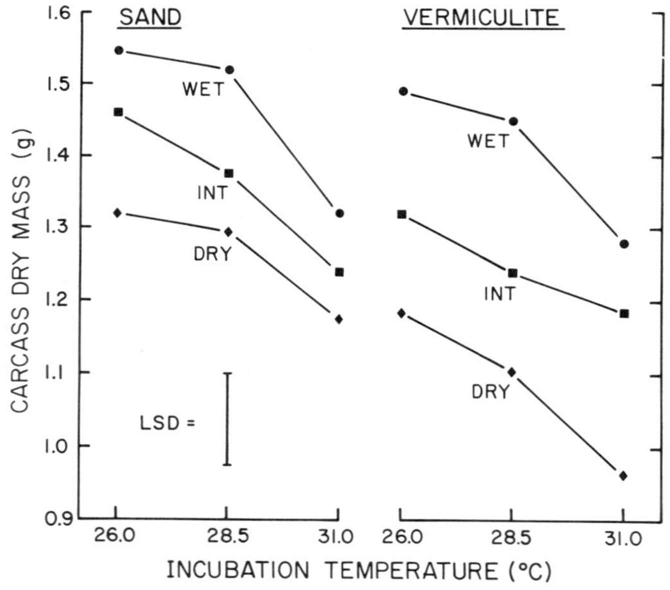

FIGURE 2. Mean values for dry masses of carcasses from Snapping Turtles (*Chelydra serpentina*) hatching at different temperatures and water potentials on substrates of sand and vermiculite (from Packard et al. 1987). Residual yolk was removed from carcasses before they were dried and weighed. For other labeling, see the caption to Figure 1.

Development to the point of hatching generally occurs more slowly at lower temperatures than at higher ones (see Packard and Packard 1988, for references). The longer incubation at lower temperatures usually combines with higher overall metabolism to cause hatchlings at low temperatures to have larger bodies (Figure 2) and smaller masses of residual yolk (Figure 3) than hatchlings incubated at high temperatures (Gutzke and Packard 1987; Gutzke et al. 1987; Packard et al. 1987, 1988; Phillips et al. 1990; Webb et al. 1986, 1987; Whitehead 1987; Whitehead and Seymour 1990; Whitehead et al. 1990). Thus, embryos developing at different temperatures differ in the degree to which they convert food reserves into tissue, with embryos at lower temperatures being more effective in this regard than embryos at higher temperatures. The point to emphasize, however, is that reptiles hatching at different temperatures commonly differ appreciably in size and physiological condition. Survival of these animals over the neonatal period may thereby be affected.

The behavior of hatchlings may also be influenced in subtle ways by the temperatures at which they developed as embryos. For instance, hatchlings of several species of snakes performed behavioral tests in the laboratory better when they developed at intermediate or high temperatures than when they developed at low temperatures (Burger 1989, 1990). Unfortunately, these findings are difficult to interpret, because many of the behaviors chosen for study (for example, ability to resist falling from the inside of a glass tube) have no clear relation to questions of survival and fitness in neonatal animals.

Moreover, Siamese Crocodiles (*Crocodylus siamensis*) that hatched from eggs incubated at 32°–33°C selected higher temperatures in a thermal gradient than did animals hatching from eggs incubated at 27°–28°C (Lang 1987). This difference in behavior may reflect irreversible effects of temperature on gene expression in the developing embryo, or it may simply be a result of thermal acclimation during later stages of embryogenesis. Another possibility is that the difference is secondary to effects of temperature on sexual differentiation (Gutzke and Crews 1988). In any event, resultant differences in thermal physiology have important implications for energy metabolism and growth by neonatal animals.

In the same vein, American Alligators that hatched at temperatures of 30.6°C and 31.7°C grew faster than neonates that emerged from eggs at 29.4°C and 32.8°C in an experiment in which all the animals were raised in controlled environmental chambers at 30°C (Joanen et al. 1987). The differences in growth were not related to variation in body size of neonates (see below), so the results were entirely unexpected. Unfortunately, the published account of this work omits some important details of experimental protocol that are needed to evaluate the findings. For instance, it is not clear if hatchlings were housed individually for the duration of the study, or if they were maintained in groups. If they were kept in groups (which probably was the case; see Joanen and McNease 1987), it is important to know if all hatchlings from a particular temperature were housed together, or if hatchlings from different treatments were intermixed. The answers to these questions are critical, because animals held in different tanks under nominally identical conditions would nonetheless be expected to differ in growth (and in other facets of their physiology and behavior), because of random, undetected variation in conditions inside the several chambers (Hurlbert 1984).

The preceding generalizations concerning long-term effects of temperature on general metabolic activity and on the morphology and physiology of hatchlings are based on studies that were performed in the laboratory and that used constant temperatures for incubation. Although average temperature commonly varies among nests in the wild, substantial variation in temperature also occurs within individual nests over a daily cycle (Packard and Packard 1988). Possible effects of such cycles in temperature have not been examined, and data presently are not available to verify that temperature regimes in nature elicit responses from embryos similar to those observed in the laboratory. Thus, predictions based on the laboratory investigations need to be tested explicitly in natural settings.

Moisture

Our interpretation of the available evidence leads us to believe that reptilian embryos that develop in eggs with flexible, porous shells (for example, many turtles and most lepidosaurians) are profoundly affected by the wetness of the environment in which they incubate. Embryos that develop in relatively moist environments have higher rates of metabolism (as judged by both the rate of oxygen consumption and the rate of depletion of nutrients from the yolk) and growth than do embryos that develop in relatively dry conditions (Gettinger et al. 1984; Janzen et al. 1990; Miller and Packard 1992; Morris et al. 1983; Packard and Packard 1986, 1989*a*; Vleck 1991). Moreover, embryos that develop in moist settings usually remain in their eggs longer before hatching than do embryos that develop in dry environments (Packard et al. 1985, 1987, 1989, 1991; Phillips et al. 1990). The higher rate of growth and longer incubation period act together to cause embryos in wet environments to attain larger size by the time of hatching than embryos in dry environments (Figure 2) (Gutzke and Packard 1986; Gutzke et al. 1987; Packard et al. 1982, 1985, 1987, 1989, 1991; Vleck 1991).

Conversely, the amount of residual yolk available to support metabolism of animals during the neonatal period is less in hatchlings from wet environments than in those from dry ones (Figure 3)

(Gutzke and Packard 1986; Gutzke et al. 1987; Packard et al. 1985, 1987, 1988; Vleck 1991). We recognize that evidence from some investigations is at variance with this generalization (for example, Packard and Packard 1987; Thompson 1990; Tracy 1980), but suspect that the contradictory findings result primarily from shortcomings in experimental design instead of important differences in the physiological responses of embryos to the availability of water (Packard and Packard 1986).

Embryos that develop in eggs with hard, rigid shells (for example, those of crocodilians, many turtles, dibamid lizards, and some geckos) are largely unaffected by the moisture regime of the environment in which they develop. Neither their metabolism nor their rate of growth seems to be affected appreciably by the hydric environment (Gettinger et al. 1984; Packard and Packard 1991), except perhaps under conditions of extreme dryness (Grigg 1987; Manolis et al. 1987). Moreover, these animals hatch after essentially the same period of incubation irrespective of the moisture regime (Packard et al. 1981). Consequently, in these species, animals that hatch in wet and dry environments are similar in size (Packard et al. 1981; Packard and Packard 1991; Webb et al. 1986) and physiology (Packard and Packard 1990).

This "insensitivity" of embryos in eggs with rigid shells probably does not reflect on any important difference between these embryos and those of other reptiles in their physiological responses to the availability of water. Instead, the lack of response to the hydric environment probably results from the buffering of water exchanges by the relatively impervious eggshell (Dunson 1982; Dunson and Bramham 1981; Packard et al. 1979; Tracy 1982). Eggs with rigid shells tend not to lose large quantities of water to dry environments, nor to gain large quantities of water from wet ones (Packard et al. 1981). Consequently, the amount of water inside eggs does not change appreciably over the course of incubation, and embryos have access to similar reservoirs of water irrespective of the hydric environment in which they develop.

It is not presently known how the amount of water inside an egg intervenes in the physiology of reptilian embryos to modulate their metabolism and the duration of their incubation. One possible explanation is that the blood volume and circulatory performance of embryos are linked to the size of the water reserve inside eggs and, thus, to water exchange by eggs (Packard 1991). Circulatory-transport capacity of embryos presumably declines as the size of the water reserve declines, so that transport of oxygen also is diminished. By this hypothesis, metabolism is limited by the availability of oxygen to cells, and growth, in turn, is a function of the level of sustained metabolism (Asson-Batres et al. 1989; Stock and Metcalfe 1987; Tullett and Burton 1987). Moreover, hatching supposedly is stimulated when diminished delivery of oxygen to a critical tissue, such as the brain, causes intracellular oxygen pressure to fall to a critical, threshold level (Packard 1991).

The water relations of reptilian embryos have been studied primarily under controlled conditions in the laboratory. Although these investigations have documented profound effects of the hydric environment on developing embryos, the ecological relevance of these laboratory studies has yet to be demonstrated. Indeed, some investigators have suggested that conditions used in laboratory experiments bear little resemblance to those actually occurring in natural nests (Ackerman 1991; Ackerman et al. 1985; Ratterman and Ackerman 1989), and have implied that the physiological capacity revealed by embryos in the laboratory is not realized in nature. Thus, studies need to be performed on eggs and embryos in natural nests to assess the degree to which results of laboratory investigations can be extrapolated to the wild.

Gas Tensions

Three studies have examined effects of sublethal hypoxia (or hypercarbia) on the metabolism and growth of embryonic reptiles. In the first of these, eggs of sea turtles (*Caretta caretta* and *Chelonia mydas*) were incubated in glass containers that were vented to the atmosphere through columns of dry sand varying in height (Ackerman 1981). The tensions of oxygen in the containers consequently were determined by a complex interplay between the rate of oxygen consumption by developing embryos and the rate of inward diffusion of the gas through the columns of sand. Variation among containers in height of the column of sand resulted in some containers that had high gas conductances (that is, short columns of sand), while other containers had low conductances (tall columns).

Embryos in containers that had relatively low gas conductances responded to the resultant hypoxia (the extent of which was unfortunately not reported) with reductions in their rate of growth and with increases in their length of incubation. Moreover, hatchlings from eggs subjected to hypoxia were smaller than those emerging from eggs exposed to normoxia, while the residual yolk in animals from the hypoxic treatment was larger than that of animals emerging in normoxia. Taken together, these findings indicate that hypoxia inhibits metabolism and growth by embryos and that it thereby retards development. The inhibition of metabolism presumably resulted from reductions in the rate of delivery of oxygen to individual cells (Connett et al. 1990), whereas the delay in hatching probably indicates that a longer period of time was required for embryos to attain a developmental stage at which they could hatch successfully.

Although results of the investigation with sea turtles conform to expectations based on studies of numerous other vertebrates, they nonetheless are at variance with results of other studies on embryonic reptiles. For example, gas exchange by embryonic American Alligators was impaired in one study by covering part of their eggshell with lacquer or aluminum tape (Deeming and Ferguson 1991). The resulting hypoxia caused late embryos to be smaller than controls in three of the experimental groups, but larger than controls in the fourth. Moreover, in a second study, eggs of a Slider (*Pseudemys* [=*Trachemys*] *scripta*) were incubated in gas mixtures that had substantially lower concentrations of oxygen than did the atmospheric air (Etchberger et al. 1991). Although survival by these turtle embryos was reduced at the lowest gas concentrations (nominally 5% and 8%), no effect of the treatments was detected on length of incubation in the survivors or in their size at hatching. Thus, hypoxia unexpectedly failed to influence metabolism or growth of embryonic alligators and slider turtles.

Although hypoxia may have the potential to inhibit embryonic metabolism and growth in some reptiles, hypoxic conditions in nests are probably the exception rather than the rule. Nests of most reptiles are buried relatively shallow (if, indeed, they are buried at all), and they contain relatively small numbers of metabolically active embryos. Consequently, the cumulative demand for oxygen usually is small, and oxygen diffuses through air spaces in the soil fast enough to prevent a serious depletion of this gas from the atmosphere surrounding incubating eggs (Christian and Lawrence 1991; Lutz and Dunbar-Cooper 1984; Thompson 1981). Thus, the low levels of hypoxia that may occur in natural nests are probably insufficient to impair metabolism and growth by embryos.

In some sea turtles and crocodilians that deposit large clutches of eggs in relatively deep hole-nests, however, embryos in later stages of incubation may consume oxygen faster than it can be replenished by diffusion through the soil (Ackerman 1977; Maloney et al. 1990; Whitehead 1987). The resultant hypoxia may be sufficient to inhibit metabolism and growth by embryos (Whitehead 1987). Thus, specific instances may occur in which hypoxia (or the associated hypercarbia) affects development of embryos in nature.

Significance of Induced Variation

Large hatchlings with small residual yolks emerge from eggs incubated under conditions of low temperature, high water potential, and high oxygen tension. Conversely, small hatchlings with large residual yolks emerge from eggs maintained under the reverse conditions: high temperature, low water potential, and low oxygen tension. It is important to determine if this environmentally induced variation in the size of the body and residual yolk of hatchlings is ecologically important or if it is ecologically neutral. This question is not trivial, because more than 90% of the statistical variance in body size of Snapping Turtles (*Chelydra serpentina*) that hatched in a laboratory study resulted from environmental modulation of the physiology of developing embryos and a similar proportion of variance may result from such modulation in nature (Packard 1991).

Large hatchlings of several lizards (Ferguson and Bohlen 1978; Ferguson and Fox 1984; Ferguson et al. 1982; Fox 1978), snakes (Jayne and Bennett 1990), and turtles (Swingland and Coe 1979) have been shown to survive the neonatal period better than small hatchlings in the same cohort. Although this finding is consistent with the view that environmentally induced variation in body size in neonatal reptiles is ecologically important, none of the studies in question demonstrated that the variation in body size in hatchling cohorts actually resulted from variation in the physical environment to which eggs were exposed during development. Thus, the investigations may have demonstrated a survival advantage to large hatchlings that emerged from large, high-quality eggs rather than to large animals that hatched in cool, moist, well-oxygenated environments (Sinervo 1990; Sinervo and Huey 1990).

Vleck (1988) performed an elegant study that addresses this point. Briefly, he incubated eggs of the Striped Plateau Lizard (*Sceloporus virgatus*) on both wet and dry media in the laboratory, marked the hatchlings for individual identification, and then released the animals into the wild. Regular censuses revealed that large hatchlings from eggs incubated on wet substrates survived better over the period of observation than did small hatchlings from eggs incubated on dry media. Thus, the large size attained by animals incubated in wet environments conferred a clear benefit during the neonatal period. This finding provides strong support for the general proposition that environmentally induced variation in the body size of hatchling reptiles affects their survival.

Large hatchlings (or neonates) are superior to small hatchlings in locomotion (Jayne and Bennett 1990; Miller et al. 1987; Sinervo 1990; Sinervo and Huey 1990) and in competition for food (Froese and Burghardt 1974). The superior locomotor ability of large hatchlings may enable them to evade predators that cannot be escaped by small hatchlings (Barrows and Schwarz 1895), and greater success in acquiring food may allow large animals to grow faster than small ones (Froese and Burghardt 1974). Rapid growth presumably enables larger animals to pass more quickly than can smaller animals through the range of body size in which hatchlings are most vulnerable to predation, and rapid growth may also enable large hatchlings to attain larger size at maturity than can be achieved by small animals in the cohort (Halliday and Verrell 1988). A large size at reproductive maturity presumably translates into greater fecundity for females and higher mating success for males (Halliday and Verrell 1988).

On the other hand, small hatchlings that emerge in warm, dry, and/or hypoxic environments have larger masses of residual yolk to sustain them during the neonatal period. Additionally, these animals also have lower requirements for nutrients (for maintenance) by virtue of their smaller size. If neonates emerge from their nests at a time of year when food is in short supply, small hatchlings may be better equipped to survive than are large hatchlings. We are unaware, however, of evidence supporting this possibility. Moreover, the conditions leading to formation of smaller hatchlings are conditions that result also in reductions in hatching success (Figures 1–3). Thus, hatching at a small size probably is a reflection of incomplete buffering of physiology in embryos, and is not an outcome that is generally advantageous.

The relative benefits of large size versus large (residual) yolk need to be assessed experimentally, however. The experiments should be performed in natural or semi-natural settings so as to yield results that are clearly relevant ecologically.

Methods for Incubating Eggs

Given that temperature, water potential, and oxygen tension have the potential to affect embryonic metabolism and growth in most species of oviparous reptiles, we need to determine which practices and procedures should be adopted for incubating eggs of rare or endangered species to achieve the highest possible hatching success and to produce the most vigorous hatchlings. We believe that large hatchlings generally are "better" than small hatchlings, and emphasize again that conditions that yield the largest hatchlings generally yield the highest hatching success as well (Figures 1 and 2). Thus, we focus on means for producing the dual result of high hatching success and large size.

This result can be attained rather easily. Both water potential and oxygen tension can be readily maintained within favorable limits without an investigator knowing the exact value assumed by either variable. Indeed, only incubation temperature needs to be monitored regularly and to be controlled fairly precisely.

We routinely incubate eggs in plastic storage boxes filled to approximately half their capacity with moistened vermiculite. The type of container used to hold eggs is largely a matter of personal preference, and any container will suffice as long as it has a lid or cover that will allow the humidity of enclosed air to approach saturation (Packard et al. 1981). Even plastic bags have been used successfully (Zweifel 1961).

We use vermiculite (Terralite™, grade 3) as a medium for incubating eggs. Individual particles of this grade of vermiculite provide numerous points of contact for transport of liquid water between substrate and eggshells (Tracy et al. 1978), yet the medium also contains numerous air-filled spaces that facilitate gaseous diffusion (Flegg 1953). Moreover, vermiculite is clean and easy to work with, and it is readily obtained from commercial sources throughout the world.

We prepare substrates by mixing approximately equal masses of water and dry vermiculite. The water potential that results is between –100 kPa and –200 kPa (Figure 4). The substrate is not saturated, so air spaces remain in the medium and gas exchange by embryos is enhanced. At the same time, however, ample water is available for uptake by incubating eggs. This range of water potential will permit absorption of sufficient water by eggs with porous, flexible shells (Gutzke and Packard 1987; Packard et al. 1987; Phillips et al. 1990), but usually will not enable eggs with rigid shells to imbibe so much water that they swell and crack (Packard et al. 1981; Packard and Packard 1989*b*, 1991). We caution that different brands (or grades) of vermiculite will require different amounts of water to produce the same range in water potential, so substrates other than Terralite™, grade 3, will have to be calibrated before they are used.

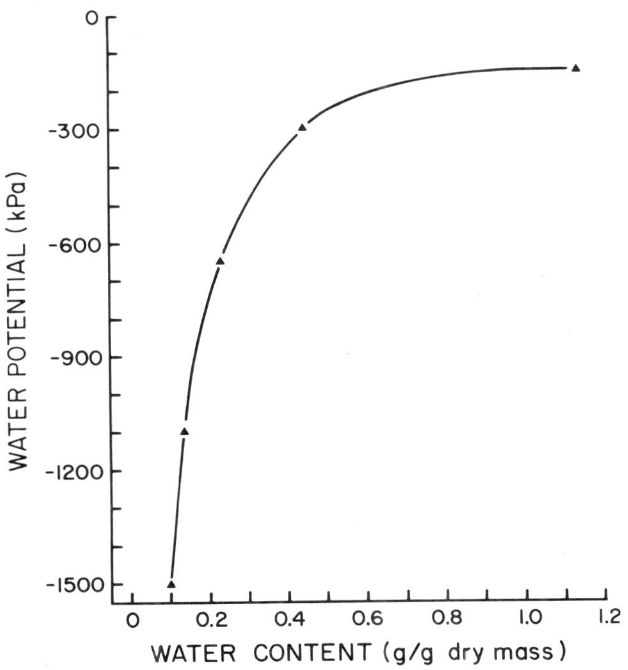

FIGURE 4. Water retention curve for vermiculite (Terralite™, grade 3) at 29°C (from Packard and Packard 1987). Note that fairly substantial changes in water content of wet vermiculite elicit only minor changes in water potential.

As a rule, we limit the number of eggs in a container so that the total mass of the eggs does not exceed one-half the total mass of water in the substrate. This practice, when coupled with weekly opening of the container to inspect the eggs (and to remove those that have putrified), assures that the oxygen tension of the enclosed air does not fall to a level that could inhibit metabolism of embryos (Packard and Packard 1984). We also preserve the orientation of the eggs at oviposition to prevent embryos from coming to lie beneath their yolk (Ewert 1985; Limpus et al. 1979; Parmenter 1980).

We recommend that eggs with flexible shells be half-buried in the substrate and that eggs with rigid shells be placed in small depressions in the medium. This step should assure that sufficient surface is available for absorption of water. Eggs incubated in this manner occasionally will absorb too much water, however, and will swell and crack or rupture, particularly if the incubation temperature is below 28°C. If periodic inspection reveals that some eggs in a group have swelled to the point of cracking, further cracking usually can be prevented simply by reducing the amount of contact between eggs and the medium. This step will reduce the uptake of water by eggs from the substrate (Packard 1991).

Each container should be weighed periodically (with the eggs), and sufficient water should be added to the substrate on these occasions to return the mass of the system to its original level. This procedure admittedly does not compensate for water that has been absorbed by eggs. However, water potential of wet vermiculite is relatively insensitive to small changes in the amount of water in the medium (Figure 4), so water potential should not depart appreciably from the desired level if overall mass of the system is maintained. We recommend that the water be at the same temperature as the incubator when adjustments are made to avoid the risk of thermal shock to embryos. As an alternative to rehydrating substrates, new media can be prepared periodically.

Temperature will need to be measured and controlled in the chamber or room where the eggs are incubated. Maintenance of the appropriate temperature may be necessary in species with ESD to assure that hatchlings of the appropriate sex are produced (Paukstis and Janzen 1990). Additionally, the temperature should be maintained in the lower part of the range of acceptable temperatures to produce hatchlings of large size (Figure 2). The exact temperature that is selected will depend on what is known about temperature tolerances for embryos of the species of interest.

Summary

Environmentally-induced variation in the metabolism and growth of embryonic reptiles has the potential to elicit substantial variation in the size and vigor of hatchlings, both in the laboratory and in the field. When eggs are incubated under conditions leading to generally high survival of embryos, the size of the hatchlings is positively related to water potential and oxygen tension, and negatively related to temperature. Large hatchlings probably survive better than small hatchlings in a cohort. Consequently, knowledge of conditions for incubation is important to ecologists detailing the demography of populations in the field, and control of these conditions is important to conservationists propagating endangered species in captivity. Eggs can be hatched successfully in programs of captive husbandry simply by incubating them on damp vermiculite in covered, plastic storage boxes. Some attention must be paid to temperature for incubating the eggs of species with environmental sex determination to assure that hatchlings of the appropriate gender are produced, but neither water potential nor oxygen tension needs to be managed rigorously to obtain large, vigorous hatchlings.

Acknowledgments

This review was drafted while Gary C. Packard enjoyed the hospitality of P. C. Withers and his colleagues at the University of Western Australia, and while John A. Phillips was a visiting scientist at the Etosha Ecology Institute, Namibia. We thank G. Kuchling for helpful discussions of problems encountered in management programs, and K. Miller and M. J. Packard for critically reviewing drafts of the manuscript. Preparation of this review was supported in part by the National Science Foundation (DCB 88–16123 to Gary C. Packard, BNS 90–00100 to John A. Phillips).

Literature Cited

Ackerman, R. A. 1977. The respiratory gas exchange of sea turtle nests (*Chelonia*, *Caretta*). Respir. Physiol., 31: 19–38.

—. 1981. Growth and gas exchange of embryonic sea turtles (*Chelonia*, *Caretta*). Copeia, 1981: 757–765.

—. 1991. Physical factors affecting the water exchange of buried reptile eggs, p. 193–211. *In* D. C. Deeming and M. W. J. Ferguson (eds.), Egg Incubation: Its Effects on Embryonic Development in Birds and Reptiles. Cambridge Univ. Press, Cambridge, UK.

Ackerman, R. A., R. C. Seagrave, R. Dmi'el, and A. Ar. 1985. Water and heat exchange between parchment-shelled reptile eggs and their surroundings. Copeia, 1985: 703–711.

Alho, C. J. R., T. M. S. Danni, and L. F. M. Padua. 1985. Temperature-dependent sex determination in *Podocnemis expansa* (Testudinata: Pelomedusidae). Biotropica, 17: 75–78.

Asson-Batres, M. A., M. K. Stock, J. F. Hare, and J. Metcalfe. 1989. O_2 effect on composition of chick embryonic heart and brain. Respir. Physiol., 77: 101–109.

Aulie, A., T. I. Kanui, and G. M. O. Maloiy. 1989. The effects of temperature on oxygen consumption of eggs and hatchlings of the Nile crocodile (*Crocodylus niloticus*). Comp. Biochem. Physiol., 93A: 473–475.

Barrows, W. B., and E. A. Schwarz. 1895. The Common Crow of the United States. Bull. United States Dept. Agr. Div. Ornithol. Mammal., 98 pages.

Bull, J. J. 1985. Sex ratio and nest temperature in turtles: comparing field and laboratory data. Ecology, 66: 1115–1122.

—. 1987. Temperature-sensitive periods of sex determination in a lizard: similarities with turtles and crocodilians. Jour. Exp. Zool., 241: 143–148.

Bull, J. J., and R. C. Vogt. 1979. Temperature-dependent sex determination in turtles. Science, 206: 1186–1188.

—. 1981. Temperature-sensitive periods of sex determination in emydid turtles. Jour. Exp. Zool., 218: 435–440.

Bull, J. J., T. Wibbels, and D. Crews. 1990. Sex-determining potencies vary among female incubation temperatures in a turtle. Jour. Exp. Zool., 256: 339–341.

Burbidge, A. A., G. Kuchling, P. J. Fuller, G. Graham, and D. Miller. 1990. The Western Swamp Tortoise. Department of Conservation and Land Management, Como, Western Australia. vi, 14 pages.

Burger, J. 1989. Incubation temperature has long-term effects on behaviour of young pine snakes (*Pituophis melanoleucus*). Behav. Ecol. Sociobiol., 24: 201–207.

—. 1990. Effects of incubation temperature on behavior of young black racers (*Coluber constrictor*) and kingsnakes (*Lampropeltis getulus*). Jour. Herpetol., 24: 158–163.

Charnier, M. 1966. Action de la temperature sur la sex-ratio chez l'embryon d'*Agama agama* (Agamidae, Lacertilien). Comp. Rend. Soc. Biol., 160: 620–622.

Christian, K. A., and W. T. Lawrence. 1991. Microclimatic conditions in nests of the Cuban iguana (*Cyclura nubila*). Biotropica, 23: 287–293.

Connett, R. J., C. R. Honig, T. E. J. Gayeski, and G. A. Brooks. 1990. Defining hypoxia: a systems view of V_{O_2}, glycolysis, energetics, and intracellular P_{O_2}. Jour. Appl. Physiol., 68: 833–842.

Cree, A., and C. Daugherty. 1990. Tuatara sheds its fossil image. New Sci., 1739: 22–26.

Crews, D., T. Wibbels, and W. H. N. Gutzke. 1989. Action of sex steroid hormones on temperature-induced sex determination in the snapping turtle (*Chelydra serpentina*). Gen. Comp. Endocrinol., 76: 159–166.

Deeming, D. C., and M. W. J. Ferguson. 1989. The mechanism of temperature dependent sex determination in crocodilians: a hypothesis. Amer. Zool., 29: 973–985.

—. 1991. Reduction in eggshell conductance to respiratory gases has no effect on sex determination in *Alligator mississippiensis*. Copeia, 1991: 240–243.

Dunson, W. A. 1982. Low water vapor conductance of hard-shelled eggs of the gecko lizards *Hemidactylus* and *Lepidodactylus*. Jour. Exp. Zool., 219: 377–379.

Dunson, W. A., and C. R. Bramham. 1981. Evaporative water loss and oxygen consumption of three small lizards from the Florida Keys: *Sphaerodactylus cinereus*, *S. notatus*, and *Anolis sagrei*. Physiol. Zool., 54: 253–259.

Etchberger, C. R., J. B. Phillips, M. A. Ewert, C. E. Nelson, and H. D. Prange. 1991. Effects of oxygen concentration and clutch on sex determination and physiology in red-eared slider turtles (*Trachemys scripta*). Jour. Exp. Zool., 258: 394–403.

Ewert, M. A. 1985. Embryology of turtles, p. 75–267. *In* C. Gans, F. Billett, and P. F. A. Maderson (eds.), Biology of the Reptilia, Vol. 14. John Wiley and Sons, New York.

Ewert, M. A., and C. E. Nelson. 1991. Sex determination in turtles: diverse patterns and some possible adaptive values. Copeia, 1991: 50–69.

Ferguson, G. W., and C. H. Bohlen. 1978. Demographic analysis: a tool for the study of natural selection of behavioral traits, p. 227–243. *In* N. Greenberg and P. D. MacLean (eds.), Behavior and Neurology of Lizards. U. S. Dept. Health, Education, and Welfare, National Institute of Mental Health, Rockville, Maryland.

Ferguson, G. W., K. L. Brown, and V. G. DeMarco. 1982. Selective basis for the evolution of variable egg and hatchling size in some iguanid lizards. Herpetologica, 38: 178–188.

Ferguson, G. W., and S. F. Fox. 1984. Annual variation of survival advantage of large juvenile side-blotched lizards, *Uta stansburiana*: its causes and evolutionary significance. Evolution, 38: 342–349.

Ferguson, M. W. J., and T. Joanen. 1982. Temperature of egg incubation determines sex in *Alligator mississippiensis*. Nature, 296: 850–853.

—. 1983. Temperature-dependent sex determination in *Alligator mississippiensis*. Jour. Zool., 200: 143–177.

Fitch, H. S., and A. V. Fitch. 1967. Preliminary experiments on physical tolerances of the eggs of lizards and snakes. Ecology, 48: 160–165.

Flegg, P. B. 1953. The effect of aggregation on diffusion of gases and vapours through soils. Jour. Sci. Food Agric., 4: 104–108.

Fox, S. F. 1978. Natural selection on behavioral phenotypes of the lizard *Uta stansburiana*. Ecology, 59: 834–847.

Froese, A. D., and G. M. Burghardt. 1974. Food competition in captive juvenile snapping turtles, *Chelydra serpentina*. Anim. Behav., 22: 735–740.

Gettinger, R. D., G. L. Paukstis, and W. H. N. Gutzke. 1984. Influence of hydric environment on oxygen consumption by embryonic turtles *Chelydra serpentina* and *Trionyx spiniferus*. Physiol. Zool., 57: 468–473.

Grainger, J. N. R. 1956. Effects of changes of temperature on the respiration of certain Crustacea. Nature, 178: 930–931.

Grigg, G. C. 1987. Water relations of crocodilian eggs: management considerations, p. 499–502. *In* G. J. W. Webb, S. C. Manolis, and P. J. Whitehead (eds.), Wildlife Management: Crocodiles and Alligators. Surrey Beatty and Sons, Chipping Norton, New South Wales, Australia.

Gutzke, W. H. N., and D. Crews. 1988. Embryonic temperature determines adult sexuality in a reptile. Nature, 332: 832–834.

Gutzke, W. H. N., and G. C. Packard. 1986. Sensitive periods for the influence of the hydric environment on eggs and hatchlings of painted turtles (*Chrysemys picta*). Physiol. Zool., 59: 337–343.

— 1987. Influence of the hydric and thermal environments on eggs and hatchlings of bull snakes *Pituophis melanoleucus*. Physiol. Zool., 60: 9–17.

Gutzke, W. H. N., G. C. Packard, M. J. Packard, and T. J. Boardman. 1987. Influence of the hydric and thermal environments on eggs and hatchlings of painted turtles (*Chrysemys picta*). Herpetologica, 43: 393–404.

Gutzke, W. H. N., and G. L. Paukstis. 1983. Influence of the hydric environment on sexual differentiation of turtles. Jour. Exp. Zool., 226: 467–469.

Halliday, T. R., and P. A. Verrell. 1988. Body size and age in amphibians and reptiles. Jour. Herpetol., 22: 253–265.

Hochachka, P. W., and G. N. Somero. 1984. Biochemical Adaptation. Princeton Univ. Press, Princeton, New Jersey. xx, 537 pages.

Hurlbert, S. H. 1984. Pseudoreplication and the design of ecological field experiments. Ecol. Monogr., 54: 187–211.

Janzen, F. J., G. C. Packard, M. J. Packard, T. J. Boardman, and J. R. zumBrunnen. 1990. Mobilization of lipid and protein by embryonic snapping turtles in wet and dry environments. Jour. Exp. Zool., 255: 155–162.

Janzen, F. J., and G. L. Paukstis. 1991. Environmental sex determination in reptiles: ecology, evolution, and experimental design. Quart. Rev. Biol., 66: 149–179.

Jayne, B. C., and A. F. Bennett. 1990. Selection on locomotor performance capacity in a natural population of garter snakes. Evolution, 44: 1204–1229.

Joanen, T., and L. McNease. 1987. Alligator farming research in Louisiana, USA, p. 329–340. *In* G. J. W. Webb, S. C. Manolis, and P. J. Whitehead (eds.), Wildlife Management: Crocodiles and Alligators. Surrey Beatty and Sons, Chipping Norton, New South Wales, Australia.

Joanen, T., L. McNease, and M. W. J. Ferguson. 1987. The effects of egg incubation temperature on post-hatching growth of American alligators, p. 533–537. *In* G. J. W.

Webb, S. C. Manolis, and P. J. Whitehead (eds.), Wildlife Management: Crocodiles and Alligators. Surrey Beatty and Sons, Chipping Norton, New South Wales, Australia.

Lang, J. W. 1987. Crocodilian thermal selection, p. 301–317. *In* G. J. W. Webb, S. C. Manolis, and P. J. Whitehead (eds.), Wildlife Management: Crocodiles and Alligators. Surrey Beatty and Sons, Chipping Norton, New South Wales, Australia.

Lang, J. W., H. Andrews, and R. Whitaker. 1989. Sex determination and sex ratios in *Crocodylus palustris*. Amer. Zool., 29: 935–952.

Leshem, A., A. Ar, and R. A. Ackerman. 1991. Growth, water, and energy metabolism of the soft-shelled turtle (*Trionyx triunguis*) embryo: effects of temperature. Physiol. Zool., 64: 568–594.

Limpus, C. J., V. Baker, and J. D. Miller. 1979. Movement induced mortality of loggerhead eggs. Herpetologica, 35: 335–338.

Lutz, P. L., and A. Dunbar-Cooper. 1984. The nest environment of the American crocodile (*Crocodylus acutus*). Copeia, 1984: 153–161.

Maloney, J. E., C. Darian-Smith, Y. Takahashi, and C. J. Limpus. 1990. The environment for development of the embryonic loggerhead turtle (*Caretta caretta*) in Queensland. Copeia, 1990: 378–387.

Manolis, S. C., G. J. W. Webb, and K. E. Dempsey. 1987. Crocodile egg chemistry, p. 445–472. *In* G. J. W. Webb, S. C. Manolis, and P. J. Whitehead (eds.), Wildlife Management: Crocodiles and Alligators. Surrey Beatty and Sons, Chipping Norton, New South Wales, Australia.

Miller, K., and G. C. Packard. 1992. The influence of substrate water potential during incubation on the metabolism of embryonic snapping turtles (*Chelydra serpentina*). Physiol. Zool., 65: 172–187.

Miller, K., G. C. Packard, and M. J. Packard. 1987. Hydric conditions during incubation influence locomotor performance of hatchling snapping turtles. Jour. Exp. Biol., 127: 401–412.

Morreale, S. J., G. J. Ruiz, J. R. Spotila, and E. A. Standora. 1982. Temperature-dependent sex determination: current practices threaten conservation of sea turtles. Science, 216: 1245–1247.

Morris, K. A., G. C. Packard, T. J. Boardman, G. L. Paukstis, and M. J. Packard. 1983. Effect of the hydric environment on growth of embryonic snapping turtles (*Chelydra serpentina*). Herpetologica, 39: 272–285.

Mrosovsky, N., P. H. Dutton, and C. P. Whitmore. 1984. Sex ratios of two species of sea turtle nesting in Suriname. Canadian Jour. Zool., 62: 2227–2239.

Muth, A. 1980. Physiological ecology of desert iguana (*Dipsosaurus dorsalis*) eggs: temperature and water relations. Ecology, 61: 1335–1343.

Packard, G. C. 1991. Physiological and ecological importance of water to embryos of oviparous reptiles, p. 213–228. *In* D. C. Deeming and M. W. J. Ferguson (eds.), Egg Incubation: Its Effects on Embryonic Development in Birds and Reptiles. Cambridge Univ. Press, Cambridge, UK.

Packard, G. C., and M. J. Packard. 1984. Coupling of physiology of embryonic turtles to the hydric environment, p. 99–119. *In* R. S. Seymour (ed.), Respiration and Metabolism of Embryonic Vertebrates. W. Junk Publishers, Dordrecht, The Netherlands.

—. 1987. Water relations and nitrogen excretion in embryos of the oviparous snake *Coluber constrictor*. Copeia, 1987: 395–406.

—. 1988. The physiological ecology of reptilian eggs and embryos, p. 523–605. *In* C. Gans and R. B. Huey (eds.), Biology of the Reptilia, Vol. 16. Alan R. Liss, New York.

—. 1990. Growth of embryonic softshell turtles is unaffected by uremia. Canadian Jour. Zool., 68: 841–844.

Packard, G. C., M. J. Packard, and L. Benigan. 1991. Sexual differentiation, growth, and hatching success by embryonic painted turtles incubated in wet and dry environments at fluctuating temperatures. Herpetologica, 47: 125–131.

Packard, G. C., M. J. Packard, and G. F. Birchard. 1989. Sexual differentiation and hatching success by painted turtles incubating in different thermal and hydric environments. Herpetologica, 45: 385–392.

Packard, G. C., M. J. Packard, and T. J. Boardman. 1982. An experimental analysis of the water relations of eggs of Blanding's turtles (*Emydoidea blandingii*). Zool. Jour. Linn. Soc., 75: 23–34.

Packard, G. C., M. J. Packard, and W. H. N. Gutzke. 1985. Influence of hydration of the environment on eggs and embryos of the terrestrial turtle *Terrapene ornata*. Physiol. Zool., 58: 564–575.

Packard, G. C., M. J. Packard, K. Miller, and T. J. Boardman. 1987. Influence of moisture, temperature, and substrate on snapping turtle eggs and embryos. Ecology, 68: 983–993.

—. 1988. Effects of temperature and moisture during incubation on the composition of hatchling snapping turtles (*Chelydra serpentina*). Jour. Comp. Physiol., B, 158: 117–125.

Packard, G. C., T. L. Taigen, M. J. Packard, and T. J. Boardman. 1981. Changes in mass of eggs of softshell turtles (*Trionyx spiniferus*) incubated under hydric conditions simulating those of natural nests. Jour. Zool., 193: 81–90.

Packard, G. C., T. L. Taigen, M. J. Packard, and R. D. Shuman. 1979. Water-vapor conductance of testudinian and crocodilian eggs (Class Reptilia). Respir. Physiol., 38: 1–10.

Packard, M. J., and G. C. Packard. 1986. Effect of water balance on growth and calcium mobilization of embryonic painted turtles (*Chrysemys picta*). Physiol. Zool., 59: 398–405.

—. 1989*a*. Environmental modulation of calcium and phosphorus metabolism in embryonic snapping turtles (*Chelydra serpentina*). Jour. Comp. Physiol., B, 159: 501–508.

—. 1989*b*. Mobilization of calcium, phosphorus, and magnesium by embryonic alligators (*Alligator mississippiensis*). Amer. Jour. Physiol., 257: R1541–R1547.

—. 1991. Sources of calcium, magnesium, and phosphorus for embryonic softshell turtles (*Trionyx spiniferus*). Jour. Exp. Zool., 258: 151–157.

Parmenter, C. J. 1980. Incubation of the eggs of the green sea turtle, *Chelonia mydas*, in Torres Strait, Australia: the effect of movement on hatchability. Australian Wildl. Res., 7: 487–491.

Paukstis, G. L., W. H. N. Gutzke, and G. C. Packard. 1984. Effects of substrate water potential and fluctuating temperatures on sex ratios of hatchling painted turtles (*Chrysemys picta*). Canadian Jour. Zool., 62: 1491–1494.

Paukstis, G. L., and F. J. Janzen. 1990. Sex determination in reptiles: summary of effects of constant temperatures of incubation on sex ratios of offspring. Smithsonian Herpetol. Inform. Serv., 83: 1–28.

Phillips, J. A., A. Garel, G. C. Packard, and M. J. Packard. 1990. Influence of moisture and temperature on eggs and embryos of green iguanas (*Iguana iguana*). Herpetologica, 46: 238–245.

Pieau, C. 1982. Modalities of the action of temperature on sexual differentiation in field-developing embryos of the European pond turtle *Emys orbicularis* (Emydidae). Jour. Exp. Zool., 220: 353–360.

Ratterman, R. J., and R. A. Ackerman. 1989. The water exchange and hydric microclimate of painted turtle (*Chrysemys picta*) eggs incubating in field nests. Physiol. Zool., 62: 1059–1079.

Schwarzkopf, L., and R. J. Brooks. 1985. Sex determination in northern painted turtles: effect of incubation at constant and fluctuating temperatures. Canadian Jour. Zool., 63: 2543–2547.

—. 1987. Nest-site selection and offspring sex ratio in painted turtles, *Chrysemys picta*. Copeia, 1987: 53–61.

Sinervo, B. 1990. The evolution of maternal investment in lizards: an experimental and comparative analysis of egg size and its effects on offspring performance. Evolution, 44: 279–294.

Sinervo, B., and R. B. Huey. 1990. Allometric engineering: an experimental test of the causes of interpopulational differences in performance. Science, 248: 1106–1109.

Standora, E. A., and J. R. Spotila. 1985. Temperature dependent sex determination in sea turtles. Copeia, 1985: 711–722.

Stock, M. K., and J. Metcalfe. 1987. Modulation of growth and metabolism of the chick embryo by a brief (72-hr) change in oxygen availability. Jour. Exp. Zool., Suppl. 1: 351–356.

Swingland, I. R., and M. J. Coe. 1979. The natural regulation of giant tortoise populations on Aldabra Atoll: recruitment. Philos. Trans. Royal Soc. London, B, 286: 177–188.

Thompson, M. B. 1981. Gas tensions in natural nests and eggs of the tortoise *Emydura macquarii*, p. 74–77. *In* C. B. Banks and A. A. Martin (eds.), Proceedings of the Melbourne Herpetological Symposium. Zool. Board Victoria, Parkville, Victoria, Australia.

—. 1990. Incubation of eggs of tuatara, *Sphenodon punctatus*. Jour. Zool., 222: 303–318.

Tokunaga, S. 1985. Temperature-dependent sex determination in *Gekko japonicus* (Gekkonidae, Reptilia). Dev. Growth Differ., 27: 117–120.

Tracy, C. R. 1980. Water relations of parchment-shelled lizard (*Sceloporus undulatus*) eggs. Copeia, 1980: 478–482.

—. 1982. Biophysical modeling in reptilian physiology and ecology, p. 275–321. *In* C. Gans and F. H. Pough (eds.), Biology of the Reptilia, Vol. 12. Academic Press, London.

Tracy, C. R., G. C. Packard, and M. J. Packard. 1978. Water relations of chelonian eggs. Physiol. Zool., 51: 378–387.

Tullett, S. G., and F. G. Burton. 1987. Effect of two gas mixtures on growth of the domestic fowl embryo from days 14 through 17 of incubation. Jour. Exp. Zool., Suppl. 1: 347–350.

Vleck, D. 1988. Embryo water economy, egg size and hatchling viability in the lizard *Sceloporus virgatus*. Amer. Zool., 28: 87A.

—. 1991. Water economy and solute regulation of reptilian and avian embryos, p. 245–259. *In* D. C. Deeming and M. W. J. Ferguson (eds.), Egg Incubation: Its Effects on Embryonic Development in Birds and Reptiles. Cambridge Univ. Press, Cambridge, UK.

Vogt, R. C., and J. J. Bull. 1984. Ecology of hatchling sex ratio in map turtles. Ecology, 65: 582–587.

Webb, G. J. W., A. M. Beal, S. C. Manolis, and K. E. Dempsey. 1987. The effects of incubation temperature on sex determination and embryonic development rate in *Crocodylus johnstoni* and *C. porosus*, p. 507–531. *In* G. J. W. Webb, S. C. Manolis, and P. J. Whitehead (eds.), Wildlife Management: Crocodiles and Alligators. Surrey Beatty and Sons, Chipping Norton, New South Wales.

Webb, G. J. W., D. Choquenot, and P. J. Whitehead. 1986. Nests, eggs, and embryonic development of *Carettochelys insculpta* (Chelonia: Carettochelidae) from northern Australia. Jour. Zool., B, 1: 521–550.

Webb, G. J. W., and H. Cooper-Preston. 1989. Effects of incubation temperature on crocodiles and the evolution of reptilian oviparity. Amer. Zool., 29: 953–971.

Webb, G. J. W., and A. M. A. Smith. 1984. Sex ratio and survivorship in the Australian freshwater crocodile *Crocodylus johnstoni*. Symposium Zool. Soc. London, 52: 319–355.

Whitehead, P. J. 1987. Respiration of *Crocodylus johnstoni* embryos, p. 473–497. *In* G. J. W. Webb, S. C. Manolis, and P. J. Whitehead (eds.), Wildlife Management: Crocodiles and Alligators. Surrey Beatty and Sons, Chipping Norton, New South Wales.

Whitehead, P. J., and R. S. Seymour. 1990. Patterns of metabolic rate in embryonic crocodilians *Crocodylus johnstoni* and *Crocodylus porosus*. Physiol. Zool., 63: 334–352.

Whitehead, P. J., G. J. W. Webb, and R. S. Seymour. 1990. Effect of incubation temperature on development of *Crocodylus johnstoni* embryos. Physiol. Zool., 63: 949–964.

Wilhoft, D. C., E. Hotaling, and P. Franks. 1983. Effects of temperature on sex determination in embryos of the snapping turtle, *Chelydra serpentina*. Jour. Herpetol., 17: 38–42.

Yntema, C. L. 1979. Temperature levels and periods of sex determination during incubation of eggs of *Chelydra serpentina*. Jour. Morphol., 159: 17–27.

Yntema, C. L., and N. Mrosovsky. 1982. Critical periods and pivotal temperatures for sexual differentiation in loggerhead sea turtles. Canadian Jour. Zool., 60: 1012–1016.

Zarrow, M. X., and C. M. Pomerat. 1937. Respiration of the egg and young of the smooth green snake, *Liopeltis vernalis* (Harlan). Growth, 1: 103–110.

Zweifel, R. G. 1961. Another method of incubating reptile eggs. Copeia, 1961: 112–113.

❦

❦ Packard, G. C., and J. A. Phillips. 1994. The importance of the physical environment for the incubation of reptilian eggs, p. 195–208. *In* J. B. Murphy, K. Adler, and J. T. Collins (eds.), Captive Management and Conservation of Amphibians and Reptiles. Society for the Study of Amphibians and Reptiles, Ithaca (New York). Contributions to Herpetology, volume 11.

Conservation of Commercially Important Reptiles Today: An Analysis Based on Crocodilians

Peter Brazaitis* and Mark Wise**

Introduction

THE MOVEMENT TO DEFEND AND PRESERVE THE world's wildlife, including unfamiliar or perhaps even unlikable animals, such as crocodilians, is not new. Crocodilians have gone from the precipice of being a critically endangered group of species in the 1950s to partial recovery in the 1960s and 1970s. They face the perils of renewed threats in the new era of deregulation and commercialization in the 1990s. Is the incentive to profit from wildlife overshadowing our need to protect wildlife?

In the 1950s and 1960s, affluent nations rapidly moved towards prosperity and economic development. The ability to gain access to remote regions with regular air service and to transport goods and materials swiftly over great distances increased dramatically. So did the ability to change the environment around us and to consume natural resources. New technologies allowed us to become more efficient predators. Wildlife was high on the menu, and a virtually uncontrolled commercial pet industry flourished with the influx of great numbers of new and exciting species. The commercial trade in exotic wild animal skins and manufactured products reaped significant profits at minimal expense. These activities often disregarded any regulations or effects on wild populations. The attitude was to take and sell as many animals as possible of a profitable species, alive or dead. When the animal was no longer available in quantities that made it commercially viable, commerce moved on to another species.

Crocodilians have historically been prime targets for use and abuse. Vilified as "man-eaters," they are often considered undesirable wildlife. Many people may see a crocodilian primarily as a pair of shoes, and only secondarily as a living part of our wildlife heritage (Figure 1). Their skins make them valuable for the manufacture of luxury products. It is thought that the trade in crocodilian skins for manufactured products alone exceeds two million skins a year.

In the tourist trade, stuffed hatchling crocodilians are favorite curios that are proffered for sale in great numbers. In the 1960s the pet industry sold millions of live animals for home aquariums. One wholesale pet dealer in New York City, regularly visited by Peter Brazaitis, imported more than 10,000 hatchling South American caimans a week for distribution. Twenty percent of the hatchling caimans shipped from South America arrived dead

*Central Park Wildlife Center
Wildlife Conservation Society
830 Fifth Avenue
New York, New York 10021, USA

**St. Augustine Alligator Farm
Route A1A South, P.O. 9005
St. Augustine, Florida 32084, USA

Current address:
11 Madeira Drive
St. Augustine, Florida 32084, USA

Acronyms used in this chapter:

AAZPA	American Association of Zoological Parks and Aquariums
CAG	Crocodilian Advisory Group
CFR	Code of Federal Regulations
CITES	Convention on International Trade in Endangered Species of Wild Fauna and Flora
ESA	Endangered Species Act of 1973
IUCN	International Union for the Conservation of Nature and Natural Resources
SSP	Species Survival Plan
Tb	Body temperature
TIAS	Treaties and other International Acts Series
TRAFFIC	Trade Records Analysis of Flora and Fauna in Commerce
USC	United States Code

from overcrowding and the adverse temperatures that they experienced en route. At that time there were hundreds of wholesale dealers and thousands of retail pet outlets. Only a fraction of the animals initially captured survived transit and the poor care purchasers generally offered, either through ignorance or overt neglect. Unfortunately, with increased populations and subsequent deregulation by wildlife authorities, the pet trade in the American Alligator (*Alligator mississippiensis*) is once again surfacing, albeit at lower levels than before.

The Need for Protection

The history of crocodilian utilization is well known. Crocodilians most often come from poor, developing countries with remote borders. These countries usually cannot afford the cost of sufficient wildlife law-enforcement personnel and equipment, and the monitoring and control programs that are needed in order to be effective. On the other hand, wildlife products, often luxury items, find ready markets in wealthy countries more concerned with profit than with conservation. The great numbers of baby crocodilians and skins in trade year after year, often in the millions annually, were cited by wildlife industries as proof that there were plenty of animals and that inexhaustible numbers remained available in the wild and were unhurt by utilization. By 1967, all of the commercially utilized species of crocodilians were in serious decline. Most of the 23 crocodilian species were either critically endangered or seriously threatened.

FIGURE 1. The Yacare Caiman (*Caiman yacare*) of central South America is one of the mainstays of the commercial leather trade. Although reduced in numbers, it is still found in suitable habitat. Listed in CITES Appendix II and as an endangered species in the United States in June 1970, it has continued to be harvested in great numbers, despite national prohibitions on commercial harvest.

By the late 1960s, most industrialized countries had achieved a comfortable level of prosperity. They could afford conservation. They began to take a global view and turned their concerns toward the world conservation of natural resources, the environment, and endangered or threatened species—topics of which nearly everyone (at almost all age levels) became aware. Many developing countries were the first to sound a cry for help. They were, however, often powerless to stem the flow of wildlife through their borders. The commercial trade in wildlife and wildlife products—whether it involved whales, primates, fish, parrots, spotted cats, crocodilians, or other reptiles—had long-established national and international networks that started with the purchase of legal and illegal animals or skins from local hunters. With a very limited presence of wildlife enforcement and routine corruption by poorly paid customs and wildlife officials, live animals and skins were easily moved out of endemic countries and into international trade, where their origins became lost in a system well designed for processing contraband. It is apparent that routes for the illegal trade in birds and crocodilian skins, even today, closely parallel the trade routes of other forms of contraband, including illicit drugs.

CITES (TIAS 8249) was implemented in 1975 and has been enforced since 1977. Trade in commercially utilized species that are listed in Appendix I, II, or III can be regulated through a system of permits and documents for the import, export, and re-export of listed species. Although commercial trade in Appendix I species is prohibited, Appendix II and III species can be commercially traded upon issuance of the appropriate permits; this fact is widely misunderstood. There are now 112 signatory countries that have agreed to abide by the provisions of the CITES treaty.

CITES itself has no enforcement or policing powers. Thus, each signatory nation adopted the CITES provisions and the protection of foreign species in its wildlife regulations. The United States passed the Endangered Species Act of 1973 (ESA; 16 USC 1538[a]–[B]; 50 CFR, part 17). Violation of CITES provisions (CITES; 16 USC 1538[c]; 50 CFR, part 23) therefore became a violation under national law. Under the ESA, however, the United States could list any additional species as endangered or threatened at its own discretion.

The Lacey Act was passed in 1900 and outlawed the interstate traffic in birds and other animals that might be taken illegally in their state of origin. It was later amended and expanded to include wildlife taken in violation of foreign law, as well as state law. In 1981, the Lacey Act and the Black Bass Act were combined into a single, powerful law-enforcement tool. This 1981 enhancement authorized the forfeiture of illegal fish, wildlife, or plants on a strict liability basis. Civil penalties were increased from US$5,000 to $10,000 per violation, and the criminal penalty section of the Lacey Act was expanded to include felony provisions.

CITES empowered national wildlife authorities throughout the world and obligated them to enforce the wildlife regulations of foreign countries as their own regulations. The authority of sovereign countries to include the protection of species deemed to be of particular concern, and that may occur outside of the countries' borders, is being seriously challenged today.

Based on an initiative of the Wildlife Conservation Society, World Wildlife Fund/Trade Records Analysis of Flora and Fauna in Commerce (TRAFFIC) became the world auditing agency for wildlife and plants in trade, and began to keep track of the numbers. While it was possible to smuggle contraband species out of a country, airway bills, customs declarations, and export and import permits were required in order to receive them in other countries. TRAFFIC record keeping allowed conservationists to ask questions, such as: if only up to 460,000 crocodilian skins received legal documentation to leave exporting countries, how could an estimated 1.5 to 2 million skins be received by other countries from the same sources (Brazaitis 1989, 1990; Gaski and Hemley 1988; Hemley and Caldwell 1986; Luxmoore 1990)? The receiving countries, often centers of manufacturing and fashion where skins and products brought high revenues, or where a pet market flourished, were often affluent countries that had well-developed wildlife law-enforcement agencies and trained staff. The effect of such auditing shook the foundations of the commercial trade in wildlife.

Regulations were slowly modified with the common goal of determining what best served the conservation and preservation of species. Funding for surveys of wild populations to assess their status was readily available through public institutions and wildlife agencies. Wildlife agencies within the United States Government could fund or undertake studies on which wildlife management and conservation decisions could be made.

Retail prices for reptilian species in the pet trade soared. Some species immediately rose in market value upon being designated as endangered or threatened. Stringent regulation and diminished populations caused many sources for wild-caught species to dry up. Many countries listed indigenous species for special protection. India, for example, listed the Common Cobra (*Naja naja*) and Indian rat snakes (*Ptyas*) as protected species in an effort to stem the decimation of populations of these valuable rodent-eating species by the snakeskin leather trade. Species were targeted for concern as threatened or endangered. Critical habitats and conservation problems were addressed through a variety of national and international forums. The age of captive management and reproduction programs for significantly threatened and endangered species had begun.

Captive Breeding and Reintroduction

The American Association of Zoological Parks and Aquariums (AAZPA) and independent zoological institutions embarked on a road toward wildlife conservation that included comprehensive breeding programs and strategies. The Species Survival Plan (SSP) was developed, under which endangered or threatened species were targeted for collaborative captive-breeding programs. Special advisory groups further helped counsel and develop multinational strategies for captive-breeding programs for critically endangered species. The AAZPA Crocodilian Advisory Group (CAG) emerged as the leader in coordinating and developing captive-breeding programs in zoological institutions.

Problems developed, however. In 1992, William Ziegler of the Miami Metro Zoo reported to the CAG that 31 United States institutions were holding 4,760 crocodilians, which, according to Ziegler, represented 26 species and subspecies (including 10 endangered species), and they successfully hatched

979 eggs that year. As the captive propagation of crocodilians in zoos successfully increases, however, the available space to place and raise offspring to maturity decreases. Many zoos have enlarged their facilities for crocodilians to accommodate their success, or have acquired new facilities to expand breeding programs. Reintroduction of captive-bred animals into protected natural areas is possible with some species. Few zoo specimens are of known origin, however, and reintroduction of individuals of a wide-ranging species from one region into another could be biologically irresponsible.

India is a leader in captive-breeding and reintroduction programs for the Mugger Crocodile (*Crocodylus palustris*) and Gharial (*Gavialis gangeticus*), which include use of DNA technologies and the ability to characterize individuals and populations. A Venezuelan effort for the critically endangered Orinoco Crocodile (*C. intermedius*) is also in place and is highly successful, with start-up assistance from the Wildlife Conservation Society. The St. Augustine Alligator Farm, St. Augustine, Florida (Figure 2), and the Atagawa Tropical Plant and Crocodile Garden, Atagawa, Japan, are the largest zoological crocodilian breeding facilities in the world that do not involve the commercial skin and meat trade. Unfortunately, for many species there may no longer be suitable protected habitat remaining for reintroduction. Such may be the case for the Chinese Alligator (*Alligator sinensis*), whose survival in the immediate future appears to depend on captive-breeding programs operated by zoological institutions and local alligator farms (Behler et al. 1982; Behler and Joanen 1982; Watanabe 1983, 1986). If reintroduction habitat does exist for many species, it may continue to be heavily hunted by both legal and illegal interests for the commercial skin trade. Thus, commercial incentives may negate the benefit of reintroduction programs aimed at maintaining biodiversity.

FIGURE 2. An Indian Gharial (*Gavialis gangeticus*) basks in a breeding facility at the St. Augustine Alligator Farm, St. Augustine, Florida.

Threats to Species

While the Chinese Alligator may be a prime example of the result of habitat loss on species decimation, habitat loss may well be a major component in the decline of wild populations of more common, perhaps non-commercial species. This illustrates the fallacy of placing all of our conservation eggs in a commercially oriented basket. The combination of adverse environmental factors and poorly controlled commercial utilization may herald the death knell for some populations of Black Caiman (*Melanosuchus niger*), Broad-snouted Caiman (*Caiman latirostris*), Common Caiman (*C. crocodilus*), and Dwarf Caiman (*Paleosuchus* species).

Recent studies on toxic-metal contamination of wild Brazilian crocodilians, conducted by Myrna E. Watanabe and her colleagues at Manhattan College in New York City, show that at least 50 percent of the Brazilian caiman population in all size classes carry lead levels of over 0.5 parts per million (M. E. Watanabe, pers. comm.), a level considered to be of serious concern in aquatic ecosystems (Walsh et al. 1977). More than 30 percent of the individuals carry substantially higher levels (up to 84 ppm). There also is concern that caimans may be contaminated with mercury as a result of gold mining operations.

Unfortunately, wildlife authorities today are under such intense pressure to deregulate species for utilization that they may base regulatory measures on cursory site estimates of current populations, regardless of actual population depletion and vulnerability (Thorbjarnarson 1992), or of the implications of pollution and adverse environmental trends. Cursory reports and anecdotal comments that some populations may still be common in some regions could be sufficient for the entire species to be downlisted to a lesser status and thus further subject the species to commercial utilization. Such is the case under consideration by the United States Fish and

Wildlife Service involving the Yacare Caiman (*Caiman yacare*) of central South America (Figure 1). Listed as a United States endangered species, Yacare Caiman are still found in substantial numbers in some suitable habitats. Populations have followed a consistent pattern of depletion in many areas, however, and may be, at best, stable in others. All caiman populations are highly vulnerable to a variety of adverse commercial and environmental pressures (Thorbjarnarson 1992); they suffer from a lack of comprehensive natural history data, insufficient protection and management programs for wild populations, and from inadequate monitoring and control of their commercial use.

In a letter to the United States Fish and Wildlife Service in 1991, Alberto Yanosky of the El Bagual Ecological Reserve, Argentina, reported that the Yacare Caiman is more endangered than the Broad-Snouted Caiman in Argentina, and voiced concern that increased hunting of one species could have grave implications for the other. Field surveys conducted by P. Brazaitis, G. Rebelo, and C. Yamashita throughout Brazil have indicated disproportionately large numbers of small animals in many regions, and the total absence of the Common Caiman and Black Caiman in a number of regions where they had been present recently. Such information suggests that caiman populations may be in more serious trouble than can be ascertained by simple one-time head counts. F. Wayne King of the International Union for the Conservation of Nature and Natural Resources (IUCN) Crocodile Specialist Group also reported observations of many small caimans in surveys he conducted in Bolivia, where caimans are exhaustively hunted as well.

Politics and Public Relations

Aside from biological considerations, however, economic and political incentives play a major role in downlisting species. The Yacare Caiman is of paramount importance to supply the needs of the crocodile leather trade. Equally important to the economic needs of the trade is to strip animals, such as the Yacare Caiman, of their protected status as United States endangered species, and to open United States markets to additional imports and expanded commercial utilization. Doing so will inevitably increase the illegal taking and decimation of possibly three other endangered species in range countries: Broad-snouted Caiman, Black Caiman, and possibly the Rio Apaporis Caiman (*C. crocodilus apaporiensis*).

Crocodilians are fast-growing and require specific environmental conditions, social space, and diets. They are not "pet items" for the home aquarist. Thus, diverting surpluses of zoo-produced offspring from breeding programs to the pet trade is unacceptable. Making zoo animals available for the hide and skin industry is even more unacceptable. Both pose serious public relations problems and are counter-productive to the image and goals that zoological institutions wish to achieve. Alternatively, closely controlled captive-breeding and collaborative reintroduction programs that include habitat protection and public education may be the most costly programs to institute. They may also, however, be the programs most apt to save crocodilian species for the future.

In the past, limited facilities and resources allowed zoological institutions to concentrate on developing breeding protocols only for targeted species and to focus their captive-propagation efforts on critically endangered crocodilians. But in the 1980s, the commercial skin industry began to invest heavily in commercial farms and ranches, and to lobby for more sympathetic regulation.

Ineffective Controls

Product tagging, initially implemented in 1973 to control the flow of illegal skins into product manufacturing, was soon rescinded. The presence of identifying skin tags placed on American Alligators and several valuable crocodile species (*Crocodylus*) was not mandated during the processing of skins—from skinning, through manufacture, and into products—nor were tags required for importation. Caiman skins were not required to bear identifying, traceable tags of any kind to enter into the trade. This alone facilitated the continued illegal taking of endangered Black Caiman, Broad-snouted Caiman, and possibly the remaining Rio Apaporis Caiman. Although identifying tags are attached to the tip of the tail in a part of the body that is left unfinished and is not used in the manufacture of products (Figure 3), tanners successfully argued that the tags damaged tanning machinery. The result was that the commercial skin trade was successful in negating the key tool required by law enforcement

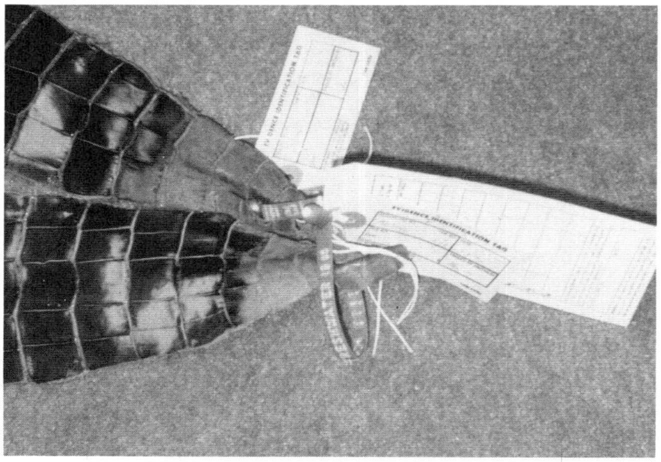

FIGURE 3. Identifying tags are affixed to the tip of the tail on American Alligator (*Alligator mississippiensis*) skins for export out of the United States. This identification must be maintained in place to the point of manufacture into products and coupled with appropriate product marking if we are to monitor and control the traffic in protected and endangered species.

authorities to effectively monitor skin and product trafficking and to prosecute violators. The illegal trade has flourished, taking advantage of the inability to track and identify the origins of individual skins and the products made from them.

Newly adopted international tagging regulations (CITES Convention, March 1992, Kyoto, Japan; Anonymous 1992) may continue the problem and perhaps facilitate the increased illegal harvesting of wild populations that include endangered species. Consumers and importers may be misled into believing that all caiman skins in the trade are rigidly controlled and from legitimate origins. This is not so. While it is true that all "legally" exported skins will now bear an identifying tag when they are exported out of the country of origin, re-exported skins that have been subject to "substantial processing and manufacturing" (tanned skins that have been subjected to substantial tanning and manufacturing) are excepted (Anonymous 1992*a*), and product marking and monitoring continue to be lacking. Furthermore, illegally acquired skins can still be trans-shipped from one South American country to another, and eventually receive tags and export documents as legal skins, as is now commonplace. Illegally acquired skins can remain undetected in trade once they are tanned and fabricated into products.

Both Singapore and Italy, centers for the traffic in caiman skins from South America, continue to be major sources for illegal skins. On 26 June 1992, the CITES Standing Committee issued a recommendation that no member states should either accept permits or certificates issued by Italy, or issue certificates for shipments to Italy. Reasons given were the absence of laws and adequate regulations; absence of penalties for violators of CITES agreements; inadequacy of border controls on imports, exports and transit shipments; and the issuance of CITES documents not in accordance with the CITES Convention. The United States Fish and Wildlife Service, however, did not adopt the recommended suspension of trade with Italy. In fact, it moved to downlist the Yacare Caiman and open the United States to imports of skins and products made from these animals, even though Yacare Caiman are the principal type of crocodilian skin most often re-exported from Italy. CITES has recommended similar trade suspensions from Bolivia, Paraguay, and recently from Thailand (from 21 April 1991 to 2 April 1992). Bolivia and Paraguay are well known as sources of Yacare skins as well.

As research funding for crocodilians declined in the late 1980s, the industry began to encourage financial dependence of crocodilian research on commercial funding. Today, most crocodilian research is conducted in the interest of commercial utilization and is supported by industrial funding. Research on non-commercial species suffers from a lack of adequate funding. In an atmosphere of economic recession, governments and many conservationists alike adopted the concept of "sustained utilization" (Thorbjarnarson 1991, 1992). The New Order of preserving species would depend largely on their value as dead, commercially saleable products.

Commercialized Conservation

With no lack of investment funds and the availability of cheap labor and materials, the industry embarked on a road of large-scale captive propagation for some of the more valuable endangered and threatened species. These included the Nile Crocodile (*Crocodylus niloticus*), New Guinea Crocodile (*C. novaeguineae*), Saltwater Crocodile (*C. porosus*), and Siamese Crocodile (*C. siamensis*). Species that do not have a high commercial interest, however, such as the Dwarf Caiman (*Paleosuchus palpebrosus*), Smooth-fronted Caiman (*P. trigonatus*), and Dwarf Crocodile (*Osteolaemus tetraspis*) have received little or no attention and can suffer whatever fate the loss of habitat might offer. Zoological institutions must operate under strict oversight by the public, professional umbrella organizations, and animal welfare regulations, but farms and ranches can engage in years of poor animal care, low production and high mortalities (especially during start-up), and virtually no minimum standards for allowable mortalities or husbandry. Replacement animals may be readily available from wild populations in some developing countries that lack or have very limited effective wildlife law-enforcement capabilities (Thorbjarnarson 1992).

The State of Louisiana alligator program is a model exception that requires high standards of maintenance and care, and the humane treatment of animals. Establishments are carefully monitored and are regularly inspected. Violators receive heavy penalties and their facilities are placed under seizure. At the present time, the alligator leather trade secures legitimate raw materials from ranches and farms, and from wild populations under sanctioned harvest quotas.

Ranches are enterprises that draw on wild populations annually for eggs and young, raising them to slaughter size in about three years. They range from well-funded, efficient operations to poorly funded and managed operations. While some heavily invested ranches actively rear hatchlings, other ranches on land with naturally occurring wild populations of crocodilians may do little more than take down their cattle ranching signs and replace them with signs proclaiming themselves caiman ranches. Such was the case observed by the CITES research team conducting surveys of crocodilians in the Pantanal region of southern Brazil in 1987. Ranches may purport to preserve wild populations by being dependent on them for an ongoing source of animals, thus making the wild population important to protect. These ranches, however, can also draw excessively on wild populations for eggs and young. When wild populations suffer from declining production due to natural nest flooding or pollution, some unscrupulous ranches may continue to harvest eggs and young to meet production quotas. As many as 50 to 80 percent of nests may be destroyed by flooding in any given year (G. Rebelo, pers. comm.) or may succumb to dry-season stresses (Thorbjarnarson 1991); these losses, because they are due to the weather, are unpredictable. Many eggs are destroyed by harsh handling in transport from wild nests to incubators.

Numerous wild-caught hatchlings may not feed and, if they do, are sometimes fed nutrient-poor diets. Brazaitis, Yamashita, and Rebelo observed these conditions at government-owned—and some privately owned—caiman ranches in southern Brazil. Elias Monteiro, a Brazilian farmer, reports that some caimans are purposely fed calcium-poor diets in an attempt to rear animals that lack ventral osteoderms, in the hopes that this will result in a more supple skin that can be more readily tanned (J. Enzinna, pers. comm.). Lack of calcium is a dietary deficiency that is well known to cause serious health problems. Profit is the incentive for ranches and farms to operate as cheaply as possible and to produce a given number of animals of commercial size in as short a time as possible. Ranching operations are located in regions where the animals naturally occur, and so are often remote and poorly supported logistically. The ranches may be exposed to minimal oversight. Only a strong management and law-enforcement program may prevent such abuses. On the plus side, ranching theoretically should promote the protection of the habitat and wild populations as a source of animals or eggs. All too often, however, other overriding environmental and economic problems continue to facilitate the loss of habitat and populations. The result is that as the habitat continues to disappear and the populations decline, ranches simply go out of business.

Farms, on the other hand, initially utilize adult breeding stock from the wild, including nuisance animals. Most offspring that are produced are raised to slaughter size and harvested, while a number are raised to maturity to reproduce themselves. Farms may be the product of considerable financial investment and reflect relatively good levels of animal care, or, in some cases, may also become poorly operated consumers of wild populations. There are no universally applied international standards of operation. Animals less than one year of age on some commercial farms and ranches in developing countries may experience up to 50 percent mortality from disease and poor nutrition. A 25 percent or higher mortality for incubating eggs is not uncommon. High-technology/low-mortality farms have

FIGURE 4. The state-operated Rockefeller Wildlife Refuge, in Grand Chenier, Louisiana, which has pioneered research on the husbandry of the American Alligator (*Alligator mississippiensis*) and the effective protection and conservation of wild populations in the United States. Coupled with a strong law-enforcement component, this model program led to the full recovery of the American Alligator in less than 20 years.

operated in the United States (Figure 4), Australia, Zimbabwe, and South Africa, and have contributed significantly to our knowledge of the captive reproduction of several endangered species of high commercial interest. Heavily invested farms with effective production, operating out of economic necessity, should theoretically mean low losses from animal mortality. In order to protect investments from competition with cheaply acquired wild-killed skins, farming interests may discourage the taking of wild populations. Many countries include the caveat in their management protocols that five percent of the animals produced in captive breeding or rearing operations must be returned to the wild. Few programs have ever actually done so, however, citing the reason that the wild populations do not require such return. Survivorship data for released animals are lacking for most species. While zoological parks and programs in India for the captive breeding of endangered species have used advanced molecular-genetic techniques to maintain genetic diversity, commercial farms for endangered species are more concerned with increasing skin and meat production.

Legal skins account for less than one-quarter of the skins in trade or about 360,000 skins from all crocodilian species worldwide. In 1991, 25,977 skins originated from commercial captive-breeding farms, 103,303 came from ranches drawing on wild populations, and 229,887 were taken directly from wild populations (Luxmoore 1991). The remainder of the 1.5 to 2 million skins estimated to be in the trade were contraband—that is, taken from threatened, endangered, or protected species and populations.

Caiman Skin "Explosion"

Colombia recently announced that its government was sanctioning the export of skins from about 80 newly developed "farms" for the Common Caiman (*Caiman c. crocodilus*) and the Dusky Caiman (*C. c. fuscus*), subspecies native to Colombia (F. W. King, pers. comm.). Colombia cites no interest in Yacare Caiman in any regulation, although thousands of skins of this central South American species often are exported illegally through Colombia. Colombia's intent is to export 650,000 caiman skins a year in the coming years. Whole, raw caiman skins from the farms are estimated by the industry to be able to bring US$35 a skin, reflecting an estimated net profit of $27 on each skin.

Ted Joanen of the Louisiana Department of Wildlife and Fisheries analyzed the support data (pers. comm.). To reach Colombia's proposed export goals, under optimum high-technology conditions, Joanen calculated that an estimated 5.7 million pounds of farm-reared *Tilapia* fish (the proposed food base) would be required to feed breeding stock and to rear animals to commercial size. This translates to 4 million pounds of fish per 100,000 animals that are raised to one meter in length. According to Joanen, 3,000 acres of caiman and *Tilapia* ponds would be required, in addition to ponds for rearing the tens of thousands of young caiman of different size classes for up to three years. Farming and ranching require long-term investments and provide insecure future profits. In contrast, wild-killed animals require little investment, but yield quick profits at current market prices. Skins from illegally killed wild animals are indistinguishable from skins of farm- or ranch-raised animals. Thus, rather than supplant the illegal taking of wild populations, these sanctioned sources of caiman skins can easily become part of the problem. The economics of the caiman skin market create the incentive to quickly draw directly on the wild populations to bolster profits and augment production quotas—that is, to process wild-acquired skins through farms for export as farmed skins. The higher the price paid for skins labeled as farm products, the greater the incentive to sell wild-caught skins as "farmed." The United States Fish and Wildlife Service has received numerous import documents indicating that Colombia has had a long history as a source for illegal skins. These skins often originate elsewhere in South America, where there is a well-established infrastructure for the trade in contraband.

Colombia has neither a management nor law-enforcement program for the protection of wild populations and the smuggling of contraband from adjoining countries into and out of Colombia is well known. Management and control of the harvesting of wild populations were reported to be impossible, due to bandit activity and the drug trade in rural areas (F. W. King, pers. comm.). Therefore, among those wishing to stimulate the legal caiman trade, farming has become the "conservation" method of choice for these species in Colombia. The status of wild populations is as yet undocumented. There are no minimum standards for farm animal care or husbandry, other than government licensing, in most countries and Colombia is no exception. In an effort to control the illegal trade, skins emanating from Colombian farms are to be tagged for export if they are whole skins. Flank pieces and tail pieces would be put together and tagged if they represented the pieces of a whole animal. Although this system of group-item tagging may be practical for purposes of trade, it may be inadequate for wildlife law-enforcement and monitoring purposes.

Present international tagging and monitoring protocols lack the ability to effectively monitor both the legal and illegal traffic in crocodilians. Seventy percent of the wildlife products that come into the United States arrive through the Port of New York. In a report by TRAFFIC U.S.A. (Gaski and Hemley 1988), 60 United States Fish and Wildlife Inspectors processed 9,500 shipments containing over 1.1 million individual products between 1984 and 1986. Present proposals by the United States Fish and Wildlife Service to partially deregulate some races of caiman (Yacare Caiman) while increasing partial regulation of others (Dusky Caiman and Common Caiman), coupled with the problems of species identification of hides and products and similarity of appearance, are viewed as further compromising law-enforcement and monitoring capability.

Brazil, too, is promoting about 25 Yacare Caiman farms and ranches in the Pantanal regions of the states of Mato Grosso and Mato Grosso do Sul. Only one or two farms currently have technology capable of producing skins. Most of the Pantanal is used for cattle ranching, and the wild caiman populations occur on those ranches. Thus, all Yacare Caiman in Brazil are "ranched." There is no national ability nor infrastructure, however, to prevent the taking and smuggling of wild caiman skins, including those of critically endangered Black Caiman and Broad-snouted Caiman from throughout Brazil. Such smuggling is commonplace throughout most of Brazil.

Illegal Trade Competition

Legitimate farming and ranching efforts are further compromised when harvest quotas for skins taken directly from wild populations also are sanctioned in the same country or region. Brazil is resisting efforts by commercial traders to promote the harvesting of their wild populations in competition with controllable ranching efforts. Under a harvest quota system, CITES authorizes the export of a given number of skins taken from the wild population each year, based on governments' recommendations. One country, however, may do little more than a cursory estimate of crocodilian populations, cite attacks on humans, and receive a harvest quota, while another may develop a highly efficient and elaborate system for population assessment and continual annual monitoring under a well-enforced program. Good examples of the latter are the crocodilian programs of the United States, Australia, Zimbabwe, and South Africa. Venezuela uses the National Guard to enforce crocodilian management (Thorbjarnarson 1991).

Many quotas are issued on the basis of trial and error. If quotas do not appear to hurt the populations, they are often increased in the following years. Only animals of a certain size may be taken at certain times of the year in order to limit the taking of females at breeding times. Harvest quotas are most abusive to wild populations in the absence of a strong, established, and effective law-enforcement presence. Lack of national wildlife law-enforcement capabilities results in animals being taken year round and stored illegally for future sale. Undersized animals may also be taken and others may be lost to hunters after being wounded. Many skins deteriorate under hot tropical conditions in storage and often are not counted in the quota. A great number of skins may leave the country to enter the same market through smuggling, while only legitimately exported skins are recorded under the quota. The first legal quota for caiman skins out of Venezuela in 1982 (Gaski and Hemley 1988) was far exceeded by actual exports. Bolivia was prohibited from trading in caiman by CITES in the 1980s because of repeated violations.

It must be emphasized that farms and ranches cannot compete economically with cheaply acquired wild-caught or widely available illegal skins. Already the effect of the infusion of millions of legal and illegal caiman skins, sold as manufactured products at retail to an unwitting public as farmed, high-quality American Alligator and legitimately captive-reared crocodile, is driving these heavily invested operations out of business. Alligator and crocodile skin prices have dropped since 1990 from US$57 per foot to the present $25 per foot (T. Joanen, pers. comm.). Survival of high-technology/low-mortality farming is often based on the premise that each animal will bring about US$150 to $200 at harvest. Thus, farming in the United States, which draws minimally on wild populations, is intended to supplant both the illegal trade and the drain on wild populations. This kind of legal farming, however, is being destroyed by the new conservation strategy of sustained utilization of wild populations under recommendations that originally promoted farming. Nile Crocodile farmers in Africa face the same threat. Besides Colombian and Brazilian initiatives, an additional one million legally sanctioned caiman skins are soon expected to enter trade from Bolivia, Guyana, Paraguay, Venezuela, and other Latin American countries, in addition to the continuing illegal trade. At a recent meeting of the IUCN Crocodile Specialist Group in Colombia, CITES representatives reported that an estimated 900,000 illegal skins were thought to be stockpiled by the industry, possibly awaiting the availability of documentation that would suggest they came from legitimate sources.

One cannot help being somewhat skeptical of claims made by the crocodilian skin-trade industry. Those advocating the legal trade promise that less than 200 farms and ranches around the world, in poor and developing countries that are beset with limited economic and technological capabilities and competing with a well-established system of illegal trade, will increase the number of legal skins in trade from the present 200,000 a year to at least two million skins annually. And they will do all of this, the industry assures us, without exploiting wild populations. If this is true, then the efforts of our zoological parks to breed endangered species—which produce only about 1,000 animals a year—pale by comparison.

Sustainable Utilization

We are told that protectionism for wild animals does not work, particularly for crocodilians, and that sustainable utilization is the conservation wave of the future. But the commercially motivated concept of sustainable utilization, grounded on the premise that wild animals only can survive based on their economic value when utilized, also has failed to prevent the abusive exploitation and continued decimation of whales for a variety of products, elephants for their ivory (Bolze 1992), and rhinoceroses for their horns. Sustainable utilization can benefit isolated regions and a small number of people, but can be detrimental to a species overall. Indeed, after 20 years of protecting many crocodilians, we still have an estimated 1.5 million illegal skins in trade annually. The failure to eliminate or substantially curtail the illegal trade cannot be attributed to the policies of protection, however, but rather to the failure to implement adequate law-enforcement and management programs to monitor and control the trade. To date, the illegal trade has been facilitated by the inability to monitor the transport of illegal skins and skin products. The exotic leather industry has done virtually nothing to police itself (Brazaitis 1991). While engaging indiscriminately in both legal and illegal trade, it has tried to make the consumption of wildlife more palatable to the public by leading them to believe that any product on a retail shelf is from a farmed, ranched, or an otherwise legally acquired animal. The profit incentive is immense.

The Market

Illegal caiman skins are often tanned and manufactured into products in Southeast Asia using cheap labor, then are exported to Europe and re-exported as European-manufactured products. Other skins are imported directly into Italy and re-exported as tanned skins to manufacturers or are manufactured into products that are then exported. South American caiman are commonly misrepresented as genuine and legal American Alligator or as New Guinea or Nile crocodiles. Caiman skin products are marketed under designer names at prices of up to US$5,000 for an average-sized handbag. Genuine, farmed American Alligator and other crocodile products command similar or only slightly higher prices, despite the vast difference between the price and quality of the raw and tanned material. While a raw caiman belly skin may have cost US$2 to $25 in South America in 1990, the same size genuine crocodile or alligator skin may have cost $250 in comparison (Anonymous 1991). Consumers are led to believe that these products are manufactured from high-quality legally farmed alligators and crocodiles. This marketing strategy is not only highly profitable, but considerably more palatable than telling the consumer that the product was made from second-rate cheap skins, was probably taken in violation of national laws, that the skins may represent an endangered species, and that they came from the killing of animals from wild populations. Typical misleading trade names are "Caiman Alligator," "Caiman Crocodile," "Crocodile," "Genuine Alligator," or "Alligator." Consumers cannot tell the difference and, in many cases, neither can buyers for the retail stores (Brazaitis 1991).

There is no such thing as a slight stimulation of international trade in a wild species. Trade means developing a market that is sufficiently large to make it internationally profitable, and the raw material must be available in future years to ensure returns on investments. The cycle begins when a species that can have commercial value is identified and sources for the raw or live material are available. Long- and short-term contracts are signed to ensure procuring of raw skins, the processing or tanning of the material, and the manufacturing of the materials into products. In the skin trade, this process takes place several years before actual products made from the species are available on the market for sale to consumers. The catalyst that makes it work is product promotion.

Once the amount of available raw material is guaranteed, product designs and fashion styles are created. Seasonal trends are targeted. The consumer is groomed to buy a product line at the time when the product and the fashion created for it can be placed on the market. Generally, this is orchestrated to take place at peak buying and fashion-introduction seasons, such as spring and fall periods. The fashion trend continues as long as the amount of raw material can sustain the stimulated demand.

When declining populations are cited, we often hear the question: how could a species, such as a crocodilian, be threatened when the industry can continually count on receiving the same tens of thousands of skins each year? The answer is that successful markets set increasing annual demands. The demand is then met to satisfy the market and maintain profits. Trade numbers do not immediately decline because, as local population numbers decline, collectors work farther afield, push into more remote and otherwise inaccessible regions, and work harder to acquire skins. When the utilization of a species appears profitable, the trade immediately attracts increasing numbers of people into the field for the collection of the animals. The gradual decline of commercially utilized species is often deceptive and finally precipitous. While local people and biologists working in the field may see regional population declines taking place, corrective action may come slowly.

In the case of crocodilians, before any punitive actions occurred, several cries for help had to be heard. The problems of the illegal skin trade had to be exposed to public scrutiny by the media; consumer education literature, such as "The Illegal Skin Trade" booklet was produced (by the Central Park Wildlife Center of the Wildlife Conservation Society; Brazaitis 1991); and an outcry from legitimate alligator and crocodile farmers and the standing committee of the IUCN Crocodile Specialist Group had to occur. Then CITES finally implemented a sanction on trade with Italy, effective as of 26 June 1992 and lifted in February 1993. Such sanctions have only been called for three times since CITES was implemented in 1973. Bolivia, Paraguay, and Thailand continue to be keys in the traffic in illegal skins and endangered species. Reluctance to initiate such sanctions is particularly evident during periods of economic hardship, when the protection of wildlife may be relegated to lesser importance than business incentives.

The greater the hardship and the need for foreign exchange, the greater is the incentive to commercially utilize wildlife populations as a low-cost, high-profit, easily available public resource. The raw material is virtually free for the taking and brings relatively high profits. The result is that at the precipitous point at which the species cannot sustain the combined environmental pressures and harvesting, the effort to fill the market demand or the mechanisms to halt the destruction are not able to react quickly enough, and the species is suddenly decimated. When the amount of legally available raw materials, including those produced by farms and ranches, becomes insufficient to supply the stimulated market demand (which quickly occurs), the demand is met with illegally obtained skins at the expense of wild populations.

In 1979, when legal American Alligator skins appeared on the market after a lapse of ten years, the trade was stimulated by fashion promotions that brought with them increases in imports of other species. In the 1980s the infusion of up to several hundred thousand legal Venezuelan caiman skins again stimulated the demand beyond the availability of raw materials and the illegal traffic in skins, including those of endangered species from South America and Asia, soared. Today, the stage is set for the cycle to begin once again.

In Kyoto, Japan, in 1992, CITES adopted a global tagging resolution for crocodilian skins in trade. While all skins of all species will be required to bear identifying tags on export from countries of origin, substantially processed and manufactured skins and all manufactured products continue to be excluded from new tagging mandates. These are the tanned skins and products that find their ways through several re-exporting countries that have extensive histories of processing contraband wildlife and pose the most difficult problems in species identification for wildlife law-enforcement and monitoring agencies.

More meaningful resolutions might have included a complete system of tagging and monitoring of skins and subsequently manufactured products from origin to consumer. Stringent trade and monitoring controls, with revocation of import/export licenses for repeat violations, could eliminate the incentive for traders to look at penalties as part of the cost of doing business. International standards for the inspection of farms and ranches and the humane treatment of animals would reduce mortalities. Provision of sufficient funding and training for wildlife law enforcement, as well as developing an international communication system for quickly identifying problems and repeat violators would also ameliorate current problems.

Summary

The trade status of species should be based on the completion of comprehensive ecological and population studies, not just on cursory population estimates. Effective conservation and management programs for wild populations and habitats in producing countries should be implemented. Trade bans with any producing country that lacks *effective* protection of wild populations and habitats need to be implemented.

However palatable new tagging protocols may make the purchase of products to the consumer, we, once again, may have fallen far short of implementing regulations to protect wild populations of crocodilians. Present worldwide trade practices (Luxmoore 1990) place priority on the use of wild animals, which undermines captive-propagation programs and encourages the further utilization of wild populations. The illegal trade and the wholesale taking of wild populations continue to proliferate. If United States imports are any example, improper and inaccurate international documentation for hides and products are commonplace. Endangered and non-endangered species, illegally acquired skins, classic American Alligator and other crocodile skins, as well as poor-quality caiman skins, all appear at random with documentation of every description. Skins continue to be trans-shipped through different countries and are re-exported again and again to obfuscate their origins.

These are grave times for conservation around the world. There is minimal funding for wildlife conservation, but ecological devastation is imminent without it—devastation for which future generations will have to pay. Crocodilian conservation is possible without trading the world's wildlife heritage for the profit incentives of a few. The Government of India, with that country's enormous rural population, has nevertheless managed a successful crocodile conservation, breeding, and reintroduction program, which over the past 15 years has involved two out of the three potential human-eating species, without commercial interests.

The major portion of crocodilian conservation funds and expertise should be directed into crocodilian ecology and natural history studies and the development of national parks and protected refuges where our children can be taught to appreciate and enjoy all wildlife, including crocodilians. The AAZPA, along with the Wildlife Conservation Society and private organizations, such as the St. Augustine Alligator Farm, have taken leadership roles in this critical effort. We cannot be content with the meager—though important—successes of our highly focused captive-breeding and conservation programs, while wild populations and their habitats around the world are relegated to uncertain conservation strategies that are dependent on commercial incentives. We should not forget that commercial incentives for crocodilians are dictated by the whims of luxury and fashion (Brazaitis 1989). We must learn to look closely at today's conservation programs, dissect and expose their fallacies, and strip them of the euphemisms and hyperbole that make them superficially palatable. We must separate the financially expedient programs and direct our real efforts towards serving the best interests of wild populations and their habitats. The principle of killing wildlife populations to preserve them—sustained utilization—does not withstand the glare of public or scientific scrutiny. Protecting wildlife is not an ugly term. It simply has been expeditiously put out of vogue and is not profitable.

Acknowledgments

We thank William Conway, Wildlife Conservation Society, and Richard Lattis, Central Park Wildlife Center, for their important comments and help. Special thanks are due to the St. Augustine Alligator Farm, William Donato and John Meehan of the Law Enforcement Division of the United States Fish and Wildlife Service, Lawrence, New York; Robin Lepore of the Office of the Solicitor, United States Fish and Wildlife Service, Newton Corners, Massachusetts; and Lisa Burianek, New York State Department of Law Environmental Protection Bureau, Albany. A special note of thanks goes to Myrna E. Watanabe, for reviewing and editing the manuscript, and to the editors of this volume for their patience.

Literature Cited

Anonymous. 1991. Trade. Crocodile Spec. Group Newsl., 10(3): 19.

—. 1992. CITES report. Crocodile Spec. Group Newsl., 11(1): 13–17.

Behler, J. L., P. Brazaitis, and T. Joanen. 1982. The Chinese alligator (*Alligator sinensis*) its status and propagation in captivity. Zool. Garten, 52: 73–77.

Behler, J. L., and T. Joanen. 1982. Captive management of the Chinese alligator. Ann. Proc. Amer. Assoc. Zool. Parks Aquar., 1982: 424–429.

Bolze, D. 1992. The ivory trade and conserving the African elephant. WCI Policy Report Number 1, Wildlife Conservation International, New York Zoological Society, New York. 16 pages.

Brazaitis, P. 1989. The trade in crocodilians, p. 196–199. *In* C. A. Ross (ed.), Crocodiles and Alligators. Golden Press, Silverwater, New South Wales, Australia.

—. 1990. Trade in crocodilian hides and products in the USA. TRAFFIC (USA), 10: 4–5.

—. 1991. The Illegal Skin Trade. Consumer education booklet. Central Park Zoo, New York Zoological Society, New York. 6 pages.

Gaski, A. L., and G. Hemley. 1988. The ups and downs of the crocodilian skin trade. TRAFFIC (USA), 8: 1–16.

Hemley, G., and J. Caldwell. 1986. The crocodile skin trade since 1979, p. 398–421. *In* Crocodiles, Proc. Working Meeting, IUCN/SSC Crocodile Specialist Group, Caracas Venezuela, Sept. 1984. Internatl. Union Cons. Nature, Publ., Caracas, Venezuela.

Luxmoore, R. 1990. Current issues in the world crocodilian skin trade. TRAFFIC(USA), 10: 2.

—. 1991. Trade. Crocodile Spec. Group Newsl., 10(2): 21–22.

Thorbjarnarson, J. B. 1991. An analysis of the spectacled caiman (*Caiman crocodilus*) harvest program in Venezuela, p. 217–235. *In* J. G. Robinson and K. H. Redford (eds.), Neotropical Wildlife Use and Conservation. Univ. Chicago Press, Chicago, Illinois.

—. 1992. Crocodiles: an action plan for their conservation. *In* H. Messel, F. W. King, and J. P. Ross (eds.), Internatl. Union Cons. Nature, Gland, Switzerland.

Walsh, D. F., B. L. Berger, and J. R. Bean. 1977. Residues in fish, wildlife, and estuaries: mercury, arsenic, lead, cadmium, and selenium residues in fish, 1971–73—National Pesticide Monitoring Program. Pesticides Monitoring Jour., 11: 5–34.

Watanabe, M. E. 1983. The Chinese alligator: is farming the last hope? Oryx, 17: 176–181.

—. 1986. A change of fortune for the Chinese alligator. Anim. Kingd., 89: 34–39.

Brazaitis, P., and M. Wise. 1994. Conservation of commercially important reptiles today: an analysis based on crocodilians, p. 209–221. *In* J. B. Murphy, K. Adler, and J. T. Collins (eds.), Captive Management and Conservation of Amphibians and Reptiles. Society for the Study of Amphibians and Reptiles, Ithaca (New York). Contributions to Herpetology, volume 11.

Caecilians (Amphibia: Gymnophiona) in Captivity

Marvalee H. Wake*

Introduction

Caecilians are relatively easy to care for in captivity, if due attention is paid to their well-being. Because so little is known of their biology, people who maintain them should keep careful notes of their activities. All observations are useful as we learn more about these fascinating animals. In this chapter, I consider aspects of the general biology of caecilians relevant to raising them in captivity. I then discuss details of their maintenance based on the few notes in the literature and particularly on my own experience during 25 years of having taken care of many species in my laboratory.

General Biology of Caecilians

Caecilians are elongate and limbless; most lack a tail entirely, and in those that have one, the tail may be only 25 mm long in an animal that measures 300–600 mm in total length (TL). The vent is at the posterior end of the body. The head is flattened and rather broad, and the eyes are small and covered by skin, or by skin and bone. Between the eye and the nostril lies a structure unique to caecilians, the tactile and chemosensory tentacle, which is extended and retracted as the animal uses it to sense its environment. The body is encircled by rings, or annuli; more primitive caecilians have greater numbers of annuli per body segment. In many species, small dermal scales are embedded in the annuli. (See Duellman and Trueb "1986" [1985], for a general summary of caecilian morphology with many references.)

The reproductive biology of many caecilians is highly derived, in contrast to that of other amphibians. More primitive caecilians lay eggs and have free-living larvae, as is the case with most frogs and salamanders. Several caecilian species are direct developers; that is, the egg clutch is laid on land, and fully metamorphosed juveniles hatch from the egg membrane. In contrast to frogs and salamanders, however, many species of caecilians are live-bearers, giving birth to juveniles after long gestation periods. For example, *Dermophis mexicanus* and *Gymnopis multiplicata* have a gestation period of 11 months (Wake 1972, 1980, 1983), and the gestation periods of *Typhlonectes compressicauda* are seven to nine months (Exbrayat and Laurent 1983; Exbrayat et al. 1981, 1983), during which the female provides nutrients to the fetuses in her oviducts (Wake 1977*a*, 1977*b*, 1980, 1982; Delsol et al. 1986; Welsch et al. 1977). All caecilians apparently have internal fertilization, effected by the male extruding the posterior part of its cloaca, as a specialized intromittent organ, and inserting it into the vent of the female to transfer sperm (Tonutti 1931, 1932, 1933; Taylor 1968; Wake 1972, 1977*a*, 1977*b*). There is, however, virtually nothing known of mate selection or courtship in these animals.

One of the reasons we lack useful observation is that most caecilians are fossorial; that is, they burrow in soil or litter. Only one family is aquatic, or semi-aquatic, and can, therefore, be more easily observed in captivity. Caecilians live throughout most tropical regions, and can be found from southern Mexico to Argentina in the Western Hemisphere, in most of tropical Africa, India, Sri Lanka, and from Southeast Asia to southern China and the Philippines. Habitat degradation is a major prob-

*Department of Integrative Biology,
and Museum of Vertebrate Zoology
University of California
Berkeley, California 94720, USA

Acronym used in this chapter:

TL Total length

lem for these amphibians, because the low- to mid-land tropical forests that they occupy are being converted to monoculture farm land, thus progressively restricting their habitats. Caecilians are not found (thus far) on Madagascar or Australia, but they can be found on the granitic Seychelles Islands, where they have spread extensively.

The phylogenetic relationships of caecilians are not yet resolved, and are under investigation by several workers. Currently, six families are recognized (Duellman and Trueb "1986" [1985]; Nussbaum and Wilkinson 1989). The Rhinatrematidae of northwestern South America are the most primitive caecilians, based on a number of features of morphology and life history (Nussbaum 1977). The Ichthyophiidae of southeast Asia share several features with the Rhinatrematidae, but are different in other characteristics. These two families are the sister-group to the "higher" caecilians (Nussbaum 1979; Duellman and Trueb "1986" [1985]; Wilkinson 1991). The latter include four families, the Uraeotyphlidae of India, the Scolecomorphidae of East and West Africa, the Typhlonectidae (the aquatic and semi-aquatic group) of northwestern South America, and the nearly pan-tropical Caeciliaidae, which several workers consider a paraphyletic group (Wake 1982; Nussbaum and Wilkinson 1989).

All caecilians have the same general elongate cylindrical shape, but their mature adult size varys. One miniature species, *Idiocranium russelli*, is sexually mature at 90 mm TL (Wake 1986). The largest species of caecilians are in the genus *Caecilia* and reach 1600 mm TL (Dunn 1942; Taylor 1968). Caecilians seem to eat almost anything that crawls under the soil, in litter, or on the ground, or burrows in mud or sticks on floating objects: earthworms, termites, orthopteran instars, coleopteran larvae (and pupae [Wake 1978]), anoline lizards (Moll and Smith 1967), and baby mice (C. Gans, pers. comm.) (summarized in Wake 1980, 1983). Some caecilians have been reported to specialize on certain kinds of prey, but this seems to occur in situations in which the particular prey item is super-abundant, such as earthworms in the rich soil of coffee fincas (Wake 1980). Most caecilians appear to be generalized feeders. They are preyed upon by snakes and some birds (see Taylor 1968). Their skin secretions, however, are toxic to some animals (Moodie 1978), including humans (M. H. Wake, pers. observ.).

Maintenance in Captivity

Terrestrial Caecilians

There are few comments in the literature that allude to captive maintenance of caecilians. Breckenridge and Jayasinghe (1979) and Breckenridge et al. (1987) raised *Ichthyophis glutinosus* from eggs through larvae to adulthood in the laboratory. They placed the eggs in a small tank that contained moist soil with a little water at one end of the tank. Larvae were reared in a tank, through which water was made to flow very gently. The water was about 8 cm deep and contained water plants. Moist soil with moss filled about a third of the tank. The tank was cleaned periodically and the soil was kept moist. Larvae were fed on bloodworms (larvae of *Chironomous* spp.) initially, and larger caecilian larvae and adults were fed earthworms. The authors attempted to simulate natural conditions in the laboratory. Exbrayat and Laurent (1983) kept *I. kohtaoensis* in plastic boxes with a substrate of moist peat. They used a 12-hour photoperiod at 29°–30°C. They fed the animals twice a week with pieces of thawed fish and earthworms. The animals were maintained for three years on this regimen.

In my experience, many species of terrestrial caecilians have done well in plastic boxes that are large enough to permit good freedom of movement and are filled with about 10 cm of moist, friable, rich, organic soil. The soil should have a near-neutral pH; caecilians do not do well in very acidic soil. Excess peat and redwood bark should be avoided, though they hold moisture well. A secure lid, perforated with small holes, should cover the container. I tape the lid to the tank for two reasons: caecilians are escape artists, and the lid helps to conserve the highly preferred humidity (70–80%). I also tape to the lid a card that identifies the animals, the place where they were collected, and their length and weight when they came into the lab. I note on the card each time the animals are fed, and the kind and number of food items. I also record any notes about the animals, such as their health and development. A temperature and light regimen, similar to that of the natural habitat of the species, suits captive specimens best. When a general regimen is needed for several taxa, I maintain them at 24°–27°C with 14 hours of light and 10 hours of darkness. I usually keep my animals in an environmental chamber so that temperature is well regulated. Soil should be either replaced or autoclaved every few months, and its moisture should be monitored so that it is humid, but not saturated.

Terrestrial caecilians usually condition readily to feeding in captivity. Earthworms of appropriate size for the size of the animal are often the preferred diet. After feeding is established, worms can be supplemented with termites and other insects, if the animal chooses to eat them. I have found that several species reject mealworms. I usually feed my animals weekly or twice a week, the same day and time each week. Most caecilians quickly grow accustomed to the feeding time, and animals can be lured out of their burrows simply by waving a worm over the burrow entrance. Drop the worm, and the animal will seize it. Hungry caecilians, if there is more than one in a good-sized tank, compete for their food, often biting each other, so it is important to supply enough food at an appropriate frequency. There are no rules for this; you establish your own by observing your animals. Number of prey items and frequency of feeding is predator- and prey-size dependent. Periodically, perhaps every three months, a vitamin and mineral supplement should be injected into the prey items before feeding.

Aquatic Caecilians

Several workers have commented in the literature on maintaining the aquatic *Typhlonectes compressicauda*. Murphy et al. (1977) kept a pair in a 91 × 45 × 45 cm aquarium with 40 cm of water at 23° ± 2°C. A subgravel filter was used, and plastic plants were placed in the tank. A light-dark cycle of 9.5 hours light, 14.5 hours dark was used. The animals were fed worms (*Lumbricus* sp.) twice a week, with shrimp and strips of beef heart occasionally offered. Food was held in front of the animals with forceps, and moved to simulate live prey. Leiman-Henley (1993) used a similar regimen. Exbrayat and Laurent (1983) report keeping nine *Typhlonectes* in a 200-l tank, and several pairs in 25-l plastic boxes. The bottoms of the containers were covered with gravel and the water was continuously filtered. Water temperature was 29°–30°C, the same as that of the natural habitat. Exbrayat and Laurent (1983) noted the characteristics of the water in the laboratory, and compared them with those of the stream where the animals were collected: a pH of 5 was the same in the laboratory as in the field, hardness was 1 degree in the field and 59 in the laboratory, calcium ions were less than 5 mg/l in nature and 420 mg/l in the laboratory, NaCl was 25 mg/l in nature and 200 in the laboratory, and a trace of nitrites was found in the laboratory water. They used a 12 hour photoperiod. Their animals were fed twice a week with pieces of thawed fish. Billo et al. (1985) kept their *Typhlonectes* in similar conditions. They used 100-l aquaria with a water depth of 13–16 cm and a temperature of 25°C. They fed their animals two or three times per week with pieces of trout.

I have found that aquatic caecilians are easy to maintain in captivity. Typhlonectids, usually *Typhlonectes natans*, appear in aquarium and pet stores with some regularity. I urge caution to those who are interested in caecilians and who wish to buy aquatic caecilians through the retail trade; animals are coming into the United States illegally, often without the knowledge of the retail store owner. Several South American countries, including Colombia, the source of many typhlonectids, have disallowed the import of animals, except for freshwater, tropical fish. Typhlonectids, however, are often collected while seining for fish, then imported as "black eels," or "rubber eels," so that they appear to be fish, rather than amphibians. Be aware that retailers must check the sources of their material, so that they are not liable to substantial penalties for selling illegally imported animals. State fish and game agencies are aware of the problem, so protect yourselves, and especially the animals.

Typhlonectids thrive in large aquaria (75 l or more) filled two thirds with water, and with good filtration systems. A gravel substrate, rocks, or other structures (for hiding places), and living vegetation are appropriate, but not necessary; typhlonectids do quite well without them. In fact, if the animals are not feeding well or are having other problems, I would remove everything except the water, the filter, and the heater, and change the water and clean the other components. I use a water temperature of 25°–28°C. Filters should be cleaned, and charcoal, cotton, and other materials replaced weekly. Tanks should be covered with a glass plate so that the temperature is maintained and the water does not evaporate too readily. The lid should be secured with tape or a large weight. I have had animals three times the size of the aperture between lid and tank wall (the diameter of the filter tube and the heater conduit) escape by forcing up the glass plate cover. They are so strong that they can rise 15 cm above the water level, gain purchase on the tank rim with their heads, and then wriggle out of the tank. They can move clumsily on a floor or other substrate, but desiccate quickly; they do not rehydrate well.

Aquatic caecilians feed well on tubifex, pieces of earthworms, or whole worms, diced raw chicken liver, and/or diced chicken heart. I prefer to initially feed my animals liver and heart as soon as possible, because it is a rich diet for them. Newborns feed readily on small (bite-sized) pieces of heart and liver, though they handle the food items more clumsily, foraging the tank bottom with open mouths as soon as they are aware that food items are present. Again, a vitamin and mineral supplement should be injected into the food items periodically. Typhlonectids respond to a regular feeding schedule, as do terrestrial caecilians.

Typhlonectids are live-bearers, and often give birth in captivity (Heinroth 1915; Barrio 1969; Exbrayat and Laurent 1983; Murphy et al. 1977; Billo et al. 1985; Leiman-Henley 1993). Two to 12 young are born, usually with their large gills still attached; the gills are shed within a day or two of birth. I have observed female caecilians "carry" their newborn, lifting the young on their backs, to the surface of the water to take their first breaths. Most caecilians, in contrast to many other amphibians, obtain relatively little oxygen through their skins (Sawaya 1941, 1947; Mendes 1941, 1945; Toews and MacIntyre 1977; Bennett and Wake 1974; Wood et al. 1975); both terrestrial and aquatic animals are primarily air-breathers. Typhlonectids pose an interesting buoyancy problem; they have one lung that is developed to extend virtually the entire length of the body, and in many species, in contrast to terrestrial caecilians, develop the other lung quite extensively. The animals go to the surface of the water to breathe, and then, with the lungs full of air, swim easily to the bottom of the tank, where they spend much of their time. Many minutes to hours later, they again poke their nostrils out of the water for another breath.

Disease Treatment

Caecilians do become diseased occasionally. Terrestrial caecilians get the equivalent of "red leg," which is indicated by engorgement and dilation of the blood vessels of the skin, especially visible on the venter of the animal. I have had good success treating animals by placing them in a clean, plastic box lined with moist paper towels, leaving crumpled towels for them to hide under, and by adding 10 ml of penicillin-streptomycin solution (Sigma Chemicals). I spray it with a syringe on the animal and on the moist paper toweling. I sometimes add 5 ml of gentamycin, a fungicide, as well. Aquatic caecilians are often imported with a heavy infestation of parasites, especially nematode eggs, which are laid under their skins. As the eggs develop, lumps appear on the skin, and these open as the worms hatch and make their way out of the host, forming open lesions in the skin that quickly become infected with fungus. I have treated animals successfully by adding 10 ml of gentamycin to the water of the tank every 24 hours.

Summary

Caecilians can be easily maintained in captivity, *if* one is willing to care for them properly. They must be observed frequently—ideally several times a day. While they must not be handled (because they experience stress readily), direct observation allows the recognition of problems, and the recording of behavior. Finally, as previously mentioned, we need all the information we can obtain about these still little-known animals. Those of us interested in maintaining and observing such unusual and interesting amphibians can contribute much to our knowledge of their biology.

Acknowledgments

I especially thank Harry Greene, University of California at Berkeley, for delivering the oral version of this paper at the Society for the Study of Amphibians and Reptiles symposium in honor of Roger Conant, held at the joint meeting of the SSAR and the Herpetologists' League, at Pennsylvania State University, in August, 1991. I thank James Murphy and Kraig Adler for including me in the symposium on maintaining amphibians and reptiles in captivity. I, too, wish to express my appreciation to Roger Conant for his lifetime of work in promoting the study of amphibians and reptiles. I am grateful to all of my colleagues who have aided me in obtaining living caecilians, and to the National Science Foundation for supporting my research on these animals and the importance of their biology to questions in evolutionary morphology, biology, and systematics.

Literature Cited

Barrio, A. 1969. Observaciones sobre *Chthonerpeton indistinctum* (Gymnophiona, Caecilidae) y su reproduccion. Physis, 28: 499–503.

Bennett, A. F., and M. H. Wake. 1974. Metabolic correlates of activity in the caecilian *Geotrypetes seraphini*. Copeia, 1974: 764–769.

Billo, R. R., J. O. Straub, and D. G. Senn. 1985. Vivipare Apoda (Amphibia: Gymnophiona), *Typhlonectes compressicaudus* (Duméril and Bibron, 1841): Kopulation, Tragzeit, und Geburt. Amphibia-Reptilia, 6: 1–9.

Breckenridge, W. R., and S. Jayasinghe. 1979. Observations on the eggs and larvae of *Ichthyophis glutinosus*. Ceylon Jour. Sci., 13: 187–202.

Breckenridge, W. R., S. Nathanael, and L. Periera. 1987. Some aspects of the biology and development of *Ichthyophis glutinosus* (Amphibia: Gymnophiona). Jour. Zool. London, 211: 437–449.

Delsol, M., J.-M. Exbrayat, J. Flatin, and M. Gueydan-Baconnier. 1986. Nutrition embryonnaire chez *Typhlonectes compressicaudus* (Duméril et Bibron, 1841), amphibien apode vivipare. Mem. Soc. Zool. France, 43: 39–54.

Duellman, W. E., and L. Trueb. "1986" [1985]. Biology of Amphibians. McGraw Hill, New York. xvii, 670 pages.

Dunn, E. R. 1942. The American caecilians. Bull. Mus. Comp. Zool., Harvard Univ., 91: 339–540.

Exbrayat, J.-M., M. Delsol, and J. Flatin. 1981. Premières remarques sur la gestation chez *Typhlonectes compressicaudus* (Duméril et Bibron, 1841), amphibien apode vivipare. Comp. Ren. Acad. Sci. Paris, 292: 417–420.

Exbrayat, J.-M., M. Delsol, and J. Lescure. 1983. La viviparité chez *Typhlonectes compressicaudus*, amphibien apode. Bull. Soc. Herpetol. France, 26: 23–24.

Exbrayat, J.-M., and M.-T. Laurent. 1983. Quelques observations concernant le maintien en élevage de deux amphibiens apodes: *Typhlonectes compressicaudus* et un *Ichthyophis*. Reproduction de *Typhlonectes compressicaudus*. Bull. Soc. Herpetol. France, 26: 25–27.

Heinroth, O. 1915. Geburt von *Typhlonectes natans* (Blindwühle) im Aquarium (Briefliche Mitteilung an den Herausgeber). Blatter für Aquarien- und Terrarienkunde, 1915: 34–35.

Leiman-Henley, L. 1993. Observations on a captive-born litter of typhlonectid caecilians. Herpetol. Rev., 24: 146–147.

Mendes, E. G. 1941. Sobre a respiração (esofágica, traqueal, e cutûnea) do *Siphonops annulatus* (Amphibia-Gymnophiona). Bolet. Fac. Fil. Cien. Let. Univ. São Paulo, 1941: 283–304.

—. 1945. Contribuição para a fisiologia dos sistemas respiratório e circulatório de *Siphonops annulatus* (Amphibia–Gymnophiona). Bolet. Fac. Fil. Cien. Let. Univ. São Paulo, 1945: 25–67.

Moll, E. O., and H. M. Smith. 1967. Lizards in the diet of an American caecilian. Nat. Hist. Misc., Chicago Acad. Sci., 187: 1–2.

Moodie, G. E. E. 1978. Observations on the life history of the caecilian *Typhlonectes compressicaudus* (D. and B.) in the Amazon basin. Canadian Jour. Zool., 56: 1005–1008.

Murphy, J. B., H. Quinn, and J. A. Campbell. 1977. Observations on the breeding habits of the aquatic caecilian *Typhlonectes compressicaudus*. Copeia, 1977: 66–69.

Nussbaum, R. A. 1977. Rhinatrematidae: a new family of caecilians (Amphibia: Gymnophiona). Occas. Pap. Mus. Zool. Univ. Michigan, 682: 1–30.

—. 1979. The taxonomic status of the caecilian genus *Uraeotyphlus* Peters. Occas. Pap. Mus. Zool. Univ. Michigan, 687: 1–20.

Nussbaum, R. A., and M. Wilkinson. 1989. On the classification and phylogeny of caecilians (Amphibia: Gymnophiona), a critical review. Herpetol. Monogr., 3: 1–42.

Sawaya, P. 1941. Contribuição para o estudo da fisiologia do systema circulatório do anfíbio *Siphonops annulatus* (Mikan). Bolet. Fac. Fil. Cien. Let. Univ. São Paulo, 1941: 207–270.

—. 1947. Metabolismo respiratório de anfíbio Gymnophiona, *Typhlonectes compressicauda* (Dum. et Bibr.). Bolet. Fac. Fil. Cien. Let. Univ. São Paulo, 1947: 51–56.

Taylor, E. H. 1968. Caecilians of the World. A Taxonomic Review. Univ. Kansas Press, Lawrence, Kansas. xiv, 848 pages.

—. 1972. Squamation in caecilians with an atlas of scales. Univ. Kansas Sci. Bull., 49: 989–1164.

Toews, D., and D. MacIntyre. 1977. Respiration and circulation in an apodan amphibian. Canadian Jour. Zool., 56: 998–1004.

Tonutti, E. 1931. Beitrag zur Kenntnis der Gymnophionen. XV. Das Genitalsystem. Morphol. Jahrb., 68: 151–292.

—. 1932. Vergleichende morphologische Studien über Enddarm und Kopulations-organe. Morphol. Jahrb., 70: 101–130.

—. 1933. Beitrag zur Kenntnis der Gymnophionen. XIX. Kopulationsorgane bei weiteren Gymnophionenarten. Morphol. Jahrb., 72: 155–211.

Wake, M. H. 1972. Evolutionary morphology of the caecilian urogenital system. Part IV. The cloaca. Jour. Morphol., 136: 353–366.

—. 1977*a*. Fetal maintenance and its evolutionary significance in the Amphibia: Gymnophiona. Jour. Herpetol., 11: 379–386.

—. 1977*b*. The reproductive biology of caecilians: an evolutionary perspective, p. 73–101. *In* D. H. Taylor and S. I. Guttman (eds.). The Reproductive Biology of Amphibians. Plenum Publ., New York.

—. 1978. Ontogeny of *Typhlonectes obesus*, with emphasis on dentition and feeding. Pap. Avulsos Zool. (São Paulo), 12: 1–13.

—. 1980. Reproduction, growth, and population structure of the Central American caecilian *Dermophis mexicanus*. Herpetologica, 35: 244–256.

—. 1982. Diversity within a framework of constraints: reproductive modes in the Amphibia, p. 87–106. *In* D. Mossakowski and G. Roth (eds.). Environmental Adaptation and Evolution, a Theoretical and Empirical Approach. Gustav Fischer Verlag, Stuttgart.

—. 1983. *Gymnopis multiplicata*, *Dermophis mexicanus*, and *Dermophis parviceps* (soldas, suelda con suelda, dos cabezas, caecilians), p. 400–401. *In* D. Janzen (ed.). Costa Rican Natural History. Univ. Chicago Press, Chicago.

—. 1986. The morphology of *Idiocranium russelli* (Amphibia: Gymnophiona), with comments on miniaturization through heterochrony. Jour. Morphol., 189: 1–16.

Welsch, U., W. Muller, and C. Schubert. 1977. Elektronenmikroskopische und histochemische Beobachtungen zur Fortpflanzungsbiologie viviparer Gymnophionen (*Chthonerpeton indistinctum*). Zool. Jahrb., Anat., 97: 532–549.

Wilkinson, M. 1991. The phylogenetic position of the Rhinatrematidae (Amphibia: Gymnophiona): evidence from the larval lateral line system. Amphibia-Reptilia, 13: 74–79.

Wood, S. C., R. B. Weber, G. M. O. Maloiy, and K. Johanson. 1975. Oxygen uptake and blood respiratory properties of the caecilian *Boulengerula taitanus*. Respir. Physiol., 24: 355–363.

❦ Wake, M. H. 1994. Caecilians (Amphibia: Gymnophiona) in captivity, p. 223–228. *In* J. B. Murphy, K. Adler, and J. T. Collins (eds.), Captive Management and Conservation of Amphibians and Reptiles. Society for the Study of Amphibians and Reptiles, Ithaca (New York). Contributions to Herpetology, volume 11.

Procedures for Setting Up and Maintaining a Salamander Colony

Edward J. Maruska*

Introduction

During the summer of 1970, I was engaged in photographing some of our local salamanders. Needing a specimen of Red Salamander (*Pseudotriton ruber*), I asked a local herpetologist if he might be able to collect a specimen for me. He did, and his only admonition was that I should be certain to get my photograph quickly, as the specimen would not live long in captivity. Herein would lie a challenge that would keep me engrossed in the study and maintenance of amphibians for many years to come. I am delighted to report, more than two decades later, that the salamander in question is not only still alive in the Cincinnati Zoo's salamander colony, but it has reproduced several times.

Because of the state of the art, captive maintenance and reproduction of many salamander species is now practical, as long as certain guidelines are followed. Properly cared for, salamanders will thrive for years (Snider and Bowler 1992).

How to Set Up a Salamander Colony

There is a relative paucity of information on setting up a salamander colony for propagation or laboratory studies. The importance of proper husbandry in the successful keeping and breeding of salamanders cannot be overemphasized. Too much emphasis, however, has often been placed on the necessity to duplicate the natural habitat of the species as closely as possible. In a zoo or museum setting, where there is a limited number of species and specimens to maintain, this might be appropriate. In a laboratory setting, however, where large numbers of animals are maintained for scientific study or breeding, simplicity in maintenance should be the desired goal. Unlike frogs and toads, salamanders are more tolerant of, and may even thrive better in, cramped quarters.

The first consideration when setting up a colony is how to provide optimal conditions for survival by creating the right environment. Many salamanders have a dual life style, with aquatic as well as terrestrial stages. Some species, however, are wholly terrestrial, while others live a totally aquatic life, breathing through gills. Often, only the larvae of some species are aquatic while, conversely, some newt species have both aquatic and terrestrial adult phases. Some species of salamanders retain larval characteristics (paedogenesis), and these neotenous forms do not transform and will mature and reproduce in this state. Thus, the first decision is whether to create an aquatic or terrestrial home for the chosen species.

Still-Water (Lentic) Forms

Aquatic species and lentic larvae of terrestrial species are best kept in low glass bowls, or, for the larger species, in aquaria (Figure 1). Anchor Hocking squat fish globes (distributed by Belknap Hardware, Louisville, Kentucky, in 1 quart, 1 gallon, and 2 gallon sizes) work nicely.

One of the essentials of keeping aquatic salamanders is to establish and maintain suitable water conditions. "Water from either a natural source or a treated source (e.g., municipal water supply), is never a pure substance, but a suspension and solution of various organic and inorganic constituents .... The overall concentrations of these substances in a supply of water [are] conveniently grouped together under the term 'water quality.' This in-

*The Cincinnati Zoo and Botanical Garden
3400 Vine Street
Cincinnati, Ohio 45220-1399, USA

FIGURE 1. Enclosures for salamanders living in still water. (A, upper) Large tanks for holding *Proteus anguinus* and *Cryptobranchus alleganiensis*. The plastic containers on moveable platforms at left hold water for aging; the small appliance in the foreground is a water-chilling unit. (B, lower) Small tanks for holding *Typhlomolge rathbuni* and neotenic species of *Eurycea* (top row, with sponge filters), *Ambystoma mexicanum* (middle row, with gravel bottoms), and species of *Pachytriton* (bottom row). Containers with water for aging and a charcoal filter are located below the counter at right. This room is maintained at about 22°C.

cludes all aspects of the water (e.g., pH, inorganic salts, organic compounds, organic waste products and dissolved gases)" (Odum 1984).

Apart from the temperature differences, the requirements for a quality water system for salamanders are much the same as for exotic aquarium fish: a reliable oxygen supply and an efficient filter system. Under-gravel filters are modeled after the principle of bacterial decomposition of wastes. A short time after introduction of the specimens into a newly established aquarium, layers of nitrifying bacteria (*Nitrobacter*) build up in the gravel, and as the water is pumped through, these beneficial bacteria convert ammonia and nitrate to less harmful nitrites. It is important to change the water frequently in a newly established aquarium until the nitrifying bacteria multiply throughout the gravel. With large salamanders, it is advisable, even after the aquarium gravel is "seeded" with bacteria, to change 10% of the water periodically (at least twice per week) to avoid ammonia build up. An under-gravel filter used in conjunction with either a power head, siphon, or a corner or box filter works best with aquatic species.

In addition to the standard methods of aquarium filtration, the Cincinnati Zoo also uses an activated carbon filtration unit attached to the water intake in one of its amphibian rooms (Bruner Water Filter, Milwaukee, Wisconsin; model 16 FF). We routinely dechlorinate our tap water using a chemical dechlorant—De Chlor—commonly used in the pet fish industry (Weco Products, Inc., Long Beach, California 90813). Tap water can also be dechlorinated by adding a few crystals of sodium thiosulfate per four liters (4.75 g per 60 liters) (Humphrey 1962).

Facilities located in geographic areas with high levels of water contamination may have to resort to unpolluted pond water for hatching and rearing of larvae. Mattison (1982) provides a formula for producing artificial pond water if suitable water is not obtainable from natural sources (see Appendix to this chapter, solution 1).

The term pH is used to express the acidity or alkalinity of any substrate. The pH scale extends from 0 (acid) to 14 (alkaline), with 7 being the neutral position. Most species of salamanders favor neutral water (pH 6.5–7.5). There are commercially available kits to detect acidic water conditions. High acid conditions (low pH) in the aquatic salamander's environment are to be avoided. Under certain acidic conditions amphibian eggs may fail to hatch, due to calcium imbalances in the developing embryos. The larvae of some salamander species will not survive in acidic water, and adults may also suffer skin irritations and deterioration of the external gills.

Some species with unusual life cycles require special techniques. For example, North American newts (*Notophthalmus*) have aquatic larvae, but transform into a terrestrial phase before transforming into breeding adults. Treat the aquatic phases of newts the same as other aquatic species, except that pieces of floating cork bark should be added onto which the adults may crawl.

As a substrate, we use various sizes of aquarium gravel. In feeding, large salamanders may accidentally ingest gravel, which may have life-threatening implications. This can be prevented by using a large gravel size or large pebbles as a substrate, or by keeping the animals in a tank devoid of gravel altogether, relying on external filtration in place of under-gravel filters.

Flowing-Water (Lotic) Forms

Stream, brook, and river salamanders present additional challenges to captive maintenance and reproduction. Swift-water or cave species, such as *Andrias*, *Cryptobranchus*, *Necturus*, *Proteus*, *Gyrinophilus* (neotenic forms), and *Typhlomolge*, require a higher aeration or agitation of their environment, due to the high oxygen content of the moving water in which they naturally live. Hellbenders (*Cryptobranchus alleganiensis*) in distress from low oxygen levels weave from side to side in an attempt to extract oxygen from a poorly aerated environment by using their wrinkled, highly vascularized skin.

One method of reducing the need for oxygen in lotic forms is to reduce the temperature of the environment, thereby slowing down the metabolic rate of the animals and, correspondingly, the need for more oxygen. A general rule is that the warmer the conditions are, the greater the need for higher aeration or agitation of water (for lotic species).

Low oxygen content of water may also have a detrimental effect on the eggs of these species as well. For example, a Tennessee Cave Salamander (*Gyrinophilus palleucus*) laid 70 eggs at the Cincinnati Zoo in 1984. Many of the eggs were fertile, but the majority of the eggs were lost to a secondary fungal infection probably resulting from oxygen deprivation (Maruska 1986). One method of hatching the eggs of lotic salamanders under semi-controlled conditions is to utilize a cloth-covered, wooden frame to house the eggs. The frame is then weighted and placed in an unpolluted stream until the eggs hatch.

Brook species of aquatic newts, such as the Old World salamandrids *Euproctus* and *Neurergus*, require shallow water and numerous hiding places.

Our refrigerated, flowing-water salamander tanks are about 95 cm long, 60 cm wide, and 35 cm high. The walls are composed of double-strength window glass. Each unit is refrigerated via a cooling coil, which is cast into a fiberglass-reinforced, epoxy resin base. This results in the even cooling of the entire tank. The alcove areas of the tank provide the salamanders with eddies so that they can get out of the constant flow of the current when they desire. The interior bottom of the aquarium is a perforated plastic, which supports the gravel and provides the system with a typical under-gravel filtration.

We have also constructed larger flow-through tanks for Japanese Giant Salamanders (*Andrias japonicus*) (Figure 2) built along a similar design.

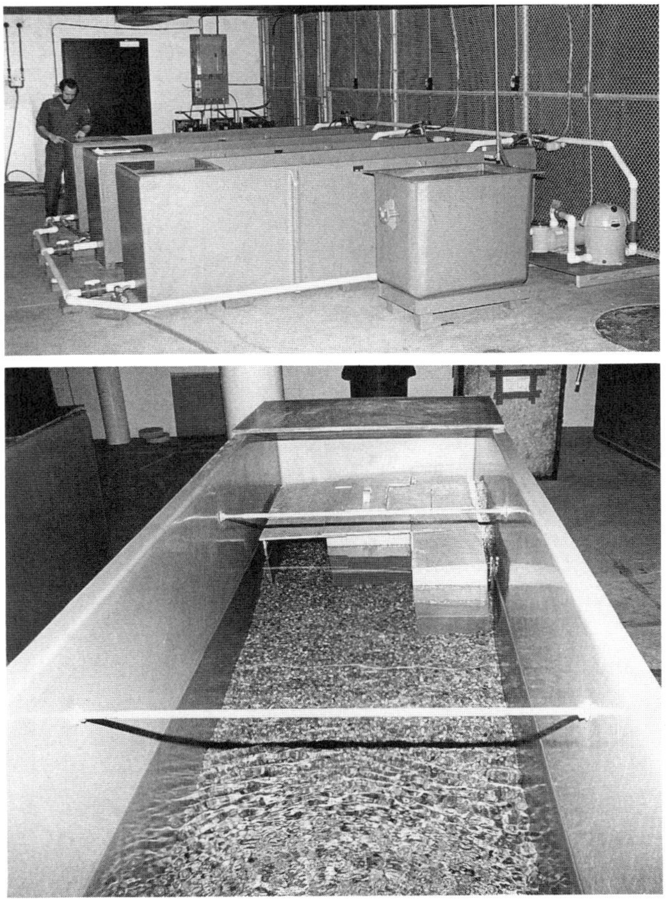

FIGURE 2. Enclosures for salamanders living in flowing water. (A, upper) Exterior of tanks for *Andrias japonicus* showing flow-through system, chilled-water pump at right, and water reservoir in small tank in foreground. (B, lower) Interior of tank showing artificial cave at end for seclusion.

Terrestrial and Arboreal Forms

Terrestrial species of salamanders can be maintained in a terrarium with earth, forest plants, and wood rot (crumbled wood from decaying logs): a slice of the animal's natural habitat enclosed in glass (Maruska 1989). This style of management for amphibians may be attractive for private collectors or zoo exhibition, but is not at all practical where large numbers of animals have to be serviced by persons engaged in other activities. Plain aquaria (with glass and commercially available perforated metal tops [Figure 3]) can be utilized for larger specimens, or those species that require some ventilation and less moisture.

We have been more successful in maintaining members of the neotropical bolitoglossines when we provide some ventilation through the use of wire top containers, as opposed to glass or plastic. An explanation for our success might be that, although most *Bolitoglossa* are tropical and are found in humid areas, many species are semi-arboreal and perhaps are subjected to greater air movement than are the more terrestrial salamanders. Another species that we have kept well ventilated is *Echinotriton andersoni* of Japan and Taiwan, but for different reasons. This species is terrestrial, but lives in a drier atmosphere and has an almost toad-like skin texture that prevents excessive dehydration. By providing a somewhat drier substrate and some ventilation, experience shows that this species can thrive under captive conditions.

The most satisfactory receptacles for rapid and convenient care of terrestrial urodeles are plastic shoe and sweater boxes (Figure 3). The boxes can be stacked on top of each other, and large numbers of salamanders can be held in a relatively small space and serviced quickly and efficiently. Some salamander species, however, require more air circulation than can be provided in a plastic container. For these species we utilize aquaria with screen-mesh lids.

For terrestrial species that require a wet environment, a substrate of gravel can be utilized with a modified underground filter, but this method requires a great deal of maintenance. At the Cincinnati Zoo, we have also used wood rot, a natural material, since salamanders can often be collected inside old logs. This material, however, does have the disadvantage that the animals burrow into it; they are often difficult to see without sifting through several centimeters of substrate.

On occasion, we have used local tap water for a variety of adult terrestrial salamanders with no apparent ill effect, and chlorinated water may even be a benefit by serving as a bactericide. Although our municipal water supply works well for our salamanders, I do not feel that we can generalize for all situations. Indeed, even our chlorinated water will destroy eggs and may damage the delicate external gills in some species. Depending on location, it is best to have one's local water tested. Distillation units are costly, but readily available from scientific supply houses (Beltz 1989).

When one is dealing with a large number of salamanders, the best substrate, by far, is unbleached paper toweling. Several layers can be placed on the bottom of the container, and additional crumpled towels can be placed on top, either saturated or wrung out, moist but not wet (depending on the moisture needs of the species). The

FIGURE 3. Enclosures for terrestrial and arboreal salamanders. In top row, aquaria with screen-mesh lids and moist, crumpled paper toweling inside, for species of *Hynobius*, *Phaeognathus hubrichti*, and some neotropical bolitoglossines. In bottom row, plastic shoe and sweater boxes, with some holes drilled in the lids and moist, crumpled paper toweling inside, for various plethodontids and small ambystomatids. The white container at right holds water for aging. This room is maintained at about 14°C.

salamanders tend to burrow into the crumpled paper, which affords them security (Figure 3). For additional security, a hiding box, broken flower pot, or piece of cork bark can be utilized. We have successfully maintained the red eft, or terrestrial stage of the North American newt *Notophthalmus*, for four years by using a damp paper towel substrate.

Behavioral Interactions

Except for the Japanese Giant Salamander, we have not witnessed any territoriality among the myriad of salamander species we have maintained at the Cincinnati Zoo. The only problems resulting in conflict among conspecifics seem to arise at feeding time when one or more of the animals may attempt to eat the same food item. Both larval and adult life stages of salamanders are carnivorous, and they will consume any prey item they can overpower, which may include other salamanders. Therefore, it is prudent to keep only animals of similar sizes together. Raxworthy (1989), however, reported that breeding male *Triturus vittatus* damage each other's crests and tails, and must be kept singly. Overcrowding should be avoided in order to prevent stress and relieve problems with poor sanitation and resulting diseases. Wherever possible, salamanders should be kept individually, but as a guide we recommend 1 to 3 specimens of a small species per plastic shoe box, 2 to 3 moderate-sized salamanders per plastic sweater box or 40-liter aquarium. We have successfully maintained individual animals for over 20 years in this manner.

Newly hatched larvae can be maintained in glass bowls of 1–4 liters, depending on larval size, with 6 to 8 per bowl. Gradually, they can be dispersed to larger bowls as the animals grow. Overcrowded and underfed larvae will attack each other's gills and limbs, resulting in missing limbs and, in some cases, totally limbless larvae.

Large male specimens of *Andrias japonicus* may be aggressive towards conspecifics, and should only be put together in specially constructed breeding units (Figure 2). At the Asa Aquarium in Hiroshima, Japan, research was conducted on injuries suffered due to fighting by captive Japanese Giant Salamanders (Kuwabara et al. 1980). Field studies indicated that large numbers of injured giant salamanders were observed during the spawning season, which is from the latter part of August to mid-September. In their captive facilities, however, most injuries occurred after the spawning season, from late September to November, and most of it was caused by males. Male Hellbenders (*Cryptobranchus alleganiensis*) in natural surroundings have been reported to be extremely territorial during the breeding season (Nickerson and Mays 1972). This behavior should be considered when setting up breeding arrangements for captives.

Food and Feeding

Larvae and adult salamanders are strictly carnivorous, and the size and type of prey is generally the only constraint on what they can or will eat. In nature, they consume a wide variety of live prey, depending on the size and age of the specimen. This may range from microscopic aquatic life and various arthropods to small vertebrates and, in some species, may include other salamanders. Some plethodontids have highly projectile tongues (e.g., *Hydromantes* and *Bolitoglossa*); these taxa are more specialized in their feeding behavior and prey largely on arthropods.

Under ideal conditions, captive salamanders should be offered a variety of prey items to choose from, thus assuring a well-balanced diet. If only a restricted range of prey items can be offered, then the food should be sprinkled periodically with a vitamin/mineral preparation or a good grade of bone meal. Beltz (1989) lists a variety of invertebrate food items (crickets, mealworms, earthworms, waxworms, fly larvae/maggots, and fruit flies), describes how to acquire and raise them, and also notes the best methods for preparing to feed them (i.e., priming the food sources with nutritious food and vitamin/mineral additives). I would add that white worms (*Enchytraeus albidus*, up to 2 cm in length) also make excellent food items, and cultures can be purchased from tropical fish dealers and can be fed to terrestrial, as well as aquatic, species.

For larval salamanders, infusoria tablets (and instructions for its culture) can be purchased from tropical fish dealers, and are an excellent food for newly hatched larvae of small species. Hatchling brine shrimp (*Artemia salinis*) can also be used to feed a variety of species of newly hatched salamander larvae. As the larvae grow, they can be offered medium or large brine shrimp and fresh water fleas (*Daphnia*, a tiny crustacean), which can be cultured or purchased from tropical fish shops.

For large aquatic salamanders, like *Cryptobranchus*, crayfish are a preferred food item. They will, however, accept both live and dead fish like most large aquatic salamanders. Live guppies and goldfish are utilized as food, and, although somewhat costly to feed, they will save food-preparation time where manpower is a consideration. Feeding minnows may create a serious parasite problem for salamanders. Jiro Kobara (pers. comm.) reports that Japanese Giant Salamanders, when offered chunks of horse mackerel, ate reluctantly, but the animals' appetites and condition improved when offered live loaches. At the Cincinnati Zoo, we offer our Japanese Giant Salamanders only live, large feeder goldfish (keeping the goldfish with the salamanders at all times); to date, our husbandry problems with this species have been minimal.

Commercial "trout chow," augmented with beef liver, is being used as a food source in some colonies of axolotls, but I am somewhat dubious about the long-term implications of such a diet. This method of feeding would also appear to be labor intensive.

Diseases of Salamanders

The husbandry of salamanders is not difficult, particularly if one has knowledge of the species in its natural environment. If an artificial environment that meets the needs of the species—such as a correct temperature range, proper humidity, balanced nutrition, as well as proper sanitation—is met, few problems can be expected. If, however, the conditions become unsatisfactory through overcrowding, sporadic feeding, poor diet, or the accumulation of solid and dissolved wastes, problems may occur. Amphibians are particularly vulnerable to unsanitary conditions because of their thin, moist skin. By its very nature, skin is both a respiratory and osmoregulatory organ, and hence, particularly sensitive to toxins and other contaminants.

One method to lessen the chance for the introduction of disease or parasites into a colony is to institute strict quarantine procedures. All incoming animals should be held in quarantine for a predetermined period of time. Decisions on appropriate quarantine should be made on a case-by-case basis. In an amphibian room, a quarantine area can be as simple as the lowest shelf in a rack which can be serviced last to prevent contamination of other animals, or as complex as a separate room or facility in which newly-arrived animals can be kept. In any case, one must use proper sanitary measures to prevent the spread of disease.

In Cincinnati, we use a minimum of 30 days of quarantine for all incoming amphibians that appear healthy, and longer if they are diseased. Routine sanitation can be augmented with the periodic use of a dilute solution of a hydrogen peroxide-containing liquid bleach such as Clorox (1 part Clorox to 30 parts water), or of any other brand of household bleach as a disinfectant. Containers should be dipped in or swabbed with this solution, and then thoroughly rinsed and neutralized using sodium thiosulfate or De Chlor before returning the animals to their containers.

Amphibian diseases have been reviewed by several authors (Reichenbach-Klinke and Elkan 1965; Elkan 1976; Marcus 1981) and this chapter does not permit dealing with detailed descriptions of them, except for brief mention of those most commonly infecting captive salamanders (but see also Jacobson, this volume, page 109).

(1) Viral Diseases. Very little is known regarding viruses that might invade salamanders or what maladies they might cause. Several viruses have been isolated from frogs, the most important being Lucké's tumor virus, which is widely studied in cancer research.

(2) Bacterial Diseases. Some of the more commonly dealt with gram-negative bacteria in amphibian colonies are *Aeromonas*, *Proteus*, *Pseudomonas*, *Acinetobacter*, *Mimia*, *Salmonella*, and *Citrobacter*.

(3) Mycotic Diseases. Mycotic (fungal) diseases are usually secondary invaders and are opportunistic when the animal is stressed by a bacterial disease, or when improper sanitation is practiced. *Basidiobolus*, *Cladosporium*, *Hormiscium*, and *Phialophora* are some of the principal fungi affecting amphibians (Elkan 1976). The parasitic *Saprolegnia* commonly infects amphibian eggs, debilitated larvae, or adults of aquatic or terrestrial salamanders, producing a cottony growth on skin or gills.

(4) Protozoan Parasites. A variety of external and internal parasites has been encountered in salamanders in our laboratory. Many amphibians are infected to some degree by protozoans which com-

monly live symbiotically with their hosts (Elkan 1976). Unless there are massive infestations, protozoans generally do not seem to be a problem with captive amphibians. *Entamoeba* has been isolated from a wide variety of amphibians; they occur in their digestive tracts and occasionally encyst in the liver. Colonies of *Vorticella* may plague larval and juvenile salamanders by clustering on the rachises of the gills (Brothers 1977).

(5) Helminth Parasites. Endoparasitic worms occur in salamanders and, in a natural state, they probably live in equilibrium with their hosts. *Acanthocephala* (thorny-headed worms, which attach themselves to mucosa of the gut), nematodes (round worms), trematodes (flukes), platyhelminths (flat worms), and cestodes (tapeworms), have all been implicated in the parasitism of amphibians (Yamaguti 1971), but scant information is available in the literature regarding helminths that parasitize salamanders. Trematodes (*Batrachycoelium*) commonly live in the intestinal tract of salamanders (Duellman and Trueb "1986" [1985]). Dyer and Brandon (1973) reported numerous species of *Brachycoelium* in 25 species of North American salamanders. Tuff and Huffman (1977) provided an index to the genera of amphibian hosts for helminths.

(6) Arthropod Parasites. Freshly collected neotenic *Ambystoma dumerilii* arrived at the Cincinnati Zoo infested with the parasitic copepod *Argulus* (fish louse). Duhon (1989*a*, 1989*b*) reported *Trichodina* and other fish parasites on axolotls (*Ambystoma mexicanum*) at the Indiana University Axolotl Colony.

Treatment of Diseases

"Considering the wealth of information dealing with the physiology, biochemistry, genetics, developmental biology, and even behavior of amphibians, it is incredible that almost nothing of a practical nature is known about amphibian medicine" (Nace et al. 1974). These authors continued by elaborating on the fact that "entire books deal with the classification of amphibian infections and infestations, while therapy and prevention are usually dispensed with within a few pages."

At the Cincinnati Zoo's amphibian colony, we maintain a large number of salamander species, and we have identified several recurrent disease syndromes that will require further laboratory analyses before reliable treatment can be prescribed, but two of these disease syndromes can be described here. One that occasionally occurs in the maintenance of the plethodontids *Ensatina* and *Bolitoglossa*, and to a lesser extent in some species of *Plethodon*, is excessively dry, flaking skin, abdominal subcutaneous hemorrhaging, and in severe cases, skin ulcerations accompanied by difficulties in skin shedding; near death, tail autotomy will often occur. Despite our various attempts at treatment, the disease has always proved fatal. The disease may be similar to the dreaded "Molchpest" affecting newts, as described by Reichenbach-Klinke and Elkan (1965).

Another disease syndrome that we see also occurs in various plethodontid species in which portions of limbs or tail or, in some cases, the mandible, become necrotic. The infected area may progress and continue to necrose until the infected limb or tail slough, or almost literally "melt" away. We have suspected a mycotic or bacterial invasion to be responsible, however, to date, we have not been able to isolate the causative agent. By improving the proper moisture requirements (damp, but not wet), and increasing the ventilation, however, both of these diseases have been reduced in our salamander colonies.

Van Duijn (1973) covers a wide range of bacterial and viral diseases and parasites that are known to infect fish. Some of the treatments that he discusses for the control of diseases and parasites in fish can be modified for treatment of salamanders. For anyone maintaining a large number of amphibians, his book will prove to be a valuable reference.

The maintenance of a large axolotl colony for scientific research studies at Indiana University, Bloomington, Indiana, originally under the direction of R. R. Humphrey and now continued by George M. Malacinski, has contributed a wealth of information on the diseases and the treatment of diseases in the Mexican Axolotl and, by extrapolation, those of other salamanders. Malacinski has kindly granted permission to include in this chapter some of the primary information, as originally published in the *Axolotl Newsletter* issued by the Indiana University Axolotl Colony. Brothers (1977) gives a brief description of diseases that affect axolotls in the Indiana University colony and their treatment, along with the antibiotics used (Tables 1–2).

Duhon (1989*a*) reports that specific knowledge of the organism responsible for a disease and tests indicating sensitivity to a particular antibiotic are the ideal way to treat it. This information, however, is not often available for amphibians, and a trial-and-error approach must be used. It is most likely that opportunistic gram-negative bacterial pathogens will be implicated in many cases, and because of this, aminoglycosides are the drugs of choice, including some of the following: chloramphenicol, tetracycline and gentamycin (Duhon 1989*a* and pers. comm.). Subsequent use of amikacin at 5 mg per kg of body weight, injected intraperitoneally at 48-hour intervals, has had excellent results. Some of the other treatments developed at the Cincinnati Zoo are listed in Table 3.

TABLE 1. Disease organisms, main symptoms, and treatments of common diseases in axolotls (modified from Brothers 1977).

	Larvae, Juveniles, and Some Adults
Vorticella (ciliate protozoans)	*Symptoms*: Clusters of colonies on rachises of gills during early stages of infection. *Treatment*: Immerse in 100% Modified Holtfreter's Solution (see Appendix) or 100% Steinberg's Solution (see Appendix) for 3–5 days; cover bowls to prevent evaporation. In cases of heavy infestation, immerse in dilute sodium hydroxide solution for 10 minutes on each of 3 days (see Table 2). Since larvae are routinely kept in 20% Modified Holtfreter's, a further modification is to combine these treatments with nitrofurazone (2 days) followed by methylene blue-acriflavine treatment (2 days) (see Table 2).
Mold infections	*Symptoms*: Cottony patches on skin. *Treatment*: Immerse in solution of Tropicure (General Developments Corp., Milwaukee, Wisconsin 53217) consisting of 1 ml for 500 ml of Modified Holtfreter's Solution (see Appendix). Immerse larvae for 10–15 minutes, adults for 20–30; repeat for 3–5 days. Maintain animals in 100% Modified Holtfreter's for 3–5 days. Some molds, particularly unicellular ones, are best treated with potassium permanganate (see Table 2). Gently swab the infected area, using cotton-tipped swabs for gills and gauze pads for the body.
	Large Juveniles and Adults
Aeromonas (bacteria)	*Symptoms*: Small red splotches over body. Infectious and lethal. *Treatment*: Tetracycline injections (refer to liquamycin in Table 2). Cosa-terramycin in the water may also be used (see Table 2).
Actinomycetes bacteria ("Red plague")	*Symptoms*: Diffuse redness over entire body; lethal within 24 h after first appearance. Highly infectious; believed to be transmitted by contact with specimens from wild populations. *Treatment*: Gentamycin injections plus nitrofurazone (2 days) followed by methylene blue-acriflavine treatment (see Table 2). All adult and large juvenile axolotls (8 months or older) should be injected and treated simultaneously. Repeat gentamycin injections every 48 h until 3 injections have been given to each animal.
Salmonella–Shigella (bacteria)	*Symptoms*: Lack of appetite, listlessness, and perhaps some diarrhea. Infectious. *Treatment*: All adults and large juveniles should be treated simultaneously. Gentamycin is the most effective antibiotic (see Table 2 for application); also use nitrofurazone (2 days) followed by methylene blue-acriflavine (3 days) in the water (see Table 2). For very severe cases, after the axolotl is injected, wrap its body loosely in damp paper towels and put it back into bowl containing Modified Holtfreter's Solution (see Appendix) filled to a depth of 3 cm; place in 8–10° C cold room for 3–5 days.
Pseudomonas (bacteria)	*Symptoms*: Some loss of appetite. Ulceration of abdominal epidermis. If untreated, infection will spread into body cavity. Somewhat infectious. *Treatment*: Swab infected area with potassium permanganate solution (see Table 2); repeat every 2–3 days for 2 weeks. Injection of gentamycin will protect against secondary infections (see Table 2). Nitrofurazone (1 day per week) followed by methylene blue-acriflavine (3 days per week) treatments in the animal's water are also helpful (see Table 2).
Blister disease	*Symptoms*: Large, fluid-filled swelling on top of head. Certain strains of axolotls are more apt to contract this disease than others. Not fatal. *Treatment*: Trim away loose skin and expose the area; penicillin G powder is then sprinkled on the affected area, which will heal in 1–2 weeks. Small blisters or those that do not rupture often disappear without treatment.

TABLE 2. Antibiotics and other agents for treatment of common diseases in axolotls (modified from Brothers 1977).

	Treatments by Injection
Gentamycin (Schering Corp.)	Antibiotic with broad spectrum of activity. When in doubt, this is antibiotic of choice. Useful for treating infections of Actinomycetes bacteria, *Salmonella,* and *Shigella,* but less effective for *Pseudomonas*. *Dose*: 1.8 mg for full-grown, adult axolotl (average about 140 g), injected intramuscularly; repeat every 48 h if necessary. Adjust dose for smaller animals.
Liquamycin (Pfizer Corp.)	An oxytetracycline hydrochloride useful for treating infections of *Salmonella, Shigella,* and *Aeromonas*. *Dose*: 4.1 mg for full-grown, adult axolotl (average about 140 g), injected intramuscularly; repeat every 48 h if necessary. Adjust dose for smaller animals.
Bicillin fortified (Wyeth Corp.)	An aqueous suspension of benzathine penicillin G (150,000 IU[1]/cc) and procaine penicillin G (150,000 IU/cc) useful for infections of gram-positive bacteria. *Dose*: Dosage is a total of 25,000 IU for a full-grown axolotl (average about 140 g). Prepare from 2 cc of stock plus 10 cc of sterile saline; inject 0.5 ml of this working solution intramuscularly.
	Treatments Administered in the Water
Cosa-terramycin (Pfizer Corp.)	A fortified, soluble powder of oxytetracycline hydrochloride useful for infections of susceptible gram-positive and gram-negative bacteria. *Dose*: 250 mg for 2 liters. Change solution every 24 h, preferrably every 12 h. Duration of treatment 3 days.
Furacin (Water Mix, Veterinary) (Eaton Veterinary)	A solution of nitrofurazone useful for topical bacterial infections. *Dose*: 250 mg for 2 1/2 liters. Duration of treatment 2 days. This solution may cause diarrhea.
Methylene blue-Acriflavine	A stock solution of methylene blue (0.0075%) plus acriflavine (0.045%) useful for external fungal and bacterial infections. *Dose*: Dilute 1 cc of stock solution to 2 liters of the Modified Holtfreter's Solution (see Appendix). Duration of treatment 2–5 days.
NaOH	A solution of dilute NaOH useful for infections of protozoans. *Dose*: Ten drops of 0.1 M NaOH per liter of water. Duration of treatment 10 minutes.
Potassium permanganate	A solution of potassium permanganate, useful for infections of *Pseudomonas* and molds. *Dose*: 1 g for 100 cc of distilled water. The affected area is gently swabbed with this solution and the animal then placed into 50% or 100% Modified Holtfreter's Solution (see Appendix). This treatment may be repeated every 2–3 days.

[1]International units

In addition, we routinely increase the salinity of the water for aquatic amphibians when treating them with antibiotic baths by using Amphibian Ringer's Solution 10–20% (see Appendix, solution 2), Holtfreter's Solution 10–100%, or Modified Holtfreter's Solution 10–20% (see Appendix, solution 3) (use of preferred solution depends on the administered therapy). This technique increases water osmolarity, which results in a rapid diffusion of electrolytes. We also use Ringer's/Holtfreter's Solution baths in treating skin injuries and combating mycotic infections.

At the Indiana University Axolotl Colony, Brothers (1977) reports the prophylactic use of Steinberg's Solution at a concentration of 10–20% (see Appendix, solution 4) for amphibian eggs and larvae.

Captive Propagation

In any attempt to propagate a species of salamander, it is necessary to have rudimentary knowledge of the animal's natural history, including to what degree it is aquatic or terrestrial, its overall distribution, and, if possible, the elevation and/or water temperature where it was collected. To successfully breed a species, not only may the necessary captive accommodations vary from species to species, including a range of temperatures (i.e., cooling down for a period of time), foods, and feeding schedules, but it may also be necessary to trigger (i.e., a dry period, followed by artificial rain, seasons, and light cycles) variations in the different physiological rhythms in order to induce courtship and eventual mating. The influence of light, humidity, and temperature on salamander breeding behavior is still not understood for the majority of species. Too much or too little variation in these parameters may be responsible for the failure of many species to complete their life cycles in captivity.

The importance of temperature in the breeding of amphibians has not been studied in detail for many species. Bachman (1969) stated that salamanders as a group are adapted to a much narrower range of temperature preferences than are frogs. An improper temperature range for salamanders may cause stress, and pathogenic organisms normally present in the environment may then become virulent (Crawshaw 1992). Laszlo (1979) dealt with the complexity of thermal requirements of amphibians and reptiles in captivity.

For the purpose of salamander maintenance and breeding we have utilized a series of ranges of temperatures that are suitable for keeping a wide variety of salamander species. Temperate, high-altitude forms can be maintained between 13–18°C, whereas tropical, high-altitude forms from as high as the tree line are best kept at 16–21°C.

The majority of temperate forms, excluding cave-dwelling species, fit nicely into the above temperate ranges. Tropical and subtropical salamanders (*Pseudoeurycea* and *Bolitoglossa*) may prefer somewhat warmer temperatures. This, however, will again be dependent on the elevation at which the animals were collected. Cloud- or moss-forest species may prefer 18–24°C, while tropical lowland forms will fare better at temperatures of 24–28°C. Spermatocytes and oocytes are present throughout the year in most subtropical and tropical salamanders, so the animals may be maintained at a constant temperature year round. With temperate species, however, a cool-down period of 4 to 6 weeks at temperatures as low as 8°C, to first suppress and then promote gonadal development, is recommended.

TABLE 3. Disease treatments developed for salamanders at the Cincinnati Zoo. These procedures were developed empirically by the zoo's herpetological and veterinary staffs.

	Antibiotics for Fungal and Bacterial Infections[1]
Sulfa Bath (Tetra Werke)	Sulfamethazine, sulfadiazine, sulfathiazole. *Dose*: Add 4–5 cc of Sulfa Bath per liter of water in which salamander is held. Sulfa Bath is added to tank every other day for 5–7 treatments; animal remains in this solution until next treatment. Used successfully for axolotls and many semi-aquatic salamanders.
Ridrot (Tetra/Terrafauna) and Iodine	PVT-iodine complex. *Dose*: These two drugs work well together when applied to bacterial lesions. Just enough antibiotic should be used to cover the lesions for 5–15 minutes at a time. These drugs are used in conjunction with Sulfa Bath.
Ditrim (Syntex Corp.)	Trimethoprim and sulfadiazine. *Dose*: Animals are injected (24% sterile injection) intramuscularly (dosage 15–20 mg per kg body weight) every other day for 5–7 treatments. This treatment is used only in more severe cases where circulating blood levels of drug are needed.
Baytril (Haver/Mobay)	Enrofloxacin. *Dose*: This excellent new antibiotic has been used successfully for aquatic salamanders. Animals are injected intramuscularly (dosage about 4 mg per kg body weight) every other day for 5–7 treatments.
	Treatment for Parasites[1] (presence determined by fecal examination)
Panacur (Hoechst-Roussel)	Fenbendazole. *Dose*: This is a broad-spectrum de-worming treatment. It is administered orally (dosage about 100 mg per kg body weight) and repeated in 10–14 days.
Flagyl (Searle Corp.; Liomont Co.)	Metronidazole. *Dose*: This can be used for flagellates and other protozoans. It is administered orally (dosage 10 mg per kg body weight) and only once.

[1]Crawshaw (1992), Nace et al. (1974: 115–126), and Zimmermann (1983: 48–56) described additional treatments for fungal, bacterial, and parasitic infections.

Determining Sex

Except for some species of newts, where there is a remarkable sexual dimorphism during the breeding season, most salamander species demonstrate only subtle secondary sexual characteristics during the breeding season. In many ambystomatid salamanders, the male's cloaca is swollen with an increase in the size of the cloacal glands lateral to the vent. The female has a somewhat broader and shorter head, the abdomen is more rounded because of the presence of ovarian eggs, and the cloaca is less swollen. In sexually active salamandrids, the cloacal region of the breeding male exhibits a swollen glandular area, and upon close examination small papillae will be found inside the vent. The female's abdomen is more rounded and the cloacal area not swollen. David Sever has published a long series of papers on cloacal morphology of salamanders (cited in Sever 1994).

Nuptial excrescences are found on the inner sides of the hind limbs of sexually active male *Notophthalmus;* these keratinous structures function to grip the female. The forelimbs of male *Pleurodeles* have similar structures during the breeding season.

Most male salamanders of the genus *Plethodon* have circular or oblong mental glands on their chins. In many species the breeding male's elongated premaxillary teeth protrude through the upper lip and the lip may possess enlarged protuberances, or cirri (Noble 1931). In some male plethodontid salamanders, the cloaca is swollen at the posterior end. In the females of some of the smaller, more delicate species, ovarian eggs may be seen through the transparent skin of the abdomen. To sex some of the larger species (i.e., *Andrias* and *Cryptobranchus*), laparoscopy has been used with success (Kramer et al. 1983).

Oviposition

Creating the proper environment for the gravid female to deposit her eggs is often overlooked when attempting to breed salamanders. This may vary from species to species (i.e., rock surfaces, twigs, sphagnum moss, live plants, etc.). Failure to provide the proper laying site may result in the female reabsorbing her eggs. Shoop (1960) noted that one of the environmental features in determining a laying site in *Ambystoma talpoideum* was the presence of twigs or similar structures in the water to which the animals could anchor the eggs. Females of *Plethodon cinereus* seem to prefer coniferous wood rot in which to lay their eggs, while those of *Hemidactylium scutatum* choose sphagnum. Females of *Necturus* fasten their eggs underneath the surface of a rock. In captivity, *Typhlomolge rathbuni* females anchor their eggs seemingly at random to pieces of gravel or to the aquarium airlift tube (E. J. Maruska, pers. observ.). Females of *Cynops pyrrhogaster* wrap their eggs individually in the leaves of aquatic plants.

Knowledge of the natural history of a species that one is attempting to propagate, or those of related species, will aid in setting up an environment that will induce captive females to oviposit. For example, the neotenic *Eurycea neotenes* has been reproduced in captivity, based on observations in nature showing that females lay eggs in aquifers. Roberts et al. (in press) developed a technique in which a meter-long plastic tube filled with limestone shards was attached to a tank; water flows through the tube and into the tank, thus creating an artificial aquifer in which the females lay their eggs.

Hormone-induced Reproduction

Within the past decade there have been tremendous advances in amphibian husbandry as zoo herpetoculturists devote more time and resources to solving the problems of controlled reproduction. Hormone-induced breeding has been achieved in numerous species of anurans, but the technology has not been widely developed in urodeles, despite the fact that much has been learned in recent years about salamander hormones (for review, see Moore, this volume, page 125).

There are two types of hormones that have been readily used for amphibians: pituitary extracts and synthetic gonadotropin hormones. In recent years, releasing hormones (giving the pituitary a pulse, which in turn stimulates the secretion of gonadotropins) have been used in a variety of vertebrates. They show much potential for hormone-induced reproduction in a wide variety of amphibian species, but hormones should only be considered when it is difficult to elicit breeding or egg deposition using natural means. Even with the use of hormone treatment, subtle changes in captive environmental conditions must be achieved to reach reproductive physiological readiness of the salamander. Only when the proper condition of the immediate surroundings, including wet and dry periods (i.e., a dry period followed by artificial rain), changes in photoperiod and temperature, or fluctuations in humidity are satisfied, may hormonal induction be of aid in obtaining fertilized eggs (Beach 1951).

The testes of many salamanders demonstrate seasonal variation. The timing of sperm development differs from species to species and the duration of sperm storage may also show considerable variation (see Moore, this volume, page 125). It is important to note that in males of *Cryptobranchus alleganiensis* and *Necturus maculosus*, spermatogenesis is prenuptial, and sperm are produced shortly before animals spawn (Norris and Jones 1987). This is an important consideration if hormone-induced breeding is attempted with these species.

In Vitro Fertilization

In ambystomatid salamanders, the techniques of in vitro fertilization are used widely under standard laboratory conditions. Humphrey (1962) described use of follicle-stimulating hormone (FSH) which will elicit the production of eggs that can be used to produce large numbers of offspring from a limited number of parent stock.

Anesthesia

When it becomes necessary to anesthetize an animal for surgery or sexing, the animal should be fasted for one week before treatment to reduce the likelihood of regurgitation and possible aspiration (Kramer et al. 1983). The anesthetic we use is MS 222 or Finquel (tricane methanosulfonate; Ayerst Co., New York City). The normal effective concentration is an aqueous solution of 0.03% to 0.05%. For a large salamander (i.e., *Cryptobranchus*) three grams of powder are dissolved in five liters of dechlorinated water at room temperature (20°C), and the animal is placed in the solution. Anesthesia usually occurs 20–25 minutes after introduction, when the specimen fails to right itself when placed on its back, or does not respond to stimulation.

Summary

Noteworthy advances in amphibian husbandry have occurred in recent years. If we are to accomplish sustained multigenerational captive reproduction of endangered Amphibia, we must understand their nutritional requirements, photoperiods, optimal temperature and humidity requirements, and the myriad variations in reproductive modes of the diverse families and species.

The establishment and maintenance of a comprehensive salamander collection at the Cincinnati Zoo and Botanical Garden is described. This collection has been an ongoing research project for the past 30 years, and our experience may be helpful in allowing the reader to avoid many pitfalls that might be encountered.

Acknowledgments

George M. Malacinski (Indiana University Axolotl Colony) and Mark K. Campbell (Cincinnati Zoo Veterinary Department) helped develop the tables. I am also grateful to Peter Strimple, Johnny R. Arnett, and Kraig Adler for their help with the manuscript.

Literature Cited

Bachman, K. 1969. Temperature adaptions of amphibian embryos. Amer. Nat., 103: 115–130.

Beach, F. A. 1951. Instinctive behavior: reproductive activities, p. 387–434. *In* S. S. Stevens (ed.), Handbook of Experimental Psychology. John Wiley & Sons, New York.

Beltz, E. 1989. Reptile and amphibian care in captivity. Bull. Chicago Herpetol. Soc. 24(11): supplement.

Brothers, A. J. 1977. Instruction for the care and feeding of axolotls. Axolotl Newsletter, Indiana Univ., 3: 9–16.

Crawshaw, G. J. 1992. Amphibian medicine, p. 1219–1230. *In* R. W. Kirk and J. D. Bonagura (eds.), Current Veterinary Therapy, volume XI. W. B. Saunders Co., Philadelphia.

Duhon, S. T. 1989*a*. Disease of axolotls, p. 264–269. *In* J. B. Armstrong and G. M. Malacinski (eds.), Developmental Biology of the Axolotl. Oxford Univ. Press, New York.

—. 1989*b*. Disease control in a large colony of axolotls. Herpetopathologica, 1: 105-108.

Duellman, W. E., and L. Trueb. "1986" (1985). Biology of Amphibians. McGraw-Hill Book Co., New York. xix, 670 pages (paperback edition 1994 by Johns Hopkins Univ. Press, Baltimore, Maryland).

Dyer, W. G., and R. A. Brandon. 1973. Helminths of three sympatric species of cave-dwelling salamanders in southern Illinois. Trans. Illinois State Acad. Sci., 66: 23–29.

Ebert, J. D. 1957. Department of Embryology, p. 297–355. *In* Year Book 56. July 1, 1956–June 30, 1957. Carnegie Inst. Washington, Washington.

Elkan, E. 1976. Pathology in the Amphibia, p. 273–312. *In* B. Lofts (ed.) Physiology of the Amphibia, volume 3. Academic Press, New York.

Humason, G. L. 1967. Animal Tissue Techniques (second edition). W. H. Freeman, San Francisco. ix, 569 pages.

Humphrey, R. R. 1962. Mexico axolotls, dark and mutant

white strains: care of experimental animals. Bull. Philadelphia Herpetol. Soc., 10(2/3): 21-28.

Kuwabara, K., T. Inoue, F. Wakabayashi, K. Ashikaga, N. Suzuki, and J. Kobara. 1980. The study on the protection of Japanese giant salamanders *Megalobatrachus japonicus* in Hiroshima Prefecture. Observation on the reproductive behavior in the stream of Matsuzai-gawa. Asa Zool. Park, Hiroshima, 22: 55–66.

Kramer, L., B. L. Dresser, and E. J. Maruska. 1983. Sexing aquatic salamanders by laparoscopy. Proc. Amer. Assoc. Zoo Veterinarians, Tampa, 1983: 192–194.

Laszlo, J. 1979. Notes on thermal requirements of reptiles and amphibians in captivity, p. 24–40. *In* Proceedings of the 3rd Annual Reptile Symposium on Captive Propagation and Husbandry. Zool. Consortium, Thurmont, Maryland.

Marcus, L. C. 1981. Veterinary Biology and Medicine of Captive Amphibians and Reptiles. Lea & Febiger, Philadelphia. xii, 239 pages.

Maruska, E. J. 1986. Amphibians: review of zoo breeding programmes. Internatl. Zoo Yearbook, 24–25: 56–65.

—. 1989. Husbandry and propagation of salamander species at the Cincinnati Zoo. Spec. Publ. Northern California Herpetol. Soc, 5: 1–10.

Mattison, C. 1982. The Care of Reptiles and Amphibians in Captivity. Blanford Press, Poole, Dorset, UK. 304 pages.

Nace, G. W., D. D. Culley, M. B. Emmons, E. L. Gibbs, V. H. Hutchison, and R. G. McKinnell. 1974. Amphibians. Guidelines for the Breeding, Care, and Management of Laboratory Animals. Nat. Acad. Sci., Washington, D.C. ix, 153 pages.

Nickerson, M. A., and C. E. Mays. 1973. The hellbenders: North American "giant salamanders." Milwaukee Public Mus., Publ. Biol. Geol., 1: viii, 1–106.

Noble, G. K. 1931. The Biology of the Amphibia. McGraw-Hill Book Co., New York. xiii, 577 pages (reprinted 1954, Dover Publ., New York).

Norris, D. O., and R. E. Jones (eds.). 1987. Hormones and Reproduction in Fishes, Amphibians, and Reptiles. Plenum Press, New York. xxvi, 613 pages.

Odum, R. A. 1984. Water quality: an often overlooked parameter for the amphibian enclosure, p. 33–58. *In* S. McKeown and F. Caporaso (eds.), Proceedings of the 8th Annual Herpetological Symposium on Captive Breeding and Husbandry. Zool. Consortium, Thurmont, Maryland.

Raxworthy, C. J. 1989. Courtship, fighting, and sexual dimorphism of the banded newt, *Triturus vittatus ophryticus*. Ethology, 81: 148–170.

Reichenbach-Klinke, H., and E. Elkan. 1965. The Principal Diseases of Lower Vertebrates. Academic Press, New York. Book II: Diseases of Amphibians. xii, 209–384 pages; book III: Diseases of Reptiles. xii, 385–600 pages (reprinted T. F. H. Publ. Company, Neptune City, New Jersey).

Roberts, D. T., D. M. Schleser, and T. L. Jordan. In press. Notes on the captive husbandry and reproduction of the Texas salamander, *Eurycea neotenes*, at Dallas Aquarium. Herpetol. Rev.

Sever, D. M. 1994. Comparative anatomy and phylogeny of the cloacae of salamanders (Amphibia: Caudata). VII. Plethodontidae. Herpetol. Monogr., 8: 276–337.

Shoop, C. R. 1960. The breeding habits of the mole salamander, *Ambystoma talpoideum* (Holbrook) in southeastern Louisiana. Tulane Stud. Zool., 8: 65–82.

Snider, A. T., and J. K. Bowler. 1992. Longevity of Reptiles and Amphibians in North American Collections (second ed.). Soc. Study Amphib. Reptiles, Oxford (Ohio), Herpetol. Circ., 21: 1–44.

Tuff, D. W., and D. G. Huffman. 1977. An index to the genera of hosts in Yamaguti's Systema Helminthum. Texas Jour. Sci., 28: 161–191.

Van Duijn, C., Jr. 1973. Diseases of Fishes (third ed.). C. C. Thomas, Springfield, Illinois. 372 pages.

Yamaguti, S. 1971. Synopsis of Digenetic Trematodes of Vertebrates. Keigaku Publ. Co., Tokyo. 2 volumes.

Zimmermann, E. 1983. Breeding Terrarium Animals. T.F.H. Publ. Company, Neptune City, New Jersey. 384 pages.

•

Appendix

For convenience, details for production of the various solutions mentioned in the text are given in the section that follows, including references to the appropriate literature.

Solution 1: Artificial Pond Water (from Mattison 1982: 122).

Make two stock solutions as follows:

Stock A:	Stock B:
175 g NaCl	5 g $NaHCO_3$
35 g $CaCl_2$	2 liters distilled water
2 liters distilled water	

Add 20 ml of solution A and 20 ml of solution B to 5 liters of distilled water to make artificial pond water.

Solution 2: Amphibian or Ringer's Solution (from Humason 1967: 411).

Mix in 1 liter of water:

6.6 g NaCl (pure, granulated canning salt)
0.15 g KCl
0.15 g $CaCl_2$
0.2 g $NaHCO_3$

Solution 3: Holtfreter's Solution and Modified Holtfreter's Solution (from Brothers 1977: 15).

Stock A:	Stock B:
3.5 g NaCl	0.2 g $NaHCO_3$
0.05 g KCl	500 ml glass-distilled H_2O
0.1 g $CaCl_2$	
500 ml glass-distilled H_2O	

The stocks should be sterilized separately. After cooling, they should be mixed in 1:1 proportions.

100% Modified Holtfreter's Solution: Holtfreter's Solution plus 204 mg $MgSO_4 \cdot 7H_2O$ per liter.

Solution 4: Steinberg's Solution (from Brothers 1977: 15, as modified from Ebert 1957: 348).

Stock Solution:	Formula:	Per liter:
17.0% NaCl	17 g/100 ml	20 ml
0.5% KCl	2.5 g/500 ml	10 ml
0.8% $Ca(NO_3)_2 \cdot 4H_2O$	4 g/500 ml	10 ml
2.05% $MgSO_4 \cdot 7H_2O$	10.25 g/500 ml	10 ml
1.00 N HCl	(for pH 7.4)	4 ml
Tris buffer	Trizma Base (reagent grade)	560 mg
Glass-distilled H_2O		946 ml

❦

❦ Maruska, E. J. 1994. Procedures for setting up and maintaining a salamander colony, p 229–242. *In* J. B. Murphy, K. Adler, and J. T. Collins (eds.), Captive Management and Conservation of Amphibians and Reptiles. Society for the Study of Amphibians and Reptiles, Ithaca (New York). Contributions to Herpetology, volume 11.

Model Programs for Reproduction and Management: Ex Situ and In Situ Conservation of Toads of the Family Bufonidae

Robert R. Johnson*

Introduction

There are an estimated 335 living species in the family Bufonidae (Duellman and Trueb "1986" [1985]), which has more species in peril than any other family of amphibians (Johnson 1990*a*). The family is cosmopolitan, diverse, contains live bearers as well as the largest and smallest of anurans, and includes species with distributions that may span continents or be restricted to one mountain-top cloud forest. Many species of Bufonidae are explosive breeders (Wells 1977) and are often the first to invade and colonize new or disturbed habitats.

As a result of the recent focus on the interplay of natural and anthropogenic causes of asynchronous population fluctuations, it is evident that many species are forced beyond the threshold of recovery by the speed and extent of anthropogenic environmental changes. As habitats recover from anthropogenic impacts, bufonid reintroduction and conservation programs may serve as models for the recovery of other anuran species. Recent conservation efforts for several bufonid species (*Peltophryne lemur, Bufo houstonensis, B. baxteri*, and *B. calamita*) include captive breeding as part of the recovery plans. Model amphibian-conservation programs may be enhanced by considering components of the following bufonid-management techniques selected for the variety and intensity of in situ and ex situ management.

*Metro Toronto Zoo
P. O. Box 280
West Hill, Ontario M1E 4R5, Canada

Acronyms used in this chapter:

AAZPA American Association of Zoological Parks and Aquariums
SSP Species Survival Plan

Model Programs

The conservation of amphibian biodiversity increasingly involves cooperation between field researchers and managers of small populations. For example, captive populations can provide a source of captive-bred animals for controlled laboratory research, studies on reproductive behavior, and as population reservoirs that are carefully managed to be returned to the wild. The International Union for the Conservation of Nature and zoo advisory groups provide reintroduction guidelines and review captive-release programs. Several case histories (see Greig 1979; and a collection of papers published in *Endangered Species Update Special Issue*, vol. 8, no. 1, 1990) have provided cross-species guidelines and a forum for review of ex situ conservation strategies and other aspects of restoration ecology. Many researchers, however, have remained cautious (Dodd 1991). Habitat and species management can only succeed when good use is made of the field data that are essential for the development of model in situ and ex situ conservation programs.

Imagine that a field researcher has identified a patch of forest in which ten species of anurans are in decline. The forest was once contiguous with surrounding forests, but has slowly become a remnant patch. If trends continue, all ten species face extinction. Some species are still relatively abundant, some are in decline, and a few have fallen below the minimum viable population size and are doomed to extinction if present trends continue. The decision is made to remove a founder population from the latter class for captive breeding. All animals would be on loan to the breeding institution and remain the property of the country of origin and subject to recall at any time. Ideally, ecological studies prior to collection of the specimens have identified temperature requirements, chemistry of natal ponds, habitat use, and other environmental variables. These are important factors in acclimating animals for captive breeding, and must be considered when releasing or translocating animals to new breeding sites within or outside of historic breeding areas. Conservation programs are then developed in conjunction with scientific advisors in the country of origin. Long-term breeding programs (that is, those of 100 years in duration, with a minimum loss of genetic diversity of the original population) initially require 20 to 30 founder animals. Short-term strategic programs can accommodate more animals since a return to the wild is contemplated within the generation time of the species. It is envisioned that offspring from captive breedings will, with approval of the government, be sent to individuals conducting scientific research on this species without having any impact on the wild populations.

Zoo-based ecological, nutritional, genetic, and reproductive physiology research would also improve the husbandry and breeding protocols to ensure long-term survival of the wild founders and the wild population itself. If warranted, the species may be considered for inclusion in the American Association of Zoological Parks and Aquariums (AAZPA) Species Survival Plan (SSP). An appointed studbook keeper would be responsible for maintaining current records on the status and location of the captive population. A propagation group and a species coordinator would ensure that an effective population size is managed so that all genetic contributions are retained in the population, and that no single genetic line is over-represented. This will be important if releases to the wild of other than eggs or tadpoles are to occur, because one captive breeding, without the high mortality associated with wild populations, might result in genetic swamping from the offspring of a single genetic line. The ultimate success for SSP participants will be the delisting of a species from intensive captive breeding programs when its continued survival in the wild has been assured.

Once the decision is made to intervene and manage a species in decline, it is no longer appropriate to be apologetic about exchanging genetic material between wild and captive populations in order to maintain the genetic integrity of the population as a whole. It is estimated that managing genetic diversity for 200 years requires 600 animals. It is obvious that priorities must be established in dealing with the most threatened of the 4,000 species of amphibians in any but short-term conservation programs. With a generation time of three to eight years, one may question just how realistic the long-term, captive self-sustainability of small anuran populations really is.

To establish the founder population, tadpoles would be collected from different ponds, if the population was considered stable enough to wait for individuals to mature for captive breeding. If tadpoles are only available from one pond, the collection of eggs or hatchling tadpoles from separate egg masses would increase the likelihood that founders were unrelated. Otherwise, sampling should be from different tadpole aggregations within one pond, because sibling recognition (Waldman and Adler 1979) may result in the existence of sibling tadpole associations. Of course, this sampling technique does not guarantee that unrelated animals are being obtained, but would approximate chance intra-population breeding encounters.

The removal of tadpoles over two or three reproductive episodes might also ensure unrelated females, since many bufonids do not have sufficient lipid stores to be represented at each breeding episode. The removal of tadpoles would be within the expected rate of loss due to mortality in the larval form, and avoids the removal of reproductively mature animals that had managed to survive the period of relatively high juvenile mortality. In other words, we would take care to ensure that no individual's genetic contribution would be removed from the population. If possible, animals already in managed or captive research programs would be utilized without removing additional animals from the wild. For example, widely dispersed and often single-animal laboratory populations of *Xenopus gilli* are proposed as sources of founders for captive breeding of this threatened South African pipid frog.

There is no consensus as to the demographic advantages of introductions at various developmental stages. The transfer of eggs or tadpoles has several advantages. They can be released in substantial numbers and selective processes would be the same as for their wild counterparts. There may be other advantages in releasing tadpoles, because it is possible that prior larval experience with the natal ponds is necessary for the toads to relocate migratory routes to and from this important resource. Rearing to the toadlet stage before release necessitates cropping the initial population to a manageable number. Of course, if space is available elsewhere, tadpoles can be distributed to a number of institutions for captive rearing so that 1,000 toadlets might be raised at five different zoos. Raising this many for release, however, would genetically swamp the wild population and is the second reason for cropping initial numbers. The 80% reduction in number approximates the mortalities of tadpoles in the wild, so that survival of the 1,000 toadlets would be similar to the number leaving natal ponds in the wild.

The rarer individuals, in our hypothetical species assemblage, have a narrowly defined niche and are naturally rare, closed-canopy species. Due to low genetic variability, or perhaps a skewed demographic structure, they are at this time vulnerable to the speed of environmental change. The more abundant species include those that usually exploit disturbed habitats on the edge of the forest tract. Rare, deep-forest species might be relocated to another patch of primary forest, or held until the factors responsible for their decline are remedied. Some of these may exploit natural clearings or openings in the canopy, and might respond to anthropogenic clearings and pool formation (such as along roads for example). Recovery for these animals would be more likely than for those which avoid clearings and utilize pools in closed-canopy forests.

Meanwhile, the local community has been involved in controlling fires, removing trees on a sustainable basis, and developing a local school education program. Schoolchildren are planting trees along the forest perimeter so that the edge is protected and the forested area is actually increasing each year. The interior remnant remains as a habitat reserve, the regenerated or secondary forest serves as a local resource with wildlife, trees, and plants harvested on a sustainable basis, and the planted areas serve as a buffer to reduce anthropogenic changes on the core habitats and the impact of edge species.

Once the cause of the decline is understood, the quality of the habitat can be improved, or critical requirements, such as water supplies, can be restored. Edge species that are tolerant of disturbance can be reintroduced once the disturbances (such as logging and fires) have gone and secondary growth is occurring. Other, less tolerant species, may be reintroduced once the secondary growth has stabilized. These represent long-term conservation strategies.

Captive breeding may not preserve all species. By integrating ex situ recovery and in situ protection and restoration, we may lose, for example, four of our ten hypothetical species, and two may still be in peril. There would be four species existing in the wild, however, where none would have existed before. More importantly, there is now a functional ecosystem capable of sustaining wildlife and a successional habitat.

Despite the hypothetical nature of the preceding example, the recent removal of all adult *Philautus romeri* (a rhacophorid frog) from three small islands, which are destined to be developed for a new airport in the Hong Kong harbor, demonstrates the necessity of preparing for an increased incidence of short-term holding and ex situ breeding until wild habitats have been secured or restored.

Management Alternatives

Habitat degradation or fragmentation will increase our dependency on techniques utilized to manage small populations. The importance of this residual captive population is proportional to the size and range of isolated wild populations. Conservation programs for four bufonid toads exemplify a range of management options that have integrated ex situ and in situ population-conservation initiatives. The Houston Toad (*Bufo houstonensis*) and Natterjack Toad (*B. calamita*) represent species with relatively stable wild populations. Ex situ management of these species highlights the importance of public education and less-intensive breeding techniques that are possible in artificial, outdoor habitat recreations or restorations. The Wyoming Toad (*B. baxteri*) and Puerto Rican Crested Toad (*Peltophryne lemur*) ex situ management programs will be examined in more detail and in some respects represent parallel programs in which components of each may be applicable for both threatened species.

Houston Toad

The Houston Toad's decline in abundance and distribution may be attributed to drought and a subsequent loss of habitat from land development (United States Fish and Wildlife Service 1984). The continued loss of habitat has suppressed the recovery of Houston Toad populations during wet years, when range expansion might be expected. Habitat is fragmented and populations are isolated, so that the historical decline of *Bufo houstonensis* populations may be indicative of the loss of habitat and general degradation of the deep-sand woodland and savannah ecosystem in this area of Texas (A. Price, pers. comm.).

Significant populations of the Houston Toad have been identified in Bastrop State Park, where ponds constructed as water reservoirs for forest fire prevention and as stock ponds have been important factors in the continued survival of this species (Figure 1). Andrew Price, of Texas Parks and Wildlife Department, is currently documenting critical habitat and ecology of wild populations in protected areas, such as Bastrop State Park. Intensive study of two breeding populations includes the collection of temperature and rainfall data and implanting passive transponders into all individuals that enter the pond so that data concerning reproduction, time in pond, longevity, and growth can be collected. Local land-use practices which affect the toad are being monitored with the expectation that toads can be accommodated on private lands adjacent to the park.

FIGURE 1. Houston Toads bred in these man-made ponds in Bastrop State Park, Texas (February 1991).

Captive populations of the Houston Toad, at Houston Zoo, were used as a source of toadlets and tadpoles in an attempt to establish satellite populations in the Attwater Prairie Chicken Refuge in southeastern Texas. To date there is no evidence that released toadlets and tadpoles have survived or reproduced. It now appears that *B. houstonensis* is excluded from this area by other species of *Bufo*, although this site is adjacent to extant *B. houstonensis* populations. In fact, it has been suggested that coastal prairie at the Attwater Refuge is marginal habitat for *B. houstonensis*, although it appears to be similar to the preferred savannah ecotype (A. Price, pers. comm.). Although toads are maintained at Houston Zoo, further releases are not contemplated. The initial ex situ programs have focused attention on this species until such time as the status and stability of wild populations could be established. The recent decision to construct migration tunnels under roadways adjacent to Bastrop Park (*Wall Street Journal*, 30 July 1990) has once again focused attention on the plight of this species.

Natterjack Toad

Management of *Bufo calamita* in the United Kingdom has focused on improving the quality of toad habitat by constructing and rehabilitating breeding ponds, and by preventing the continual fragmentation of toad populations and heathland in general. The progression from heathland to woodland and the cooling of some ponds in the resulting shade has facilitated the expansion of Common Toad, *B. bufo*, into ponds occupied previously by the warm-water-dwelling Natterjack Toad, *B. calamita* (Beebee 1983).

Dune habitats have been destroyed for seaside developments, and in other dune areas the successional acidification of oligotrophic breeding ponds of the Natterjack Toad is being addressed by removing peat buildup. Tree cover is being reduced, but emphasis is now on restoring breeding ponds (T. J. C. Beebee, pers. comm.), some of which encompass 8,000 square meters in the dune slack basins. Ponds are shelved with shallow gradients of 10–20 degrees and with midsummer depths of no more than 50 cm.

Although some translocations of artificially reared toadlets into constructed ponds have been successful, initial attempts at reintroductions of Natterjack Toads have failed, primarily due to the acidity at chosen release sites. This emphasizes the need to characterize the critical habitat and the importance of field work prior to release. Criticism of these attempts centers around the loss of translocated toads, although many were transferred from doomed populations. Management options to increase survival of eggs and tadpoles includes the control of invertebrate and vertebrate predators so that the numbers that might be reasonably expected to die from natural predation can be recruited for translocation. Captive breeding and release is ideally suited to situations in which there are limited numbers of animals that can be used for translocation without some impact on the source population.

In perhaps the best example of ex situ breeding potential, Marwell Zoo, in the United Kingdom, has reconstructed a large walk-in outdoor heathland habitat in which Natterjack Toads (and sand lizards) will be released as part of their captive-breeding program. Such habitat simulations are important both for cycling adult toads and to prepare naive captive-bred toads for release to the wild. Ideally, these habitat reconstructions are located in the country of origin and are as near the release site as possible.

The limited acceptance of new breeding ponds by Natterjack Toads requires further study as to why particular ponds are accepted or overlooked (Podloucky 1989; Schlupp et al. 1989). The short-term loss of learned behaviors, such as knowledge of migration routes and critical habitat for feeding, hibernation, or egg-laying, is likely to be far more critical than genome loss (Western 1986).

Wyoming Toad

The Wyoming Toad, *Bufo baxteri*, is in need of immediate assistance from both in situ and ex situ conservation programs. Recovery objectives include (1) a stable and secure existing population, (2) the creation of five new populations of 100 adult toads each, and (3) the elimination of the imminent threat of extinction. Due to the sudden and continued decline of this species in their only known breeding site, Mortenson Lake, a captive population would ensure a backup population in the event of extinction of the species in the wild, and provide a source of animals to establish satellite populations. Wyoming Game and Fish Department currently holds adults and juveniles, and juveniles are currently being maintained at Cheyenne Mountain Zoo in Colorado Springs.

Historically, all known populations of the Wyoming Toad have been found within 48 km of Laramie, Wyoming. Flood plain breeding sites have been eliminated by diverting river water to supply the demand of water rights, and runoff from pasture irrigation has increased the salinity of many ponds (pers. observ.). The effects of aerial spraying of a pesticide (Baytex) to control mosquitos has not been extensively investigated, but no longer occurs over known breeding sites (United States Fish and Wildlife Service 1991).

The only known population of the Wyoming Toad was discovered at Mortenson Lake in 1987. From a population numbering in the thousands, the most recent counts have only found 155 adult animals. Combined with high adult mortalities, reproduction has been steadily declining. Adult mortalities of more than 80% have occurred each year in 1991 and 1992 (S. Corn, pers. comm.). In 1990, drought forced the owner of the lake to lower water levels in order to irrigate fields. With the assistance of the Nature Conservancy, the purchase of Mortenson Lake and the surrounding land will ensure control of water levels in the lake. In 1991, only three females bred, and developing tadpoles were in constant threat as water levels receded in the reservoir. Quick action by Wyoming Game and Fish Department and United States Fish and Wildlife Service officials to maintain lake water levels, and actually pump water into the tadpole foraging areas, was required to protect the developing tadpoles. Breeding in 1991 was restricted to tire ruts in the mud, and two depressions in the lakeside marsh that were caused by boats stored there over the winter

FIGURE 2. Wyoming Toads bred in these depressions made by stored boats, adjacent to Mortenson Lake (June 1991).

(Figure 2). Any increase in shallow, open-water areas might provide additional egg-laying sites. No reproduction occurred at Mortenson Lake in 1992 (S. Corn, pers. comm.).

In a bold attempt at reintroduction, female and juvenile Wyoming Toads are being maintained in captivity, and overwintered for four months at temperatures that are slowly reduced to 5°C, with a relative humidity of 78% (D. Kwiatkowski, pers. comm.). The strategy is to utilize these overwintered females and wild males, collected at Mortenson Lake, for reproduction and to place the eggs at the Lake George introduction site. Once a male is located from Mortensen Lake in the spring, it will be paired with the female within a breeding "cage" at Lake George, the site of previous toad breeding. It is anticipated that toads which survive to reproductive age will return to their natal lake, and that this will be the first indication of potential success in this effort at re-introduction. In 1992, this method resulted in tadpoles at the Lake George site, despite the fact that toads did not breed at the Mortenson Lake site.

The involvement of some of these Wyoming Toads, overwintered in captivity, in a captive-breeding program might expand the population at a rate faster than if they were left in the wild. Surplus captive animals could be the focus of research projects and could be used to establish satellite populations. Ex situ programs parallel in situ recovery objectives. If necessary, an ecological substitute or closely related surrogate species can be used to answer some of the questions related to survival in the target species. None of these ex situ programs affect the in situ conservation efforts and they may contribute to our understanding of the causes of decline.

The translocated adult breeding was the only breeding of this species in 1992. At present levels of mortality (approaching 80%) in the wild population, captive breeding is the only means of producing enough animals to maintain the demographic structure of the wild population and to ensure at least one backup population in the wild.

Puerto Rican Crested Toad

The recovery of the Puerto Rican Crested Toad, *Peltophryne lemur,* in the wild must include (1) continued protection of the one remaining breeding pond in the Guánica Forest Reserve, (2) captive propagation for release in constructed ponds, (3) public education, (4) research on critical habitat, ecology, post-reproductive movement, and (5) the genetic separation of two known populations. The return of captive-bred animals to the wild is the primary focus of *P. lemur* conservation programs (Johnson 1990*b*). The Puerto Rican Crested Toad conservation program could be re-assessed in ten years if satellite populations are established both from wild translocations and captive-bred releases. In the program's tenth year as an SSP of the AAZPA, captive populations of toads are maintained at 13 zoos, and the Department of Biology Center for the Propagation of Endangered Species at the University of Puerto Rico, Humacao. Toads of this species have been bred at the Metro Toronto, Buffalo, and Cincinnati Zoos.

FIGURE 3. (A, left) In the southern part of their range, Puerto Rican Crested Toads bred in this single seasonal pond; (B, right) Puerto Rican Crested Toads in northern Puerto Rico only bred in man-made cattle troughs, such as the one in this photograph.

The Puerto Rican Crested Toad breeds in one pond on the southwestern coast (Figure 3A) and in no more than four man-made cattle troughs in the northwest (Figure 3B). Original estimates of a southern population of 3,000 toads have been revised to 300, and, in the north, no more than 25 have been recorded. The Puerto Rican Department of Natural Resources now considers the northern population to be extirpated, because none have been seen since 1989 despite suitable breeding conditions (J. Moreno, pers. comm.). Preliminary data (A. Goebel, pers. comm.) suggest that these populations have significant differences in mitochondrial DNA that reflect their geographical separation. The disappearance of the northern population represents a significant loss of genetic diversity for this species. The remaining, smaller population is vulnerable to catastrophic loss.

In the south, Puerto Rican Crested Toads breed in the Tamarindo section of the Guánica State Forest. The breeding pond is located in a precarious location within 100 meters of the sea and could be breached or inundated by heavy seas during severe storms or hurricanes. The site serves as a parking lot for users of a nearby beach during the dry season and is closed during breeding episodes. In fact, until 1984, the flooded parking area was regularly drained by well-meaning employees of the nearby town of Guánica. As a result there was not enough water remaining for the tadpoles to complete their 18-day (range 15–25) larval period before metamorphosing. Recruitment to the Guánica population during this period was not possible and the only other breeding pond was destroyed by a hurricane in 1985 (M. Canals, pers. comm.).

The importance of the discovery of a breeding population of Puerto Rican Crested Toads in Guánica Forest by Miguel Canals cannot be underestimated, nor can the series of actions he initiated to secure this site for subsequent breedings. The ditch, which drained the flooded parking area in which the toads bred, was dammed. A series of posts prevented cars from driving into the breeding area, and from destroying vegetation used by the toads during egg laying, and, during the three-week breeding period, the road to the parking lot was closed to prevent contamination of the water. A public information campaign through local schools and newspapers has resulted in local acceptance of the changes which have occurred in this high-use area to ensure the survival of the toad. The survival of the Puerto Rican Crested Toad thus far has been dependent to a large extent on the good will of the citizens of Guánica, and on the efforts of Jorge Moreno, of the Department of Natural Resources, and Miguel Canals, the department's forest manager.

Amphibians have colonized dry habitats because they are adapted to conserve body fluids by forming a protective cocoon of shed skin (Loveridge and Craye 1979), by increasing blood-urea levels (Katz and Gabbay 1986), or through drought-avoidance by aestivating in humid underground chambers, usually in rock. In many instances these conditions are required to stimulate egg maturation, or to maintain a full complement of eggs in readiness for a brief period of reproduction. The microenvironments utilized by aestivating amphibians are not well studied, and their re-creation in captivity remains a challenge. Amphibians migrate if components of their critical habitat are spatially separated (Sinsch 1990). It is apparent that we cannot underestimate the importance of site fidelity. The range of homing ability coincides with the natural migratory range of the species. Intraspecific variation suggests that orientation behavior is adapted to special habitat features. Studies of temperate bufonid activity may help in understanding the behavior of tropical bufonids in which annual spatial and temporal behaviors may not be synchronized.

Bufo bufo may subdivide its annual migration to breeding ponds into a fall segment that occurs during periods of favorable weather and a second migration that is concluded in the spring (Sinsch 1990). Non-reproductive toads hibernate in the summer range. This habitat segregation would reduce competition for hibernation sites. To complete migration in a non-random way, Sinsch has suggested a two-step process. Mapping determines the position of the toad relative to its destination, and compassing determines direction to reach the destination. In some cases, piloting by using visual or acoustic cues may be utilized. Given the sophistication of orienting behavior, we must also consider the importance of landmarks in the captive environment. Toads are constrained by evaporative water loss. Males, however, have a lower threshold for migration and move at every opportunity, often under less-than-optimum conditions. Females move only under more optimum conditions. As a result, there tends to be more males present, although the same number of females may breed, and varying numbers breed each year in correlation with the number of opportunities for migration. Because favorable conditions for migration occur sporadically, those hibernating or aestivating at some distance may not reach the natal ponds in a single trek. As a result, there is a series of waves of migrants represented at the pond in an accumulative manner. If conditions are not favorable, some migrating animals may never reach the breeding pond. One can envision that in a series of poor years a proportion of the population at some given range may not contribute to recruitment for several years.

If we use *B. bufo* as a model, we might expect the Puerto Rican Crested Toad to approach breeding sites in accumulative stages that coincide with periods of rainfall. Those within one kilometer reach the pond first, and those at distances up to three kilometers may not reach the pond at all that year if there are not repeated episodes of rainfall. Miguel Canals (pers. comm.) has noted that about 18 cm of rainfall over a short period, or several episodes of rainfall totaling the same amount, are required for *P. lemur* to appear in the breeding ponds. During the 1990 breeding episode, in which 300 toads emerged, warm water welled up into the beachside breeding pond. It would appear that this water was still running out from the surrounding hills several days after rainfall. It may be speculated that, as this water backs up, toads continue to appear from increasing altitudes. The large amounts of rainfall that accompany tropical depressions may result in mass emergence. Just such an emergence occurred following Hurricane Hugo in 1984, when a total of about 33 cm of rain fell within 24 hours and an estimated 3,000 Puerto Rican Crested Toads emerged to breed. It is not known whether the toads responded to moisture percolating through their underground retreats, to water backing up in subterranean channels in the hills that surround the breeding pond, or to the sound of water striking the ground.

Site fidelity may be recognized in natal ponds, home ranges, and hibernation/aestivation sites. This fidelity is easily understood in cases in which there are no alternative sites. There are many accounts of amphibians crossing one pond to breed in another. It has been suggested that at least some amphibians utilize corridors, within which they migrate in a straight line (Shoop and Doty 1972). Toads have selected some man-made ponds as alternative breeding sites if forced to breed there at least once (Podloucky 1989). Range expansion, however, can only occur when new sites are selected. In fact, some breeding ponds may be secondary sites, with preferred sites unavailable due to annual weather changes or habitat alteration (such as lowering of water tables).

The loss of a breeding pond for the Puerto Rican Crested Toad occurred during Hurricane Hugo in 1984. Water seemingly exploded out of the hills and washed out a pond at Guánica Hills, and all of the toads that were breeding at it. Since that time, no toads have used this site, although it is only one kilometer away from the primary breeding site, and well within the migratory range of this species. It is just such short-term or stochastic events, perhaps superimposed on long-term change, that cause local declines and extirpations.

Environmental stimuli, such as photoperiod, temperature, and rainfall, are expressed physiologically by the secretion of reproductive hormones into the blood stream. An amphibian becomes sensitized to secondary, and then tertiary, behavioral stimuli that did not previously stimulate a response (Schiøtz 1973). For example, male calls only stimulate the females after they have experienced a rise in temperature and an increase in rainfall. Our challenge is to recognize those factors responsible for stimulating or facilitating reproduction, and then re-create these in captivity in a sequence that approximates the thresholds encountered in the wild. Therein lies the importance of field data over captive husbandry data. In this regard, aestivation, breeding, and husbandry protocols (Devison 1991; Johnson and Paine 1989; Paine 1985) have been developed after extensive review of field data. For example, just prior to metamorphosis, water temperatures are raised to 28°C to simulate the rise in water temperature measured in ponds in the field. Water levels are reduced to increase the size of beach areas, which also corresponds to a similar situation observed in the field. These beach areas are used extensively by newly metamorphosed Puerto Rican Crested Toads to bask and to breathe without having to swim to the surface.

Despite exposure to dehydrating conditions, newly metamorphosed Puerto Rican Crested Toads will move en masse out of the water. This behavior occurs in captivity, despite the availability of fresh water. In the wild, this behavior has obvious advantages as toadlets must seek refuge from lethal water and ground temperatures, and in some cases deteriorating water conditions in a drying pond. Clumping behavior is common in many bufonids (Duellman and Trueb "1986" [1985]) as it was for the Puerto Rican Crested Toad. The mass of toadlets represents a reduced ratio of surface area to volume and has obvious advantages in the dehydrating conditions of the Guánica environment. Typically, 15–30 toadlets will clump in one mass under any available object and will conform to the shape of the space under the shelter. In captivity, halved coconut shells can be completely filled with toadlets, and in the field many clumps have been observed, particularly under limestone rocks. In addition, spontaneous clumping in open areas without shelter has been observed in captivity. Leaf-litter postures have also been observed both in captivity and the field.

Newly metamorphosed Puerto Rican Crested Toads seek refuge as soon as they leave the water. This has adaptive advantage in the wild, as ground temperatures exceed 45°C around the drying breeding ponds in Puerto Rico. A single mass of toadlets in one clump reduces the ratio of surface area to body mass with a corresponding reduction in evaporative water loss. Clumping under small rocks was observed around the breeding pond and this may represent a critical factor in juvenile mortality. In fact, most of these refuges were occupied by *B. marinus* prior to the emergence of *P. lemur*. This may provide evidence of the critical impact the introduced bufonid has on juvenile mortality in the island endemic.

Radio Tracking and Strategies for Amphibian Release Programs

Release and translocation programs for amphibians are not, as yet, well developed. When 3,000 newly metamorphosed Puerto Rican Crested Toads were released in 1988, the only evidence of survivorship came from the discovery in 1989 of two animals released as part of a group of 640, and sightings of toads in 1992 and 1993 in western Guánica. Emphasis has now shifted to the release of tadpoles. The small size of released toadlets makes follow-up on the success of introductions or releases difficult, but nonetheless important. To date, the only measure of success has been the presence or absence of toadlets at release sites. Intensive monitoring now occurs for the first three weeks after release and monthly thereafter.

Twelve captive-bred, adult Puerto Rican Crested Toads were outfitted with a radio transmitter carried in a dorsal harness (Johnson, in press) to determine habitat use and survival of captive raised toads. Toads moved up to 60 meters in the first night after release. Mongoose predation was a significant factor on the survival of adult, captive-raised toads.

FIGURE 4. (A, left) During the study of post-reproductive movement by a Metro Toronto Zoo research team, Puerto Rican Crested Toads carried this radio transmitter in its specially designed harness; (B, right) Puerto Rican Crested Toads sought refuge in limestone holes and crevices such as the one shown in this photograph. Leaf litter was removed to reveal opening.

After waiting two years before there was enough rainfall to stimulate emergence and reproduction, a research team from Metro Toronto Zoo tracked post-reproductive movements of ten wild Puerto Rican Crested Toads for 20 days (Figure 4A). As expected, these toads utilize crevices and solution holes in the limestone as daytime retreats from the dehydrating effects of ground temperatures which approach 45°C during the day (Figure 4B). Toads migrated up to two kilometers during our study period. After a three-day period of activity in which the distance traveled averaged 150 metres per 24-hour period for all toad movements (daily individual movement ranged from 15 to 500 meters), toads settled into an area, and movement was reduced to an average of six metres per night. During the period of reduced movement, toads often returned to the same refuge.

Data on pH, salinity, calcium content, and temperature of the breeding ponds were collected at Guánica by a Metro Toronto Zoo research team in 1990. It is essential that the chemistry and ecological characteristics of the breeding ponds be characterized. First, a pond profile would allow managers to maintain its essential character given sudden or long-term changes that may adversely affect the present population of Puerto Rican Crested Toads. Second, the need to identify existing ponds suitable for toad reproduction is imperative. Failing this, it will be necessary to construct breeding ponds that mirror the conditions of the existing breeding sites.

In the south, it is anticipated that new ponds, whether naturally formed during rains or man made to fill during rain, would receive tadpoles of Puerto Rican Crested Toads from two sources. Some tadpoles would be translocated from the present breeding pond to adjacent ponds outside the migratory range of the crested toad, and a second pond would receive captive-bred tadpoles returned to Puerto Rico for release. In 1993, 12,000 tadpoles were returned for release in a newly constructed pond. Tadpole releases into new ponds are now the highest priority and, given the numbers involved, represent the greatest chance of successful establishment of satellite populations. Identifying future release sites remains a high priority for the recovery of this species.

Given the prolific reproductive output of amphibians, there is a very real possibility of genetically swamping wild populations, if releases represent the contribution of a small number of founders. To reduce this possibility, it may be necessary to utilize offspring from as many founder animals as possible by equalizing the representation from each breeding pair of Puerto Rican Crested Toads, and to release tadpoles, which is the life-stage with the highest mortality.

Puerto Rican Crested Toads intended for release should be acclimated to the conditions of the release environment. Post-metamorphic migration away from the breeding pond requires further study to determine its importance in relocating breeding ponds. Post-metamorphic movements may orient the toadlet to its new environment and provide a "map" so that the toad can later return to its natal pond for breeding.

Captive breeding and translocations of Puerto Rican Crested Toads should not replace the need to restore habitat or protect existing ponds and breeding populations. Providing satellite ponds so that a core population can naturally extend its range in times of natural surplus of animals is preferable to utilizing naïve captive-bred animals. The relative merits of utilizing numerous tadpoles or fully grown, but naïve, toads (Johnson and Paine 1989) requires further field trials to determine the life-stage at which the animal is most likely to survive to replace itself. The long-term survival of the crested toad is dependent upon protection of existing breeding sites and establishment of satellite populations.

More recently, Metro Toronto Zoo has funded the production of 2,000 posters that have been distributed throughout Puerto Rico. The posters have illustrations which aid in distinguishing between the endemic Puerto Rican Crested Toad and the introduced Giant Toad (*Bufo marinus*), and provide contacts that are to be notified if crested toads are seen. This is part of a program to locate additional populations, and to increase awareness of this species and other threatened species in Puerto Rico.

The success rate for non-game translocations, such as that for Puerto Rican Crested Toads, will be low until trials can be conducted and analyzed. A period of relatively poor establishment must be anticipated, and these should not have a negative effect on consideration of this species for further introduction attempts (Johnson 1990*b*). The release of captive-bred animals and habitat restoration are management tools that will increasingly be the last resort for any number of species. The potential of success in release programs must be considered as only one management strategy among others in stemming the rapid and catastrophic loss of amphibian species diversity.

Summary

These four programs illustrate management options that are required as a result of environmental change. Some degree of management is required until the causes of decline are fully understood. Many bufonids quickly exploit changing and altered habitats. Although they are quick to exploit new sources of water, the natural recruitment of self-sustaining populations to newly created habitats must be measured over several generations.

We may well ask what these four programs contribute to preserving anuran biodiversity. In an analysis of amphibians bred in captivity (Johnson 1990), it is apparent that, in the last five years, only 1.6% of amphibian species have been bred in captivity, and most of these only once. The selection of animals for conservation programs on the basis of their rarity emphasizes those species that have a restricted range, endemics, and specialists who are interested in that species (Western 1986). If action is taken to reverse degradation of wild habitat, these sensitive species may be preserved. Disturbed, secondary, and reconstituted habitats, however, are likely to be the legacy of our impact on ecosystems. Common species may also be considered in light of their role in ecosystem energetics and the self-contained processes responsible for ecological integrity.

It is important to consider the ecological role of the anuran. It is not enough to preserve a genome without prospects for a "place" for evolutionary change. Emphasis could be placed on increased awareness of amphibian populations, and appropriate in situ conservation strategies within preserves set aside for other species. For example, rather than "rescuing" amphibians from Atlantic coastal forest in Brazil, it may be more appropriate to ensure the protection of existing populations and the environments they rely on as part of the Golden Lion Tamarin recovery plan. We are still faced, however, with the decision as to whether it is more appropriate to protect faunal assemblages in large reserves, or amphibian biodiversity in a large number of smaller reserves that represents more ecotypes.

The design of reserves must account for the impact of gradual environmental changes and shifts in the distribution of ecosystems preserved within the reserve boundary; reserves must be large enough to preserve a species and the ecological processes that guarantee its long-term survival (Frankel 1983). If conservation in this sense implies the preservation of a species' habitat, then ex situ species conservation can best be managed through the exchange of genetic material between the wild and the captive population. The focus on these captive populations would not replace the emphasis on wild populations. The managers of small populations, whether in situ or ex situ, must work in tandem with national conservation strategies at the local and national level.

The short-term preservation of biodiversity may be achieved through captive-breeding programs, but in the long term, it is the preservation of in situ ecological processes that will determine the fate of the population. Even in short-term programs, however, the loss of learned behaviors involving, for example, migration routes and critical habitats for feeding, hibernation, or egg-laying, is likely to be more significant than longer term concerns over the loss of rare alleles (Western 1986). To avert the full impact of a crisis, it is an advantage to have prior knowledge of the reproductive behavior, physiology, nutrition, and genetics of the captive population, before it is necessary to take into captivity a critically low threshold number of wild animals. Keeping captive populations in large habitat simulations (as Marwell Zoo is doing for *Bufo calamita*) might preserve behaviors suited to the environment from which the animal has come. This is a priority for short-term conservation programs. With appropriate genetic exchange, captive and wild populations would share genetic profiles.

Field workers must be relied upon for data that will help to identify species of special concern, and that may benefit from captive propagation. These programs may be considered as conservation field trials. The integration of in situ and ex situ conservation strategies can only be developed by the testing of hypotheses, with each program contributing to the development of amphibian conservation and management options in an accumulative way.

Acknowledgments

Frederick Paine, Miguel Canals, Jorge Moreno, Dianne Devison, Anna Goebel, Thomas Thorne, Don Kwiatkowski, Stephen Corn, Andrew Price, Paul Edgar, Trevor Beebee, David Withers, and Robert Wiese shared data and provided information from unpublished sources. Metro Toronto Zoo, and Wyoming Game and Fish provided support for field work. John Carnio, Dianne Devison, and two anonymous reviewers provided helpful comments. James Murphy provided encouragement and a forum for the sharing and growth of new ideas and strategies.

Literature Cited

Beebee, T. J. C. 1983. The Natterjack Toad. Oxford Univ. Press, Oxford. 159 pages.

Devison, D. 1991. Management program and breeding of the Puerto Rican crested toad at Metro Toronto Zoo, p. 53–59. *In* Proceedings of the Sixteenth American Association of Zoo Keepers Conference, New Orleans, Louisiana.

Dodd, C. K. 1991. Relocation, repatriation, and translocation of amphibians and reptiles: Are there conservation strategies that really work? Herpetologica, 47: 336–350.

Duellman, W. E., and L. Trueb. “1986” (1985). Biology of Amphibians. McGraw-Hill, New York. 670 pages.

Frankel, O. H. 1983. The place of management in conservation, p. 1–14. *In* C. M. Schonewald-Cox et al. (eds.), Genetics and Conservation. Benjamin/Cumming, London, UK.

Greig, J. C. 1979. Principles of genetic conservation in relation to wildlife management in southern Africa. South African Jour. Wildl. Res., 1979: 57.

Johnson, R. R. 1990*a*. American Association of Zoological Parks and Aquariums Amphibian Taxon Advisory Group report. Oklahoma City, Oklahoma. Unpublished Manuscript.

—. 1990*b*. Release and translocation strategies for the Puerto Rican crested toad. Captive propagation and reintroduction: a strategy for preserving endangered species. Endang. Species Update Spec. Issue, 8: 54-57.

—. In press. Radiotracking anurans using an external harness. Herpetol. Review.

Johnson, R. R., and F. L. Paine. 1989. The release of captive bred Puerto Rican crested toads: captive management implications and the cactus connection, p. 962–967. *In* Proceedings of the American Association of Zoological Parks and Aquariums Regional Conference, Wheeling, West Virginia.

Katz, U., and S. Gabbay. 1986. Water retention and plasma and urine composition in toads under burrowing conditions. Jour. Comp. Physiol., B, 156: 735

Loveridge, J. P., and G. Craye. 1979. Cocoon formation in two species of southern African frogs. South African Jour. Sci., 75: 18.

Paine, F. 1985. Husbandry, management, and reproduction of the Puerto Rican crested toad, p. 59–75. *In* Proceedings of the Eighth International Herpetological Symposium. Zool. Consorium, Thurmont, Maryland.

Podloucky, R. 1989. Protection of amphibians on roads—examples and experiences from Lower Saxony, p. 15–27. *In* T. E. Langton (ed.), Amphibians and Roads. ACO Polymer Products, Shefford, UK.

Schiøtz, A. 1973. Evolution of anuran mating calls, p. 311–319. *In* J. L. Vial (ed.), Evolutionary Biology of the Anurans. Univ. Missouri Press, Columbia.

Schlupp, I., M. Kietz, R. Podloucky, and F. M. Stolz. 1989. Pilot project Braken: preliminary results from the resettlement of adult toads to a substitute breeding site, p. 127–133. *In* T. E. Langton (ed.), Amphibians and Roads. ACO Polymer Products, Shefford, UK.

Shoop, C. R., and T. L. Doty. 1972. Migratory orientation by marbled salamanders near a breeding area. Behav. Ecol., A, 7: 131–136.

Sinsch, U. 1990. Migration and orientation in anuran amphibians. Ethol., Ecol., Evol., 2: 65–79.

Stone, M. D. 1991. Wyoming Toad Recovery Plan. United States Fish and Wildlife Service, Denver, Colorado. 28 pages.

United States Fish and Wildlife Service. 1984. Houston Toad Recovery Plan. United States Fish and Wildlife Service, Albuquerque, New Mexico. 73 pages.

—. 1991. Wyoming Toad Recovery Plan. United States Fish and Wildlife Service, Denver, Colorado. 28 pages.

Waldman, B., and K. Adler. 1979. Toad tadpoles associate preferentially with siblings. Nature, 282: 611–613.

Wells, K. D. 1977. The social behavior of anuran amphibians. Anim. Behav., 25: 666–693.

Western, D. 1986. The role of captive populations in global conservation, p. 13–20. *In* K. Benirschke (ed.), Primates. The Road to Selfsustaining Populations. Springer-Verlag, New York.

❦

❦ Johnson, R. R. 1994. Model programs for reproduction and management: ex situ and in situ conservation of toads of the family Bufonidae, p. 243–254. *In* J. B. Murphy, K. Adler, and J. T. Collins (eds.), Captive Management and Conservation of Amphibians and Reptiles. Society for the Study of Amphibians and Reptiles, Ithaca (New York). Contributions to Herpetology, volume 11.

Reproductive Strategies, Breeding, and Conservation of Tropical Frogs: Dart-Poison Frogs and Malagasy Poison Frogs

Elke Zimmermann* and Helmut Zimmermann**

Introduction

The neotropical dart-poison frogs (family Dendrobatidae) and the Malagasy poison frogs (genus *Mantella*, family Ranidae) share traits that distinguish them from all other extant frog taxa. These frogs are small in size (ranging from about 2–5 cm), diurnal, often brightly colored with interesting patterns, and can synthesize unusual toxic alkaloids in their skin for protection against predators (Duellman and Trueb 1986 [1985]; Daly et al. 1987). Furthermore, they display a highly elaborated courtship and terrestrial oviposition behavior. These attributes make them among the most interesting of tropical anurans to the public and to scientists and frog herpetoculturists world-wide. Until recently, this broad interest had led to mass exportation of these frogs from their countries of origin and few specimens survived in captivity. Since 1987, dart-poison frogs of the genera *Dendrobates* and *Phyllobates* have been listed by the Convention on International Trade in Endangered Species (CITES), in its Appendix 2. As a result, commercial trade in wild-caught dendrobatid frogs has declined. Trade in the genus *Mantella*, especially with Malagasy golden frogs (*Mantella aurantiaca*), however, has subsequently increased.

More than 130 species of dart-poison frogs of the genera *Allobates*, *Colostethus, Dendrobates*, *Epipedobates, Minyobates*, *Phobobates*, and *Phyllobates* and about eight different species of Malagasy poison frogs of the genus *Mantella* have been described (Zimmermann and Zimmermann 1988; Glaw and Vences 1992*a*). All occur in tropical rain forests, often with patchy distributions and fairly restricted ranges; these species include, for example, *Dendrobates azureus* (Hoogmoed 1969), *D. speciosus* (Jungfer 1985; Edwards et al. 1988), *Epipedobates pulchripectus* (Weygoldt 1983), and *Mantella aurantiaca* (Arnoult 1966; Zimmermann and Hetz 1992). The deforestation of tropical rain forests—which is occurring at a rate of about 250,000 km^2/year (Myers 1985)—is the most dire threat to these species, which are adapted to rain forests.

In this chapter, we focus on four major topics that are important in establishing species survival programs for tropical frogs. We draw on our experience of the last two decades of studying the behavior and reproduction of 35 dendrobatid and five mantelline species, both in the field and in captivity. In particular, we review the main reproductive strategies evolved in these frogs as an adaptation to their habitats to ensure survival of offspring; discuss how breeding can contribute in preserving them in captivity; present the first data on the decline of these frogs, based on field studies in Ecuador and in Madagascar; and review four areas in which measures for the future protection of these endangered anurans must be taken.

* Faculty of Biology
University of Konstanz
Universitätstrasse 10
D–78435 Konstanz, Germany

Mailing address:
German Primate Center
Kellnerweg 4
D–37077 Göttingen, Germany

** Abraham-Wolf-Strasse 39
D-70597 Stuttgart 70, Germany

Acronyms used in this chapter:

AARA Association des Amis des Reserves d'Andasibe
CITES Convention on International Trade in Endangered Species
DFG Deutsche Forschungsgemeinschaft
DGHT Deutsche Gesellschaft für Herpetologie und Terrarienkunde
WWF World Wide Fund for Nature

TABLE 1. Major reproductive patterns of dart-poison frogs and Malagasy poison frogs.

I. REPRODUCTION RESTRICTED TO SEVERAL MONTHS PER YEAR

(1) *Reproductive success dependent upon location of oviposition sites on banks beside flowing water. Oviposition sites limited. Tadpole-rearing sites and food for tadpoles both unlimited.*

Males compete for calling sites and oviposition sites (such as dark caves or holes on the banks of rivulets or swamps) through the use of territorial calls and fighting. They attract females through the use of advertisement calling. Male sexual interference (that is, sperm competition) takes place during mating. Females do not compete with each other. Females recognize mates on the basis of advertisement calls and probably through visual cues (such as color and pattern). Females select mates on the basis of courtship activity and oviposition sites. There is no amplexus (see Figure 1 for courtship behavior). There is no transport of tadpoles. Tadpoles hatch after development of internal gills, and they wriggle into the water beneath the oviposition site on their own. Tadpoles are nonaggressive and are herbivorous. They are subject to the crowding effect (conspecific tadpole growth inhibited by high density). Taxa using this reproductive strategy are *Mantella aurantiaca, M. betsileo, M. crocea,* and *M. madagascariensis.*

II. REPRODUCTION THROUGHOUT THE YEAR

(2) *Reproductive success dependent upon proximity of oviposition sites to larger bodies of water or to flowing water, and on transport of tadpoles overland to water. Oviposition sites limited. Tadpole-rearing sites and food for tadpoles unlimited.*

Males compete for calling sites and oviposition sites (such as dark caves or holes on the banks of rivulets or swamps) through the use of territorial calls and fighting. They attract females through the use of advertisement calling. Male sexual interference (sperm competition) takes place during mating. Females do not compete with each other. Females recognize mates on the basis of advertisement calls, and select mates on the basis of courtship activity and oviposition site. Cephalic amplexus by males terminates courtship (see Figure 2 for courtship behavior). Brood-care by males includes clutch attendance, clutch moistening, and the transport of tadpoles to water. Tadpoles are nonaggressive and are omnivorous. They are subject to the crowding effect. Taxa using this reproductive strategy are *Epipedobates anthonyi, E. boulengeri–espinosai* complex, *E. tricolor, E. bilinguis, E. parvulus, E. pictus,* and *E. pulchripectus.*

(3) *Reproductive success independent of proximity of oviposition sites to larger bodies of water or to flowing water, but dependent on transport of tadpoles overland to smaller bodies of water. Oviposition sites unlimited. Tadpole-rearing sites and food for tadpoles limited.*

Males compete through advertisement calling; there is no further inter-male sexual competition for mates. Females compete with each other through sexual interference during mating by clasping and pressing down on courting females. Females recognize mates on the basis of advertisement calls. Males and females both choose mates. For males to lead females to oviposition sites, males require stroking by their mates. Females select mates according to the males' advertisement calling activity and/or courtship activity. There is no amplexus (see Figure 3 for courtship behavior). Brood-care by males includes irregular moistening of clutch and the transport of tadpoles to water. Tadpoles are omnivorous and are (a) nonaggressive (and subject to the crowding effect); or (b) aggressive in times of food scarcity. Taxa using reproductive substrategy (a) are *Phyllobates bicolor, P. terribilis, P. lugubris,* and *P. vittatus*; and taxa using substrategy (b) are *Dendrobates auratus, D. azureus, D. leucomelas,* and *D. tinctorius.*

(4) *Reproductive success independent of proximity of oviposition sites to larger bodies of water or to flowing water, but dependent on the transport of tadpoles to phytotelmata (plants with open water reservoirs). Oviposition sites unlimited. Tadpole-rearing sites and food for tadpoles limited.*

Male competition takes place through advertisement calling, fighting, and defense of territories with phytotelmata. Females recognize mates on the basis of advertisement calls and select mates on the basis of courtship activity and tadpole-rearing sites. Females do not compete with each other. There is no amplexus during mating (see Figure 4 for courtship behavior).

Substrategy (a) involves male brood-care, including irregular clutch-moistening and the transport of tadpoles to phytotelmata; the feeding of eggs to tadpoles by females is induced by the courtship activity of male at tadpole-rearing site; tadpoles are omnivorous and are aggressive. Substrategy (b) involves brood-care by females, including irregular clutch-moistening, the transport of single tadpoles to their own water-filled rearing site in phytotelmata, and weekly feeding of each larva by the female's own unfertilized eggs until metamorphosis is completed (at about 3 months); tadpoles are specialized egg eaters and are nonaggressive. Inhibition of conspecific tadpole growth if artificially transported to same water-filled axil of phytotelmata. Taxa using reproductive substrategy (a) are *Dendrobates imitator,* and taxa using substrategy (b) are *D. arboreus, D. granuliferus, D. histrionicus, D. lehmanni, D. pumilio,* and *D. speciosus.*

Reproductive Strategies of Dart-Poison Frogs and Malagasy Poison Frogs

Dart-poison frogs and Malagasy poison frogs display a prolonged breeding period in the field, as well as under captive conditions (Silverstone 1975; Wells 1981; Zimmermann 1986; Razarihelisoa 1988; Zimmermann and Zimmermann 1988; Summers 1992; Glaw and Vences 1992*a*). Whereas dart-poison frogs may reproduce throughout the whole year if sufficient food, oviposition sites, and mates are available, reproduction in Malagasy poison frogs is seasonally dependent and lasts for about four months, a period which corresponds to the rainy season in Madagascar. To date, there is no information on whether annual changes in photoperiodicity trigger reproduction, as occurs in other Malagasy vertebrates (Perret 1992). In contrast to most other anurans, dendrobatids and Malagasy poison frogs have developed highly complex reproductive strategies. Four major patterns can be found and these most probably have evolved as an adaptation to limited resources (Zimmermann and Zimmermann, in press; see Figures 1–4 and Table 1 for illustration).

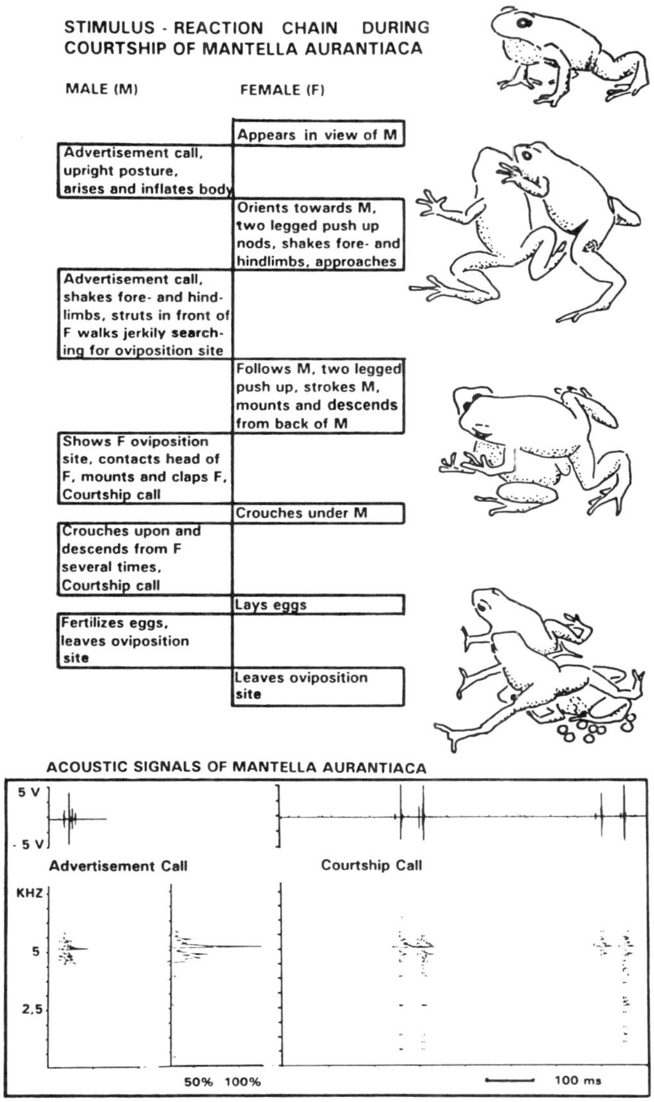

FIGURE 1. Schematic display of stimulus-reaction chain during courtship of *Mantella aurantiaca*. Advertisement calls are produced at a rate of one to three calls per second.

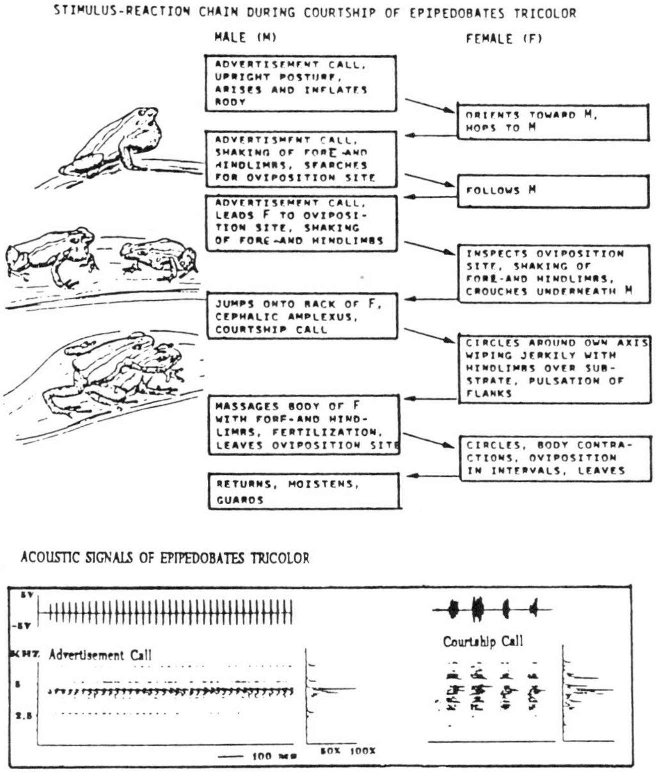

FIGURE 2. Schematic display of stimulus-reaction chain during courtship of *Epipedobates tricolor*.

Captive Breeding of Dart-Poison Frogs and Malagasy Poison Frogs

Ecological requirements should be considered when keeping dart-poison frogs and Malagasy poison frogs in captivity. Size of the terrarium depends upon the species, its size, its behavior, and the number of frogs maintained (Zimmermann 1979, 1982, 1986, 1992).

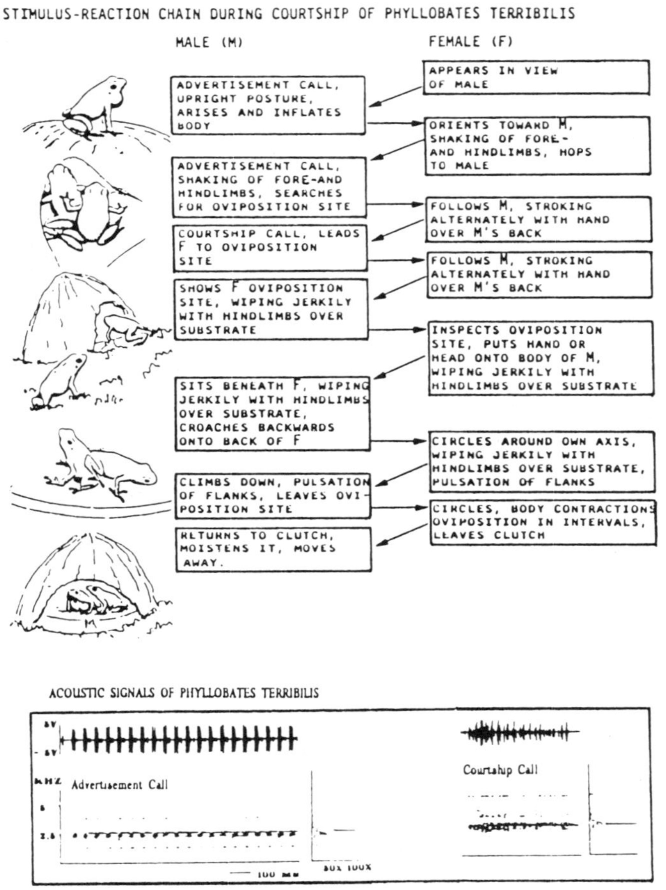

FIGURE 3. Schematic display of stimulus-reaction chain during courtship of *Phyllobates terribilis.*

Dart-Poison Frogs. Most dendrobatids may be maintained in small heterosexual groups of an equal sex ratio in warm, moist terrariums (see Figure 5 for illustration). The environment within the terrarium can be improved by covering the interior walls with cork and by planting tropical plants, such as commercially grown *Philodendron, Scindapsus, Ficus,* bromeliads, and orchids. Moist oak leaves or petri dishes under coconut halves turned cutside down are used by most dendrobatids as oviposition sites. Details of terrarium construction and furnishings are fully described by Zimmermann (1979, 1986, 1992). Dendrobatids of different species with distinct reproductive behavior may be kept and bred together if enough space, oviposition sites, and food is available. The maintenance of closely related taxa with similar reproductive behavior should be avoided, as hybridization resulting in sterile offspring may occur (Zimmermann and Zimmermann 1988).

Malagasy Poison Frogs. Aside from *Mantella laevigata* (Glaw and Vences 1992*b*), all the other known species of *Mantella* live on the banks of swamps or rivulets, where they oviposit in dark caves among roots or stones or in dark holes dug out by themselves or by crabs (H. Zimmermann, pers. observ.). They may be kept and bred successfully as heterosexual groups with an equal sex ratio in moist terraria. The terrarium should contain water to a depth of about 1 to 2 cm. The walls can be lined with sheets of cork that may or may not be in contact with the water. Several dark tunnels and small caves should be made available (see Figure 6 for illustration).

Males and females of most dendrobatids and of species in the genus *Mantella* are difficult to distinguish from one another as they are similar in size and morphology. Females may be somewhat larger

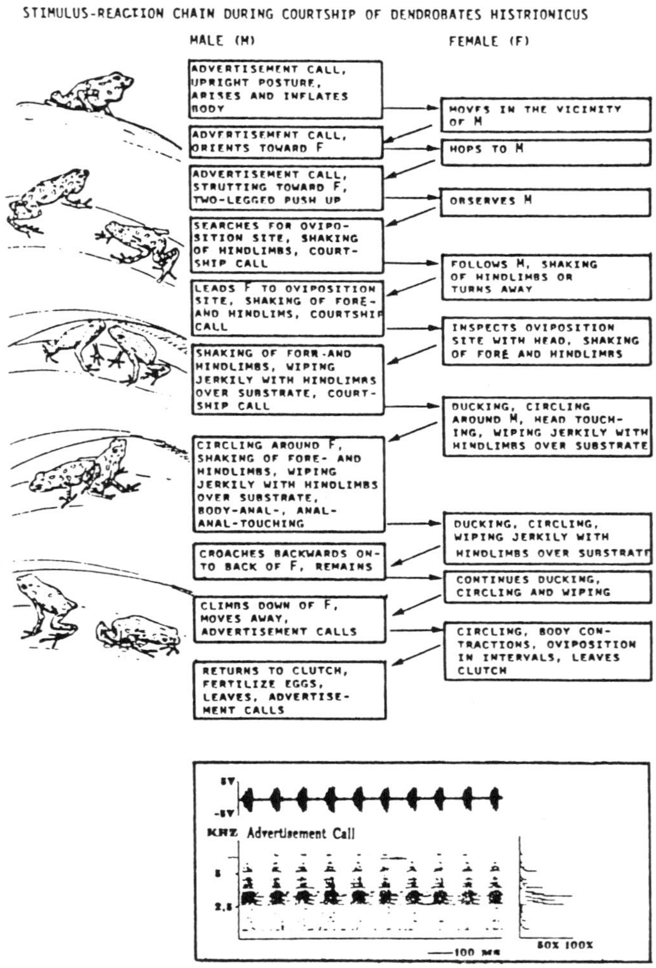

FIGURE 4. Schematic display of stimulus-reaction chain during courtship of *Dendrobates histrionicus.*

in size than males (see also Table 2). Males of some dendrobatid taxa may have broader digits than females and may possess vocal folds. The most reliable feature to separate mature males from females is calling behavior. Only adult males are able to produce calls, whereas females of all taxa are mute.

Clutches and/or tadpoles may be reared in a terrarium. Artificial rearing, however, usually is more successful. Clutches should be kept moist until the tadpoles hatch from their gelatinous covering, which takes about two to three weeks at temperatures between 20° and 25°C, irrespective of species. Conditions for raising tadpoles are dependent upon tadpole feeding, space requirements, and their level of aggression. Oak leaves or water plants should be provided as shelters for all taxa. Herbivorous tadpoles of the same and even of different clutches can be reared in the same water container by feeding them with algae and commercially available dry fish food. In omnivorous tadpoles, cannibalism may occur. Tadpoles often attack, kill, and feed on nonsibling larvae when they are put in the same water container. Weaker siblings may also be cannibalized in times of food scarcity. Omnivorous tadpoles should therefore be raised as sibling groups or singly and with an abundance of food (such as commercially available fish food). Tadpoles kept in breeding terraria feed on detritus and small invertebrates in their water sites. Oophagous tadpoles should be reared singly. A small drop of fresh chicken egg yolk should be provided every second day. The water has to be renewed about five hours after feeding. We have found that these tadpoles cannot digest any item other than chicken egg yolk or the eggs of their mother.

FIGURE 5. An example of a moist tropical terrarium for keeping and breeding of dart-poison frogs (specifically *Epipedobates tricolor*); here males defend small territories (marked by broken lines and by letters A to F), whereas females (symbolized by I, II, III) stay on the ground.

Tadpole development in dendrobatids and the genus *Mantella* ranges from between two and six months and depends upon the species, food availability, tadpole density, and temperature.

After metamorphosis is completed, froglets should be transferred to moist terraria. Froglets of the Malagasy poison frogs, as well as those of oophageous dendrobatid species, can be fed with springtails (*Collembola*). They can ingest newly hatched crickets and fruit flies after a few weeks, as do newly metamorphosed froglets of all the other taxa. Sexual maturity is reached 4 to 18 months after metamorphosis, depending on the species, food availability, frog density, and temperature.

Detailed information about the main reproductive characteristics of 35 dendrobatid species and four species of *Mantella*, acquired by breeding them in captivity, is summarized in Table 2.

Field Studies on Ecuadorian Dart-Poison Frogs and Malagasy Poison Frogs

In most Latin American countries, poison-dart frogs are protected by national nature-protection laws. Malagasy poison frogs are protected by the Malagasy nature-protection law, as are all Malagasy

FIGURE 6. Moist tropical terrarium for keeping and breeding of Malagasy poison frogs. Artificial caves are shown in cutaway views.

wildlife. In addition, trade in dendrobatid frogs of the genera *Dendrobates* and *Phyllobates* is regulated by CITES. In Germany, commercial trade in dendrobatids and Malagasy poison frogs is further restricted by national laws. How effective are these regulations? Do they really help to preserve endangered populations or species?

We have done field studies in Ecuador since 1984 and in Madagascar since 1988 with the primary aim of studying the ecology and behavior of these anurans in their natural environment. We report here on the field situation of two representative species: Ecuadorian populations of *Dendrobates histrionicus*, one of the most specialized of dendrobatids, which requires access to phytotelmata (water-filled bromeliads) for successful reproduction; and the endemic Malagasy Golden Frog (*Mantella aurantiaca*), which is known to occur at only a single locality within the eastern rain forest of Madagascar and which requires access to swamps of *Pandanus* for reproduction.

Dendrobates histrionicus is distributed in a large variety of morphs in tropical lowland rain forests of the western slopes of the Andes from Colombia to Ecuador. Both pristine rain forests and secondary growth vegetation with a high abundance of bromeliads typify their habitats (Zimmermann 1989, Zimmermann and Zimmermann, in press). Males are territorial and defend small areas (including some oviposition and tadpole-rearing sites) against other males. As with all of these anurans, males attract females by producing advertisement calls while sitting at exposed sites within their territories. Gravid females respond by phonotaxis. A highly complex courtship ceremony follows, often lasting several days. The male leads the female through his territory and passes several potential spawning (for example, tunnels made by leaves on the ground or in the vegetation) and tadpole-rearing sites (for example, bromeliads). The female inspects these sites and then often leaves to search for another male until she finally deposits her clutch.

The reason that the female is so particular may be because she presumably will have to spend a large amount of energy in brood care. She transports each tadpole individually on her back to a water-filled bromeliad leaf axil where she then feeds it regularly once a week with infertile eggs (about 3–7 eggs per tadpole) until metamorphosis is complete (Zimmermann and Zimmermann 1981, Zimmermann 1990). To feed the tadpole, she climbs backwards into the bromeliad leaf axil. When the tadpole recognizes its mother, it displays a begging behavior. The tadpole swims in a circle with trembling movements of the tail and then wriggles upon its mother's back again and again. These tactile stimulations seem to induce oviposition. Our laboratory studies show that a female may have five reproductive clutches per year and may care for as many as four tadpoles from one clutch simultaneously, each deposited in different axils of the same bromeliad.

This unique reproductive strategy, which is well adapted to phytotelmata, and the highly specialized oophageous larvae are very vulnerable to habitat disturbances by humans. We learned how dire this threat was during our field studies on dart-poison frogs in Ecuador. The most southerly distribution of

TABLE 2. Synopsis of breeding data on dart-poison and Malagasy poison frogs. Personal observations by the authors are marked "pers. obs."

Species	Mean length adults (mm) Male	Mean length adults (mm) Female	Age at sexual maturity (in months)	Longevity (in years)	Eggs per clutch (maximum number)	References
			DENDROBATIDAE			
Colostethus palmatus	27	35	—	—	29	1
saulii	17	19	—	—	30	2
species	23	26	—	—	11	pers. obs.
talamancae	22	28	12	—	33	3
trinitatis	23	31	7	—	35	4, pers. obs.
Allobates femoralis	28	33	10	6	20	5, pers. obs.
Dendrobates arboreus	21	22	—	—	7	6
auratus	28	30	15	6	8	7, 8, 9
azureus	33	37	10	—	5	7,10
fantasticus	23	25	6	—	4	11, pers. obs.
histrionicus	28	30	10	4	9	12
imitator	17	19	8	3	2	13, 14, 15
lehmanni	28	30	10	4	9	12
leucomelas	30	32	16	10	8	16
pumilio	19	21	10	4	9	17, 18, pers. obs.
"quinquevittatus"	15	16	8	3	9	19, 20, 21
reticulatus	14	16	7	3	2	15, 20
speciosus	27	29	—	—	9	22, 23, pers. obs.
tinctorius	38	40	—	11	7	7, 24, 25, pers. obs.
variabilis	16	17	8	3	6	14, 15, 26
Epipedobates anthonyi	21	23	11	4	25	3, 15
azureiventris	24	27	—	—	14	27
"boulengeri"	21	23	12	4	20	15, pers. obs.
bilinguis	18	20	—	—	13	28, 29
parvulus	23	25	12	—	16	29, pers. obs.
pictus	19	21	10	3	30	15, 29, pers. obs.
pulchripectus	23	25	12	5	20	15, 29, pers. obs.
tricolor	22	26	9	13	30	30, 31
Phobobates bassleri	34	40	—	—	35	32, pers. obs.
silverstonei	38	40	—	—	—	33, pers. obs.
trivittatus	35	40	—	—	34	34, pers. obs.
Phyllobates bicolor	40	41	—	—	17	3, 15
lugubris	23	25	10	5	15	35, 15
terribilis	32	35	12	8	20	36, 37, 38
vittatus	26	29	10	5	15	15, 35, 39
			RANIDAE: MANTELLINAE			
Mantella aurantiaca	20	23	12	6	140	40
crocea	18	23	11	4	110	40, pers. obs.
madagascariensis	22	25	—	4	49	41, pers. obs.
viridis	24	30	—	5	—	40, pers. obs.

REFERENCES: 1. Lüddecke 1974; 2. E. Schröder, pers. comm.; 3. Zimmermann 1989; 4. Krintler 1982; 5. Weygoldt 1980*a*; 6. Jungfer 1988; 7. Polder 1973–1975; 8. Senfft 1936; 9. Zimmermann 1974; 10. Kneller 1982*b*; 11. Kneller 1983; 12. Zimmermann and Zimmermann 1981; 13. Kneller 1982*a*; 14. Schulte 1986; 15. Zimmermann and Zimmermann 1988; 16. Zimmermann and Zimmermann 1980; 17. Graeff and Schulte 1980; 18. Weygoldt 1980*b*; 19. Lescure and Bechter 1982; 20. Zimmermann and Zimmermann 1984; 21. Schulte 1981*b*; 22. Beutelschiess and Beutelschiess 1983; 23. Jungfer 1985; 24. Ensinck 1980; 25. Weygoldt 1982; 26. Zimmermann and Zimmermann, in press; 27. Kneller and Henle 1985; 28. Jungfer 1989; 29. Weygoldt 1983; 30. Schmidt 1981; 31. Zimmermann 1983; 32. Schulte 1981*a*; 33. Schulte 1979; 34. Henzl 1986; 35. Zimmermann 1982; 36. Myers et al. 1978; 37. Zimmermann and Zimmermann 1985; 38. Beutelschiess and Beutelschiess 1986; 39. Broodman 1974; 40. Zimmermann 1992; 41. Zimmermann 1986.

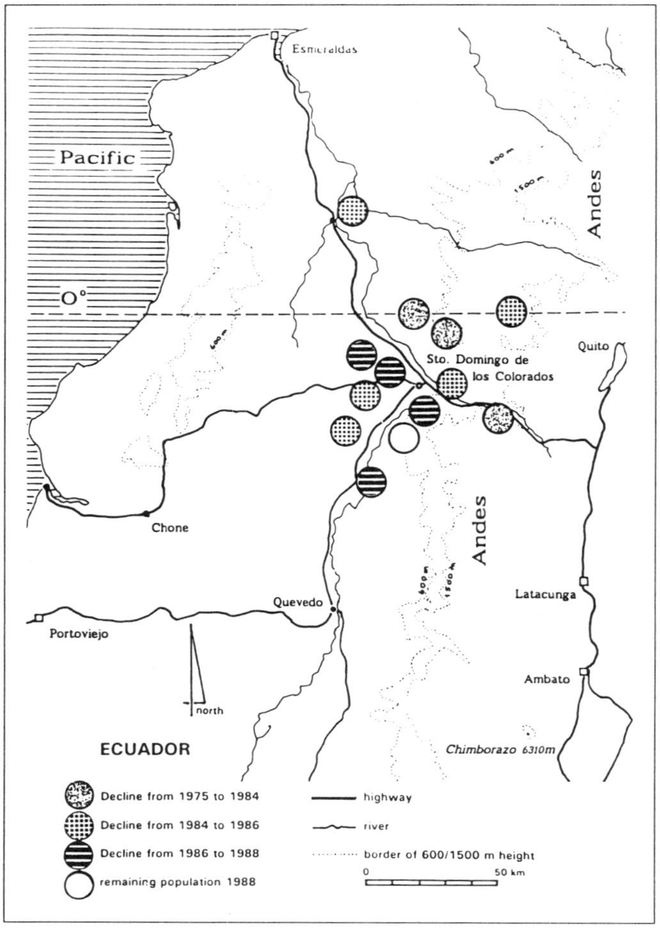

FIGURE 7. Map illustrating the decline of populations of *Dendrobates histrionicus* around Santo Domingo de los Colorados, Province Pichincha, Ecuador. Thirteen populations marked by circles were recorded by Silverstone in 1975. Today, all are gone but one.

this interesting species occurs south of the small town of Santo Domingo de los Colorados, Pichincha Province, Ecuador. *D. histrionicus* shares its habitat with another dendrobatid frog, a species of the *Epipedobates boulengeri–espinoisai* complex. Whereas the former inhabits bushes and trees covered with bromeliads, the latter lives on the ground, preferring areas covered by stones and dead leaves. We intended to study populations of *D. histrionicus* in the same habitats over several years and had selected sites where intact breeding populations were found by Silverstone in 1975 (Zimmermann 1989; see also Figure 7). When we started our field study in 1984, however, three of the 13 populations described by Silverstone had disappeared completely. Two years later, in 1986, an additional five populations were decimated, another was gone two years later in 1988, and a further four populations were finally lost. A single population, with its self-sustaining capacity probably endangered, remained isolated in oil palm monocultures. The Pacific tropical wet-forest region of Ecuador formerly supported a diverse biota rich in endemic species (Dodson and Gentry 1978). It is now the norm that pristine forests are logged. These areas, together with agricultural land that was traditionally used by the native people, have been converted almost completely into monocultures, with pineapple, banana, or oil palm plantations erasing the original habitat of almost all of the original rain forest–adapted wildlife. Reintroduction of captive-bred frogs in such cases would be a hopeless project.

Malagasy Golden Frogs (*Mantella aurantiaca*), with their bright yellow to red color, are one of the most spectacular Malagasy frogs. They inhabit a small area in the pristine montane forest in eastern Madagascar, around the village of Andasibe. During the rainy season (from about December to March), males defend small calling sites with nearby oviposition caves at the border of a swampy area called "Marais de Torotorofotsy." Since 1988, field studies have been conducted to gain more information about the geographic range, biology, and status of this species. The data collected on its reproduction confirmed earlier data gained by breeding Malagasy Golden Frogs in captivity (see Zimmermann 1992 for details).

Furthermore, the data revealed that Malagasy Golden Frogs are indeed restricted to a limited range (Figure 8), where they are concentrated on *Pandanus* vegetation. Their exploitation for trade might cause an enormous threat to these populations. Likewise, there is an additional threat due to the rapid destruction of the forest area around Andasibe. According to Green and Sussman (1990), much of this forest region will be destroyed during the next three decades if clearing activities continue at the current pace. In addition, the swamp of *Pandanus* in the vicinity of the village of Andasibe is to be drained (H. Zimmermann, pers. observ.). As a consequence, the Malagasy Golden Frog populations, which formerly were distributed along the border of the swamp of Torotorofotsy (Arnoult 1966) are now isolated from each other and clumped as remnants of the swamp of *Pandanus* in their northeastern range. Reintroduction in this case is also not feasible, because there are no habitats left in which Malagasy Golden Frogs could survive.

These two examples illustrate that laws for the protection of species and for trade regulation are useful as a preliminary step in the conservation of species. Effective species protection requires much more, however, such as a detailed knowledge about the life history and ecosystem of the species studied, as well as—most importantly—habitat protection in harmony with the needs of the indigenous human population.

Suggestions for Effective Protection

Declines in tropical frog populations can be found almost everywhere around the globe, although in most cases reliable, long-term monitoring studies are usually lacking (Baringa 1990; Blaustein and Wake 1990; Wake 1991). One major cause for this decline appears to be the enormous growth of the human population with all its attendant side effects on the world's atmosphere and ecosystem. Immediate action for the protection of as much of the biodiversity as possible is urgently needed. It is important not only for ethical reasons, but also for our own survival in the future as part of the ecosystem of this planet. Therefore, collaborative efforts are required involving private, scientific, and political groups.

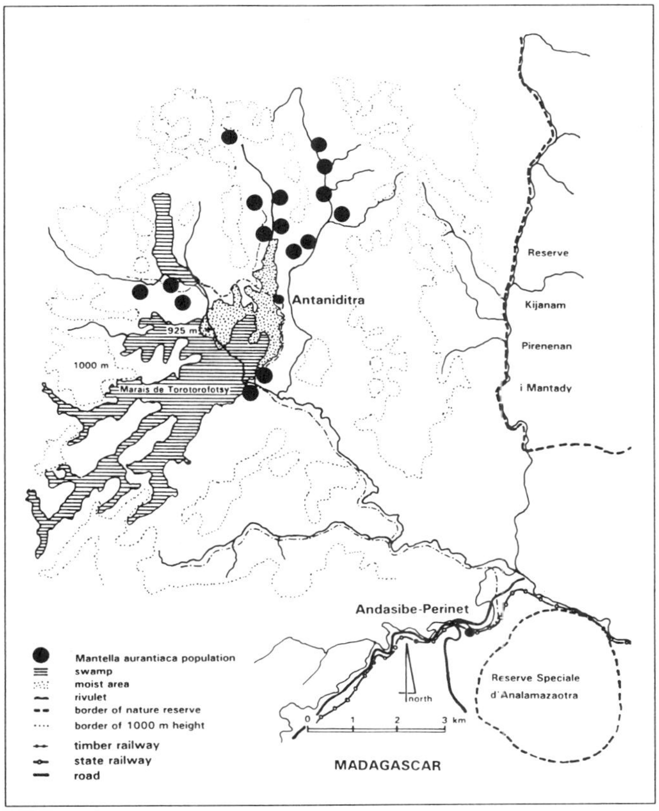

FIGURE 8. Map illustrating the distribution of populations of the Malagasy Golden Frog (*Mantella aurantiaca*) in the swamp remnants of *Pandanus* of the "Marais de Torotorofotsy," near the village of Andasibe, eastern Madagascar, in 1993. The whole area south of these populations has had its habitats of autochthonous forest cleared out.

What has been done and what must be done for effective protection of tropical wildlife, such as the endangered neotropical dart-poison frogs and Malagasy poison frogs? Four major actions are being undertaken simultaneously, as follows.

Habitat Protection

Habitat protection is a vital need, and requires the largest amount of landscape possible and the prospect of creating a network of protected areas. In Ecuador and Colombia, private individuals, nature conservation institutions, the Awa Indians, and the national governments are collaborating to protect a 530,000 ha area of pristine rain forest with a rich fauna and flora (Tobar Donoso Project), including *Dendrobates histrionicus.*

In Madagascar, the Deutsche Gesellschaft für Herpetologie und Terrarienkunde (DGHT) Anuran Specialist Group is working with World Wide Fund for Nature (WWF)–Madagascar and other nature-protection agencies (for example, Association des Amis des Reserves d'Andasibe [AARA]), as well as with the government and the indigenous population to enlarge the nature reserve "Kijanam Pirenenan i Mantady" towards the west, so that the remnants of the Malagasy Golden Frog habitats will be protected (Interim Report, 1992, of the DGHT Anuran Specialist Group. "Species Survival Project, Malagasy Golden Frog").

Long-Term Field Studies

Long-term field studies on the life history, geographic distribution, population variability, and biodiversity of habitats (managed by various scientific and private groups) have just begun to increase our knowledge of the life history of tropical frogs (Schlüter 1984; Donnelly 1989; Andreone 1991; E. Samec, pers. comm. 1992; Glaw and Vences 1992*a*:

Brust 1993). Such data will give us the ability to assess, for example, the degree of decline and the disappearance of populations and their possible causes, and to improve conservation programs for these frogs in the near future.

Breeding Programs

Breeding programs for dendrobatids and Malagasy poison frogs were initiated and are presently coordinated by species coordinators of the DGHT Anuran Specialist Group. Their aim is to enlarge our present knowledge of the taxonomy, behavior, physiology, genetics, and breeding of these frogs, and to enhance the possibility for exchanging animals of known origin for the establishment of self-sustaining populations in captivity.

Figure 9 demonstrates an example of the breeding records of members of this group. From 1989 to 1991, more than 3,900 individuals of 27 different species of dendrobatids and more than 340 individuals of two different species of *Mantella* were bred successfully and most dendrobatids were bred over multiple captive generations.

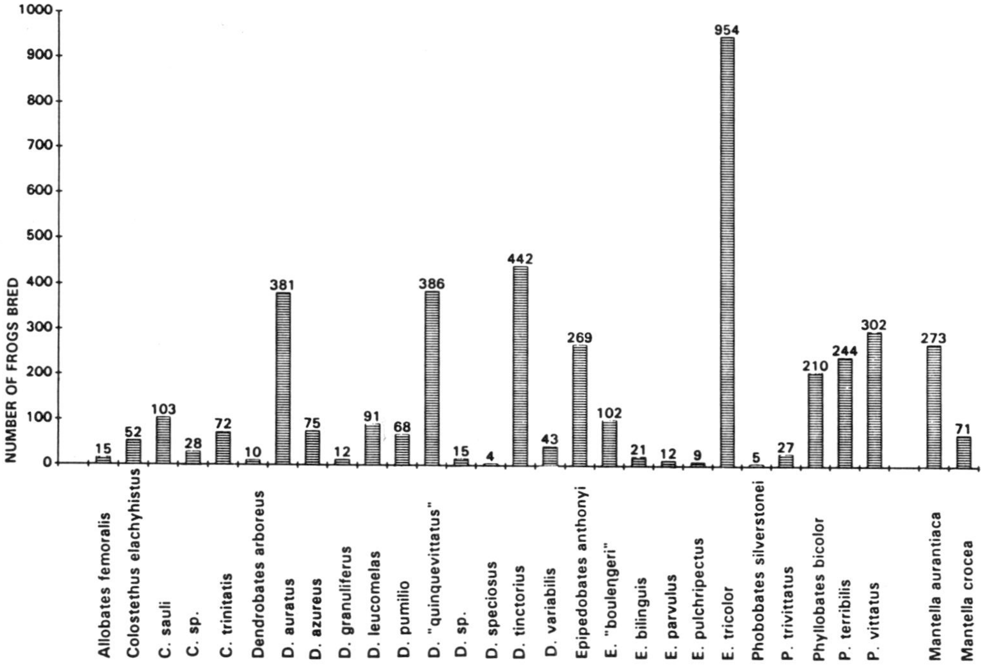

FIGURE 9. Review of 27 species of dart-poison frogs and of two species of Malagasy poison frogs (*Mantella*) bred by members of the DGHT Anuran Specialist Group, 1989–1991.

Regulation of Trade

Efforts should be undertaken to regulate the trade in all dendrobatid frogs and all Malagasy poison frogs. Species with very restricted geographic ranges (for example, *Mantella aurantiaca*) should be put on Appendix I of CITES. Limited capture of wildborn specimens should be possible for scientific purposes as well as for establishing breeding colonies by responsible zoos, laboratories, and amateur breeders.

Only if these efforts are strengthened and financially supported will these unique poison frogs of the tropics survive.

Summary

Reproductive strategies, breeding, and conservation of tropical frogs are outlined here using case studies of neotropical poison-dart frogs (Dendrobatidae) and Malagasy poison frogs (Ranidae: Mantellinae). Husbandry and captive breeding of 35 dendrobatid and four matelline species are reviewed as are their major reproductive patterns. First data on the decline of these frogs are presented, based on field studies in Ecuador and in Madagascar. Measures for future protection require habitat protection, long-term field studies, establishment of breeding programs, and regulation of trade.

Acknowledgments

We wish to express sincere thanks for financial or logistical support during our studies to the Society for the Study of Amphibians and Reptiles, the Deutsche Forschungsgemeinschaft (DFG), the participants of the symposium at Pennsylvania State University (August 1991) for stimulating discussions, the DGHT Anuran Specialist Group and the Bundesverband für fachgerechten Natur- und

Artenschutz for supporting field studies in Madagascar, the Ministere de la Production Animal et des Eaux et Forêts (Antananarivo and Andasibe, Madagascar) for permission to conduct field studies, E. del Pino and Dr. T. de Vries (Universidad Católica del Ecuador, Quito) and the Colorado Indians (Chigüilpe, Ecuador) for their help during our field studies in their country, the International Union for the Conservation of Nature (Gland, Switzerland), WWF–Madagascar, and AARA for their support in Madagascar, and members of the DGHT Anuran Specialist Group for fruitful collaboration and stimulating discussion.

We would also like to thank Mauvis Gore for polishing the English version of this manuscript. The paper also profited from comments by and discussions with Peter Narins, James B. Murphy, Kraig Adler, and two anonymous reviewers.

Literature Cited

Andreone, F. 1991. Conservation aspects of the herpetofauna of Malagasy rain forests. Zool. Soc. "La Torbiera" Sci. Rep., 1: 1–45.

Arnoult, J. 1966. Contribution à l'étude de batraciens de Madagascar. Écologie et développement de *Mantella aurantiaca* Mocquard, 1900. Bull. Mus. Hist. Nat. Paris, 37: 931–940.

Barinaga, M. 1990. Where have all the froggies gone? Science, 247: 1033–1034.

Beutelschiess, J., and C. Beutelschiess. 1983. *Dendrobates speciosus*– ein Rubin im Terrarium. Herpetofauna, 4: 6–8.

—. 1986. Beobachtungen an *Phyllobates terribilis* im Terrarium. Sauria, 8: 7–11.

Blaustein, A. R., and D. B. Wake. 1990. Declining amphibian populations: a global phenomenon? Trends Ecol. Evol., 5: 203–204.

Broodmann, D. 1974. Die Pflege und Zucht von *Phyllobates lugubris*. Aquar. Terrar. Zeitschr., 27: 136–141.

Brust, D. G. 1993. Maternal brood care by *Dendrobates pumilio*: a frog that feeds its young. Jour. Herpetol., 27: 96–98.

Daly, J. W., C. W. Myers, and N. Whittaker. 1987. Further classification of skin alkaloids from neotropical poison frogs with a general survey of toxic/noxious substances in the Amphibia. Toxicon, 25: 1023–1095.

Dodson C. H., and A. H. Gentry. 1978. Flora of the Rio Palenque Science Center, Los Rios, Ecuador. Selbyana, 4: 1–628.

Donnelly, M. A. 1989. Effects of reproductive resource supplementation on space-use patterns in *Dendrobates pumilio*. Oecologia, 81: 212–218.

Duellman, W. E., and L. Trueb. 1986 (1985). Biology of Amphibians. McGraw Hill, New York. xii, 670 pages.

Edwards, M. W., J. W. Daly, and C. W. Myers. 1988. Alkaloids from Panamanian poison frog, *Dendrobates speciosus*. Jour. Natur. Prod., 51: 1188–1197.

Ensinck, F. H. 1980. De kweek van *Dendrobates tinctorius*. Lacerta, 38: 102–106.

Glaw, F., and M. Vences. 1992*a*. A Field Guide to the Amphibians and Reptiles of Madagascar. M. Vences and F. Glaw Verlags GbR, Cologne. xii, 331 pages.

—. 1992*b*. Zur Biologie, Biometrie und Färbung bei *Mantella laevigata*. Sauria, 14: 25–29.

Graeff, D., and R. Schulte. 1980. Neue Erkenntnisse zur Brutbiologie von *Dendrobates pumilio*. Herpetofauna, 2: 17–23.

Green, G. M., and R. W. Sussman. 1990. Deforestation history of the eastern rain forests of Madagascar from satellite images. Science, 248: 212–215.

Henzl, M. 1986. Freilandstudie an *Dendrobates trivittatus* in Peru. Jahrestagung der Deutschen Gesellschaft für Herpetologie und Terrarienkunde, Basel. Rundbrief, 91: 2.

Hoogmoed, M. S. 1969. Notes on the herpetofauna of Surinam III. Zool. Meded., 12: 133–141.

Jungfer, K. H. 1985. Beitrag zur Kenntnis von *Dendrobates speciosus*. Salamandra, 21: 263–280.

—. 1988. Froschlurche von Fortuna, Panama. herpetofauna, 56: 6—12.

—. 1989. Pfeilgiftfrösche der Gattung *Epipedobates* mit rot granuliertem Rücken aus dem Oriente von Ecuador und Peru. Salamandra, 25: 81–98.

Kneller, M. 1982*a*. Die Fortpflanzung von *Dendrobates reticulatus* im natürlichen Lebensraum und im Terrarium. Das Aquarium, 135: 148–151.

—. 1982*b*. Erfolgreiche Nachzucht des blauen Pfeilgiftfrosches *Dendrobates azureus* (Hoogmoed, 1969). Herpetofauna, 4: 6–9.

—. 1983. Beobachtungen an *Dendrobates fantasticus* in natürlichen Lebensraum und im Terrarium. Herpetofauna, 5: 15–18.

Kneller, M., and K. Henle. 1985. Ein neuer Blattsteigerfrosch (Salientia: Dendrobatidae: *Phyllobates*) aus Peru. Salamandra, 21: 62–69.

Krintler, K. 1982. *Colostethus trinitatis*, ein interessanter Frosch von der Insel Tobago. Herpetofauna, 4: 22–26.

Lescure, J., and R. Bechter. 1982. Le comportment de reproduction en captivité et la polymorphisme de *Dendrobates quinquevittatus* Steindachner (Amphibia, Anura, Dendrobatidae). Rev. Fr. Aquariol., 8(1981): 107–118.

Lüddecke, H. 1974. Ethologische Untersuchungen zur Fortpflanzung von *Phyllobates palmatus*. Doctoral Dissertation, University of Mainz. 206 pages.

Myers, C. W., J. W. Daly, and B. Malkin. 1978. A dangerous toxic new frog (*Phyllobates*) used by Embera Indians of western Colombia, with discussion of blowgun fabrication and dart poisoning. Bull. Amer. Mus. Nat. Hist., 161: 307–365.

Myers, N. 1985. Die Sinkende Arche. Georg Westermann, Braunschweig. xii, 252 pages.

Perret, M. 1992. Environmental and social determinants of sexual function in the male lesser mouse lemur (*Microcebus murinus*). Folia Primatol., 59: 1–25.

Polder, W. N. 1973–1975. Pflege und Fortpflanzung von *Dendrobates azureus* und anderer Dendrobatiden. Aquar. Terrar. Zeitschr., 1: 28–32; 7: 244–249; 9: 319–323; 11: 389–392; 12: 424–428.

Razarihelisoa, M. 1988. Ecologie et éthologie des amphibiens terrestres et en doges dans differents types d'écosystèmes à Madagascar, p. 41–45. *In* L. Racotovao, V. Barre, and J. Sayer (eds.), L'Équilibre des Ecosystèmes Forestiers à Madagascar. Actes d'un Séminaire International. International Union for the Conservation of Nature and Natural Resources, Gland, Switzerland.

Schlüter, A. 1984. Ökologische Untersuchungen an einem Stillgewässer im tropischen Regenwald von Peru unter besonderer Berücksichtigung der Amphibien. Doctoral Dissertation, Univ. Hamburg. 300 pages.

Schmidt, U. 1981. *Dendrobates tricolor* (Boulenger 1899)–eine wertvolle Bereicherung unserer Tropenterrarien. Herpetofauna, 11: 18–24.

Schulte, R. 1979. *Dendrobates silverstonei* (Myers und Daly, 1979), ein neuer Giftfrosch aus Peru. Herpetofauna, 1: 24–30.

—. 1981*a*. *Dendrobates bassleri*–Freilandbeobachtungen, Haltung und Zucht. Herpetofauna, 3: 23–28.

—. 1981*b*. *Dendrobates quinquevittatus*; Ökologie, Haltung und Zucht. Herpetofauna, 3: 24–28.

—. 1986. Eine neue *Dendrobates*-Art aus Ostperu (Amphibia: Salientia: Dendrobatidae). Sauria, 8: 11–20.

Senfft, W. 1936. Das Brutgeschäft des Baumsteigerfrosches (*Dendrobates auratus* Girard) in Gefangenschaft. Zool. Gart., 8: 122–131.

Silverstone, P. A. 1975. A revision of the poison-arrow frogs of the genus *Dendrobates* Wagler. Bull. Los Angeles County Mus. Nat. Hist., 21: 1–55.

Summers, K. 1992. Dart-poison frogs and the control of sexual selection. Ethology, 91: 89–107.

Wake, D. B. 1991. Declining amphibian populations. Science, 253: 860.

Wells, K. D. 1981. Parental behavior of male and female frogs, p. 184–197. *In* R. D. Alexander and D. Tinkle (eds.), Natural Selection and Social Behavior. Chiron Press, New York.

Weygoldt, P. 1980*a*. Zur Fortpflanzungsbiologie von *Phyllobates femoralis* (Boulenger) im Terrarium (Amphibia: Salientia: Dendrobatidae). Salamandra, 16: 215–226.

—. 1980*b*. Complex brood care and reproductive behavior in captive poison-arrow frogs, *Dendrobates pumilio* O. Schmidt. Behav. Ecol. Sociobiol., 7: 329–332.

—. 1982. Durch Nachzucht erhalten: der Färberfrosch *Dendrobates tinctorius*. Aquar.-Mag., 16: 6–13.

—. 1983. Durch Nachzucht erhalten: drei Arten aus der *Phyllobates pictus* Gruppe. Aquar.- Mag., 17: 566–572.

Zimmermann, E. 1986. Breeding Terrarium Animals. T.F.H. Publ., Neptune City, New Jersey. 384 pages.

—. 1990. Behavioral signals and reproduction modes in the neotropical frog family Dendrobatidae, p. 61–73. *In* W. Hanke (ed.), Biology and Physiology of Amphibians. Gustav Fischer, New York.

Zimmermann, E., and H. Zimmermann 1982. Soziale Aktionen, Brutpflege und Zucht des Pfeilgiftfrosches *Dendrobates histrionicus*. Salamandra, 18: 150–167.

—. In press. Pfeilgiftfrösche- Tropische Froschlurche mit aussergewöhnlichem Fortpflanzungsverhalten. Naturwiss. Rundschau.

Zimmermann, H. 1974. Die Aufzucht des Goldbaumsteigers *Dendrobates auratus*. Aquar.-Mag., 8: 526–531.

—. 1979. Tropical Frogs. T.F.H. Publ., Neptune City, New Jersey. 93 pages.

—. 1982. Durch Nachzucht erhalten: *Phyllobates vittatus* und P. *lugubris*. Aquar.-Mag., 16: 109–112.

—. 1983. Durch Nachzucht erhalten: *Phyllobates tricolor*. Aquar.-Mag., 17: 17–22.

—. 1989. Conservation studies on the dart-poison frogs Dendrobatidae in the field and in captivity. Internatl. Zoo Yearbook, 28: 31–44.

—. 1992. Nachzucht und Schutz von *Mantella crocea*, *Mantella viridis* und des madagassischen Goldfröschchens *Mantella aurantiaca*. Zeitschr. Kölner Zoo, 35: 165–171.

Zimmermann, H., and S. Hetz. 1992. Vorläufige Bestandsaufnahme und Kartierung des gefährdeten Goldfröschchens, *Mantella aurantiaca*, im tropischen Regenwald Ost-Madagaskars. Herpetofauna, 14: 33–34.

Zimmermann, H., and E. Zimmermann. 1980: Durch Nachzucht erhalten: der Baumsteiger *Dendrobates leucomelas*. Aquar.-Mag., 14: 211–217.

—. 1981. Sozialverhalten, Fortpflanzungsverhalten und Zucht der Färberfrösche *Dendrobates histrionicus* und *D. lehmanni* sowie einiger anderer Dendrobatiden. Zeitschr. Kölner Zoo, 24: 83–99.

—. 1984. Durch Nachzucht erhalten: Baumsteigerfrösche *Dendrobates quinquevittatus* und *D. reticulatus*. Aquar.-Mag., 18: 35–41.

—. 1985. Zur Fortpflanzungsstrategie des Pfeilgiftfrosches *Phyllobates terribilis* Myers, Daly and Malkin, 1978. Salamandra, 21: 281–297.

—. 1988. Etho-taxonomie und zoogeographische Artengruppenbildung bei Pfeilgiftfröschen (Anura: Dendrobatidae). Salamandra, 24: 125–160.

Zimmermann, E., and H. Zimmermann. 1994. Reproductive strategies, breeding, and conservation of tropical frogs: dart-poison frogs and Malagasy poison frogs, p. 255–266. *In* J. B. Murphy, K. Adler, and J. T. Collins (eds.), Captive Management and Conservation of Amphibians and Reptiles. Society for the Study of Amphibians and Reptiles, Ithaca (New York). Contributions to Herpetology, volume 11.

Captive Management and Breeding of Dendrobatid and Neotropical Hylid Frogs at the National Aquarium in Baltimore

John F. Cover, Jr.,* Sandra L. Barnett,* and Robin L. Saunders*,**

Introduction

Dendrobatid frogs (Family Dendrobatidae) are generally terrestrial and diurnal, and often have high population densities in the wild (Myers and Daly 1976). These attributes make them well-suited for field work, and easily caught for captive studies. Moreover, the striking colors of many dendrobatids have long made them popular both with hobbyists and zoos and aquariums. Not surprisingly, there is a large body of literature on the captive care and breeding of the dendrobatids (Cover and Wisnieski 1989; Heselhaus 1988; Schulte 1980; Senfft 1936; Weygoldt 1980, 1984; Zimmermann 1986; Zimmermann 1989; Zimmermann and Zimmermann 1981).

In contrast, hylid frogs (Family Hylidae) are primarily nocturnal and arboreal. Females can be particularly difficult to find because they do not advertise their position by calling as do males. The rarity of females in captive collections, as well as the difficulty in keeping and breeding some species, may explain the paucity of literature on the husbandry of this family of frogs (Miller 1984; Odum et al. 1984; Schulte 1980; Zimmermann 1986).

In this chapter, we discuss techniques currently used at the National Aquarium in Baltimore (NAIB) to maintain and breed dendrobatid and neotropical hylids. To date, we have kept 25 species of dendrobatids, with repeated, successful captive breeding of 19 species (a 20th species, *Dendrobates granuliferus*, has produced only one offspring). We have kept 21 species of neotropical hylids, with successful breeding in four of the five species in which breeding has been attempted (Tables 1 and 2).

Husbandry Procedures

Housing

Proper cage enrichment is a key factor in the successful maintenance and breeding of dendrobatids and hylids. Cover and Wisnieski (1989) provide a detailed description of caging and lighting for dendrobatids at NAIB (Figure 1). Similarly enriched, but larger (greater than 40 cm in height) enclosures are utilized for hylid frogs.

Live, broadleaf potted plants (including *Aglaonema commutatum, A. roebelini, Philodendron oxycardium, Epipremnum aureum, Peperomia obtusifolia, Spathiphyllum* sp., and *Syngonium podophyllum*), various species of bromeliads (for obligate oophagous dendrobatids), cork bark, and vines and branches (for hylids) are added to the enclosures to provide hiding and perching areas, and oviposition sites. Care is taken to intersperse relatively open areas among well-planted ones so that the frogs can easily hunt their insect prey. Breeding huts, made from the plastic bottoms of two-liter soda bottles, are added to dendrobatid tanks for use in hiding and oviposition (Cover and Wisnieski 1989).

---

*National Aquarium in Baltimore
501 East Pratt Street, Pier 1
Baltimore, Maryland 21202, USA

***Current address:*
Cincinnati Zoo and Botanical Gardens
3400 Vine Street
Cincinnati, Ohio 45220, USA

Acronyms used in this chapter:

NAIB	National Aquarium in Baltimore
OD	Outside diameter

Lighting

The tanks are illuminated with all-aluminum fluorescent light fixtures fitted with polished aluminum reflectors (Duro-Test Lighting, Secaucus, New Jersey). Each fixture holds two lights—one 40-watt full-spectrum light (Vita-Lite, Duro-Test Corp., Fairfield, New Jersey) and one 40-watt ultraviolet light (Black Light, General Electric, Cleveland, Ohio). The lights are located approximately 8 cm above the screened top of the frog enclosures. The lighting is controlled by timers, with a 12-hour on-off cycle. A skylight provides additional light in the main breeding room.

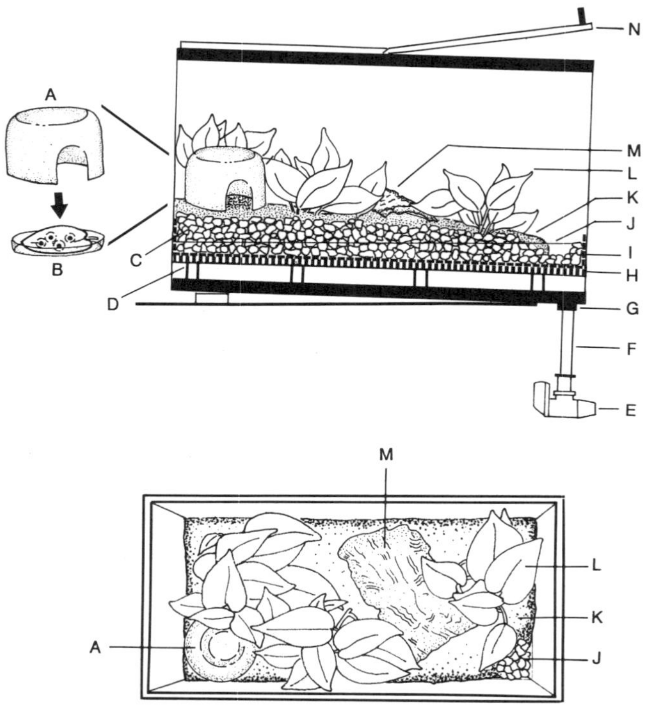

FIGURE 1. Lateral (upper) and aerial (lower) views of a 38-liter frog enclosure at National Aquarium in Baltimore. (A) plastic hiding box/breeding hut, (B) petri dish with egg-covered plastic leaf, (C) pea gravel, (D) plastic bio-filter ring (2.5 cm OD [outside diameter]), (E) plastic stopcock, (F) soft plastic tubing (1.8 cm OD), (G) plastic drain nipple (2.5 cm OD), (H) plastic "egg-crate" grate, (I) fiberglass window screening, (J) shallow pool located over front corner drain, (K) moist sheet moss, (L) live, potted plant with base of pot resting on fiberglass screening, (M) cork bark cave/feeding platform, (N) plastic-hinged, vinyl-framed lid inset with fiberglass screening. Notice in upper figure that the aquarium is tipped toward the drain end by means of a small block beneath the opposite end.

Temperature

The breeding colony is divided between two rooms. Lowland species of frogs, regardless of age, and immature frogs of most highland species are kept in the "warm" room (main breeding room), which ranges in temperature from 23–26°C, depending on the time of day and the season. Highland species are kept in an air-conditioned room maintained at 23°C. With the exception of several highland species of dendrobatids (*Dendrobates speciosus, Epipedobates espinosai, E. tricolor*), all frog eggs are incubated in the warmer room, and their larvae are raised there. Eggs of some species, which thrive as adults in the cooler room (*Dendrobates fantasticus, D. imitator*), fail to hatch or have exceedingly prolonged development time when incubated in the cooler room.

Misting

The frog enclosures are misted daily from a hose. They are completely emptied through the floor drain (Figure 1) and rinsed once a week.

The water in our frog rooms is municipal water from local reservoirs, delivered at 23°C. Chlorine is removed by passing the water through four 74-cm Chemical Filters (Lifegard model AF–93T, Rainbow Plastics Filter Div., El Monte, California) packed with activated charcoal.

Food and Feeding

Stomach-content analyses of wild-caught dendrobatids suggest that they feed on a wide variety of small invertebrates, primarily ants (Donnelly 1991; Silverstone 1975, 1976). At NAIB, adult dendrobatids are fed every other day a diet that alternates between newly hatched to one-week-old crickets (*Acheta domestica*) and flightless fruitflies (*Drosophila* spp.). Immature dendrobatids and adults housed in large groups are fed daily, and the diet alternates between crickets and fruitflies. Very small dendrobatid froglets (approximately 10 mm in snout-vent length) are housed on leaf litter, which is collected locally. The litter naturally contains an array of tiny invertebrates, such as springtails (Order Collembola), which the froglets eat.

Crickets are both cultured in-house and purchased from a commercial supplier. The crickets are maintained on a high-calcium (8%) commercial cricket diet (Zeigler Brothers, Inc., Gardners, Pennsylvania) to rectify their naturally poor calcium-to-phosphorous ratio (Allen and Oftedal 1989). Crickets are dusted with a multiple vitamin supplement (Nekton-Rep, Nekton-USA, Inc., Clearwater, Florida) and one of two mineral supplements (Nekton-MSA, Nekton-USA, Inc., Clearwater, Florida; D-Ca-Fos, Fort Dodge Lab., Inc., Fort Dodge, Iowa) if the crickets are fed the Ziegler diet for less than 48 hrs prior to being fed to the frogs.

The fruitfly colony is maintained on a commercial media (Instant *Drosophila* Medium, Formula 4–24, Carolina Biological Supply Co., Burlington, North Carolina). Fruitflies have a poor calcium-to-phosphorous ratio (Allen 1989), as do crickets, and currently are dusted prior to being fed to the frogs.

Stomach-content analyses of wild-caught neotropical hylids indicate that they feed on a wide variety of invertebrates, primarily orthopterans (Duellman 1978).

At NAIB, hylids are fed 2-week to 4-week-old crickets (*Acheta domestica*) three times per week. Newly metamorphosed hylids also are fed fruitflies (*Drosophila* spp.) once per week. Because the crickets are fed to the frogs many hours before they are consumed, a shallow dish of Ziegler's cricket diet is kept in each hylid tank. That way, crickets can continue to eat the diet (and thereby maximize their nutritional value to the frogs) until they themselves are eaten.

Larval hylids and dendrobatids (except obligate oophagous species) are fed daily on a blend of commercial fish food, which is, by weight: 69% Tetra Marin Flake Food (TetraWerke, Ulrich Baensch GmbH, Melle, Germany), 14% Aquarian Tropical Fish Flakes (Mardel Lab., Inc., Glendale Heights, Illinois), 7% Ziegler Chloro-Flake Food (Ziegler Bros., Inc., Gardners, Pennsylvania), 7% Nekton-MSA, and 3% Nekton-Rep. Currently, Aquarian Vitamin and Mineral Flakes (Mardel Lab., Inc.) are used ecluusively. The flake food is supplemented on alternate days with partially cooked spinach.

Larvae of obligate oophagous dendrobatids (*Dendrobates granuliferus, D. histrionicus, D. pumilio, D. speciosus*) are raised by their female parent. She provides unfertilized nutritive eggs for her young to eat (Weygoldt 1980; Zimmermann and Zimmermann 1981; Brust 1993).

Veterinary Care

Specimen health is monitored daily by visual checks. At least once a week, a "head count" is taken of all the occupants in each tank. Individuals exhibiting abnormal behavior, weight loss, or other signs of ill health (for example, dull skin, skin lesions, or cloudy eyes) are examined by the veterinary staff and treated as necessary. A detailed medical log is kept of all treatments. Generally, frogs are kept in their home tank for treatment, to minimize stress. If isolation from the group is required, the sick frog is housed in an enriched tank, again to minimize stress.

Necropsies are performed on all frogs that die for reasons other than traumatic injury.

Quarantine

All new acquisitions are placed in quarantine tanks that are isolated from the established collection. The tanks are identical in size and enrichment to our permanent housing. "Sterile" enclosures, consisting of a moist paper towel substrate and a few plastic plants and hiding boxes, were abandoned several years ago. We observed that animals housed in these stark environments had higher rates of illness and death than did animals housed in enriched environments.

When a frog enclosure is emptied, all organic materials move with the occupants, or the enrichment is discarded. The tank is disinfected with 10% solutions of household bleach or Nolvasan (Aveco Co. Inc., Fort Dodge, Iowa), and thoroughly rinsed with hot tap water. Iodine-based disinfectants (e.g., Betadine) are highly toxic to frogs, and are never used (Stoskopf et al. 1985).

At least three stool samples are collected (each spaced at least one week apart), from each tank of new arrivals. The fecal samples are screened for pathogenic organisms. Medical treatment is administered only when the staff veterinarian deems the parasitic load to be at a pathogenic level.

Sex Determination

Sex determination is essential in creating successful breeding units, as well as in assembling nonbreeding groups that minimize stress. Sex identification in dendrobatid frogs is described in detail by Cover and Wisnieski (1989).

Duellman (1970) describes sexual dimorphism in hylid species, which includes size (females are larger), coloration, and the presence of enlarged nuptial pads, spines, and glands in reproductively active males.

Captive Propagation

Captive reproduction of dendrobatids and neotropical hylids occurs throughout the year, similar to reproduction of tropical anurans in the wild (Duellman and Trueb "1986" [1985]).

Dendrobatid Frogs

In our experience, dendrobatids usually breed better when maintained in pairs rather than in groups. In the latter case, reproduction is often hindered by preoccupation with territorial defense, and egg cannibalism by cage-mates.

Spawning is initiated in dendrobatids by increasing the humidity in the enclosure. This is accomplished by covering the lid with clear plastic sheeting and increasing the frequency of misting. Proper oviposition sites are essential to successful reproduction. Without such sites, frogs may fail to deposit eggs, or may do so at sites ill-suited to development of the eggs. Techniques used in captive breeding of dendrobatids vary according to the species and their individual life histories. The species maintained at NAIB fit into three categories: breeding-hut spawners, leaf spawners, and obligate oophagous species (Table 1). Each is managed differently.

Most breeding-hut spawners prefer to deposit their eggs on a flat, plastic leaf set in a petri dish,

TABLE 1. Captive breeding of dendrobatid frogs at the National Aquarium in Baltimore (incubation and rearing occurred in "warm room" at 23°–26°C, unless otherwise indicated).

Species	Clutch size			Time to hatching (days)			Time to metamorphosis[1] (days)		
	Mean	Range	n[2]	Mean	Range	n[3]	Mean	Range	n[4]
Breeding hut spawners									
Colostethus talamancae	—	—	—	—	—	—	—	—	—
Dendrobates auratus	6.4	1–13	51	14.8	7–23	162	46.4	37–74	114
Dendrobates azureus	4.7	1–9	139	15.4	5–21	251	70.5	39–108	185
Dendrobates fantasticus	4.6	1–8	74	14.0[5]	7–30	231	74.1	37–160	101
Dendrobates imitator	2.5	1–5	43	12.6[5]	6–26	72	48.9	40–78	37
Dendrobates tinctorius	5.9	2–9	9	15.4	11–21	30	63.1	55–76	18
Dendrobates variabilis	9.0	3–18	18	15.4[5]	6–22	78	63.0	26–89	62
Phyllobates bicolor	13.5	7–21	32	13.8	7–19	91	42.5	34–54	15
Phyllobates lugubris	11.2	4–20	13	10.9	5–22	51	39.9	38–47	8
Phyllobates vittatus	15.0	5–24	10	10.1	7–13	47	45.5	35–54	11
Obligate oophagous species									
Dendrobates granuliferus	5.5	5–6	2	—	—	—	—	—	—
Dendrobates histrionicus	6.3	3–8	11	—	—	—	—	—	—
Dendrobates pumilio	6.7	2–16	37	10.0	9–12	16	—	—	—
Dendrobates speciosus	9.0	8–10	8	13.0[6]	10–14	12	—	—	—
Leaf spawners									
Dendrobates reticulatus	5.0	2–13	5	15.0	7–18	9	60.0	45–68	6
Epipedobates anthonyi	18.3	8–33	8	11.5	6–16	30	—	—	—
Epipedobates azureiventris	10.6	4–17	12	9.0	5–12	57	38.1	26–86	39
Epipedobates espinosai	14.0	12–16	4	13.0	9–15	39	30.0	28–31	6
Epipedobates pictus	23.3	20–28	3	13.1	7–20	47	—	—	—
Epipedobates tricolor	18.0	10–24	4	15.3	15–16	15	—	—	—

[1]Metamorphosis is defined as the emergence of forelimbs
[2]Number of clutches
[3]Number of eggs hatched
[4]Number of larvae metamorphosed
[5]Eggs incubated in either "cool room" (23°C) or "warm room" (23–26°C)
[6]Eggs incubated in "cool room" only (23°C)
— Data not recorded

which is partially filled with dechlorinated tap water. The dish is set inside a breeding hut (Figure 1). The huts are checked for eggs every other day, and fresh dishes are put in the huts at each check. If eggs are found, they are incubated. The leaf-and-petri dish assembly is placed on a bed of soggy aquarium-filter floss (polyester fiber) in a bowl that is covered with plastic wrap. Water is added to the petri dish, as needed, to keep the lower edge of the egg mass constantly moist. When the eggs hatch, cannibalistic species (which includes many species of *Dendrobates*) are placed in individual rearing bowls (Pyrex 175 ml custard cups or Pyrex 300 ml deep pie dishes, Corning, Inc., Corning, New York). The larvae are fed daily, after each is moved to a clean bowl of aged water.

In contrast, non-cannabilistic species, such as those of the genera *Epipedobates* and *Phyllobates*, are reared in community aquariums. Conspecifics of different bloodlines are kept in separate tanks. The larvae are fed daily. Water quality is maintained by a 10–20% weekly water change and by circulating the tank water through a sponge filter (Goldfish Dirt Magnet, Jungle Corp., Cibolo, Texas) or less frequently, through an activated charcoal canister filter (Magnum 330, Marineland Aquarium Products, Chatsworth, California). A layer of fine aquarium gravel over a sub-floor grate prevents the larvae from being drawn into the filter.

Not all breeding-hut spawners deposit their eggs in a petri dish. *Dendrobates imitator*, which typically breeds on vertical surfaces (Zimmermann and Zimmermann 1988), usually deposits its eggs on the inside wall of the hut. *Dendrobates fantasticus* prefer to deposit its eggs on the top of broad leaves that pressed up against the roof of the hut or another leaf. Eggs that are not laid on plastic leaves are easily transferred to them by hand. The eggs are then incubated in the manner described above.

Leaf-spawning dendrobatids deposit their eggs on the upper surface of broad flat leaves. We usually remove the eggs and artificially incubate them using the method described above. Occasionally, the eggs are left in the home tank. There, the male parent tends the eggs and, upon hatching, transports the larvae to the tank pool. The larvae continue their development there, without parental involvement. The larvae feed on pool algae, and on a daily feeding of fish flake food. It is important to allow a substantial build-up of algae in the pool for this method of tadpole rearing to succeed.

Oophagous dendrobatids typically deposit their eggs on the upper surface of their tank bromeliad, or on adjacent broadleaf vegetation. We do not artificially rear the young of obligate oophagous frogs, but depend instead on the female parent to tend the eggs and feed (with unfertilized nutritive eggs) the developing larvae.

Hylid Frogs

To stimulate spawning in hylids, we create a very moist, humid environment preceded by a period of low humidity and moisture. A high-moisture environment is created by covering the enclosure with

TABLE 2. Captive breeding of neotropical hylid frogs at the National Aquarium in Baltimore (incubation and rearing occurred in "warm room" at 23°–26°C).

Species	Clutch size			Time to hatching (days)			Time to metamorphosis[1] (days)		
	Mean	Range	n[2]	Mean	Range	n[3]	Mean	Range	n[4]
Leaf spawners									
Agalychnis callidryas	113.0	82–144	2	—	4–7	128	43.0	38–53	25
Phyllomedusa hypochondrialis	57.5	28–87	2	—	7–10	112	38.0	34–48	36
Phyllomedusa tarsius	422.0	324–520	2	—	7–10	861	59.0	48–97	200
Pool breeders									
Smilisca phaeota	559.0	300–750	3	14.8	2–3	1700+	28.0	25–30	600

[1]Metamorphosis is defined as the emergence of forelimbs
[2]Number of clutches
[3]Number of eggs hatched
[4]Number of larvae metamorphosed
— Data not recorded

plastic sheeting, raising the water level in the pool, and simulating rainfall. The latter is accomplished in one of two ways: (1) the enclosure is fitted with a standpipe and then misted overhead with a hose (using tempered, dechlorinated water) for several hours daily, or (2) a recirculating canister filter is connected to the enclosure, with the return hose directed through an overhead drip pan.

The hylid frogs bred thus far at NAIB are either pool-spawners (*Smilisca phaeota*) or leaf-spawners (*Agalychnis callidryas, Phyllomedusa hypochondrialis, P. tarsius*) (Table 2). The leaf-spawners typically deposit their eggs on broad leaves that overhang standing water. The leaves (with eggs attached), are then removed and suspended over water in a covered jar. Hatching is stimulated by misting the clutch with a spray bottle. Readiness to hatch is evident by the partial breakdown in the jelly mass, heightened movement of the embryos, and the loss of the embryos' external gills. The larvae drop into the water when they are free of their egg case.

The newly hatched larvae are transferred to an aquarium to complete their development. Water quality is maintained using the same protocol established for our tanks of dendrobatid larvae, that is, a 10–20% weekly water change, and use of a sponge filter or an activated charcoal canister filter. The larvae are fed a daily meal of fish flake food.

The pool-spawning hylids deposit their eggs directly into the shallow pool of their enclosure. The eggs and larvae are left in the pool to complete their development. The larvae feed on pool algae and a daily meal of fish flake food. Water quality is maintained in the pool by circulating the water through an activated charcoal canister filter.

Larvae are removed from their rearing container (custard cups, aquarium, or terrarium pool) as soon as all four legs emerge. While dendrobatid larvae often remain in the water for up to several days after all legs emerge, newly metamorphosed hylids often drown if they cannot leave the water within a few hours.

Summary

Based upon our experience in breeding 19 species of dendrobatids and four species of neotropical hylids, we believe that the following parameters are most important for successful breeding:

(1) Proper social grouping;

(2) Frequent feeding and proper nutrition (particular care must be paid to preserving the nutritional value of insect prey for nocturnal frogs, because the prey may not be eaten for many hours after being placed in the frog enclosures);

(3) High humidity and/or, in the case of hylids, the provision of artificial rainfall that follows a relatively dry period;

(4) Well-enriched housing, with proper oviposition sites.

Although we have been successful in breeding many species of dendrobatid frogs, the captive-born young differ from their wild-born counterparts in at least one important respect. The captive-born animals do not produce any of the defensive alkaloids found in the wild-born animals (Daly et al. 1980, 1992). This phenomenon could undermine future conservation efforts that include introduction of captive-born frogs into the wild. To date, the skins of captive-born hylids have not been examined for the presence of the chemical defenses that might occur in wild-caught specimens.

Acknowledgments

The Servicio de Fauna Silvestre of Costa Rica, the Instituto Nacional de Recursos Naturales Renovables of Panama, and the Ministerio de Agricultura y Ganaderia of Ecuador and of Peru, are gratefully acknowledged for permission to collect the specimens upon which our breeding program is founded. We also wish to thank the staff and volunteers of the National Aquarium in Baltimore for their assistance and support of our efforts. The authors are grateful to the following individuals for providing specimens and for sharing information: John Daly (National Institutes of Health), Jack Frenkel (University of Kansas), Anthony Wisnieski (Baltimore Zoo), Charles Nishihira, and Rainer Schulte.

Literature Cited

Allen, M. E. 1989. Nutritional Aspects of Insectivory. Michigan State Univ., East Lansing, Michigan. Doctoral Dissertation. xiii, 205 pages.

Allen, M. E., and O. T. Oftedal. 1989. Dietary manipulation of the calcium content of feed crickets. Jour. Zoo Wildlife Med., 20: 26–33.

Brust, D. G. 1993. Maternal brood care by *Dendrobates pumilio*: a frog that feeds its young. Jour. Herpetol., 27: 96–98.

Cover, J. F., Jr., and A. P. Wisnieski. 1989. Captive maintenance and propagation of poison-dart frogs (Anura: Dendrobatidae) at the National Aquarium in Baltimore, p. 465–472. *In* L. J. Boyd (ed.), American Association of Zoological Parks and Aquariums 1989 Annual Conference Proceedings. Publ. Amer. Assoc. Zool. Parks Aquar., Wheeling, West Virginia.

Daly, J. W., C. W. Myers, J. E. Warnick, and E. X. Albuquerque. 1980. Levels of batrachotoxin and lack of sensitivity to its action in poison-dart frogs (*Phyllobates*). Science, 208: 1383–1385.

Daly, J. W., S. I. Secunda, H. M. Garraffo, T. F. Spande, A. Wisnieski, C. Nishihira, and J. F. Cover, Jr. 1992. Variability in alkaloid profiles in neotropical poison frogs (Dendrobatidae): genetic versus environmental determinants. Toxicon, 30: 887–898.

Donnelly, M. A. 1991. Feeding patterns of the strawberry poison frog, *Dendrobates pumilio* (Anura: Dendrobatidae). Copeia, 1991: 723–730.

Duellman, W. E. 1970. The Hylid Frogs of Middle America. Univ. Kansas Mus. Nat. Hist. Monogr., 1: 1–753.

— (ed.). 1978. The biology of an equatorial herpetofauna in Amazonian Ecuador. Univ. Kansas Mus. Nat. Hist. Misc. Publ., 65: 1–352.

Duellman, W. E., and L. Trueb. "1986" (1985). Biology of Amphibians. McGraw Hill, New York. xvii, 670 pages (paperback edition 1994, Johns Hopkins Univ. Press, Baltimore).

Heselhaus, R. 1988. Pfeilgiftfrösche. Eugen Ulmer GmbH, Stuttgart, Germany. 99 pages (English edition 1994, Ralph Curtis Books, Sanibel, Florida).

Miller, T. J. 1984. Notes on a breeding of the red-eyed tree frog, *Agalychnis callidryas*, p. 34–42. *In* P. J. Tolson (ed.), Proceedings of the 7th Annual Reptile Symposium on Captive Propagation and Husbandry. Zool. Consortium, Thurmont, Maryland.

Myers, C. W., and J. W. Daly. 1976. Preliminary evaluation of skin toxins and vocalizations in taxonomic and evolutionary studies of poison-dart frogs (Dendrobatidae). Bull. Amer. Mus. Nat. Hist., 157: 177–262.

Odum, R. A., J. M. McClain, and T. C. Shely. 1984. Hormonally induced breeding and rearing of White's treefrog, *Litoria caerula* (Anura: Pelodryadinae), p. 42–53. *In* P. J. Tolson (ed.), Proceedings of the 7th Annual Reptile Symposium on Captive Propagation and Husbandry. Zool. Consortium, Thurmont, Maryland.

Schulte, R. 1980. Frösche und Kröten. Eugen Ulmer GmbH, Stuttgart. 240 pages.

Senfft, W. 1936. Das Brutgeschäft des Baumsteigerfrosches (*Dendrobates auratus* Girard) in Gefangenschaft. Zool. Gart. Leipzig, 8: 122–131.

Silverstone, P. A. 1975. A revision of the poison-arrow frogs of the genus *Dendrobates* Wagler. Los Angeles Co. Nat. Hist. Mus. Sci. Bull., 21: 1–55.

—. 1976. A revision of the poison-arrow frogs of the genus *Phyllobates* Bibron *in* Sagra (Family Dendrobatidae). Los Angeles Co. Nat. Hist. Mus. Sci. Bull., 27: 1–53.

Stoskopf, M. K., A. P. Wisnieski, and L. Pieper. 1985. Iodine toxicity in poison-arrow frogs, p. 86–88. *In* M. S. Silberman and S. D. Silberman (eds.), Proceedings—1985—Annual Meeting American Association of Zoo Veterinarians. Publ. Amer. Assoc. Zoo Veterin., Philadelphia.

Weygoldt, P. 1980. Complex brood care and reproductive behavior in captive poison-arrow frogs *Dendrobates pumilio* O. Schmidt. Behav. Ecol. Sociobiol., 7: 329–332.

—. 1984. Beobachtungen aus Fortpflanzungsbiologie von *Dendrobates pumilio* Schmidt, 1857 im Terrarium (Salientia: Denbrobatidae). Salamandra, 20: 112–120.

Zimmermann, E. 1986. Breeding Terrarium Animals. T.F.H. Publ., Neptune City, New Jersey. 384 pages.

Zimmermann, H. 1989. Conservation studies on the 'dart-poison' frogs Dendrobatidae in the field and in captivity. Internatl. Zoo Yearbook, 28: 31–44.

Zimmermann, H. and E. Zimmermann. 1981. Sozialverhalten, Fortpflanzungsverhalten und Zucht der Farberfrösche *Dendrobates histrionicus* und *D. lehmanni* sowie einiger anderer Dendrobatiden. Zeitschr. Kölner Zoo, 24: 83–99.

—. 1988. Etho-taxonomie und zoogeographische Artengruppenbildung bei Pfeilgiftfröschen (Anura: Dendrobatidae). Salamandra, 24: 125–160.

❦

❦ Cover, J. F., Jr., S. L. Barnett, and R. L. Saunders. 1994. Captive management and breeding of dendrobatid and neotropical hylid frogs at the National Aquarium in Baltimore, p. 267–273. *In* J. B. Murphy, K. Adler, and J. T. Collins (eds.), Captive Management and Conservation of Amphibians and Reptiles. Society for the Study of Amphibians and Reptiles, Ithaca (New York). Contributions to Herpetology, volume 11.

Reproduction in Captive Neotropical Musk and Mud Turtles (*Staurotypus triporcatus*, *S. salvinii*, and *Kinosternon scorpioides*)

J. Michael Goode*

Introduction

Many aspects of natural history can be better and more accurately observed in captives than in free-living animals. The number of observations possible, however, is limited by the number of specimens which can be maintained. Procedures and management practices in the collection of reptiles at the Columbus Zoo have been developed to promote the keeping of small groups of reproductive animals, such as turtles, under consistently replicated, yearly conditions which enable the compilation of several years' results into a larger, albeit artificial, sample of observations of an identified group.

The neotropical turtle genus *Staurotypus* was reviewed by Iverson (1985*a*), and its component species, the Mexican Giant Musk Turtle, *S. triporcatus*, and the Pacific Giant Musk Turtle, *S. salvinii*, were reviewed by Iverson (1985*b*) and Dean and Bickham (1983), respectively. Most attention has been directed towards aspects of these species other than natural history, and relatively few reports concern the reproduction or growth of either species (Ewert 1985; Ewert and Legler 1978; Schmidt 1970). Reproduction in the genus *Kinosternon* has been reviewed recently by Iverson et al. (1991), and there are a few reports which deal with the species treated here, including nesting, reported by Álvarez del Toro (1982, as *K. cruentatum*), and a report on the nominate subspecies of the currently recognized species (*K. scorpioides*) in Venezuela by Sexton (1960).

Details of caging, diets, and related techniques for maintaining turtles have been presented elsewhere (Goode 1991). All breeding specimens of the three species of turtles were fed a varied diet ad libitum 3–5 times weekly. No differences in reproductive output related to diet have been apparent during the years reported here (1978–1991), even though minor changes in diet composition occurred. The emphasis was placed upon consistent yearly replication of environmental factors in the captive conditions, particularly those ("exogenous proximal factors" as discussed by Moll 1979) involving caging temperatures (27°C air, 23°C water, with minor variation), photoperiod (approximating the annual light/dark cycle at 20°N Latitude), and relative humidity (60–80% in the caging units year round).

Most egg clutches were deposited overnight in nesting sites provided in the cages, recovered the following morning, and weighed and measured prior to incubation. The incubation of eggs in the reptile department was largely uncontrolled, with eggs placed in sealed containers, using the standard 1:1 (by mass) mixture of vermiculite to tap water as a medium. Incubation temperatures were determined by the selected areas of the reptile collection building in which the eggs were kept, and varied widely. Incubation times also varied widely as a result. In eggs produced prior to 1988, *S. triporcatus* incubation times were 97–298 days, with a mean of 150.5 days ($n = 272$); *S. salvinii* were 130–415 days,

*Columbus Zoo
9990 Riverside Drive, Box 400
Powell, Ohio 43065, USA

Acronyms used in this chapter:

AF	Annual fecundity
C	Clutch of unknown size
CF	Clutch frequency
CL	Carapace length
CS	Clutch size
CZ	Columbus Zoo, original group specimen 1
FW	Fort Worth Zoo, original group specimen 2
LC	Larger clutch
RACM	Relative annual clutch mass
RCM	Relative clutch mass
s	Standard deviation
SC	Smaller clutch
SH	The Shed, Inc., original group specimen 3

with a mean of 246.8 days (n = 127); and *K. scorpioides cruentatum* were 84–248 days, with a mean of 165.7 days (n = 103). Eggs of the three species generated since 1988 have been produced mainly to respond to requests, and have been included in reports by other investigators (Ewert and Nelson 1991; Ewert 1991).

Groups have been compared statistically by means of pairwise t-tests.

Results and Discussion

Mexican Giant Musk Turtle (Staurotypus triporcatus)

Eighty-nine clutches were produced by females of *Staurotypus triporcatus* in the years 1981–1991. Fifty-seven of these were produced by three females (the "original group" in the following discussion), including two wild-caught, but long-term, captives: specimen 1 (designated CZ) which remained 335 mm in straight-line carapace length (CL) throughout the period, and which was obtained commercially on 6 July 1970, and specimen 2 (FW) which was provided on breeding loan from the Fort Worth Zoo on 26 July 1981 and grew from 309 to 329 mm CL during the period 1981–1991. The third original female (SH) was obtained commercially as a recently collected specimen on 10 August 1984. While this animal grew from 220 mm CL at accession to 295 mm CL in 1991, neither growth nor size at egg laying caused significant variation in clutch production (see below). An additional 32 clutches were produced by five females hatched and raised in the collection. This "progeny group" in the following discussion consisted of three clutchmates hatched on 14 July 1980 and two unrelated specimens hatched on 4 and 18 March 1982. Females were housed with various males throughout the period; females of the original group were maintained separately from each other. Not all females were housed in potential reproductive situations at all times, and only years in which eggs were produced are considered to be nesting years for the females. A total of 34 nesting years (21 for the original group and 13 for the progeny group) is here reported.

TABLE 1. Growth in *Staurotypus triporcatus*.

Age (post-hatching)	Number of specimens	Size range (mm CL)	Mean
1 year	36	54–90	67.8
2 years	24	68–127	92.0
3 years	13	75–180	131.3
4 years	12	117–192	152.1
5 years	10	153–222	189.0
6 years	9	182–253	217.4
7 years	9	214–278	245.0
8 years	7	244–292	263.0
9 years	7	278–318	301.0

Hatchlings varied in carapace length from 35 to 48 mm after assumption of normal shell contour following eclosure. Subsequent growth of the animals maintained in the collection is shown in Table 1. Attainment of secondary sexual characters by males (longer, thicker preanal tail and greater tail length) generally occurred in faster-growing specimens at a younger age and was fairly rapid. Three males became sexually dimorphic late in their third year, but never at sizes below 110 mm CL; all became dimorphic by the beginning of their fifth year, at a size of 150 mm CL. Callosities on the inner aspect of the thigh have appeared in conjunction with the onset of tail length and girth increases. Progeny-group females produced their first clutches late in their eighth year (7 years 184 days, 7 years 287 days, and 7 years 310 days) and early in their ninth year (8 years 81 days) at sizes ranging from 248–283 mm CL. An additional progeny female did not lay until her tenth year, at 319 mm CL. All progeny females were well above the smallest size observed at egg laying in the series (220 mm CL, 1 clutch of 12 eggs).

No consistent sexual dimorphism in size has been noted, with both males and females of unrelated clutches surpassing 300 mm CL, and with specimens of both sexes at 335 and 339 mm CL for the largest male and female, respectively, approaching the reported maximum CL for the species of approximately 380 mm (Neill and Allen 1959).

Nesting for each group of turtles, and reproductive output for each season are summarized in Table 2. Observed nesting seasons, the period spanning the first and last laying date of the nesting year, were 40–333 days, with an overall mean for the original and progeny groups combined of 180.1 days (n = 14), separated by non-nesting seasons of 93–234 days, with a mean of 186.9 days (n = 12).

TABLE 2. Nesting and reproductive output in *Staurotypus triporcatus*.

Nesting season	Number of			Nesting season		Days prior to next clutch	Clutch size		Clutch frequency per female	Annual fecundity per female
	Females	Clutches	Eggs	Inclusive dates	Days		Range	Mean		
Original females										
1981/82	2	2	25	18 Oct–16 Dec	59	184	12–13	12.50	1.0	12.5
1982/83	2	5	56	18 Jun–6 Feb	212	208	9–15	11.20	2.5	28.0
1983/84	2	5	53	12 Sep–23 Mar	192	231	9–14	10.60	2.5	26.5
1984/85	3	9	95	18 Sep–20 Mar	183	234	5–14	10.55	3.0	31.7
1985/86	3	3	25	9 Nov–19 Dec	40	233	4–14	8.33	1.0	8.3
1986/87	2	5	44	9 Aug–19 Feb	194	189	4–12	8.80	2.5	22.0
1987/88	2	9	106	27 Aug–20 Apr	236	140	7–16	11.78	4.5	53.0
1988/89	2	7	84	7 Sep–19 Apr	224	171	7–18	12.00	3.5	42.0
1989/90	2	7	72	16 Aug–13 Feb	180	212	5–16	10.28	3.5	36.0
1990/91	1	5	45	19 Sep–15 Apr	219	—	6–10	9.00	5.0	45.0
Total	21	57	605	(Mean)	(173.9)	(200.2)		(10.61)	(2.71)	(28.8)
Progeny females										
1987/88	1	3	6	14 Jan–23 Mar	68	194	1–4	2.00	3.00	6.0
1988/89	3	4	24	3 Oct–20 Mar	168	93	1–8	6.00	1.25	8.0
1989/90	4	9	70	21 Jun–20 May	333	154	2–9	7.78	2.25	17.5
1990/91	5	16	109	21 Oct–22 May	213	—	2–13	6.81	3.20	21.8
Total	13	32	209	(Mean)	(195.5)	(147.0)		(6.53)	(2.46)	(16.1)
Combined original and progeny females										
Total	34	89	814	(Mean)	(180.1)	(186.9)		(9.15)	(2.62)	(23.9)

Combining all years into a single nesting season, laying dates spanned the 336 day period 18 June through 20 May. However, 84 of 89 clutches (94.4%) were produced in the 249 day period 18 August through 24 April. As noted in Table 2, clutch frequency (CF) for individual females was 1–5 clutches per season in the original group of three females and 1–4 in the progeny group. Clutch size (CS) was 4–18 eggs per clutch in the original group and 1–13 in the progeny group. Mean annual fecundity (AF) ranged from 8.3–53.0 eggs per season per female in the original group and 6.0–21.8 in the progeny group. Mean performances of the original group, consisting of various combinations of the three females in different seasons aggregating to 21 female-nesting-years, were variable (means of CF 2.71, CS 10.61, and AF 28.81). Mean performance of the progeny group includes great variation in individual performance, as the animals matured and increased reproductive output through the four seasons, and was lower due to the inclusion of early and relatively unproductive seasons (means of CF 2.46, CS 9.15, and AF 23.94).

In the original group of turtles, size is not believed to be an influence on egg production. Although a positive correlation of clutch size to body size of egg-laying females has been established in many diverse taxa, the relationship is often obscured or overridden by other factors (Wilbur and Morin 1988). In a series of *Kinosternon subrubrum*, Gibbons et al. (1982) noted that body size explained only 3% of the observed variation in clutch size. Two of our original females of *S. triporcatus* did not increase in carapace length appreciably during the nesting seasons (specimens CZ and FW), while the third (SH) grew from 220 mm CL in 1984 to 295 mm CL in 1991. The first clutch laid by the latter animal (12 eggs in 1984), however, was equal in number to the first clutch of the largest, non-growing specimen (CZ) and was exceeded only in the fourth consecutive year of egg laying. The fourth of seven consecutive seasons was the most productive (5 clutches, 59 eggs). The largest clutch size observed was produced by the intermediate-sized specimen (18 eggs by FW) which also showed the highest mean clutch size for the series (11.16 eggs).

Congdon and Tinkle (1982) showed that, in a temperate species having an annual brumation, resources used in egg production were provided both by stored resources and resources obtained from the environment during egg production. Management practices for these captives provided food so that neither nutrition nor cost of obtaining resources ("foraging efficiency") was limiting for egg production. Stored resources remained at a high level throughout egg production as subjectively appraised by the "fleshiness" of the animals remaining much more pronounced than the state observed in recently collected specimens. They were fat and remained fat no matter how many eggs they produced. Additionally, they were fed ad libitum 3–5 times weekly throughout the nesting period. Indications that the quality of the nutritional content was not lacking included the absence of nutritional disease in the adults during multi-seasonal egg production and the continued viability of hatchlings from eggs of later consecutive seasons. Influences of body size on clutch size other than limitation of volume, involving size-related differences in obtaining or storing resources, are negated by the absence of resource limitation.

Clutch size and clutch frequency for each female in the original group are shown in Table 3. Mean clutch size for the three animals did not differ significantly ($p > 0.3$ in each of three paired comparisons. Mean clutch frequency, however, was significantly higher in specimen SH than in CZ (3.28 versus 2.33 clutches/season respectively, $p < 0.01$) and approached significance in relation to FW ($0.1 > p > 0.05$). Although both clutch size and clutch frequency varied widely interseasonally and among individuals, the greater variation in clutch frequency among individuals, as opposed to the variation in clutch size, is in accord with the observation of Gibbons (1982), who states that clutch frequency is the more important source of variation in interseasonal differences in egg production.

TABLE 3. Individual clutch sizes and clutch frequencies in *Staurotypus triporcatus* (original group females).

Female	Number of clutches	Clutch size: Range	Mean	s[1]
FW	20	5–18	11.16	3.453
CZ	14	5–14	10.69	2.398
SH	23	4–16	10.22	4.909
Total	57	4–18	10.61	3.129

Female	Number of seasons	Clutch frequency: Range	Mean	s[1]
FW	8	1–4	2.71	0.888
CZ	6	1–4	2.33	1.106
SH	7	1–5	3.28	1.484
Total	21	1–5	2.71	1.277

[1]Standard deviation

Wide variation was apparent in individual performances in regard to both clutch size within seasons and clutch frequency between seasons. The series of 57 clutches includes 34 pairs of clutches produced consecutively by a female. These were scored solely on the basis of the later clutch being larger (+), smaller (–), or equal to (=) the earlier clutch. While clutch size increased and decreased with approximately the same frequency (+47%, –41%, =12%) in the sample, the variation was not without pattern. Clutches of less than mean clutch size for the female were predominantly followed by larger clutches (+71%, –23%, =6%), while clutches of more than the mean clutch size were predominantly followed by smaller or equally sized clutches (+28%, –56%, =17%). Similarly, 17 pairs of consecutive seasons by individual females showed clutch frequency increases and decreases of 47% and 35% (=18%), while clutch frequency of seasons following those in which clutch frequency was below the mean for the female predominantly increased (+87.5%, –12.5%) and clutch frequency of seasons following those in which clutch frequency was above the mean predominantly decreased (+11%, –56%, =33%).

While it is indicated that some influences tend to stabilize clutch size and clutch frequency within an extremely variable system, no isolation of those influences is apparent in this series. The impact of the wide range of variation, however, has been to restrict the level of significance in the treatment of results in the sample sizes available. As some actual correlations may be obscured by this, which would become apparent in larger samples having identical qualities, I have presented some values which are insignificant, but approach significance ($0.1 > p > 0.05$).

The 57 clutches of the original group were produced on 21 occasions of a female reproducing in a season. Because conditions were consistently repli-

TABLE 4. Clutch size and clutch frequency in *Staurotypus triporcatus* (original group females).Data are grouped according to number of clutches per year (for example, CF 2, two clutches per year with separate data for first and second clutch). Ordinal position (1st, 2nd, etc.) denotes sequence of laying by individual females; in some instances, clutches are grouped for statistical comparisons (see text).

Clutch group	Number of clutches	Range of clutch size	Mean	s[1]
Clutch Frequency 1 (CF-1)	5	4–14	10.00	3.847
Clutch Frequency 2 (CF-2)	8	4–15	9.00	3.295
1st clutch	4	7–12	9.33	2.055
2nd clutch	4	4–15	8.75	3.961
Clutch Frequency 3 (CF-3)	18	5–18	10.89	2.908
1st clutch	6	5–12	8.60	2.417
2nd & 3rd clutches	12	9–18	11.83	2.544
2nd clutch	6	9–14	11.00	1.732
1st & 2nd clutches	12	5–14	9.09	2.391
3rd clutch	6	9–18	12.67	2.925
Clutch Frequency 4 (CF-4)	16	5–16	11.50	3.082
1st clutch	4	5–16	9.75	4.206
2nd clutch	4	12–14	13.75	1.098
1st & 2nd clutches	8	5–14	11.75	3.667
3rd clutch	4	9–12	10.00	1.225
4th clutch	4	9–16	12.50	2.500
3rd & 4th clutches	8	9–16	11.25	2.332
Clutch Frequency 5 (CF-5)	10	6–14	10.40	2.417

[1]Standard deviation

cated, and size of animals and availability of resources were consistently above a limiting level, egg production in various years can be aggregated or compared. Clutch size in relation to clutch frequency is presented in Tables 4 and 5 in different assessments. Table 4 shows the 21 nestings grouped by clutch frequency, with all clutches laid singly grouped as CF 1, and those laid as two clutches per season grouped as CF 2 and divided into first and second clutches, etc. Clutches laid as CF 2 were smaller than those laid as CF 1 (mean CS 10.00 versus 9.00, $p < 0.05$). Those laid as CF 3 were larger than CF 2 (mean CS 10.89 versus 9.00, $p < 0.025$). Clutches laid as part of group CF 3 increased in size sequentially, although not all increments were significant, but either aggregation of two clutches within CF 3 was significantly different from the third. The CF 3 and CF 4 groups were not significantly different from each other. An anomalous but significant decrease occurred between the second and third subgroups of CF 4 (mean CS 13.75 versus 10.00, $p < 0.05$), although aggregates of the first-second and third-fourth subgroups did not differ (mean CS 11.75 versus 11.25, $p > 0.4$). Only two series of CF 5 were produced, thus clutch groups are not warranted. While the clutch size of CF 5 was not significantly smaller than CF 4, neither was it significantly larger than CF 1.

Nestings of the original group females are also aggregated into a single composite of 21 reproducing females in Table 5. This table presents the laying history of 21 series of clutches produced by females in various years, and includes 21 females producing one clutch, 16 which produced a second, 12 which produced a third, etc. Classes representing first, second, etc. clutches (noted in Table 5 as "1st clutch—all CF," "2nd clutch—all CF," etc.) are divided into two columns: subgroups of clutches which were followed by a subsequent clutch (column "Preceding Clutch," noted as "1st of CF 2–5, 2nd of CF 3–5," etc.) and clutches which were not followed by a subsequent clutch (column "Last Clutch," noted as "CF 1, 2nd of CF 2," etc.)

Clutch size increased from first to second clutch in all CF classes (mean CS 9.63 versus 10.94, $p < 0.05$) but did not change significantly from the second to the fourth class (mean CS 10.94 versus 11.75 versus 11.33, $p > 0.2$). The preceding and last clutch size did not differ in the first clutches (mean CS 9.50 versus 10.00, $p > 0.4$), but approached significant differences in the second and third. However, the preceding clutch size was larger in the second (mean CS 11.67 versus 8.75, $0.1 > p > 0.05$) while last clutch size was larger in the third (mean CS 10.88 versus 12.67, $0.1 > p > 0.05$). Last clutch size was significantly larger in the fourth (mean CS 12.50 versus 9.00, $p < 0.05$) and in the aggregate of preceding third and fourth, as opposed to the aggregate of the last third and fourth (mean CS 12.60 versus 10.38, $p < 0.05$). Means of aggregates of preceding first and second clutch sizes and preceding third and fourth clutch sizes were not significantly different (mean CS 10.50 versus 10.38, $p > 0.4$), but means of aggregates of last first-second and last third-fourth were (mean CS 9.44 versus 12.60, $p < 0.05$).

TABLE 5. Clutch size and proximal laying history of *Staurotypus triporcatus* (original group females). Data are grouped according to ordinal position of clutches as laid by individual females. For each group: *n* is the number of clutches, followed by range of clutch sizes, mean, and standard deviation in parentheses.

Ordinal position of clutch	Preceding clutches	Last clutches
First clutch—all CF n=21,4–14, 9.63, (3.280)	First clutch of CF 2–5 n=16, 5–13, 9.50, (3.044)	CF 1 n=5, 4–14,10.00, (3.847)
	First clutch of CF 2–5, Second of CF 3–5 n=28, 5–13, 10.50, (2.886)	CF 1 & Second of CF 2 n=9, 4–15, 9.44, (3.947)
Second clutch—all CF n=16, 4–15, 10.94, (3.009)	Second clutch of CF 3–5 n=12, 8–14, 11.67, (2.173)	Second clutch of CF 2 n=4, 4–15, 8.75, (3.960)
Third clutch—all CF n=12, 9–18, 11.75, (2.586)	Third clutch of CF 4–5 n=6, 9–16, 10.88, (1.771)	Third clutch of CF 3 n=6, 10–18, 12.67, (2.924)
	Third of CF 4, Fourth of CF 5 n=8, 8–14, 10.38, (1.798)	Third clutch of CF 3, Fourth of CF 4 n=10, 9–18, 12.60, (2.764)
Fourth clutch—all CF n=6, 9–16, 11.33, (2.687)	Fourth clutch of CF 5 n=2, 8–10, 9.00, (1.00)	Fourth clutch of CF 4 n=4, 9–12, 12.50, (2.500)

The relationships in Table 5 indicate that clutch size and clutch frequency did not vary independently, and that proximal laying history of the female was correlated to clutch size. While no insight is provided regarding factors involved in clutch size of first clutches, in this series the mean of the first clutches did not differ significantly from the mean of the entire series (9.63 versus 10.22, $p > 0.2$). The following model is consistent with relationships of subsequent clutches:

(1a) If second clutch is small (in this series smaller than the first or the mean for the series), clutch production stopped with the second clutch.

(1b) If second clutch is large (in this series larger than the first or the mean for the series), clutch production continued with a third clutch.

(2a) If third clutch is large, clutch production stopped with the third clutch.

(2b) If third clutch is small, clutch production continued with a fourth clutch.

(3a) If fourth clutch is large, clutch production stopped with the fourth clutch.

(3b) If fourth clutch is small, clutch production continued with a fifth clutch.

Correlation of this model to relationships in clutch size and clutch frequency in Table 4 are shown in Table 6. In this table, the designation C refers to a clutch of unknown size, but reflecting

TABLE 6. Correlation of model for predicting further clutches based on clutch size, clutch frequency, and laying history in *Staurotypus triporcatus*. All observations refer to the data in Table 4, except as noted. Additional symbols in this table: C clutch of unknown size, LC larger clutch, SC smaller clutch.

Clutch freq.	Predictions from model	Observations
CF 1	C	CF 1
CF 2	C—SC	mean CS of (CF 1 > CF 2 < CF 3)
		$\frac{\text{(mean CS of CF 2)} \times 2}{\text{(mean CS of CF 3)} \times 3} = 55\%, < 66.6\%$
CF 3	C—LC—LC	mean CS of CF 3 (1st < 2nd < 3rd)
		$\frac{\text{(mean CS of CF 3)} \times 3}{\text{(mean CS of CF 4)} \times 4} = 71\%, \ngtr 75\%$
CF 4	C—LC—SC—LC	mean CS of CF 4 (2nd > 3rd)
		$\frac{\text{(mean CS of CF 4)} \times 4}{\text{(mean CS of CF 5)} \times 5} = 88\%, > 80\%$
CF 5	C—LC—SC—SC—C	mean CS of CF 5 < CF 4
		mean CS of preceding 2nd > preceding 3rd or 4th (Table 5)
		$\frac{\text{(mean CS preceding 3rd)} \times 2}{\text{(mean CS preceding 2nd)} \times 3} = 61\% < 66.6\%$ (Table 5)

the qualities of first clutches in Table 5, in that subgroups of C do not differ significantly from each other. LC and SC are clutches that are, respectively, larger and smaller than each other or C. The model provides most favored compositions of CF from 1–5. These compositions explain (from Table 4) the lower mean clutch size of CF 2 relative to CF 1 and CF 3, the incremental increase in mean clutch size of first, second, and third subgroups of CF 3, the larger mean clutch size of the second relative to the third subgroup of CF 4, and the decrease in mean clutch size of CF 5 from CF 4.

Ratios of mean clutch size of CF 2–5 can be estimated with the assumption that C is intermediate to LC and SC. These are CF 2 < 66.6% of CF 3, CF 3 > 75% of CF 4, and CF 4 > 80% of CF 5, and are included in the table with calculations from values in Table 4. The mean clutch size of the aggregate of the second of CF 3–5 (LC-LC-LC, 11.67) was larger than the mean clutch size of the second of CF 2, third of CF 4 and fourth of CF 5 (SC-SC-SC, 9.30, $p < 0.025$). The ratio of mean clutch size of preceding third clutches to preceding second clutches (SC-SC: LC-LC-LC) was less than 66.6% (Table 5).

The model does not hold up as well for CF 5 clutch size, with 3 of 10 clutches in the two series not meeting prediction. In CF 2–4, the model is accurate for clutch size in 36 of 42 clutches (86%), although only 8 of the 14 series are entirely as predicted.

The effect of this relationship of clutch size, clutch frequency, and laying history is a disproportionate stepped increase in fecundity, particularly in CF 1 through CF 4. A female producing two clutches produces more eggs than a female producing a single clutch, but less than twice as many. A female producing three clutches produces more than three times as many eggs as a female producing a single clutch, and more than 150% of the number produced by a female producing two clutches. A female producing four clutches produces more than four times as many eggs as a female laying a single clutch, and more than twice the number of eggs produced by a female laying two clutches. While a constant rate of increased clutch size with increased clutch frequency would produce (assuming 1 as mean and first CS) the ratio 1:2:3:4 as clutch frequency increased from 1 to 4; the actual results in this series approximated 1:1.8:3.3:4.4.

Multiple clutches in the original series encompassed 36 internesting intervals (internesting interval: the period in days between successive laying dates by a female within a season). These ranged from 32 to 93 days with a mean of 52.8 and did not differ statistically among the three females. As included in Table 7, internesting interval did not vary significantly in clutches laid as CF 2, 3, and 4 (53.5–55.0, $p > 0.45$). While the internesting interval of CF 5 was numerically shorter, the difference was not significant (mean 48.7 versus 55.0, $p < 0.15$). Relative to laying history, internesting interval was shorter, but not significantly so, prior to all last clutches than prior to all second clutches (mean 57.2–50.3). However, when aggregated into ordinal

TABLE 7. Internesting interval in *Staurotypus triporcatus*.

	Internesting interval			
	Number	Range	Mean	s[1]
Female				
CZ	8	36–93	58.75	17.086
FW	12	39–90	51.30	12.187
SH	16	32–93	53.00	16.598
Clutch frequency				
CF 2	4	39–70	53.50	13.684
CF 3	12	36–93	55.30	17.665
CF 4	12	42–85	55.00	12.409
CF 5	10	32–93	48.70	18.295
After first clutches	12	39–93	57.20	20.785
Before last clutches	12	37–58	50.30	8.003
Laying history				
1st-2nd clutches	16	39–93	56.69	19.081
2nd-3rd clutches	12	36–85	54.58	13.244
3rd-4th clutches	6	32–56	46.00	8.226
Clutch size				
Preceding CS < mean	16	32–93	60.50	20.068
Preceding CS > mean	19	36–66	48.60	8.405
Following CS < mean	13	36–93	50.00	8.849
Following CS < mean	17	32–85	52.10	13.176

	Clutch size			
Internesting interval	Number	Range	Mean	s[1]
very long intervals[2]	10	8–15	9.90	2.119
very short intervals[3]	12	6–15	11.58	2.871

[1]standard deviation
[2]very long intervals defined as greater than the mean internesting interval plus $^{S}/_{2}$
[3]very short intervals defined as less than the mean internesting interval minus $^{S}/_{2}$

classes, the internesting interval separating third and fourth clutches was significantly shorter than the internesting interval separating first and second clutches (mean 56.7 versus 46.0, $p < 0.05$), although neither increment between the two was significant. As shown in Table 7, the internesting interval was also shorter prior to larger clutch sizes, as the internesting interval preceding clutches of less than mean clutch size was longer than the internesting interval preceding clutches of more than mean clutch size (mean internesting interval 60.5 versus 48.6, $p < 0.05$). Intervals following small and large clutches did not differ (mean internesting interval 50 versus 52.1, $p > 0.45$). Conversely, clutch size of clutches following very long internesting intervals (defined as greater than mean internesting interval + s/2) was smaller than the clutch size of clutches following very short internesting intervals (defined as less than mean internesting interval – s/2), although not significantly so (average CS 9.90 versus 11.58, $0.1 > p > 0.05$).

Little has been reported on internesting intervals in turtles; most information is based on relatively isolated observations. Gibbons (1983), in a discussion of clutch production in *Kinosternon subrubrum*, speculated that observed variation in the internesting interval was a result of environmental factors delaying oviposition of one clutch while a second clutch continued to develop as follicles. This would result in compensation between adjacent internesting intervals, with the one becoming longer while the next was shortened, and also assumes that ovulatory interval approximates the mean internesting interval. In this series, this is supported by the similarity of means of internesting intervals of individual females and clutch frequency classes, with the relatively shorter mean internesting intervals of CF 4 and 5 resulting from the inclusion of more intervals bounded both before and after by other intervals than first or last internesting interval in the higher clutch frequency. Also, the means of each series of internesting intervals (those separating clutches laid by a single female in a season) ranged only from 45.5 to 69.5 days ($n = 12$). The assumption that follicles are produced at an interval approximating the mean internesting interval, however, requires that, in this series, fully developed eggs be retained for periods of up to 38 days (mean internesting interval 55 days, maximum internesting interval 93 days) without adversely affecting viability. Furthermore, no environmental effects that would cause the female to delay oviposition are apparent in the captive series. The relationship of shorter internesting intervals preceding larger clutches, however, indicates that the rate of production has some association with the number of eggs produced, and cannot act upon fully formed oviducal eggs. In the absence of evidence of differential utilization of ovulated eggs, it is probable that variation in rate occurs in ovulation and vitellogenesis. While speculative, such an adaptation would enhance "bet hedging" in the number of eggs produced, by allowing variation in the timing of oviposition related to the factors that influence the number of eggs.

As noted above, laying dates were clustered in the central portion of the nesting season, and clutch size was larger. In the aggregate of the 57 clutches laid by the original group, clutch size of clutches laid 9 October–28 January ($n = 21$, mean 11.80) was larger than clutches laid prior to 8 October ($n = 13$, mean 8.4, $p < 0.005$) or those laid after 29 January ($n = 13$, mean 9.9, $p < 0.025$). As shown in Table 8, initial laying dates of individuals producing one or two clutches per year were generally later than initial laying dates of individuals producing three or more clutches. Clutches laid early in the season were predominantly first clutches of more productive seasons, while seasons of lower clutch frequency began later, with smaller clutch size of these included in the period of the high clutch size of second clutches of three or more clutches. This timing produced the largest clutches of more productive seasons, and the entire production of less productive seasons, within a limited and simultaneous period beginning in late November.

TABLE 8. Laying dates and their relationship to clutch frequency in *Staurotypus triporcatus*.

	Laying date of initial clutch		
Clutch frequency	Number	Range	Mean
CF 1	5	18 Oct–19 Dec	20 Nov
CF 2	4	9 Aug–15 Jan	26 Oct
CF 3	6	18 Jun–10 Nov	10 Sep
CF 4	4	16 Aug–7 Nov	17 Sep
CF 5	2	19 Sep–28 Oct	8 Oct
CF 3–5 combined		18 Jun–10 Nov	21 Sep
CF 1–5 combined		18 Jun–19 Dec	18 Oct

TABLE 9. Mean clutch egg mass, individual variation, and clutch size in *Staurotypus triporcatus*.

Female	Number of clutches	Mean clutch egg mass (g)		
		Range	Mean	s[1]
CZ	14	11.53–22.25	17.16	2.988
FW	20	14.32–18.21	16.69	1.735
SH	23	13.00–18.21	15.45	1.531
CF 1–4	13	14.32–18.21	16.21	1.352
CF 5	10	13.00–16.60	14.45	1.261
Clutch size				
4–8	17	13.23–21.58	17.31	2.254
9–12	25	13.54–20.00	15.87	3.074
13–18	15	13.00–22.25	15.82	2.179

[1]Standard deviation

Egg size and mass varied considerably in the entire series laid by the original group, with sizes of 37–50 mm in length and 20–27 mm in width and masses of 10.8–23.0 g. Mean size and mass for the 605 eggs was 43.16 × 24.85 mm, 16.24 g. Eggs were not tracked individually through incubation. On the basis of plural or complete hatching of clutches, however, it is known that eggs as small as 39 mm length or 23 mm width or 12.3 g and as large as 48 mm length or 29 mm width or 19.5 g, produced viable hatchlings. Clutches were generally consistent in egg size and mass, with few varying more than 2 mm in either dimension or 2 g in mass within the clutch. In the following consideration of relationship of egg size, the means for each clutch are used as the unit of size, with these units grouped into various populations. In this way, egg size represents the "packaging" of reproductive output, but does not include direct indication of the allocation of resources into different egg sizes, as each clutch, irrespective of clutch size, is given equal weight as an instance of the production of a particular egg size.

As shown in Table 9, mean egg size for the entire series of female SH was significantly smaller than the other females (15.45 versus 17.16 and 16.69 g, $p < 0.025$). This animal, showing the most growth, and presumably the youngest of the three, was also the most productive, and produced the only series of CF 5 (two occasions). As included in Table 9, egg size of the clutches laid as CF 5 was smaller than that of CF 1–CF 4 clutches (mean 14.45 versus 16.21 g, $p < 0.005$) laid by female SH, and egg size of CF 1–4 clutches of SH was not significantly different from that of CF 1–4 clutches of females FW and CZ (mean 16.21 versus 16.69 and 17.16 g, $p > 0.35$).

Eggs of category CS 4–8 were larger than those of CS 9–12 (mean 17.31 versus 15.87 g, $p < 0.05$), while those of CS 9–12 did not differ from those of CS 13–18 (mean 15.87 versus 15.82 g, $p > 0.45$). As indicated above, egg size varied with clutch frequency, as shown in Table 10. Eggs laid as CF 5 were smaller than those laid as CF 4, or than the aggregate of CF 3 and 4 (mean 14.45 g, as opposed to 16.99 and 16.52 g, $p < 0.05$). Although eggs laid as CF 3 were numerically smaller (mean 15.25 g) than CF 1, 2, or 4, the differences were not significant. Nor was egg size significantly different in aggregates of CF 1–2 and CF 3–4 (mean 17.19 and 16.52 g, $p > 0.05$). Changes in egg size did not parallel changes in clutch size, with no difference in egg size of CF 1, 2, and 3 while clutch size was lower in category CF 2 than in either CF 1 or 3. Similarly, egg size was smaller in CF 5 than in CF 4, while clutch size of the two groups did not differ significantly.

Egg size in relation to laying history is summarized in Table 11. Although egg mass decreased incrementally in the first through fifth clutches (means 17.08, 16.56, 15.71, 15.08, 13.87 g), no individual decrease is significant. Clutches grouped (as in Table 5) into preceding and last clutches of each class showed a similar incremental decrease in size, without significant changes at any particular grouping. In the first through third clutches, the preceding clutches were larger than the last clutch, but not significantly so in any case (mean 17.25 versus 17.02, 17.12 versus 16.38, 16.09 versus 15.25 g, $p > 0.25$) nor in the aggregate of the three classes. In all

TABLE 10. Mean clutch egg mass and clutch frequency in *Staurotypus triporcatus*.

Clutch frequency group	Number of clutches	Clutch egg mass (g)			Mean clutch size
		Range	Mean	s[1]	
CF 1	5	13.33–22.25	17.25	3.198	10.00
CF 2	8	15.49–18.44	17.16	1.175	9.00
CF 1&2	13	13.33–22.25	17.19	2.252	
CF 3	18	11.53–19.00	15.25	3.885	10.89
CF 4	16	14.44–21.58	16.99	2.048	11.50
CF 3&4	34	11.53–21.58	16.52	2.080	
CF 5	10	13.00–16.00	14.45	1.123	10.40

[1]Standard deviation

TABLE 11. Mean clutch egg mass and laying history in *Staurotypus triporcatus*.

Clutch frequency group	Number of clutches	Mean clutch egg mass (g)			Mean clutch size
		Range	Mean	s[1]	
All first	21	13.25–22.25	17.08	2.488	9.63
CF 1	5	13.25–21.58	17.02	2.189	10.00
preceding	16	13.33–22.25	17.25	3.198	9.50
All second	16	13.71–18.63	16.56	1.534	10.94
2nd of 2	4	15.49–18.63	16.38	1.569	8.75
preceding	12	13.71–18.63	17.12	1.269	11.67
All third	12	11.53–20.00	15.71	2.168	11.75
3rd of 3	6	11.53–17.90	15.25	1.993	12.67
preceding	6	13.00–20.00	16.09	2.258	10.88
All fourth	6	13.67–17.33	15.08	1.183	11.33
4th of 4	4	14.44–15.55	15.64	1.055	12.50
preceding	2	13.67–17.33	13.96	0.290	9.00
Fifth	2	13.14–14.60	13.87	0.730	9.50
All clutches					
1st & 2nd	38	13.25–22.25	17.07	2.123	
3rd & 4th	27	11.53–20.00	15.56	1.953	
CF 2 through CF 4 only					
1st & 2nd	33	13.25–22.25	16.85	2.239	
3rd & 4th	14	11.53–20.00	15.84	1.953	

[1]Standard deviation

classes, egg size was smaller than in groups preceding them but the decrease was significant only in the preceding second clutch—all third clutch pairing (mean 17.25 versus 16.56, 17.12 versus 15.71, 16.09 versus 15.08, 13.96 versus 13.87 g). Decrease in egg size from the fourth to fifth clutches reflects the inclusion of clutches of category CF 5 as 2 of 6 clutches in the fourth and 2 of 2 clutches in the fifth. Although the fifth clutches were of smaller size than fourth clutches (mean 13.87 versus 15.08 g, $p > 0.05$), they were not of smaller size than eggs of preceding fourth clutch (mean 13.87 versus 13.96 g, $p > 0.45$), and preceding fourth clutches were smaller than the class of fourth clutches which includes them (mean 13.96–15.08 g, $p < 0.05$).

Aggregates of all first and second clutches were larger than all third and fourth clutches (mean 17.07 versus 15.56 g, $p < 0.05$), which included eggs laid as CF 1 in the first grouping and eggs laid as 1st through 4th of CF 5 in both groupings. Excluding these, however, leaving only eggs laid as CF 2–4, first and second clutches were not significantly smaller than third and fourth clutches (mean 16.85 versus 15.83 g, $p > 0.05$).

While few incremental changes were significant, decrease in egg mass through the series was significant when several increments are spanned, particularly so as the mean egg size of preceding clutches was slightly larger than last clutches in all but those preceding the fifth clutches. As an example, while all first clutches (mean 17.08 g) were not larger than all second (mean 16.56 g) or all third (mean 15.71 g), they were significantly larger than all fourth (mean 15.08 g, $p < 0.05$); while preceding first clutches (mean 17.25 g) were not larger than all second (mean 16.56 g) they were significantly larger than all third (mean 15.71 g, $p < 0.05$); and, while all second clutches were not larger than all third (mean 16.56 versus 15.71 g, $p > 0.10$), preceding second clutches were larger (mean 17.12 versus 15.71 g, $p < 0.05$). The decrease in egg mass in clutches laid, as preceding fourth and fifth clutches, was great enough to be significant as an incremental change. Despite the correlation of larger egg mass in clutches less than CS 9, changes in egg mass relative to clutch frequency and laying history did not parallel changes in clutch size, and were apparently masked by the similarity of egg mass in clutches larger than CS 9.

Egg sizes in the first years of breeding differed from later years. Eggs of the first four and six clutches (two and three seasons) of females CZ and FW, however, were smaller than later eggs (mean 14.76 g as opposed to 16.14 g, $p < 0.025$), while eggs of the first five clutches of SH were larger than later eggs (mean 17.15 g versus 16.14 g $p > 0.05$). This may reflect the relatively higher productivity of female SH compared to FW and CZ in early and late years (mean CF of SH 1.66–4.50; mean CF of CZ and FW 2.00–2.75), or may also be associated with a smaller clutch size in female SH in early years (mean 8.2) as opposed to those of CZ and FW (mean 12.25).

Eggs produced by the progeny group were less massive than those produced by the original group, with means for the two series (see Table 9 and 12) of 14.30 and 16.14 g, $p < 0.025$. While eggs of the fourth season were smaller than those of the third, or of the aggregate of the first, second, and third seasons ($p < 0.05$), all eggs produced in that season were laid by female 1980A, which had the smallest individual egg mass. Although the 1980A mean of 13.42 g was not significantly less than the 1980B mean of 14.08 g ($p > 0.15$), it was smaller than the

1980C mean of 14.29 g and larger groups, as well as the overall mean (mean 14.30 g, $p < 0.05$). That this is the sole effect for the decrease in mean egg mass in the fourth season is indicated by the similarity of eggs produced by 1980A in first, second, and third seasons (n = 30, mean 13.27 g), and in the fourth season (mean 13.56 g, $p > 0.35$). Individual variation in the progeny series is greater than in the original group (2.43–1.71 g), which is also true of variations in individual egg sizes (range 10–24 g as opposed to 10.8–23.0 g). Smaller egg mass in the progeny as a group, and in female SH relative to CZ and FW, however, may reflect an association of egg mass and age, as SH was a considerably younger specimen (assumed on the basis of growth) than the long-term captives CZ and FW.

The pattern of variation in egg mass is consistent with the effect of resource availability limiting the investment in each egg (smaller egg mass in larger clutches, smaller egg mass in last as opposed to preceding clutches). However, it is also consistent with a strategy where environmental conditions which favor additional resource allocation to reproduction also favor decreased allocation of resources to each offspring produced. In this series, egg size decreased in larger and later clutches in the absence of limitation of resources, as judged by clutch production itself, and indicates the latter explanation.

TABLE 12. Egg mass in *Staurotypus triporcatus* (progeny group).

		Egg mass (g)		
Season	Number	Range	Mean	s[1]
First	35	10.6–21.0	14.62	3.089
Second	54	10.0–17.2	14.28	1.921
Third	49	13.0–17.0	14.58	1.095
Fourth	32	12.0–24.0	13.56	3.937
1st–3rd	138	10.6–21.0	14.48	1.924
Female				
1980A	62	10.0–24.0	13.42	3.021
1980B	18	13.5–16.1	14.08	2.354
1980C	43	10.6–17.2	14.29	1.634
1982D	20	12.0–17.0	14.60	1.356
1982E	28	12.0–21.0	15.85	2.687
Total	170	10.0–24.0	14.30	2.602

[1]Standard deviation

As a whole, egg size decreased with increased productivity in any aspect, although obscured by the individual variation of the females. Eggs laid in small, single clutches were of larger mass than eggs laid in larger, or more frequent (or successive) clutches. Differences in egg mass with laying history, however, were relatively greater than differences associated with clutch frequency classes, indicating that the effects were more cumulative during the nesting season than causative prior to the nesting season. The numerical decrease in the mean masses of clutches, laid as various clutch frequency classes, reflect the inclusion of later (and subsequent) clutches in each class, and do not indicate that first clutches of what would be CF 3, 4, or 5 were smaller than first clutches of what would be single or CF 2 clutches.

The three female *Staurotypus triporcatus* in the original group showed a marked increase in annual fecundity in their first years of reproduction, which is similar to observations on a variety of turtles of other species in our collection and breeding program. The data for *S. triporcatus* (summarized in Table 13) were not concurrent in time, but were concurrent with regard to the length of time that the animals were in breeding situations in our collection (1981 to 1985 for female CZ and FW, 1984 to 1988 for SH). The similarity of changes in their first four seasons is indicative of the consistency of captive conditions provided the animals. Clutch size decreased numerically, but not significantly in the first three seasons (mean CSs 11.25, 10.16, and 9.14); while clutch frequency increased incrementally, with the increase becoming significant from the first to third seasons (mean CFs 1.33, 2.00, and 2.33). Mean annual fecundity increased insignificantly in the first three seasons (15.00, 20.33, and 21.33 eggs). While not significant in the small sample size at hand, the increase from 15 to 21 eggs per year represents a 40% increase in the number of eggs put into the ground as a result of slightly smaller clutches laid with a higher frequency in a comparison of first and third years. Both clutch size and clutch frequency increased significantly from the third to the fourth seasons (9.14 versus 11.17 and 2.33 versus 4.00) resulting in a significant increase in mean annual fecundity (21.33 versus 44.66 eggs). Simultaneously, internesting intervals decreased. Only eight internesting intervals are available in the first through third seasons, but as

TABLE 13. Seasonal egg production in *Staurotypus triporcatus* (original group). For each group of data: n is sample size, followed by the mean, range, and standard deviation in parentheses.

	First season	Second season	Third season	Fourth season
Clutch size	n=4, 11.25, 8–13, (1.902)	n=6, 10.16, 4–15, (3.463)	n=7, 9.14, 4–14, (3.043)	n=12, 11.17, 5–14, (2.544)
Clutch frequency	n=3, 1.3, 1–2, (0.471)	n=3, 2.0, 1–3, (0.816)	n=3, 2.3, 2–3, (0.471)	n=3, 4.0, 3–5, (0.816)
Mean annual fecundity	n=3, 15.00, 12–20, (3.599)	n=3, 20.33, 4–34, (11.897)	n=3, 21.33, 11–36, (10.656)	n=3, 44.66, 34–59, (10.530)
Internesting interval	64	39–93	47–70 n=8, 57.13, 39–93, (17.424)	n=9, 48.4, 39–66, (8.447)

an aggregate, these are significantly longer than the nine internesting intervals in the fourth season (mean 57.1 versus 48.4, $p < 0.025$).

This pattern, of increased clutch size and clutch frequency with decreased internesting interval, was reported in an earlier, more general treatment, involving the several species in which it has occurred in our collection (Goode, 1991), and was attributed to acclimation effects on captives. While this may be true to some extent, the pattern is also consistent with the mechanism of a "bet hedging" reproductive strategy (Stearns, 1976), in which reproductive animals do not necessarily maximize progeny at each reproductive bout, but may in some instances conserve available resources for later reproductive output. Inherently, this involves producing the greatest reproductive output when environmental conditions are most favorable, and less reproductive output when environmental conditions are less favorable. While conditions provided to the animals in this series were fairly constant, the pattern becomes consistent with a "bet hedging" model if the period of environmental favorability which determines fecundity is not assumed to be within a particular season, but of multiseasonal duration, or cumulative from one season to the next. In the series shown in Table 13, annual fecundity in the first three seasons increased as a result of increased clutch frequency, but with a decrease in clutch size. Using the notation for clutch size relative to clutch frequency in Table 6, this reflects a shift from a predominance of C in the first season (CF 1.33) to a predominance of C–SC in the third season (CF 2.33). Increased clutch size in the fourth season reflects the change to a predominance of C–LC–SC–LC (CF 4.00) spanning the disproportionate increase in clutch size from CF 2 to CF 3 and higher. In the series comprising Table 13, clutch positions (as in Table 5) for the first three seasons include 71.5% C or SC and 28.5% LC; while the fourth season includes 50% LC and 50% C and SC.

Reproductive output of the progeny group was much lower than that of the original group, although they were well above the smallest size at egg laying observed (248–319 mm CL as opposed to 220 mm CL of female SH at production of 12 eggs) and were in some cases larger than female CZ or FW. As shown in Table 14, fecundity of the progeny group, also aggregated into first, second, etc., seasons of reproduction and not concurrent in time, increased from mean annual fecundity 7.8 in the first season to 16.33 in the third. Only one record is available for the fourth season, in which annual fecundity was 34.00. Analysis is limited by the small sample and extreme variation of the observations but it is obvious that fecundity increased from first to second

TABLE 14. Seasonal egg production in *Staurotypus triporcatus* (progeny group). For each group of data: n is sample size, followed by the mean, range, and standard deviation in parentheses.

	First season	Second season	Third season	Fourth season
Clutch size	n=10, 4.33, 1–7, (2.539)	n=13, 4.92, 2–8, (1.891)	n=6, 8.16, 5–13, (2.478)	n=3, 11.33, 9–11, (1.886)
Clutch frequency	n=5, 1.7, 1–2, (0.748)	n=5, 2.4, 2–8, (1.102)	n=3, 2.0, 2	n=1, 3.0, 3
Mean annual fecundity	n=5, 7.8, 5–13, (2.786)	n=5, 11.8, 2–18, (5.268)	n=3, 16.3, 12–22, (4.182)	n=1, 34.0, 34.0

seasons primarily as a result of increased clutch frequency, and from second to third seasons primarily as a result of increased clutch size, while increases from third to fourth season involved both clutch size and clutch frequency. Only the fourth season clutches fit the model shown in Table 6, in which C–LC–LC is predicted and 10–10–14 eggs were produced. In first through third seasons, clutches predicted as C have a mean clutch size of 5.23 (n = 13, range 1–9), while those predicted as SC had a mean of 5.00 (n = 12, range 4–13). However, the four clutches predicted as LC had a mean clutch size of only 4.25 (range 4–5). Only 15 internesting intervals occurred in the progeny group. The two in the fourth season (37 and 42) were, with one exception (41 in first seasons), shorter than all internesting intervals in the first through the third seasons.

Pacific Giant Musk Turtle (Staurotypus salvinii)

Specimens of *Staurotypus salvinii* produced 129 clutches in the years 1984 through 1991. Five females (the "original group" in the following discussion), obtained commercially on 26 January and 19 March 1984, produced 105 clutches. This group was reduced by one female prior to the 1988/89 season and by another prior to the 1989/90 season. An additional 24 clutches were produced in the years 1988 through 1991 by two females received as recent hatchlings on 10 December 1981 and 2 October 1982, and raised in the collection. These turtles were on breeding loan from the Maryland Center for Herpetological Research. The progeny females were maintained individually, as in the original *S. triporcatus* females (see above), and clutch production was recorded individually. Because relatively few records for the original group were individual, all observations for those turtles were combined.

Neonates varied in carapace length from 22 to 36 mm at hatching, and subsequent growth of these turtles raised in our collection is presented in Table 15. With a single exception, all progeny retained in the collection, which were hatched from eggs laid prior to 1988, have been males. This anomaly in a species shown to have heterogametic sex determination (Bull et al. 1974) was investigated in this series of eggs and reported elsewhere (Ewert and Nelson 1991). Males of *S. salvinii* are sexually dimorphic in tail length, girth of preanal tail, and presence of callosities on the hind legs as early as one year of age (70 mm CL), and all of our turtles were obviously dimorphic at the end of their second year (or at a size of approximately 100 mm CL). Specimens have been observed to evert their penis at 14 and 15 months of age. As in *S. triporcatus*, the attainment of secondary sexual characters was rapid in some specimens, with originally unsexable examples becoming obviously dimorphic within a three month period. Two females of the progeny group produced their first clutches at ages of 6 years, 73 days and 6 years, 352 days, and at 188–146 mm in carapace length. The latter carapace length is the smallest size for which egg laying has been observed in our turtles. Both of our females, however, were undoubtedly well past maturation at the time of their first breeding, and were not placed with males until the year prior to those clutch productions. Sachsse and Schmidt (1976) reported reproduction in sibling specimens in the female's third year. Reproduction of both of our progeny females in their first season was greater than the output of the original females in their first season (see below).

Nesting seasons are presented in Table 18. The first season of the original group, extending 312 days from 24 June through 2 May, encompassed all later seasons of both groups. In the aggregate, however, 120 of 130 clutches (95%) were laid in the 209 day period from 8 August through 5 March. Nesting seasons (n = 10) averaged 224.7 days, while intervening non-nesting seasons averaged 137.0 days.

Egg production for both the original and progeny groups is summarized in Table 16. Clutch size was 1–9 in the original, and 2–7 in the progeny group, with respective means of 5.17 and 5.13. Annual

TABLE 15. Growth in *Staurotypus salvinii*.

Age (post-hatching)	Number of specimens	Size range (mm CL)	Mean
1 year	34	37–96	68.2
2 years	26	58–136	89.1
3 years	12	75–138	103.5
4 years	8	90–134	109.0
5 years	6	114–145	123.4
6 years	5	131–161	152.0
7 years	3	143–184	167.0
8 years	2	164–198	181.0

TABLE 16. Nesting seasons, clutch size, clutch frequrency, and fecundity in *Staurotypus salvinii*.

Nesting season	Number of			Nesting season		Days prior to	Clutch size			Clutch frequency	Annual fecundity
	Females	Clutches	Eggs	Inclusive dates	Days	next clutch	Range	Mean	s[1]	per female	per female
Original group											
1984/85	5	13	45	24 Jun–2 May	312	184	2–7	3.46	1.278	2.6	9.0
1985/86	5	19	95	24 Jul–23 Feb	236	186	3–7	5.00	1.451	3.8	19.0
1986/87	5	19	111	28 Aug–31 Jan	156	180	5–8	5.84	0.933	3.8	22.0
1987/88	5	23	133	30 Jul–30 Jan	184	193	4–9	5.79	1.322	4.0	26.6
1988/89	4	16	86	11 Aug–18 May	279	84	4–8	5.73	1.181	4.0	21.5
1989/90	3	6	30	10 Aug–2 May	264	107	1–9	5.00	2.769	2.0	10.0
1990/91	3	9	43	17 Aug–22 May	216	—	1–7	4.77	1.618	3.0	14.3
Progeny group											
1988/89	2	6	29	28 Nov–18 May	171	84	3–7	5.00	1.414	3.0	14.5
1989/90	2	9	48	10 Aug–2 Apr	235	177	4–7	5.33	0.942	4.5	24.0
1990/91	2	9	46	26 Sep–9 Apr	194	—	2–7	5.11	1.099	4.5	20.5
Combined original group											
	30	105	543		235.3	139.2		5.17	1.218	3.5	18.1
Combined progeny group											
	6	24	123		200.0	130.5		5.13	1.218	4.0	20.5

[1]Standard deviation

fecundity and mean clutch frequency are derived from the numbers of females and numbers of clutches for each season and known only as means for the season in the original group. Seasonal mean annual fecundity ranged from 9.0–26.6 (mean 18.1) in the original and from 14.5–24.0 (mean 20.5) in the progeny group. Mean clutch frequency ranged from 2.0–4.0 (mean 3.5) in the original and from 3.0–4.5 (mean 4.0) in the progeny group. The initial years of the original group show the pattern of increased mean annual fecundity, clutch size, and clutch frequency as discussed in regard to *S. triporcatus*. Increases in clutch size from first to second seasons (mean 3.46 versus 5.00, $p < 0.01$) and from second to third seasons (mean 5.00 versus 5.84, $p < 0.025$) and increase in clutch frequency from first to second seasons (mean 2.6 versus 3.8) resulted in mean annual fecundity increases of 9.0 versus 19.0 versus 22.0. Subsequent interseasonal changes were not statistically significant as increments; decreases, however, spanning several seasons were significant (for example, 1987/89–1990/91, mean CS 5.79 versus 4.77, $p < 0.05$).

Results from the progeny group were similar to the original group of females, with the exception of having a more productive first year (approximating the second year of the original group). In addition to the similarity of mean clutch size (5.13 versus 5.17), the mean annual fecundity of the combined second and third season of the progeny group was similar to the combined mean annual fecundity of the most productive seasons of the original group (1986/87, 1987/88, and 1988/89, 23.5–23.57). While few conclusions can be drawn from this, it is indicated that the progeny females were larger and older than the sizes or ages that limited clutch frequency or clutch size. Higher first season fecundity in the progeny than in the original group may be related to the long term stability of the progeny animals in the captive environment prior to being placed in reproductive situations, as compared to the relatively recently collected specimens in the original group.

Clutch size was smaller in the early and late extremes of the nesting season. In the aggregate of the original group into a single nesting year, 17 clutches laid prior to 17 November and 11 clutches laid after 14 February were smaller than clutches laid in the central portion of the season (mean CS early 4.75, late 3.44, central 5.63, $p < 0.05$). In the small number of observations on the progeny group, clutch size declined slightly with laying history, as: first clutches ($n = 6$) mean CS 5.5, second clutches ($n = 6$) mean CS 5.8, third clutches ($n = 6$) mean CS 4.8, fourth clutches ($n = 4$) mean CS 4.75 and fifth clutches (n = 2) mean CS 4.5. While not directly observed in the original group, clutch size relative to laying dates indicates larger clutch size in third and fourth clutches than in first and second clutches. In the 1985/86 and 1986/87 seasons (both mean CF 3.8) and in the 1987/88 and 1988/89 seasons (both mean CF 4.0), it can be assumed that first and second clutches were predominantly in the early half of the laying dates; while third and fourth clutches were predominantly in the second half of laying dates. In aggregates of the two sets of seasons, early clutches were smaller than late clutches (1985/86–1986/87: n = 36 clutches, mean CS 4.77 versus 6.05, $p < 0.055$ and 1987/88–1988/89: n = 38 clutches, mean CS 4.17 versus 6.50, $p < 0.005$). The two seasons, which had mean clutch frequencies of less than 3.0 (1984/85: mean CF 2.6; 1989/90: mean CF 2.0), consisted of larger clutches in the early half of laying dates (1984/85: n = 13, mean CS 4.17 versus 3.00, $p < 0.005$ and 1989/90: n = 6, mean CS 6.00 versus 4.00, $p < 0.05$). This pattern indicates a similarity to the egg production pattern of *S. triporcatus* as noted in Table 5, such that seasons, in which mean clutch frequency was less than 3.00, had a predominance of clutches laid in C–SC patterns, while seasons, in which CF was 3.00 or more, had a predominance of larger clutches in later layings (C–LC–LC or C–LC–SC–LC).

In the progeny group, clutches laid as CF 3 had a mean clutch size of 5.5, those laid as CF 4 had a mean clutch size of 5.5, and those laid as CF 5 had a mean clutch size of 5.3 (n = 2 in each). In the original group, an increase of clutch size with increased clutch frequency, at least up to CF 4, is indicated in differences between seasons. Four seasons having mean clutch frequency more than 3.5 (1985/86–1986/87: mean CF 3.8 and 1987/88–1988/89: mean CF 4.0) had an overall mean clutch size of 5.51. Three seasons having mean clutch frequencies less than 3.5 (1984/85: mean CF 2.6, 1989/90: mean CF 2.0, and 1990/91: mean CF 3.00) had an overall mean clutch size of 4.21 ($p < 0.01$).

Internesting intervals in the progeny group were 20–114 days, with a mean (n = 18) of 57.6. While not directly observed in the original group, internesting intervals can be estimated by the minimal periods in which $n + 1$ clutches were produced by n females. These periods for each season were 29–63 days with a mean of 44.7 days.

Egg size and mass for each season are summarized in Table 17. In the original group of females, sizes were 26 to 43.5 mm length, 19 to 26 mm width,

TABLE 17. Egg size and mass in *Staurotypus salvinii*.

Season	Number of			Clutch size	Egg size (mm)		Egg mass (g)		
	Females	Clutches	Eggs		Range	Mean	Range	Mean	s[1]
Original group									
1984/85	5	13	45	3.46	26.0–40.0 × 19.0–26.0	32.53 × 20.16	5.0–15.0	8.72	2.916
1985/86	5	19	95	5.00	30.5–43.0 × 19.0–25.0	37.43 × 22.58	6.8–12.2	10.21	1.592
1986/87	5	19	111	5.84	32.0–42.0 × 20.0–23.0	37.26 × 21.34	8.1–13.2	10.35	1.465
1987/88	5	23	133	5.79	33.0–44.0 × 19.0–24.0	36.96 × 21.13	7.8–13.8	10.39	1.441
1988/89	4	16	86	5.73	31.5–42.0 × 20.0–23.0	39.30 × 22.51	8.1–12.8	10.58	1.062
1989/90	3	6	30	5.00	35.0–43.5 × 20.5–23.0	39.55 × 19.23	9.0–13.0	10.87	0.876
1990/91	3	9	43	4.77	34.5–43.0 × 20.5–23.0	39.15 × 21.33	9.0–14.1	10.85	1.389
Progeny group									
1988/89	2	6	29	5.00	35.0–40.0 × 20.5–23.0	37.35 × 21.15	9.2–14.3	10.43	0.830
1989/90	2	9	48	5.33	36.5–40.0 × 20.0–22.0	40.38 × 21.74	9.9–12.0	11.54	0.905
1990/91	2	9	46	5.11	35.0–43.0 × 20.5–43.0	39.84 × 21.78	9.0–14.5	11.81	1.158
Combined original group									
	30	105	543	5.17		37.15 × 21.39		10.34	1.252
Combined progeny group									
	6	24	123	5.13		39.46 × 21.61		11.37	1.029

[1]Standard deviation

and 5 to 14.1 g (means of 37.15 × 21.39 mm, 10.34 g). In the progeny group, sizes were 35 to 43 mm length, 20 to 23 mm width, and 9 to 14.5 g (means of 39.46 × 21.61 mm, 11.37 g). While eggs were not tracked individually through incubation, it is known that eggs as small as 30.5 mm length or 19 mm width or 7.0 g, or as large as 42 mm length or 25 mm width or 12.5 g, have produced viable hatchlings. Eggs of the first season (1984/85) were smaller than all subsequent years, and smaller than the mean for the group (8.72 versus 10.21 g, $p < 0.01$). From the 1985/86 through 1990/91 season, egg mass increased consistently. While no single increment of consecutive seasons is significant ($p > 0.1$), increments spanning two or three seasons are significant (for example, 1985/86–1988/89: 10.21 to 10.58 g, $p < 0.005$; 1987/88–1989/90: 10.39 to 10.87 g, $p < 0.05$). Eggs of the progeny group were larger than those of the original group (mean 11.37 versus 10.34 g, $p < 0.005$). In the progeny group, egg mass increased significantly from the first to second, and from the second to third seasons (mean 10.43 versus 11.54, $p < 0.005$; versus 11.81, $p < 0.05$). No relationship is apparent in the incremental increase in egg size in both series. In the original group, egg mass increased consistently while associated with increases, decreases and stability in mean clutch size and mean clutch frequency.

Egg mass was less in larger clutches, although the relationship is obscured by the variation in egg size from season to season. Table 18 presents egg mass relative to clutch size for the original series. Mass of eggs laid as clutch size 1–4 did not differ as a group from those laid as clutch size 7–9 in the entire series. The removal of the eggs laid in 1984/85 (which were, as a season group, smaller than all others) from the clutch size 1–4 group, however, produced a grouping in which egg size of the CS 1–4 group was significantly larger than CS 5 (mean 11.55 g versus 10.41 g, $p < 0.025$) and in which the clutch size was larger. Eggs of each season are also subgrouped into large and small clutch size, but the class of eggs laid as CS 5 are in the larger CS group in the 1984/85–1985/86 seasons and in the smaller CS group in later seasons, reflecting increased mean clutch size in the seasons. The 1989/90 and 1990/91 seasons are aggregated to increase sample size. Eggs of small clutch size were larger in all cases, but only significantly so in four of the six. Similar subgroups of each season, based upon laying date, revealed no significant differences in any season between masses of eggs laid in the early and late parts of the season (CF variation in CS).

Red-checked Mud Turtle (Kinosternon scorpioides cruentatum)

Specimens of this species produced 160 clutches in the years 1978 through 1991. The subspecies considered here ranges from Tamaulipas (Mexico) to Honduras (Iverson 1991). A mature pair (obtained commercially on 28 May 1968) and an additional male and two females (obtained commercially on 9 March 1977) produced seven clutches erratically in the years 1978 through 1983. These clutches are not considered in the following, but did produce the progeny females later added to the breeding group. Two additional pairs were obtained commercially on 14 February 1984 by export from Honduras and presumably were collected there. These five females constituted the breeding group in the 1984/85 and 1985/86 seasons. Three progeny females (one hatched on 19 September 1978; two hatched on 30 March 1981) were added to the group prior to the 1986/87 season. Two of the original females were removed; and four additional progeny females (hatched on 14 January, 18 January, 6 June, and 2 August 1982) were added prior to the 1987/88 sea-

TABLE 18. Egg mass and clutch size in *Staurotypus salvinii*.

	Clutch size	Number of clutches	Mean	s[1]
1984/85–1990/91	7–9	21	10.35	0.942
	6	23	10.50	1.365
	5	35	10.41	1.614
	1–4	24	10.76	1.632
1985/86–1990/91	1–4	15	11.55	0.864
1984/85	2–3	8	9.13	1.775
	5	5	8.13	2.198
1985/86	3–4	8	11.06	1.451
	5–8	11	9.53	1.634
1986/87	5	9	10.59	1.103
	6–9	10	10.34	1.062
1987/88	4–5	9	10.91	1.643
	6–9	14	10.31	1.025
1988/89	4–5	8	10.78	1.643
	6–9	8	10.61	1.341
1989/90–1990/91	4–5	9	11.88	1.033
	6–9	6	10.27	0.790

[1]Standard deviation

son. Two progeny females (hatched on 30 March 1981 and 18 January 1982) were removed prior to the 1988/89 season. One original female (obtained on 14 February 1984) and one progeny female (hatched on 19 September 1978) were removed; and two additional progeny females (hatched on 31 August and 25 October 1982) were added prior to the 1989/90 season. All females in the group in 1989/90 remained in the group through 1990/91 but several additional females were housed in the group for varying lengths of time, and as a result the group size is not known.

Size of females were 122–146 mm in carapace length with means for each season of 130.4 to 134.1 mm. Changes in mean size of breeding animals resulted primarily from addition and removal of different sized specimens, and little growth was shown by any breeding animals. Smallest size at egg laying observed in the group was 122 mm CL (one of the 1984 females) which grew only from 122–124 mm CL in the period 1984–1991. The largest clutch size recorded for this specimen was five eggs (on three occasions).

Individual nesting seasons are included in Table 19, and together encompassed the 315 day period from 9 August to 14 June. Length of seasons ranged from 69 to 263 days (with a mean of 188.9 days) and were separated by non-nesting periods, which ranged from 98 to 254 days, with a mean of 173.2 days. Mean dates of the nesting season were 20 October through 27 April. Clutch production was clustered in the central portion of the nesting seasons, with 144 of 154 (93.5%) clutches produced in the 212 day period from 21 October to 21 May.

Temperature dependent sex determination has been reported in this species, and confirmed in eggs of this series (Ewert and Nelson 1991). Due to incubation conditions, all progeny from eggs laid prior to 1988, which have been raised to maturity, have been females. Hatchlings ranged from 29–37 mm CL shortly after leaving the egg, and subsequent growth of specimens retained in the collection is shown in Table 20. Minimum size and age observed at nesting was 132 mm CL and 5 years, 117 days, but this is considerably larger than the minimum observed in the series (122 mm CL). Progeny females reached a mean length which surpassed the minimum nesting size in the latter part of their third year (3 years, 6 months to 4 years posthatching). Growth slowed considerably after the fifth year, with no individuals increasing more than 4 mm CL in the ages 5 to 9 years. While few records of male growth are available, the minimum size at which dimorphic characters became distinguishable was 118 mm CL (4 years, 87 days) in a progeny male and 122 mm CL in a wild collected male. Growth of progeny from this series has been shown to be comparable, although more variable, than sizes of wild-caught specimens ($n = 52$) assignable to second through fifth year age classes on the basis of carapacial annuli (Goode 1991).

While growth as an increase in carapace length of females has slowed or ceased after the fifth or sixth year, females in this age group continue to show changes in the configuration of the shell over time, which increase the bulk of the animal without necessarily increasing the linear dimensions of carapace length, shell height, or width of the carapace or plastron. Growth resulting in a greater convexity

TABLE 19. Nesting seasons and egg laying in *Kinosternon scorpioides cruentatum*.

Season	Number of Females	Number of Clutches	Number of Eggs	Nesting season Inclusive dates	Nesting season Days	Days prior to next clutch	Mean clutch frequency	Clutch size Range	Clutch size Mean	Clutch size s[1]	Mean annual fecundity
1984/85	5	5	10	19 Dec–26 Feb	69	164	1.00	1–3	2.00	0.632	2.0
1985/86	5	11	34	9 Aug–20 Mar	223	254	2.22	1–5	3.09	1.564	6.8
1986/87	8	13	31	29 Nov–27 Mar	118	155	1.63	1–4	2.38	0.923	3.6
1987/88	10	30	81	29 Aug–19 May	263	98	3.00	1–5	2.70	1.295	8.1
1988/89	8	26	106	25 Aug–29 Mar	216	220	3.25	2–7	4.07	1.662	13.2
1989/90	8	26	85	31 Oct–5 Jun	217	148	3.25	1–6	3.26	1.287	10.6
1990/91	—	42	133	10 Nov–14 Jun	216	—	—	1–8	3.16	1.617	—
Total		153	480	(Mean)	(188.9)	(173.2)			(3.14)		

[1]Standard deviation

of the sides of the rear portion of the carapace, and a shift in the site of maximum shell height to the rear creates a more bulbous configuration in the rear portion of the carapace. In two extreme conditions, the three carapacial keels are not detectable on the rear portion of the carapace, or the area lying between the outer keels, including the midline keel, is depressed in relation to the curve formed by the sides of the carapace. Although difficult to quantify, the result is an increase in the potential volume within the carapace and plastron in the rear portion of the animal. This shell configuration has been observed in some, but not all, males known to have been in excess of eight years age and that showed no significant growth over periods of several years. While this pattern of change of shape in the carapace complicates consideration of reproduction in relation to carapace length, it has also been, to say the least, less than helpful in the identification of examples of this taxon.

Clutch production in our *Kinosternon scorpioides cruentatum* for each season is summarized in Table 19. An egg-laying female was identified only in 43 of the 153 clutches and, unlike the original series of *Staurotypus salvinii*, records do not involve all females in each season in reproduction. Clutch frequency, calculated from the number of females in the group, must be considered only as a minimum value of group performance. Clutch size ranged from 1–8, with an overall mean of 3.14. Clutch frequency, for the first six seasons, ranged from (minimally) 1.63–3.25, with a mean of 2.52. Mean clutch size for seasons varied insignificantly from 2.00–3.09 in the first four seasons (mean CS 2.00–3.09–2.38–2.70, $p > 0.05$). However, mean clutch size in the fifth season was significantly higher than that of the seasons preceding or following it (2.70–4.07–3.26, $p < 0.05$). Although productivity of the females is only estimated, it is supportive of a pattern of increased fecundity, similar to that of *Staurotypus* in that both seasonal increases in mean clutch size (1987/88–1988/89) and the large but insignificant increase from 1984/85–1985/86 (2.00–3.09, $p > 0.05$) occurred in the years in which all females were in at least their second year in the conditions at hand.

In seasonal performance, clutch size increased with increased clutch frequency. Mean clutch size for the aggregate of the 1984/85–1987/88 seasons, in which mean clutch frequency was 2.11, was significantly smaller than mean clutch size of the aggregate of the 1988/89 and 1989/90 seasons, in which mean clutch frequency was 3.05 (mean CS 2.64 versus 3.11, $p < 0.005$). Clutch size did not vary regularly with laying date, however, as would be predicted if clutch size increased or decreased with laying history. In the aggregate of 1984/85 and 1985/86, in which mean clutch frequency was 1.38, clutch size did not differ in early and late clutches (before and after the midpoint of laying dates)(mean CS 2.38 versus 2.50, $p > 0.35$). In the aggregate of 1986/87 and 1987/88 (mean CF 2.66), early clutches were smaller than late clutches (mean CS 2.35 versus 3.20, $p < 0.05$), indicating an increase in CS from first to second and third clutches. However in the aggregate of 1988/89 and 1989/90, in which mean clutch frequency was 3.05, early and late clutches did not differ significantly, and decreased slightly (mean CS 3.77 versus 3.54, $p > 0.3$). While late clutches in this aggregate were not significantly larger than late clutches laid with mean clutch frequency of 2.66 (mean CS 3.54 versus 3.20, $p > 0.2$), early clutches in the latter grouping were much larger (mean CS 3.77 versus 2.35, $p < 0.005$). In the absence of identification of laying females no cause for this is apparent.

Minimal internesting intervals recorded, on the basis of the few observations of identified nesting females, were 32 and 35 days. Egg size was 26.5–37 mm length, 11–22 mm width and 3.8–9.1 g (means for 476 eggs, 17.9 × 31.6 mm and 6.44 g). Eggs as small as 12 mm width, 29 mm length and 4.4 g, and as large as 21 mm width, 34 mm length and 8.2 g produced viable hatchlings.

TABLE 20. Growth in female *Kinosternon scorpioides cruentatum.*

Age (post-hatching)	Number of specimens	Carapace length Range (mm)	Carapace length Mean
At hatching	67	27–36	33.0
6 months	29	44–68	58.2
1 year	28	50–87	69.1
1 year, 6 months	25	57–104	83.6
2 years	20	66–116	96.2
2 years, 6 months	16	78–118	101.7
3 years	13	86–125	107.0
3 years, 6 months	12	99–134	116.5
4 years	10	109–142	130.4
4 years, 6 months	10	117–145	132.3
5 years	8	122–145	134.0
5 years, 6 months	5	122–152	136.0

Mean egg size for each season is summarized in Table 21. Eggs laid in the first two seasons (1984/85 and 1985/86) were larger than eggs laid in the ensuing three seasons (mean 6.82, 6.83–6.24, 6.17–6.33 g, $p < 0.05$). Egg mass increased in the last two seasons (1989/90 and 1990/91). Although incremental increases were not significant, eggs of 1989/90 were significantly larger than those of 1986/87 (mean 6.56–6.24 g, $p < 0.05$). Mass of eggs relative to clutch size is also summarized in Table 21. No incremental decreases in mean egg mass by clutch size were significant, although the decrease from CS 3 to CS 4 approached that level (mean 6.42–6.16 g, $p > 0.05$). Aggregates of eggs laid as CS 1–3 were significantly larger than eggs laid as CS 4–6 (mean 6.49–6.17 g, $p < 0.05$). Interseasonal changes in egg mass did not parallel changes in mean clutch size entirely, as the absolute minimum mean egg mass occurred in the season preceding the largest mean clutch size, and in a season having a lower mean clutch size than three others (1987/88: mean CS 2.70, 6.17 g; 1989/89: mean CS 4.07, 6.33 g; 1989/90: mean CS 3.25, 6.56 g; 1990/91: mean CS 3.15, 6.45 g). However, the overall trend of small clutches in the early seasons having larger egg mass than larger clutches in later seasons is apparent. Age, independent of size, of the nesting females may also have been a factor. The large decrease in mean egg size in the third season occurred with the addition of young animals to the group, and although animals were added in subsequent years, the ages of those specimens were generally older in later seasons.

TABLE 21. Egg mass by season, and clutch size in *Kinosternon scorpioides cruentatum*.

Season	Number of eggs	Egg mass (g) Range	Mean	s[1]
1984/85	10	5.5–7.5	6.82	0.908
1985/86	32	5.4–8.2	6.83	0.979
1986/87	31	3.8–7.9	6.24	1.083
1987/88	78	4.8–9.0	6.17	0.979
1988/89	106	5.2–9.1	6.33	0.850
1989/90	85	5.0–8.1	6.56	0.709
1990/91	132	4.8–9.0	6.45	1.188
Clutch size				
1–2	125	4.7–8.3	6.58	0.993
3	126	4.8–9.0	6.42	0.999
4	88	4.9–9.1	6.16	0.979
5	95	3.8–9.0	6.20	0.992
6	42	5.5–8.1	6.12	0.605

[1]Standard deviation

Summary

Seasonally, reproductive patterns of the three species were very similar. Females of *Staurotypus triporcatus* and *S. salvinii* produced eggs in the 336-day period from 18 June to 20 May and the 312-day period from 24 June to 2 May, respectively, while those of *Kinosternon scorpioides cruentatum* produced eggs in the 312-day period from 9 August to 14 June. While the lengths of these periods are consistent with a year-round, acyclic reproduction, the clustering of laying dates of each species also indicates a seasonality in each. Females of *S. triporcatus* and *S. salvinii* produced 95% of their clutches in 249-day (18 August to 24 April) and 209-day (8 August to 5 March) seasons, respectively, while *K. s. cruentatum* females produced 94% in a 212-day (21 October to 21 May) season. Individual nesting seasons for the three had respective means of 180.1, 224.7, and 188.9 days. The three species were maintained under similar conditions in these series, and they also occur in proximity to each other in northern Central America and may be adapted to similar climatic regimes. A determination as to whether the similarities in reproductive seasonality are an artifact of captivity or a reflection of similar adaptation must await information from wild populations.

Problems in the correlation of rates of growth and maturation in captive and free-living specimens have been discussed by Zug (1991), and certainly apply to these observations. Both *S. salvinii* and *K. s. cruentatum* were maintained non-reproductively until well past maturation, as indicated by size at egg laying and by performance in their first year, in comparison to the case in *S. salvinii*. Progeny of *S. triporcatus*, however, appeared to have matured (as measured by the capability to produce fertile eggs) two to three seasons prior to the capability of production of clutches commensurate with their size relative to older females. While this may reflect artificially rapid growth in that form, growth of progeny *K. s. cruentatum* has been shown to be comparable to wild-collected specimens through the fifth year posthatching.

Body size of the female has been shown to be positively correlated with clutch size at the population level in many species of turtles. The correlation at the population level, however, does not extend to the level of the individual. While larger animals can, and as a group do, produce larger clutches, not all individual larger females produced larger clutches than all individual smaller females. Because the animals in these series were similarly sized and the number of females was much more akin to the individual than to the population level, and because other influencing factors overshadowed the effects of size upon egg production, size is not included in the analysis of reproductive output in these series.

Interseasonal differences in egg production were not isolated in individual seasons, but occurred as multiseasonal increases in fecundity. While it is not distinguished in these series as to whether the animals responded to a particular multiseasonal duration of environmental influences with a particular rate of egg production, or whether rate of increase in egg production was cumulative in several successive seasons of consistent environmental conditions, it is indicated that the period of time that constitutes the "environmental influences" which affect reproduction are not contained within a single nesting season. Interseasonal variations of energy and resource utilization in reproduction included the rate of production of eggs and, related to clutch size and frequency, the relative investment in individual eggs. At one extreme, the animals produced one or two small clutches of large sized eggs at long intervals; at the other, they produced three, four, or five larger clutches of smaller sized eggs at shorter intervals.

Variations in annual fecundity were associated with changes in both clutch size and clutch frequency. Clutch frequency, however, was the more active variable of the two in several respects. Inherently, changes in clutch frequency had greater numerical impact upon changes in annual fecundity, but in multiseasonal increases in egg production, clutch frequency also showed largest increases one or two seasons prior to largest increase in clutch size. Clutch size also varied with clutch frequency, as shown in *S. triporcatus* and indicated more and less strongly in *S. salvinii* and *K. scorpioides cruentatum*. Clutches laid as the second of CF 2 were relatively small, while clutches laid as the second and third of CF 3, and the second and fourth of CF 4, were relatively large.

Consideration of resource utilization based upon relative egg and body masses are artificial in the groups at hand, due to the high body mass of the well-fed females in the series. However, these are useful as comparisons between similarly well-fed groups. Few records of individual mass of females after oviposition are available, and mass varied among females, and in time in regard to individual females. As an approximation of "average" mass in each species, the normal mass of a near-mean-sized female in the non-nesting season has been used as an approximation. These are: *Staurotypus triporcatus* —4200 g, *S. salvinii*—900 g, and *Kinosternon scorpioides cruentatum*—405 g.

Despite the disparity in size of adults, eggs of *S. triporcatus* and *S. salvinii* are remarkably similar in size. Eggs in this series had respective means of 16.24 and 10.69 g (43.2 x 24.9 and 37.6 x 21.4 mm) and a small overlap occurred in the ranges of eggs producing viable hatchlings (12.5–12.3 g at 42–39 mm length and 25–23 mm width). Although *S. salvinii* had only 21.4% of the average body mass of *S. triporcatus*, its mean egg mass was 62.5%. Relative clutch mass (RCM) of *S. triporcatus* in the original group (mean CS 10.71) was 4.14%; while that of *S. salvinii* (mean CS 5.36) was 6.37%. Relative annual clutch mass (RACM) for *S. triporcatus* (mean CF 2.71 in original group) was 11.22%; while that of *S. salvinii* (mean CF 3.5) was 22.28%. Overall, the average *S. triporcatus* female utilized resources equivalent to 11.2% of body mass to produce 28.8 progeny per season; while the average *S. salvinii* used resources equivalent to 22.3% of body mass to produce 18.1 progeny per season.

Reproductive investment of *K. s. cruentatum*, as calculated from this series, is artificially very low, due to the relative high body mass of the females, and the probable low mean clutch size for the series, due to the inclusion of females new to the breeding group in most seasons with resultant small clutch production. RCM, based upon mean egg mass of 6.44 g and mean clutch size of 3.14, was 4.9%. This is extremely low when compared to data from other kinosternid turtles (Iverson 1991). The calculation of mean clutch frequency on the basis of the number of females present in the group, without observation of egg production by all individuals, may artificially lower RACM even further. In the last two seasons (1988/89 and 1989/90), in which group size was static, with mean CF 3.25 in both, RACM was 16.21%. However, the smallest female in the series

(124 mm CL) was observed to produce a clutch of 5 eggs at a body mass of 337 g, for an individual RCM of 9.6%, and was in one season observed to produce at least three clutches totaling 14 eggs, for an individual RACM of 26.8%.

Acknowledgments

Thanks are due to David Blody and his staff at the Fort Worth Zoo for the loan of specimens, as well as Anthony Wisneisky for provision of hatchlings as a breeding loan. Michael A. Ewert and Brian Viets contributed discussion and counsel; two reviewers and the editors of this volume greatly improved the manuscript. In particular, gratitude is expressed to the Reptile Department staff of the Columbus Zoo, Daniel Badgley, Ronald Hatcher, Nanci Pintavalli, Jane McEvoy, and Joel Williams for assistance, discussion, and primarily for their enthusiasm, hard work, and dedication to the livestock in the department.

Literature Cited

Álvarez del Toro, M. 1982. Los Reptiles de Chiapas. Third edition. Inst. Historia Natural, Tuxtla Guitierrez, Chiapas, Mexico. 248 pages.

Bull, J. J., R. G. Moon, and J. M. Legler. 1974. Male heterogamety in kinosternid turtles (genus *Staurotypus*). Cytogenet. Cell Genet., 13: 419–425.

Congdon, J. D., and D. W. Tinkle. 1982. Reproductive energetics of the painted turtle (*Chrysemys picta*). Herpetologica, 38: 228–236.

Dean, R. H., and J. W. Bickham. 1983. *Staurotypus salvinii*. Soc. Study Amphib. Reptiles, Cat. Amer. Amphib. Reptiles, 327: 1–2.

Ewert, M. A. 1985. Embryology of turtles, p. 75–267. *In* C. Gans, F. Billett, and P. F. A. Maderson (eds.), Biology of the Reptilia, volume 14: Development A. John Wiley, New York.

—. 1991. Cold torpor, diapause, delayed hatching and aestivation in reptiles and birds, p. 173–192. *In* C. C. Deeming and M. W. Ferguson (eds.). Egg Incubation: Its Effects on Embryonic Development in Birds and Relatives. Cambridge Univ. Press, Cambridge, UK.

Ewert, M. A., and J. M. Legler. 1978. Hormonal induction of oviposition in turtles. Herpetologica, 34: 314–318.

Ewert, M. A., and C. E. Nelson. 1991. Sex determination in turtles: diverse patterns and some possible adaptive values. Copeia, 1991: 50–69.

Gibbons, J. W. 1982. Reproductive patterns in freshwater turtles. Herpetologica, 38: 222–227.

—. 1983. Reproductive characteristics and ecology of the mud turtle, *Kinosternon subrubrum* (Lacépède). Herpetologica, 39: 254–271.

Gibbons, J. W., J. L. Greene, and K. K. Patterson. 1982. Variation in reproductive characteristics of aquatic chelonians. Copeia, 1982: 776–783.

Goode, J. M. 1991. Breeding aquatic and semi-aquatic turtles at the Columbus Zoo, p. 66–77. *In* K. R. Beaman, F. Caporaso, S. McKeown, and M. D. Graff (eds.). First International Symposium on Turtles and Tortoises: Conservation and Captive Husbandry. Circle, Los Angeles.

Iverson, J. B. 1985*a*. *Staurotypus*. Soc. Study Amphib. Reptiles, Cat. Amer. Amphib. Reptiles, 328: 1–2.

—. 1985*b*. *Staurotypus triporcatus*. Soc. Study Amphib. Reptiles, Cat. Amer. Amphib. Reptiles, 362: 1–2.

—. 1991. Phylogenetic hypotheses for the evolution of modern kinosternine turtles. Herpetol. Monogr., 5: 1–27.

Iverson, J. B., E. L. Barthelmess, G. R. Smith, and C. E. de Rivera. 1991. Growth and reproduction in the mud turtle *Kinosternon hirtipes* in Chihuahua, Mexico. Jour. Herpetol., 25: 64–72.

Moll, E. O. 1979. Reproductive cycles and adaptations, p. 305–331. *In* M. M. Harless and H. Morlock (eds.). Turtles: Perspectives and Research. Wiley, New York.

Neill, W. T., and R. Allen. 1959. Studies on amphibians and reptiles of British Honduras. Publ. Res. Div. Ross Allen Reptile Inst., 2(1): 1–76.

Sachsse, W., and A. A. Schmidt. 1976. Nachzucht in der zweiten Generation von *Staurotypus salvinii* mit weiteren Beobachtungen zum Fortpflanzungsverhalten (Testudines, Kinosternidae). Salamandra, 12: 5–16.

Schmidt, A. A. 1970. Zur Fortpflanzung der Kreuzbrustschildkröte (*Staurotypus salvinii*) in Gefangenschaft. Salamandra, 6: 3–10.

Sexton, O. J. 1960. Notas sobre la reproducción de una tortuga Venezolana, la *Kinosternon scorpioides*. Mem. Soc. Cienc. Natur. La Salle, 20: 189–197.

Stearns, S. C. 1976. Life history tactics: a review of the ideas. Quart. Rev. Biol., 51: 3–47.

Wilbur, H. M., and P. J. Morin. 1988. Life history evolution in reptiles, p. 387–439. *In* C. Gans and R. B. Huey (eds.). Biology of the Reptilia. Volume 16, Ecology B. Defense and Life History. A. R. Liss, New York.

Zug, G. R. 1991. Age determination in turtles. Soc. Study Amphib. Reptiles, Herpetol. Circ., 20: 1–28.

❦ Goode, J. M. 1994. Reproduction in captive neotropical musk and mud turtles (*Staurotypus triporcatus*, *S. salvinii*, and *Kinosternon scorpioides*), p. 275–295. *In* J. B. Murphy, K. Adler, and J. T. Collins (eds.), Captive Management and Conservation of Amphibians and Reptiles. Society for the Study of Amphibians and Reptiles, Ithaca (New York). Contributions to Herpetology, volume 11.

CONSERVATION BIOLOGY OF GALÁPAGOS REPTILES: TWENTY-FIVE YEARS OF SUCCESSFUL RESEARCH AND MANAGEMENT

LINDA J. CAYOT,* HOWARD L. SNELL,**,*** WASHINGTON LLERENA,* AND HEIDI M. SNELL**,****

Introduction

REARING AND REPATRIATION PROGRAMS FOR Galápagos Tortoises (*Geochelone*) and Land Iguanas (*Conolophus*) of the Galápagos Islands were established in 1965 and 1976, respectively, to protect threatened populations from extinction. During the last 25 years, all of the tortoise and iguana populations included in these long-term programs have been saved from immediate danger. The ultimate success of the programs, however, will be determined in the future and is closely linked to the eventual eradication of introduced mammals within the Galápagos. The current status of Galápagos Tortoise and Land Iguana populations has been reviewed recently and will not be presented again here (for tortoises, see MacFarland et al. 1974; de Vries 1984; Fritts 1983, 1984; Ernst and Barbour 1989; for iguanas, see Snell 1984; Snell et al. 1984).

Since the discovery of the islands in 1535, Galápagos Tortoises have been exploited for meat, first by the buccaneers in the 17th and 18th centuries, then by whalers and fur sealers in the 19th century, and by colonists after 1832 (Townsend 1925; Slevin 1959; de Vries 1984; Hickman 1985). A conservative estimate of the number of Galápagos Tortoises removed by the American whaling fleet from 1830 to 1900 exceeds 100,000 (Townsend 1925). In the late 19th century and early 20th century research expeditions removed significant numbers of the relatively few remaining tortoises (Slevin 1959). Finally, in the first half of the 20th century, tortoises were commercially exploited for their oil (Beck 1903; Slevin *in* Fritts and Fritts 1982). Currently, a few tortoises are still killed every year by humans (H. L. Snell, pers. observ.).

As the number of Galápagos Tortoises and their exploitation by humans declined, mammals introduced by early visitors and colonists became the major threat to the tortoise populations and remain so today (Eckhardt 1972; MacFarland et al. 1974; MacFarland and Reeder 1975; Hoeck 1984). Introduced predators, primarily pigs (*Sus scrofa*), rats (*Rattus rattus*), and dogs (*Canis familiaris*), have wreaked havoc on some populations. Introduced competitors, principally goats (*Capra hircus*), but also burros (*Equus asinus*) and wild cattle (*Bos taurus*), destroy tortoise habitat. The combination of low population sizes that resulted from severe exploitation by humans and the impact of introduced mammals on these same populations has caused the extinction of at least two races and pushed several others to the edge of extinction.

Land Iguanas were not usually heavily exploited by humans, but they are much more vulnerable to introduced predators. Their demise on Santa Cruz and Isabela (Figure 1) was due primarily to nest destruction by pigs and predation of adults by feral dogs (Snell 1984; Snell et al. 1984). While the cause of extinction of Land Iguanas on Santiago is unknown (Snell et al. 1984), dogs may have been present there prior to 1900, when the extinction occurred (Kruuk 1979; Heyerdahl and Skjölsvold

* Charles Darwin Research Station
Casilla 17–01–3891
Quito, Ecuador

** Department of Biology
University of New Mexico
Albuquerque, New Mexico 87131, USA

*** Charles Darwin Foundation for the Galápagos Islands
Casilla 17–01–3891
Quito, Ecuador

**** Science Applications International Corporation
Albuquerque, New Mexico 87106, USA

1956), and may have been the primary cause. Dogs have also had severe impacts on certain populations of Marine Iguanas, *Amblyrhynchus cristatus* (Kruuk and Snell 1981).

The extinction of Land Iguanas from Baltra occurred during the late 1940s. During World War II an American airbase was constructed on Baltra and inhabited by several thousand United States servicemen and Ecuadorian support staff. While the actual mechanisms of the extinction of Land Iguanas there are disputed (Eibl-Eibesfeldt 1960; Woram 1991), it is apparent that some combination of habitat destruction, direct predation by humans, dogs, and cats, and possibly competition by feral goats caused one of the fastest known extinctions of a population of reptiles.

Tortoise Program

A rearing and repatriation program for Galápagos Tortoises (*Geochelone elephantopus*) was begun in 1965 to save the population of Pinzón. Following the establishment of the Galá-pagos National Park in 1959, surveys of the tortoise populations were begun (Figure 1). On Pinzón, only old adults were found and no juveniles. Black rats, introduced to Pinzón in the latter half of the 1800s, were eating all of the hatchlings and had apparently stopped recruitment into the population since, perhaps, the turn of the century (MacFarland et al. 1974).

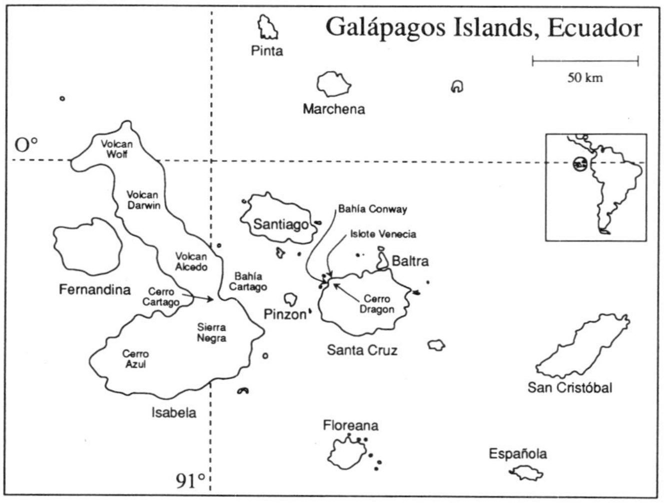

FIGURE 1. Map of the Galápagos Islands identifying localities where conservation activities of the Charles Darwin Research Station and the Servicio Parque Nacional Galápagos occur.

Over the years, other threatened populations that were included in the program, and the factors that endangered them, have been those of Santiago (small population with a majority of the animals male, nest destruction by pigs, and habitat destruction by goats), San Cristóbal (small population and nest destruction by dogs), Sierra Negra (small population, nest destruction by pigs, and predation by dogs and humans), Cerro Azul (small population, nest destruction by pigs, and predation by dogs), Santa Cruz (nest destruction by pigs), and Volcán Wolf (predation by humans) (MacFarland et al. 1974).

The tortoise population of Española, however, was so close to extinction that all tortoises on the island (12 females and 2 males) were removed to the Tortoise Breeding Center at the headquarters of the Charles Darwin Research Station and the Servicio Parque Nacional de Galápagos, where a captive-breeding program was initiated. In addition, goats had destroyed much of the vegetation, destroying the tortoises' food. The adult tortoises are maintained in captivity, and have been breeding and nesting. As with the other races, the young are reared to 3 to 5 years of age and then repatriated. The first successful hatching occurred in 1970–71. In 1977, an additional adult male was returned to the islands from the San Diego Zoo and was added to the breeding population (Fritts 1978).

Land Iguana Program

A program for Land Iguanas (*Conolophus subcristatus*) began in 1976, following the near extirpation of two populations by wild dogs (Cerro Cartago on Isabela and Cerro Dragón on Santa Cruz; Figure 1). All iguanas found in these areas were transferred to the Tortoise Breeding Center and the iguana program was begun. As with the Española tortoises, the iguanas are bred in captivity and the hatchlings reared for eventual repatriation. Unlike Galápagos Tortoises, Land Iguanas of all sizes are susceptible to predation by dogs; therefore, repatriations are only possible following effective efforts to control populations of dogs (Reynolds 1982).

Due to overcrowding in the Center at the start of the program, 38 of the Santa Cruz iguanas were moved to the small islets of Venecia on the northwestern coast of Santa Cruz in 1977 (Figure 2), where they were released in semi-captive conditions. Because Venecia lacked nesting areas, approximately 100 m^3 of soil were moved there from Santa Cruz and an artificial nesting area was built. The iguanas breed and reproduce and juveniles are then repatriated to Cerro Dragón, Isla Santa Cruz (Snell and Snell 1980; Snell and Márquez 1985).

The third population included in the iguana program is that of Baltra/Seymour Norte. The population of Land Iguanas on Baltra became extinct in the late 1940s. Approximately 70 of them, however, had been transferred to Seymour Norte (an island that apparently never had native Land Iguanas) in 1932 and 1933 (Banning 1933; Reynolds 1981; Woram 1992). By the late 1970s it appeared that there was little to no recruitment into the population on Seymour Norte and the first pair of adults was brought to the Center (Snell and Snell 1981; Snell et al. 1984). Later, this breeding population was enlarged. The objective of breeding these iguanas was the eventual repatriation of iguanas to Baltra (Cayot and Menoscal 1992).

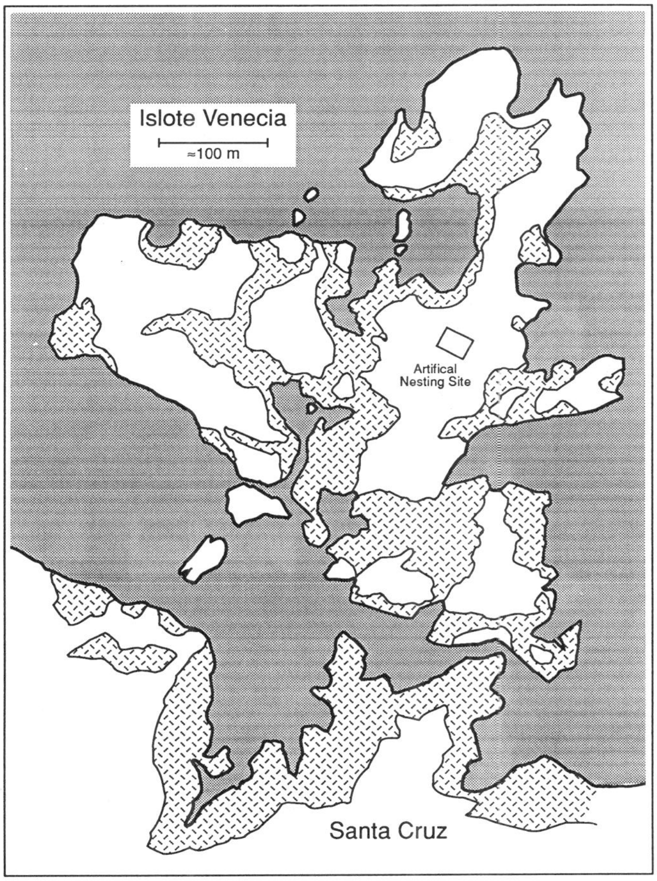

FIGURE 2. Map of Islote Venecia, the site of the semi-captive rearing program for Land Iguanas from Santa Cruz. The shaded area represents ocean waters and the dashed areas mangrove swamps. The clear areas of Venecia are the available habitat for Land Iguanas.

Methods

Four basic management strategies are involved in the recovery of Galápagos Tortoise and Land Iguana populations in Galápagos. The success of each strategy is interdependent with the others. The strategies are:

(1) Captive rearing of tortoises and iguanas, followed by repatriation to their island of origin. This strategy involves captive-breeding colonies, such as those of the Española tortoises and iguana populations of Santa Cruz, Isabela (Cartago Bay) and Baltra; and the transfer of eggs and/or hatchlings from natural nests to the Tortoise Rearing Center, which has been done with all other threatened tortoise populations (see below).

(2) Use of a semi-captive breeding colony in natural conditions, as is done with the iguanas on Islote Venecia (Santa Cruz population).

(3) Protection of tortoise nests against destruction by pigs (Santiago and Santa Cruz populations).

(4) Control and/or eradication of introduced mammals on the smaller islands and in critical tortoise and iguana areas.

Captive Rearing of Galápagos Tortoises and Land Iguanas

Breeding in Captivity. Española tortoises and the three groups of iguanas from different island populations are bred at the Center. The tortoises (1 male with 5 females and 2 males with 7 females) are permanently housed in two corrals (20 × 54 m), each with several nesting areas. They breed naturally. During the nesting season (June through December), females are checked daily for nesting activity.

Land Iguanas are normally housed individually due to their extreme aggressiveness. During the breeding season, which differs for the three populations (Snell et al. 1984), a single male is housed with one or two females in the large breeding pens (25 × 12 m), each of which contains a single nesting zone. When the female commences nesting, the male is removed to avoid potential fights over territories.

The morning following the nesting of either tortoises or iguanas, the nest is opened and the eggs are transferred to the incubators.

Transfer of Eggs and Hatchlings from the Wild. In all Galápagos Tortoise populations, except Española, eggs and hatchlings are collected from natural nests on the respective islands near the end of the incubation season and are brought to the Center. The incubation period is completed at the Center (usually for a period of a few weeks). An annual goal of 50 tortoises per population was established, based on recommendations of the Work Group on "Problems and Solutions Related to Population Genetics, Minimum Population Size, and Endogamy" of the International Workshop on the Herpetology of Galápagos in 1988.

Incubation. Initially, solar incubators were used in the Center. In the 1980s, a series of experiments were conducted to determine the optimum temperature and water potential for incubation (Snell 1985; Snell, Snell, and Tracy 1985; Snell, Snell, and Lawler 1987; Tracy and Snell 1985). The more important results of these experiments include:

(1) Galápagos Tortoises have temperature-dependent sex determination; lower temperatures produce males and higher temperatures produce females (Sancho 1988).

(2) Certain temperatures, which are different for tortoises and iguanas, result in a higher hatching success (Snell, Márquez et al. 1985; Snell, Snell, and Tracy 1985).

(3) Water potential of the substrate is critical for iguana eggs (which are soft-shelled) and less critical for tortoise eggs (which hard-shelled) (Snell 1985; Snell, Snell, and Tracy 1985).

As a result of these findings, the incubation system was changed and overall hatching success has improved. Electric incubators with thermostatic controls are now used. Tortoise eggs are incubated at a temperature of 28.5°–29.5°C and a water potential of –1100 kPa (kilopascals). This produces the highest hatching success and a male-to-female ratio of 1:2. Iguana eggs are incubated at a temperature of 30°C and a water potential of ≈ –600 kPa.

Rearing of Young. Rearing procedures for both Galápagos Tortoises and Land Iguanas have been improved over the years. Improvements for tortoises primarily have involved the physical conditions of their corrals—the most significant change has been moving them outdoors (Snell, Márquez et al. 1985; Snell et al. 1988)—while changes for iguanas have included improving both physical conditions of their cages (principally, heat lamps for the cold season) and their diet.

Upon emerging from the egg, both tortoises and iguanas are kept in dark boxes for a period of 2 to 4 weeks, which simulates the time in the natural nest chamber (MacFarland et al. 1974). Tortoises are then transferred to outdoor corrals. As of December 1990, all tortoises are reared outside on a natural substrate, so that they can receive direct sunlight. Hatchlings are kept confined in corrals with a soil substrate until they reach approximately two years of age. These corrals are covered at night to prevent predation by rats. At two years, the tortoises are transferred to adaptation corrals, which are larger areas with a natural lava substrate, where they remain until repatriation.

Iguanas are housed in completely closed cages to prevent their escape and to prevent predation by rats and cats. High mortality in recent years appears to be due to dietary problems. Because of the difficulty of maintaining a well-balanced, highly nutritious diet, particularly during periods of drought, use of a prepared diet mixed with fresh plant material was initiated in 1990 (O. T. Oftedal and L. J. Cayot, in prep.). This diet is based on one originally created for green iguanas.

Repatriation. Repatriation of both tortoises and iguanas generally takes place during the hot or rainy season when conditions are most favorable. Prior to repatriation, the animals are measured and weighed, and then permanently marked. They are transferred to their island of origin in wooden boxes, then carried to the release site. Tortoises are released either in a nesting zone or in one of the major living areas of adults. Iguanas are released near the center of distribution of the original population.

Monitoring of Repatriated Populations. To determine the success of the repatriation program, the various populations are monitored periodically. Galápagos Tortoises or Land Iguanas encountered are measured and their identification recorded. In the case of Española, the population is monitored semi-annually, with tortoise searches concentrated in the areas surrounding the two release sites. A census of the tortoise population on Pinzón was taken in 1989 and again in 1990, using a mark-recapture system. Monitoring of the other less-endangered tortoise populations is done less regularly.

The Land Iguana populations at Cerro Dragón and Cerro Cartago are monitored annually. In 1988, permanent areas were defined to take censuses of the populations. These encompass the major areas of the iguana colonies. A system of mark-recapture is used. In addition, censuses of two natural populations of iguanas are regularly done: Isla Plaza Sur (Snell et al. 1984) and Puerto Bravo, Volcan Wolf, Isabela (Snell et al. 1986). These natural populations will serve as controls for comparisons of fluctuations within repatriated populations.

Prior to any repatriation, factors originally threatening the population must be eliminated or controlled. For over-exploited populations with no introduced animals, nothing is required, because human predation has been greatly reduced (de Vries 1984). In the case of the existence of feral predators or competitors, however, the populations of these animals must either be reduced or eliminated. Population control of feral animals in the Galápagos is usually carried out by a combination of hunting and poisoning.

Semi-Captive Breeding Colony

As previously mentioned, the iguana program uses an additional "semi-captive" colony located on Islote Venecia (Figure 2), just off the northwest corner of Santa Cruz (Figure 1). Since their introduction there and the construction of an artificial nesting site in 1977, the original 38 adults have successfully reproduced. Currently, the population of Venecia is between 150 and 300 iguanas, and the first-generation offspring have begun reproducing (Snell and Márquez 1985; Márquez et al. 1986). The high degree of success at this site is possibly due to its proximity to the natural range of the iguanas introduced there. Venecia is less than 5 km from Cerro Dragón, the site of the iguana colony from which the adults were captured. Seasonal climatic patterns, vegetation, and the physical environment are practically identical. Venecia is protected from the feral dogs that devastated the Cerro Dragón population of iguanas by a 3 m wide channel separating it from Santa Cruz. Since 1985 young iguanas from Venecia have augmented the captive-produced iguanas repatriated at Cerro Dragón.

Protection of Natural Nests

In two populations of Galápagos Tortoises, those of Santa Cruz and Santiago, the primary threat to successful reproduction is destruction of nests by feral pigs (MacFarland et al. 1974). In those populations, natural nests were protected by wardens of the Servicio Parque Nacional de Galápagos who had built rock walls around them. The rocks prevent attack by the pigs, yet allow emerging hatchling tortoises to disperse naturally. Unfortunately, the 1×2 m walls probably lowered the temperature of the nests and may have influenced sex ratios of the neonates. A new method of protecting natural nests consists of covering them with 1.5 m^2 pieces of chain-link fencing, which are placed flat on the surface of the ground. Nests protected in this manner had temperatures identical to adjacent unprotected nests (Reynolds 1982). Undoubtedly some individual hatchlings are still encountered and eaten by pigs, but protecting the nests prevents losing a complete clutch in a single encounter.

Control of Feral Mammals

A program for the control or eradication of introduced mammals has coincided with that of rearing and repatriation. For Galápagos Tortoises, this has included attempts at mammal control or protection of tortoise nests. Rats have been controlled in the major tortoise-nesting zone on Pinzón; while not necessary for the survival of the repatriates, rat eradication is essential for the ultimate survival of the population. Goats, the only introduced mammal on Española, were eradicated in 1978. Control of pigs in tortoise nesting zones on Santiago and Santa Cruz is combined with the annual protection of tortoise nests. A major program to eradicate pigs on Santiago began in 1989. On San Cristóbal, nests were fenced against dogs, until their eradication in the mid–1970s. On both Sierra Negra and Cerro Azul, Isabela, dogs were eradicated in 1982, pigs are controlled in the nesting zones, and nests are protected if necessary.

Dogs were eradicated from the Land Iguana areas at Cerro Dragón, Santa Cruz and Cerro Cartago, Isabela in 1982. At both sites, cats are poisoned semi-annually. Populations of cats and dogs were reduced on Baltra prior to the first repatriation in June 1991.

Conclusions

Incubation. Advances in incubation methods in recent years have resulted in major improvements in hatching success for Galápagos Tortoises (Figure 3). Hatching success for Española tortoises averaged 19.5% from 1979–80 to 1986–87 (earlier data are less reliable). In 1987–88 and 1988–89, while the incubation experiments were in process, hatching success averaged 43.3%. In the last three years, with the incubation system established, hatching success averaged 54.4%. In terms of overall tortoise production, an average of 24.3 Española tortoises hatched annually between 1971 and 1987 (the range was 10–52), while an average of 89 per year (the range was 82–96) hatched in the last five years.

Results of incubation of Land Iguanas are more variable and show a gradual decline in hatching success (Figure 3). Hatching success of iguana eggs is usually higher than those of tortoises, however, even though tortoise eggs seem much more robust. We propose two factors that potentially contribute to the decline in hatching success of iguana eggs. The first is an apparent problem with the physical condition of captive females, which is related to diet. The second is a change in the protocol for extracting eggs from nests laid in captivity. During the years of high hatching success, eggs were removed from nests within three hours of oviposition (Snell and Snell 1980). Recently, changes in the duties of the personnel responsible for caring for iguanas has caused greater delays (often of 12 to 24 hours) in the removal of eggs. For reasons that we do not understand, eggs remaining within the captive-laid nests for longer periods of time are significantly more prone to attack by fungus during incubation (H. L. Snell, pers. observ.).

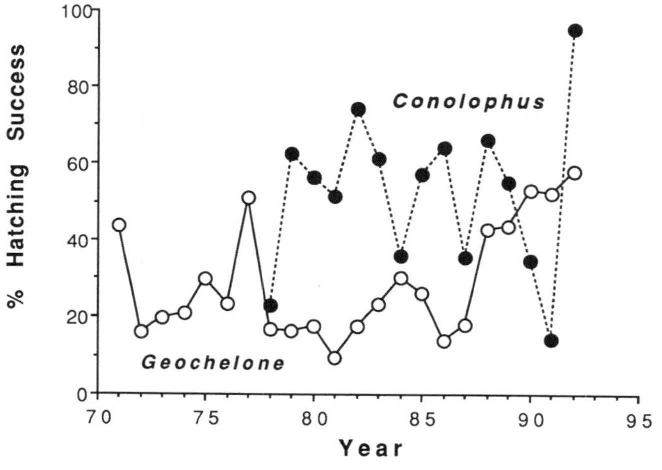

FIGURE 3. Hatching success of Galápagos Tortoise and Land Iguana eggs incubated at the Charles Darwin Research Station/Servicio Parque Nacional de Galápagos rearing and repatriation program. Solid circles represent data for Land Iguanas and hollow circles are tortoises from the Española population. Lines connect points for clarity, no relationship is implied. All points represent means of all eggs laid.

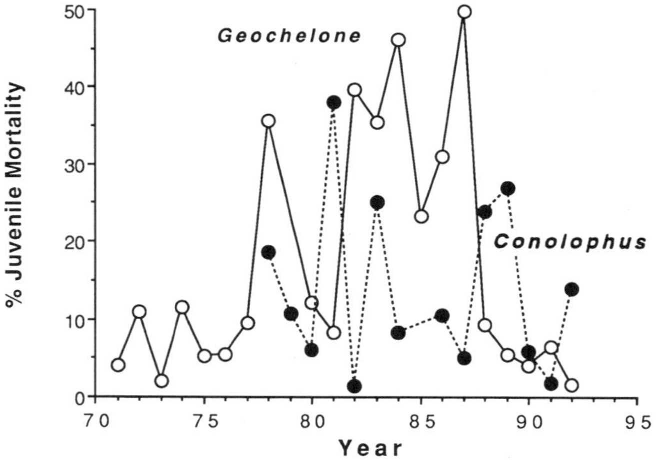

FIGURE 4. Annual Mortality of Galápagos Tortoise and Land Iguana juveniles housed at the Charles Darwin Research Station/Servicio Parque Nacional de Galápagos rearing center. Data come from all populations reared in any year. Circles and lines as in Figure 3.

Rearing. Improvements in rearing conditions have resulted in lower mortality of juvenile tortoises in the last few years (Figure 4). Annual rates of mortality of juvenile tortoises averaged 30.7% between 1980 and 1987 (earlier data are less reliable), while in the last three years mortality dropped to an average of 5.9%. Mortality remained low in 1991 and 1992.

Mortality of hatchling Land Iguanas has been equally erratic (Figure 4). In 1988 and 1989, annual rates of mortality of hatchling iguanas averaged 25.6%. Following changes in diet, average mortality dropped to below 6% per year in 1990 through 1992. Again, as in the hatching success of eggs, the mortality of tortoises is greater than that of iguanas. Much of the early mortality of tortoises, however, was due to raising them indoors (Snell, Márquez, et al. 1985, Snell et al. 1988).

Repatriation. From 1970 to 1992, there has been a steady increase in the number of Galápagos Tortoises repatriated to their island of origin (Figure 5). By the end of 1992, a total of 1415 had been released.

Tortoises have been repatriated for approximately 23 years, with an average of 62 repatriates each year. With the current goal of 50 tortoises/cohort for each tortoise taxon in the program, and a population of 400–600 in the Center at any one time, this number should be doubled within the next ten years.

A total of 390 iguanas has been repatriated from the Rearing Center to Cerro Cartago (Isabela), and 65 to Cerro Dragón (Santa Cruz). An additional 110 have been transferred from Islote Venecia to Cerro Dragón. In June 1991, 35 five-year-old iguanas were released on Baltra, making this the first time iguanas were present on that island in more than 40 years. An additional 24 were repatriated in 1992, yielding a total population of 59 iguanas on Baltra. The total number of repatriated iguanas is 710. Repatriation of iguanas has been performed for approximately ten years, yielding an average of 71 repatriates each year. Due to the dietary problems in the Center, there are few juveniles at the moment. With the use of the prepared diet, however, the numbers should increase in the near future.

The higher rate of repatriation for iguanas, as compared to that of tortoises, reflects their greater reproductive effort (Snell et al. 1984; MacFarland et. al. 1974) and the generally higher rates of hatching success and survivorship (Figures 3 and 5).

Population Status. A review of the population status of three of the more threatened populations of reptiles indicates steady improvement since the start of the rearing and repatriation program.

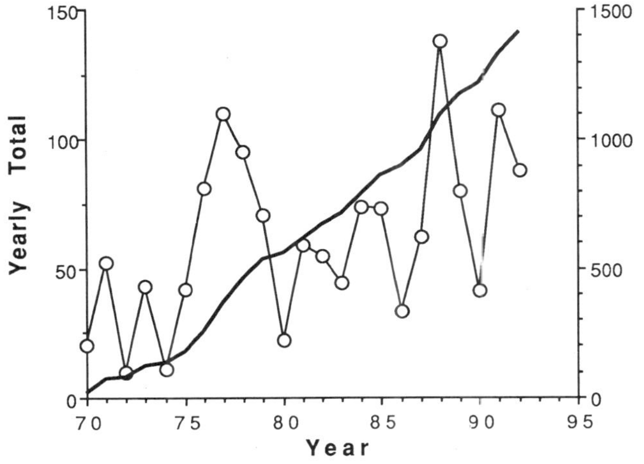

FIGURE 5. Total numbers of juvenile Galápagos Tortoises (circles) repatriated to all populations per year and the cumulative total (thick line). Note difference in scales.

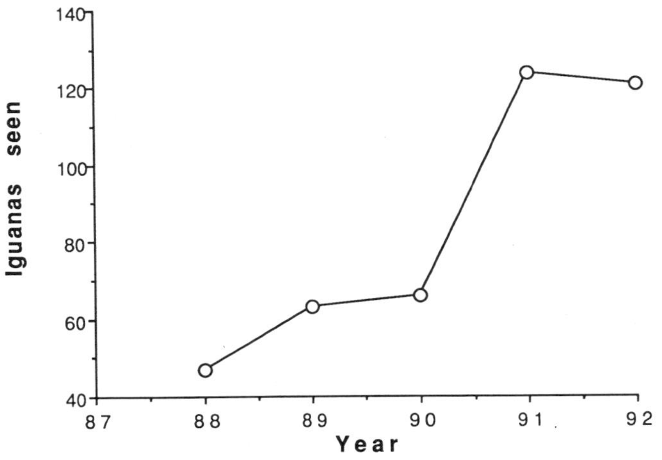

FIGURE 6. Numbers of Land Iguanas seen during annual censuses of the Cartago Bay repatriation site. While there is a slight potential for variation in census effort between years, most of the increase is due to successful repatriation and reproduction.

The tortoise population on Española, the closest to extinction in 1959, will probably be the first to be self-sustaining, and will no longer need management. Tortoises were first repatriated to Española in 1975. By November 1991, a total of 369 had been released, and an additional 211 live in the Center. Goats, the only introduced mammal on Española, were eradicated in 1978 (Hoeck 1984). In November 1990, the first hatchlings (both dead) and four attempted nests were found (Márquez et al. 1991). In June 1991, the first live hatchling was found; in November 1991, 15 nests were located and the same hatchling recaptured.

On Pinzón, the population had only a brief time before it would become extinct, because it was limited to old adults with no successful recruitment. The first repatriates (cohort 1965–66) have reached reproductive size and are now larger than the native adults. Copulation and nesting by repatriates has been recorded, but no young known to be offspring of repatriates have yet been found. A total of 184 of the 268 repatriates were observed during the tortoise censuses of 1989–90, with an estimated repatriate population of 207, giving a minimum survivorship of 68.7% and an estimated survivorship of 77.2%. Mortality of natives in the last 20 years has been high for males and relatively low for females. Although this population will never be self-sustaining until rats are eradicated, the success of the repatriation program has provided an additional 100 years or more in which to eliminate the rats.

Following the reduction in size of the feral dog population in 1982 at Cerro Cartago on Isabela, repatriations of Land Iguanas began (Reynolds 1981, 1982). To date, nearly 400 juvenile iguanas and 21 of the original group of adults taken to the Center have been repatriated. Annual monitoring trips indicate a growing population (Figure 6). Nests and juveniles are located each year, and in October 1991 a total of 124 iguanas was captured, including 26 natives that had not been observed previously. Due to the improved status of the population, the Cartago iguanas will no longer be bred in captivity. The remaining adults were repatriated in 1992, and semi-annual trips for reducing the size of the feral cat population and annual monitoring trips will be continued.

Acknowledgments

Long-term research and management programs are maintained only with the collaboration of many people. We thank the personnel and consultants of the Charles Darwin Research Station and the Servicio Parque Nacional de Galápagos, who have worked together for many years for the conservation of the giant tortoises and land iguanas of Galápagos. We gratefully acknowledge the major financial support for these programs provided by the Government of Ecuador, the Zoological Society of San Diego, the Frankfurt Zoological Society, and the World Wide Fund for Nature. In addition, the National Science Foundation (IBN-9207895 H. L. Snell), the United States Man in the Biosphere Program, the United States Agency for International Development, the Tinker Foundation, and the University of New Mexico have provided financial support for various aspects of these programs and the preparation of this manuscript.

Summary

Through the breeding, rearing and repatriation program, all of the endangered populations of Galápagos Tortoises and Land Iguanas, except that of the lone tortoise from Pinta, have been brought back from the edge of extinction. The long-term goal of establishing self-sustaining populations that do not require intervention by humans is not likely in the immediate future, except for the tortoise population of Española and hopefully the iguana population of Baltra. The establishment of self-sustaining populations on other islands is not only dependent on the demonstrated success of the repatriation program but also on the ultimate success in the eradication of introduced mammals.

The longevity and relatively old age at sexual maturity of both Galápagos Tortoises and Land Iguanas makes the need for long-term studies more important than in the recovery of many other species. Survival of the repatriates, as shown on Pinzón, is not enough. Successful reproduction and recruitment into the population is required.

Galápagos is an ideal site for successful repatriations. First, the longevity of both Galápagos Tortoises and Land Iguanas was important in the survival of the populations until protection began. Once protection of the threatened populations started, an important key to the ultimate success is the existence of habitats that are relatively free from adverse disturbances. In addition, the reptiles are reared in climatic conditions very similar to their natural conditions, and fed similar foods, both of which help them survive upon repatriation.

The current successes with the most threatened races, results of the last 25 years of management, now allow us to shift our focus to less-threatened populations. Protection of more and more populations will help achieve the ultimate goal of preserving the Galápagos ecosystem for the future.

Literature Cited

Banning, G. H. 1933. Hancock Expedition to the Galápagos Islands, 1933. General Report. Bull. Zool. Soc. San Diego, 10: 1–30.

Beck, R. H. 1903. In the home of the giant tortoise. Ann. Rep. New York Zool. Soc., 7: 160–174.

Cayot, L. J., and R. Menoscal. 1992. Land iguanas return to Baltra. Not. Galápagos, 52: 11–13.

de Vries, T. 1984. The giant tortoises: a natural history disturbed by man, p. 145–146. *In* R. Perry (ed.), Key Environments: Galápagos. Pergamon Press, Oxford, UK.

Eckhardt, R. C. 1972. Introduced plants and animals in the Galápagos Islands. BioScience, 22: 585–590.

Eibl-Eibesfeldt, I. 1960. Galápagos. MacGibbon and Kee, London, UK. 192 pages.

Ernst, C. H., and R. W. Barbour. 1989. Turtles of the World. Smithsonian Inst. Press, Washington, DC. 313 pages.

Fritts, T. H. 1978. Española tortoise returns. Not. Galápagos, 28: 17–18.

—. 1983. Morphometrics of Galápagos tortoises: evolutionary implications, p. 107–108. *In* R. I. Bowman, M. Berson, and A. Leviton (eds.), Patterns of Evolution in Galápagos Organisms. Pacific Division Amer. Assoc. Adv. Sci., San Francisco, California.

—. 1984. Evolutionary divergence of giant tortoises in Galápagos, p. 165–176. *In* R. J. Berry (ed.), Evolution in the

Galápagos Islands. Academic Press, London, UK.
Fritts, T. H., and P. R. Fritts (eds.). 1982. Race with Extinction: Herpetological Notes of J. R. Slevin's Journey to the Galápagos 1905–1906. Herpetol. Monogr., 1: 1–98.
Heyerdahl, T., and A. Skjölsvold. 1956. Archaeological evidence of pre-Spanish visits to the Galápagos islands. Amer. Antiq., 22: 1–71.
Hickman, J. 1985. The Enchanted Islands: The Galápagos Discovered. Tanager Books, Dover, New Hampshire. 169 pages.
Hoeck, H. N. 1984. Introduced fauna, p. 233–245. *In* R. Perry (ed). Key Environments: Galápagos. Pergamon Press, Oxford, UK.
Kruuk, H. 1979. Ecology and control of feral dogs in Galápagos. Tech. Rep. Charles Darwin Res. Stat., Isla Santa Cruz, Galápagos. 59 pages.
Kruuk, H., and H. L. Snell. 1981. Prey selection by feral dogs from a population of marine iguanas (*Amblyrhynchus cristatus*). Jour. Appl. Ecol., 18: 197–204.
MacFarland, C. G., and W. G. Reeder. 1975. Breeding, raising and restocking of giant tortoises (*Geochelone elephantopus*) in the Galápagos Islands, p. 13–37. *In* R. D. Martin (ed.), Breeding Endangered Species in Captivity. Academic Press, New York.
MacFarland, C. G., J. Villa, and B. Toro. 1974. The Galápagos giant tortoises (*Geochelone elephantopus*) Part I: Status of the surviving populations. Biol. Conser., 6: 118–133.
Márquez, C., G. Morillo, and L. J. Cayot. 1991. A 25-year management program pays off: repatriated tortoises on Española reproduce. Not. Galápagos, 51: 17–18.
Márquez, C., H. L. Snell, H. M. Snell, S. Rea, M. Wilson, and F. Cepeda. 1986. The ten year struggle to save the endangered land iguanas. Not. Galápagos, 44: 9–11.
Reynolds, R. 1981. Land iguanas on North Seymour Island. Not. Galápagos, 34: 17–18.
—. 1982. Some observations on the captive management of Galápagos tortoises and land iguanas at the Darwin Station and suggestions for the future, p. 115–119. *In* Informé Anual 1982: Estación Científica Charles Darwin. Charles Darwin Foundation, Quito.
Sancho A., A. C. 1988. Influencia de la Temperatura de Incubación en el Sexo y Parámetros para el Reconocimiento del Sexo de la Tortuga Gigante de Galápagos (*Geochelone elephantopus*) e Histologíca de la Gonada Juvenil de la Iguana Terrestre (*Conolophus subcristatus*). Thesis for Licenciatura Degree, Pontificia Universidad Católica del Ecuador, Quito, Ecuador. 165 pages.
Slevin, J. R. 1959. The Galápagos Islands: a history of their exploration. Occ. Pap. California Acad. Sci., 25: 1–150.
Snell, H. L. 1984. Evolutionary Ecology of Galápagos Land Iguanas (*Conolophus*). Doctoral Dissertation, Colorado State University, Fort Collins, Colorado. 142 pages.
—. 1985. Investigation of optimal conditions for incubating eggs of Galápagos giant tortoises (*Geochelone elephantopus*) and land iguanas (*Conolophus subcristatus*). Tech. Rep. Charles Darwin Res. Stat., Isla Santa Cruz, Galápagos, Ecuador. 25 pages.
Snell, H. L., and C. Márquez. 1985. Chequeo de Venecia con la posibilidad de una repatración de iguanas a Bahía Conway y Cerros Montura y Dragón. Tech. Rep. Charles Darwin Res. Sta., Isla Santa Cruz, Galápagos, Ecuador. 4 pages.
Snell, H. L., C. Márquez, and S. Rea. 1988. Informe final del experimento de crianza de galapaguitos. Tech. Rep. Charles Darwin Res. Stat., Isla Santa Cruz, Galápagos, Ecuador. 22 pages.
Snell, H. L., C. Márquez, S. Rea, H. M. Snell, and F. Llerena. 1985. Un experimento sobre condiciones mejores para la crianza de los galapaguitos recien nacidos. Tech. Rep. Charles Darwin Res. Stat., Isla Santa Cruz, Galápagos, Ecuador. 10 pages.
Snell, H. L., and H. M. Snell. 1980. 1979 annual report, land iguana conservation program, p. 36–51. *In* U. Eberhardt (ed.), Annual Report of the Charles Darwin Research Station. Charles Darwin Foundation, Quito.
—. 1981. Rare land iguana breeds in captivity. World Wildl. Fund Monthly Rep., August 1981: 1–2.
Snell, H. L., H. M. Snell, and H. E. Lawler. 1987. Effects of the incubation environment on the eggs, hatchlings, and neonatal growth rates of *Sauromalus varius*: progress report. Tech. Report Arizona-Sonora Desert Mus., Tucson, Arizona. 5 pages.
Snell, H. L., H. M. Snell, and C. R. Tracy. 1984. Variation among populations of Galápagos land iguanas (*Conolophus*): contrasts of phylogeny and ecology, p. 185–207. *In* R. J. Berry (ed.), Evolution in the Galápagos Islands. Academic Press, London, UK.
—. 1985. Behavioral and morphological adaptations by Galápagos land iguanas (*Conolophus subcristatus*) to water and energy requirements of eggs and neonates. Amer. Zool., 25: 1009–1018.
Snell, H. M., H. L. Snell, and K. Flies. 1986. A permanent quadrant for estimating long-term fluctuations in land iguana populations at Puerto Bravo, Isabela. Tech. Rep. Charles Darwin Res. Stat., Isla Santa Cruz, Galápagos, Ecuador. 5 pages.
Townsend, C. H. 1925. The Galápagos tortoises in their relation to the whaling industry: a study of old logbooks. Zoologica, 4: 55–135.
Tracy, C. R., and H. L. Snell. 1985. Interrelations among water and energy relations of reptilian eggs, embryos, and hatchlings. Amer. Zool., 25: 999–1008.
Woram, J. M. 1991. Who killed the iguanas? Not. Galápagos, 51: 12–17.
—. 1992. That first iguana transfer. Not. Galápagos, 51: 20–22.

Cayot, L. J., H. L. Snell, W. Llerena, and H. M. Snell. 1994. Conservation biology of Galápagos reptiles: twenty-five years of successful research and management, p. 297–305. *In* J. B. Murphy, K. Adler, and J. T. Collins (eds.), Captive Management and Conservation of Amphibians and Reptiles. Society for the Study of Amphibians and Reptiles, Ithaca (New York). Contributions to Herpetology, volume 11.

HUSBANDRY OF CAPTIVE DAY GECKOS (*PHELSUMA*): PAST, PRESENT, AND FUTURE

TIMOTHY L. TYTLE*

Introduction

EVER SINCE THE LIZARD GENUS *PHELSUMA* WAS first named by J. E. Gray in honor of the Dutch worm researcher Murk van Phelsum, and the beauty of these lizards became known to Europeans, there has been an increasing desire by both public institutions and private individuals to acquire and, more recently, to maintain and propagate the many day geckos of this genus.

Except for a few species of *Phelsuma* that were introduced into East Africa, two species that were introduced into the Hawaiian Islands, and an additional species native to the Bay of Bengal, all members of the genus are confined to Madagascar, or to a number of smaller, well-dispersed Indian Ocean Islands. These include the Comoro Islands (located northwest of Madagascar), the Seychelles Islands (north of Madagascar), and the Mascarene Islands (east of Madagascar).

Despite numerous revisions, taxonomic confusion in this genus persists. Depending upon which taxonomy is used, up to 70 taxa of *Phelsuma* can now be recognized. With the exception of several recently described taxa, the works of Mertens (1962, 1966 plus his many later additions) form the basis for the most modern classification of these lizards, though several other researchers have also had significant input to the present taxonomic status of this genus (Rendahl 1939; Loveridge 1942; Börner 1972; Cheke 1982; Gardner 1987).

*323 NW 16th Street
Oklahoma City, Oklahoma 73103, USA

Acronym used in this chapter:

TSD Temperature-dependent sex determination

Reproductive Physiology

It was not until the 1970s that more than isolated attempts were made to maintain and reproduce members of the genus *Phelsuma*. Based primarily on the presence or absence of well-developed femoral pores, most day geckos can be easily sexed. Healthy, reproductively active females usually produce one or two hard-shelled eggs, and lay clutches as frequently as every two to three weeks. Although adult males make hardy captives, reproductively active females often develop spastic paralysis and "floppy jaws," and hatchlings frequently develop kinks in their vertebral columns. Radiographic examination of these lizards reveal diffuse demineralization, in addition to scoliosis (Tytle 1986). These abnormalities are remarkably similar to rickets as observed in humans. Furthermore, when the radiographs of deformed day geckos are compared to those of healthy, reproductively active individuals, dramatic differences are noted. Not only are the skeletons of the healthy lizards mineralized, but retro-otic calcium deposits can often be observed in the females (Tytle 1986). The size of these deposits was found to be quite variable, but appeared to fluctuate during the year, becoming smaller during periods of maximum egg deposition. These calcium deposits, referred to as endolymphatic glands, are sometimes radiographically discernible in adult males, but infrequently reach a size that can be detected externally. When adequate calcium supplementation was provided to affected day geckos in the form of powdered cuttlebone or oyster shell, the advancement of skeletal deformities was arrested, and skeletal remineralization and calcium deposition into the endolymphatic glands ensued.

There has long been a keen awareness of calcium metabolism and its importance in reptilian husbandry (Langerwerf 1980; Frye 1981; Tytle 1986).

Reproductively active *Phelsuma* in my possession are provided with a dish of powdered calcium (Rep-Cal, Los Gatos, California) and spent *Phelsuma* egg shells. It is interesting to note that only reproductively active females showed interest in these shells and, furthermore, that their eagerness to eat the shells can be used as a crude indicator of their reproductive activity (Tytle 1990).

Sex Ratios

Once reproductive success was obtained, several *Phelsuma* species were found to have a heavily skewed sex ratio under captive conditions. Sean McKeown, working extensively with captive-husbandry techniques in *Phelsuma*, has bred animals which have produced offspring of both sexes from seven different taxa of *Phelsuma* from the Seychelles, Mauritius, Réunion, and Madagascar (some for multiple generations). His breeding of long term, captive *P. g. guimbeaui*, however, have produced females almost exclusively (McKeown 1989, 1993), and I have independently had the same results among more than 30 offspring of the same taxon. I have also not produced males in *P. lineata pusilla* among more than 30 sexable offspring. Similar findings have been reported with *P. guentheri* (at the Jersey Wildlife Preservation Trust) where, among over 50 offspring (in 1978–1979), only three males were identified (Bloxam and Tonge 1980).

Researchers have questioned whether these heavily female-skewed, captive-bred populations are a function of environmental temperature during a critical phase of egg incubation. Over the years, most turtles, all crocodilians, and several lizard taxa have been shown to exhibit temperature-dependent sex determination (TSD) (Bull 1983; Lang et. al. 1989; Ewert and Nelson 1991). TSD has also been shown to be important in some species of geckos (E. Wagner *in* Bull 1980; Tokunaga 1985, 1989; Bull 1987*a*). In investigations of TSD in geckos, research on *Eublepharis macularius* (Leopard Gecko) by Bull (1987*a*, 1987*b*) is most frequently quoted. He found the sex of offspring in this species to be heavily temperature-dependent; only females were produced at a constant incubation temperature of 26°C, an equal sex distribution was produced at 29.5°C, and a predominance of males was produced at 32°C.

Larry Talent, of Oklahoma State University, has investigated TSD in *P. madagascariensis grandis* at constant incubation temperatures of 26°C, 28°C, and 32°C, and has failed to produce a single male. A single male, however, was produced in a group of eggs initially incubated at 32°C, and then changed to 28°C (L. Talent, pers. comm.). As mentioned earlier, Sean McKeown and I have also incubated *Phelsuma g. guimbeaui* at several constant temperatures without producing a male. The etiology of heavily skewed sex distribution in favor of females in some *Phelsuma* species has yet to be understood.

Incubation Periods

Another interesting phenomenon arising from captive *Phelsuma* husbandry has been the much longer incubation periods, as compaired with those of other taxa, found in all indigenous species on the Seychelles Islands that have thus far been studied. The tabulated results of early reproductive success, at an incubation temperature of 28° ± 2°C, in the combined collections of Thomas Digney and myself, show longer incubation periods in Seychelles Island *Phelsuma* than in similar-sized Mascarene Island and Malagasy taxa (Digney and Tytle 1983). Specifically, *P. sundbergi*, a large Seychelles species, which is comparable in size to *P. madagascariensis*, has a significantly longer incubation period. These differences appear to apply to the two smaller Seychelles species investigated (*Phelsuma astriata* and *P. longinsulae pulchra,* the latter often referred to as *P. sundbergi longinsulae*) which seem to have longer incubation periods than do their Malagasy and Mascarene Islands counterparts. The numbers are small, but the trend is apparent. More recent data, not presented here, substantiate these trends. The etiology for this difference, however, remains a mystery.

Coloration and Diet

One of the reasons, if not the major reason, behind the popularity of the day geckos of the genus *Phelsuma* is their strikingly beautiful colors. While color degradation has not been noted in *Phelsuma madagascariensis grandis*, many other members of the genus have, unfortunately, fairly consistently reproduced drab offspring as compared to wild-caught or outdoor-managed counterparts. I have found this phenomenon to be particularly evident in *P. comorensis*, *P. guimbeaui*, and *P. standingi*. These captive-reproduced individuals, however, appear healthy, are long-lived, and produce viable offspring. The reason or reasons for the drab color in some species of captive-reproduced *Phelsuma* is not known. The introduction of broad-spectrum lighting in the form of Vita Lites and black lights does not appear to have had a major effect, nor has the addition of a variety of dietary supplements, such as nectar and carotene. To accurately determine the factor or factors influencing pigmentation, I suggest a study with a highly controlled set of environmental and dietary factors in a large-colony setting. Such a study would be complicated, because accurate objective determination of color intensity in such lizards is difficult when the color patterns within the same subspecies are often variable, and the color within a single animal varies greatly with stress.

Research on the herpetoculture of lizards of the genus *Phelsuma* has already been initiated in both Europe and the United States to develop a complete, formulated, powdered diet which would negate the need for live prey (L. Talent, pers. comm.). In Europe, experimentation is currently in progress which concentrates on a Lorikeet bird diet with a variety of additives.

In the United States, Larry Talent has conducted extensive experimentation with a complex powdered dietary supplement. At present, the diet is composed of powdered crickets combined with pure carbohydrates and a variety of vitamins and minerals (L. Talent, pers. comm.). Talent is currently utilizing *P. madagascariensis grandis* as a large *Phelsuma* model and *P. dubia* as a small study model. His results to date, while far from complete, have been suggestive. Specifically, he has found that the extremely hardy *P. dubia* can be maintained solely on the powdered diet for at least two generations with no ill effects in egg production, egg viability, growth rates, or morphology. In *P. madagascariensis grandis*, however, while offspring can be successfully raised and maintained on this diet, no viable eggs have yet been produced (L. Talent, pers. comm.). Talent has been slowed in his research by the complexity of the diet, and, therefore, needs to test a large variety of formulas on larger lizard colonies for extended periods of time.

Summary

What I have set forth here is a brief overview of selected aspects of the herpetoculture of the genus *Phelsuma*. Early husbandry problems with spastic paralysis and skeletal deformities have been largely overcome with calcium and, more recently, vitamin D_3 supplementation. There remains a dilemma in resolving the skewed sex distribution in some species. While *Phelsuma* of the Seychelles Islands have been found to have a longer incubation period, once recgonized this presents only a minor husbandry problem. Although well known to experienced *Phelsuma* breeders, the exact etiology of color degradation in the offspring of some *Phelsuma* species bred indoors is as yet not fully understood; however, an effective powdered diet for Day Geckos may soon be realized.

Literature Cited

Bloxam, Q., and S. Tonge. 1980. Maintenance and breeding of *Phelsuma guentheri* (Boulenger, 1885) p. 51–62. *In* S. Townson (ed.), The Care and Breeding of Captive Reptiles. British Herpetol. Soc., London.

Börner, A. R. 1972. Revision der Geckonidengattung *Phelsuma* (Gray, 1825). Privately published, Cologne. 145 pages.

Bull, J. J. (ed.). 1980. Sex determination in reptiles. Quart. Rev. Biol., 55: 3–21.

—. 1983. Evolution of Sex Determining Mechanisms. Benjamin Cummings Publ. Co., Menlo Park, California. 316 pages.

—. 1987*a*. Temperature-sensitive periods of sex determination in reptiles. Validity of sex diagnosis in hatchling lizards. Canadian Jour. Zool., 65: 1421–1424.

—. 1987*b*. Temperature-sensitive periods of sex determination in a lizard: similarities with turtles and crocodilians. Jour. Exp. Zool., 241: 143–148.

Cheke, A. S. 1982. *Phelsuma* (Gray, 1825) in the Seychelles and neighboring islands: a reappraisal of their taxonomy and description of two new forms. Senckenb. Biol., 62: 181–198.

Digney, T., and T. L. Tytle. 1983. Captive maintenance and propagation of the lizard genus *Phelsuma*, p. 141–156. *In* D. L. Marcellini (ed.), 6th Annual Reptile Symposium on Captive Propagation and Husbandry. Zool. Consortium, Thurmont, Maryland.

Ewert, M. A., and C. E. Nelson. 1991. Sex determination in turtles: diverse patterns and some possible adaptive values. Copeia, 1991: 50–69.

Frye, F. L. 1981. Biomedical and Surgical Aspects of Captive Reptile Husbandry. Veterinary Med. Publ. Co., Edwardsville, Kansas. 456 pages.

Gardner, A. S. 1987. The systematics of the *Phelsuma*

madagascariensis group of day geckos (Reptilia: Gekkonidae) in the Seychelles. Zool. Jour. Linnean Soc., 91: 93–105.

Lang, J. W., H. Andrews, and R. Whitaker. 1989. Sex determination and sex ratios in *Crocodylus palustris*. Zoo, 29: 935–952.

Langerwerf, B. A. 1980. The successful breeding of lizards from temperate regions. *In* S. Townson (ed.), The Care and Breeding of Captive Reptiles. British Herpetol. Soc., London.

Loveridge, A. 1942. Revision of the Afro-Oriental geckos of the genus *Phelsuma*. Bull. Mus. Comp. Zool., Harvard Univ., 89: 439–482.

McKeown, S. 1989. Breeding and maintenance of the Mauritius Lowland Forest Day Gecko (*Phelsuma g. guimbeaui*) at the Fresno Zoo, p. 116–122. *In* P. J. S. Olney and P. Ellis (eds.), International Zoo Yearbook, volume 28. Zool. Soc. London, London.

—. 1993. The General Care and Maintenance of Day Geckos. Herpetocult. Library Spec. Edit., Advanced Vivarium Systems, Lakeside, California. 143 pages.

Mertens, R. 1962. Die Arten und Unterarten der Geckonengattung *Phelsuma*. Senckenb. Biol., 43: 87–127.

—. 1966. Die nichtmadagassischen Arten und Unterarten der Geckonengattung *Phelsuma*. Senckenb. Biol., 47: 85–110.

Rendahl, H. 1939. Zur Herpetologie der Seychellen. I. Reptilien. Zool. Jahrbuch. Abt. Syst., Ökol. Geograph. Tiere, 72: 157–328.

Tokunaga, S. 1985. Temperature-dependent sex determination in *Gekko japonicus* (Gekkonidae, Reptilia). Dev. Growth Differ., 27: 117–120.

—. 1989. Temperature-dependent sex determination and life history of *Gekko japonicus* (Reptilia: Gekkonidae). Abstract, First World Congress of Herpetology, September 1989, University of Kent at Canterbury, UK.

Tytle, T. L. 1986. Calcium metabolism in the lizard genus *Phelsuma*, a preliminary report, p. 175–183. *In* F. Caporaso, S. McKeown, and K. H. Peterson (eds.), 9th International Symposium on Captive Propagation and Husbandry. Zool. Consortium, Thurmont, Maryland.

—. 1990. Day Geckos: *Phelsuma*. The captive maintenance and propagation of day geckos. Vivarium, 2: 15–19, 29.

❦ Tytle, T. L. 1994. Husbandry of captive day geckos (*Phelsuma*): past, present, and future, p. 307–310. *In* J. B. Murphy, K. Adler, and J. T. Collins (eds.), Captive Management and Conservation of Amphibians and Reptiles. Society for the Study of Amphibians and Reptiles, Ithaca (New York). Contributions to Herpetology, volume 11.

Long-Term Breeding Program with the Giant Day Gecko (*Phelsuma madagascariensis*) at the National Zoological Park

Béla J. Demeter* and Geoffrey F. Birchard**

Introduction

We have maintained a colony of giant day Geckos (*Phelsuma madagascariensis grandis*) at the National Zoological Park since 1973. Early reproductive success with this species, including a description of the management program, growth data, and nutritional problems of this group, has been reported (Demeter 1976). Since the publication of this work, several excellent reviews of *Phelsuma* husbandry have appeared (Bloxam and Vokins 1978; Digney and Tytle 1983; Tytle 1989; McKeown 1993). Long-term studies of captive colonies are lacking, however, from this body of work.

Recently we compiled data on our long-term (18 years) captive colony, which provide detailed information on the growth, development, and reproductive biology of this species in captivity. The founding lizards of this colony consisted of 1 male and 3 females, all wild-caught. Over time we added 30 (10 males, 20 females) mostly captive-bred animals to the colony to diversify breeding stock. In all we have had over 120 births at our facility. The current colony numbers 25 (7 males, 18 females) animals.

*Department of Herpetology, National Zoological Park
Washington, D. C. 20008, USA

**Department of Biology, George Mason University,
Fairfax, Virginia 22030, USA

Acronyms used in this chapter:

ANOVA	Analysis of variance test
GE-BL	General Electric blacklight
NCSS	Number Cruncher Statistical System
SD	Standard deviation
SVL	Snout-to-vent length
UV	Ultraviolet light
UVB	Ultraviolet B

S. Tong (pers. comm.) of the Jersey Wildlife Preservation Trust, Channel Islands, UK, has observed a marked decline in the reproductive output of the Jersey *Phelsuma guentheri* colony over the past six years. Townsend and Cole (1985) have also indicated that their colonies of *Cnemidophorus* were experiencing lineage senescence (see Porter et al., this volume, page 91). In this chapter, we discuss whether our data show indications of decreased fecundity and egg viability in our *Phelsuma* colony. We also discuss changes in dietary and lighting protocols that have been implemented since Demeter's earlier report (1976).

Methods

All records kept since the establishment of the colony of *Phelsuma madagascariensis grandis* in 1973 were examined, and data were extracted on egg and hatchling measurements and dates, and growth and chronological information on dams and sires. Over the 18 years of this colony's existence, different levels of effort have been expended in breeding animals. Data, however, were uniformly collected.

Eggs were always taken from cages as soon as discovered and artificially incubated on a variety of substrates. Moisture content was not measured, but extremes were avoided. Incubation temperatures were recorded with a Schultheis thermometer and ranged from 26° to 32°C. Eggs were measured to the nearest millimeter with calipers and weighed on an Ohaus triple-beam balance to the nearest 0.1 g. Snout-to-vent lengths were taken on the ventral surface of geckos with a ruler and weight measured with an Ohaus balance to the nearest 0.1 g.

Statistical analyses were performed using an NCSS computer package. Differences among groups were assessed with a Student's *t* test or one-way ANOVA. Relationships between variables were assessed with least-squares regression analysis. A *p* value of less than 0.05 was considered significant.

Maintenance of Animals

Lighting

Our colony of *Phelsuma madagascariensis grandis* has been kept under artificial lighting year-round with a 12/12 light-dark cycle, as described by Demeter (1976). Ambient light also illuminates the room from windows on two sides.

In 1983 we participated in a study (Allen 1989) to determine the effects of different dietary levels of calcium and Vitamin D on two geckos (*Eublepharis macularius* and *P. madagascariensis grandis).* Fifteen hatchling grandis were assigned to four experimental dietary groups and one control group. The control group was maintained under two 1.2-m-long fluorescent fixtures that held one black light (General Electric BL-40) and one broad-spectrum bulb (General Electric Chroma-50). The bulbs were hung 20 cm from the cage tops and were on a 10/14 light-dark cycle. The three lizards in the control group did not experience any mortality in the course of the study and showed optimal growth for this species. Radiographs revealed well-mineralized bones and no evidence of pathology.

The experimental groups of *grandis* were maintained under ambient room-light conditions that were identical to those of the *Eublepharis* (that is, no bulbs directly over cages and standard fluorescent lighting from fixtures in the 5 m-high ceilings). Dramatic mortality occurred in the experimental *Phelsuma* groups in spite of the fact that some animals were fed on diets supplemented with both calcium and vitamin D_3. All of these *Phelsuma* grew poorly and upon necropsy were found to have soft and pliable bones, including the mandible and maxilla. There was no mortality in any of the *Eublepharis*, although those fed suboptimal levels of calcium and vitamin D_3 exhibited signs of calcium and/or vitamin D_3 deficiency (M. E. Allen, pers. comm.).

These findings suggest that *grandis* require significant amounts of ultraviolet (UV) light to synthesize vitamin D. Apparently, this species did not absorb sufficient amounts of vitamin D or calcium from the diet provided. This is consistent with Townsend and Cole's (1985) observations that some species of lizards require more ultraviolet light than others. From this comparison of a diurnal (*Phelsuma madagascariensis*) and a nocturnal (*Eublepharis macularius*) species, we suggest that differences in vitamin D and calcium metabolism may correlate with activity period.

The optimal quantity and form of UV radiation that are necessary for keeping *grandis* in captivity through multiple generations has still not been determined. Tytle (1989) stated that he was able to raise hatchling *Phelsuma* successfully under standard fluorescent fixtures. We have found that a combination of broad-spectrum fluorescent bulbs in concert with an ultraviolet bulb (GE BL) in either a 3:1 or 1:1 ratio has produced good results in the propagation of these animals. For juvenile geckos the distance of the bulbs from the animals is probably critical and the lamps should be no more than 20 cm from the top of the cage. Gehrmann (1987) indicates that decreasing the distance of these bulbs to the cage from 30 to 15 cm can increase the UVB irradiance by a factor of 3 to 4.

Diet

Prior to 1985 we offered our Giant Day Geckos oyster shells, ad libitum, as a supplemental source of calcium. Since Allen's (1989) work on *Eublepharis,* we have simplified our dietary procedures. Our *Phelsuma madagascariensis grandis* are now fed twice weekly, about five crickets per feeding per adult. In addition to being dusted with a vitamin and mineral powder (Pervinal), crickets are fed a high calcium/vitamin D_3 diet (Allen and Oftedal 1989). No other calcium supplement is currently being offered. Fresh fruit, usually oranges, is offered to the lizards biweekly. Cages are heavily misted every day (twice per day in the winter, due to drier conditions caused by heating the building) to provide drinking water and to increase humidity.

Growth and Reproduction

Figure 1A shows that *Phelsuma madagascariensis grandis* of both sexes grow rapidly during their first 20 months. After 20 months, female growth plateaus while males continue to grow for about a year longer before growth slows. Both sexes level off at a very stable plateau at a nearly constant weight for the duration of their lifespan of approximately ten years.

The earlier plateau in growth by female *grandis* is correlated with reproductive maturity. Egg-laying begins immediately after females reach sexual maturity at about 20 months. The fact that female growth plateaus earlier than that of males might be consistent with the hypothesis that ingested energy is directed into reproduction (egg production) and away from growth.

Female *grandis* typically produce their first clutch at approximately 20 months (Figure 1B) and consistently produce eggs for the remainder of their lives. The largest number of egg clutches are produced by animals that are 3 to 5 years of age. Females can reproduce into the tenth year, but in our colony, many females died at an earlier age. The peak years of egg production may reflect an artifact of colony management. Efforts directed to this species propagation program were initially high and with time (and success) were reduced.

Bloxam and Vokins (1978) recorded that the egg-laying peak for *P. guentheri* was in June and the egg-laying season was from February to October. These estimates were made on the basis of data that were compiled over a two-year period. Tytle (1989)

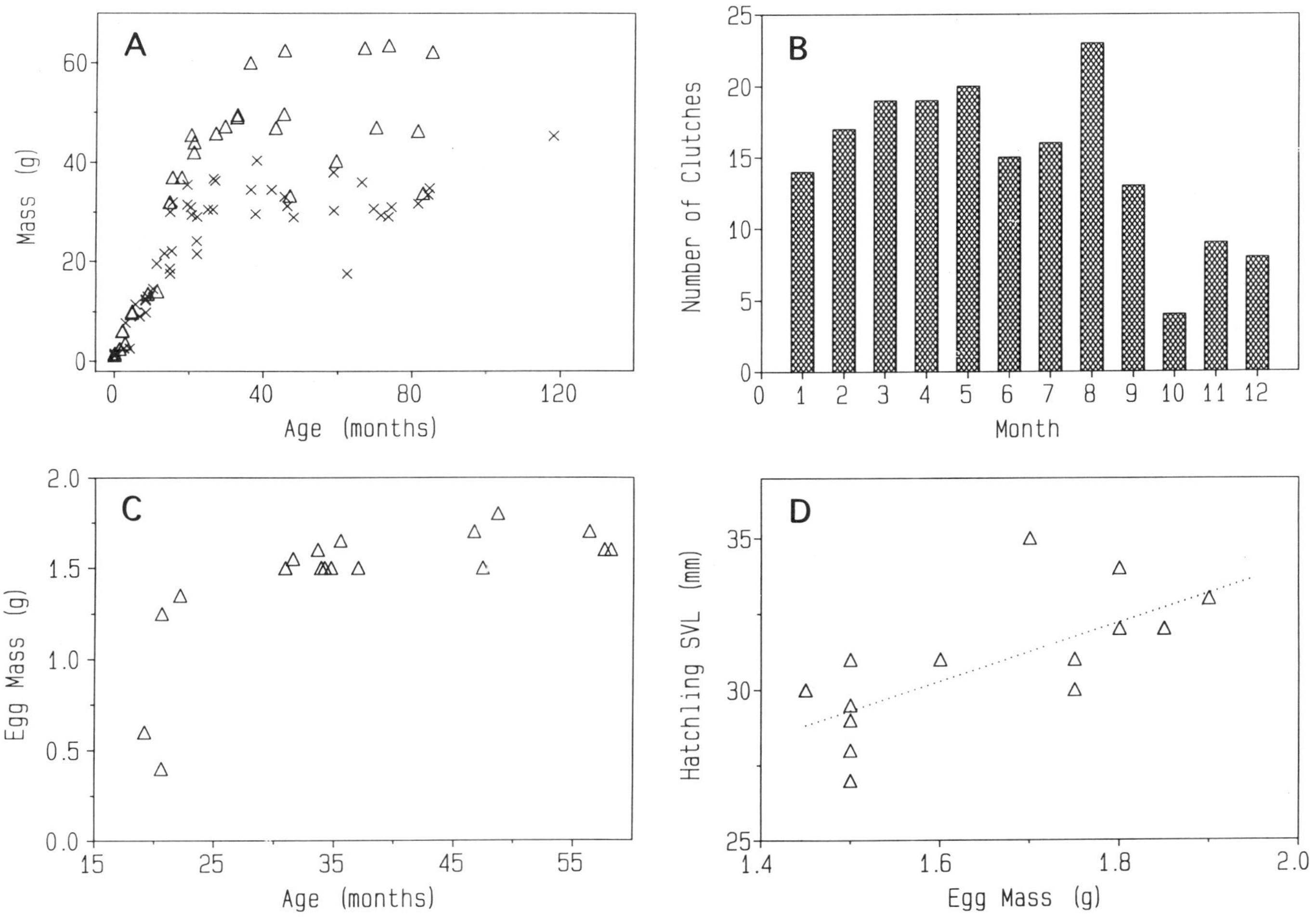

FIGURE 1. (A) *Phelsuma madagascariensis grandis* mass as a function of age. X females, Δ males, $n = 34$ for males, $n = 54$ for females. (B) Egg laying as a function of month in *grandis*. Differences between months were not significant. (C) Egg mass as a function of age in two sibling *grandis* born in captivity. (D) Hatchling snout-vent length as a function of egg mass in *grandis*. The equation for the regression line is SVL = 14.79 + 9.68 (mass), $r = .70$, $p < 0.05$, $n = 16$. Only 14 data points are shown, since two pairs were identical.

TABLE 1. Egg characteristics of *Phelsuma madagascariensis grandis* bred at the National Zoological Park.

Characteristic	Number	Mean	Range	SD
Egg mass (g)[1]	102	1.54	0.4 – 2.0	0.32
Egg mass (g)[2]	70	1.57	1.1 – 1.9	0.17
Egg length (mm)	108	14.60	12.05 – 18.40	1.77
Egg width (mm)	106	13.50	10.05 – 15.90	0.91

[1]All eggs [2]Fertile and calcified eggs only

states that in colonies in the United States, peak egg-laying for *Phelsuma* takes place between March and November, although he did not present data to support these observations.

Our data (Figure 1B) show that egg-laying in *grandis* occurs throughout the year. Although there is a tendency for egg production to decline from October to December, there was no statistical evidence of a specific egg-laying season for *Phelsuma* in captivity under the conditions described above.

Table 1 summarizes the characteristics of *grandis* eggs. Note that there is little variation between the total number of eggs for which weights were taken (n = 102) and hard eggs (n = 70), at least in mass. There has been no measurable change in egg mass, egg size, or fertility over the life of the colony. Overall fertility is 63.6% (n = 264, 96 infertile). There is some trend towards decreased fertility in the first eggs laid by a female, but this was not statistically significant. Uncalcified eggs (n = 51) were all infertile and represented 22.7% of all eggs produced. Of the eggs produced without a sire (n = 17), 11 (64.7%) were uncalcified.

Figure 1C shows the mass of eggs laid by two sibling female *grandis*. It appears that eggs laid early are smaller than eggs laid later in life. A clutch of eggs represents approximately 10% of the body weight of an average female. A female can lay up to six clutches of two eggs in one year. Eggs from later clutches (that is, the third clutch and greater) tend to be uniform in size. This is typical of some species that lay eggs, including birds. Unlike snakes, which continue to grow throughout life and produce larger or more eggs with age, *Phelsuma* stops growing and egg size remains constant.

The mean incubation period for eggs of *grandis* incubated at 31°C was 41.6 days (n = 10, SD = 2.2, range = 38–44 days). The physical characteristics of hatchlings are shown in Table 2. Hatchling size was found to increase with increasing egg mass (Figure 1D). The relationship between hatchling snout-to-vent length (SVL) and egg mass is shown in Figure 1D. A positive correlation between egg mass and neonate mass has been observed previously in reptiles (Packard and Packard 1988). The production of larger offspring has been suggested to increase neonatal fitness (see, for example, Miller et al. 1987; Packard and Packard 1988). It has been suggested that this results from changes in performance, such as increases in ability to capture prey or locomotor performance.

Discussion

These data present information on a long-term captive colony of *Phelsuma madagascariensis*. We were unable to discern any changes in reproductive effort and/or pattern with time in this population. Several significant variables were changed over the years that preclude us from drawing an overall conclusion regarding the effects of captivity on fecundity and egg viability in this species.

Our breeding strategy consisted of introducing new stock into the colony whenever it was available to increase genetic diversity. We also back-crossed animals to earlier generations when possible to maintain founder representation. While this may be a sound approach to management of a captive colony, it makes it extremely difficult to make direct comparisons between generations.

This points to a common problem inherent in herpetological husbandry. Sound management does

TABLE 2. Hatchling characteristics of *Phelsuma madagascariensis grandis* hatched at the National Zoological Park.

Characteristic	Number	Mean	SD
Mass (g)	24	1.2	0.2
Snout-vent length (mm)	22	31.9	10.0
Total length (mm)	19	61.0	14.7

not always lead to sound research. Useful data are difficult to obtain in addressing the long-term effects of captivity in lizards. We suspect that there may be some deleterious effects in keeping *Phelsuma* over multiple generations; anecdotal evidence is consistent with this hypothesis. The challenge remains, however, to document this phenomenon and ascertain those factors affecting it.

Porter et al. (this volume, page 91) suggest that the reproductive drop in their colonies of *Cnemidophorus* may be a result of the presence of the commercial pesticide, Thiram, which has been found to occur in the chicken mash that was fed to the insects that were then used for lizard food. This is an intriguing hypothesis that merits further investigation. It would be premature, however, to rule out other elements, either genetic or environmental, that may adversely influence our ultimate success in propagating these animals.

Summary

Nearly two decades of work with *Phelsuma madagascariensis grandis* have enabled us to obtain critical information pertaining to growth, longevity, sexual maturity, and other reproductive parameters of this gecko. Lighting, dietary, and other husbandry regimens described herein have been developed through both trial-and-error and experimental design. We feel confident about these techniques in rearing these animals. Although questions remain about long-term consequences of captivity in this species, we feel the data presented here can serve as a reliable baseline for anyone contemplating future work with this species.

Literature Cited

Allen, M. E. 1989. Nutritional Aspects of Insectivory. Doctoral Thesis, Michigan State University, East Lansing, Michigan. 125 pages.

Allen, M. E., and O. T. Oftedal. 1989. Dietary manipulation of the calcium content of feed crickets. Jour. Zoo Wildl. Med., 20: 26–33.

Bloxam, Q., and M. Vokins. 1978. Breeding and maintenance of *Phelsuma guentheri* (Boulenger, 1885) at the Jersey Zoological Park. Jour. Jersey Wildl. Preserv. Trust, 15: 82–91.

Demeter, B. J. 1976. Observations on the care, breeding and behaviour of the giant day gecko (*Phelsuma madagascariensis*) at the National Zoological Park, Washington. Internatl. Zoo Yearbook, 16: 130–133.

Digney, T., and T. Tytle. 1983. Captive maintenance and propagation of the lizard genus *Phelsuma*, p. 141–156. *In* D. Marcellini (ed.), Proceedings of the 6th Annual Reptile Symposium on Captive Propagation and Husbandry. Zoological Consortium, Thurmont, Maryland.

Gehrmann, W. H. 1987. Ultraviolet irradiances of various lamps used in animal husbandry. Zoo Biol., 6: 117–127.

McKeown, S. 1993. The General Care and Maintenance of Day Geckos. Advanced Vivarium Systems, Lakeside, California. 143 pages.

Miller, K., G. C. Packard, and M. J. Packard. 1987. Hydric conditions during incubation influence locomotor performance of hatchling snapping turtles. Jour. Exp. Biol., 127: 401–412.

Packard, G. C., and M. J. Packard. 1988. The physiological ecology of reptilian eggs and embryos, p. 523–605. *In* C. Gans and R. B. Huey (eds.), Biology of the Reptilia, Volume 16. Alan R. Liss, New York.

Townsend, C. R., and C. J. Cole. 1985. Additional notes on the requirements of captive whiptail lizards (*Cnemidophorus*), with emphasis on ultraviolet radiation. Zoo Biol., 4: 49–55.

Tytle, T. 1989. The captive maintenance and propagation of day geckos. Vivarium, 2: 15–19, 29.

❦ Demeter, B. J., and G. F. Birchard. 1994. Long-term breeding program with the giant day gecko (*Phelsuma madagascariensis*) at the National Zoological Park, p. 311–315. *In* J. B. Murphy, K. Adler, and J. T. Collins (eds.), Captive Management and Conservation of Amphibians and Reptiles. Society for the Study of Amphibians and Reptiles, Ithaca (New York). Contributions to Herpetology, volume 11.

HUSBANDRY AND REPRODUCTION OF THE PREHENSILE-TAILED SKINK, *CORUCIA ZEBRATA*

JOHN D. GROVES*

Introduction

THE LIZARD FAMILY SCINCIDAE IS A GROUP OF wide-ranging lizards in both temperate and tropical regions. Their world-wide distribution has exposed them to a variety of ecological situations which have resulted in adaptations to these varying conditions. Most skinks are small, primarily terrestrial, insectivorous lizards with elongated and depressed bodies, small legs, and small, flattened heads. Some members of this family, particularly those that occur in Australia and the Pacific region, are large and show a greater variety of ecological adaptations in body form and behaviors.

One of the most unusual members of this interesting group of lizards is the Prehensile-tailed Skink, *Corucia zebrata*, a large, poorly known, endemic lizard of the Solomon Islands. Very little has been reported about this large skink since its original description by Gray (1855). Early accounts give brief descriptions of its habitat (Guppy 1887), food and feeding behavior (Kinghorn, 1928), morphological adaptations (Schmidt 1932), predation (Loveridge 1946), and other general remarks (Schmidt and Inger 1957). McCoy (1980) briefly summarized available information about this skink in the wild and, more recently, Parker (1983) expanded on this knowledge and presented a detailed summary of its behavior.

Although *C. zebrata* has been maintained in captivity in European and American zoos, very little has been published concerning its requirements in captivity. Honegger (1975, 1985) described his experience with this species and provided information on food, reproduction, and diseases. Bowler (1981) briefly discussed a successful captive colony of this skink at the Philadelphia Zoological Garden. More recently, Wright (1991) published a popular account, based largely on Bowler (1981), on various aspects of this species in captivity. This chapter reports on the biology and behavior of *C. zebrata* in a long-term, reproductively active colony, and compares this information with what has already been reported for the species.

Origin and Management of the Philadelphia Colony

In December 1972, the Philadelphia Zoological Garden received an adult male Prehensile-tailed Skink from a local animal dealer. In April 1973, a juvenile female was obtained from the same dealer. In September 1973, an additional adult male and three adult females were received from the Chester Zoo in the United Kingdom. The latter four lizards were reportedly from Bougainville in the Solomon Islands. Additional skinks have been added periodically to this group as a result of loans, trades, and captive reproduction. In 1989 an additional 11 wild-caught individuals were added to the group for the purpose of diversifying its genetic composition. A complete genealogical history of each colony has been maintained. Only four specimens do not have complete histories, due to the difficulties in identifying adult parents. Identification of each specimen has been maintained by photographic methods and records of various morphological characters.

*Philadelphia Zoological Garden
3400 West Girard Avenue
Philadelphia, Pennsylvania, 19104, USA

Current address:
North Carolina Zoological Park
4401 Zoo Parkway
Asheboro, North Carolina 27203, USA

The original breeding group was divided into two colonies, each consisting of one male with two compatible females. An additional male and two females were later added to form a third colony in 1979. Additional modifications to the colonies have occurred throughout the years to accommodate births, mortalities, the distribution of progeny to other zoos, and the return of breeding-loan individuals. Colonies have contained from three to five unrelated adults. Less aggression and more reproduction, however, have been observed in the colony that has continued as one male and two females. Juveniles were left in all colonies after 1979 without increasing aggression until male juveniles became four years old. At that time adult males and their male young would fight, causing us to separate these apparently maturing juveniles. A total of 71 Prehensile-tailed Skinks have been recorded in five colonies between 1972 and 1990.

A variety of enclosures have been used to house Prehensile-tailed Skinks at the Philadelphia Zoological Garden. These range from medium-sized aquariums (56 l), which are used to isolate individual specimens for medical reasons, to large enclosures (measuring $1.52 \times 1.52 \times 1.52$ m), which are used in both on-exhibit and in off-exhibit holding facilities. Larger enclosures contain a variety of tree limbs for climbing purposes. Hollow logs have been added, because this species lives in hollow logs in the wild, and it was believed that they would provide security for the lizards.

Due to interspecific aggression, it is often difficult to establish groups of animals. Large, tall enclosures have proven to be the best type of housing for *C. zebrata*. The height of the enclosure enables the lizards to use a variety of climbing perches and to space themselves more effectively, thus reducing aggression early during periods of introduction.

Substrates have included small round stones, licorice root mulch, cedar mulch, and newspaper. Stones were discontinued due to difficulty in keeping them clean. Mulches were also discontinued (even though this was the best substrate, because it helped maintain proper humidity), due to roach problems in the off-exhibit holding enclosures. Newspaper has proven to be good as a floor covering, because it is easily replaced and affords the skinks additional hiding places.

Water was provided in the exhibit in a recessed fiberglass floor pool with a diameter of about 20 cm and a depth of 35 cm. Skinks in off-exhibit holding enclosures were given suitably sized water bowls, depending on the size of the enclosure. Water is readily used by the skinks for drinking and soaking. Soaking aids in shedding their skins, and may also assist in defecation, since fecal material is often found in the water containers.

Environmental conditions on- and off-exhibit were similar. The only difference was that the original breeding colony, maintained on exhibit, received a 12-hour photoperiod with eight hours of ultraviolet radiation. Since 1979, all colonies have been maintained off-exhibit. They are not given ultraviolet radiation, and receive an eight-hour photoperiod. Temperatures in each group vary between 26.7° and 29.4°C, with relative humidity between 60% and 68%.

Sexing of specimens has been difficult, and has been based on the size of adults (females are somewhat larger and more robust than the males) and behavioral differences noted between the sexes (females are more aggressive than males). The use of sexing probes has not been successful with this species.

Diet

Although no field studies on the food and feeding behavior of the Prehensile-tailed Skink have been undertaken, some observations of food items have been reported. Kinghorn (1928) reported that the contents of one stomach contained a mass of circular leaf particles. Honegger (1975) stated that the preferred food of this species are the epiphytic plants of the genera *Piper* and *Epipremnum*. Parker (1983) listed the leaves and fruit of the epiphytic vine *Scindapsus* and a wild pepper vine (*Piper* sp.) as favorite foods of this species on Bougainville. Of eight specimens that I examined at the Bishop Museum (BM) in Honolulu, Hawaii, in 1982, six (BM 2223, 3133, 3360–3362, 3365) contained the remains of leaf particles and small fruit seeds. One stomach (BM 33133) also contained a large mass of nematodes.

These observations, and the observations of Honegger (1975) and Bowler (1981) on captive specimens, suggest that this species is herbivorous. The stomach of this species contains two chambers (Iverson 1982), much like that of herbivorous iguanids, which also suggests a herbivorous diet.

The basic diet of the Prehensile-tailed Skinks at the Philadelphia Zoo consists of chopped or diced apples, oranges, bananas, carrots, kale, romaine lettuce, spinach, and hard-boiled eggs. Liquid multivitamins, bone meal, and oyster-shell flour are mixed into the basic diet for proper supplementation. Food is offered twice weekly. For several years, some animal protein, consisting of minced horse meat, small mice, and dead chicks, was also offered as part of the diets. Crickets were sometimes given and were chased and eaten in *Varanus*-like fashion.

Honegger (1975) expressed surprise with the statement in a manuscript by Uwe Peters of the Taronga Zoo (Australia) that worms and insects were a part of this lizard's diet, and questioned whether this was an unusual circumstance. My observations suggest that insects and other small animals may be part of this lizard's diet in the wild. That insect and other animal remains have not been recovered in the stomachs of museum specimens may merely reflect the small sample size and relatively rapid digestion of animal proteins.

Fecal material is often eaten by lizards of this species in captivity. Honegger (1975, 1981, 1985) mentioned this behavior in his captives at the Zurich Zoo. Kinghorn (1928) reported that this species lives in groups of three in a single tree hollow, with only the topmost individual emerging to eat leaves, while the other two individuals eat only the excrement of the other lizard. Parker (1983) was unable to directly confirm Kinghorn's report, but did state that he had heard identical stories of this behavior from natives of six different language groups on Bougainville Island. Coprophagy has been observed in the Philadelphia colonies, but only from the floor of their enclosures, and not from their water containers. Coprophagic behavior may be important for the transferring of cellulose-digesting gastrointestinal fauna and flora from adult skinks to the juveniles, as has been reported for some herbivorous iguanid species (Iverson 1982; Troyer 1982).

Keratophagy has been observed in the Philadelphia colonies and in Honegger's (1985) group. On one occasion I observed a female skink in colony A eat the still-attached dead skin from the back of another female. Normally, however, skinks would eat pieces of dead, dry skin off the floor of their enclosures.

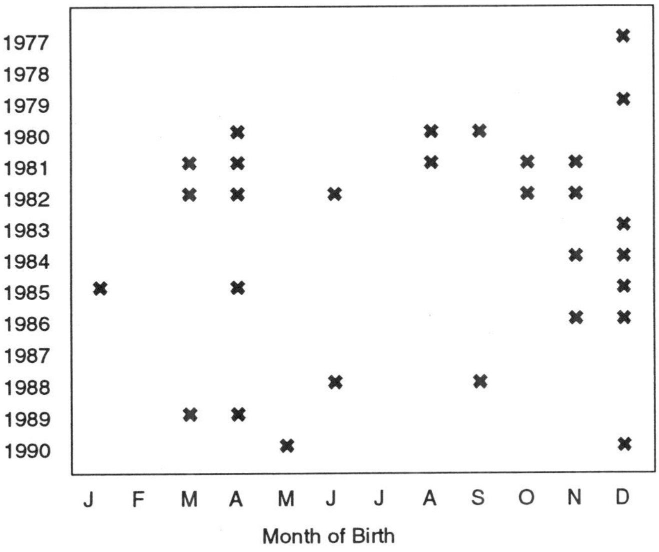

FIGURE 1. Monthly distribution of *Corucia zebrata* births at the Philadelphia Zoological Garden (1977–1990).

Reproduction

Reproduction of the Prehensile-tailed Skink has been reported by Bowler (1981), Honegger (1975, 1985), and Parker (1983). Breeding occurs throughout the year, with one or two young being born at a time. Courtship behavior, which is not often observed, has been reported by Bowler (1981), Honegger (1985), and Nichols (1985), and consists of the male approaching the female from the side, biting her in the pelvic region and then moving anteriorly. The male eventually grasps the female's shoulder or neck and alternately strokes the female's sides with his forefeet. The hindfeet stroke the female's pelvic region, causing her to raise it for insertion of a hemipenis. Courtship behavior has occurred both during the day and at night.

Bowler (1981) reported the births of ten viable young (one of which died three months after birth) in the Philadelphia colonies from December 1977 to July 1981. Between that time and December 1990, an additional 34 young have been produced at Philadelphia, including ten second-generation births, the first of which occurred in 1982 (Groves 1982). Births have occurred in every month except February and July (Figure 1). Stillbirths and neonatal deaths have been high. Of a total of 44 neonates born, 26 have either been stillborn or have died within 31 days of birth (59%). Among these, six were stillbirths and 20 were neonatal deaths. All of the young that died at birth or during the neonatal period had extensive amounts of unabsorbed yolk (14.1 and 21.8 g in two specimens) that had usually ruptured within the body cavity. Honegger (1985) reported 21 births of Prehensile-tailed Skinks at the Zurich Zoo in an 11-year period and had 7 stillbirths (33%). He did not report any neonatal deaths. Wright (1991) reported mummified fetuses and stillbirths as common among recently imported females. It is likely that these high percentages of stillbirths and neonatal deaths are an artifact of captivity.

Sexual maturity in this species is reached between the fourth and fifth years of age. Three captive-bred females have produced young at 49 months, 55 months, and 57 months of age. A captive-bred male sired his first young at four years, nine months of age. The fact that young males must be separated from adult males in their colonies at four years of age also indicates that they have matured at this time.

Gestation in this species has not yet been adequately determined, because copulatory behavior is not often observed. From records at the Philadelphia Zoological Garden, gestation appears to be between six and eight months in duration. During this period, females become progressively more aggressive towards human intruders. The aggressiveness lasts for several weeks after giving birth. Honegger (1985) gives a gestation period of approximately six months for his groups in Zurich. Wright (1991), however, states that gestation periods of up to 11 months have been reported in the literature.

Of the 44 births of Prehensile-tailed Skinks at the Philadelphia Zoological Garden during the period between 1977 and 1990, 18 have been single births and 13 have been twin births. Twin births may be genetically determined by the female. Of 16 females that have given birth, seven females have produced twins. Two second-generation females, which were twins themselves, produced mostly twins. One male that had bred with one of these twin females was later placed with other females. These pairs, however, did not produce twins.

The young are born in membranous sacs, which are eaten by the female parent. Living neonates tend to hide beneath any cover in their enclosures or in available hollow logs. Honegger (1985) reports similar behavior by his neonates, but also states that the females and juveniles are very aggressive during this time. Juveniles at the Philadelphia Zoological Garden have not been aggressive at birth, although the females remain very aggressive for several weeks after birth, apparently protecting their young. Juveniles shed their natal skin within a day, and begin feeding approximately ten days after birth. I have, on several occasions, observed females nudge and/or push their young to food in what appeared to be an attempt to start them to feed. Honegger (1985) did not report this behavior, but indicated that females and their young were hard to separate during the early life of the neonates.

Young that were born from 1977 to 1980 were always separated from the adults shortly after birth, but in later years were allowed to remain with the adults in their colonies. Although Honegger (1985) reported cannibalism of young in his group, no cases of cannibalistic behavior of neonates have been observed in the Philadelphia colonies.

Medical Histories

A variety of common ailments has been experienced, all of which are normal with captive lizards. These include chronic dermatitis, bites caused by cagemates, and necrotic stomatitis. Most of these medical problems have not resulted in the death of the animal, but were severe enough to warrant aggressive veterinary treatment. More serious medical problems which have caused deaths have been amoebiasis, peritonitis (caused by intestinal perforation), eggbinding, pancreatic adenocarcinoma, hepatitis, bacterial dermatitis, and abscesses of the lung and liver. These medical issues were not chronic throughout the colonies of skinks, and were mostly detected during necropsies. Honegger (1975) reported *Salmonella* infestations and amoebic dysentery in his group of Prehensile-tailed Skinks.

The most recurrent medical problem in this group of skinks has been malabsorption of yolk by recently born lizards. This has led to a high stillbirth and neonatal death rate. Most of these individuals were born during the cooler parts of the year (November to April); gestating females may not have had adequate warmth to develop their young properly. Although few measurements of the newborn young were taken, it is obvious from published sources that these young were among the smallest recorded. Honegger (1975) reported a neonate that had a snout-to-vent length of 15.5 cm, and a tail length of 18.2 cm. Its weight was 125 g. Parker (1983) provided measurements of two newborn skinks. One had a total length of 33 cm, and the other had a snout-to-vent length of 17.8 cm, and a tail length of 17.5 cm. Three neonates that died in the Philadelphia colonies within three days of birth had snout-to-vent lengths of 11.0 to 23.1 cm and tail lengths of 11.5 to 14.0 cm. Five dead neonates ranged in weight from 27.5 to 84.7 g.

Longevity

The Prehensile-tailed Skink is a long-lived species. The average longevity at the Philadelphia Zoological Garden (not including neonatal deaths) is seven years, six months. The longest-lived individuals are two specimens (one male and one female) that were obtained as adults in September 1973 from the Chester Zoo. Both of these lizards are still living and have lived together since their arrival. They have also been the most productive pair in the entire group, producing three sets of twins and one single birth. Honegger (1985) stated that the longevity record at the Zurich Zoo was a female from Guadalcanal that lived for seven years and 11 months.

Summary

Several colonies of Prehensile-tailed Skinks (*Corucia zebrata*) have been maintained for the last 18 years at the Philadelphia Zoological Garden. A total of 44 births, including ten second-generation births, have occurred. Stillbirths and early neonatal mortality is high (59%). Breeding occurs throughout the year, with one to two young born after a gestation period of 6–8 months. Behaviors of the females suggest some parental care. Average longevity in this colony is seven years, six months, and the longest-lived individual is approaching 18 years.

The skinks are best housed in large, tall enclosures. Hollow logs are used for retreats and appear to facilitate reproduction. The diet consists of mixed fresh fruits and vegetables, which is supplemented with multi-vitamins, bone meal, and oyster shell flour. The young are raised with the adults. The optimal group size and composition to reduce aggression appears to be one male with two females and their young.

Acknowledgments

Many people and institutions have assisted with the development and management of the colonies of Prehensile-tailed Skinks at the Philadelphia Zoological Garden throughout the past 18 years. These include many staff members, both past and present. I would like particularly to thank the keepers in the Reptile Department who have cared for these lizards. They include Sarah Cunius, Charles Ripka, Thomas Nichols, Joyce Parker, Daniel Christman, George Lutman, Dawn Lavoie, and William Altimari. Kevin Bowler began this colony at Philadelphia and was responsible for its early development. Martin Kupersmith provided valuable information on the habits and habitats of this skink during the early years and provided several specimens on loan. Alan A. Ziegler and Carla H. Kisinami of the Bernice P. Bishop Museum in Honolulu, Hawaii, are thanked for their assistance during and after my visit to the museum. P. M. C. Stevens of the Chester Zoo, in Chester, UK, was very helpful in providing valuable specimens and information concerning his captive colonies of skinks.

I would also like to thank the following who provided assistance during the preparation of this manuscript: William Altimari, Elizabeth Bahner, Virginia Pierce, Pat Farina, Karl Kranz, Robert McLear, and Kevin Wright. I would also like to thank Roger Conant who has had a major role in the development of my career, particularly for bringing me to the Philadelphia Zoological Garden.

Literature Cited

Bowler, J. K. 1981. Captive reproduction of the prehensile-tailed skink at the Philadelphia Zoo, p. 192–194. *In* Proceedings of the American Association of Zoological Parks and Aquariums 1981 Annual Conference. Amer. Assoc. Zool. Parks Aquar., Wheeling, West Virginia.

De Vosjoli, P. 1993. The General Care and Maintenance of Prehensile-tailed Skinks. Herpetocult. Library, Lakeside, California. 56 pages.

Gray, J. E. 1855. A new genus of fish-scaled lizard (*Scissosare*) from New Guinea. Proc. Zool. Soc. London, 1855: 217–218.

Groves, J. D. 1982. Second generation prehensile-tailed

skink born. Amer. Assoc. Zool. Parks Aquar. Newsl., 23: 18.

Guppy, H. B. 1887. The Solomon Islands and Their Natives. Swan Sonnenschein, Lowery and Co., London. xvi, 384 pages.

Honegger, R. 1975. Beitrag zur Kenntnis des Wickelskinkes *Corucia zebrata*. Salamandra, 11: 27–32. [A contribution to the knowledge of the prehensile-tailed skink *Corucia zebrata*. English translation by Paul Gritis, published in Bull. Chicago Herpetol. Soc., 22: 34–37].

—. 1985. Additional notes on the breeding and captive management of the prehensile-tailed skink (*Corucia zebrata*). Herpetol. Rev., 16: 21–23.

Iverson, J. B. 1982. Adaptation to herbivory in iguanine lizards, p. 60–76. *In* G. M. Burghardt and A. S. Rand (eds.), Iguanas of the World. Noyes Publ., Park Ridge, New Jersey.

Kinghorn, J. R. 1928. Herpetology of the Solomon Islands. Rec. Australian Mus., 16: 123–178.

Loveridge, A. 1946. Reptiles of the Pacific World. Macmillan, New York. xii, 259 pages (reprinted 1974 by Society for the Study of Amphibians and Reptiles).

McCoy, M. 1980. Reptiles of the Solomon Islands. Wau Ecology Inst., Wau, Papua New Guinea. vi, 80 pages.

Moser, K. 1992. The prehensile-tailed skink, *Corucia zebrata* Gray: care, behavioral observations and reproduction, p. 85–89. *In* P. D. Strimple and J. L. Strimple (eds.), Contributions in Herpetology. Greater Cincinnati Herpetol. Soc., Cincinnati, Ohio.

Nichols, T. J. 1985. Courtship and copulatory behavior of captive skinks *Corucia zebrata* at the Philadelphia Zoo. Zoo Review (Philadelphia Zool. Garden), 2: no pagination.

Parker, F. 1983. The prehensile-tailed skink (*Corucia zebrata*) on Bougainville Island, Papua New Guinea, p. 435–440. *In* A. G. J. Rhodin and K. Miyata (eds.), Advances in Herpetology and Evolutionary Biology: Essays in Honor of E. E. Williams. Museum of Comparative Zoology, Harvard University, Cambridge, Massachusetts.

Schmidt, A. A. 1991. Zur Haltung und Fortpflanzung des Wickelskinks *Corucia zebrata* Gray, 1855. Salamandra, 27: 238–245.

Schmidt, K. P. 1932. Reptiles and amphibians from the Solomon Islands. Field Mus. Nat. Hist., Zool., 18: 175–190.

Schmidt, K. P., and R. F. Inger 1957. Living Reptiles of the World. Doubleday and Co., New York. 287 pages.

Troyer, K. 1982. Transfer of fermentative microbes between generations in herbivorous lizard. Science, 216: 540–542.

Wright, K. 1991. The Solomon Island Skink. Reptile Amphib. Mag., 1991(March/April): 10–19.

Note Added in Proof

Two additional papers on the husbandry of the Prehensile-tailed Skink, which appeared after this contribution was written and accepted for publication, are worth mentioning (Schmidt 1991; Moser 1992). Both articles contain information that is similar to that in this chapter. A more recent publication has also appeared that provides more detailed information for the pet keeper (De Vosjoli 1993).

❦

❦ Groves, J. D. 1994. Husbandry and reproduction of the prehensile-tailed skink, *Corucia zebrata*, p. 317–322. *In* J. B. Murphy, K. Adler, and J. T. Collins (eds.), Captive Management and Conservation of Amphibians and Reptiles. Society for the Study of Amphibians and Reptiles, Ithaca (New York). Contributions to Herpetology, volume 11.

Old World Chameleons in Captivity: Growth, Maturity, and Reproduction of Malagasy Panther Chameleons (*Chamaeleo pardalis*)

Gary W. Ferguson*

Introduction

Old world chameleons (family Chamaeleonidae) are listed on Appendix II of CITES and are considered threatened by much of the conservation community (Dodd 1982). Their unusual adaptations for climbing and leading an arboreal existence, as well as their attractive coloration, have made them popular subjects for captivity (Bustard 1989; DeVosjoli 1990*a*, 1990*b*; Ferguson and Blades 1991; Schmidt et al. 1989) and targets for heavy exploitation by the pet trade (Dodd 1982). Despite the popularity of chameleons, very few field studies exist on any of the 130-or-so species (Bourgat 1970; Burrage 1973; Lin and Nelson 1981).

Chameleons are arboreal, insectivorous, metachromatic, and mostly oviparous; aside from these facts, virtually nothing is known of their life history and social behavior in the field. Much more basic field information on potentially threatened species must be generated before meaningful conservation can be accomplished—other than protection of natural areas containing chameleons, curbing wholesale exportation, and establishing captive colonies.

Considering the exploitation of chameleons and the fact that many species are restricted to rapidly disappearing ecosystems, such as the rain forests of Madagascar (Brygoo 1971, 1978; Jenkins 1987; Raxworthy 1988), captive propagation seems justified from at least two points of view. First, captive propagation of a few hardy, attractive species coupled with export restrictions might divert popular interest from exploitation of wild-caught specimens. Mortality of wild-caught chameleons is extremely high due to mishandling during capture, transient housing, and shipping. Most wild chameleons carry heavy parasite loads and this, combined with stress of handling, crowding, dehydration, and improper temperatures, is more than many individuals can tolerate (Bustard 1989; DeVosjoli 1990*a*, 1990*b*; Ferguson and Blades 1991; Schmidt et al. 1989). Death of recent imports, even seemingly robust animals, is frequent and unpredictable. Few people interested in keeping chameleons would pass up a healthy captive-raised or head-started animal, if offered a choice between this and a wild-caught animal of uncertain survivability.

Second, the Malagasy and African forests contain most of the described forms of chameleons (Brygoo 1971, 1978; Hillenius 1959). Tropical forest ecosystems are rapidly disappearing (Jolly and Lanting 1987; Raxworthy 1988). Development of husbandry technology using chameleons from various habitats seems to be an important priority. When species become threatened to the point at which captive-rescue operations are needed, it is too late to embark on studies to investigate temperature, nutritional, and other environmental requirements.

---

*Department of Biology
Texas Christian University
Fort Worth, Texas 76129, USA

Acronyms used in this chapter:

ANOVA	Analysis of variance
CITES	Convention on International Trade in Endangered Species of Fauna and Flora
kPa	Kilopascals
SVL	Snout-to-vent length
UVA	Ultraviolet A

These are better conducted while the species are abundant and adequate material for experimentation is available.

Captive Management: State of the Art

Despite the heavy mortality of imported chameleons, enough survive and do well in captivity to perpetuate a popular interest in chameleons. A few institutions and private individuals have bred them and a very few have reported success past the first captive generation (Van Mater 1971; Schmidt et al. 1989; McKeown 1991). Some of the species reported to be hardy in captivity are: *Chamaeleo jacksonii, C. dilepis, C. bitaeniatus, C. ellioti, C. hoehnelii, C. pardalis, C. montium,* and *Bradypodion pumilis* (Bustard 1989; DeVosjoli 1990*a*, 1990*b*; Ferguson and Blades 1991; Schmidt et al. 1989).

Several factors seem to correlate with successful maintenance of healthy specimens (Bustard 1989; DeVosjoli 1990*a*, 1990*b*; Ferguson and Blades 1991; Schmidt et al. 1989). These include social isolation, vines and branches for climbing, proper ambient temperature that is appropriate to the species, frequent misting or a hygienic drip system for watering, exposure to proper light (artificial or natural depending on the species), meticulous hygiene, a diet that consists of a variety of insect species with nutrient supplements, and proper nesting substrate for oviparous females. When success is reduced, especially with captive reproduction or survival of captive-produced hatchlings, experts differ as to the causes. Opinions usually center around factors such as nutritional imbalance, improper lighting (artificial versus natural), air circulation, or heavy vegetation (whether or not chameleons need this for security).

An additional problem relates to egg husbandry. Many oviparous chameleons have prolonged egg incubation periods. These may last up to a year and include a diapause or resting period (Bons and Bons 1960; Blanc 1974). Artificial incubation environments that are near the tolerated extreme for certain factors may permit egg survival, but prolong this resting period. Fertile eggs may remain in apparent healthy condition for over a year without developing into the advanced embryonic stages, as I have observed in eggs of *C. lateralis*. This phenomenon has also been observed in *C. oustaleti* (David Grow, Todd Risley, pers. comms.).

Given the diversity of environments that chameleons inhabit (from dry subtropical desert to tropical rain forest to high, mountain grassland), there is likely to be considerable species specificity in temperature, light, and nutritional requirements. Experimental work is needed on a variety of species to define species-specific or population-specific requirements and tolerance for these factors and to determine if requirements or tolerances can be predicted from general knowledge of the natural habitat of a species or population.

The Panther Chameleon (Chamaeleo pardalis)

Of the 14 chameleon species maintained in my laboratory over the past 15 years, the hardiest and easiest to work with so far has been the Malagasy Panther Chameleon. This is one of the larger chameleons. Males sometimes exceed 50 cm in total length and approach 200 g in mass; females reach 35 cm and approach 60 g in mass when gravid. The Panther Chameleon is distributed along the warm, humid coast of northern and northeastern Madagascar and has been introduced onto Réunion Island (Brygoo 1971).

The natural history and general ecology of the Panther Chameleon has been thoroughly studied on Réunion Island (Bourgat 1970) and observed elsewhere (Brygoo 1971; Schmidt et al. 1989; Raxworthy 1988; G. W. Ferguson, pers. observ.). The species is very abundant in disturbed habitat throughout its Malagasy range (G. W. Ferguson, pers. observ.) and may inhabit the canopy of undisturbed forest (Raxworthy 1988). Males and females are very colorful during the breeding season, which may last from three months on Réunion (Bourgat 1970) to nine months or more on the coastal island of Nosy Bé in the northwestern part of its range. In captivity, females from Nosy Bé cycle continuously and produce a clutch of 15–40 eggs every 6–8 weeks. Males from Nosy Bé may retain their bright colors, but may show short periods (one to two months) of quiescence of sexual behavior. Juveniles of all sizes, except recent hatchlings, were discovered on Nosy Bé in May 1991. This suggests prolonged seasonal reproduction in the field as well.

The coloration and some of the anatomical features (for example, details of the head morphology or ornamentation) of male Panther Chameleons, varies geographically (Brygoo 1971; Bourgat 1970;

Schmidt et al. 1989). In the north, males tend to have brighter facial colors (yellows and reds) and emphasize varying shades of green more than in the southern parts of their range. Those of the southern portion of the east coast emphasize darker shades, but can rapidly change to brilliant orange, yellow, or red. Nonbreeding females are nondescript gray or brown with faint blotches and vertical bars of dark color. When sexually receptive, they assume a uniform orange or pink coloration, which rapidly changes to a dark brown or black with bold orange or pink blotches after they have bred and become nonreceptive.

A Study of Growth in Captive Chamaeleo pardalis

In August 1988, a half-grown male Panther Chameleon from Nosy Bé Island was obtained from a commercial dealer in reptiles. In March 1989, a recently collected adult non-gravid female was obtained. A clutch of 15 fertile eggs was obtained from her on 24 May 1989. Apparently these eggs were sired by a wild male before capture of the female. The captive pair was bred on 21 June 1989 and the female deposited 22 fertile eggs (possibly sired by a combination of sperm from the captive male and stored sperm). The female was bred and deposited eggs nine more times until 8 October 1990, when she died with a prolapsed uterus while attempting to deposit her tenth clutch of eggs. She was bred not only to the male mentioned above, but also to a male from Ambanja, a male from Diégo Suarez, and one of her sons produced by her first clutch of eggs. Viability of her eggs decreased with successive clutches (Table 1).

Twelve offspring from her first two clutches and four additional specimens hatched at another facility were selected for a study of growth under ad libitum feeding conditions. The feeding rates, growth, maturity, and reproduction of this cohort and the husbandry techniques used during this period are reported below.

Husbandry Techniques Used

An adult male and female were maintained singly, each in 130-liter aquaria standing on end. A wooden wall was constructed to fit in the open side and included a service door (30 × 15 cm), which consisted of a wooden frame covered with 6-mm mesh for ventilation. Attached to the inside of the wooden wall was an incandescent fixture and a 45-cm fluorescent fixture. A 25-watt bulb with a hardware-and-cloth covering produced an elevated cage temperature during the day (about 27°–29°C). A 15-watt Vita-lite (Durotest) was inserted into the fluorescent fixture to enhance cage lighting and provide a small amount of ultraviolet irradiation (mostly UVA; see Gehrmann 1987). The bottom of the terrarium was substrate-free. A plastic sweater box was fitted into the bottom and provided a catch-basin for feces. A potted tropical plant (*Pothos* sp.) was placed in the cage in a small plastic water-containment pan. A dead branch placed into the terrarium rested on wooden strips glued to the glass

TABLE 1. Fertility and viability of eggs produced by original female *Chamaeleo pardalis* from 4 May 1989 to 10 July 1990.

Date laid	Clutch number	Number of eggs	Number fertile*	Number hatched
24 May 1989	1	15	15	12
26 July 1989	2	22	22	17
14 September 1989	3	22	22	0
3 November 1989	4	29	27	3
25 December 1989	5	29	21	20
7 February 1990	6	20	0	0
30 March 1990	7	29	26	0
17 May 1990	8	29	21	4
10 July 1990	9	21	19	5

*Non-fertile eggs were those significantly smaller than average and spoiling within 10 days of being laid. Most fertile eggs that failed to hatch survived to term (7–9 months).

sides of the cage. It provided perches for the chameleon and support for the plant. Food (such as mealworms, superworms, and crickets with the hind legs removed) was introduced three times weekly into a 237-ml plastic cup that hung from a branch or from the mesh of the service door. A vitamin-and-mineral powder, composed of one-half Reptivite (Zoo Med) and one-half $CaCO_3$, covered the bottom of the cup and was changed with each feeding. Water dropped onto the plant in such a way to be caught by the plant's containment pan. The drip system consisted of medical saline-drip bottles or bags suspended outside of the terrarium with the tube threaded through a hole in the wooden door and hung from the ceiling of the enclosure. Water dripped for about 15 minutes, three times per week. Lights were controlled with a timer on a 12-hour photoperiod. The cages were next to a west-facing window, but did not receive direct sunlight.

For mating, the female was either moved to the cage of the male, or vice versa, or both were put on a stick or plant outside of the enclosure. The pair were left together for six to eight hours. Usually the pair mated twice during this period. Two weeks after mating, a pan of substrate, composed of one-half potting soil and one-half sand, was placed in the bottom of the enclosure of the female and left until nesting. The substrate mass measured 30×30×15 cm. The female usually began digging immediately and laid her clutch within two to three days.

Eggs were removed, weighed, numbered with a felt-tipped pen, and set up in moistened vermiculite (–200 kPa [kilopascals], 1:1 water-to-dry-vermiculite ratio by mass). All eggs were moved to fresh vermiculite approximately every two months. Incubation temperature varied. Most eggs were incubated at room temperatures, which ranged from daily fluctuations of 19°–23°C to 22°–26°C, depending on the season. One half of each clutch was incubated at a constant 28°C for a portion of the incubation period (Table 2).

The constantly elevated temperature influenced the incubation period in a peculiar way (Table 2). If this was imposed during the last quarter of incubation there was no effect (Table 2, clutch 1). If it was imposed during the latter trimester of incubation

TABLE 2. Incubation duration, incubation temperature, and hatchling sex ratio for three clutches of eggs of original female *Chamaeleo pardalis*. While not rigorously controlled, incubation water potential varied from –200 to –400 kPa. Parentheses after days indicates number of temperature readings averaged. Temperatures are in degrees C.

Characteristic	Clutch 1			Clutch 2			Clutch 5		
	Days	Mean temperature		Days	Mean temperature		Days	Mean temperature	
		Minimum	Maximum		Minimum	Maximum		Minimum	Maximum
Incubation									
Initial	177 (4)	20	26	114 (3)	20	26	258 (19)	21*	27
Terminal	53 (2)	19*	28	128 (6)	19*	28			
Mean incubation duration for eggs at variable temperatures	230 days			237 days			236 days		
Mean incubation duration for eggs subjected to constant 28°C during terminal portion of incubation	230 days			211 days			308 days		
Hatchling males:females	5:7			8:10			13:6		

*Indicates that half of the clutch was incubated at a constant 28°C for the remaining period of incubation.

(Table 2, clutch 2), it accelerated hatching. If imposed during the entire period (Table 2, clutch 5), however, it prolonged incubation by two months. Healthy hatchlings were produced under both conditions, but about one-third of those incubated at the elevated temperature had developmental abnormalities (mostly a shortened tail).

Sex of hatchlings can be recognized by thickness of the tail base, with about 70% accuracy. Male hatchlings have a tailbase measuring 1.6–2.0 mm (as measured from dorsal to ventral sides with vernier calipers); for females, the tailbase measurement is 1.3–1.6 mm. Mass and snout-to-vent length (SVL) of lizards was measured biweekly throughout the study. Mass was measured using a top-loading digital balance (Ohaus). SVL was estimated with a plastic ruler by letting the chameleon perch along the edge. Pulling on the lizard's tail stimulated full extension of its spine.

Hatchlings were set up singly in small plastic terraria of about 1.3 liters. A small branch of heavenly bamboo (*Nandina* sp.) was placed in each terrarium as a perch. An opaque vial (5 cm high × 1.8 cm diameter) was placed in each terrarium as a food container. Water was provided by misting the walls of the terrarium twice daily. No substrate was provided and cages were thoroughly cleaned every two weeks. As the lizards grew they were placed in larger terraria with basically the same design. As they became large enough to tip over the vial by standing on it, the vial was taped to the floor of the terrarium and a vial of a smaller diameter was inserted. The larger vial served as a receptacle for the smaller, which could be easily removed each day to exchange old insects for new and to be cleaned. The 16 terraria were placed on a raised shelf directly under a fluorescent fixture containing two 40-watt Vita Lites. The cage was left uncovered, allowing the light rays to contact the lizard directly for about the first two months of life. After that, a plastic lid, with 1 × 10 mm slots separated by one mm of plastic, separated the light from the lizard and noticeably reduced the irradiance reaching the lizard. When the lizards climbed onto the underside of the lid their body was about 15 cm from the light bulbs.

The temperature of the cage array was monitored daily with four minimum-maximum thermometers that were placed on the shelf next to the cages. Mean high temperatures varied from 30.2°C (SD = 0.8, n = 11) in January through March to 31.5°C (SD = 0.8, n = 11) from April through June. Mean high temperature from July through September was 30.6°C (SD = 0.7, n = 13). Mean low temperatures varied from 20.8°C (SD = 0.8, n = 11) in January through March to 22.3°C (SD = 0.9, n = 13) from July through September. Mean low temperature from April through June was 21.9°C (SD = 1.0, n = 11). Periodically, the interior temperature of each cage was monitored by inserting a thermocouple wire attached to a Wescor thermocouple reader. There were no major thermal gradients within the cages and internal cage temperature closely matched the reading of the closest thermometer.

Maximum ambient temperature varied from 2° to 3°C among the thermometers of the array on any given day. To equalize these position effects, cages were systematically rotated to a new position each day. Because there was no "hot spot" near or within the cages, one can justifiably assume lizard body temperature matched air temperature. Occasional cloacal temperature readings verified this assumption.

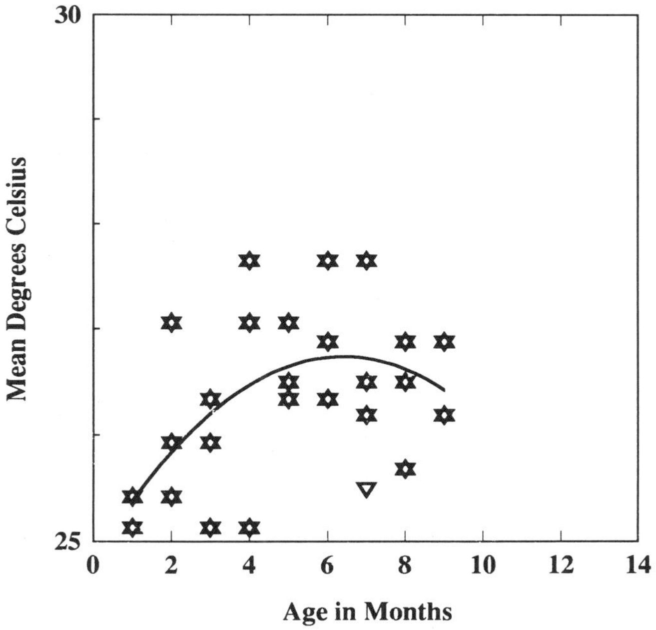

FIGURE 1. Age in months versus mean environmental temperature during that age for 16 Panther Chameleons. There are 16, mostly overlapping values for each age. Males are inverted open triangles, females are open triangles.

Four of the hatchlings used in the study hatched in November 1989, six hatched in January 1990, and six hatched in March 1990. A slight seasonal trend in environmental temperature occurred (Figure 1) such that the laboratory was slightly cooler at the beginning and at the end of the study.

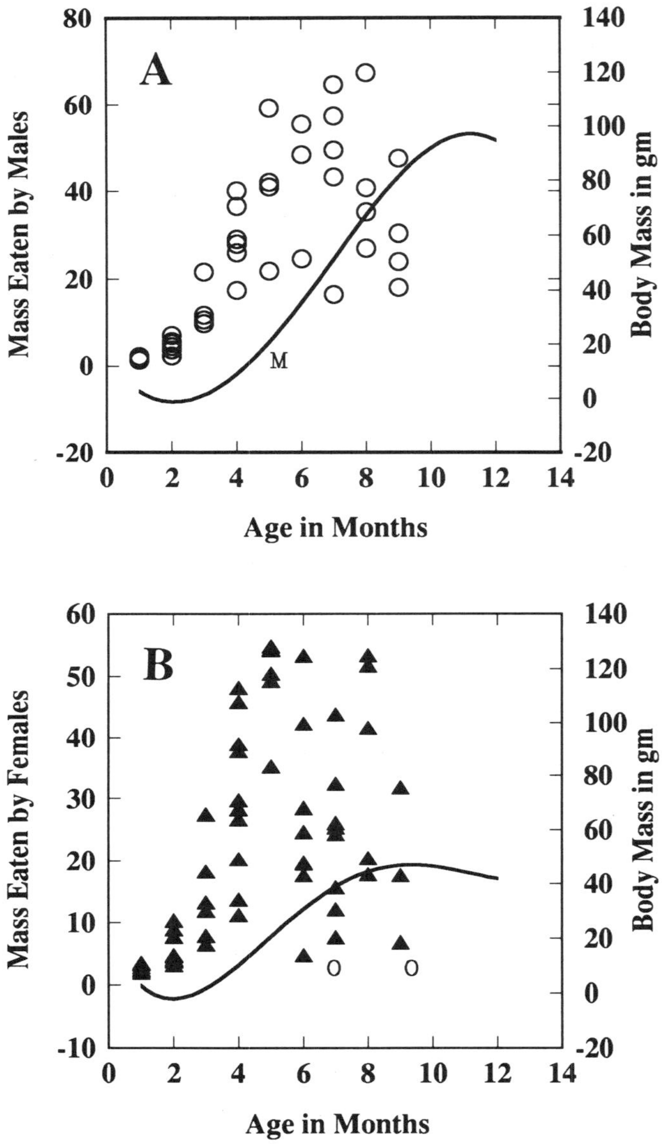

FIGURE 2. Age in months versus mass of insects eaten by 6 male (A) and 10 female (B) Panther Chameleons. The solid lines are growth curves (age versus mass) from Figure 4 for comparison. Each symbol represents feeding data for an individual; O male, ▲ female. There are overlapping values that are not discernible on the graphs. M, in panel A, indicates average age of first mating. O, in panel B, indicates average age of oviposition for clutch one and clutch two. While there seem to be differences in mass eaten for males versus females, these were not statistically significant (repeated measures ANOVA, no interaction between male and female values).

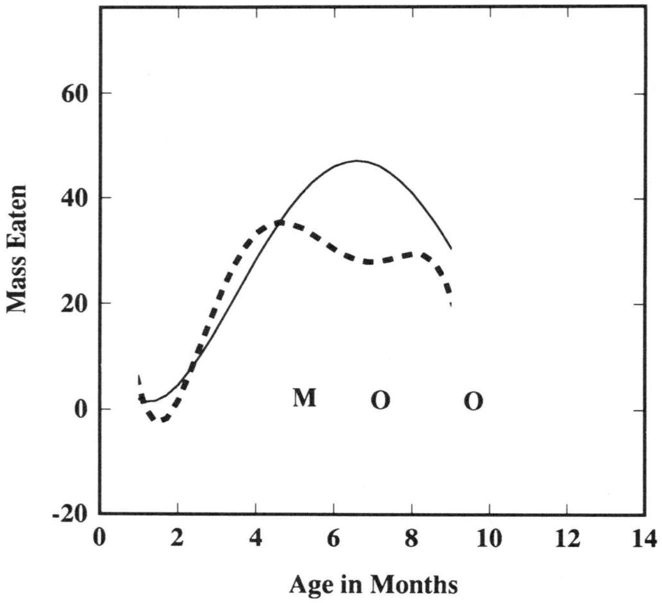

FIGURE 3. Polynomial feeding curves for Panther Chameleons generated from the data shown in Figure 2. Solid line is for males; dotted line is for females. M indicates average age of first mating. O indicates average age of oviposition for clutches one and two.

Lizards were fed appropriate-sized crickets or mealworms throughout the experiment. After reaching mature size, superworms (*Zophobas* sp.) were sometimes substituted for mealworms. During the first two months, lizards were fed crickets that were only one-third grown (average weight was 4 mg). After that period, equal numbers of larger crickets (average weight was 0.25 g) and medium mealworms (average weight was 0.04 g) were offered three to five times per week in quantities sufficient to result in a residual at the next feeding. New and residual insects were weighed each feeding day to assess ad libitum feeding rates. All growth data were compiled into LOTUS 123 files. All graphs were plotted using SIGMAPLOT (Jandel Corp.), which also generated the polynomials fitted to the points. All statistical analyses including repeated-measures ANOVA's were generated using SYSTAT Inc. (Evanston, Illinois; program MGLH).

Feeding Rates and Growth

Chameleons began feeding within three days of hatching. The amount of food eaten increased during growth and reached a peak at four to five months for females and about six to seven months for males (Figures 2 and 3). The ratio of mass of food eaten to lizard body mass reached its peak during the third month, after which it dropped rapidly as sexual maturity approached (Figure 2). From the first through the fourth month, the chameleons were

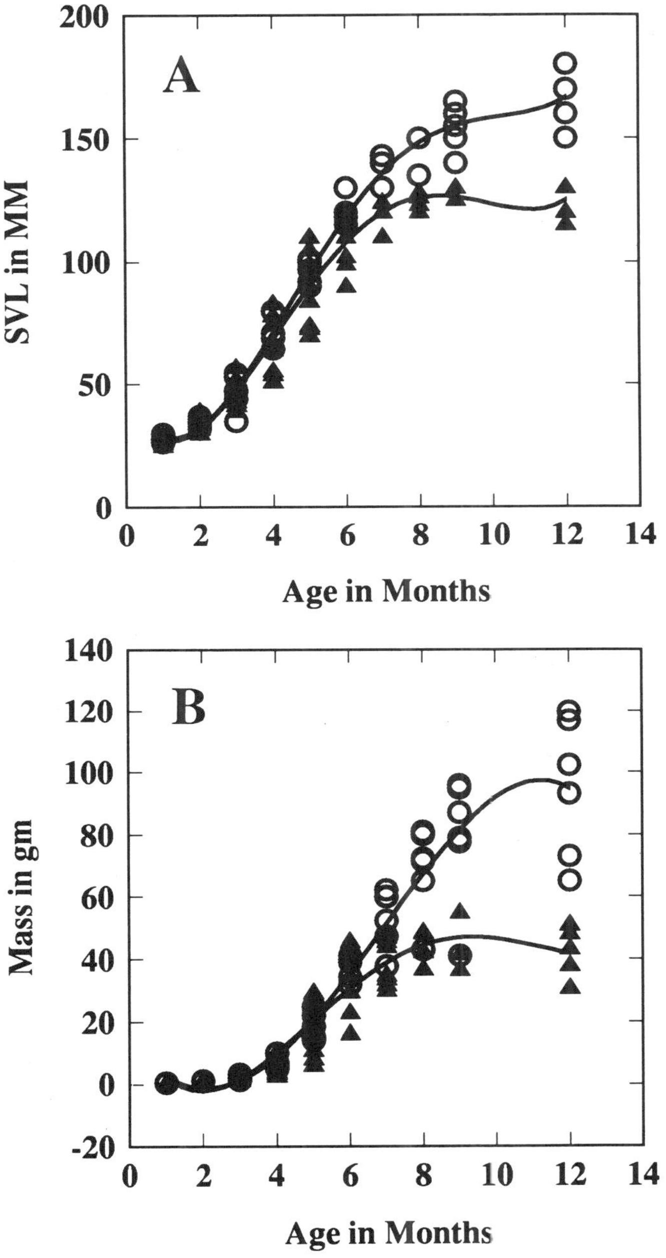

FIGURE 4. Age versus SVL (A) and mass (B) for 16 Panther Chameleons. O male; ▲ female. Lines are polynomial curves fitted to the points. Male and female curves are significantly different (repeated measures ANOVA, probability of no interaction between male and female values <0.001.)

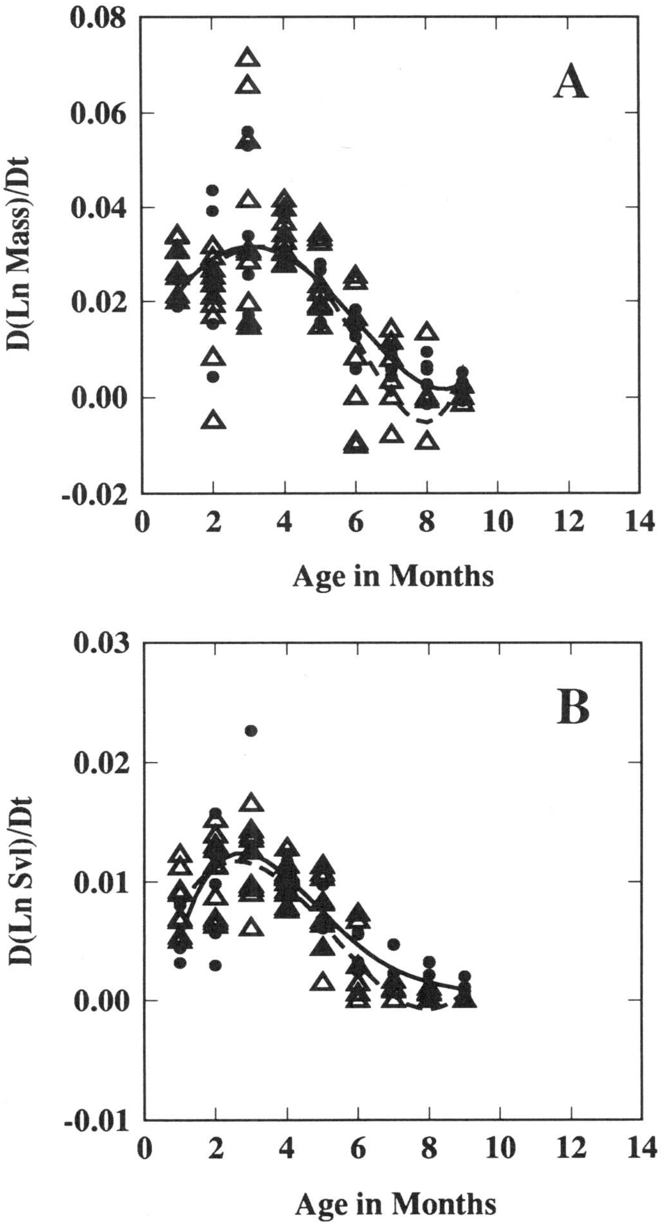

FIGURE 5. Age versus size-specific growth rate (see Andrews 1982) in Panther Chameleons; (A) mass specific growth; (B) SVL-specific growth. ● male; Δ female. Solid line fits male points; dotted line fits female points. Male and female curves differ significantly (repeated measures ANOVA probability of no interaction between male and female values <0.001).

eating from four to six times their body mass per month (Ferguson 1991). As females became reproductively active their food intake began to cycle; they fed voraciously when undergoing vitellogenesis and greatly reduced food intake when gravid (Figure 2).

Females and males grew at equivalent rates during their first six months or until females reached a minimum mature size of slightly over 130 mm SVL (Fig 4). After six months, growth of the females rapidly approached zero while that of males continued at decreasing rates throughout the next several months (Figures 4 and 5).

Because of the slight variation of temperature during the study, a multiple regression was performed to test the effects of amount of food utilized and temperature on growth during the second month (Table 3). While food mass eaten was a strong predictor of growth, the minor temperature differences throughout the study period made no significant contribution to the variance.

Sexual maturity was indicated by sexually dimorphic color, courtship, copulation, and the production of fertile eggs. Age of maturity was six months for both males and females, despite the submaximal size of the males (130 mm SVL). Fertility of the first clutch was high (164, or 79%, of first-clutch eggs were fertile, out of a total of 206 first-clutch eggs). Of the 164 fertile eggs, however, only six hatched. Most of the others reached full development, but failed to hatch. Full-term embryos appeared normally proportioned, but several had very soft heads. It is unclear why they failed to hatch, but nutritional imbalance related to calcium metabolism is probably the cause. Experiments studying the effect of vitamin D, ultraviolet light, and calcium content of food are needed. One problem with currently used supplements may be the high level of vitamin A present in these supplements. In chickens, massive dietary supplementation of vitamin A interferes with the uptake of vitamin E—another fat-soluble vitamin—from the gut (Frig and Bronz 1983). This inhibitory effect could apply to all fat-soluble vitamins, such as vitamin D, in reptiles as well as chickens. Alternatively, the vitamin D or calcium supplementation used in this study may have been sufficient for growth, but insufficient for viable egg production.

Summary

There is justification for the establishment of captive colonies of Old World chameleons. Due to the diverse environments that chameleons inhabit there is likely to be considerable variation in light, nutritional, and enclosure requirements. Studies of these requirements for a diversity of chameleon species is an urgent prerequisite for the establishment of captive colonies. Guidelines for experimental studies must be generated by observations of chameleons in the field and monitoring of relevant environmental requirements. Trial-and-error study by both professional and amateur keepers also can contribute much to our knowledge (see, for example, Buckley 1991).

While sustained multi-generational reproduction is not yet highly successful for chameleons, the Panther Chameleon and a few other species seem highly adaptable to current captive environments. As knowledge of chameleon natural history increases, and as husbandry technology develops through trial-and-error and experimental study, more spe-

TABLE 3. Multiple regression of amount of food eaten (variable 1) and temperature (variable 2) versus growth during the second month after hatching ($n = 16$) in *Chamaeleo pardalis*. Model is $Y = a+b\times1+c\times2$; b and c are regression coefficients for variables 1 and 2, respectively, and t is a parameter used to evaluate the probability of similarity of two or more samples. R^2 indicates the proportion of the variance of dependent variable explained by the two independent variables (total = 1.0).

Dependent variable	Independent variable 1	Independent variable 2	R^2 of model
Mass increase during month 2	Mass of food eaten b = 0.235 t = 5.93 $p < 0.001$	Mean temperature during month 2 (program did not enter variable); no significant contribution to variance	0.72
Snout-to-vent increase during month 2	b = 1.74 t = 3.94 $p < 0.002$	c = −0.36 t = −0.26 No significant contribution to variance	0.57

cies should prove captive-hardy and candidates for sustained captive propagation. The high reproductive potential of most chameleon species should facilitate the rapid establishment of large thriving colonies as our knowledge increases.

Acknowledgments

I thank Douglas and Matthew Ferguson for help during this study. Ronald Tremper provided prime specimens to start my colony. Financial support for the study was by the Texas Christian University Department of Biology and the Texas Christian University Research Fund.

Literature Cited

Andrews, R. M. 1982. Patterns of growth in reptiles, p. 273–320. *In* C. Gans (ed.). Biology of the Reptilia, volume 13D. Academic Press, London.

Blanc, F. 1974. Table de développement de *Chamaeleo lateralis* Gray 1831. Ann. d'Embryol. Morphogen., 7: 99–115.

Bons, J., and N. Bons. 1960. Notes sur la reproduction et le développement de *Chamaeleo chameleon* (L.). Bull. Soc. Sci. Nat. Phys. Maroc., 40: 323–335.

Bourgat, R. 1970. Recherches écologiques et biologiques sur le *Chameleo pardalis* Cuvier 1829 de l'Isle de la Réunion et de Madagascar. Bull. Soc. Zool. France, 95: 259–268.

Brygoo, E. R. 1971. Reptiliens Sauriens Chamaeleonidae. Genre *Chamaeleo*. Faune Madagascar, 33: 1–138.

—. 1978. Reptiliens Sauriens Chamaeleonidae. Genre *Brookesia* et complément pour la genre *Chamaeleo*. Faune Madagascar, 47: 1–173.

Buckley, R. 1991. Experiments with habitat trees: notes on the captive management of reptiles. Vivarium, 3: 10–18, 28–30.

Burrage, B. R. 1973. Comparative ecology and behavior of *Chamaeleo pumilis pumilis* and *Chamaeleo namaquensis* (Sauria: Chamaeleonidae) Ann. South African Mus., 61: 1–158.

Bustard, R. 1989. Keeping and breeding oviparous chameleons. British Herpetol. Soc. Bull., 27: 1–16.

DeVosjoli, P. 1990*a*. True Chameleons. Part I: Husbandry. Advanced Vivarium Systems, Lakeside, California. 36 pages.

—. 1990*b*. True Chameleons. Part II: Notes on Popular Species, Diseases and Disorders. Advanced Vivariums Systems, Lakeside, California. 29 pages.

Dodd, C. K. 1982. Kenya's Kinyonga may be in trouble. Defenders, 57: 19–25.

Ferguson, G. W. 1991. Ad-libitum feeding rates, growth and survival of captive-hatched chameleons (*Chamaeleo pardalis*) from Nose Bé Island, Madagascar. Herpetol. Rev., 22: 124–125.

Ferguson, G. W., and J. Blades. 1991. Keeping old-world chameleons in captivity. Vivarium, 3: 18–29.

Frig, M., and J. Bronz. 1983. Relationship between vitamin A and vitamin E in the chick. Internatl. Jour. Vitamin Res., 54: 125–133.

Gehrmann, W. H. 1987. Ultraviolet irradiances of various lamps used in animal husbandry. Zoo Biol., 6: 117–127.

Hillenius, D. 1959. The differentiation within the genus *Chamaeleo* Laurenti 1768. Beaufortia, 8: 1–92.

Jenkins, M. D. 1987. Madagascar: An Environmental Profile. International Union for the Conservation of Nature and Natural Resources, Cambridge, UK. 374 pages.

Jolly, A., and F. Lanting. 1987. Madagascar: a world apart. Natl. Geogr., 171: 148–183.

Lin, J.-Y., and C. E. Nelson. 1981. Comparative reproductive biology of two sympatric tropical lizards *Chamaeleo jacksonii* Boulenger and *Chamaeleo hoehnelii* Steindachner (Sauria: Chamaeleonidae). Amphibia-Reptilia, 1: 287–311.

McKeown, S. 1991. Second-generation panther chameleons at the Chaffee Zoo. Amer. Assoc. Zool. Parks Aquar. Commun., 1991: 14.

Raxworthy, C. J. 1988. Reptiles, rainforest and conservation in Madagascar. Biol. Conserv., 43: 181–211.

Schmidt, W., K. Tamm, and E. Wallikewitz. 1989. Chamaleons: Drachen unserer Zeit. Herpetologischer Fachverlag, Munster. 112 pages.

Van Mater, J. 1971. The natural history of two generations of *Chamaeleo jacksonii* in captivity. Herpetology, 5: 1–23.

❦ Ferguson, G. W. 1994. Old World chameleons in captivity: growth, maturity, and reproduction of Malagasy panther chameleons (*Chamaeleo pardalis*), p. 323–331. *In* J. B. Murphy, K. Adler, and J. T. Collins (eds.), Captive Management and Conservation of Amphibians and Reptiles. Society for the Study of Amphibians and Reptiles, Ithaca (New York). Contributions to Herpetology, volume 11.

Ecological and Nutritional Management of the Endangered Piebald Chuckwalla (*Sauromalus varius*) in Captivity

Howard E. Lawler,* Thomas R. Van Devender,* and James L. Jarchow*

Introduction

In the past decade, the number of large iguanid lizards which have been declared as endangered or threatened by the United States Fish and Wildlife Service and the Convention on International Trade in Endangered Species (CITES) has increased at an alarming rate. Many populations have decreased as the result of loss of habitat, use by indigenous peoples as food or tourist commodities, wanton destruction, and over-exploitation for the animal trade (Fitch and Henderson 1977; Fitch et al. 1982).

Large, insular iguanids may benefit from development of captive and quasi-captive propagation and management techniques which maintain genetic integrity and provide opportunities for continuing research. Management protocols have been proposed or developed for *Conolophus* (F. Cepeda Proaño, pers. comm. 1983; H. Snell, pers. comm. 1983), *Ctenosaura* (Fitch et al. 1982), *Cyclura* (Castro and Duval 1979; Duval 1983; Crutchfield 1982), *Iguana* (Fitch and Henderson 1977; Fitch et al. 1982; Werner and Miller 1984; Werner 1988), and *Sauromalus* (Lawler and Jarchow 1986). Captive-management plans for iguanids must consider, among other things, social, spatial, and territorial requirements, and specialized herbivorous diets.

Sauromalus varius, the largest of 11 taxa in the genus, which reaches a maximum total length of over 600 mm (Case 1982), is endemic to Isla San Esteban in the Gulf of California, Sonora, Mexico. Case (1982) estimated the entire insular population at 4,500 animals. The population appears to be concentrated in Arroyo Lemantur, a wide, shallow canyon that supports a relatively dense desertscrub, with more food resources than the nearly barren slopes. *S. varius* is listed as endangered under the endangered species acts of Mexico and the United States, and is included in CITES Appendix I. These designations are based primarily on documented occasional use as food by Mexicans and Seri Indians, and commercial exploitation for the pet trade (Anonymous 1979). By all indications, commercial exploitation is the only serious threat to *S. varius*. Significant degradation of habitat and increased use for food are not likely in the future. Simple protection from commerce should ensure its perpetuity.

The management techniques reported here are based on empirical analysis of *S. varius* behavior, ecology, and dietary selection on Isla San Esteban and at the Arizona-Sonora Desert Museum (ASDM). The analysis of the nutritional values of plant food was initiated as a potential tool in applied captive management, rather than as basic research. The preliminary data presented here are inconclusive, and primarily intended to demonstrate the importance of such analysis in the formulation of captive diets for herbivorous lizards.

Arizona-Sonora Desert Museum Colony

A colony of *Sauromalus varius* has been maintained at the Arizona-Sonora Desert Museum since 1977. In 1981, we recognized the limitations inherent in managing *S. varius* solely in a mixed-species

*Arizona-Sonora Desert Museum
2021 North Kinney Road
Tucson, Arizona 85743, USA

Acronyms used in this chapter:

ADF	Acid detergent fiber
ASDM	Arizona-Sonora Desert Museum
CITES	Convention on International Trade in Endangered Species
L	Lignin
NDF	Neutral detergent fiber
PVC	Polyvinyl chloride

lizard exhibit, and began development of a comprehensive plan for management of the captive population (Lawler and Jarchow 1986). The primary areas of concern are diet and nutrition, pathology and veterinary care, social organization and behavior, spatial requirements, and genetics (H. E. Lawler, in press).

An off-display, outdoor facility for propagation and study was designed and constructed in 1982 to improve the potential for reproductive success and expanded genetic diversity. Before designing the enclosure, we visited Isla San Esteban to assess the habitat for features utilized by the lizards.

The Sonoran desertscrub on Isla San Esteban, in the Central Gulf Coast biogeographic subdivision, is similar in many respects to that of the Arizona Upland subdivision in the Tucson Mountains near the museum, with many chuckwalla food plants in common (Turner and Brown 1982). In Arroyo Lemantur, on Isla San Esteban, chuckwallas use small caliche caves along arroyo banks and spaces among large boulders on open slopes as refuges from inclement weather. Adults are frequently seen basking near the entrances to these retreats, which may be excavated by the lizards several meters into the arroyo banks.

The ASDM enclosure is located on a site where edible native plants are present. Additional native shrubs and grasses were planted to increase potential forage and cover. The enclosure features a concrete block perimeter wall, subdivided into separate areas for *S. varius* and *S. hispidus* (Spiny Chuckwalla), another species endemic to Islas San Lorenzo Norte and Sur, Isla Angel de la Guarda, and several small satellite islands in the Gulf of California. A primary objective was to provide as much space as possible while retaining managerial access to the animals. The population structure and social biology of *S. varius* are very different from those of *S. obesus*. Agonistic behavior is typically limited to early spring, when males apparently establish a linear dominance hierarchy, and June, when females establish and defend a temporary nesting territory (Lawler and Jarchow 1986). The space (10.5 m × 9.9 m) has proven adequate to manage enough animals to comprise a social unit (Brattstrom 1974; Carpenter 1967; Prieto and Ryan 1978). The 1 m high wall is based on a concrete footing 30 cm deep. The interior surface is skirted with sheet-metal flashing to preclude escape by climbing. Surface area is increased by a number of large rocky outcrops positioned away from the walls and the primary refuge building.

The concrete block refuge building is 2 m high × 1.9 m × 1.3 m (about 5 m^3) and the entire entrance side of the building is an insulated door, which allows complete access. The top is constructed of foam-insulated fiberglass, which can be lifted off for thorough dismantling and cleaning. This feature has proven invaluable in relieving periodic blooms of the mite *Hirstiella pyriformis* (Newell and Ryckman 1964). Lizards enter the refuge structure through PVC tubes, which are 12.7 cm in diameter, and lead from the exterior to enclosed individual wooden retreat boxes. No more than two tubes lead to a box, thus enabling segregation among the colony according to individual refuge-site selection. An individual lizard generally returns to the same retreat, except during peak summer activity, when selection appears more random. The building is buried to the edges of the top with rocky soil, and capped with larger more stable rocks; only the retreat tubes and the keeper access door are exposed.

To approximate the maritime, subtropical desert climate of the island, the building is heated in winter to interior temperatures of 12°–18°C with a thermostat-controlled 750–1500-watt space heater. The lizards normally have free access to the outside, except during brief periods when freezes are forecast. In that event, the retreat tubes are plugged with insulating material to prevent exit, and to improve heat retention. Throughout much of the year, daily communal basking occurs; the most popular sites are on top of the shelter building and on the surrounding slopes. Rocky outcrops, away from the building, are occupied during the warmer months (April through September), usually by males. These features seem to provide respite for subordinate animals during periods of agonistic behavior, and correspond to the temporary refuges occupied in the arroyos of Isla San Esteban. Based on observations of heavy sea mists that frequently blanket Isla San Esteban, a timer-controlled misting system was installed to increase ambient humidity, thus reducing evaporative body water loss from the lizards. This feature is especially important from May to early July, when relative humidity drops below 10% in southern Arizona.

Since 1981, a breeding colony of eight males and 13 females has been assembled at ASDM. Some of the original 1981 founders (and their progeny) are part of a small group collected in 1977 by Sylber (1985). In 1985, a second colony of two males and three females was collected from the wild, and established at Centro Ecológico de Sonora in Hermosillo. This group had not reproduced by the end of 1992.

A total of 205 progeny, representing ten maternal lines, has been produced in the ASDM enclosure through 1992. Females construct nesting burrows in the natural enclosure substrate, usually in open areas near the walls. Hatching in these subterranean nests has been 95–100% successful. In a few cases, however, progeny were unable to dig to the surface due to compaction of the soil during summer rains. The problem was apparently resolved by filling the nesting sites to a depth of approximately 60 cm with a more friable soil mixture of 1:3 sand to soil. Genealogical records are maintained to insure maximum genetic variability. Progeny not needed for the ASDM program are provided to collaborators participating in *S. varius* conservation, to scientific institutions for research, or to zoological institutions for educational public exhibition. Investigation of captive parental relationships and genetic variability in wild and captive populations of *S. varius* are in progress under the direction of Llewellyn Densmore at Texas Tech University (see Densmore et al., this volume, page 343).

Isla San Esteban Study Area

Sauromalus varius is endemic to Isla San Esteban, a deep-water island, 43 km^2 in area, which rises to 531 m in elevation and is located in the midriff island series of the Gulf of California. The Central Gulf Coast Sonoran desertscrub on the island is dominated by cacti, especially Cardón (*Pachycereus pringlei*), Cholla (*Opuntia ciribe*), and Pitahaya Agria (*Stenocereus gummosus*), and desert trees and shrubs, including Brittlebush (*Encelia farinosa*), elephant trees (*Bursera microphylla, B. hindsiana*), Foothills Paloverde (*Cercidium microphyllum*), Honey Mesquite (*Prosopis glandulosa*), Ironwood (*Olneya tesota*), and Sangrengado (*Jatropha cuneata*; Felger and Lowe 1976). Limited areas of saltscrub communities, which are dominated by Saltbush (*Atriplex barclayana*), occur in areas inland of high cobble beaches.

Natural Diet

A vital aspect of captive wildlife management is provision of a diet that is nutritionally appropriate for the physiology of the species. As with other herbivorous reptiles, dietary regimens for captive iguanids have usually been formulated with more attention given to palatability than nutritional content. The diets of free-ranging animals in natural habitats offer the best clues to their nutritional needs.

Schmidt (1922) reported flowers of the giant Cardón and leaflets of leguminous plants in the stomachs of *Sauromalus varius*. Norris and Dawson (1964) observed *S. varius* feeding on *Opuntia* flowers, and noted the resinous sap of *Jatropha* on the snouts and lips of adults. Case (1982) reported that 70% of the diet of *S. varius* consisted of the fruits and flowers of Cholla. He also observed *S. varius* eating the flowers of Foothills Paloverde, Honey Mesquite, and Ironwood, and the flowers and fruits of Pitahaya Agria.

Hansen's (1974) microhistological analyses of dung of *S. obesus* from Arizona demonstrated the utility and potential of determining diet from scats. Sylber's (1988) quantitative macroscopic analyses of 375 *S. varius* fecal pellets, collected in 1979–1980, documented a broader diet of 22 species of plants, including forbs (annual and herbaceous perennial dicots, which total 36% of total diet) and grasses (1.2%). The plant parts eaten included seeds and fruits (46%), flowers (10%), leaves (36%), and stems (7%). Differences in the results of the Case and Sylber studies may be related to site differences, great differences in the availability of summer annuals in response to highly variable rainfall, and differences in analytical methods. Honey Mesquite and Ironwood are primarily restricted to the main channel of Arroyo Lemantur, while Cholla stands are densest on flats to the west.

Examination of scats we collected in Arroyo Lemantur in June 1985 and September 1990 showed that leaves of Desert Rose Mallow (*Hibiscus denudatus*), Honey Mesquite, and Ironwood, and fruits of Cholla, which were all previously reported, were commonly consumed. Samples were collected from sites where *S. varius* were observed basking or feeding, or from the entrances to their retreats, to minimize inclusion of scats of the sympatric iguanid *Ctenosaura hemilopha conspicuosa*. Fecal pellets in the samples were identical to those produced by captive *S. varius*. Fecal pellets of the omnivorous *C. h. conspicuosa* often differ in size, shape, and the abundance of insect remains, lizard scales, and bones (H. E. Lawler and T. R. Van Devender, pers. observ.). Previously undocumented diet items revealed in the 1985 and 1990 scat analyses were Cardón fruits, and the fruits and leaves of a cucurbit vine (*Vaseyanthus insularis*). A number of pellets were composed predominantly of blades and stems of Six-weeks Threeawn (*Aristida adscensionis*), possibly mixed with Six-weeks Grama (*Bouteloua barbata*) and Six-weeks Needle Grama (*B. aristidoides*). Sylber (1988) only reported traces of grasses in his samples and did not specifically identify them.

Chemical Analyses of Food Plants

To learn more about the significance of these plants in the diet of *Sauromalus varius*, we collected 17 samples of 14 species for analyses of nutrient and mineral content (Table 1). Six samples were collected in June 1985, five in September 1990, and six in April 1992. Samples of Six-weeks Threeawn (the entire plant) and Cholla (the whole fruit and the fruit with seeds removed) were taken in both 1985 and 1990. Leaves of Honey Mesquite were analyzed in 1985 and 1992. Fresh samples were sealed in plastic bags and transported on ice to the University of Arizona. In the Nutritional Analysis Laboratory, the samples were initially weighed before and

TABLE 1. Nutritional analyses of plants in the diet of *Sauromalus varius* on Isla San Esteban, Sonora, Mexico. Percentages of moisture and dry matter for total sample; others of dry matter. Percentages of potentially important nutrient sources in **bold**. Key: ADF acid detergent fiber, CC cell content (100 – NDF), CE cellulose, CP crude protein (% Nitrogen × 6.25), DM dry matter, HC hemicellulose (NDF – ADF), LI lignin, LP lipids, M moisture, NDF neutral detergent fiber. Life forms: AN annual, CC columnar cactus, CT cactus, GA annual grass, HP herbaceous perennial, HV herbaceous vine, SB subshrub, SH shrub, T tree. *September 1990, **April 1992; others June 1985.

Common name	Species	Life form	Material	Water		Cell content			Fiber					
				M	DM	CP	CC	LP	NDF	ADF	CE	HC	LI	L:ADF
			NATIVE PLANTS											
Ironwood	*Olneya tesota*	T	Leaves	50.2	**49.8**	14.7	**62.9**	—	**37.1**	26.7	16.3	10.4	10.4	0.39
Baja Guayacán**	*Viscainoa geniculata*	SH	Leaves	**66.1**	33.9	**17.3**	**65.0**	**10.7**	**35.0**	27.9	20.8	7.1	6.4	0.23
Honey Mesquite	*Prosopis glandulosa*	SH	Leaves	43.3	**46.7**	**19.4**	**58.0**	—	42.0	**30.5**	**25.7**	**11.5**	**4.8**	**0.16**
Honey Mesquite**	*Prosopis glandulosa*	SH	Leaves	53.1	**46.9**	**20.3**	**59.0**	8.1	41.0	**32.7**	**24.4**	8.3	15.1	0.46
Tinta**	*Stegnosperma halimifolium*	SH	Leaves	**79.8**	20.2	9.4	**83.4**	**16.2**	**16.6**	13.6	10.6	3.0	**3.3**	0.24
Desert Rose Mallow	*Hibiscus denudatus*	SB	Entire plant	40.8	**59.2**	9.6	42.2	—	57.8	**31.4**	**26.2**	**26.4**	**5.2**	**0.17**
Cardón	*Pachycereus pringlei*	CC	Fruit	**65.0**	35.0	8.6	32.0	—	68.0	**48.0**	**40.6**	20.0	7.4	**0.15**
Cholla	*Opuntia ciribe*	CT	Whole fruit	**72.0**	28.0	3.6	**58.2**	—	41.8	29.3	22.1	12.5	7.1	0.43
Cholla*	*Opuntia ciribe*	CT	Fruit, no seeds	**87.3**	12.7	5.3	**75.6**	—	**24.4**	14.0	10.0	10.4	**4.8**	0.34
Six-weeks Grama*	*Bouteloua barbata*	GA	Entire plant	**65.3**	34.7	**16.2**	36.8	—	63.2	**34.2**	**28.8**	**29.0**	**3.0**	**0.09**
Six-weeks Needle Grama*	*Bouteloua aristidoides*	GA	Entire plant	**62.9**	37.1	9.8	33.8	—	66.2	**36.1**	**31.5**	**30.1**	**4.5**	**0.12**
Six-weeks Threeawn	*Aristida adscensionis*	GA	Entire plant	14.5	**85.5**	5.7	26.8	—	73.2	**37.5**	**34.6**	**35.7**	**2.9**	**0.08**
Six-weeks Threeawn*	*Aristida adscensionis*	GA	Entire plant	**67.0**	33.0	11.4	28.8	—	71.2	**38.9**	**33.7**	**32.3**	**3.1**	**0.08**
Woody Nievitas**	*Cryptantha racemosa*	HP	Entire plant	54.7	**45.3**	5.8	**71.5**	**14.7**	**28.5**	**33.8**	?	–5.3	**3.3**	**0.10**
Desert Passion-flower**	*Passiflora arida*	HV	Leaves, fruit	**61.1**	38.9	**16.3**	**53.6**	**28.7**	46.4	**34.0**	21.6	**12.4**	7.5	0.22
Cucurbit Vine*	*Vaseyanthus insularis*	HV	Entire plant	**88.0**	12.0	**21.8**	**69.8**	—	**30.2**	20.4	12.3	9.8	**3.3**	**0.16**
Rock Daisy**	*Perityle emoryi*	AN	Entire plant	**76.8**	23.2	9.7	**68.6**	**13.4**	**31.4**	24.4	17.4	7.0	**3.8**	**0.16**
			PRODUCE											
Alfalfa	*Medicago sativa*	AN	Entire plant	10.3	—	**17.3**	—	—	31.4	—	—	—	—	—
Carrot	*Daucus carota*	HP	Root	**88.2**	—	8.4	—	—	8.5	—	—	—	—	—
Collard	*Brassica oleracea*	AN	Leaves	**90.9**	—	**32.7**	—	—	6.1	—	—	—	—	—
Mustard	*Brassica juncea*	AN	Leaves	**89.5**	—	**28.5**	—	—	10.5	—	—	—	—	—

after oven-drying at 50°C, and again after drying at 100°C to measure water content, and then ground to pass through a 0.5 mm screen in a cyclone grinder. The presence of crude protein, neutral detergent fiber (NDF), calcium, and phosphorus was determined using a Technicon Autoanalyzer. The presence of cellulose, hemicellulose, lignin, and acid detergent fiber (ADF) was determined according to table 1 in Goering and Van Soest (1970). The 1992 samples were analysed for lipids. Similar nutritional analyses have been conducted for plants in the diet of *Odocoileus hemionus crooki* (Desert Mule Deer) and *Ovis canadensis mexicana* (Desert Bighorn Sheep) in Arizona Upland Sonoran desertscrub habitats in Arizona (Seegmiller et al. 1990 and references therein), and *Gopherus flavomarginatus* (Bolson Tortoise) (Adest et al. 1989).

As part of the nutritional analyses, calcium and phosphorus were measured in the 1985 samples and ash content in the 1990 samples. Residues from the 1992 nutritional analyses were analysed for calcium, iron, magnesium, phosphorus, potassium, sodium, and zinc in the Soil, Water, and Plant Analysis Laboratory (Table 2). Samples were prepared by means of acid extraction (digestion) using nitric acid and hydrogen peroxide in a microwave oven. Iron and zinc were analyzed using the ascorbic acid colorimetric method. Others used inductively coupled plasma.

The results show that all of the plants have some nutritional value, either water, nutrients, or minerals (Table 1). Moisture content ranged from 88.0% in the Cucurbit Vine to 14.5% in dried Six-weeks Threeawn. Excluding the latter sample, all samples had more than 40% water; 14 samples had greater than 50%. A September 1990 sample from living Six-weeks Threeawn (67.0%), and those for Six-weeks Grama (62.9%) and Needle Grama (65.3%), demonstrate that living annual grasses are a good source of moisture. In contrast to summer activity of

TABLE 2. Mineral content of potential food plans of *Sauromalus varius* on Isla San Esteban, Sonora, Mexico. Elements: Ca calcium, Fe iron, K potassium, Mg magnesium, Na sodium, P phosphorus, Zn zinc. Most values are percentages of dry matter; Fe and Zn in parts per million. *September 1990, **April 1992; other samples June 1985. Scientific names in Table 1.

Common name	Ash	Ca	P	Ca:P	K	Na	Mg	Fe	Zn
				NATIVE PLANTS					
Ironwood	—	4.70	0.04	118.0	—	—	—	—	—
Baja Guayacán**	16.2	2.44	0.15	16.3	2.18	0.42	0.80	79.9	23.9
Honey Mesquite	—	1.10	0.12	9.3	—	—	—	—	—
Honey Mesquite**	6.1	0.93	0.17	5.5	1.36	0.03	0.42	60.3	59.8
Tinta**	19.9	3.01	0.55	5.5	2.51	1.54	1.19	86.4	19.9
Desert Rose Mallow	—	1.10	0.44	2.5	—	—	—	—	—
Cardón	—	3.40	0.11	31.2	—	—	—	—	—
Cholla	—	19.3	0.07	204.6	—	—	—	—	—
Cholla*	23.2	—	—	—	—	—	—	—	—
Six-weeks Grama*	9.8	—	—	—	—	—	—	—	—
Six-weeks Needle Grama*	6.6	—	—	—	—	—	—	—	—
Six-weeks Threeawn	—	0.48	0.12	4.0	—	—	—	—	—
Six-weeks Threeawn*	10.3	—	—	—	—	—	—	—	—
Woody Nievitas**	19.8	3.40	0.20	17.0	2.22	0.43	1.00	148.0	29.7
Cucurbit Vine*	24.4	—	—	—	—	—	—	—	—
Desert Passionflower**	8.5	1.28	0.20	6.0	2.22	0.03	0.24	464.0	34.0
Rock Daisy**	19.0	1.78	0.23	7.4	2.89	1.86	0.60	227.0	11.1
				PRODUCE					
Alfalfa	1.64	0.26	6.3	—	—	—	—	—	—
Carrot	0.28	0.27	1.0	—	—	—	—	—	—
Collard	1.70	0.57	3.0	—	—	—	—	—	—
Mustard	1.74	0.48	3.6	—	—	—	—	—	—
Tomato	3.00	0.34	8.8	4.46	0.70	690.0	62.0	—	—

S. varius, individuals of *S. obesus tumidus*, in the Silver Bell and Waterman mountains west of Tucson, in the northeastern Sonoran Desert, aestivate in the arid foresummer from late May until the summer rains begin in mid-July, and do not eat dried grasses (T. R. Van Devender and H. E. Lawler, unpubl. data). Although Cholla fruits had moisture contents of 72.0% with seeds, and 87.3% without seeds, the thick epidermis of Chollas may hinder extraction of moisture. Moisture in the leaves of trees and shrubs (40.8–66.1%) may be easier to utilize. Tinta (*Stegnosperma halimifolium*), a large shrub occasionally found along arroyos, has succulent leaves with very high water content (79.8%).

Other nutritional components of diet items are expressed as percentages of the dry matter to evaluate them independently of variable water content. Surprisingly, Cholla fruits, a common food, have few nutrients and high levels of calcium. Plants with relatively high protein content, the primary source of amino acids, include the cucurbit vine (21.8%), Honey Mesquite (19.4–20.3%), Baja Guayacán (*Viscainoa geniculata*; 17.3%), Desert Passionflower (*Passiflora arida*; 16.3%), Six-weeks Grama (16.2%), and Ironwood (14.7%). These values are similar to those for typical wet-season forage consumed by *Gopherus flavomarginatus* at the Mapimí Reserve in northeastern Durango, Mexico (Adest et al. 1989). The other live grasses (9.8 and 11.4%), Desert Rose Mallow (9.6%), Rock Daisy (*Perityle emoryi*; 9.7%), and Tinta (9.4%) had moderate amounts of protein. Lowest protein contents were found in cactus fruits (3.6 to 8.6%), dead Six-weeks Threeawn (5.7%), and Woody Nievitas (*Cryptantha racemosa*; 5.8%).

Another principal dietary component in plants is fiber. The amount of useful energy in fiber depends on its structure and the ability of the animals to digest it. Nutritional analyses estimate fiber in several ways. By measuring NDF and ADF, the relative contents of cellulose, lignin (L), and hemicellulose can be determined. NDF is a measure of cell-wall content, and an inverse indication of useful energy, because the remainder of the dry matter (cell contents) includes proteins, fats, starches, and sugars. Lignin is the most indigestible fiber. The L-to-ADF ratio is an estimate of how much of the cell-wall fiber is potentially digestible by animals that utilize microbial fermentation. A high L-to-ADF ratio indicates that the cell wall is not easily fermented; plants with low ratios are easily digested. Ruminants, such as the Desert Mule Deer, pass food quickly through a relatively short digestive tract to extract soluble proteins, fats, and minimal cellulose. Those with longer compartmentalized digestive tracts can extract more energy from cellulose through microbial fermentation. Studies of *Iguana iguana* imply that herbivorous iguanids are nearly as efficient as ruminants in degrading hemicellulose and cellulose by fermentation to provide an energy source (Troyer 1984).

The high NDF of grasses (63.2 to 73.2%) and Cardón (68.0%) indicates low cell content of nutrients and energy. The spines of Cardón are not easily digested and the seeds pass largely intact. Tinta (16.6%), Cholla fruits without the woody seeds (24.4%), Woody Nievitas (28.5%), cucurbit vine leaves and stems (30.2%), and Rock Daisy (31.4%) contain the greatest cell-content energy, while Baja Guayacán (35%), Ironwood (37.1%), and Honey Mesquite (42.0%) are intermediate. The L-to-ADF ratio for grasses (0.08 to 0.12) indicates that the cell-wall fiber is easily fermented, while Cholla fruits (0.34 and 0.43), Ironwood (0.39), and the 1992 samples of Honey Mesquite (0.46) are more difficult.

Mineral content in the 1985 and 1990 samples was measured on a dry-matter basis (percentage ash, Table 2). Values for the annual grasses were 6.6 to 10.3%. Cholla fruits without seeds (23.2%) and the cucurbit vine (24.4%) had high mineral content. The minerals in Cholla fruit are likely to be inert calcium oxalate crystals in the epidermis. In the 1985 samples, calcium values were high for Cholla with seeds (19.3%) and Ironwood leaves (4.7%). The preliminary mineral analyses point out several important nutritional considerations. Calcium greater than 0.4% is considered adequate for most livestock forage (Minson 1990). With the exceptions of Desert Rose Mallow (0.44) and Tinta (0.55), all of the samples were low in phosphorus. Calcium-to-phosphorus ratios ranging from 2.5 to 204.6 are greater than the 1.2 to 2.0 in ideal livestock feed. Excessive calcium in livestock forage exacerbates phosphorus deficiency (Minson 1990). The samples all contained adequate magnesium, although Tinta (1.19%) and Woody Nievitas (1.0%) were high. Sodium was accumulated to high levels in Rock Daisy (1.86%) and Tinta (1.54%). Iron levels were not excessive.

Although these data are preliminary, they illustrate the menu of nutrients in plant foods available to *S. varius* in the highly variable maritime desert environment of Isla San Esteban. High humidity and the prevalence of food plants with more than 40% water may allow general activity and feeding in the summer, when mainland *S. obesus* are aestivating. Eating a variety of different plants through the year balances any short-term nutritional deficiencies. Staples in drier periods include Cholla fruits in the flats, and Honey Mesquite and Ironwood leaves along arroyo banks. Cholla fruits have (1) high moisture content that may not be easily extracted because of thick epidermis, (2) low protein content, (3) low fiber content with useful energy, but low digestibility, and (4) extremely high mineral content (23.2%), including calcium (14.3%). In contrast, Honey Mesquite and Ironwood leaves have (1) moderate water, (2) high protein, and (3) moderate fiber and useful energy. The fiber is moderately digestible in Honey Mesquite leaves, but less so in Ironwood. The winter-spring annual Rock Daisy has high water content, moderately high fiber and useful energy, easily digested fiber, but relatively low (9.7%) crude protein and high sodium (1.86%) levels.

The other plants observed in *S. varius* scats reflect exploitation of seasonal resources. Annual grasses with (1) moderate water when green, (2) moderate protein, (3) high fiber content and relatively little digestible energy, and (4) easily fermented cell walls can be abundant in winter-spring or summer-fall rainy seasons. The cucurbit vine is an excellent food with (1) high water, (2) high protein, (3) low fiber and a lot of useful energy, and (4) moderately fermentable cell walls but high mineral content. Other seasonal plants not sampled in this study, including annual and herbaceous perennial dicots (such as amaranths, euphorbs, legumes, and mustards), flowers of trees and shrubs (such as Brittlebush, Foothills Paloverde, Honey Mesquite, and Ironwood), and cacti (Cholla and Pitahaya Agria) are likely to be important in the diet as well. The annuals in particular are high in water and protein, easily digestible, and may provide additional nutrients. Abundance of seasonal food plants may well be the key to the ability of the lizards to accumulate the lipids they require for successful reproduction.

Captive *S. varius* at ASDM consume native plants that grow in the enclosures or are provided as cuttings, which include the leaves, flowers, and bean pods of Foothills Paloverde, Ironwood, and Velvet Mesquite (*Prosopis velutina*), the leaves and flowers of acacias (*Acacia constricta, A. greggii*) and Brittlebush, and the fruit of Saguaro (*Carnegiea gigantea*, June-July). Because native food plants are not usually available in sufficient quantity throughout the long feeding season, moist leafy alfalfa hay from bales, grated carrot, and collard or mustard greens (*Brassica oleracea* and *B. juncea*) are provided an average of 2 to 5 days per week during the spring, summer, and fall. Bell peppers, broccoli, cut green beans, or zucchini squash are occasionally included in small amounts. Commercial produce is reduced or eliminated when native plants are available in sufficient quantity, and suspended entirely from November through February. Blue Grama (*Bouteloua gracilis*), Bush Muhly (*Muhlenbergia porteri*), and Six-weeks Threeawn, grown in 60 cm^2 flats, were offered in rotation, with little or no consumption.

Dietary regimens for herbivorous reptiles in captivity can be refined by a better understanding of feeding strategies and nutrient flow in the wild. Further studies are needed to refine our understanding of seasonal and annual nutritional intake, and to determine actual nutritional requirements of *S. varius*. Controlled-feeding studies are planned to determine more precisely the nutritional benefits that *S. varius* derives from various foods.

Summary

A captive colony of eight males and 13 females of *Sauromalus varius* (Piebald Chuckwalla) was established at the Arizona-Sonora Desert Museum in 1981. A 10.5 m × 9.9 m enclosure for breeding and behavioral observation was established after observing wild animals in their natural habitat. Supplementary heat in winter and humidity (using misters) in early summer compensate for the colder winter and drier early summer climate in Tucson, more closely simulating the milder maritime climate of Isla San Esteban. The breeding program has been very successful with 139 progeny in nine maternal lines hatched to date. A second colony of two males and three females was established at Centro Ecológico de Sonora in 1985, though this group has not yet reproduced. Captive parental relationships, and genetic variability in captive and wild populations are being assessed using molecular techniques by Llewellyn Densmore and his students at Texas Tech University.

To provide a rational basis for dietary planning for captive animals, the nutritional value of natural diets on Isla San Esteban has been studied. Case (1982) and Sylber (1988) have documented 22 species of plants which are eaten by *S. varius*. Our observations and scat analyses indicated that Cardón fruits and cucurbit vine leaves and fruit were also eaten, increasing the known plant species used as food to 24. We found that *S. varius* was eating dead annual grasses, including Six-weeks Threeawn, in June, when mainland *S. obesus* are in aestivation. High relative humidity on a marine island apparently contributes to extended summer activity and utilization of additional food resources. The kinds of foods eaten are highly dependent on seasonal and annual climatic fluctuations in an inherently variable desert climate.

We analyzed 17 samples of 14 species of plants identified in scats for nutritional content at the University of Arizona. Residues of six samples were analyzed for biologically important minerals. The results indicate that the food plants available to *S. varius* on Isla San Esteban are a rich nutrient menu; every plant has something of value, but a variety of plants must be eaten for a healthy diet. The amount of moisture, protein, fiber (of differing degrees of digestibility), and minerals varies with plant species and seasonal condition of the plant. Only dried Six-weeks Threeawn had less than 40% water; 11 samples were greater than 60%. Although Cholla fruits are high in moisture, they have little nutritional content, and are extremely high in calcium, which is probably due to inert calcium oxalate crystals in the epidermis. The ability of *S. varius* to consume a substance that is toxic to many animals, calcium oxalate, without apparent ill effect, needs study. Ironwood leaves are a good protein source, but have high calcium content and cell-wall fiber that is difficult to digest. Annual grasses, such as Six-weeks Grama, Six-weeks Needle Grama, and Six-weeks Threeawn, are moderately good sources of water and protein when green. Low levels of phosphorus in food plants and high calcium-to-phosphorus ratios raise the possibility that phosphorus may be a limiting element.

Additional research is needed to evaluate the dietary importance of other plants, especially dicot herbs and the flowers of various cacti, trees, and shrubs. The abundance of ephemeral plants in years with exceptional rainfall from winter through spring may well allow the accumulation of sufficient lipids in the body to facilitate reproduction. It is clear that the nutritional content of native plant foods is very different than commercially available produce. Data on native plant foods will be used to reevaluate the diets of the ASDM captives. We feel that basic observation and study of the animal in the wild and in enclosures replicating the natural habitat is invaluable in developing successful long-term captive-management programs for large iguanids, such as *S. varius*.

Acknowledgments

We thank the following individuals for numerous courtesies, guidance, information, and material support in various aspects of this project. Field assistance and/or logistical support was provided by: (México) Carlos Castillo, Carlos Galindo, Manuel García, Guillermo Lara, Rogelio Molina, Dinorah Retes, and José Maria Ruíz of El Centro Ecológico de Sonora, J. Mario Cirett-Galán of Secretaría de Desarrollo Urbano y Ecología in Hermosillo, and Bernardo Villa of Universidad Nacional Autónoma de México in Ciudad México; (United States) Kent Beaman, A. Dale Belcher, L. Lee Grismer, Steven F. Hale, Brent Martin, and Robert Perrill. Special appreciation is due Wilfrido Contreras Dominguez and Graciela de la Garza García, Secretaría de Desarrollo Urbano y Ecología, for permits issued in 1985 and 1990, respectively. Ted J. Case, Fausto Cepeda Proaño, C. Kenneth Dodd, Jr., Charles H. Lowe, Howard Snell, and Thomas Wiewandt provided information and valuable discussion. At the University of Arizona, R. Spencer Swingle, Department of Animal Sciences, provided nutritional analyses of food plants and invaluable help in their interpretation, and Anita L. Hayden and Janik F. Artiola, Department of Soil and Water Science, analyzed the mineral content of the samples. We are grateful to Hugh McCrystal and the ASDM herpetological staff for their diligence in caring for the lizards in captivity. The propagation and research facility, much of the field work, and mineral and nutrient analyses were funded by the Roy Chapman Andrews Research Fund of the Arizona-

Sonora Desert Museum. Elkan Morris and David L. Hardy provided auxiliary funding and personal assistance for expeditions to Isla San Esteban in 1983 and 1985, respectively. Richard Montanucci, Robert Espinoza, and two anonymous reviewers critically reviewed the manuscript and provided many helpful comments. We thank Lauray Yule and Linda Pierce for their invaluable assistance in preparing the manuscript.

Literature Cited

Adest, G. A., G. L. Aguirre, D. J. Morafka, and J. V. Jarchow. 1989. Bolson tortoise (*Gopherus flavomarginatus*) conservation: II. Husbandry and reintroduction. Vida Sylvestre Neotrop., 2: 14–20.

Anonymous. 1979. San Esteban Island Chuckwalla under review. Endang. Species Tech. Bull., 4: 6.

Brattstrom, B. H. 1974. The evolution of reptilian social behavior. Amer. Zool., 14: 35–49.

Carpenter, C. C. 1967. Aggression and social structure in iguanid lizards, p. 87–105. *In* W. W. Milstead (ed.), Lizard Ecology, a Symposium. Univ. Missouri Press, Columbia.

Case, T. J. 1982. Ecology and evolution of the insular gigantic chuckwallas, *Sauromalus hispidus* and *Sauromalus varius*, p. 184–212. *In* G. Burghardt and A. Rand (eds.), Iguanas of the World: Their Behavior, Ecology, and Conservation. Noyes Publ., Park Ridge, New Jersey.

Castro, C. S., and J. Duval. 1979. Reproduction en captividad de iguanas del genero *Cyclura*. Zoodom, 3: 12–18.

Crutchfield, T. E. 1982. Courtship and nesting behavior in *Cyclura nubila lewisi*, p. 54–56. *In* Proceedings of the 5th Reptile Symposium on Captive Propagation and Husbandry. Zool. Consortium. Thurmont, Maryland.

Duval, J. J. 1983. Recommendations for the captive management of West Indian rock iguanas (*Cyclura*), p. 181–196. *In* Proceedings of the 6th Reptile Symposium on Captive Propagation and Husbandry. Zool. Consortium, Thurmont, Maryland.

Felger, R. S., and C. H. Lowe. 1976. The island and coastal vegetation and flora of the northern part of the Gulf of California. Los Angeles Co. Nat. Hist. Mus. Contr. Sci., 285: 1–59.

Fitch, H. S., and R. W. Henderson. 1977. Age and sex differences, reproduction and conservation of *Iguana*. Milwaukee Public Mus. Contrib. Biol. Geol., 13: 1–21.

Fitch, H. S., R. W. Henderson, and D. M. Hillis. 1982. Exploitation of iguanas in Central America, p. 397–417. *In* G. M. Burghardt and A. S. Rand (eds.), Iguanas of the World: Their Behavior, Ecology, and Conservation. Noyes Publ., Park Ridge, New Jersey.

Goering, H. K., and P. J. Van Soest. 1970. Forage Fiber Analyses. United States Dept. Agricult. Handbook no. 379, 20 pages.

Hansen, R. M. 1974. Dietary of the chuckwalla, *Sauromalus obesus*, determined by dung analysis. Herpetologica, 30: 120–123.

Lawler, H. E. In press. Applications of field herpetology in captive management programs for endangered herpetofauna. *In* Proceedings of the 1990 Conference on Herpetology in North American Deserts. Los Angeles Co. Mus.

Lawler, H. E., and J. L. Jarchow. 1986. A captive management plan for large iguanine lizards using the Isla San Esteban chuckwalla *Sauromalus varius* Dickerson as a model, p. 137–164. *In* Proceedings of the 9th International Herpetology Symposium on Captive Management and Propagation. Zool. Consortium, Thurmont, Maryland.

Minson, D. J. 1990. Forage in Ruminant Nutrition. Academic Press, San Diego, California. 483 pages.

Newell, I. M., and R. E. Ryckman. 1964. *Hirstiella pyriformis* sp. n. (Acari, Pterygosomidae), a new parasite of lizards from Baja California. Jour. Parasitol., 50: 163–171.

Norris, K. S., and W. R. Dawson. 1964. Observations on the water economy and electrolyte excretion of chuckwallas (Lacertilia, *Sauromalus*). Copeia, 1964: 638–646.

Prieto, A. A., and M. J. Ryan. 1978. Some observations of the social behavior of the Arizona chuckwalla, *Sauromalus obesus tumidus* (Reptilia, Lacertilia, Iguanidae). Jour. Herpetol., 12: 327–336.

Schmidt, K. P. 1922. The amphibians and reptiles of Lower California and the neighboring islands. Bull. Amer. Mus. Nat. Hist., 56: 607–707.

Seegmiller, R. F., P. R. Krausman, W. H. Brown, and F. M. Whiting. 1990. Nutritional composition of desert bighorn forage in the Harquahala Mountains, Arizona. Desert Plants, 10: 87–90.

Sylber, C. K. 1985. Eggs and hatchlings of the yellow giant chuckwalla and the black giant chuckwalla in captivity. Herpetol., Rev., 16: 18–21.

—. 1988. Feeding habits of the lizards *Sauromalus varius* and *S. hispidus* in the Gulf of California. Jour. Herpetol., 22: 413–424.

Troyer, K. 1984. Structure and function of the digestive tract of a herbivorous lizard *Iguana iguana*. Physiol. Zool., 57: 1–8.

Turner, R. M., and D. E. Brown. 1982. Sonoran desertscrub. Desert Plants, 4: 212–217.

Werner, D. I. 1988. The effect of varying water potential on body weight, yolk and fat bodies in neonate green iguanas. Copeia, 1988: 406–411.

Werner, D. I., and T. J. Miller. 1984. Artificial nests for female green iguanas. Herpetol. Rev., 15: 57–58.

Lawler, H. E., T. R. Van Devender, and J. L. Jarchow. 1994. Ecological and nutritional management of the endangered Piebald Chuckwalla (*Sauromalus varius*) in captivity, p. 333–341. *In* J. B. Murphy, K. Adler, and J. T. Collins (eds.), Captive Management and Conservation of Amphibians and Reptiles. Society for the Study of Amphibians and Reptiles, Ithaca (New York). Contributions to Herpetology, volume 11.

A Molecular Approach for Determining Genetic Variation in Captive and Natural Populations of the Piebald Chuckwalla (*Sauromalus varius*)

Llewellyn D. Densmore, III,* Erika D. Pliler,* and Howard E. Lawler**

Introduction

The genus *Sauromalus* Duméril includes at least four species, *S. ater, S. hispidus, S. obesus,* and *S. varius* (see Etheridge [1982] for references concerning revisions), that are found in desert regions of southwestern United States, western Mexico, the eastern portion of the peninsula known as Baja California Sur, and on various islands in the Gulf of California. Two of these species, *S. hispidus* and *S. varius*, are found as gigantic insular forms. The Piebald Chuckwalla (*S. varius*), described by Dickerson (1919), is a threatened, endemic species that is naturally occurring only on Isla San Esteban in the Gulf of California, Sonora, Mexico. Over the last several decades, there have been a number of primarily ecological or behavioral studies of *S. varius* (Case 1982), and as reported elsewhere (Lawler et al., this volume, page 333) this work continues.

Although the levels of genetic variation that exist in captive populations of species (endangered or common), as compared to the levels present in the wild, have been, and remain, a critical question for zoo and wildlife personnel and for private breeders, very little is known about it. It is assumed that the amount of genetic variation would be lower in a captive population, if for no other reason than sampling error, but we do not know the level at which this becomes a problem. In other words, given a genetic bottleneck (such as almost always occurs in captive populations), at what level of genetic diversity does inbreeding depression set in, and can the potential for phenotypic problems associated with inbreeding be monitored, predicted, and, it is hoped, avoided in captive-propagation programs. This problem obviously becomes even more critical when dealing with rare and/or endangered species.

The largest captive population of *S. varius* is housed at the Arizona–Sonora Desert Museum (ASDM) in Tucson, Arizona. Reproductive and rearing success has been achieved through the development of spacious outdoor enclosures (not on public display) that house the founders and a majority of the progeny (Lawler and Jarchow 1985). These facilities now include smaller enclosures in which designated breeding stock can be isolated from the general population for propagation to produce desired genetic representation (H. E. Lawler, in press).

* Department of Biological Sciences
and Biotechnology Institute
Texas Tech University
Lubbock, Texas 79409, USA

** Arizona-Sonora Desert Museum
2021 North Kinney Road
Tucson, Arizona 85743, USA

Acronyms used in this chapter:

ACD-B	Acid-citrate-dextrose solution B
ASDM	Arizona–Sonora Desert Museum
bp	Base pairs
dNTP	Deoxy nucleotide triphosphates
EDTA	Ethylenediaminetetraacetic Acid
NTSYS	Numerical Taxonomy and Multivariate Analysis System
PAUP	Phylogenetic Analysis Using Parsimony
PCR	Polymerase Chain Reaction
PHYLIP	Phylogeny Inference Package
RAPD	Random amplified polymorphic DNA
SAHN	Sequential Agglomerative Hierarchical and Nested method
SDS-Urea	Sodium Dodecyl Sulfate-Urea
SIMINT	Similarity for Interval Data
Taq	*Thermus aquaticus*
TREE	Tree Display
UPGMA	Unweighted pair groups averaging
UV	Ultraviolet light

Until 1983, all specimens were housed in a mixed Sonoran Desert lizard exhibit at the museum entrance. No records are available prior to 1981 that pertain to either specimen identification or reproduction. Because the listing of the species as endangered under the United States Endangered Species Act further restricted prospects for acquiring new stock from the wild, we elected to consider the entire group as founders in efforts to develop a viable, captive gene pool. Relationships among animals present in 1981 are not known, but some are suspected to be progeny of the Sylber project mentioned below (Sylber 1985) or of undocumented breeding at ASDM before 1981.

The original 1981 colony (9 specimens) may have included some or all of the two males and two females collected by Charles Sylber in 1974 (Sylber 1985) and/or their progeny that were donated to ASDM in 1979. Four additional specimens, also originating from the Sylber project, were donated to the ASDM colony by Lester Harris, of Loma Linda University, in 1983. In 1985, three males and one female, presumably wild-caught, confiscated animals, were provided by the Arizona Game and Fish Department. Keith Klemme kindly loaned one male and three female wild-caught specimens in 1989.

This group of founders (8 males and 13 females) has produced some 133 progeny representing nine maternal blood lines. Careful records and pedigrees have been kept for the members of this colony; these should eventually allow determination of genetic variation in an entire captive lizard population, as well as tests of hypotheses for the inheritance of specific genetic markers. At the current time, however, we do not even have working estimates of genetic diversity in either the captive or natural populations.

This chapter is a preliminary assessment of variation at the molecular level for wild-caught versus captive-bred populations of *S. varius*, and is a part of the comprehensive study of *varius* biology, which was initiated by the Arizona–Sonora Desert Museum in collaboration with El Centro Ecológico de Sonora (Hermosillo), the Rio Grande Zoological Park (Albuquerque, New Mexico), and the University of New Mexico. Initially we intended to use standard DNA fingerprint analyses (Jeffreys et al. 1985*a*, 1985*b*) to address this problem, employing Southern transfer and hybridization of hypervariable mini-satellite markers in the nuclear genome and using similar techniques to determine variation in mitochondrial DNAs among different individuals. Although partially successful, our results were inconsistent, and due to the limited amounts of tissue available, the need to replicate experiments several times threatened to rapidly exhaust our DNA samples—an especially serious problem for the wild-caught animals. These problems led us to try a recently described rapid method that uses Polymerase Chain Reaction (PCR) technology.

Random Amplified Polymorphic DNA (RAPD) markers amplified using *Taq* polymerase in a DNA Thermal Cycler can be detected with standard DNA-staining techniques following electrophoretic separation on agarose gels (Welsh and McClelland 1990, Williams et al. 1990). The RAPD technique is a rapid, reasonably inexpensive, and relatively simple way to generate fingerprint data. Furthermore, it requires nanogram or smaller amounts of target DNA. This preserves the sample and allows numerous replicate experiments to be performed to verify electrophoretic patterns and to recover as much information as possible from the comparisons.

In this chapter, we report the results of our initial efforts to assess genetic variation among different individual Isla San Esteban Chuckwallas using RAPD markers, an interpretation of these results, and their expected impact on future work. In addition, we also identify technical problems that we and others have found with RAPD analyses and discuss how they were dealt with.

Materials and Methods

Blood samples were collected from 16 individuals at the Arizona–Sonora Desert Museum during late July of 1990 using caudal puncture (as described in Gorzula et al. 1976). These animals are hereafter designated as "museum" or "M." A sample of 16 additional animals from Isla San Esteban was collected during early September 1990; these individuals are designated as "island" or "I." All blood was collected in exactly the same manner for both groups of samples, using acid-citrate-dextrose solution B (ACD-B) as an anticoagulant. Total DNA was isolated using SDS-Urea, as described in Densmore and White (1991). This rapid method produces very high quality DNA that is suitable for cloning, Southern transfer and hybridization, and PCR analyses.

The reagents used in the PCR reaction are those included in the Perkin Elmer-Cetus kit. They are *Taq* polymerase (replicase that functions optimally at higher temperature, which is isolated from the thermophyllic bacterium, *Thermus aquaticus*), the four deoxy nucleotide triphosphates (dNTPs), an optimum reaction buffer (supplied by Perkin Elmer-Cetus), and magnesium chloride (about 1.5 µm). To this "master mix" is added, in approximately a 1:10 ratio, a quantity of tetramethylammonium chloride, which effectively makes A:T base pairs bind as strongly as C:G base pairs, increasing primer binding efficiency (Wood et al. 1985). The master mix is then placed on a UV light box (300 nm) for about 2 minutes. This procedure effectively destroys any contaminating DNA. To an aliquot of this mixture the primer(s) and target DNA are added. We have found that by doing preliminary checks of concentration of both the primers and target DNAs, we can ensure optimum reaction conditions. Optimum reaction concentrations are approximately 2 µM for primer and 2.5 ng target DNA in 25 µl reaction mix.

Once the reagents are mixed, we overlay them with one drop of mineral oil and put the samples in the Perkin Elmer-Cetus DNA Thermal Cycler. PCR amplification is divided into three stages: (1) a denaturing step, in which the hydrogen bonds holding together the double-stranded DNA are broken; (2) an annealing step, in which added primer seeks out and binds to its complement; and (3) an extension step, in which the temperature-stable replicating enzyme recognizes the primer and incorporates complementary dNTPs in the 5'–3' direction. The amount of dNTPs added and thus the size of the amplified fragment vary with extension time. This series of three events constitutes one cycle and generally 25–45 cycles are needed to amplify the product to detectable levels (that is, visualized on ethidum bromide-stained agarose gels).

Double-stranded PCR amplification typically employs specific primers 23 to 28 bases in length. By using primers of this size, a high degree of specificity for the target sequence can be gained. In practice, the amplified sequence is usually 200–3000 base pairs (bp) in length (by altering conditions, such as extension times, much longer amplifications are possible), and represents a single sequence that is flanked by the two primers.

The shorter RAPD primers are *not* added in pairs. Only one primer is added, but the smaller size of the primer essentially increases the copy number of sequences that are complementary to it in the target DNA (the probability of any randomly generated sequence occurring in a genome is 4^n, where n is the number of bases in the sequence), so that some primer molecules will bind in relatively close proximity on opposite strands in both orientations. Under these conditions, the region between the primers bound in opposite orientations will amplify. In practice, multiple fragments are normally generated during a profile of amplification cycles using this method, and comparison of fragments among individuals has revealed considerable polymorphism (Welsh and McClelland 1990, Williams et al. 1990). The three RAPD primers used in this study were randomly generated oligonucleotides of ten bases each. The primer sequences were as follows: MA1–5' TGCTCACTGA 3'; MA2–5' TGGACACTGA 3'; MA3–5' TTGCGTCCAA 3'.

In the present study, the following conditions were used for RAPD amplifications: to denature the target DNA, 94°C for one minute; to anneal primers to the denatured DNA, 35°C for one minute; for extension (catalyzed by *Taq* polymerase), 72°C for two minutes. This cycle is repeated 45 times. The change in temperature from extension to the next denaturation step and from denaturation to annealing is reached as quickly as the thermal cycler will allow. The instrument is programmed, however, to take four minutes to go from the annealing to extension steps (from 35° to 72°C). This gradual change (called "ramping") insures that the short primers remain bound to as many sites as possible by allowing *Taq* polymerase to extend each primer a few bases (at a slightly lower efficiency), thus stabilizing them as the temperature increases to 72°C.

After amplification, the sample fragments were compared, following electrophoresis on 1.5% vertical agarose gels (buffer system: TAE–0.04 M tris-acetate, 0.001 M EDTA). Fragment bands were visualized by staining in ethidum bromide (5 µl of 10 mg/ml in 100 ml agarose) and were destained in 0.001 M $MgSO_4$. Size standards, both *Hind* III digested lambda DNA, and 100 bp ladders (Promega), were run with the samples to allow estimation of fragment size. Samples were each amplified several times and run on different gels to verify fragment migration and identity. Fragments were then scored as 1 or 0, depending on the presence or absence of bands in a particular fragment size class.

These presence/absence data were subjected to similarity analysis followed by SAHN clustering and a UPGMA phenogram was produced (SIMINT, SAHN, and TREE, NTSYS, version 1.5 [Rohlf 1989]). In addition, this distance data set was clustered using the neighbor-joining method of Saitou and Nei (1987) and a phenogram was produced (neighbor in PHYLIP, version 3.4 [Felsenstein 1991]). Finally, cladistic analyses were performed using Wagner Parsimony followed by consensus tree construction (PAUP, version 3.0n [Swofford 1991]) so that possible phylogeographic evaluations could be made (Avise et al. 1987).

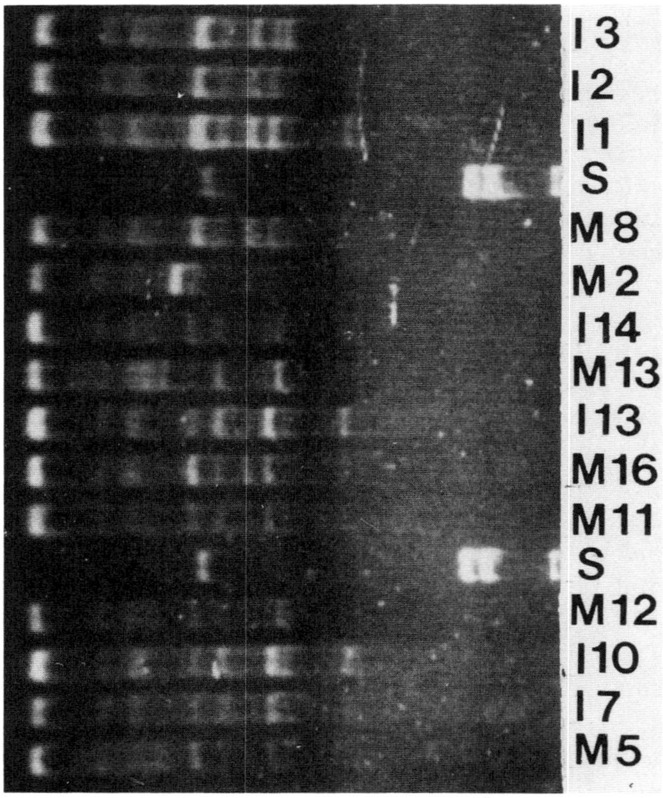

FIGURE 1. PCR products detected following amplification using the MA3 primer. Gel is 1.5% agarose. Sample to lane correspondence as follows: lanes with M and a number correspond to a particular museum lizard (1–16); island animals indicated in the same way by an I; S refers to the *Hind* III digested lambda DNA size standard.

Results and Discussion

It was very clear from the beginning of this study that almost all of the chuckwallas shared a high percentage of fragment bands for each of the three sets of amplifications (for example, with each primer). Occasionally, some bands could be attributed to artifactual amplification; there can be high-enough levels of contaminating DNA in the *Taq* polymerase to allow its unwanted amplification when using short oligonucleotide primers. Generally these spurious amplification products represent bacterial DNA, perhaps present from the isolation of the polymerase. The UV treatment mentioned above minimizes this problem. Because a negative control (all of the reagents minus the target DNA) is included in every set of analyses, electrophoretically resolved bands that might be deemed artifactual (that is, shared not only by samples, but also present in the negative control lane) were not scored or considered in any further analysis. A gel that illustrates the typical patterns of amplified products of both island and museum animals is presented in Figure 1.

Fifty-two different fragment bands were identified from 30 individuals in the three sets of amplifications. These 52 characters were scored as present (1), absent (0), or missing (?)—for example, when data were not resolvable—and ordered into a 30 × 52 matrix (Appendix 1). This matrix of characters was then analyzed in several ways (see below).

To determine the amount of phylogenetic or phylogeographic information in the data set, a heuristic search using tree bisection and reconnection (from PAUP) was initially performed. Ten replicates of the search were done with individuals added in random order in each of the ten replications. This analysis produced 20 equally parsimonious trees of 154 steps. Although certain ingroup affinities noted below were supported in all trees, consensus analyses (strict, 50% majority rule, and Adams) only offered fair resolution for this data set. The Random Trees option of PAUP was then used to estimate how much phylogenetic information might reside in this data set. This program randomly chose 10,000 trees, fitted the data to the trees, and determined the skewness (g_1 statistic) of the tree-length distribution. The relationship between g_1 and the amount of phylogenetic signal has recently been demonstrated (Hillis 1991; Huelsenbeck 1991), and although the g_1 statistic is affected by tree topology and several other parameters, it appears that optimal g_1 values are generally less than −0.34 (Hillis 1991). The g_1 values for these data were only about −0.2, which suggests that the probability of always finding phylogenetically optimal trees is low. This provides an explanation for the large number of trees recovered, even though certain "clades" were resolved consistently.

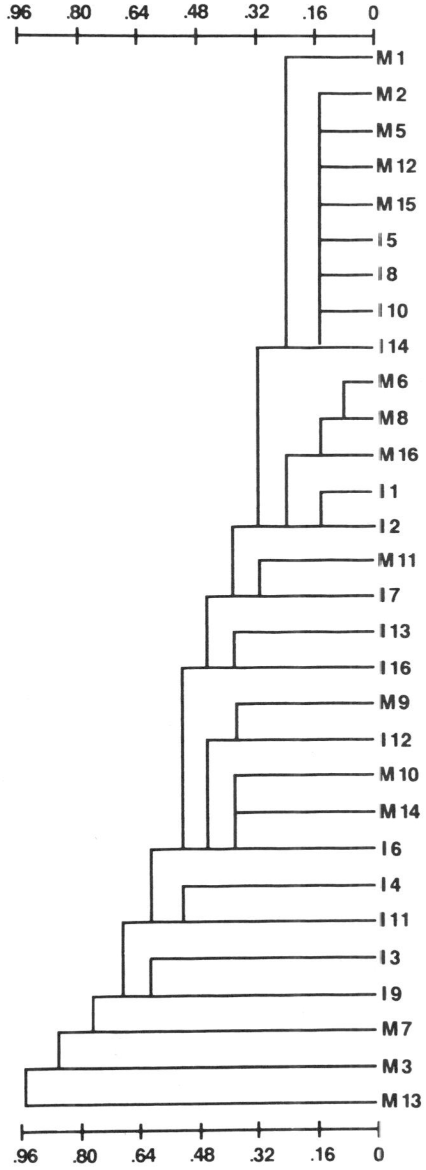

FIGURE 2. A consensus phenogram produced by clustering averge taxonomic distances using SAHN (see text for details), with the tree generated by UPGMA. Samples labeled as in Figure 1. Data used to generate this phenogram from Appendix I.

Two kinds of phenetic analyses were used to determine degrees of similarity among the different individual lizards. Distances were first calculated using the SIMINT option of NTSYS. This program uses discrete data (for example, presence/absence) to generate an average taxonomic distance between each of the individuals (or taxa). These distances were clustered using a SAHN (combined sequential, agglomerative, heirarchical, and nested methods from Sneath and Sokal [1973]) method, and a phenogram was then produced using the unweighted pair groups averaging (UPGMA) method. Six equally supported trees were found from which a consensus tree was generated (Figure 2). This analysis, which assumes equal evolutionary rates, was successful in distinguishing many of the lizards from one another. Several regions of the tree, however, were still unresolved. Especially problematic was the region in the upper part of the phenogram (Figure 2) that includes M2–I14. Also difficult to resolve was the region that includes M10–I6.

The algorithm of Saitou and Nei (1987) called "Neighbor-Joining" was then used to cluster the average taxonomic distances calculated above by SIMINT. This PYHLIP program constructs a tree by successive clustering pairs of individuals that minimize the total branch length at each stage of clustering. Once clustered, a single tree was then generated by the UPGMA analysis as above. The phenogram generated by this method (Figure 3) assumes no constant evolutionary rate, and therefore gave the highest degree of resolution of any analysis that we performed, resolving each of the problematic areas of the consensus phenogram (Figure 2) discussed above. The algorithm appears to be particularly suited for use with fingerprint data. Jonathan Longmire (pers. comm.) found that it was more successful for recovering "correct" tree topologies from DNA fingerprint data for several groups of birds (when relationships were known from several other sets of data) than any other clustering method (but also see Hillis et al. 1994).

When the technical problems that can lead to amplification artifacts are resolved and an optimal clustering method is used, differences among almost all individuals could be identified; that is, no two individuals shared *all* of the same fragment patterns for all three amplifications. Observing this kind of polymorphism is especially important in the captive-propagated ASDM animals. These results suggest that there is good reason to expect that these animals still retain a high degree of variability.

There appears to be a genetically based inheritance for at least some of the RAPD products (Welsh and McClelland 1990; Williams et al. 1990; see, however, Ellsworth et al. 1993); unlike restriction fragment length polymorphisms and variable nonterminal repeats, RAPD products may or may not include coding regions. Because of this (as of yet undetermined level of) inheritance, it might also be expected that many of the museum specimens should share more RAPD products (due to having more recent common ancestry with other museum specimens) with each other, rather than with the recently collected island (or museum) animals. This prediction appears to be at least partially supported. Close inspection of the phenograms produced by either phenetic analyses, while differing somewhat in topology, clustered many of the island animals together and many of the museum animals together (Figures 2 and 3).

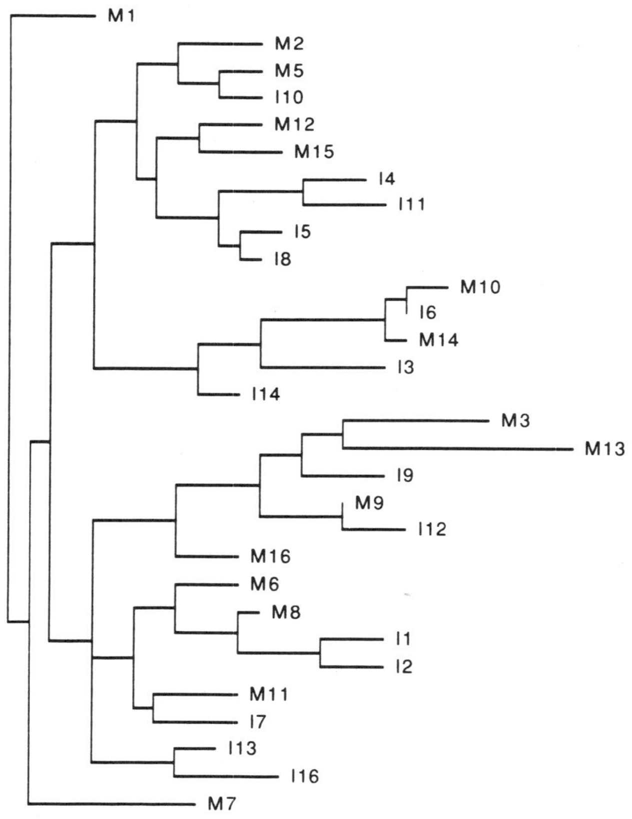

FIGURE 3. Unrooted phenogram produced by neighbor-joining clustering of average taxonomic distances with the tree produced using UPGMA. Samples labeled as in Figure 1. Data used to generate this phenogram from Appendix I.

There were a number of cases, however, in which museum and island animals were clustered closely together (Figures 2 and 3; for example, M11 and I7 or I9 and M12). This could be due to artifact, resulting from random changes in target DNA sequences complementary to the primers, or might even reflect subtle differences in DNA concentration (Ellsworth et al. 1993). Either of these situations could lead to amplification of fragments of similar mobility, suggesting shared characters. It is also possible, however, that these shared bands represent homologous sequences. If these animals were not close relatives (and given the level of RAPD variation that we have found in both the island and museum animals this does not seem to be a necessity), then it is not unlikely that some of the recently collected island forms might share as many fragments with some captive-bred animals as they do with other island lizards. How much population subdivision occurs in this species is not known, nor is the amount of migration. Therefore merely collecting sympatric animals does not necessarily mean that they share very similar genetic backgrounds.

It is more likely, however, that a change in a DNA sequence that is complementary to a primer would result in the loss of a previously common fragment, and would lead to separation of animals. If there were one or more base substitutions (or insertions, deletions, or crossover events) in a region of the target sequence that is critical to primer binding, then the two previously complementary sequences might never bind and there would be no fragment amplified in that region. While this is probably the major mechanism for divergence of these sequences, it might also reflect nothing more than a sampling error, and lead to "clusters" that were not real. This kind of problem could be minimized by adding analyses of other short primers (effectively increasing the size of the data set) and/or by using other sources of rapidly evolving amplification products (for example, certain mitochondrial DNA sequences). Studies of this kind are currently underway in the senior author's laboratory.

We have also resampled all of the museum animals used in this study, as well as many of the adult individuals in the captive population (more than 50 animals). Verification of an individual's identity and pedigree is critical for these analyses, and we wish to compare the amplification products of DNAs isolated from a second blood collection of these animals before concluding that the amplification patterns represent genetically inherited markers or estimating absolute levels of variation in the populations. This second sample of DNA from each of the lizards will also be valuable for assessing any potential differences in RAPD patterns due to artifact. As Ellsworth et al. (1993) have noted, technical and interpretative problems must be fully resolved before clear patterns of genetic inheritance can be demonstrated from RAPD data. We will also be making another trip to Isla San Esteban to collect a larger, more representative population sample of the island lizards.

Summary

We have shown that PCR products, amplified using so-called RAPD markers, vary among different wild-caught and captive-reared San Esteban Island lizards. Although preliminary, these data indicate that different individuals can be distinguished and when presence/absence data are scored, can be clustered according to similarity. The neighbor-joining method of Saitou and Nei (1987) was found to be the most sensitive method of analysis, and generated a single tree that resolved most animals. We have noted that while many of the museum animals clustered most closely together, as did many of the island forms, sometimes museum animals shared more amplification products with island lizards. The observation of considerable variation among the museum lizards (that is, all are essentially identifiable as distinct from one another) suggests that there still exists a considerable amount of genetic variability in the captive population and that there has not yet been critical (or at least detectable) inbreeding depression.

Having demonstrated that individual variation exists, with increased sampling we can now approach questions about population subdivision and movement or permanent migration from one part of the island to another. Increasing the museum and island sample sizes will also allow estimation of the actual level of genetic variation in this species and compare it to what is present in the total captive population. Resampling the same museum animals will indicate whether the condition of the animal or random effects do not alter the amplification products and will go far towards establishing the genetic basis for these kind of data. Furthermore, once we have RAPD and mitochondrial DNA fingerprint data for all of the museum animals, we will then be able to suggest which lizards should be mated to maintain a level of variation that approaches that found in the wild. Finally, using other PCR primers to amplify specific mitochondrial and nuclear products to be used in sequencing or restriction endonuclease analyses, we will be able to address a number of systematic questions, such as which other species of *Sauromalus* are most closely related to *S. varius* and ultimately how *Sauromalus* is related to other iguanid lizards at the molecular level. In summary, this study represents only the first of many efforts that will employ these and other molecular markers to address numerous topics concerning the systematics, evolution, and population biology of *S. varius*.

Acknowledgments

We wish to thank several individuals for assisting us on this project. Kent Beaman, Dale Belcher, Carlos Castillo, L. Lee Grismer, Stephen Hale, Guillermo Lara, Bob Purkiss, Thomas R. Van Devender, and P. Scott White were on the expedition and helped to collect animals and their blood samples on Isla San Esteban. James L. Jarchow, Bob Purkiss, and P. Scott White collected blood from the animals in the captive population at Arizona–Sonora Desert Museum. Robert Owen, P. Scott White, and especially Kevin Bowers helped in data analysis and with comments on an earlier version. Stephanie Kain transcribed and entered data, and she and Mark Grimson assisted with the figures.

Finally, we wish to acknowledge the many contributions that Roger Conant has made to herpetology over his long career. We thank him for his popular works that have introduced so many persons to the field, as well as his many scientific efforts. This work was supported in part by the Texas Advanced Research Program (award 00036440140) and Texas Tech University.

Literature Cited

Avise, L. C., J. Arnold, R. M. Ball, E. Bermingham, T. Lamb, J. E. Neigel, C. A. Reeb, and N. C. Saunders. 1987. Intraspecific phylogeography: the mitochondrial DNA bridge between population genetics and systematics.

Ann. Rev. Ecol. Syst., 18: 489–522.

Case, T. J. 1982. Ecology and evolution of the insular gigantic chuckwalla, *Sauromalus hispidus* and *Sauromalus varius*, p. 184–211. *In* G. M. Burghardt and A. S. Rand (eds.), Iguanas of the World: Their Behavior, Ecology, and Conservation. Noyes Publ., Park Ridge, New Jersey.

Densmore, L. D., and P. S. White. 1991. The systematics and evolution of the Crocodilia as suggested by restriction endonuclease analysis of mitochondrial and nuclear ribosomal DNA. Copeia, 1991: 602–615.

Dickerson, M. C. 1919. Diagnoses of twenty-three new species and a new genus of lizards from lower California. Bull. Amer. Mus. Nat. Hist., 41: 461–477.

Ellsworth, D. L., K. D. Rittenhouse, and R. L. Honeycutt. 1993. Artifactual variation in randomly amplified polymorphic DNA banding patterns. BioTechniques, 14: 214–217.

Etheridge, R. E. 1982. Checklist of iguanine and Malagsy iguanid lizards, p. 7–37. *In* G. M. Burghardt and A. S. Rand (eds.), Iguanas of the World: Their Behavior, Ecology, and Conservation. Noyes Publ., Park Ridge, New Jersey.

Felsenstein, J. 1991. PHYLIP (Phylogeny Inference Package) Version 3.4. Dept. Genetics SK–50, Univ. Washington, Seattle, Washington. 308 pages.

Gorzula, S., C. L. Arocha-Pinango, and C. Salazar. 1976. A method of obtaining blood by vein puncture from large reptiles. Copeia, 1976: 838–839.

Hillis, D. M. 1991. Discriminating between phylogenetic signal and random noise in DNA sequences. *In* M. M. Miyamoto and J. Crafcraft (eds.), Phylogenetic Analysis of DNA Sequences. Oxford Univ. Press, Oxford, UK.

Hillis, D. M., J. P. Huelsenbeck, and C. W. Cunningham. 1994. Application and accuracy of molecular phylogenies. Science, 264: 671–677.

Huelsenbeck, J. P. 1991. Tree-length distribution skewness: an indicator of phylogentic information. Syst. Zool., 40: 257–270.

Jeffreys, A., V. Wilson, and S. L. Thein. 1985*a*. Hypervariable 'minisatellite' regions in human DNA. Nature, 314: 67–73.

—. 1985*b*. Individual-specific 'fingerprints' of human DNA. Nature, 316: 76–79.

Lawler, H. E., and J. L. Jarchow. 1985. A captive management plan for large iguanine lizards using the Isla San Esteban chuckwalla, *Sauromalus varius* Dickerson as a model, p. 137–164. *In* S. McKeown, F. Caporaso, and K. H. Peterson (eds.), Proceedings of the 9th International Herpetological Symposium on Captive Management and Propagation. Zool. Consortium, Thurmont, Maryland.

Rohlf, F. J. 1989. NTSYS (Numerical Taxonomy and Multivariate Analysis System) Version 1.50. Exeter Publ., Sertauket, New York. vi, 185 pages.

Saitou, N., and M. Nei. 1987. The neighbor-joining method: a new method for reconstructing phylogenetic trees. Molec. Biol. Evol., 4: 405–425.

Sneath, P. H. A., and R. R. Sokal. 1973. Principles of Numerical Taxonomy. W. H. Freeman, San Francisco, California. vi, 359 pages.

Swofford, D. L. 1991. PAUP: Phylogenetic Analysis using Parsimony, Version 3.0n. Illinois Nat. Hist. Surv., Champaign, Illinois. viii, 123 pages.

Sylber, C. K. 1985. Eggs and hatchlings of the yellow giant chuckwalla and the black giant chuckwalla in captivity. Herpetol. Rev., 16: 8–21.

Welsh, J., and M. McClelland. 1990. Fingerprinting using PCR with arbitrary primers. Nucleic Acids Res., 18: 7213–7219.

Williams, J. G. K., A. R. Kubelik, K. J. Livak, H. A. Rafalski, and S. V. Tingey. 1990. DNA polymorphism amplified by arbitrary primers are useful as genetic markers. Nucleic Acids Res., 18: 6531–6535.

Wood, W. I., J. Gitshcier, L. A. Lastey, and R. M. Lawn. 1985. Base composition-independent hybridization in tetramethyl ammonium chloride: a method for oligonucleotide screening of highly complex gene libraries. Proc. Natl. Acad. Sci. USA, 82: 1585–1588.

Appendix

Random amplified polymorphic DNA fragments scored as discrete characters.
1 = presence of fragment; 0 = absence of fragment;
? = fragment not resolvable after amplification of DNA.

	MA1 MA2 MA3
M1	00000000000000100000000??????????????100011010001000
M2	0000000000101101000000000000010001000001111110011010
M3	0001010111111000000100001000000011000001000110011010
M5	00000000000011100000000??????????????101011011011010
M6	0000000001001000100000000000010100000101011110011010
M7	0000000000110000000000010001010101010100000110011010
M8	0000001011001000000000000000010011000100011110011010
M9	0000010101000000000000000000000000001001000110001010
M10	1000010101101000000000000000100101000???????????????
M11	0000000001000000100000000000000011000100111010001110
M12	0000000000001010000000000000000100000001110010111010
M13	0011000101001100000011001001000000001001100011001110
M14	1000010100101000000000000000000100001001010011011010
M15	0000000000001000000000000000000011000001010110101010
M16	0000000101110100000000000000010010000101011110011010
I1	0000001000001000011001000000000001000100011010011010
I2	0000001000001000011000000000010010000111011010011010
I3	1010100001100000000000000000000000001110111010011010
I4	0000000000000100010000000000000010100000000011100010
I5	0000000000001100010000000000000001000???????????????
I6	1000010101101000000000000000000100000???????????????
I7	0100001100000000100000000000000001000100111110011010
I8	0000000000000100010000000000001000000000011010011010
I9	0000000001010000000000011000000010001111100110011010
I10	0000000000001001000000000000000001000100011011011010
I11	0000000010000100000000000000000000100000000111001000
I12	0000010101000100000000010000000000000???????????????
I13	0000000001010010000000100000000001000101011100010110
I14	0000000000101010000000000000000001001100110111011010
I16	0000010001001000010000100001010001000???????????????

❦ Densmore, L. D., III, E. D. Pliler, and H. E. Lawler. 1994. A molecular approach for determining genetic variatin in captive and natural populations of the Piebald Chuckwalla (*Sauromalus varius*), p. 343–351. *In* J. B. Murphy, K. Adler, and J. T. Collins (eds.), Captive Management and Conservation of Amphibians and Reptiles. Society for the Study of Amphibians and Reptiles, Ithaca (New York). Contributions to Herpetology, volume 11.

THE REPRODUCTIVE MANAGEMENT OF THE INSULAR SPECIES OF *EPICRATES* (SERPENTES: BOIDAE) IN CAPTIVITY

PETER J. TOLSON*

Introduction

NINE SPECIES OF INSULAR BOAS, OF THE GENUS *Epicrates,* inhabit the Greater Antilles and the Bahama Islands. Endemic taxa are found on Cuba (*E. angulifer*), Hispaniola (*E. fordii* and *E. gracilis*), Jamaica (*E. subflavus*), Puerto Rico (*E. inornatus*), and the Little Bahama Bank (*E. exsul*). *Epicrates chrysogaster*, *E. monensis*, and *E. striatus* have more scattered distributions on the southern Bahamas, the Puerto Rico Bank, and Hispaniola and the Great Bahama Bank, respectively. Although some *Epicrates* species apparently coexist quite well with humans under certain conditions, others have not fared well since the arrival of Europeans. The nearly complete deforestation of the West Indies, in concert with the arrival of exotic mammals, such as the Black Rat (*Rattus rattus*), House Cat (*Felis catus*), and Indian Mongoose (*Herpestes auropunctatus),* have adversely affected boa populations on many islands. Three of the six Antillean species of *Epicrates* are currently endangered: *E. inornatus*, *E. subflavus*, and *E. monensis*.

For many years, zoological parks have recognized the precarious position of wild populations of *Epicrates*, and have directed considerable resources towards their propagation in captivity (see Murphy and Guese 1977; Huff 1980; Bloxam 1982). Members of this genus exhibit striking morphological diversity and significant differences in ecological requirements and reproductive timing (Tolson 1992; Tolson and Henderson 1993). Laboratory studies (see Tolson et al. 1985; Tolson 1992; Teubner 1986) have demonstrated that both proximate environmental factors and social interactions are important for successful reproduction of *Epicrates* in captivity, and careful attention to the requirements of individual species is necessary for successful, long-term propagation programs. The Toledo Zoological Gardens has a ten-year history of effort in this sphere, and is the only institution to have maintained all nine and reproduced seven of the insular species in its collection.

Materials and Methods

Housing

Epicrates are housed in large exhibit cages, as well as in smaller holding cages. In holding areas, smaller species, such as *E. fordii*, *E. gracilis*, and *E. monensis*, are caged in standard aquaria measuring 50 × 25 × 25 cm (Tolson 1989). Larger species, such as *E. angulifer*, *E. inornatus*, and *E. subflavus*, are housed in either 44.5 × 122 × 65.5 cm or 41 × 90.5 × 46.5 cm standard aquaria, depending on the size of the snake. Neonates are kept in plastic shoeboxes. The substrate in holding cages is generally newspaper, although paper toweling is used in shoeboxes. Breeding cages have a substrate of number 20 sand, which is covered with dead leaves, and exhibit cages have substrates of soil or cypress bark mulch, which are covered with dead leaves. As these snakes are nocturnal, daytime refugia are a necessity. Commercially available hide boxes, such as those provided by B. J. Specialties Company (2802 Melody Lane, Columbia, Missouri 65203) or Fuhrman Diversified, Inc. (905 A South 8th Street, LaPorte, Texas 77571), are used in holding areas. Hollow logs, rock piles, or similar retreats are used in exhibit cages.

*Toledo Zoological Society
2700 Broadway
Toledo, Ohio 43609, USA

Acronyms used in this chapter:

PTLs	Plasma testosterone levels
SVL	Snout-to-vent length
TL	Tail length

Feeding

Epicrates are opportunistic predators and feed on a wide variety of prey, including rodents (Gundlach 1880; Sheplan and Schwartz 1974), birds (Sheplan and Schwartz 1974; Tolson 1988), bats (Hardy 1957; Rodriguez and Reagan 1984), lizards (Henderson et al. 1987; Tolson 1988), and frogs (Henderson et al. 1987). Neonate and juvenile *Epicrates* feed nearly exclusively on lizards, switching to endothermic prey at approximately two years of age (Henderson et al. 1987). At the Toledo Zoological Gardens, juvenile *Epicrates* are fed *Anolis carolinensis* or *A. cristatellus*. Neonates of small species of *Epicrates*, such as *E. fordii*, *E. gracilis*, and *E. monensis*, are fed live 0.5–1.0 g *A. carolinensis* for the first one to two months, then larger prey as growth progresses. Juvenile *Epicrates* can usually be induced to accept newborn mice, using the scent-transfer techniques described by Ross and Marzec (1990). Neonate *E. angulifer*, however, will usually feed readily on 3.0–5.0 g juvenile mice shortly after birth. Young *Epicrates* are able to kill and eat prey items in the wild which are very large in proportion to their own size, yet some neonates in captivity will steadfastly refuse to eat.

If tube feeding is indicated (for example, because of a loss of body mass equivalent to more than 33% of the birth weight), a high calorie (about 28 calories per gram) dietary supplement, such as Nutri-cal (Evsco Pharmaceuticals, Buena, New Jersey 08310), is given by tube twice per week. Experience at the Toledo Zoological Gardens has indicated that neonate body-mass losses in excess of this amount nearly always end in death.

Adult snakes are fed laboratory mice or rats, although some adult *E. fordii*, *E. gracilis,* and *E. monensis* prefer *Anolis* sp. Food is usually offered weekly, except during the reproductive season. Many individual *Epicrates* are reluctant to feed during courtship, and some females will cease feeding during pregnancy. It is important, therefore, to ensure that snakes are in a good nutritional state at the onset of the breeding season. Females are allowed to accumulate significant body mass (short of outright obesity) prior to breeding. A female with a snout-to-vent length (SVL) of about 1 m, for example, would be kept at a body mass of approximately 250 g. Males are kept at leaner body masses. Females are fed throughout the reproductive season, including the period just prior to parturition, if they are inclined to accept food. Smaller food items are given to the females as the mass of the developing young increases.

Proximate Environmental Factors

At the Toledo Zoological Gardens, attempts have been made to reproduce the climatic regimes of the islands inhabited by *Epicrates*. These data are available through the United States Weather Bureau or other sources (for example, see Briscoe 1966) This strategy translates into providing a nighttime temperature drop to lows of 20°–25°C from November through April. This winter temperature drop is essential for reproduction (see Teubner 1986). Daytime temperatures fluctuate from 28°–30°C. Relative humidity is allowed to drop to about 40% from November to February, and then is gradually increased to above 80% in May through September by the use of free-standing humidifiers. Increases in humidity seem to enhance reproductive activity (Huff 1978, 1980; Teubner 1986). Access to water is usually restricted to one day per week from November through February. Day length is maintained at 12 hours throughout the year.

Social Manipulations

Off-display snakes are housed individually, except during the breeding season, when single pairs are kept together. On occasion trios (2 males, 1 female) are placed together to stimulate courtship, or two males are placed together prior to the introduction of the female (see Huff 1980). After combat (Tolson 1983) or when courtship commences, the subordinate male is removed. Males usually indicate that they are ready to commence courtship by the onset of restlessness. In *Epicrates*, this activity translates into continual prowling around the cage during the day. The onset of male reproductive condition is also signaled by shedding of the hemipenial epithelium. Shed independently from the rest of the epidermis, it is often found in the water bowl or on the cage substrate. Mengden et al. (1980) noted that shedding of the epithelial layer of skin of the hemipenis has been observed in *Eunectes notaeus*, *Sanzinia madagascariensis*, and "others," but make no mention of any correlation with reproductive activity.

When a male is determined to be in breeding condition, he is kept isolated in one of the breeding cages for three to five days. After this short period of acclimation, the female is introduced. Disturbance of the pair is kept to a minimum through the breeding period, but females are weighed once per month. Any courtship activity or copulation is noted.

Management of Pregnancy

Females are isolated approximately 120 days after the first copulation. It is essential that they be provided with a thermal gradient generated by a supplemental heat source (with multiple refugia along it) throughout pregnancy. Buden (1975) associated scale anomalies, exhibited by a litter of *Epicrates chrysogaster*, to the air-conditioned holding facilities in which their mother was kept during her gestation. Tolson (1988) reported that wild *E. monensis* maintain body temperatures of 30°–33°C while basking during pregnancy. The cages are packed with sphagnum moss or dead leaves to a depth of 5 cm as parturition approaches. This additional substrate provides refuge for the neonates after birth. In captivity, females may devour living young after birth (Tolson 1992).

Care of Neonates

Newborn *Epicrates* are weighed, snout-to-vent length (SVL) and tail length (TL) are measured, and the offspring are then placed in individual shoeboxes with a hide box and a small water bowl. Food is offered after the first shed, which usually occurs one to five days after birth.

Results

Reproductive Timing

Courtship commences in February for most insular *Epicrates*, but there are two notable exceptions. For *E. fordii*, courtship often begins in late December or early January, while the Cuban Boa, *E. angulifer*, normally courts in May or June. Species differences notwithstanding, there may be considerable variation in the onset of reproductive timing within a given species, both from year to year in a single population, or within a given year among different populations (Tolson 1992). It is likely that differences in local climatic conditions are the source of this variation. Reproduction in most species of *Epicrates* appears to be biennial (Huff 1980; Tolson 1983), but some populations, both captive and wild, may reproduce annually under certain conditions (Bloxam 1982; Tolson 1992).

Reproductive Behavior

Courtship behavior is initiated by the male, and is usually very intense and prolonged, often lasting for two or three weeks or more (Tolson 1980). Courtship follows the typical boid pattern, with extensive stimulation by the male, using the pelvic spurs. Courtship behavior in *Epicrates* was described by Tolson (1980), and was broken down into four phases following the nomenclature of Gillingham et al. (1977): Tactile-Chase, Tactile-Alignment, Tail-Search, and Intromission and Coitus. Tolson (1980) reported that *Epicrates* courtship was characterized by prolonged concertina-like tail-search movements with extensive spur use by the male. Multiple copulations are common.

Reported gestation periods for insular *Epicrates* range from 132 days to as long as 252 days (Tolson 1992; Nowinski 1977). The usual gestation period is about 150 days when a supplemental heat source is provided for the gravid female. Duration of the gestation period is dependent to a great degree on the thermoregulatory activities of the female.

There is considerable size diversity within this genus, ranging from the smallest species, *E. fordii* (maximum SVL about 1 m), to the largest, *E. angulifer* (maximum SVL about 4 m). Accordingly, there are trenchant body-mass, SVL, and litter-size differences among the young of the various species. *Epicrates fordii*, *E. gracilis*, and *E. monensis* have litter sizes of 2–10 young, with body masses of 3.5–6.5 g. *Epicrates chrysogaster* and *E. exsul* have litter sizes of 2–23 young, with body masses of 4.5–8.4 g (Buden 1975; Tolson 1992). *Epicrates inornatus*, *E. striatus*, and *E. subflavus* have litter sizes of 6–51 young, with body masses of 11.3–21.7 g (Grant 1933; Tolson 1992). *Epicrates angulifer* is a species with truly large neonates having body masses in excess of 200 g. Litter sizes in smaller adult *E. angulifer* (SVL about 2 m) usually range from 3–10 young. No data exist for litter sizes of females larger than 3.0 m, but litter sizes are potentially much higher. Litter size in all species of *Epicrates* is usually a function of female body size; the larger the female of any given species, the larger the litter size. A trend appears in captive *E. monensis*, wherein body mass and SVL of neonates also seems to be positively correlated with female SVL. Reproductive longevity for *Epicrates* may approach 20 years (Tolson 1991).

Discussion

Ample male-female interaction is necessary for successful reproduction. Unless sufficient courtship occurs, females may reabsorb ovarian follicles. Tolson et al. (1985) demonstrated that female *Epicrates angulifer* kept isolated from males do not complete follicular maturation and do not ovulate. Teubner (1986) reported that male *E. striatus* kept isolated from females do not show increased levels of plasma testosterone as the reproductive season commences. The cases of false pregnancy reported (Huff 1980) may be partially due to insufficient courtship by the male. This problem is exacerbated if the male is removed from the female prematurely. Increasing body girth of a female in a breeding situation is not necessarily an indication of pregnancy, only the development of ovarian follicles.

Dominant males may inhibit reproduction of smaller males. Teubner (1986) reported that dominant male *E. striatus* have mean plasma testosterone levels (PTLs) significantly higher than subordinate males. When the alpha males are removed, and beta males continue to have access to females, the PTLs of the beta males increase and they commence courtship. The significance of this finding is that it may not be the best strategy to place smaller or less aggressive males into a group breeding situation if reproduction from that male is desired. If males are allowed to remain together in a group situation during the reproductive season, care must be taken to prevent injury to the subordinate males. Bite wounds—including severe lacerations—may occur during combat. Occasionally, a larger female snake may behave aggressively toward a male. An instance occurred at the Toledo Zoological Gardens, in which an adult female *E. inornatus* killed and consumed her male cage mate during the reproductive season. A similar incident occurred with a pair of *E. subflavus* exhibited at the Columbus Zoological Gardens (J. M. Goode, pers. comm.)

Summary

Zoo-based research on plasma sex steroid hormone levels and on ultrasonographic monitoring of follicular growth in females has demonstrated that both proximate environmental factors and social interactions are important for successful captive reproduction of insular species of *Epicrates*. At the Toledo Zoological Gardens, West Indian boas are kept under seasonal climatic regimens which approximate environmental conditions in the wild and are housed in social groups which facilitate the male combat and extended courtship necessary for long-term, successful, reproductive programs for these species. By providing these conditions, we have been able to reproduce seven insular species of *Epicrates* held in our collections.

Acknowledgments

I am particularly indebted to Valerie Hornyak and the other members of the staff of the Department of Herpetology, Toledo Zoological Gardens, for extraordinary dedication and support of the Zoo's *Epicrates* breeding programs. I also gratefully acknowledge the pioneering work on the captive reproduction of *Epicrates* by Thomas A. Huff, which was generously shared and provided the impetus for later reproductive studies. Reproductive research on *E. monensis* was supported by the Institute of Museum Services (Conservation Project Support Grants IC–70095–87 and IC–90453–89).

Literature Cited

Bloxam, Q. M. C. 1982. Über Haltung and Zucht der Jamaika-Schlankboa (*Epicrates subflavus*) im Jersey Zoo. Zeitscr. Kolner Zoo, 25: 133–137.

Briscoe, C. B. 1966. Weather in the Luquillo Mountains of Puerto Rico. Inst. Trop. Forestry, United States Forest Ser. Res. Pap. ITF– 3: 1–250.

Buden, D. W. 1975. Notes on *Epicrates chrysogaster* (Serpentes: Boidae) of the southern Bahamas, with description of a new subspecies. Herpetologica, 31: 166–177.

Gillingham, J. C., C. C. Carpenter, B. J. Brecke, and J. B. Murphy. 1977. Courtship and copulatory behavior of the Mexican milk snake, *Lampropeltis triangulum sinaloae* (Colubridae). Southwest. Nat., 22: 187–194.

Grant, C. 1933. Notes on *Epicrates inornatus* (Reinhardt) Copeia, 1933: 224–225.

Gundlach, J. 1880. Contribucion á la Erpetologia Cubana. G. Monteil, Havana. 99 pages.

Hardy, J. R. 1957. Bat predation by the Cuban boa, *Epicrates angulifer* (Bibron). Copeia, 1957: 151–152.

Henderson, R. A., T. A. Noeske-Hallin, J. A. Ottenwalder, and A. Schwartz. 1987. On the diet of the boa *Epicrates striatus* on Hispaniola, with notes on *E. fordi* and *E. gracilis*. Amphibia-Reptilia, 8: 251–258.

Huff, T. A. 1978. Breeding the Puerto Rican boa at the Reptile Breeding Foundation. Internatl. Zoo Yearbook, 18: 96–97.

—. 1980. Captive propagation of the subfamily Boinae with emphasis on the genus *Epicrates*, p. 125–139 *In* J. B. Murphy and J. T. Collins (eds.), Reproductive Biology and Diseases of Captive Reptiles. Soc. Study Amphib. Reptiles, Oxford, Ohio, Contrib. Herpetol., 1.

Mengden, G. A., C. G. Platz, R. Hubbard, and H. Quinn. 1980. Semen collection, freezing, and artificial insemination in snakes, p. 71–78. *In* J. B. Murphy and J. T. Collins (eds.), Reproductive Biology and Diseases of Captive Reptiles. Soc. Study Amphib. Reptiles, Oxford, Ohio, Contrib. Herpetol., 1.

Murphy, J. B., and R. K Guese. 1977. Reproduction in the Hispaniolan boa *Epicrates fordii fordii* at Dallas Zoo. Internatl. Zoo Yearbook, 17: 132–133.

Nowinski, B. 1977. Voortplanting van de Cubaanse boa, *Epicrates angulifer*, in het terrarium. Lacerta, 35: 144–147.

Rodriguez, G. A., and D. P. Reagan. 1984. Bat predation by the Puerto Rican boa, *Epicrates inornatus*. Copeia, 1984: 219–220.

Ross, R. A., and G. Marzec. 1990. The Reproductive Husbandry of Pythons and Boas. Inst. Herpetol. Res., Stanford, California. 270 pages.

Sheplan, B. R., and A. Schwartz. 1974. Hispaniolan boas of the genus *Epicrates* (Serpentes: Boidae) and their Antillean relationships. Ann. Carnegie Mus., 45: 57–143.

Teubner, V. A. 1986. Endocrine and behavioral aspects of the reproductive cycle of the Haitian boa (*Epicrates striatus*). Doctoral Dissertation, Univ. Toledo, Toledo, Ohio. 86 pages.

Tolson, P. J. 1980. Comparative reproductive behavior of four species of snakes in the boid genus *Epicrates*, p. 87–97. *In* R. Hahn (ed.), Proceedings of the 4th Annual Reptile Symposium on Captive Propagation and Husbandry. Zool. Consortium, Thurmont, Maryland.

—. 1983. Captive propagation and husbandry of the Cuban boa, *Epicrates angulifer*, p. 285–292. *In* R. Hahn (ed.), Proceedings of the 6th Annual Reptile Symposium on Captive Propagation and Husbandry. Zool. Consortium, Thurmont, Maryland.

—. 1988. Critical habitat, predator pressures, and management of *Epicrates monensis* on the Puerto Rico Bank: a multivariate analysis. United States Dept. Agric. Forest Serv. Gen. Tech. Rep., RM–166: 228–238.

—. 1989. Breeding the Virgin Islands boa *Epicrates monensis granti* at the Toledo Zoological Gardens. Internatl. Zoo Yearbook, 28: 163–167.

—. 1991. *Epicrates* (West Indian Boa). Reproductive longevity. Herpetol. Rev., 22: 100.

—. 1992. The reproductive biology of the neotropical boid genus *Epicrates* (Serpentes: Boidae), p. 165–178. *In* W. C. Hamlett (ed.), Reproductive Biology of South American Vertebrates. Springer-Verlag, New York.

Tolson, P. J., and R. W. Henderson. 1993. The Taxonomy and Natural History of West Indian Boas. R and A Publishing, Ltd., Portishead, UK. 124 pages.

Tolson, P. J., T. A. Reichard, J. M. Terry, C. S. Roberts, and D. H. Clifford. 1985. Effects of courtship on follicular growth and development in the Cuban boa, *Epicrates angulifer* (Serpentes: Boidae). Abstract Soc. Study Amphib. Reptiles / Herpetol. League Ann. Meeting, Tampa, Florida.

❦

❦ Tolson, P. J. 1994. The reproductive management of the insular species of *Epicrates* (Serpentes: Boidae) in captivity, p. 353–357. *In* J. B. Murphy, K. Adler, and J. T. Collins (eds.), Captive Management and Conservation of Amphibians and Reptiles. Society for the Study of Amphibians and Reptiles, Ithaca (New York). Contributions to Herpetology, volume 11.

HUSBANDRY OF LONG-TERM CAPTIVE POPULATIONS OF BOID SNAKES (*EPICRATES*, *CORALLUS*, AND *CHONDROPYTHON*)

TROOPER WALSH*

Introduction

IN EARLY 1976, THE NATIONAL ZOOLOGICAL PARK (NZP) began to assemble breeding groups of *Epicrates cenchria* (Brazilian Rainbow Boas), *Corallus canina* (Emerald Tree Boas), and *Chondropython viridis* (Green Tree Pythons). We currently maintain some of the largest captive-breeding populations of these snakes anywhere in the world, and have produced a total of 722 offspring from these three species. This includes 20 litters of *E. cenchria* (361 neonates), ten litters of *C. canina* (101 neonates), and 24 clutches of *C. viridis* (260 young). Third-generation breeding is now common for all species. Our bloodlines are diverse, and include some founder stock and many captive lines.

Over the years, our work has generated a tremendous amount of data and a number of publications (Walsh 1976, 1977, 1978*a*, 1978*b*, 1979, 1981, 1983; Van Mierop et al. 1982; Walsh and Davis 1983). In recent years other zoo herpetologists and private breeders of reptiles have published accounts of their experiences with these species (Blake 1992; Murphy et al. 1978; Ross and Marzec 1990; Tepedelen 1989; Weidner 1986; Zulich 1984, 1990).

The purpose of this chapter is to update our 15-year history with these animals, focusing on new material that is critical to long-term population management. The subjects covered are: (1) physical conditioning and thermal cycling to induce breeding, (2) care of gravid females and egg incubation, and (3) husbandry techniques for the rearing of offspring.

*Department of Herpetology
National Zoological Park
Washington, D. C. 20008, USA

Acronym used in this chapter:

NZP National Zoological Park

Physical Conditioning and Thermal Cycling to Induce Breeding

Temperature cycles are the primary environmental cues that we control and manipulate to stimulate breeding behavior in all three species. We try to provide a six- to nine-month period of minimal day/night temperature fluctuations for a "pre-breeding/conditioning" phase. During this time, the animals are provided with a diurnal thermal gradient, which ranges from 25°C to 34°C, with a nightly low that averages 23°C. To induce breeding, the night-time lows are allowed to drop below 16°C for four to as much as 12 weeks. Daytime high temperatures remain about the same during this period. As long as the animals have the opportunity to warm themselves in the day, health problems are not experienced.

Courtship and breeding behaviors develop soon after cooling begins. Males usually stop feeding when cooled, while females may eat regularly through ovulation. In the live-bearing snakes (*Epicrates* and *Corallus*), gravid females may infrequently accept small food items throughout gestation.

Taken alone, the cooling process we use to stimulate breeding may not be any more important to reproduction than the more stable temperatures of the pre-breeding/conditioning period. Both conditions seem equally important for long-term, successful propagation, with change acting as the trigger. When providing thermal cycles and gradients, it is also useful to note where specimens position themselves in relation to specific temperature zones. For instance, individuals of *Chondropython* that are provided with a daytime thermal gradient in the pre-breeding period generally seek out temperatures around 27°C. When nighttime cooling is initiated and females prepare to ovulate, they will seek out cooler temperatures. When gravid, the females will seek warmer temperatures. When cycling these reptiles to breed, the animal's behavior is a good indicator of what to do next with temperature regimens.

All three boids have produced young or eggs in every season of the year at the NZP. The *Chondropython* have produced fertile eggs in every month except September. The ability to manipulate reproductive cycles is of benefit with regard to maintenance of young. By choosing when to breed particular individuals of a given species, we can control when, and how many, young are produced.

It is possible to breed females year after year in all three species. We currently choose, however, to give females a year off between breedings. This seems particularly important with the live bearers, which may not feed for over six months while gravid. Our experience with breeding females annually shows a reduction in fecundity and condition of the female. In some breeding females, prolapsed cloacae, reduced muscle tone, and premature death may result.

With *Chondropython,* we have experimentally tried to double-clutch females in the same way that some commercial breeders of reptiles do with colubrids. To accomplish this, the first clutches were pulled for artificial incubation, and females were fed heavily while being subjected to a condensed pre-breeding/conditioning cycle. All six clutches from these females hatched and produced normal young. In two instances, however, females prolapsed soon after laying their second clutches, and in a third case, a female lost all of her teeth when allowed to brood the second clutch. It is suspected that the third female experienced a form of calcium depletion. To this day, three years later, the now-retired female has no teeth.

Care of Gravid Females and Egg Incubation

Thermal gradients are provided for gravid boids at all times. Gravid snakes display physical and behavioral changes, such as seeking heat, altered feeding patterns, restlessness, and general posterior swelling. It is important not to confuse ovulation with signs of pregnancy. The appearence of quick-developing, localized, mid-abdominal bloating of females is associated with ovulation. Obviously it is critical to maintain the sexes together at this time, as well as to continue with nightly cooling. Failure to distinguish between ovulation and conception may result in no young if males are removed and/or cooling cycles are interrupted prematurely.

In the late 1970s, we set up two gravid *Corallus canina* in special brooding cages to monitor the position of the females in relation to four temperature zones. Results indicated the gravid snakes preferred warm temperatures that averaged 31°C for most of the gestation period. Over the last few weeks prior to parturition, however, the females sought out cooler regions that averaged 28°C.

More casual and recent observations of other gravid *Corallus, Chondropython,* and *Epicrates* show similar temperature preferences, all of which appear different from those of males and non-gravid females. Failure to provide an adequate thermal gradient for these gravid boids, or too high or too low an ambient temperature during the latter stages of pregnancy, may result in deformed and/or stillborn young.

It appears that *Chondropython* eggs go though a similar change with regard to thermal needs, as do developing young in live-bearing *Corallus*. During the early 1980s, L. H. S. Van Mierop (in conjunction with the NZP) determined the optimum incubation temperatures for *Chondropython* eggs by monitoring brooding females on eggs (Van Mierop et al. 1982). During the first six weeks, females maintained clutch temperatures around 31.5°C. In the last week, clutch temperatures were allowed to drop to an average of 29°C. It appears that eggs that are kept too warm in the last few days result in dead, full-term fetuses. This is a very common problem experienced by many breeders of *Chondropython*, particularly those using artificial incubation.

In our experience and from discussions with other breeders, it is widely agreed that *Chondropython* eggs are one of the more difficult python eggs to hatch on a consistent basis. The eggs are relatively thin shelled, and are sensitive to handling, extreme temperatures, or excessive moisture. In recent years at the NZP, we have had excellent success hatching *Chondropython* eggs using both maternal and artificial incubation. Regardless of the incubation method, it may be beneficial to let females brood their eggs for several days to allow the clutch to "form up." During this time, the delicate shells harden, which gives the vascular system of the egg a stronger framework. This brief period of maternal incubation also allows infertile or dead eggs to solidify and become less of a threat to good eggs. The eggs require an atmosphere of high humidity, but succumb quickly to contact with excess moisture, thus indicating the possible need for dry nesting and incubating media in humid climates.

Husbandry Practices for Offspring

Among the three species, housing and husbandry needs of the neonates vary considerably. *Epicrates cenchria* neonates are the easiest of these species to get started and maintain. Offspring do well when set up in large groups, and feed voraciously on young rodents after their first shed. *Corallus canina* may also be housed communally. Due to a more complicated feeding regimen, however, it may be advisable to use individual cages. Because of the large size of newborn *Corallus* and their very slow metabolism, food is rarely offered until the young are three to four weeks old. Many *Corallus* prefer live, young adult mice over baby mice or dead food for their first meals. Juvenile *Corallus* are fed at the NZP about once every two weeks, depending on defecation cycles.

Because of their nervous nature and ability to injure each other, we set up young *Chondropython* individually. Problem feeders are common. One of our more successful tricks for stubborn eaters involves slitting open a freshly killed bird and placing dead newborn mice in the body cavity to be warmed and scented. Within any given clutch, problem feeders will readily accept baby mice prepared in this fashion. We have never had a baby *Chondropython* starve to death at the NZP, but holdouts of up to three months occasionally occur.

Most breeders are aware of a condition in captive-raised *Chondropython* that is commonly referred to as the "kinky-tail syndrome." Our experience indicates that this condition probably results from inappropriate handling of young animals, and not genetic flaws or bone disease, as has been suggested. Since the mid–1980s, the NZP has employed a policy of minimal physical contact with *Chondropython* throughout their first year. Cages are set up to be worked on without disturbing the animals. If specimens do have to be moved, they are encouraged to crawl onto a new perch with gentle prods, rather than being pulled from an old perch. The point is to avoid the animal anchoring its prehensile tail and experiencing unnatural stress to the vertebrae. Finally, it is NZP policy not to probe *Chondropython* for sex determination until they are at least a year old and more able structurally to withstand restraint. Since we initiated these "hands off" policies eight years ago, no animals have displayed the "kinky-tail syndrome."

Summary

The National Zoological Park has some of the largest captive-breeding populations of Brazilian Rainbow Boas, Emerald Tree Boas, and Green Pythons in the world. Over the past 15 years, nearly 800 offspring have been produced of these three species. This success has been due to the attention paid to thermal cycling, care of gravid females, and rearing of young. Breeding in all three species is stimulated by allowing nighttime temperatures to drop from an average of 23° to 16°C. Thermal gradients are provided for all species at all times; this is especially important for gravid females whose thermal needs change during gestation. The housing and husbandry needs for neonates vary considerably among the three species. Rainbow Boas are the easiest to get started and maintain, while Green Tree Pythons are the most difficult. These three species are specialized in their habits, but all make hardy and productive captives if careful attention is paid to their needs.

Acknowledgments

I would like to thank Dale Marcellini, Curator of Herpetology at the National Zoological Park, for reviewing the manuscript. Appreciation is also extended to Ann Walsh for help in the preparation of this paper.

Literature Cited

Blake, H. 1992. The green tree python (*Chondropython viridis*). Vivarium, 3: 19–22.

Murphy, J. B., D. G. Barker, and B. W. Tryon. 1978. Miscellaneous notes on the reproductive biology of reptiles. 2. Eleven species of the family Boidae, genera *Candoia*, *Corallus*, *Epicrates* and *Python*. Jour. Herpetol., 12: 385–390.

Ross, R. A., and G. Marzec. 1990. The Reproductive Husbandry of Pythons and Boas. Inst. Herpetol. Res., Stanford, California. 270 pages.

Tepedelen, K. 1989. Captive propagation of the emerald tree boa (*Corallus caninus*), p. 77–80. *In* R. L. Gowen (ed.), Proceedings of the Northern California Herpetological Society's Conference on Captive Propagation and Husbandry of Reptiles and Amphibians, Davis, California. Spec. Publ. 5.

Van Mierop, L. H. S., T. Walsh, and D. L. Marcellini. 1982. Thermoregulation in *Chondropython viridis*, p. 265–274. *In* D. L. Marcellini (ed.), Proceedings of the Sixth Annual Reptile Symposium on Captive Propagation and Husbandry. Zool. Consortium, Thurmont, Maryland.

Walsh, T. 1976. Reptile reproduction with respect to simulated environmental cycles. Anim. Keeper Forum, 3: 69–70.

—. 1977. Husbandry and breeding of *Chondropython viridis*. Natl. Assoc. Sound Wildlife Prog. Jour., 1: 10–17.

—. 1978*a*. Husbandry and breeding of *Corallus canina*. Unpubl. manuscript. Natl. Zool. Park, Washington, D.C. 26 pages.

—. 1978*b*. Thermal preferences of gravid *Corallus canina*. Unpubl. manuscript. Natl. Zool. Park, Washington, D.C. 13 pages.

—. 1979. Further notes on the husbandry and breeding of *Chondropython viridis*, p. 102–111. *In* R. A. Hahn (ed.), Third Annual Reptile Symposium on Captive Propagation and Husbandry. Zool. Consortium, Thurmont, Maryland.

—. 1981. Breeding the green tree python and the emerald tree boa, p. 111–116. *In* R. Pinney (ed.), The Snake Book. Doubleday & Co., Garden City, New York.

—. 1983. Revealing the family secrets of herptiles. Zoogoer, 12: 17–20.

Walsh, T., and R. Davis. 1983. Husbandry and breeding of *Epicrates cenchria* at the National Zoological Park, p. 108–114. *In* P. J. Tolson (ed.), Proceedings of the Seventh Annual Reptile Symposium on Captive Propagation and Husbandry. Zool. Consortium, Thurmont, Maryland.

Weidner, T. M. 1986. Captive reproduction of emerald tree boas, *Corallus caninus* Linnaeus, p. 127–134. *In* C. H. Peterson (ed.), Proceedings of the Tenth International Herpetological Symposium on Captive Propagation and Husbandry. Zool. Consortium, Thurmont, Maryland.

Zulich, A. 1984. Captive breeding, husbandry, and neonatal care of the green tree python, *Chondropython viridis*, with emphasis on maternal incubation of the eggs, p. 114–118. *In* R. A. Hahn (ed.), Proceedings of the Eighth Annual Herpetological Symposium on Captive Propagation and Husbandry. Zool. Consortium, Thurmont, Maryland.

—. 1990. Green tree python. Reptile Amphib. Mag., 1990 (Sept.–Oct.): 2–6.

Walsh, T. 1994. Husbandry of long-term captive populations of boid snakes (*Epicrates*, *Corallus*, and *Chondropython*), p. 359–362. *In* J. B. Murphy, K. Adler, and J. T. Collins (eds.), Captive Management and Conservation of Amphibians and Reptiles. Society for the Study of Amphibians and Reptiles, Ithaca (New York). Contributions to Herpetology, volume 11.

THE SPECIES SURVIVAL PLAN FOR *CROTALUS DURISSUS UNICOLOR*: A MULTIFACETED APPROACH TO CONSERVATION OF AN INSULAR RATTLESNAKE

R. ANDREW ODUM* AND MATTHEW J. GOODE**

Introduction

THE AMERICAN ASSOCIATION OF ZOOLOGICAL Parks and Aquariums (AAZPA) Species Survival Plan (SSP) program for the Aruba Island Rattlesnake, *Crotalus durissus unicolor*, was initiated in 1982. Since that time, the SSP program has evolved from a captive-based propagation effort to a broad, field-based approach which encompasses the many issues that are involved in the conservation of this insular rattlesnake. The main goal of the SSP is to conserve and protect the animal in its natural environment. Captive populations of *C. d. unicolor* are maintained to support wild populations, not as a replacement for wild populations. As reservoirs of genetic and demographic material, captive populations can be used to reinforce, revitalize, or reestablish wild populations (Foose 1983; Ballou and Foose, in press).

The success of any SSP program requires overcoming problems associated with the conservation of the organisms. Many issues encountered in managing an SSP program are not apparent at its initiation. For this reason, SSP programs must respond to new situations and challenges that invariably arise through the term of the program, and appropriate reactions must be implemented. In some cases, the original program goals may be altered or abandoned, and new goals may be established.

Occasionally, opportunities arise that allow significant advances in taxon conservation. Such opportunities may include political, proprietorship, or economic changes, designation of critical habitat, release and relocation opportunities, or enhanced specimen availability for captive-propagation programs. SSP conservation programs must be adaptable to such unforeseen situations as they arise, so that, when possible, any opportunity that may improve the prospects of survival of the endangered taxon is exploited.

This paper is an overview of our efforts to conserve *Crotalus durissus unicolor* through the SSP of the AAZPA. Some problems and issues that have been addressed to date include: (1) a limited number of founders for the captive population, (2) ophidian *Paramyxovirus* epidemics, (3) a lack of information about the population status and life history of the snake, (4) inadequate genetic references to monitor the status of the captive population through successive generations, and (5) questions concerning the future of this endemic form on Aruba Island, off the northwestern coast of Venezuela.

This chapter is organized into two parts. First, we describe ex situ efforts to manage a captive population in the United States, as well as an overview of work completed to overcome the problem of ophidian *Paramyxovirus*. Our goal is to maximize the

*Department of Herpetology
Toledo Zoological Society
2700 Broadway
Toledo, Ohio 43609, USA

**5971 East 18th Street
Tuscon, Arizona 85711, USA

Acronyms used in this chapter:

AAZPA	American Association of Zoological Parks and Aquariums
F	Inbreeding coefficient
FGE	Founder Genome Equivalents
H_e	Heterozygosity
OPV	Ophidian *Paramyxovirus*
PHVA	Population and Habitat Viability Assessment workshop
SSP	Species Survival Plan
ST	Studbook number

genetic diversity of wild populations, and to cope with the pathogen that has had a substantial negative impact on the demographics of the captive population. This disease complicates any attempt for future release of animals on Aruba Island. Secondly, we describe in situ work on Aruba that includes field research, and a public relations and education campaign for *unicolor* on Aruba Island.

Captive Population

Genetic and Demographic Management

As with individual SSP programs in general, the science used to manage a propagation scheme has evolved. A more detailed methodology of the demographic and genetic analysis of an SSP population has been omitted from this paper. In the early 1980s, the dominant basis for genetic management relied upon founder contribution. By the mid-1980s, retaining founder genomes became the principal emphasis. This was later refined with the concept of Founder Genome Equivalents (FGE) (Lacy 1989), which is defined as the number of new, unrelated, wild-caught animals required to maintain the genetic diversity which is found in the present captive population. Methods for choosing breeding pairs included "maximum avoidance of inbreeding" (Flesness 1977), equalization of founder contribution (Foose et al. 1986), the Founder Importance Coefficient (FIC) (J. D. Ballou, pers. comm., 1989), and the Mean Kinship (MK) (Ballou and Lacy, in press). In implementing the *Crotalus durissus unicolor* SSP program, we have followed these developments and refinements in propagation schemes, and are currently using Mean Kinship and inbreeding as the basis for choosing breeding pairs.

An overall genetic goal for the captive population of the *unicolor* SSP has been established to maintain 90% of the expected genetic diversity of the wild population (defined as the amount of the expected heterozygosity in a random breeding population, H_e) for a period of 200 years (Soulé et al. 1986). For captive animals, a carrying capacity of 250 individuals was established. The genetic-retention goal and carrying-capacity goals are based on a compromise between minimizing the loss of genetic diversity, and maintaining a manageable captive population size that is not at high risk of extinction from deterministic and stochastic events. SSP population size for any single taxon must be limited so that a maximum number of taxa can be accommodated in the limited captive space available. Limitations on the SSP carrying capacity were made to minimize the impact on other species competing for captive space.

Since 1982, a captive population database has been maintained in the International Studbook for the Aruba Island Rattlesnake (Peterson 1992). This database was computerized, using software specifically developed for the *unicolor* SSP program in an xbase language (Borland International) for IBM-compatible personal computers (Odum 1990). An xbase language was selected because it allowed easy data manipulation and translation into other formats for genetic and demographic analysis.

Initial genetic analysis (using Lacy 1991; Mace 1986) of the captive population in 1982 established the effects of unmanaged breeding within the population. Founder contribution was heavily skewed (calculated to be 60%) for one individual founder (Figure 1), and a large portion of the captive population was inbred (inbreeding coefficient, $F > 0.25$). Only 67.5% of the expected wild gene diversity (H_e) was found in the captive population. This was far below the 90% goal of the program, which required a minimum of 20 founders (H_e = 97.5%) at its initiation (computer model of Ballou 1989). The actual number of Founder Genome Equivalents (FGE) for the population in 1982 was 1.537.

To correct this problem, actions were taken to improve the skewed founder contributions and maximize FGE. By 1991, the FGE were increased to

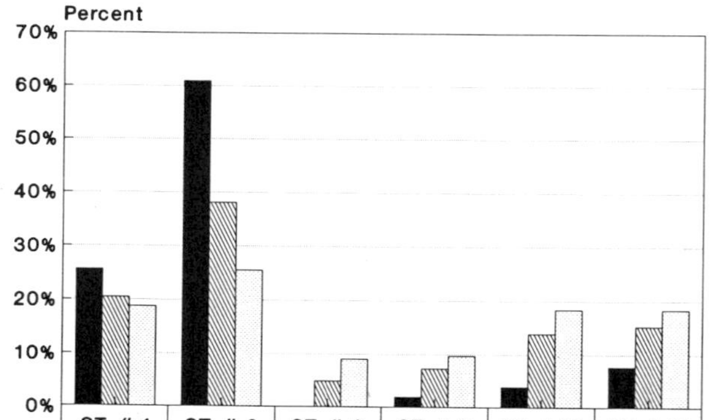

	ST # 1	ST # 2	ST # 3	ST # 5	ST # 13	ST # 14
1982	25.642%	60.896%	0%	1.923%	3.846%	7.692%
1988	20.441%	38.134%	4.878%	7.279%	13.974%	15.294%
1991	18.827%	25.474%	9.068%	9.754%	18.444%	18.434%

FIGURE 1. Founder representation of each founder (indicated by studbook number, ST) for the captive population.

3.165 (Figure 2) through selective breeding, as well as through the removal of surplus animals, which were from over-represented founders of unknown pedigrees, or which had an inbreeding coefficient (F) greater than 0.25. This is reflected by the increase of expected heterozygosity (H_e) to 86.2%. Although this was a substantial improvement over the H_e at the program's initiation, additional, unrelated founding stock would have been required to achieve our overall genetic goals.

To support the AAZPA conservation efforts, ten additional, unrelated, potential founders were imported into the United States in 1989. With the inclusion of these new, wild-caught animals in the SSP program, the potential H_e in the captive population increased to 96.5%. In 1991, another ten potential founders were imported, bringing the potential H_e to 97.9%. The inclusion of these new animals has made the goal of 90% H_e in 200 years feasible.

A method to compare the actual heterozygosity to the calculated H_e in future captive generation of *unicolor* was needed. As part of the field-research project (mentioned below), blood was collected from 25 wild-born individuals as a genetic reference. In the future, the heterozygosity in the captive population can be compared to the amount of heterozygosity in this base sample. This will make it possible to determine the effectiveness of the breeding schemes employed within the SSP program.

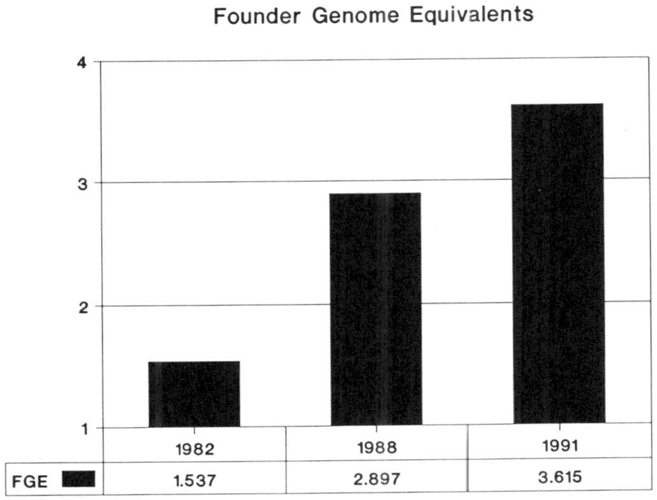

FIGURE 2. Gene diversity sampled in the descendant captive population measured in Founder Genome Equivalents (FGE).

Paramyxovirus

Preliminary demographic analysis of the captive population in 1983 identified ophidian *Paramyxovirus* (OPV) as a significant factor affecting the longevity of *Crotalus durissus unicolor* in American zoos. At several institutions, epidemics resulted in considerable mortality. Although no statistical evaluation has been performed, *unicolor* appears to be especially susceptible to this disease. Thus, we explored ways to protect the captive population from this virulent pathogen.

Ophidian *Paramyxovirus* was first identified as the cause of death of a group of *Bothrops moojeni* in Switzerland in the 1970s (Fölsch and Leloup 1976). Since that time, OPV has been implicated in many epidemics in captive snakes throughout the world. It has been identified in most major herpetological collections in United States zoos. Reptiles are easily transportable, as reflected in the huge numbers imported into the United States (Dodd 1986), which results in the establishment of OPV as a pandemic pathogen in captive collections.

Steps to protect the captive population of *unicolor* from OPV were initiated. This pathogen is a virus that is not directly eliminated through antibiotic therapy, and no anti-viral drugs have yet been tested. Little is known of the long-term pathology of this disease, and once an animal has been exposed, it may die, or perhaps harbor the virus indefinitely. Our initial approach to protect captives focused first on immunization by vaccination prior to exposure, rather than on post-exposure management.

Prior to 1988, no vaccination studies had been performed on a snake. During 1988 and 1989, killed-OPV-vaccine trials took place at the Houston Zoo in a cooperative effort with the University of Florida, Gainesville (Jacobson et al. 1991). Twenty-three *Crotalus atrox* were used as a model for viperid snakes. The products tested included three killed-virus preparations: one without, and two with adjuvants, and a control inoculant. Test animals were bled at two-week intervals and antibody response to the vaccine was measured by hemaglutination inhibition. Jacobson's study established that snakes can respond to a killed-virus vaccine by producing antibodies, although these responses were not identified in all test animals. The response, when it occurred, was minimal and transient. No live-virus challenges were made on this study group of *atrox*.

The development of an effective vaccine will probably be a long-term effort that will require many additional product trials. Because the effectiveness of any preparation may be species-specific, it will be necessary to test vaccines on *unicolor*. SSP surplus *unicolor* have been set aside for future vaccine trials. One trial has already been performed. This was a preliminary study that tested a modified live vaccine (J. Flanagan, pers. comm.), and resulted in the death of one *unicolor* that received the test product. Additional product tests are scheduled to take place in 1993 or 1994.

Other studies to determine an incubation period of the OPV disease were performed at the Toledo Zoo in 1990–1991. Results determined an incubation period of 70 days from exposure to morbidity (R. A. Odum and M. Lloyd, unpubl. data). A carrier state was also identified in which animals showed some clinical signs of the disease, and were infectious. One animal remained infectious for approximately one year before its death. Jacobson plans future studies, including trials of several other vaccine products, and the development of a new test for direct identification of OPV in tissue samples.

In Situ Conservation

Field Work

In 1982, a literature search revealed that there were few published data about the wild population of *Crotalus durissus unicolor* on Aruba. The most recent information available was from several herpetologists at zoos, who visited the island and did not find any *unicolor* after substantial searching. To learn more about the status of the wild population, and to obtain life-history data for this taxon, a one-year field project was initiated in late 1988. It is not the intent of this chapter to present detailed findings of this field work (R. A. Odum and M. J. Goode, in prep.). The following is a brief preliminary overview of our findings.

During this project, observations of free ranging *unicolor* included courtships ($n > 10$) and copulations ($n = 4$). Data were obtained from approximately 40 *unicolor*. Study animals were obtained by intensive ground searching, as well as by receiving specimens collected by Arubans. Radiotelemetry was used to monitor several wild-caught specimens for movements, intraspecific interactions, and habitat preference. Several gravid females were also held in captivity to obtain data on brood size, neonate size, and neonate sex ratio. Data were also collected from wild-caught animals that were being held in captivity on Aruba.

Through interviews, information was also obtained from Aruban citizens about sightings and incidental take of *unicolor* which proved invaluable in determining the current range. Our research established that *unicolor* is still found on Aruba in reasonable numbers, and that the wild population is breeding successfully.

Public Relations and Education

Public relations and education programs began on Aruba in conjunction with the field-research project in 1988–1989. A primary focus of this campaign was to increase the awareness of the Aruban people of their native fauna, with particular emphasis on the native rattlesnake. Adult Arubans were the target group for the public relations campaign, and school-age children were the target group for the education program.

The campaign established contacts with local media. Numerous stories were published in newspapers and magazines (in Dutch, in Papiamentu [the local Aruban language], and in English), and radio and television interviews were broadcast. Lectures were also given to social groups on the island. A great deal of interest was shown by Arubans toward the "American snake experts" working on the island. The researchers became well known to the general public, and were frequently recognized by local people, who were usually happy to express their opinions with regard to the rattlesnake.

Although no formal surveys were taken, there was an increased awareness by Arubans of the existence of the rattlesnake through the course of this public relations campaign. This awareness seemed to be accompanied by a generally positive attitude towards the snake. Most people did not perceive the rattlesnakes as a threat, and many people felt that the animal had a right to exist. A great deal of time was spent talking to people to establish and reinforce positive points of view about the natural environment of Aruba.

In addition to this public relations campaign, we made efforts to contact and talk to school groups on Aruba. This education program focused on grade-school and middle-school students. Because the fate of the Aruban ecosystem ultimately lies in future generations of citizens and leaders of Aruba, it was felt that these groups could have a significant impact on the long-term conservation strategy for *Crotalus durissus unicolor*. These young age-groups were usually more receptive to new ideas. Through numerous lectures, it is hoped that the probability of the survival of *unicolor* on Aruba will increase through the next century.

Summary

The Aruba Island rattlesnake Species Survival Plan is an ongoing effort to advance the conservation of this insular form, and to protect its critical habitat. We have made significant advances toward the long-term conservation of *Crotalus durissus unicolor* on Aruba (see Table 1). In February 1992, an International Symposium and a Population and Habitat Viability Assessment (PHVA) workshop were conducted on Aruba. These meetings were a cooperative effort of the AAZPA SSP, the IUCN–World Conservation Union Captive Breeding Specialist Group, and the Aruba Department of Agriculture, Husbandry, and Fishes.

The meetings were a continuation of the multifaceted approach to the many conservation issues regarding *unicolor*. They included a general symposium to review the available data on *unicolor*, a snake envenomation workshop for medical professionals, a teachers' workshop to demonstrate techniques for teaching conservation issues to students, and the PHVA. The location (Aruba Island) for the meetings was specifically chosen to involve as many local residents as possible. Attending the meetings were members of Aruba government agencies, FINAPA (national parks), STIMARUBA (an active conservation organization on Aruba Island), and Arubans with an interest in conservation, as well as a number of American and Dutch conservation workers with expertise in a variety of biological disciplines.

The PHVA has resulted in the formulation of an Action Plan that was prepared by the workshop attendees (Aruban, Dutch, and American). The Action Plan focusses on both the captive and wild populations and will address habitat utilization

TABLE 1. Action Plan Summary for the Aruba Island Rattlesnake, *Crotalus durissus unicolor*, devised during the Population and Habitat Viability Assessment workshop in February 1992.

Wild population

1. Designate current "Preservation Zone" as National Park.
2. Designate remaining *unicolor* habitat adjacent to the National Park as a "Conservation Management Zone." Proposals for development in this area should be reviewed to assess the impact on the rattlesnake prior to alteration of habitat.
3. Recognize the endangered status of *unicolor* and afford the snake legal protection on Aruba.
4. List *unicolor* in Appendix II of CITES.
5. Continue education programs for educators, adults, and school children about conservation and the value of *unicolor* in the ecosystem.
6. Control importation of exotic species.
7. Reduce the probability of extinction of the wild population to less than 1% for the next 100 years.
8. Manage the wild population for a minimum of 1000 animals greater than one year of age.
9. Design additional field studies of population status and population dynamics which is essential to provide quantitative data on the decline, critical threats, and to develop techniques for long term monitoring of the wild population.
10. Train Aruban biology and wildlife technicians to provide expertise for the long-term management of the National Parks and Conservation Management Zones.

Captive population

1. Maintain the captive population as a backup for the wild population.
2. Maintain a minimum of 95% of the gene diversity of the wild population indefinitely.
3. Expand the captive population to include Europe and other areas of the world.
4. Establish a captive carrying capacity of 150–200 animals in the United States.
5. Import additional unrelated animals every generation to maintain desired gene diversity.

and species management. The goal for the captive population has been changed to maintain 95% of the H_e indefinitely, as a backup for the wild population. This will require the importation of several additional animals (founders) from Aruba each generation, or approximately every ten years. A goal for the wild population was established to reduce the probability of extinction of *unicolor* during the next 100 years to less than 1%. This will be accomplished by (1) setting aside sufficient habitat on the Island as National Park and "Conservation Management Zone" to support a viable population, (2) initiating legal protection to reduce incidental take, (3) increasing education efforts for school-age and adult Arubans, and (4) using the captive population as a backup. A more complete listing of the objectives of the Action Plan is presented in Table 1.

Acknowledgments

The authors would like to thank the Houston Zoo and the Toledo Zoo for their support in these efforts. Special acknowledgment must be made to the Coastal Aruba Refining Co, N.V., a subsidiary of the Coastal Corporation of Houston, Texas, for their generous funding of the International Symposium and PHVA workshop conducted in February 1992. The authors would also like to thank Tom Barmes—without his support for this program and his personal commitment to the conservation of Aruban fauna, this work would not have been possible.

Literature Cited

Ballou, J. D. 1989. CAPTIVITY Version 2.11: Wordtech Quicksilver Dbase Compiler, Computer Software to Calculate Carrying Capacity from N_e, Generation Time, Gopulation Growth Rate, and Program Duration and Goals. National Zoological Park, Washington, D.C.

Ballou, J. D., and T. Foose. In press. Demographic and genetic management of captive populations. *In* D. Kleiman and S. Lumpkin (eds.), Wild Mammals in Captivity. Univ. Chicago Press, Chicago.

Ballou, J. D., and R. Lacy. In press. Identifying genetically important individuals for the management of genetic variation in pedigreed populations. *In* J. D. Ballou, A. Gilpin, and T. J. Foose (eds.), Population Management for Survival and Recovery. Columbia Univ. Press, New York.

Dodd, C. K. 1986. Importation of live snakes and snake products into the United States, 1977–1983. Herpetol. Rev., 17: 76–79.

Flesness, N. 1977. Gene pool conservation and computer analysis. Internatl. Zoo Yearbook, 17: 77–81.

Fölsch, D. W., and P. Leloup. 1976. Über eine verlustreich verlaufene Infektion in einen Schlangenbestand. Verhandlungsbericht des XVII. Internationalen Symposiums über die Erkrankungen der Zootiere. Akademie-Verlag (Berlin), 18: 159–166.

Foose, T. J. 1983. The relevance of captive propagation to the conservation of biotic diversity, p. 374–401. *In* C. M. Schonewald-Cox, S. M. Chambers, B. Macbride, and L. Thomas (eds.), Genetics and Conservation. Benjamin/Cummings, Menlo Park, California.

Foose, T. J., R. Lande, N. Flesness, G. Rabb, and B. Read. 1986. Propagation plans. Zoo Biol., 5: 139–146.

Jacobson, E., J. M. Gaskin, J. P. Flanagan, and R. A. Odum. 1991. Antibody responses to Western Diamondback Rattlesnake, *Crotalus atrox*, to inactivated ophidian *Paramyxovirus* vaccines. Jour. Zoo Wildlife Med., 22: 184–190.

Lacy, R. C. 1989. Analysis of founder representation in a pedigree: founder equivalents and founder genome equivalents. Zoo Biol., 8: 111–124.

—. 1991. GENES: C Program to Perform Genetic Analysis on Single Taxon Databases, Version 9.2. Brookfield Zool. Soc., Chicago, Illinois.

Mace, G. 1986. GENEDROP: Computer Software for Gene Drop Analysis. Zool. Soc. London, UK.

Odum, R. A. 1990. Studbook Management System, Version 3.0 Software. Toledo Zool. Soc. and Houston Zool. Gardens.

Peterson, K. H. 1992. International Studbook for the Aruba Island Rattlesnake, 1992 edition. Houston Zool. Gardens, Houston, Texas. 55 pages.

Soulé, M. E., M. Gilpin, W. Conway, and T. Foose. 1986. The Millennium Ark: how long a voyage, how many staterooms, how many passengers? Zoo Biol., 5: 101–113.

Odum, R. A., and M. J. Goode. 1994. The species survival plan for *Crotalus durissus unicolor*: a multifaceted approach to conservation of an insular rattlesnake, p. 363–368. *In* J. B. Murphy, K. Adler, and J. T. Collins (eds.), Captive Management and Conservation of Amphibians and Reptiles. Society for the Study of Amphibians and Reptiles, Ithaca (New York). Contributions to Herpetology, volume 11.

Artificial Refugia as a Habitat-Improvement Strategy for Snake Conservation

Robert T. Zappalorti* and Howard K. Reinert**

Introduction

Wildlife management often involves habitat manipulation to create improved living conditions for species of particular interest (Yoakum and Dasmann 1969; Yoakum 1971). For many years, such efforts have been commonly and successfully used in game and sport fish management (White 1971). With the exception of nest boxes for songbirds, however, such procedures have only recently been applied to non-game and endangered animal species.

Programs for the management of snake species have traditionally fallen under the category of "pest control," and have usually been aimed at reducing the population size or limiting the occurrence of snakes in the vicinity of human habitations (Allen 1961; Klauber 1972; Knight 1986; Brown 1993). The increasingly evident decline of amphibian and reptilian populations (Ashton 1976; Dodd 1987; Corbett 1989) has begun to emphasize the need for management techniques that can be successfully implemented to improve environmental conditions for these unpopular, but important, members of natural communities.

*Herpetological Associates, Inc.
2525 Dover Road, Bamber Lake
Forked River, New Jersey 08731, USA

**Department of Biology
Trenton State College
Hillwood Lakes, CN 4700
Trenton, New Jersey 08650–4700, USA

Acronyms used in this chapter:

ANOVA Analysis of variance
PVC Polyvinyl chloride
SE Standard error of mean

Although human population growth and its resultant destruction of habitat is considered a major factor in the decline of many wildlife species, several species of amphibians and reptiles are commonly associated with artificial structures or disturbed areas (Wilson and Porras 1983; Schwartz and Henderson 1991). The propensity of certain species to be associated with human-altered habitats led Ashton and Ashton (1981) to include such areas as a habitat category for the Florida herpetofauna. In particular, some snakes seem to have little aversion to disturbed areas (Blaesing 1979; Zappalorti and Burger 1985), and several species are commonly found in the vicinity of human habitation. Human-induced habitat changes may inadvertently provide suitable microclimatic conditions, increased or concentrated food supplies, or accessible overwintering sites (Owens 1949; Gillingham 1974).

During 1981–1982, several shed skins of Corn Snakes (*Elaphe guttata*) and Pine Snakes (*Pituophis melanoleucus*) were found at what appeared to be a natural underground refugium in southern New Jersey. Excavation of the site in July 1982 revealed that it was not natural, but synthetic. The refugium consisted of construction debris, such as lumber, metal, and rubber mats, that had been buried approximately 2 m deep in a 2.5 × 3.5 m trench. The excavation of the site yielded one Pine Snake, one Milk Snake (*Lampropeltis triangulum*), three Corn Snakes, two freshly laid clutches of Corn Snake eggs (25 eggs), and 22 shells of hatched egg from the previous years. It was apparent from these findings that a successful snake refugium had been inadvertently constructed. This led Zappalorti to purposely design and build similar structures for use by snakes. Since 1982, a total of 43 such artificial refugia have been constructed in the Pine Barrens of southern New Jersey. This chapter summarizes our continuing monitoring program of the use of these artificial structures by snakes.

Study Area

This research was conducted in a 2,833-ha area in Ocean County, New Jersey. Approximately 37% (1,043 ha) of the land had been developed as residential communities. The remaining 1,790 ha were typical coastal plain forest, dominated by Pitch Pine (*Pinus rigida*) and various oaks (*Quercus marilandica*, *Q. ilicifolia*, and *Q. velutina*). A more detailed vegetational description of the study area is given by Zappalorti and Burger (1985). General descriptions of coastal plain forests in New Jersey can be found in Forman (1979). Elevations ranged from 3 to 38 m above sea level. Approximately 20 km of sand, gravel, or paved roads traversed the area, and a 30-m wide, common right-of-way for public sewer and electric transmission lines bisected the area from east to west.

Artificial Refugia

A total of 25 refugia was constructed on the study area during 1985–1986. These were positioned from 53 m to 589 m apart (mean distance between refugia 188 m, SE 29.5 m) along 5 km of the sewer and electric right-of-way.

Each refugium (Figure 1) was constructed using 22 pressure-treated railroad ties, 14 m of 7.5-cm-diameter, perforated, plastic (PVC) pipe, 4.5 m^2 of plastic sheeting or tar paper, and several stumps, logs, and branches. After removal of surface vegetation, a 2-m-wide, 4.5-m-long, 1.8-m-deep trench was excavated. Two full-length (2.6 m) railroad ties

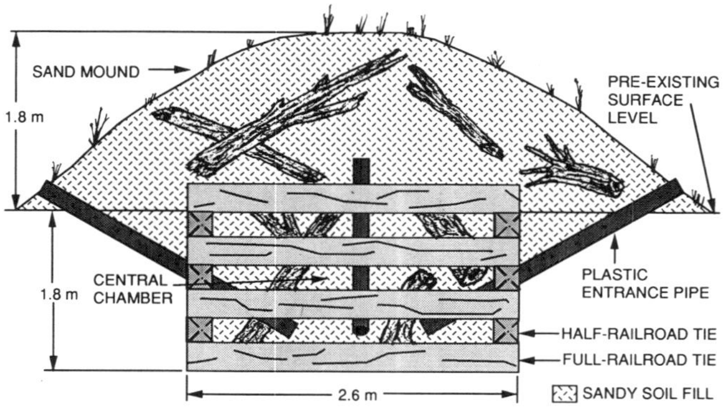

FIGURE 1. Structural design of underground refugia. Refer to adjacent text for construction details.

FIGURE 2. A completed refugium with surface shelters for snakes provided by old railroad ties.

were laid on the floor of the trench along each side, and two half-ties (1.3 m) were placed on top of the full-ties at each end to form a rectangle. The ties were secured to one another with large nails to prevent separation over time. This alternate stacking procedure of full-ties and half-ties was repeated four times to form a rectangular box. Four 3.5-m-long sections of plastic, perforated pipe (7.5 cm in diameter) were placed on each side of the structure to serve as entrances to the central chamber (Figure 1). These entrance pipes extended from the ground surface to the bottom of the chamber at an angle of approximately 35 degrees from the horizontal, and were staked in place to prevent movement. The central chamber was then filled with stumps, logs, branches, and sandy soil. The top of the structure was formed using eight ties nailed side by side and covered with plastic sheeting or tar paper to prevent water from filling the chamber during heavy rains. Finally, logs, stumps, and branches were piled on top of the structure to a height of 1 m, and the entire structure was covered with sandy soil until a mound approximately 1.8-m high was formed. Vegetation that was originally removed from the ground surface was replanted on the mound, and several logs or old railroad ties were scattered about the mound (Figure 2).

Sampling Period and Procedures

Between the spring of 1987 and the fall of 1989, the 25 refugia were subjected to 1,679 hours of observation. Systematic searches were performed at refugia during each visit. One or two observers walked slowly toward a refugium until it was clearly visible. Entrance pipes and non-vegetated areas in the vicinity were scanned with binoculars for the presence of exposed snakes. If no snakes were observed from several vantage points, the structure was slowly approached, and the area within a 10-m radius was surveyed for up to 15 minutes. The entrance pipes were checked with a flashlight.

Observations of snake activity at refugia were placed in one of the following seven categories:

(1) Ingress or egress—snakes with some portion of their body in direct contact with a refugium entrance pipe;

(2) Exposed—snakes observed in a coiled or sedentary position on the ground surface;

(3) Concealed—snakes found hidden under shelter objects, such as logs, stumps, or railroad ties;

(4) Mating—snakes of the same species and different sex found coiled together either copulating or in some phase of courtship behavior;

(5) Ovipositing—female snakes found in the process of excavating a nest burrow (Burger and Zappalorti 1991) or laying eggs;

(6) Shedding—snakes found in premolt condition (opaque), in the process of ecdysis, or observation of a shed skin; and

(7) Active—snakes observed actively crawling.

It is obvious that several of these categories are not mutually exclusive. For simplicity, each observed snake was placed in the one activity category that best represented its behavior and required the least subjectivity on the part of the observer. For example, any snake having opaque eyes or skin was placed in the "shedding" category regardless of other behavior exhibited. Repeated observations of the same specimen were not included in the following analyses.

Chi-square comparisons of behavior frequencies between species were performed in accordance with the methods of Zar (1984). Analysis of variance (ANOVA) and unplanned comparisons of mean monthly observation frequencies were performed following the methods of Sokal and Rohlf (1981).

Results

A total of 139 snakes of nine different species were observed at 17 of the 25 artificial refugia during the three-year period (Table 1). Pine Snakes comprised the greatest percentage (52.5%) of snakes observed during both overwintering (November 1 to April 30)

TABLE 1. Number of individual snakes of nine species observed at artificial refugia from 1987 through 1989.

Species	Overwintering (November 1 to April 30)	Active period (May 1 to October 31)	Total
Pine Snake (*Pituophis melanoleucus*)	40	33	73
Corn Snake (*Elaphe guttata*)	15	32	47
Racer (*Coluber constrictor*)	1	6	7
Eastern Hognose Snake (*Heterodon platirhinos*)	1	3	4
Common Garter Snake (*Thamnophis sirtalis*)	1	2	3
Milk Snake (*Lampropeltis triangulum*)	0	2	2
Common Kingsnake (*Lampropeltis getula*)	0	1	1
Eastern Ribbon Snake (*Thamnophis sauritus*)	0	1	1
Rough Green Snake (*Opheodrys aestivus*)	0	1	1
Totals:	58	81	139 individuals

and active-season periods (May 1 to October 31). Corn Snakes were the next most frequently observed species at refugia (33.8% of observed snakes). Combined, these two species accounted for 94.8% of the snakes observed to use these structures as overwintering sites, and 80.2% of the snakes observed during the active season.

Snakes were observed utilizing the structures for a broad variety of behaviors during the active season. Figure 3 illustrates the relative frequency of various behaviors exhibited by the two most commonly observed species, Corn Snakes and Pine Snakes. A Chi-square analysis (2 × 7 contingency table) indicated that the relative frequency of observed behaviors differed significantly between these two species ($\chi^2_{(6)} = 49.15, P < 0.01$). Pine snakes were most frequently observed lying exposed on the ground surface, often basking on the mound itself (Figure 4). In comparison, Corn Snakes were most frequently found under the shelter objects, such as logs, stumps, or railroad ties, that had been placed around each refugium. Both species were commonly observed entering or exiting refugia, indicating the use of these structures as active season shelters (Figure 5). In addition, ecdysis, courtship, mating, and ovipositing were observed for both species at refugia. Six clutches of Pine Snake eggs and ten clutches of Corn Snake eggs were known to be laid in refugia during the three-year study period. It is suspected, however, that nesting at refugia was more frequent than these fortuitous observations indicate. To avoid excessive disturbance, extensive

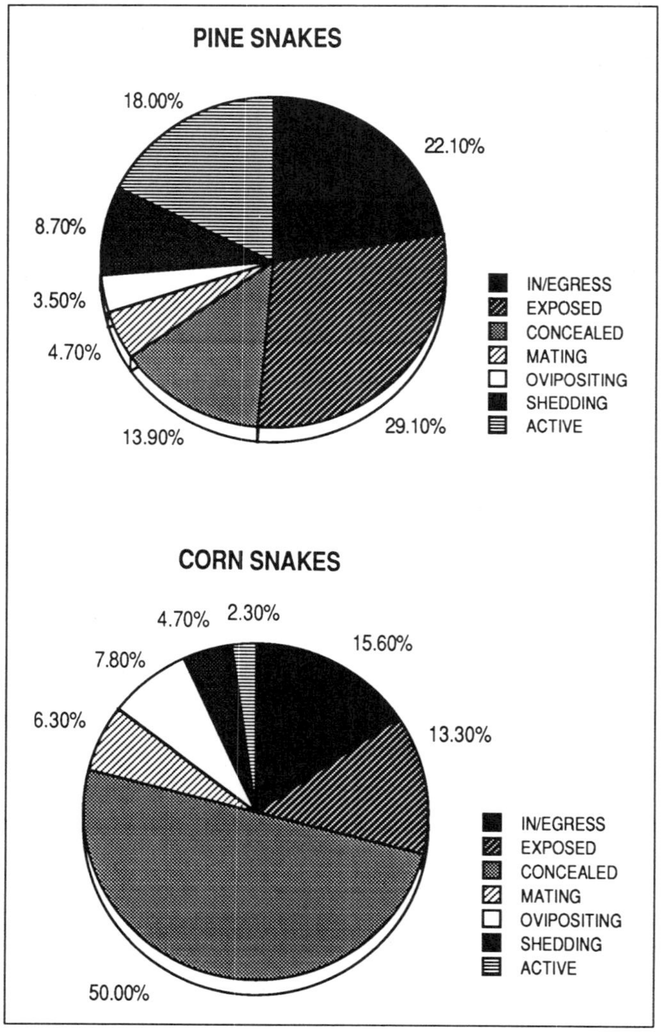

FIGURE 3. Comparison of the relative frequency of behaviors of Pine Snakes (*Pituophis melanoleucus*) and Corn Snakes (*Elaphe guttata*) observed at artificial refugia.

FIGURE 4. Two Pine Snakes (*Pituophis melanoleucus*) observed utilizing a refugium as a basking and/or foraging location.

excavations in search of eggs were not routinely performed at refugia. Egg clutches were usually discovered when neonatal snakes were observed emerging from the refugia after hatching.

Because of unequal sampling efforts during the three years, the data were transformed into "snakes observed per hour of sampling" to facilitate comparisons. A one-way ANOVA (model I) indicated that the mean monthly frequencies of observation of snakes per hour at artificial refugia differed significantly ($F_{s(7,16)} = 3.70$, $P < 0.05$). This suggests the occurrence of seasonal trends in the use of refugia. Snakes were observed with the highest frequency during the spring and fall months, as they entered or emerged from hibernation at the structures (Figure 6). Unplanned comparisons of mean monthly frequencies using the T-Method (Sokal and Rohlf 1981) indicated that, in July and August, significantly lower numbers of snakes were observed per hour than in October ($P < 0.05$). The low observation frequencies in July and August possibly resulted from either nocturnal behavior patterns or an increase in the use of surrounding woodland by snakes.

Figure 7 illustrates the frequency of observation of snakes (in snakes observed per hour of sampling) at each refugium over the three-year-study period. The number of structures exhibiting snake activity increased from five in 1987, to seven in 1988, and finally to 17 in 1989.

In addition to the snakes reported, several other species of reptiles and amphibians were observed in the vicinity (less than 10 m radius) of refugia. The most frequently observed species were Eastern Box Turtles (*Terrapene carolina*), Fence Lizards (*Sceloporus undulatus*), Ground Skinks (*Scincella lateralis*), and Woodhouse's Toads (*Bufo woodhousii*).

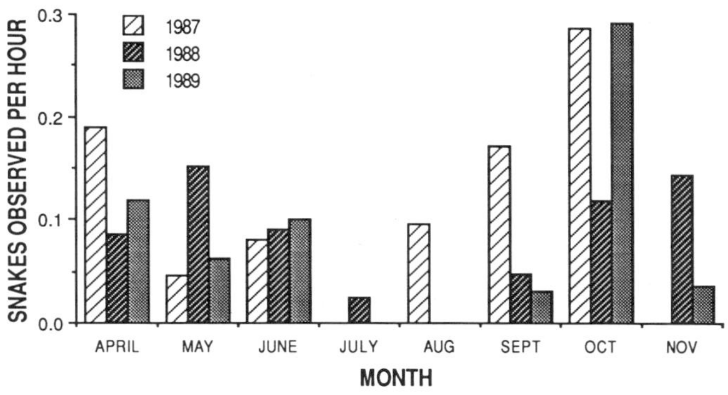

FIGURE 6. Monthly frequency of observation of snakes at artificial refugia.

FIGURE 5. A Corn Snake (*Elaphe guttata*) emerging from a refugium entrance pipe following hibernation.

Discussion

Previous investigators have constructed artificial hibernacula for a variety of experimental purposes (Goris 1971; Gillingham and Carpenter 1978). We are unaware, however, of any prior effort to design and construct refugia for use by free-ranging snakes in natural habitats. Our observations suggest that such structures may be useful as a habitat-improvement technique for snake conservation. It is clear that a large number of snakes, representing a diverse array of species, located and used our refugia within three years of their construction. The refugia have been particularly successful at attracting Pine Snakes and Corn Snakes for use as overwintering and nesting sites. Both of these species have demonstrated declining populations in New Jersey, and are officially listed as threatened (Pine Snake) or endangered (Corn Snake) by the New Jersey Department of Environmental Protection and Energy.

Natural hibernacula of Pine Snakes and Corn Snakes are usually associated with the decaying root systems of tree stumps or mammal burrows (Burger et al. 1988). Suitable hibernation sites may be a limited resource for certain snake species (Graves et al. 1986; Burger et al. 1988), and high mortality may occur during the first winter, due to the inability of hatchling snakes to locate safe refugia (Fukada 1978). Although it is presently unknown whether our artificial refugia have resulted in any increases in the population sizes through increased survival or reproductive success, they do provide suitable habitat for a wide variety of ecologically significant activities for these and other snake species.

Although a majority of the refugia have exhibited snake activity over time, it appears that the placement of a refugium may greatly influence its attractiveness to snakes and its frequency of use. Surrounding habitat and topography may play an important role in determining the activity at any particular structure. Upland habitat used by Pine Snakes as nesting areas (Burger and Zappalorti 1986) is located near several of the refugia that exhibited frequent snake activity (for example, refugia numbers 3, 5, 6, 12, 20, and 24 [Figure 7]). Refugia exhibiting little or no snake activity since their construction (for example, refugia numbers 7, 8, 17, and 18 [Figure 7]) are in the vicinity of streams and wetlands which are dominated by White Cedar (*Chamaecyparis thyoides*).

Along the right-of-way, high frequencies of snake observations occurred at approximately 1.5- to 2-km intervals. This could represent a natural spacing distance for hibernacula that may result from the relative distance to suitable nesting and foraging sites and the maximum activity ranges of members of subpopulations or kin-groups. However, detailed information on the spacing of natural refugia, or the movements and genetic relationships of snakes in the vicinity of either artificial or natural refugia, is currently unavailable. If low use continues at intermediate structures, construction efforts could be substantially reduced by building fewer refugia at greater intervals.

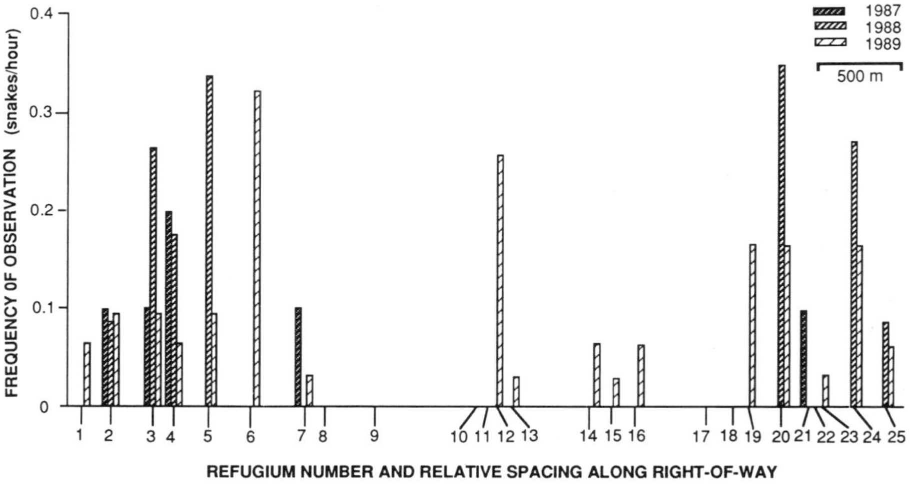

FIGURE 7. Frequency of observation of snakes at 25 artificial refugia along a 5 km public utility right-of-way. These data suggest that an increasing number of the structures were used by snakes over the three-year study period.

Summary

In an effort to improve snake habitat by providing artificial shelters, we constructed 25 subterranean refugia along a 5-km section of a sewer and electric line right-of-way in southern New Jersey. By the end of the three-year study period, snake activity had been observed at 17 (68%) of the structures. The bulk of the observations were of Corn Snakes (*Elaphe guttata*) and Pine Snakes (*Pituophis melanoleucus*). These two species utilized the refugia with high frequency for winter hibernation and for shelter, ovipositing, courtship, shedding, and basking during the active season. Seven other species of snakes (Table 1) also were observed at the structures during the study. Our observations indicate that snakes will locate and use artificial refugia which are placed in suitable habitat. Such structures may improve existing snake habitat by creating favorable sites for biologically important behaviors.

In the years since their construction, an increasing number of these structures have served as hibernacula, active-season shelters, nesting sites, and basking habitat for snakes. This suggests that the construction of artificial refugia may be an effective method for improving snake habitat. Long-term studies are currently underway in an effort to determine if the presence of artificial refugia results in an increase in snake population levels, and to compare the use of artificial refugia with that of natural refugia.

Acknowledgments

The Ocean County Utilities Authority constructed the 25 refugia as part of a mitigation plan. Jersey Central Power and Light Company (General Public Utilities) provided substantial funding for the intensive monitoring of the refugia. Authorization and necessary permits were supplied by the New Jersey Department of Environmental Protection and Energy,

Division of Fish, Game and Wildlife (Endangered and Nongame Species Program). Herpetological Associates, Inc., provided additional support, necessary supplies, and long-term funding for this project. The use of a field research station was provided by the Ocean County Planning Board and Engineering Department.

We thank J. Burger, L. Bushar, W. Callaghan, P. Danch, R. Fengya, M. Fergusson, R. Ford, M. Gochfeld, O. Heck, E. Johnson, J. Milos, P. Mooney, and P. Vargas-Zappalorti for their assistance with various aspects of this project. We are especially grateful to Gianluca Rocco and James Dowdell for their dedication to this project and for their long hours in the field monitoring refugia.

Literature Cited

Allen, R. 1961. How to Hunt the Eastern Diamondback Rattlesnake for Rattlesnake Control Programs. Publ. Ross Allen's Reptile Institute, Silver Springs, Florida. 20 pages.

Ashton, R. E., Jr. (ed.) 1976. Endangered and threatened species of amphibians and reptiles in the United States. Soc. Study Amphib. Reptiles, Herpetol. Circ., 5: 1–65.

Ashton, R. E., Jr., and P. S. Ashton. 1981. Handbook of Reptiles and Amphibians of Florida. Part One: The Snakes. Windward Publ., Miami, Florida. 176 pages.

Blaesing, M. E. 1979. Some aspects of the ecology of the Eastern Garter Snake (*Thamnophis sirtalis sirtalis*) in a semi-disturbed habitat in west-central Illinois. Jour. Herpetol., 13: 177–181.

Brown, W. S. 1993. Biology, status, and management of the timber rattlesnake (*Crotalus horridus*): a guide for conservation. Soc. Study Amphib. Reptiles, Herpetol. Circ., 22: 1–78.

Burger, J., and R. T. Zappalorti. 1986. Nest site selection by pine snakes, *Pituophis melanoleucus*, in the New Jersey Pine Barrens. Copeia, 1986: 116–121.

—. 1991. Nesting behavior of pine snakes (*Pituophis m. melanoleucus*) in the New Jersey Pine Barrens. Jour. Herpetol., 25: 152–160.

Burger, J., R. T. Zappalorti, M. Gochfeld, W. I. Boarman, M. Caffrey, V. Doig, S. D. Garber, B. Lauro, M. Mikovsky, C. Safina, and J. Saliva. 1988. Hibernacula and summer den sites of pine snakes (*Pituophis melanoleucus*) in the New Jersey Pine Barrens. Jour. Herpetol., 22: 425–433.

Corbett K. 1989. Conservation of European Reptiles and Amphibians. Christopher Helm, London. 274 pages.

Dodd, C. K., Jr. 1987. Status, conservation, and management, p. 478–513. *In* R. A. Seigel, J. T. Collins, and S. S. Novak (eds.), Snakes: Ecology and Evolutionary Biology. McGraw Hill, New York.

Forman, R. T. T. 1979. Pine Barrens: Ecosystem and Landscape. Academic Press, New York. 601 pages.

Fukada, H. 1978. Growth and maturity of the Japanese rat snake, *Elaphe climacophora*. Jour. Herpetol., 12: 269–274.

Gillingham, J. C. 1974. Reproductive behavior in the western fox snake, *Elaphe v. vulpina* (Baird and Girard). Herpetologica, 30: 309–313.

Gillingham, J. C., and C. C. Carpenter. 1978. Snake hibernation: construction of and observations on a man-made hibernaculum (Reptilia, Serpentes). Jour. Herpetol., 12: 495–498.

Goris, R. C. 1971. The hibernation of captive snakes. Snake, 3: 65–69.

Graves, B. M., D. Duvall, M. B. King, S. L. Lindstedt, and W. A. Gern. 1986. Initial den location by neonatal prairie rattlesnakes: functions, causes, and natural history in chemical ecology, p. 285–304. *In* D. Duvall, D. Müller-Schwarze, and R. M. Silverstein (eds.), Chemical Signals in Vertebrates. Volume 4. Plenum Press, New York.

Klauber, L. M. 1972. Rattlesnakes: Their Habits, Life Histories and Influence on Mankind. Volumes 1–2. Univ. Calif. Press, Berkeley, California. xxx, 1536 pages.

Knight, J. E. 1986. A humane method for removing snakes from dwellings. Wildl. Soc. Bull., 14: 301–303.

Owens, V. 1949. An overwintering colony of *Coluber c. constrictor* (Say) and *Elaphe o. obsoleta* (Say). Herpetologica, 5: 90.

Schwartz, A., and R. W. Henderson. 1991. Amphibians and Reptiles of the West Indies: Descriptions, Distributions, and Natural History. Univ. Florida Press, Gainesville. xvi, 720 pages.

Sokal, R. R., and F. J. Rohlf. 1981. Biometry. W. H. Freeman, San Francisco, California. v, 859 pages.

White, R. J. 1971. Stream improvement, p. 106–110. *In* R. D. Teague (ed.), A Manual of Wildlife Conservation. The Wildlife Society, Washington, D. C.

Wilson, L. D., and L. Porras. 1983. The ecological impact of man on the south Florida herpetofauna. Univ. Kansas Mus. Nat. Hist. Spec. Publ., 9: 1–89.

Yoakum, J. 1971. Habitat improvement, p. 74–78. *In* R. D. Teague (ed.), A Manual of Wildlife Conservation. The Wildlife Society, Washington, D. C.

Yoakum, J., and W. P. Dasmann. 1969. Habitat manipulation practices, p. 173–231. *In* R. H. Giles, Jr. (ed.), Wildlife Management Techniques. The Wildlife Society, Washington, D. C.

Zappalorti, R. T., and J. Burger. 1985. On the importance of disturbed sites to habitat selection by pine snakes in the Pine Barrens of New Jersey. Environ. Cons., 12: 358–361.

Zar, J. H. 1984. Biostatistical Analysis. Prentice-Hall, Englewood Cliffs, New Jersey. xiv, 718 pages.

Zappalorti, R. T., and H. K. Reinert. 1994. Artificial refugia as a habitat-improvement strategy for snake conservation, p. 369–375. *In* J. B. Murphy, K. Adler, and J. T. Collins (eds.), Captive Management and Conservation of Amphibians and Reptiles. Society for the Study of Amphibians and Reptiles, Ithaca (New York). Contributions to Herpetology, volume 11.

THE CONTRIBUTION OF CAPTIVE MANAGEMENT TO THE CONSERVATION OF TUATARA (*SPHENODON*) IN NEW ZEALAND

ALISON CREE,* CHARLES H. DAUGHERTY,** DAVID R. TOWNS,*** AND BARBARA BLANCHARD****

Introduction

TUATARA (*SPHENODON*) ARE LIZARD-LIKE REPtiles, endemic to New Zealand, that are of tremendous international significance as the only surviving members of the Order Sphenodontida (*sensu* Fraser 1988). They are listed as rare in the 1988 Red List (IUCN 1988) and are on Appendix I of CITES (Convention on International Trade in Endangered Species of Wild Fauna and Flora). Tuatara became extinct on the two largest islands of New Zealand following the arrival of humans at about 1000 AD, and over the last 200 years have become extinct on at least ten of New Zealand's offshore islands. They currently survive on 30 offshore islands, which are mostly uninhabited and which represent an area that is less than 0.1% of tuatara's former range. Although tuatara are fully protected by law and public access to their islands is prohibited, the remaining populations remain vulnerable to continued decline (Daugherty et al. 1992).

Much has happened since 1988 when our previous review of captive breeding of tuatara was written (Cree and Daugherty 1990). In that review, we summarized the results of past attempts at captive breeding and concluded that, although captive breeding had the potential to contribute significantly to tuatara conservation, it had yet to do so in practice. In brief, more than 100 adult tuatara have been taken into captivity over the last century, and since 1952, at least 52 of these adults have been in pairs or groups in which breeding could potentially have occurred (Cree and Daugherty 1990, and unpubl. data). Despite these attempts, no captive-bred juvenile has been raised to sexual maturity, and thus no self-maintaining captive colony exists. Prior to the mid-1980s, captive maintenance had been largely for the purpose of display; the rare instances in which young were produced were a matter for jubilation rather than a consequence of informed and deliberate management. Little was known about reproduction in the wild, and almost all captive tuatara were from the single most abundant population. Indeed, the possibility of significant variation among wild populations of tuatara was discounted in New Zealand (Dawbin 1962, 1982; Robb 1977), despite the fact that existing taxonomy recognized several subspecies (Wettstein 1931, 1943; Wermuth and Mertens 1977).

In that review, we recommended the following goals to improve the role of captive management in the conservation of tuatara: (1) a survey of all known populations of tuatara to identify unique genetic stocks and/or populations threatened with extinction; (2) a comprehensive, national manage-

---

*Department of Zoology
University of Otago, Box 56
Dunedin, New Zealand

**School of Biological Sciences
Victoria University of Wellington, Box 600
Wellington, New Zealand

***Science and Research Division
Department of Conservation, P. B. 68908
Auckland, New Zealand

****Wellington Zoological Gardens
Newtown Park
Newtown, Wellington 2, New Zealand

Acronyms used in this chapter:

CITES	Convention on International Trade in Endangered Species of Wild Fauna and Flora
IUCN	International Union for the Conservation of Nature and Natural Resources
kPa	Kilopascals
TSD	Temperature-dependent sex determination
UNEP	United Nations Environment Program
WWF	World Wide Fund for Nature

ment plan for tuatara, which incorporates the role of captive breeding in conservation; (3) an integrated program of captive management among the many institutions holding tuatara in captivity; and (4) further research in specified areas to improve the success of captive breeding.

So many of these recommendations have been implemented that an update on captive management of tuatara is opportune. In this review we first briefly summarize progress as of 1991 on the first three recommendations listed above, and then expand on the significant role that captive breeding is now playing in conservation of the different genetic stocks of tuatara that have been recently identified. We conclude by summarizing those areas in which continued improvement and research are required.

Developments in Tuatara Conservation 1988–1991

Survey of Genetic Variation and Population Status

Tuatara are found on 30 of New Zealand's offshore islands; these islands range in area from 0.4 to 3083 ha and in latitude from 35° 19' S to 41° 07' S. During the period from 1988 to 1991, surveys were made of 27 of these populations. Population status was assessed using timed capture rates and/or density estimates, and by examining size-class frequency distributions, following concern (Crook 1973) that some populations had reduced recruitment and low numbers in the presence of introduced rats (that is, the kiore, *Rattus exulans*). Blood samples and morphometric data were collected to assess geographic variation and the existing taxonomy of tuatara, and blood samples from most populations were also analyzed to determine sex-hormone concentrations, and thus levels of reproductive activity. Preliminary results have been reported (Daugherty et al. 1990, 1992; Cree, Daugherty, and Hay 1991; Cree, Daugherty, Schafer, and Brown 1991; Cree et al. 1992) and other publications are in preparation.

The most exciting finding came from genetic studies that confirm the existence of a second species of tuatara, *Sphenodon guntheri*, in addition to the more common species, *S. punctatus* (Daugherty et al. 1990). *S. guntheri* exists only on tiny (4 ha) North Brother Island in Cook Strait (Figure 1) and, ironically, had been described last century as a separate species (Buller 1877). This population was later reduced to the status of a subspecies (Wettstein 1931). Subspecific differentiation of tuatara, however, was disregarded within New Zealand (Dawbin 1962, 1982; Robb 1977). Our genetic survey also showed that the more common species *S. punctatus* was divisible into two genetic stocks (Figure 1). One, represented by 25 populations off the northeastern coast of the North Island, is the subspecies named *S. p. punctatus* (Wettstein 1931); the other, represented by four populations in western Cook Strait, appears sufficiently distinct to be considered a different subspecies (Daugherty et al. 1990), but has not yet been described. Finally, the survey showed that there were no genetic or morphological grounds for supporting the distinction of tuatara on Little Barrier Island as the subspecies *S.*

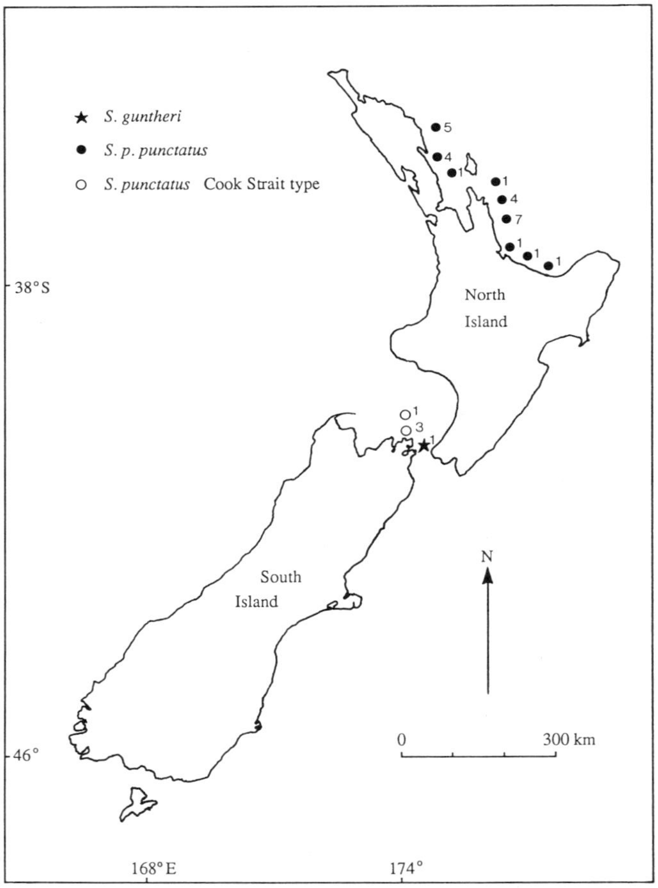

FIGURE 1. Distribution of the three extant genetic stocks of tuatara in New Zealand (after Daugherty et al. 1990). The numeral beside each symbol indicates the number of tuatara-inhabited islands covered by that symbol.

p. reischeki (Wettstein 1943); this population is indistinguishable from the surrounding *S. p. punctatus* populations (Whitaker and Daugherty 1991).

Our survey also confirmed an earlier report (Crook 1973) that populations co-existing with kiore were at risk of extinction. Four of these eight populations (three currently described as *S. p. punctatus*, plus the Little Barrier population) were in fact on the verge of extinction; they consisted of extremely low numbers (≤21 known) of adults only, many of which appeared aged (Cree, Daugherty, and Hay 1991). Tuatara on the remaining four rat-inhabited islands (all *S. p. punctatus*) were more numerous, though densities were still reduced compared with rat-free islands, and three populations showed clear evidence of recruitment failure (A. Cree, C. H. Daugherty, and J. M. Hay, unpubl. data). Plasma sex-hormone concentrations suggested that adults on most rat-inhabited islands were still reproductively active (A. Cree, C. H. Daugherty, and J. M. Hay, unpubl. data); thus, remedial actions to save these populations would not be wasted.

A National Management Plan for Tuatara

The findings described above clearly showed the urgent need for the reassessment on a national level of conservation efforts for tuatara, including captive-breeding attempts. Specifically, conservation efforts must recognize three distinct taxa of tuatara with separate reasons for, and degrees of, vulnerability (Table 1). The New Zealand Department of Conservation rapidly began planning a comprehensive recovery strategy for tuatara. The recovery plan currently exists in draft form (Cree 1990), and

TABLE 1. Current status in the wild and in captivity of genetic stocks of tuatara (*Sphenodon*) as of 1991, and recommendations for future conservation efforts (after Cree 1990; Daugherty et al. 1991).

Genetic stock	Estimated total population	Number of islands now inhabited	Number of new, wild populations recommended for establishment by 1995	Number currently in captivity			Recommended number of long-term captive populations by 1995	Current contributions of captive management to conservation
				E[1]	J	A		
Sphenodon guntheri	300	1	2	73	94	1[2]	2	Gene bank; incubation of wild-collected eggs to produce juveniles for introduction into new islands
Sphenodon p. punctatus	10,000	25	1	0	14	35	0	Temporary captive breeding of adults from four relictual populations; juveniles produced will be used to restock source or nearby islands following eradication of introduced rats
Sphenodon punctatus subspecies[3]	45,000	4	1	12	108	29	2+	Education/advocacy; research; captive-reared juveniles to be used for a reintroduction trial on an island where tuatara have become extinct

[1]E eggs, J juveniles, A adults.
[2]One aged female, probably post-reproductive.
[3]Cook Strait populations; thought to represent an unnamed subspecies of *S. punctatus* (Daugherty et al. 1990).

a team of scientists and managers from the Department of Conservation, New Zealand universities, and New Zealand zoos is helping formulate the final version of the plan and is coordinating the plan's implementation. Major five-year goals of the plan have still to be finalized; those suggested in the draft plan are listed below. Consistent with recent international recommendations (IUCN/UNEP/WWF 1991), these goals are explicitly quantified whenever possible:

(1) No further extinction of any population of tuatara should be allowed.

(2) The security and number of tuatara in all endangered populations should be enhanced.

(3) All genetic stocks (subspecies or above) should be represented by 1995 by at least two wild populations on islands capable of supporting at least 1,000 tuatara each.

(4) At least two permanent, self-sustaining captive populations should be established by 1995 for all genetic stocks found in the wild on fewer than four islands.

(5) To improve advocacy and to help redress the loss of offshore island populations of tuatara in historic times, at least one new wild population of each of the two most abundant genetic stocks of tuatara should be re-established by 1995 on islands on which controlled public access is permitted.

Captive management has a role to play in each of these recommended goals, as outlined below.

Integrated Captive Management

In 1988, prior to the geographic survey of tuatara populations, at least 34 adult tuatara and 101 juveniles were in captivity in New Zealand (Cree and Daugherty 1990). All came from a single population (Stephens Island) of the most abundant genetic stock of tuatara (the Cook Strait form of *Sphenodon punctatus*). The captive adults were spread among six institutions (2–9 adults per institution) and juveniles among 13 institutions (4–35 juveniles per institution). Clearly, significant reorganization of captive stocks was needed in order to achieve the goals of the recovery plan as noted above (see below also). To assist this, a workshop was held in 1990 for all captive-breeding institutions and a national coordinator for captive stocks of tuatara was appointed to act as a liaison among all captive-breeding institutions and the Tuatara Recovery Team (Blanchard 1991).

The Role of Captive Management in the Future Conservation of Tuatara

The Brothers Tuatara (Sphenodon guntheri)

The Brothers Tuatara (*Sphenodon guntheri*) is the rarer species of tuatara. It exists on only one island, and the population consists of only about 300 adults and uncounted juveniles (Thompson et al. 1992). In order to achieve the recommended goals of the draft recovery plan for this species, at least two new wild populations and two permanent, self-sustaining captive stocks should be established by 1995 (Table 1). Significant progress has been achieved toward these goals. Selection of appropriate islands within the geographic vicinity of North Brother Island for stocking (or restocking) with tuatara is underway by the Department of Conservation (goal 3). At least one of the new populations will be established using captive-reared (head-started) juveniles, though the source population is large enough that direct transfer of adults could be contemplated for the second new population. Establishment of new wild populations of tuatara has rarely been attempted in the past (the only known attempt, in the 1920s, was poorly documented and apparently unsuccessful), so trials are planned to establish juvenile and adult tuatara of the more common *S. punctatus* (Cook Strait form) on another island (see below) before release of *S. guntheri* on new islands is attempted.

Head-starting of juvenile tuatara for reintroduction is an attractive option, because eggs can be readily collected from wild females using hormonal induction without removing the females from the source population (Thompson et al. 1991), and the eggs can be incubated in captivity with a high degree of hatching success (Thompson 1990). So far (1988–1991), 208 *S. guntheri* eggs have been collected (Cree, Daugherty, Schafer, and Brown 1991; C. H. Daugherty, J. M. Hay, et al., unpubl. data). The eggs have been incubated in vermiculite at −400 kPa (kilopascals) using three temperature regimes: 18°C constant, 22°C constant, or a fluctuating temperature regime ranging between 18°–23°C that more closely approximates thermal conditions in natural nests. High hatching success (85.7–92.2%) has been achieved under all regimes, although significant variation in incubation length and in hatchling body length and mass is observed (Cree, Hay, et al. 1991). The significance of this variation in terms of post-hatching growth rate and survivorship is unknown. Preliminary studies on Cook Strait *S. punctatus* suggest that temperature-dependent sex determination (TSD) is unlikely in tuatara (M. B. Thompson, pers. comm.; see below), but the sex ratio of captive-reared juvenile *S. guntheri* is at present unknown.

In total, 94 hatchlings are now alive and 73 eggs are still being incubated (C. H. Daugherty, J. M. Hay, et al., unpubl. data). The eggs are incubated and hatchlings are reared indoors for several months, and then transferred in groups of 20 or more to outdoor enclosures at three New Zealand wildlife parks. The enclosures are not on public display. It is planned to release the head-started young at about 3–4 years of age, when the risks of predation, desiccation, and thermal stress in the wild are probably less than they would be for hatchlings. The time until sexual maturity and the life span of wild *S. guntheri* are unknown, but *S. punctatus* in the nearby population on Stephens Island reach maturity at about 11–13 years and can live at least 60 years (Castanet et al. 1988).

Progress has also been made in establishing long-term captive-breeding stocks of this species. One long-term captive colony of 18 hatchlings from the egg incubation program has been established in New Zealand. Because of the long lead-time until these animals reach the size of sexual maturity and the fact that successful breeding of captive-reared juveniles has never been achieved in the past (Cree and Daugherty 1990), we recommend that a second permanent captive stock is established using wild-collected adults.

The Northern Tuatara (Sphenodon punctatus punctatus)

The subspecies Northern Tuatara (*Sphenodon punctatus punctatus*) is the most widespread genetic stock of tuatara, although it is not the most numerous (Table 1). Total numbers are estimated at about 10,000 animals, spread among 25 islands. Because of this relatively large number of islands, new wild populations for security purposes (goal 3 above) and permanent captive stocks (goal 4 above) of this taxon are not required. Captive management is, however, involved in the achievement of goals 1 and 2 (above). Specifically, captive breeding of the few remaining individuals has been undertaken as a last-ditch attempt to save the four nearly extinct populations coexisting with introduced rats. Between 4 and 14 adults from each population have been transferred to outdoor captive enclosures, either at a mainland zoo (three populations) or on the source island (Little Barrier Island). Survival in situ of these populations was considered unlikely because of the low numbers and scattered distribution of the remaining adults, several of which appeared aged and in poor nutritional condition. Although direct observation of the interaction between tuatara and kiore is lacking, all data strongly support the view that kiore compete with tuatara for food, and prey on tuatara eggs and/or juveniles (Crook 1973; Whitaker 1978; Cree and Thompson 1988; Newman 1988; Newman and McFadden 1990; Towns 1991).

Our hope is that these animals can be induced to breed and that head-started young can be re-established on rat-free islands (which are, in three out of four cases, the source islands, following rat eradication) over the next 5 to 10 years. Eggs were obtained from three females from one island at the time of collection from the wild, and 14 hatchlings have been produced. Reproductive activity (as assessed by plasma sex-hormone concentrations) in the first year post-capture of the adults was reduced compared with nearby wild populations without rats (Cree, Daugherty, and Hay 1991). Possible explanations are that some individuals are post-reproductive, in poor nutritional condition, and/or suffering stress effects in captivity. Rat eradication is (as of 1991) underway on the smallest (100 ha) of the four islands and is planned for the two next largest (170–225 ha) during the next five years. Rat eradication on the fourth island, Little Barrier (3083 ha), would be extremely difficult and expensive. Although the long-term goal is to re-establish a healthy population of wild tuatara on Little Barrier, temporary release of adults and captive-reared juveniles on a smaller rat-free island nearby may be the most viable short-term option while rats remain present on Little Barrier.

The draft recovery plan also recommends reintroduction of one population of Northern Tuatara on an island where controlled public access is permitted (goal 5). At present, the only live tuatara the New Zealand public can see are a few in single-species captive displays, often in small enclosures. The opportunity to see this saurian "charismatic megavertebrate" in its natural island community, which is dominated by reptiles and seabirds, is likely to be a significant attraction that could boost public support for tuatara-conservation and island-restoration programs. An island suitable for restoration has been identified, and re-establishment of *S. p. punctatus* there could be either by direct transfer of adults from a nearby wild population, or by release of head-started juveniles from wild-collected eggs.

The Cook Strait Tuatara (Sphenodon punctatus *subspecies*)

Although found only on four islands, the Cook Strait Tuatara (*Sphenodon punctatus* subspecies) is the most numerous genetic stock of tuatara (Table 1). Most (probably 30,000 or more; Newman 1982) are on Stephens Island; the remaining three populations are small (numbers are between the tens to the low thousands). Stephens Island was the only population of tuatara represented in captivity in 1988, and although no captive group is yet self-sustaining, there are encouraging signs that some may become so (Cree and Daugherty 1990), perhaps over the next decade or so. Clearly, however, the number of captive groups (13) and individuals (135) of this genetic stock in captivity in New Zealand in 1988 were far higher than required to fulfill goal 4 of the draft recovery plan. These captive colonies have thus been considerably reorganized over the past three years. The aim is to reduce the total number of groups and individuals in captivity in New Zealand in order to make space available in zoos and wildlife parks that have experience in maintaining tuatara to rear more threatened genetic stocks. Some juveniles have been sent to zoos overseas and some have been made available for research. It is also planned to release some captive-reared juveniles and wild Stephens Island adults on an island where controlled public access can occur. Apart from the advocacy benefits, this will enable reintroduction procedures to be tested prior to the release of the rarer *S. guntheri* on other islands.

Summary of Current Conservation Activities Involving Captive Breeding

The ambitious recovery plan for tuatara described above represents a rapid turn-around from the situation ten years ago, when conservation of wild populations relied largely on restriction of public access to their islands and captive maintenance was mainly for display (Daugherty et al. 1992). Clearly, captive breeding is now seen as having an important role to play in the conservation of wild populations. Temporary captive maintenance of adults is being used to promote the survival and breeding of populations on the verge of extinction in the wild, and captive incubation of wild-collected eggs is being used to establish new, permanent, captive colonies of rare genetic stocks and to generate juvenile tuatara for reintroduction to the wild. This program thus involves close integration between in situ and ex situ conservation activities as promoted by IUCN/UNEP/WWF (1991), and reflects the increased commitment of zoos and wildlife parks in New Zealand to the conservation of endemic wildlife (Jakob-Hoff, in press). Nevertheless, much remains to be done to ensure the success of the captive-breeding components of the program. Areas of priority for future research are discussed below.

Future Research Needs

Institutions attempting to breed tuatara in captivity are in the fortunate position that a large body of information is available on the problems that have been experienced with captive husbandry of reptiles overseas (see, for example, Murphy and Collins 1980; Marcus 1981). Although this allows common husbandry problems to be anticipated, the physiology and ecology of tuatara are so unusual that solutions to such problems often require specific research on tuatara themselves.

Two areas in which research is urgently required are the nutrition of adults and juveniles, and the conditions necessary to improve juvenile health and overcome high juvenile mortality (Cree and Daugherty 1990). Nutritional studies are important because (1) obesity in adults and juveniles and growth deformities in juveniles have occurred frequently in captivity (Newman et al. 1979; A. Cree, M. Brown, et al., unpubl. data); (2) anecdotal evidence suggests that egg quality can be low in captivity (A. Cree, unpubl. data); and (3) preliminary studies on captive Stephens Island adults have revealed abnormal nutritional indices (significantly elevated plasma-cholesterol and plasma total-protein concentrations), which, in females, are also associated with abnormal plasma sex-hormone cycles (A. Cree, M. Brown, et al., unpubl. data). Captive tuatara often receive monotonous diets of high-fat insect larvae and lack certain items that are known, from studies on wild tuatara (Walls 1981), to be part of the natural diet, including plant-eating orthopteran insects (weta) and the eggs and chicks of marine-feeding seabirds. Plant-eating insects and marine-feeding seabirds could be sources of fatty acids that are potentially deficient in the diet of captive animals, and this hypothesis needs to be investigated. Marine-feeding seabirds are not part of the natural diet of many reptiles maintained in captivity overseas, and this is a good example of a case in which specific research on tuatara, based on knowledge of its unusual ecology in the wild, is important.

Although tuatara eggs can now be incubated in captivity with a high probability of hatching, success in rearing juveniles has not been as good. For instance, of 87 Stephens Island juveniles hatched in captivity from wild-collected eggs and subsequently distributed since 1986 to captive-rearing institutions in New Zealand, only 47 (54%) survived by the end of 1991 (A. Cree, unpubl. data). Apart from nutrition, as noted above, areas in which research would be valuable include the determination of optimal thermal conditions, optimal densities, and suitable lighting regimes for juveniles that are reared indoors. Densities have been unnaturally high in some captive colonies of juveniles and this has resulted in aggression and reduced growth rates (C. H. Daugherty, J. M. Hay, et al., unpubl. data). On the other hand, unnaturally high growth rates in captivity may also be harmful (W. H. Dawbin, pers. comm., *in* Newman et al. 1979). Given these observations and recent studies on juvenile alligators (*Alligator mississippiensis*) that show that high densities are associated with reduced growth rates and elevated plasma concentrations of the stress hormone corticosterone (Elsey et al. 1990), similar research to determine optimal densities and growth rates for juvenile tuatara would be extremely valuable.

Like other reptiles that bask, juvenile tuatara often show signs of metabolic bone disease when reared indoors under conditions in which the ultraviolet wavelengths of natural light that stimulate vitamin D_3 production are lacking. The levels of exposure to artificial sources of ultraviolet light reported to be beneficial for other reptiles (Townsend and Cole 1985; Gehrmann 1987) may be unsuitably high for tuatara, however, which bask only discreetly and are primarily nocturnal. Research in this area, including the use of dietary supplements of calcium and vitamin D_3, would be valuable and could profitably be carried out by overseas institutions, which are often unable to maintain tuatara in outdoor enclosures. Finally, although preliminary studies suggest that TSD is unlikely in tuatara (M. B. Thompson, pers. comm.), definitive studies are required to ensure that current egg incubation programs do not, as with past sea turtle–conservation programs (Standora and Spotila 1985), produce a highly skewed sex ratio.

Other important areas of research relate to the integration between captive-rearing programs and reintroduction attempts. How can aged adult *Sphenodon p. punctatus* be encouraged to breed in captivity to produce juveniles for reintroduction? At what age/size should captive-reared juveniles be released in the wild? What sort of monitoring should be carried out for captive-reared animals once released? How do growth rates of juveniles in captivity affect subsequent reproduction? How can island ecosystems degraded by the past presence of rats be improved to provide sufficient food for (re)introduced tuatara? These questions are just the start of what promises to be a challenging and rewarding decade of tuatara research and conservation.

Summary

Until 1988, captive breeding of tuatara (*Sphenodon*) had contributed little to the conservation of this rare and important New Zealand reptile. Numerous tuatara had been taken into captivity, but no captive-bred juvenile had ever reached sexual maturity. Virtually all captive tuatara were from the single most abundant population, and almost nothing was known about reproduction in or genetic variation among wild populations. Much has happened between 1988 and 1991. First, a survey of genetic variation among most of the 30 wild populations has revealed the existence of two species of tuatara, one of which probably has two subspecies. Second, a national recovery plan for tuatara is being prepared by the New Zealand Department of Conservation. This plan foresees a significant role for captive management in the conservation of wild populations. Captive incubation of wild-collected eggs and head-starting of juveniles are being employed to establish new wild populations of the rarer species, *S. guntheri*, and captive breeding of adults from relictual populations of the more common species, *S. punctatus*, is being used to generate juveniles for reintroduction to previously rat-inhabited islands. By these and other means it is hoped that the security of all genetic stocks of tuatara can be enhanced, and further population extinction averted. Priority areas for future research relating to captive management include nutrition of adults and juveniles, and optimal conditions for rearing healthy juveniles.

Acknowledgments

We are most grateful to curators of captive tuatara for their willingness to provide relevant information, and to D. Butler for helpful comments on the manuscript. Research referred to here on tuatara and restoration of their island habitats by the authors has been supported by Auckland Zoo, Dallas Zoo, ICI Crop Care, New Zealand Department of Conservation, New Zealand Lottery Board, Royal Forest and Bird Protection Society of New Zealand (Waikato Branch), San Diego Zoological Society, University of Otago, Victoria University of Wellington, Wellington Zoological Gardens, and WWF–New Zealand, to whom we are most grateful.

Literature Cited

Blanchard, B. 1991. Future plans for the captive breeding of tuatara. New Zealand Jour. Zool., 18: 343 (abstract).

Buller, W. L. 1877. Notes on the tuatara lizard (*Sphenodon punctatus*), with a description of a supposed new species. Trans. Proc. New Zealand Inst., 9: 317–325.

Castanet, J., D. G. Newman, and H. Saint-Girons. 1988. Skeletochronological data on the growth, age, and population structure of the tuatara, *Sphenodon punctatus*, on Stephens and Lady Alice Islands, New Zealand. Herpetologica, 44: 25–37.

Cree, A. 1990. Draft Tuatara Recovery Plan. Unpubl. Report New Zealand Dept. Conservation, Wellington. 74 pages. (see *Note Added in Proof*)

Cree, A., J. F. Cockrem, and L. J. Guillette, Jr. 1992. Reproductive cycles of male and female tuatara (*Sphenodon punctatus*) on Stephens Island, New Zealand. Jour. Zool., London, 226: 199–217.

Cree, A., and C. H. Daugherty. 1990. Captive breeding of the New Zealand tuatara: past results and future directions, p. 477–491. *In* B. L. Dresser, R. W. Reece, and E. J. Maruska (eds.), Proceedings of the Fifth World Conference on Breeding Endangered Species in Captivity. Cincinnati Zoo and Botanical Garden, Cincinnati, Ohio.

Cree, A., C. H. Daugherty, and J. M. Hay. 1991. Reproduction and conservation of rare populations of tuatara (*Sphenodon punctatus*) on offshore islands of New Zealand. *In* Proceedings of the 60th Congress of the Australian and New Zealand Association for the Advancement of Science. Section A6: Reproduction in animals. University of Adelaide, Adelaide. (University of New South Wales Library, Kensington, Australia [microfiche holding]).

Cree, A., C. H. Daugherty, S. F. Schafer, and D. Brown. 1991. Nesting and clutch size of tuatara (*Sphenodon guntheri*) on North Brother Island, Cook Strait. Tuatara, 31: 9–16.

Cree, A., J. M. Hay, C. H. Daugherty, and S. Keall. 1991. Effects of constant and variable incubation temperatures on growth of tuatara (*Sphenodon guntheri*) embryos. Proc. Physiol. Soc. New Zealand, 11: 59 (abstract).

Cree, A., and M. B. Thompson. 1988. Unravelling the mysteries of tuatara reproduction. Forest and Bird, 250: 14–16.

Crook, I. G. 1973. The tuatara, *Sphenodon punctatus* Gray, on islands with and without populations of the Polynesian rat, *Rattus exulans* (Peale). Proc. New Zealand Ecol. Soc., 20: 115–120.

Daugherty, C. H., A. Cree, J. M. Hay, and M. B. Thompson. 1990. Neglected taxonomy and continuing extinctions of tuatara (*Sphenodon*). Nature, 347: 177–179.

Daugherty, C. H., D. R. Towns, A. Cree, and J. M. Hay. 1992. The roles of legal protection versus intervention in conserving the New Zealand tuatara, *Sphenodon*, p. 247–259. *In* J. H. M. Willison, S. Bondrup-Nielsen, C. Drysdale, T. B. Herman, N. W. P. Munro, and T. L. Pollock (eds.), Science and the Management of Protected Areas. Elsevier Science Publishers, Amsterdam, Netherlands.

Dawbin, W. H. 1962. The tuatara in its natural habitat. Endeavour, 21: 16–24.

—. 1982. The tuatara *Sphenodon punctatus* (Reptilia: Rhynchocephalia): a review, p. 149–181. *In* D. G. Newman (ed.), New Zealand Herpetology. Occas. Publ. No. 2, New Zealand Wildl. Serv., Wellington.

Elsey, R. M., T. Joanen, L. McNease, and V. Lance. 1990. Growth rate and plasma corticosterone levels in juvenile alligators maintained at different stocking densities. Jour. Exp. Zool., 255: 30–36.

Fraser, N. C. 1988. The osteology and relationships of *Clevosaurus* (Reptilia: Sphenodontida). Philos. Trans. Royal Soc., (B), 321: 125–178.

Gehrmann, W. H. 1987. Ultraviolet irradiances of various lamps used in animal husbandry. Zoo Biol., 6: 117–127.

International Union for the Conservation of Nature and Natural Resources. 1988. 1988 IUCN Red List of Threatened Animals. International Union for the Conservation of Nature and Natural Resources, Gland, Switzerland. xviii, 154 pages.

International Union for the Conservation of Nature and Natural Resources/World Wide Fund for Nature. 1991. Caring for the Earth. A Strategy for Sustainable Living. International Union for the Conservation of Nature and Natural Resources, Gland, Switzerland. iv, 228 pages.

Jakob-Hoff, R. M. In press. Recent developments in the Australasian species management program. Internatl. Zoo Yearbook.

Marcus, L. C. 1981. Veterinary Biology and Medicine of Captive Amphibians and Reptiles. Lea and Febiger, Philadelphia. xii, 239 pages.

Murphy, J. B., and J. T. Collins (eds.). 1980. Reproductive biology and diseases of captive reptiles. Soc. Study Amphib. Reptiles, Oxford, Ohio, Contrib. Herpetol., 1: 1–277.

Newman, D. G. 1982. Tuatara, *Sphenodon punctatus*, and burrows, Stephens Island, p. 213–221. *In* D. G. Newman (ed.), New Zealand Herpetology. Occas. Publ. No. 2. New Zealand Wildl. Serv, Wellington.

—. 1988. Evidence of predation on a young tuatara, *Sphenodon punctatus*, by kiore, *Rattus exulans*, on Lady Alice Island. New Zealand Jour. Zool., 15: 443–446.

Newman, D. G., I. G. Crook, and L. R. Moran. 1979. Some recommendations on the captive maintenance of tuatara *Sphenodon punctatus* based on observations in the field. Internatl. Zoo Yearbook, 19: 68–74

Newman, D. G., and I. McFadden. 1990. Seasonal fluctuations of numbers, breeding, and food of kiore (*Rattus exulans*) on Lady Alice Island (Hen and Chickens Group), with a consideration of kiore: tuatara (*Sphenodon punctatus*) relationships in New Zealand. New Zealand Jour. Zool., 17: 55–63.

Robb, J. 1977. The Tuatara. Meadowfield, Shildon, UK. 64 pages.

Standora, E. A., and J. R. Spotila. 1985. Temperature dependent sex determination in sea turtles. Copeia, 1985: 711–722.

Thompson, M. B. 1990. Incubation of eggs of tuatara, *Sphenodon punctatus*. Jour. Zool., London, 222: 303–318.

Thompson, M. B., C. H. Daugherty, A. Cree, D. C. French, J. C. Gillingham, and R. E. Barwick. 1992. Status and longevity of the tuatara, *Sphenodon punctatus*, and Duvaucel's gecko, *Hoplodactylus duvaucelii*, on North Brother Island, New Zealand. Jour. Royal Soc. New Zealand, 22: 123–130.

Thompson, M. B., D. G. Newman, and P. R. Watson. 1991. Use of oxytocin in obtaining eggs from tuatara (*Sphenodon punctatus*). Jour. Herpetol., 25: 101–104.

Towns, D. R. 1991. Response of lizard assemblages in the Mercury Islands, New Zealand, to removal of an introduced rodent: the kiore (*Rattus exulans*). Jour. Royal Soc. New Zealand, 21: 119–136.

Townsend, C. R., and C. J. Cole. 1985. Additional notes on the requirements of captive whiptail lizards (*Cnemidophorus*), with emphasis on ultraviolet radiation. Zoo Biol., 4: 49–55.

Walls, G. Y. 1981. Feeding ecology of the tuatara (*Sphenodon punctatus*) on Stephens Island, Cook Strait. New Zealand Jour. Ecol., 4: 89–97.

Wermuth, H., and R. Mertens. 1977. Liste der rezenten Amphibien und Reptilien. Testudines, Crocodylia, Rhynchocephalia. Das Tierreich, 100: 1–174.

Wettstein, O. von. 1931. Rhynchocephalia, p. 1–235. *In* W. Kükenthal and T. Krumbach (eds.), Handbuch der Zoologie, volume 7. De Gruyter, Berlin and Leipzig.

—. 1943. *Sphenodon punctatus reischeki* nov. subsp. Zool. Anz., 143: 45–47.

Whitaker, A. H. 1978. The effects of rodents on reptiles and amphibians, p. 75–86. *In* P. R. Dingwall, I. A. E. Atkinson, and C. Hay (eds.), The Ecology and Control of Rodents in New Zealand Nature Reserves. New Zealand Dept. Lands Surv. Informat. Ser. 4.

Whitaker, A. H., and C. H. Daugherty. 1991. Research on the tuatara (*Sphenodon punctatus*) of Little Barrier Island, 5–12 February 1991. Unpubl. Report New Zealand Dept. Conservation, Wellington. 54 pages.

Note Added in Proof

The Department of Conservation's Tuarary Recovery Plan (Cree 1990) has now been published as:

Cree, A., and D. Butler. 1993. Tuatara Recovery Plan (*Sphenodon* spp.). Threatened Species Recovery Plan no. 9. New Zealand Department of Conservation, Wellington. 71 pages.

Rats have now been eradicated from four tuatara islands, and rat eradication is planned for a further two islands in spring 1994. For further information, see the following papers:

Towns, D. R., I. McFadden, and T. Lovegrove. 1993. Offshore islands co-operative project with ICI Crop Care Division: Phase One (Stanley Island). Sci. Res. Intern. Rep. no. 138. Department of Conservation, Wellington. 22 pages.

Towns, D. R., I. McFadden, P. Thomson, H. Robertson, and R. Colbourne. 1994. Offshore islands co-operative project with ICI Crop Care Division: Phase Two (Red Mercury Island). Sci. Res. Intern. Rep. no. 142. Department of Conservation, Wellington. 12 pages.

❦ Cree, A., C. H. Daugherty, D. R. Towns, and B. Blanchard. 1994. The contribution of captive management to the conservation of tuatara (*Sphenodon*) in New Zealand, p. 377–385. *In* J. B. Murphy, K. Adler, and J. T. Collins (eds.), Captive Management and Conservation of Amphibians and Reptiles. Society for the Study of Amphibians and Reptiles, Ithaca (New York). Contributions to Herpetology, volume 11.

The Future Role of the Private Sector in Breeding Endangered Species

Brian P. Backner*

Introduction

THAT ENDANGERED SPECIES CAN BE SAVED FROM extinction through the use of captive-breeding programs is a relatively old, but still debatable, proposition. Proven or not, worldwide habitat conversion continues to increase the number of species that could possibly benefit from such programs at a rate that far exceeds current capacity to absorb them. While estimates of endangered species of reptiles and amphibians number in the hundreds, and rise almost daily, the capacity of zoological institutions to house and care for them remains relatively constant. One estimate (Conway 1989) places worldwide carrying capacity within zoological parks at only 96 reptilian and 32 amphibian taxa under current Species Survival Plan (SSP) guidelines. Among American Association of Zoological Parks and Aquarium (AAZPA) member institutions, the estimated carrying capacity for amphibians is estimated at just 15 taxa (Johnson 1992). Given the growing inequity of the numbers indicated here, the need for increased carrying capacity would seem to be clear. Given the current worldwide economic climate, however, it would seem unlikely that a major investment could be expected from the publicly funded arena (for example, zoos and related institutions). One possible recourse is to look to qualified individuals in the private sector for the needed space and personnel.

*International Herpetological Symposium, Inc.
17 Margaret Road
Sharon, Massachusetts 02067–2419, USA

Acronyms used in this chapter:

AAZPA	American Association of Zoological Parks and Aquariums
CBSG	Captive Breeding Specialist Group
IUCN	International Union for the Conservation of Nature
PIT	Passive Integrated Transponder
SSP	Species Survival Plan
TAG	Taxon Advisory Group

Current Programs

In North America, zoological parks are involved in SSPs for several taxa of threatened or endangered reptiles and amphibians. While there exists a complex set of guidelines for determining both specimen and genetic management, the ultimate goal is to maintain 90% of the natural genetic diversity for two hundred years (Gray 1985). Working closely with the SSPs are the Taxon Advisory Groups (TAGs) of the AAZPA. It is the task of these groups to advise the Wildlife Conservation and Management Committee of the AAZPA on species to be considered for SSP status and inclusion (Behler 1989; Hudson 1989; McClain 1989; Paine and Johnson 1989; Stearns 1989).

Internationally, the Species Survival Commission of the International Union for the Conservation of Nature (IUCN) has among its committees the Captive Breeding Specialist Group (CBSG). The CBSG, acting on recommendations from its subcommittees, helps to coordinate captive breeding programs in over 35 countries. Its most recent accomplishment has been to recommend a global standard for a transponder system to allow for permanent identification of zoological specimens (Anonymous 1991). A comprehensive review of the above-mentioned organizations is available (Lawler 1992).

The Private Sector

The so-called private sector is an extremely heterogeneous group. Educational backgrounds can range from the professional with a postgraduate degree to the high school dropout. Likewise, herpetological interests are equally diverse, and may range from the collector of herpetological literature, to the animal keeper interested in a single species or an entire family, to the individual who diversifies almost to the point of chaos. Similar diversity exists in the physical plants available for the housing of captive animals, as well as in the practical experience that these individuals have in the field of animal husbandry. The extent of formal education, herpetological interest, or physical setup, however, may have little correlation with success in animal husbandry and captive breeding. Several individuals have had tremendous success over the past 20 years despite the "handicap" of no formal education in zoology or herpetology, and they have contributed invaluable information. Self-taught, these individuals have consistently demonstrated success at husbandry and breeding through astute observation and networking with other amateurs at the ever-increasing number of regional and national meetings devoted to herpetological interests within the private sector.

The extent of the private sector in North America can only be estimated. This is best done by considering the current memberships of several of the larger regional or non-professional herpetological societies: the Chicago Herpetological Society boasts a membership in excess of 1,700, the American Federation of Herpetoculturists claims greater than 2,700 members, and the International Herpetological Symposium, Inc., maintains an active mailing list of 3,800 individuals, 3,100 of which are not associated with zoological parks or academic institutions. While these organizations are not all-inclusive, and overlap in membership doubtlessly exists, it would be reasonable to use a figure of 3,000 individuals as a highly conservative estimate of the size of the private sector in the United States. The actual number may be several to ten times higher.

A crude, but possibly accurate, assessment of the extent of successful captive breeding within the private sector can be found in the number of mailings from individuals offering captive-raised reptiles and amphibians for sale. In 1991 alone, I received 38 such lists, with 24 or more species for sale. Combined, these lists represent over 200 reptilian and 40 amphibian taxa. The total number of lists received in 1991 (including those with less than 24 species for sale) well exceeded 100, indicating that the number of individuals producing captive-bred animals is not insignificant. Furthermore, if the market value for certain species is analyzed over time, the general trend indicates downward movement of prices. As the trade in reptiles is presumably subject to the laws of supply and demand, a logical conclusion is that there is an ever-increasing number of animals for sale, and that people must be successfully breeding them in captivity.

Given the tremendous diversity of interest and expertise within the private sector, it is obvious that guidelines for minimum standards need to be crafted. Furthermore, steering committees should be implemented to choose qualified individuals and follow their progress, offering assistance, encouragement, and, when indicated, remedial action. Such committees already exist, although only for the use and assistance of AAZPA member institutions; it would be relatively painless to expand the scope of these to oversee carefully chosen individuals in the private sector.

Utilization of the Private Sector in Captive Breeding Programs

The perception of a strong commercial, if not outright exploitative, tendency within the private sector has long been a point of contention with the zoological community. The private sector, with several notable exceptions, has thus been scorned and excluded from serious consideration whenever captive-breeding programs for endangered species are discussed.

A competing, and perhaps controversial, view of this situation is to harness and exploit the strong profit motive of the private sector. Given the large commitment of time and resource allocation necessary to maintain even a small colony of animals, it is unrealistic to expect any but the most affluent or altruistic persons to participate in the SSP for an endangered species and not be compensated in some manner. While this might take the form of increased recognition for some individuals, it is to be expected that monetary compensation would be the norm. The sale of surplus, captive-bred animals (but not endangered species) by AAZPA member institutions to one another is a common practice, and certainly the private sector would be expected to utilize this channel for distribution of their stock. Given the limited carrying capacity of member institutions, however, a point would be reached at which the highly successful breeder (or group of breeders) could out-produce demand and ultimately be penalized by having an ever-enlarging colony of animals for which to care. Without a legitimate outlet for the captive-bred offspring, either euthanasia or sale to "non-approved" individuals or institutions would be the likely result. Both options appear to be unacceptable. The former would result in the permanent loss of possibly needed genetic diversity; the latter in the same loss of genetic variety (although not necessarily permanently), along with possible legal ramifications in cases in which the Federal Endangered Species Act and numerous state statutes are involved. Although open to argument, it would appear that this second course would be the better choice.

Such a policy would be a great departure from accepted practice, and would require an unprecedented degree of cooperation among the zoological and academic communities, the private sector, and the governmental agencies responsible for enforcing the above-mentioned statutes. After all, it would be quite surprising the first time one would see a tuatara for sale in the local pet shop. Although an extreme example, such might have to be the case for the private sector to become involved.

Permanent Animal Identification

If the unorthodox arrangement posed by this proposition can be accepted, then the problem of specimen and genetic management can be seen to be solved in a relatively simple and straightforward manner through the use of the Passive Integrated Transponder (PIT) system. (The system chosen by the CBSG Working Group on Permanent Animal Identification is the Trovan Electronic Identification System manufactured in the United States by Infopet Identification Systems of Westlake Village, California.) The PIT tags themselves and the syringe-like implanter are simple to use and relatively inexpensive: US$20.00 for the implanter and $5.85 each for the PIT tags in lots of 25. The simple training involved to use this system and the low cost per animal would not be expected to create an undue burden for the average individual—although the cost for the hand-held scanner ($837.00) would make acquisition unlikely for all but the largest private colonies. Included in the cost of each PIT tag is the registration of the unique transponder number with the International Species Information System (ISIS).

The implantation of a unique PIT tag into captive-bred specimens is straightforward and can be accomplished in several minutes or less for each animal. The small size of the tags (2 × 11 mm) has allowed their use in all but the smallest of reptiles and amphibians (such as frogs of the family Dendrobatidae). The integrated microchip circuitry of the tag is encased in biologically inert glass, and has been used in a wide variety of species without apparent effect on behavior or physiology. The use of these PIT tags would ensure positive identification of each specimen, no matter what its ultimate fate. Animals sold into the pet trade or other alternative channels could thus be "retrieved" should the need arise. Obviously, some formula for determining exactly which animal(s) are to be sold into these alternative channels would have to be developed, and whether it should be based on genetic or other parameters would have to be determined.

An added benefit to this system could be the possible decline in trade in illegally obtained endangered species. Since each PIT tag is unique, and not reproducible, restricted access to them would make any animal without a verifiable PIT tag of suspect origin. An animal without a PIT tag could be presumed to be either illegally imported or collected, or to have had its PIT tag removed to obscure its origin. This could make the job of law enforcement officials somewhat simpler, since any animal carrying a valid PIT tag could be instantly traced.

Summary

The future role of the private sector in the breeding of rare and endangered species needs to be seriously considered, although implementation of a program, such as the one outlined in this chapter, would be highly unorthodox by current practice and be likely to encounter stiff resistance by academics, zoo professionals, and law enforcement officers. Given unabated global habitat conversion, the current status of wild populations, and the limited resources likely to be available in public zoological parks for the foreseeable future, such a radical proposal may yet become acceptable if endangered reptiles and amphibians are to survive.

Literature Cited

Anonymous. 1991. Final report on transponder system testing and product choice as a global standard for zoological specimens. Captive Species Breeding Group News, 2: 3–4.

Behler, J. 1989. Crocodilians: status, captive culture, and crocodilian advisory group recommendations. Ann. Proc. Amer. Assoc. Zool. Parks Aquar., 1989: 55–56.

Conway, W. G. 1989. The prospects for sustaining species and their evolution, p. 199–209. *In* D. Western and M. Pearl (eds.). Conservation for the Twenty-first Century. Oxford Univ. Press, New York, New York.

Gray, R. L. 1985. Captive propagation as a tool in wildlife management, p. 7–23. *In* R. L. Gray (ed.), Captive Propagation and Husbandry of Reptiles and Amphibians. Proc. Northern California Herpetol. Soc. and Bay Area Amphib. Reptile Soc., Davis, California.

Hudson, R. 1989. The need for an AAZPA lizard advisory group. Ann. Proc. Amer. Assoc. Zool. Parks Aquar., 1989: 42–54.

Johnson, R. R. 1992. AAZPA Amphibian Taxon Advisory group. Amer. Assoc. Zool. Parks Aquar., Wheeling, West Virginia. Unpublished manuscript. 15 pages.

Lawler, H. E. 1992. Advanced protocols for the management and propagation of endangered and threatened reptiles, p. 57–66. *In* M. J. Uricheck (ed.), Proceedings of the 15th International Herpetological Symposium on Captive Propagation and Husbandry. Internatl. Herpetol. Symp., Danbury, Connecticut.

McClain, J. M. 1989. Propagation of endangered snakes: past, present, future. Ann. Proc. Amer. Assoc. Zool. Parks Aquar., 1989: 67–76.

Paine, F. L., and R. Johnson. 1989. Amphibian advisory group report and recommendations. Ann. Proc. Amer. Assoc. Zool. Parks Aquar., 1989: 36–41.

Stearns, B. C. 1989. Chelonian species survival plans: present status and future directions. Ann. Proc. Amer. Assoc. Zool. Parks Aquar., 1989: 24–35.

❦

❦ Backner, B. P. 1994. The future role of the private sector in breeding endangered species, p. 387–390. *In* J. B. Murphy, K. Adler, and J. T. Collins (eds.), Captive Management and Conservation of Amphibians and Reptiles. Society for the Study of Amphibians and Reptiles, Ithaca (New York). Contributions to Herpetology, volume 11.

Directions for Future Research at Academic Institutions

Carl Gans*

Introduction

Whenever I am asked to write about the future, I develop a strong feeling that a crystal ball will be needed. Everything that I have learned and observed about human relations and the things that are inherent in the study of evolutionary biology suggests that uncertainty and unpredictability are the order of the day. Consequently, the task one faces in writing a predictive piece, such as this one, can best be fulfilled safely by generating something which might be acceptable to the audience, and which is unlikely to become too obviously wrong within the foreseeable future.

If I may restate my task, from characterizing what "will happen" to what I believe "needs to" or "should happen," it may be possible to generate a statement that meets the above criteria. It also lets me express certain personal attitudes, which I assume many readers may share, although we may not enjoy admitting them. Presumably, our aim is to assure the survival of amphibian and reptilian diversity. Specifically, we are concentrating on the study and enhancement of captive breeding efforts, and it is my task to deal with the present and future contributions of researchers in these areas who are employed by universities.

An Unexpected Revolution

Whereas I am, and have been, a university professor for much of my life, I must regretfully note that, judging from the past, the key to success in this most worthy endeavor is unlikely to derive from universities. Past successes have come primarily from other places—and I consider these successes to have been spectacular. Twenty years ago, my friend Wilfred T. Neill commented that most of the species of crocodilians would likely become extinct in the not-too-distant future (Neill, 1971). This comment has caused numerous snickers among so-called professionals, because it proved to be so patently wrong. All crocodilian species remain alive today, and their total numbers seem to have risen locally, and perhaps even globally.

In retrospect, Neill's error in prediction reflects not the success of the activities of any zoologist per se, but rather results from a revolution which could not have been predicted. This revolution has involved major changes in the attitude of the general public, which has led to an increased concern about the fate of animals, an enhancement of the popular interest in their preservation and conservation, and, most important, a parallel shift in people's willingness to pay for these endeavors. One can even state that books, such as Rachel Carson's "Silent Spring" or, to a lesser extent, Neill's "The Last of the Ruling Reptiles," have contributed to achieving this revolution in public consciousness. Fieldbooks and handbooks of faunas have furnished the public with a basis for observing and responding to changing abundance of their favorite organisms.

The revolution may well be placed at the door of television programming, which provided a showcase for the efforts of naturalists and film makers. The continued appearance in peoples' living rooms of images showing appealing, colorful, and diverse animals doing interesting things helped modify public attitudes. During the 1960s through the early 1980s, there were periods during which almost every evening included at least one animal program. These images appeared on commercial, and not just educational, programming; many were

*Department of Biology
The University of Michigan
Ann Arbor, Michigan 48109–1048, USA

not true nature films, but piggybacked animal footage onto adventure stories, zoo safaris, and such. These films were designed in each case to illustrate a story, with animals as a key component. They documented the intrinsic interest of topics in natural history, and often noted the ever-increasing threat to these organisms.

Secondary to this educational pattern have been illustrated articles in magazines—indeed the advent of many additional, colorful magazines—and the upgrading of the presentations offered by The Nature Conservancy, the Wilderness Society, the Audubon Society, and others. Then there has been the renovation of zoos, making them more pleasant to visitors, and, seemingly, to the animals, and the increasing exposure of visitors to information without critically reducing entertainment. A change in the nature of safaris has occurred, as well as the opportunity to watch animals in their natural state from Jeep, Landrover, bus, tour boat, and foot, and to participate in photo safaris, has added to earlier experiences. Even laboratory zoologists now partake of these trips, seeing them as educational vacations rather than occasions for field work. Reports by returning participants elicit positive responses, documenting the wide, popular attention. It is not surprising that even politicians and bankers are realizing that the public's interest in organisms is serious, and that it signals a greater recognition of the needs of organisms and a greater willingness to pay for these needs than ever before. Many politicians, bankers, and other such people are even joining the trips.

The Costs of Emotion

We have to remember, however, that most of the public's behavior represents responses to emotional cues. We must remember that animals which look like babies obviously attract special attention. The commitment to animals, and the willingness to pay for this commitment, thus reflects reaction to propaganda addressed to the emotions, rather than a factual understanding of the problems faced by organisms. Also, the emotion is often designed to comfort one's conscience. It may represent a sacrifice to the spirit of organisms lost for our benefit or convenience; it is remarkably similar to the selection and adoration of totem creatures in many hunting societies.

I do not wish to decry this emotional base; it has its merits. At the least, it has led to an increased investment in protection of animals, and to the potential of meaningful discussion. It does, however, also have major demerits. Emotion often lends support for seemingly good causes that really do harm. It overrides reasoned attitudes and clouds our capacity to recognize the difference. It generates intolerance for those who may not share one's views.

Clearly, the emotional response is intrinsic to the problem and leads to erroneous decisions. In the present case, there is emphasis on the cute rather than the necessary, on the easiest problems for propaganda purposes rather than the biologically most critical, on the protection of individuals rather than the maintenance of populations, and on the consideration of individual species rather than the consideration of environments. Anything that is done "for animals" is somehow applauded, because the word "animals" is commonly interpreted as meaning each individual animal, or each individual specimen.

Regrettably, there are vested interests which encourage such emotion. Perhaps the most pernicious aspect of the emotional approach is the morass that is being wished on us by the animal-welfare, or specieist, lobby. The "friends" of animals have saddled the research community with ever-more complex, expensive, and cumbersome bureaucracy, whose rule-making activities are wasting money on the spurious grounds that this will help the organisms. Even when it can be shown that the particular action is desirable for a few specimens, such procedures have commonly led to, and are leading to, enormous wastes of money, inhibition of study, and reduction in the amount of results achieved per unit expenditure. They deflect attention from enforcement procedures that would really aid the species. These approaches are the zoological equivalent of the argument that anything that could ever produce cancer, in any dosage and for any individual, must be banned—absolutely. Anything that helps any individual animal will be good. Hence the fate of a dozen salamanders taken by a student for serious study is never contrasted with the fate of one hundred thousand animals killed by clear-cutting an adjacent forest block.

Were resources infinite, the animal welfare lobby, relying on utilizing emotion rather than reasoned argument, could perhaps be tolerated more readily. I would posit that the funds being diverted do not derive from an infinite, but from a most finite, pool that is probably inadequate to start with. For instance, application of rules, which were intended for persons who work with birds and cats, to people attempting an understanding of ectotherms are increasing the cost of research by an order of magnitude. In terms of fixed dollars, they are reducing research results by more than three quarters. Yet the research results of which we speak are precisely those that might allow decisions about real conservation, about matters that are critical to the survival of species. Some of my friends become uncomfortable when I start to speak strongly about this. They attempt to compromise and urge me to accept the good intentions of those subject to emotional reasoning. I am willing to accept these intentions for many individuals; however, my experience leads me to the conclusion that the activities of these individuals are fundamentally harmful, and that they are being manipulated by a group with an agenda that proposes ultimately to close down animal research (not even to speak of all other utilization of animals).

I am convinced that research into the diversity and needs of organisms is the best, indeed the only, way that we can retain some remnants of organismic diversity for the coming generations. This requires research and educational facilities, the generation and dissemination of knowledge, and approaches which lead to broad understanding of organisms. Hence, I object to arguments that zoos are intrinsically cruel, and that museums and research facilities should be restricted (or eliminated). I object to the recent, most spectacular success of the emotional propagandists, which may be seen in the United Kingdom by the potential closing of the Regent's Park Zoo in London, and of many of the research facilities of the Natural History Museum in South Kensington.

Multidisciplinary Approaches to Conservation

None of this directly addresses the topic I was to discuss, namely the future directions for research in academic institutions. Indeed, it leaves open where we should go at this moment, and what role one may recommend for the universities. I doubt that the major contribution of universities should be a breakthrough toward, let us imagine, a different polymuctate synthesis that provides us with a novel ectotherm aphrodisiac! Some novel and useful research findings will inevitably derive from the laboratory, and I expect their generation to continue. An increased understanding of the biology of organisms will allow better decisions about conditions under which reptiles and amphibians are likely to reproduce. It will tell us more about the sizes of breeding pools, the maintenance of genetic diversity, the effect of environmental states on growth and development, and the avoidance, not just of inbreeding, but of the less obvious byproducts of domestication. Meetings, such as the one from which this symposium volume developed, and which was attended jointly by terrarists and members of the zoo, museum, and university research communities, are highly desirable in fostering communication and the complex exchange of observations and ideas.

I see the primary task of universities, however, to be the fostering of education and the teaching of how to carry out research effectively. This task remains before us, but it should transcend the rote memorization of facts, particularly facts in areas of great uncertainty. Educators, especially those in biology departments, are ideally placed to teach discernment to those who will themselves teach in turn. We have the opportunity to address future instructors in primary and high schools, future medical, dental, and veterinary biologists, and indeed also those who aim to enter zoological research as their career. Instead of being defensive about the maintenance of environmental and species diversity, we should allow the students to consider the decision-making process, and be prepared to apply (and teach) it in turn.

Another critical issue on which the universities might be able to help would be in providing multidisciplinary approaches to a better understanding of what is required for real conservation. I stress this because of the repeated demonstration that even the most successful efforts at reproduction will not be enough. Consider the Indian crocodilians, the Mugger (*Crocodylus palustris*), the Estuarine Crocodile (*C. porosus*), and the Gharial (*Gavialis gangeticus*). A quarter of a century ago, the Mugger was severely endangered, and the Gharial was just about extinct. Twenty years later, the major reproductive problems have been solved. Many Indian zoos and parks have Mugger breeding facilities. Indeed the Madras Crocodile Bank, just by itself (not counting the dozens of other endeavors), has close to ten thousand Muggers which are approaching sexual maturity. If no more animals were to be raised, this number would probably exceed the carrying capacity of the Indian streams now devoted to this organism. Estuarine Crocodiles and Gharials still have lower populations, but here too one can see times, less than a decade away, when holding facilities will have more specimens than can possibly be stocked in the areas which are suitable and can be protected (and lived with). But on the other hand, outside of these parks (and even within many of them), environmental degradation continues.

Naturally, the crocodilians represent a special case, as at least two of the Indian species have the potential of being dangerous to humans and to domestic livestock. Crocodilians, however, do not seem to be special in demonstrating the ectothermal capacity for rapid reproduction. Another special case may exist in which some tropical or other animals are of very restricted biotope and limited demands. Thus treefrogs of the high forest canopy are unlikely to survive reintroduction unless patches of forest are protected or regenerated; we need to know which trees and which commensals are critical. All of us know about the need to study the questions and problems concerning edge effects, absolute patch size, and similar matters that deserve attention in maintaining viable populations. Such organisms of narrow niche probably can only be maintained if we can have at least some level of strict protection.

There is a vast number of species, however, that could potentially coexist with humans, even in patchy situations. We will probably be unable to achieve a vast increase in absolutely protected areas. Research and education, however, might well be directed to what I like to call the rules for coexistence. Questions remain about how much forest land and how much botanical diversity must be maintained to assure survival of some percentage of local herpetofaunas, and whether the maintenance of such conditions can be encouraged by approaches other than absolute protection of the entire environment. We also need to consider whether there are educational and legislative approaches for limiting the increasing monoculture of the environment, such as tax incentives, rather than absolute protection. Even more critical is the question of whether we can find incentives for limiting the successive shifts from one type of monoculture to another, each with its mechanical and chemical attributes that further shrink the original faunas.

I have listed a series of questions that are based on zoology, but the solutions of which demand more scope than this. I see great merit to using the resources of the social sciences and the practical understanding of the fields of the law, engineering, and politics. As all of these approaches coexist on university campuses, there is the potential of starting dialogs that would lead to further research and teaching. The goodwill of the overall public still remains; the results of the environmental revolution are still with us. While this state continues, our efforts should not be diverted and restricted to enhancement of the breeding of individuals in the laboratory. A multidimensional, multidisciplinary approach must establish a theoretical and operational basis for occupying, sharing, and exploiting common environments. Such an approach should specifically address and aim to reduce the inevitable cost of these procedures. Without it, our efforts are likely to be purely cosmetic in the long run. With it, we could still help the maintenance of much now-surviving diversity. Coincidentally, this would provide Roger Conant with a demand for further editions of his field guide!

Summary

Past successes in convincing the public that many animals are interesting and appealing, and that they deserve protection, have not originated primarily in the academic community. Rather, naturalists have transmitted this message, often by coupling education with appeals to the emotions. Although achieving truly desirable aims, this risks conflation of protection of individuals and species, of the obviously cute and the biologically necessary. It has fostered a wasteful bureaucracy that addresses and limits research, rather than protecting biodiversity. Academic institutions, however, retain the option not only of educating generations of students, but also of fostering multidiciplinary approaches. One potential example is the development of patterns for sharing rather than partitioning environments among humans and members of the herpetofauna.

Literature Cited

Neill, Wilfred T. 1971. The Last of the Ruling Reptiles. Columbia Univ. Press, New York. xvii, 486 pages.

❦

❦ Gans, C. 1994. Directions for future research at academic institutions, p. 391–395. *In* J. B. Murphy, K. Adler, and J. T. Collins (eds.), Captive Management and Conservation of Amphibians and Reptiles. Society for the Study of Amphibians and Reptiles, Ithaca (New York). Contributions to Herpetology, volume 11.

Collection-Management, Captive-Breeding, and Conservation Programs in Zoo Herpetological Collections

Dale L. Marcellini*

Introduction

CONSERVATION IS ONE OF THE MAIN GOALS OF zoos, and is one of the reasons that justifies their existence. Conservation is defined in different ways by different people. Many feel that conservation is a complex global issue that deals with resource use, pollution, habitat destruction, and expanding human populations. It is apparent from the policy statements of most zoos, and from the publications of the American Association of Zoological Parks and Aquariums ("The New Ark," "Protecting the Present to Protect the Future," and "The Purposes of Zoos and Aquariums") that most people who work in and manage zoos have chosen to define conservation as the breeding of rare and endangered species in captivity. Curators are largely responsible for zoo conservation programs, and this definition is perhaps to be expected, as most of us come from a background of collecting and taking care of animals. In this chapter I will briefly explore how equating captive breeding with conservation has hampered zoo professionals in dealing with broader conservation issues in zoos, and I will suggest some ways we might change to more effectively handle these important issues.

Discussion

Zoo animal departments are involved in breeding rare, endangered, and threatened animals, and have education and public-relations programs which promote and describe these efforts in glowing terms. Thus, most curators believe that they are doing a good job with conservation. We must question, however, whether these breeding programs are really conservation, or whether they are merely preservation. Our concentration on the breeding of rare and endangered species may allow curators to delude themselves, to unwittingly act in ways which are harmful to the preservation of species in the wild, and to avoid dealing with real conservation issues in zoos. Curators of herpetology at zoos may be more guilty than bird and mammal curators of husbandry and management practices which are contrary to good conservation programs. We might ask: what are some of the things that we curators of herpetology are doing wrong?

Curators of herpetology at American zoos seem to be obsessed with species that come from outside the United States. Most large reptilian collections in the United States have a significant emphasis on rare, exotic species. This interest is evidenced by the fact that, of the six herpetological Species Survival Plans (SSP), none of them is designated for species which are found in the United States. In addition, in a survey done in 1988 by curators interested in potential species of reptiles and amphibians for SSP programs, zoo herpetology curators were asked to submit priority species for inclusion. This group identified 44 species that should definitely be included in SSP, and an additional 55 to be included if founders were available; of these 99 species, only eight were from the United States.

---

*Department of Herpetology
National Zoological Park
Washington, D.C. 20008, USA

Acronyms used in this chapter:

AAZPA	American Association of Zoological Parks and Aquariums
ISIS	International Species Information System
PETA	People for the Ethical Treatment of Animals
SSP	Species Survival Plan

Curators of herpetology at zoos still appear to be involved in stamp collecting as well, and therefore seem to value rarity above all else. Bingaman (1987) documented the collection composition of 36 zoos in the United States. She was surprised to find that over 50% of the collection of an average reptile house is comprised of species that no other zoo maintains. Bingaman's paper also provided considerable evidence for a lack of real commitment to the captive breeding of most of the rare and exotic specimens that zoo herpetariums hold. She found that in most collections, over 50% the species are represented by only one or two specimens, and that over 90% of the species are represented by six specimens or less. A brief perusal of current herpetological collections, as listed in Slavens and Slavens (1991), makes it apparent that collections share few species, and that group sizes are small. It is difficult to develop cooperative, sustained breeding programs under those conditions.

Only rarely are such programs done on a long-term basis, even with species which are bred at zoos. Many of us have had the experience of needing a specimen, and of calling a zoo known to be breeding the species, only to be disappointed by the fact that the species is no longer being bred.

One of the results of the stamp-collector mentality and lack of commitment to long-term breeding is that many of the specimens that we obtain must be wild-caught. Records of the International Species Information System (ISIS) for 1990–1991 show that at least 25% of amphibians and reptiles in zoos are wild-caught. This percentage is probably much higher, because over 25% of herpetological additions are listed as of unknown origin, and a majority of these unknowns are most likely to be wild caught. A 50:50 ratio of captive-bred to wild-caught specimens seems high, but bird and mammal collections are well over 70% captive-bred (ISIS 1990–91), even though captive husbandry for these groups is more fully understood.

As zoo curators, we justify our interest in the exotic and rare (and that the majority of our collections are stocked from the wild) by emphasizing our commitment to education and conservation. We talk about showing the zoo visitor a variety of amphibians and reptiles and their interesting and important adaptations. Rarely, however, is the zoo visitor told about these things in any effective way. In fact, many of the exotic species that are held are never even placed on exhibit. Moreover, our commitment to conserve species by breeding them in captivity and reintroducing them into the wild (as described in "Protecting the Present to Protect the Future," an AAZPA pamphlet) is often cited to justify our program's thrust, even though reintroduction may not be realistic. The difficulties of successful reintroduction for amphibians and reptiles have been documented in the symposium on which this book is based, and in three recent articles (Burke 1991; Dodd and Seigel 1991; Reinert 1991). Although some disagreement about the success of reintroduction programs exists, it is clear that reintroduction of amphibians and reptiles has had limited success. Of the six herpetological SSP species, only one, the Puerto Rican Crested Toad (*Peltophryne lemur*), has been reintroduced, with limited success (see Johnson, this volume, page 243). Even with the charismatic and much better funded mammal and bird SSP species, only eight of 46 are currently involved in reintroduction. If one of the most successful reintroduction programs (that of the Golden Lion Tamarin, *Leontopithecus rosalia*) is closely scrutinized, it becomes evident that responsible reintroduction cannot occur very often (Beck et al. 1991). Reintroduction is expensive, difficult, and often unsuccessful, even when habitat is available for the species in question.

There are many signs that the emphasis on the captive breeding of endangered species may no longer be sufficient justification for keeping these animals in captivity. Zoos are continually being attacked and challenged by People for the Ethical Treatment of Animals (PETA) and other animal-rights groups on the issue of conservation through captive breeding. The small number and limited effect of breeding and reintroduction programs for the conservation of wild populations makes zoos increasingly vulnerable. In addition, some allies of zoos in conservation, such as the National Park Service, Fish and Wildlife Service, The Nature Conservancy, World Wildlife Fund, and even the United States Congress, have begun to put increasing emphasis on ecosystem preservation, and less emphasis on species preservation. In a recent meeting, Charles Dane, Chief of the Endangered Species Office of the United States Fish and Wildlife Service, stressed the importance of zoos which show a real commitment to conservation education and the conservation of wild populations. He emphasized that captive breeding was no longer a compelling reason for the acquisition of rare and endangered species by zoos.

If zoo herpetologists can admit that captive breeding is not really conservation, because it probably never will have a significant impact on species in the wild, perhaps they can deal more effectively with conservation education in our zoos. There are a number of positive aspects to zoos that make them ideal places to teach conservation. Zoos have a large and varied clientele, which includes large numbers of children, and they have real living things that are in close proximity to visitors. Thus, they have the audience and the compelling features that can be used to create a learning atmosphere.

In spite of the obvious advantages that zoos have for education, most reptile houses make only a cursory effort at it. A few labels, some explanatory graphics, or an occasional school program is all that can be managed in the limited time available to curators and keepers. A keeper casually talking to visitors is a rarity—there simply is not enough time. Most curators say they would like to do more education, but complain that they do not have the people, time, or money. The maintenance of large, diverse collections of rare and exotic amphibians and reptiles in zoos requires many resources. If resources, such as money, space, and personnel, are limited, curators of herpetology at zoos should begin to make changes, and apply more of these scarce resources to education in the pursuit of a conservation goal.

Conclusions

Zoos need to change their emphasis from dealing only with animals to dealing more with the public. Some of the resources that are currently being using to maintain and breed rare and exotic amphibians and reptiles must be redirected to develop and run effective, thoughtful, and interactive, educational programs for zoo visitors. These programs should be aimed at developing a conservation consciousness through an appreciation and understanding of reptiles and amphibians. In addition, zoo herpetological collections and programs need to concentrate more on local species and local conservation issues. The Bog Turtle (*Clemmys muhlenbergii*) programs that some zoos are involved with are good examples. These programs involve state agencies, private conservation organizations, and even land owners, as well as zoos. It is not enough, however, to merely work with local species. It must be made clear to the visitor how people affect these animals. The visitor will be much easier to reach, involve, and educate if we deal with local species and issues that are within his or her own experience and sphere of influence. Some visitors might be stimulated to become involved and do something about local conservation problems which involve amphibians and reptiles.

Some curators of herpetology are currently working on more effective and thoughtful educational programs, and others are already deeply involved in local-species and local-conservation issues. Much more needs to be done, however, as environmental degradation continues at an accelerated pace all over the United States. If zoos are going to do more, they must change, reducing their emphasis on breeding endangered species, and increasing their emphasis on public education. Times are changing—and if zoos and zoo herpetological collections are to survive, we need to become a valued community-education resource. If we expect our efforts to have a significant impact on conservation, we must become more involved at the local environmental level.

Summary

Conservation is one of the main goals of zoo reptile houses, and yet curators act in ways which may be harmful to the conservation of species in the wild. Collections are composed largely of exotic, rare, and wild-caught species. Only rarely are breeding programs done on a long-term basis. When breeding is successful, reintroduction is almost never done. Zoo herpetologists must begin to act more responsibly in the way collections are managed, and more emphasis needs to be placed on conservation education.

Literature Cited

Beck, B., D. Kleiman, J. M. Dietz, and L. A. Dietz. 1991. Costs of a reintroduction and criteria for success: accounting and accountability in the Golden Lion Tamarin conservation program, p. 125–142. *In* J. H. W. Gipps (ed.), Beyond Captive Breeding: Reintroducing Endangered Species to the Wild. Oxford University Press, Oxford, UK.

Bingaman, L. 1987. Herpetological collection composition: recent and future. Ann. Proc. Amer. Assoc. Zool. Parks Aquar., 1987: 844–861.

Burke, R. L. 1991. Relocations, repatriations, and translocations of amphibians and reptiles: taking a broader view. Herpetologica, 47: 350–356.

Dodd, C. K., and R. A. Seigel. 1991. Relocation, repatriation, and translocation of amphibians and reptiles: are they conservation strategies that work? Herpetologica, 47:336–349.

International Species Information System. 1990–1991. Mammal, Bird, Reptile, and Amphibian Abstracts. International Species Informat. Systems, Apple Valley, Minnesota.

Reinert, H. K. 1991. Translocation as a conservation strategy for amphibians and reptiles: some comments, concerns, and observations. Herpetologica, 47: 357–363.

Slavens, F., and K. Slavens. 1991. Inventory of Live Reptiles and Amphibians in Captivity: Breeding—Longevity and Inventory. Slaveware Publ. Co., Seattle, Washington. 505 pages.

❦

❦ Marcellini, D. L. 1994. Collection-management, captive-breeding, and conservation programs in zoo herpetological collections, p. 397–400. *In* J. B. Murphy, K. Adler, and J. T. Collins (eds.), Captive Management and Conservation of Amphibians and Reptiles. Society for the Study of Amphibians and Reptiles, Ithaca (New York). Contributions to Herpetology, volume 11.

Techniques for the Capture and Restraint of Captive Crocodilians

Mark Wise*

Introduction

The capture and restraint of captive crocodilians is hazardous, even for an experienced zoo professional. It is even more so to those persons who have an interest in herpetology, but who have no experience in handling and being around these creatures. Most of us handle only a few specimens during our lifetime. Often the species handled is the American Alligator (*Alligator mississippiensis*), and even with that reptile, the capture or handling may be done only once in a lifetime. This chapter summarizes capture methods for use on captive specimens. One method may be preferred over another (especially in the case of specimens larger than 1.5 meters), but should be considered before attempting any crocodilian capture, because only some of the techniques apply to all captures, while others are more appropriate to particular situations. In dealing with crocodilians, an error in the selection of an appropriate capture technique may have grave consequences for both the captor and captive.

The St. Augustine Alligator Farm in St. Augustine, Florida, contains the world's most extensive crocodilian collection: over 3,000 specimens, representing all 22 living species. Thirteen species of crocodilians have reproduced at the St. Augustine Alligator Farm, including the successful births of over 60 Chinese Alligators (*Alligator sinensis*). Other rare species in the collection include the Gharial (*Gavialis gangeticus*), Orinoco Crocodile (*Crocodylus intermedius*), and the Black Caiman (*Melanosuchus niger*). It has been necessary for us to regularly capture and/or restrain specimens in our facility for a variety reasons, such as transferring specimens from our Ocala facility to St. Augustine, or simply collecting blood samples for research.

Because of the extensive experience gained in housing this collection, restraint and/or capture techniques have been developed which are not only safe for the captor, but will place less stress on the animal as well. Crocodilians build up lactic acid during periods of stress, such as capture, so it is of utmost importance that the specimen be captured and released with the least amount of stress to the animal. The techniques outlined in this chapter have been used in the capture of animals ranging from the smallest hatchling crocodilian to a 6-m Saltwater Crocodile (*Crocodylus porosus*).

Although many other institutions are now using chemical restraint, we have always used the methods below, and have never had a serious accident with a keeper or an injury to any specimens.

Safety

Safety measures are most important while attempting the capture of a crocodilian. Some of the most important measures are:

(1) Always keep your attention on the specimen being captured as well as other specimens in the exhibit. Sometimes another specimen in an exhibit may sneak up behind the captors and attack.

(2) Hands must never be placed within reach of the animal. Most bites occur when the hands are left within *lateral striking distance* of the jaws. All approaches should be made directly from the back over the neck area, and the captor's hands should be kept as low as possible on the approach.

*St. Augustine Alligator Farm
Route A1A South, P.O. 9005
St. Augustine, Florida 32084, USA

Mailing address:
11 Madeira Drive
St. Augustine, Florida 32084, USA

(3) Always maintain a *balanced* position, so that one is always ready to move quickly away from the specimen.

(4) Specimens should always be captured in open spaces, not only for safety, but also for the sake of the animal. Slender-snouted species may hit their jaws on walls or trees and injure themselves.

(5) If at all possible, attempt to capture the specimen by standing outside the exhibit, if it is an aggressive species. This works well if an initial rope can be secured on the specimen, because it is much safer to have a fence between the captors and the crocodilian. The rope should be tied to trees or rigid fences, in case the animal tries to move or spin. The captors may then enter the exhibit more safely to place a second rope on the animal and to proceed with the capture.

(6) Never capture the specimen on concrete. It may severely abrade the crocodilian's jaws, as well as the knees and knuckles of the captors.

(7) It is recommended that the captors grasp the jaws of all crocodiles and the Gharial only while wearing thick protection, such as leather gloves, because the sharp teeth can inflict damage even when the jaws are secured. One thrash of the head can inflict a deep laceration. I speak from experience.

(8) Always have a minimum of two persons on hand while attempting to capture a crocodilian.

(9) If a crocodilian does not need to be captured, *do not catch it.* If an enclosure needs to be entered, either to retrieve items which do not belong there or to clean it, the household garden hose becomes a useful and important tool. The hose can be used to spray the specimen gently on its eyes. This will close the eyes long enough for retrieval or clean up to be performed. *Do not take any undue chances when using this method.* This method is useful for quick maintenance operations only.

(10) A crocodilian exhibit that is entered on a regular basis should have a holding area built adjacent to the primary exhibit so that the animal can be manuevered into the area and restrained. This works well for cleaning and other maintenance, and may also provide an area for eggs to be deposited in a captive-breeding situation. A garden hose spray may be used to move difficult animals into this holding area. All new enclosures planned for crocodilians should have this holding area as part of their design.

Materials and Methods

Smaller crocodilians, those that are less than 12 cm long, may be captured by quickly grasping the reptile in the nuchal area, just behind the head. This task is normally simple for most species, but extra caution is urged with Cuban Crocodiles (*Crocodylus rhombifer*), because they are notorious for their ability to jump (even the hatchlings).

Although an experienced handler can capture nearly all species of crocodilians which are up to a meter in length by grasping them behind the neck, I do not recommend it. At a meter in length, a crocodilian is a very different animal, more muscular and stronger than a juvenile, and the chance of injury to both captor and the crocodile is increased. A safer method is the use of a simple household sponge-mop to pin the head down, much like the hook used for venomous snakes. The sponge-mop works well because it is soft, flexible, and is also stable on the slippery nuchal scales of crocodilians, while a snake hook or similar apparatus, which is hard and smooth, may slip when applied to the same area of the neck. By applying firm, yet gentle, pressure with the sponge-mop, the specimen can then be grasped firmly behind the head. The other hand can be used to support the body near the rear legs.

If the jaws of a meter-long, captured crocodilian are going to be secured by tape, the tail should be placed between the legs of the captor. This frees the second hand while the other hand is holding the neck area. The jaws may then be closed at this point by making an approach from the rear of the crocodilian's head. This should be done by staying very close to the top of the specimen's head, quickly grabbing the base of the skull, and then closing the jaws. After the jaws are secured, they should then be wiped dry by a helper, and taped using electrical tape.

For specimens ranging from one to two meters, the best method for capture is a commercially available capture-pole. These poles may be purchased from most animal-capture equipment companies. The devices are spring-loaded poles that allow the specimen to be captured from a distance. A 2-m capture-pole is recommended for crocodilians. The spring-loaded device allows the specimen to be released without ever physically handling it. The following safety regimen should be observed while using a capture-pole:

(1) Never over-tighten the noose, because this may strangle the crocodilian.

(2) Never allow the crocodilian to bite the capture-pole. It is difficult to free the pole from the closed jaws, and doing so may put a captor's hands in a compromising position while trying to free the pole from the animal's jaws. Larger crocodilians may hold the pole in their mouth, flail it back and forth, and hit the captor with it.

After the capture-pole noose is around the crocodilian's neck, a helper should approach the crocodilian from the rear. Smaller specimens may simply be grasped behind the neck. During this procedure, the capture-pole may either remain around the neck of the animal or be removed, provided the crocodilian is under control. The jaws may then be closed by approaching from the rear, moving the hand over the top of the jaws, and finally by grasping and closing the jaws with a firm grip. Remember to *never* place your arms or legs within lateral reach of the crocodilian's jaws.

For crocodilians which are 2 m in length, the captor manning the capture-pole should not remove the pole, but instead apply continual pressure by pulling on the catch pole, while a second person approaches from the rear. The second captor should place a hand firmly on the nuchal area of the crocodilian and sit on the specimen's back, always remaining alert and ready to withdraw in case the animal rotates its jaws laterally or rolls its entire body. Once firmly astride the crocodilian, the person's hand should be passed over the animal's upper jaw, moving back to front, pushing the upper jaw down onto the lower jaw and shoving both toward the ground. At this point, if the animal is still under control, the specimen's jaws should be grasped with the stronger hand and pulled upward to be wiped dry and taped.

For more aggressive specimens (particularly when persons with less skill are involved in the capture), it should be noted that there is an alternative to sitting on the back of the specimen (which may be a tremendous relief to the inexperienced). The alternative is a device called a jaw-rope, which allows the crocodilian's jaws to be cinched shut by simply pulling on the rope and closing a loop, which the captor has prepared beforehand. The jaw-rope is prepared by making a lariat-type device out of a flexible, stable rope. The jaw-rope is then gently slipped over both the upper and lower jaw of the crocodilian (just behind the mandibular symphysis), and is pulled from one end, thus forcing the jaws shut; added excitement results, however, on those occasions when the loop is not tightened quickly enough and the jaws remain partially open. To complete closing the jaws, push down on them from the top, cinching the rope at the same time. When using the jaw-rope, several safety tips are in order:

(1) Never rely entirely on the jaw rope. It is simply a device to assist in closing the jaws. If the rope appears secure, the jaws may be grabbed, then wiped dry and taped. If a crocodilian's teeth protrude laterally from its jaws, the captors should wear protective gear on their hands—even with its mouth taped, a crocodilian may quickly jerk its head and severely lacerate a captor.

(2) Use a rope that is not too large in diameter, that is flexible and strong, and that provides some friction against itself while being cinched.

(3) If needed, or if the captor feels more confident in doing so, use two jaw ropes.

(4) Some captors like to toss a wet towel over the eyes of crocodilians while they are being captured. This covers the eyes so that a crocodilian cannot see what the captor is doing. This technique sometimes works with specimens that are generally passive in nature. It is my experience, however, that in many instances, a crocodilian becomes annoyed when a wet towel is tossed over its eyes—the animal becomes disturbed and more difficult to capture. If you feel this technique might work, try it. If it does not succeed, abandon it and select another capture method.

Capture of Larger Specimens

Specimens larger than 2 m in length are much more powerful and dangerous animals than are smaller ones, and require different capture techniques. Specimens of this size should only be captured by placing nylon rope (of at least a 1-cm diameter) around the neck, followed by securing the jaws with a jaw-rope. Several additional techniques which may be used when capturing larger crocodilians are:

(1) To capture a large crocodilian, first place the rope around the neck to restrain it.

(2) Never sit on the back of a large crocodilian and attempt to hold the jaws shut—if the reptile should jerk its head or roll, you could be seriously wounded. The power generated by a large crocodilian is extraordinary.

(3) If a large crocodilian is to be dragged to a different position or pulled a short distance to an appropriate area for examination, place another rope behind the front legs. Do not pull the crocodilian by the neck rope, because this could injure it, or even break its neck—use the rope fitted behind the front legs for dragging the animal short distances. For extremely large crocodilians, two ropes behind the anterior legs may be required to provide additional room (and leverage) for pulling. Several of our specimens at St. Augustine ultimately had to be moved with tractors, and our 6-m Saltwater Crocodile had to be lifted into our exhibit with a crane.

(4) If a crocodilian is to be moved from an exhibit pool, I recommend that the water be left in the pool. Obviously, it is much easier to move a heavy crocodilian by floating it on the water, as opposed to dragging it across the floor and then up and over the steep edges of the pool. But of more importance, large crocodilians may tend to roll their bodies rapidly while being captured. If they do this, pulling them across water will not hurt, and will actually assist in the moving process. But pulling a crocodilian on concrete while it is rolling its body can injure the specimen.

(5) Cuban Crocodiles and some other species of crocodilians are very aggressive, and tend to lunge at captors. Two neck ropes are almost mandatory with these aggressive types. Such crocodilians should be secured with an initial rope on the neck that is pulled in one direction and tied to an object. The second rope should be pulled in the other direction, and the combination should restrict the forward or reverse movement of the animal.

Capture of the Slender-Snouted Forms

Snouts of the slender-jawed crocodilians are fragile and may possibly break if handled roughly. The Gharial, False Gharial (*Tomistoma schlegelii*), and the Slender-snouted Crocodile (*Crocodylus cataphractus*) are good examples of crocodilians that have snouts which must be handled with care. The Gharial has a particularly sensitive snout and will protect it by holding it high in the air. Several techniques useful for working with these slender-snouted species are:

(1) *Never* attempt to capture these slender-snouted species in a confined area. Their exhibits should not have holes in the walls or around the pools in order to prevent them from accidentally injuring their jaws.

(2) Capture slender-snouted crocodilians in their pools, because the water will slow down and absorb some of the force of the crocodilian's slashing jaws while it is being restrained and secured.

(3) Avoid the exceptionally sharp teeth of these species, because they can inflict much injury while the jaws are being secured.

(4) With the exception of the Gharial, all species of slender-snouted forms can be secured with ropes if necessary, but I prefer to use a heavy net to capture them in the water. Entangle them in the net before attempting to restrain the jaws.

Release After Capture

Release of most crocodilians is simple following their capture. Being captured is extremely stressful for a crocodilian, and release of the specimen should not elevate stress. There are several important and safe (for both the captor and the crocodilian) release techniques, such as:

(1) During the release of a large crocodilian, always position the captor close to the exhibit-entry door.

(2) If possible, all crocodilians should be released in a pool, because it cushions any thrashing or impact by the animal, and it gives the captor an advantage in swiftly exiting the enclosure when large specimens are involved.

(3) Smaller crocodilians should be released by first removing the hand that is the holding the tail and then removing the hand holding the head. Some captors sit on the back of a larger crocodilians while removing tape from the mouth. I prefer to pull the tape off while in front of the specimen, because it is too easy for a crocodilian to turn quickly and bite while the captor is still climbing from its back.

Summary and Discussion

By following these described methods, crocodilian capture and restraint can be easily and safely executed. If a captor believes that a pending capture is unsafe or beyond his or her capability, it should not be attempted. If a captor is accidentally grabbed by a crocodilian during capture, attempt to prevent the animal from rolling and twisting its body—this is a dangerous behavior when performed by larger crocodilians and can result in loss of the person's limb. With smaller animals (less than one meter) prevention of rolling may be done by simply grasping the animal with the other hand. Larger animals may be restrained by sitting on their back and driving their nuchal areas into the ground and placing one's knees under the anterior limbs of the specimen. In either instance, care must be taken not to put other body parts in jeopardy while freeing the bitten part. The second bite may be more severe than the first. In many instances, a crocodilian may bite quickly and then release. Therefore, if a bite occurs, hesitate briefly before trying any release measures. It has been the experience of the author that most bites are reflexive. If a crocodilian bites and holds on, however, almost no force or prying method will release the jaws. If the crocodilian continues to grip with its jaws, the specimen may have to be chemically sedated or, in extreme cases, euthanasia of the specimen may be in order to release the jaws.

❦

❦ Wise, M. 1994. Techniques for the capture and restraint of captive crocodilians, p. 401–405. *In* J. B. Murphy, K. Adler, and J. T. Collins (eds.), Captive Management and Conservation of Amphibians and Reptiles. Society for the Study of Amphibians and Reptiles, Ithaca (New York). Contributions to Herpetology, volume 11.

Index to Scientific Names

Names of amphibians and reptiles are in **boldface** type.

PUBLICATIONS OF THE

SOCIETY FOR THE STUDY OF AMPHIBIANS AND REPTILES

SOCIETY PUBLICATIONS may be purchased from:
Dr. Robert D. Aldridge, Publications Secretary,
Department of Biology, St. Louis University,
St. Louis, Missouri 63103, USA.
(*telephone:* area code 314, 977-3910 or 977-3916;
fax: area code 314, 977-3117).

Prices are effective through December 1995. Make checks payable to "SSAR." Shipments sent at customer's risk; however, packages can be insured at cost (see below). Overseas customers must make payment in USA funds using a draft drawn on American banks (include an additional amount to cover bank conversion charges) or by International Money Order. All persons may charge to MasterCard or VISA (provide account number and expiration date); items marked "out-of-print" are no longer available.

Shipping and Handling Costs

Shipments inside the USA: Shipping costs are in addition to the price of publications. Add an amount for shipping of the first item ($2.00 for a book costing $10.00 or more <u>or</u> $1.00 if the item costs less than $10.00) plus an amount for any additional items ($1.00 each for books costing over $10.00 and $0.50 for each item costing less than $10.00).

Shipments outside the USA: Determine the cost for shipments inside USA (above) and then <u>add</u> 4% of the total cost of the order.

Large prints (marked *): For shipments inside the USA, add $3.00 for any quantity; outside the USA, instead add $7.00 for any quantity.

Insurance costs: For shipments inside the USA, add $1.00 for each $50.00 value of order; outside the USA, instead add $2.00 for each $50.00 of value.

CONTRIBUTIONS TO HERPETOLOGY

Book-length monographs, comprising taxonomic revisions, results of symposia, and other major works. Prepublication discount to Society members.

No. 1. *Reproductive Biology and Diseases of Captive Reptiles*, by James B. Murphy and Joseph T. Collins (eds.). 1980. Results of a Society-sponsored symposium, including papers by 37 leading specialists. 287 p., illus. Paperbound. Out-of print.

No. 2. *The Turtles of Venezuela,* by Peter C. H. Pritchard and Pedro Trebbau. 1984. An exhaustive natural history covering half of the turtle species of South America. 414 p., 48 color plates (25 watercolor portraits by Giorgio Voltolina and 165 photographs of turtles and habitats) measuring 8½ x 11 inches, keys, 16 maps. Regular edition, clothbound $45.00; patron's edition, two leatherbound volumes in cloth-covered box, signed and numbered by authors and artist $300.00. (*Also*: set of 25 color prints of turtle portraits on heavy paper stock, in protective wrapper $30.00.)

No. 3. *Introduction to the Herpetofauna of Costa Rica / Introducción a la Herpetofauna de Costa Rica,* by Jay M. Savage and Jaime Villa R. 1986. Bilingual edition in English and Spanish, with distribution checklist, bibliographies, and extensive illustrated keys. 220 p., one color plate, map. Clothbound $30.00.

No. 4. *Studies on Chinese Salamanders*, by Ermi Zhao, Qixiong Hu, Yaoming Jiang, and Yuhua Yang. 1988. Evolutionary review of all Chinese species with keys, diagnostic figures, and distribution maps. 80 p., 7 plates (including 10 color photographs of salamanders and habitats). Clothbound $12.00.

No. 5. *Contributions to the History of Herpetology*, by Kraig Adler, John S. Applegarth, and Ronald Altig. 1989. Biographies of 152 prominent herpetologists (with portraits and signatures), index to 2500 authors in taxonomic herpetology, and academic lineages of 1450 herpetologists. International coverage. 202 p., 148 photographs, 1 color plate. Clothbound $20.00.

No. 6. *Snakes of the* Agkistrodon *Complex: A Monographic Review*, by Howard K. Gloyd and Roger Conant. 1990. Comprehensive treatment of 33 taxa of pitvipers included in four genera: *Agkistrodon*, *Calloselasma*, *Deinagkistrodon*, and *Hypnale*. Also includes nine supplementary chapters by leading specialists. 620 p., 33 color plates (247 photographs of snakes and habitats), 20 uncolored plates, 60 text figures, checklist and keys, 6 charts, 28 maps. Clothbound $75.00. (*Also*: separate set of the 247 color photographs of snakes and habitats [on 32 plates], in protective wrapper. $30.00; limited-edition print of the book's frontispiece illustrating snakes of all four genera, from watercolor by David M. Dennis. Signed individually by Roger Conant and the artist $25.00.)

No. 7. *The Snakes of Iran*, by Mahmoud Latifi. 1991. Review of the 60 species of Iranian snakes, covering general biology, venoms, and snake bite. Appendix and supplemental bibliography by Alan E. Leviton and George R. Zug. 167 p., 22 color plates of snakes (66 figures), 2 color relief maps, 44 species range maps. Clothbound $22.00.

No. 8. *Handbook to Middle East Amphibians and Reptiles*, by Alan E. Leviton, Steven C. Anderson, Kraig Adler, and Sherman A. Minton. 1992. Annotated checklist, illustrated key, and identification manual covering 148 species and subspecies found in region from Turkish border south through the Arabian Peninsula (including Bahrain, Qatar, and United Arab Emirates) and the Arabian (Persian) Gulf. Chapters on venomous snakes and snakebite treatment plus extensive bibliography. 264 p., 32 color plates (220 photographs), maps, text figures. Clothbound $28.00.

No. 9. *Herpetology: Current Research on the Biology of Amphibians and Reptiles.* 1992. Proceedings of the First World Congress of Herpetology (1989), with a foreword by H.R.H. Prince Philip, Duke of Edinburgh. Includes the plenary lectures, a summary of the congress, and a list of delegates with their current addresses. 225 p., 28 photographs. Clothbound $28.00.

No. 10. *Herpetology of China*, by Ermi Zhao and Kraig Adler. Comprehensive review of Chinese amphibians and reptiles, including Hong Kong and Taiwan. 522 p., 48 color plates (371 photographs), portraits, text figures, maps. Clothbound $60.00.

No. 11. *Captive Management and Conservation of Amphibians and Reptiles*, by James B. Murphy, Kraig Adler, and Joseph T. Collins (eds.). 1994. Results of a Society-sponsored symposium, including chapters by 70 leading specialists. 408 p., 35 photographs, 1 color plate. Clothbound $58.00.

FACSIMILE REPRINTS IN HERPETOLOGY

Exact reprints of classic and important books and papers. Most titles have extensive new introductions by leading authorities. Prepublication discount to Society members.

ANDERSON, J. 1896. *Contribution to the Herpetology of Arabia*. Introduction and new checklist of Arabian amphibians and reptiles by Alan E. Leviton and Michele L. Aldrich. 160 p., illus. (one plate in color), map. Clothbound $25.00.

BELL, T. 1842–1843. *Herpetology of the "Beagle."* Part 5 of Charles Darwin's classic, "Zoology of the Voyage of H.M.S. Beagle," containing descriptions of amphibians and reptiles collected on the expedition. Introduction by Roberto Donoso-Barros. 100 p., 20 plates (measuring 8½ x 11 inches), map. Paperbound $13.00, clothbound $18.00.

BOGERT, C. M., and R. MARTÍN DEL CAMPO. 1956. *The Gila Monster and Its Allies.* The standard work on lizards of the family Helodermatidae. New preface by Charles M. Bogert and retrospective essay by Daniel D. Beck. 262 p., color plate, 62 photographs, 35 text figures, index. $38.00. (*Also*: limited edition print of the book's frontispiece illustrating a Gila monster, from watercolor by David M. Dennis. Signed individually by Charles Bogert and the artist $25.00.)

BOJANUS, L. H. 1819–1821. *Anatome Testudinis Europaeae*. The standard atlas of turtle anatomy. Introduction by Alfred Sherwood Romer. 200 p., 40 foldout plates. Out-of-print.

BOULENGER, G. A. 1877–1920. *Contributions to American Herpetology*. A collection of papers (from various journals) covering North, Central, and South American species, with an introduction by James C. Battersby. Complete in 18 parts totalling 880 p., numerous illustrations, index. Paperbound. Complete set: 18 parts plus index and two tables of contents (for binding in two volumes), in parts as issued $55.00.

BULLETIN OF THE ANTIVENIN INSTITUTE OF AMERICA. Volumes 1–5, 1927–1932. Introduction by Sherman A. Minton. 575 p., 163 photographs, maps, index. Out-of-print.

CAMP, C. L. 1923. *Classification of the Lizards*. The foundation of modern lizard systematics. New preface by the author and an introduction by Garth Underwood. 220 p., 112 figures, index. Out-of-print.

CHANG, M. L. Y. 1936. *Amphibiens Urodèles de la Chine*. The classic work on Chinese salamanders, with a new checklist by Arden H. Brame. 168 p., illus., 5 plates. Out-of-print.

COPE, E. D. 1864. *Papers on the Higher Classification of Frogs*. Reprinted from Proceedings of the Academy of Natural Sciences of Philadelphia and Natural History Review. 32 p. Paperbound $3.00.

COPE, E. D. 1871. *Catalogue of Batrachia and Reptilia Obtained by McNiel in Nicaragua; Catalogue of Reptilia and Batrachia Obtained by Maynard in Florida*. 8 p. Paperbound $1.00.

COPE, E. D. 1892. *The Osteology of the Lacertilia*. An important contribution to lizard anatomy, reprinted from Proceedings of the American Philosophical Society. 44 p., 6 plates. Paperbound $4.00.

COWLES, R. B., and C. M. BOGERT. 1944. *A Preliminary Study of the Thermal Requirements of Desert Reptiles*. The foundation of thermoregulation biology, with extensive review of recent studies by F. Harvey Pough. Reprinted from Bulletin of American Museum of Natural History. 52 p., 11 plates. Paperbound $5.00.

DUNN, E. R. 1926. *Salamanders of the Family Plethodontidae*. A recognized classic treatment of the plethodontid salamanders, including tropical and European species. Introductions by David B. Wake and Arden H. Brame. 480 p., illus., 3 plates, 86 maps, index. Out-of-print.

ESCHSCHOLTZ, F. 1829–1833. *Zoologischer Atlas* (herpetological sections). Descriptions of new reptiles and amphibians from California and the Pacific. Introduction by Kraig Adler. 32 p., 4 plates (measuring 8½ x 11 inches). Paperbound $3.00.

ESPADA, M. JIMÉNEZ DE LA. 1875. *Vertebrados del Viaje al Pacifico: Batracios*. Major taxonomic work on South American frogs. Introduction by Jay M. Savage. 208 p., 6 plates, maps. Clothbound $20.00.

FAUVEL, A.-A. 1879. *Alligators in China*. Original description of *Alligator sinensis*, including classical and natural history. 42 p., 3 plates. Paperbound $5.00.

FITZINGER, L. J. 1843. *Systema Reptilium*. An important nomenclatural landmark for herpetology, including Amphibia as well as reptiles; world-wide in scope. Introduction by Robert Mertens. 128 p., index. Paperbound $15.00.

GLOYD, H. K. 1940. *The Rattlesnakes, Genera* Sistrurus *and* Crotalus. Introduction and new checklist by Hobart M. Smith and Herbert M. Harris. 300 p., plus 31 plates of photographs, index. Out-of-print.

GRAY, J. E. 1825. *A Synopsis of the Genera of Reptiles and Amphibia*. Reprinted from Annals of Philosophy. 32 p. Paperbound $3.00.

GRAY, J. E. 1831–1844. *Zoological Miscellany*. A privately printed journal, devoted mostly to descriptions of amphibians, reptiles, and birds from throughout the world. Introduction by Arnold G. Kluge. 86 p., 4 plates. Paperbound $6.00, clothbound $10.00.

GÜNTHER, A. 1885–1902. *Biologia Centrali-Americana. Reptilia and Batrachia*. The standard work on Middle American herpetology with 76 full-page plates measuring 8½ x 11 inches (12 in color). Introductions by Hobart M. Smith, A. E. Gunther, and Kraig Adler. 575 p., photographs, maps. Clothbound $50.00. (*Also*: separate set of the 12 color plates, in protective wrapper $18.00.)

HOLBROOK, J. E. 1842. *North American Herpetology*. Five volumes bound in one. The classic work by the father of North American herpetology. Exact facsimile of the definitive second edition, including all 147 plates, measuring 8½ x 11 inches (20 reproduced in full color). Introduction and checklists by Richard and Patricia Worthington and by Kraig Adler. 1032 p. Leatherbound patron's edition, out-of-print; regular edition, clothbound $60.00.

JUNIOR SOCIETY OF NATURAL SCIENCES (CINCINNATI, OHIO). 1930–1932. Herpetological papers from the society's Proceedings, with articles by Weller, Walker, Dury, and others. 56 p. Paperbound $3.00.

KIRTLAND, J. P. 1838. *Zoology of Ohio* (herpetological portion). 8 p. Paperbound $1.00.

LECONTE, J. E. 1824–1828. *Three Papers on Amphibians*, from the Annals of the Lyceum of Natural History, New York. 16 p. Paperbound $2.00.

LINNAEUS, C. 1766–1771. *Systema Naturae* (ed. 12) and *Mantissa Plantarum* (herpetological portions from both). 56 p. Introduction by Kraig Adler. Out-of-print.

LOVERIDGE, A. 1946. *Reptiles [and Amphibians] of the Pacific*. The standard review of the herpetofauna of the Pacific region including Australia and extending from Indonesia to Hawaii and the Galápagos Islands. 271 p., 7 plates, 1 double-page map, index. Out-of-print.

McILHENNY, E. A. 1935. *The Alligator's Life History*. The most complete natural history of the American alligator. Introduction by Archie Carr and a review of recent literature by Jeffrey W. Lang. 125 p., 18 photographs and a portrait. Clothbound $20.00.

McLAIN, R. B. 1899. *Contributions to North American Herpetology*. Three privately printed papers containing important distributional records and the description of a new form. 28 p., index. Paperbound $2.00.

ORBIGNY, A. D' [and G. BIBRON]. 1847. *Voyage dans l'Amérique Méridionale*. This extract comprises the complete section on reptiles and amphibians from this voyage to South America. 14 p., 9 plates measuring 8 1/2 x 11 inches. $3.00.

RAFINESQUE, C. S. 1820. *Annals of Nature* (herpetological and ichthyological sections), 4 p. Paperbound $1.00.

RAFINESQUE, C. S. 1822. *On Two New Salamanders of Kentucky*. 2 p. Paperbound $1.00.

RAFINESQUE, C. S. 1832–1833. *Five Herpetological Papers from the Atlantic Journal*. 4 p. Paperbound $1.00.

SOWERBY, J. DEC., E. LEAR, and J. E. GRAY. 1872. *Tortoises, Terrapins, and Turtles Drawn From Life*. The finest atlas of turtle illustrations ever produced. Introduction by Ernest E. Williams. 26 p., 61 full-page plates (measuring 8 1/2 x 11 inches). Clothbound $25.00.

SPIX, J. B. VON, and J. G. WAGLER. 1824–1825. *Herpetology of Brazil*. The most comprehensive and important early survey of Brazilian herpetology. Introduction by P. E. Vanzolini. 400 p., 98 plates, one in color (each measuring 8 1/2 x 11 inches), map. Clothbound $36.00.

TROSCHEL, F. H. 1850 [1852]. Cophosaurus texanus, *neue Eidechsengattung aus Texas*. 8 p. Paperbound $1.00.

TSCHUDI, J. J. VON. 1838. *Classification der Batrachier*. A major work in systematic herpetology, with introduction by Robert Mertens. 118 p., 6 plates. Paperbound $18.00.

TSCHUDI, J. J. VON. 1845. *Reptilium Conspectus*. Descriptions of new reptiles and amphibians from Peru. 24 p. Paperbound $2.00.

VANDENBURGH, J. 1895–1896. *Herpetology of Lower California*. Herpetology of Baja California, Mexico (collected papers). 101 p., 11 plates, index. Paperbound $8.00.

WAITE, E. R. 1929. *The Reptiles and Amphibians of South Australia*. Introduction by Michael J. Tyler and Mark Hutchinson. 282 p., color plate, portrait, 192 text figures including numerous photographs. Clothbound $35.00.

WIEGMANN, A. F. A. 1834. *Herpetologia Mexicana*. Introduction by Edward H. Taylor. 66 p., 10 plates (folio, measuring 10 x 14 inches). Out-of-print.

WILCOX, E. V. 1891. *Notes on Ohio Batrachians*. 3 p. Paperbound $1.00.

WILLISTON, S. W. 1925. *Osteology of the Reptiles*. Covers living and extinct forms, with introduction by Claude W. Hibbard. 304 p., 191 text figures, index. Out-of-print.

WRIGHT, A. H., and A. A. WRIGHT. 1962. *Handbook of Snakes of the United States and Canada, Volume 3, Bibliography*. Out-of-print since about 1969, this cross-indexed bibliography is a necessary companion to Volumes 1 and 2. 187 p. Clothbound $18.00.

HERPETOLOGICAL REVIEW AND H.I.S.S. PUBLICATIONS

The Society's official newsletter, international in coverage. In addition to news notes and feature articles, regular departments include regional societies, techniques, husbandry, life history, geographic distribution, and book reviews. Issued quarterly as part of Society membership or separately by subscription. All numbers are paperbound as issued and measure 8 1/2 x 11 inches. In 1973, publications of the Herpetological Information Search Systems (*News-Journal* and *Titles and Reviews*) were substituted for *Herpetological Review*; content and format are the same.

Volume 1 (1967–1969), numbers 1–9, $4.00 per number.

Volumes 2–25 (1970–1994), four numbers in each volume (except volumes 3–4, with 6 numbers each), $4.00 per number.

The following numbers are out-of-print and *no longer available*: Volume 1(number 7), 3(2, 6), 4(1), 5(1, 2), 6(1, 2, 4), 7(3, 4), and 10(2).

Cumulative Index for Volumes 1–7 (1967–1976), 60 pages, $4.00.

Cumulative Index for Volumes 1–17 (1967–1986), 90 pages, $7.00.

H.I.S.S. Publications: News-Journal, volume 1, numbers 1–6, and Titles and Reviews, volume 1, numbers 1–2 (all of 1973–1974), complete set, $10.00.

Index to Geographic Distribution Records for Volumes 1–17 (1967–1986), including H.I.S.S. publications, 44 pages, $5.00.

CATALOGUE OF AMERICAN AMPHIBIANS AND REPTILES

Loose-leaf accounts of taxa prepared by specialists, including synonymy, definition, description, distribution map, and comprehensive list of literature for each taxon. Covers amphibians and reptiles of the entire Western Hemisphere. Issued by subscription. Individual accounts are not sold separately.

CATALOGUE ACCOUNTS:

Complete set:	Numbers 1–580, $290.00.
Partial sets:	Numbers 1–190, $60.00.
	Numbers 191–410, $70.00.
	Numbers 411–580, $130.00.

INDEX TO ACCOUNTS 1–400: Cross-referenced, 64 pages, $5.00.

IMPRINTED POST BINDER: $25.00. (Note: One binder holds about 200 accounts.)

SYSTEMATIC TABS: Ten printed tabs for binder, such as "Class Amphibia," "Order Caudata," etc., $5.00 per set.

JOURNAL OF HERPETOLOGY

The Society's official scientific journal, international in scope. Issued quarterly as part of Society membership. All numbers are paperbound as issued, measuring 7 x 10 inches.

Volume 1 (1968), numbers 1–4 combined.

Volumes 2–5 (1968–1971), numbers 1–2 and 3–4 combined, $6.00 per double number.

Volume 6 (1972), numbers 1, 2, and double number 3–4.

Volumes 7–28 (1973–1994), four numbers in each volume, $6.00 per single number.

The following volumes and numbers are out-of-print and are *no longer available*: Volume 1, 2, 3, 4, 5(3, 4), 6, 7(1), 8(1), 9(1, 2, 4), 10(1, 4), 11(4), and 12(1, 2).

Cumulative Index for Volumes 1–10 (1968–1976), 72 pages, $7.00.

HERPETOLOGICAL CIRCULARS

Miscellaneous publications of general interest to the herpetological community. All numbers are paperbound, as issued. Prepublication discount to Society members.

No. 1. *A Guide to Preservation Techniques for Amphibians and Reptiles* by George R. Pisani. 1973. 22 p., illus. $3.00.

No. 2. *Guía de Técnicas de Preservación de Anfibios y Reptiles* por George R. Pisani y Jaime Villa. 1974. 28 p., illus. $3.00.

No. 3. *Collections of Preserved Amphibians and Reptiles in the United States* compiled by David B. Wake (chair) and the Committee on Resources in Herpetology. 1975. 22 p. Out-of-print.

No. 4. *A Brief Outline of Suggested Treatments for Diseases of Captive Reptiles* by James B. Murphy. 1975. 13 p. $3.00.

No. 5. *Endangered and Threatened Amphibians and Reptiles in the United States* compiled by Ray E. Ashton, Jr. (chair) and 1973–74 SSAR Regional Herpetological Societies Liaison Committee. 1976. 65 p. Out-of-print.

No. 6. *Longevity of Reptiles and Amphibians in North American Collections* by J. Kevin Bowler. 1977. 32 p. $3.00. (See also number 21.)

No. 7. *Standard Common and Current Scientific Names for North American Amphibians and Reptiles* (1st ed.) by Joseph T. Collins, James E. Huheey, James L. Knight, and Hobart M. Smith. 1978. 36 p. $3.00. (See also numbers 12 and 19.)

No. 8. *A Brief History of Herpetology in North America Before 1900* by Kraig Adler. 1979. 40 p., 24 photographs, 1 map. $3.00.

No. 9. *A Review of Marking Techniques for Amphibians and Reptiles* by John W. Ferner. 1979. 42 p., illus. $3.00.

No. 10. *Vernacular Names of South American Turtles* by Russell A. Mittermeier, Federico Medem and Anders G. J. Rhodin. 1980. 44 p. $3.00.

No. 11. *Recent Instances of Albinism in North American Amphibians and Reptiles* by Stanley Dyrkacz. 1981. 36 p. $3.00.

No. 12. *Standard Common and Current Scientific Names for North American Amphibians and Reptiles* (2nd ed.) by Joseph T. Collins, Roger Conant, James E. Huheey, James L. Knight, Eric M. Rundquist, and Hobart M. Smith. 1982. 32 p. $3.00. (See also numbers 7 and 19.)

No. 13. *Silver Anniversary Membership Directory*, including addresses of all SSAR members, addresses and publications of the herpetological societies of the world, and a brief history of the Society. 1983. 56 p., 4 photographs. $3.00.

No. 14. *Checklist of the Turtles of the World with English Common Names* by John Iverson. 1985. 14 p. $3.00.

No. 15. *Cannibalism in Reptiles: A World-Wide Review* by Joseph C. Mitchell. 1986. 37 p. $4.00.

No. 16. *Herpetological Collecting and Collections Management* by John E. Simmons. 1987. 72 p., 6 photographs. $6.00.

No. 17. *An Annotated List and Guide to the Amphibians and Reptiles of Monteverde, Costa Rica* by Marc P. Hayes, J. Alan Pounds, and Walter W. Timmerman. 1989. 70 p., 32 figures. $5.00.

No. 18. *Type Catalogues of Herpetological Collections: An Annotated List of Lists* by Charles R. Crumly. 1990. 50 p. $5.00.

No. 19. *Standard Common and Current Scientific Names for North American Amphibians and Reptiles* (3rd ed.) compiled by Joseph T. Collins (coordinator for SSAR Common and Scientific Names List). 1990. 45 p. $5.00. (See also numbers 7 and 12.)

No. 20. *Age Determination in Turtles* by George R. Zug. 1991. 32 p., 6 figures. $5.00.

No. 21. *Longevity of Reptiles and Amphibians in North American Collections* (2nd ed.) by Andrew T. Snider and J. Kevin Bowler. 1992. 44 p. $5.00. (See also number 6.)

No. 22. *Biology, Status, and Management of the Timber Rattlesnake* (Crotalus horridus): *A Guide for Conservation* by William S. Brown. 1993. 84 p., 16 color photographs. $8.00.

No. 23. *Scientific and Common Names for the Amphibians and Reptiles of Mexico in English and Spanish / Nombres Científicos y Comunes en Ingles y Español de los Anfibios y los Reptiles de México* by Ernest A. Liner. Spanish translation by José L. Camarillo R. 1994. 118 p. $12.00.

PUBLICATIONS OF THE OHIO HERPETOLOGICAL SOCIETY

OHS was the predecessor to the Society for the Study of Amphibians and Reptiles. All publications international in scope. Paperbound as issued.

Volume 1 numbers 1–4, plus Special Publications 1–2 (all 1958), facsimile reprint, out-of-print.

Volume 2 (1959–1960), four numbers, $2.00 per number; numbers 3 and 4 out-of-print.

Volume 3 (1961–1962), four numbers, $1.00 per number; numbers 1 and 3 out-of-print.

Volume 4 (1963–1964), four numbers; double number 1–2, $4.00, numbers 3 and 4 $2.00 each.

Volume 5 (1965–1966), four numbers, $2.00 per number.

Special Publications 3–4 (1961–1962), $2.00 per number; number 3 out-of-print.

OTHER MATERIALS AVAILABLE FROM THE SOCIETY

The following color prints and brochures may be purchased from the Society. (*Extra postage required; see "Shipping and Handling Costs.")

*SILVER ANNIVERSARY COMMEMORATIVE PRINT. Full-color print ($11\frac{1}{2}$ x $15\frac{1}{4}$ inches) of a Gila Monster (*Heloderma suspectum*) on natural background, from a watercolor by David M. Dennis. Issued as part of Society's 25th Anniversary in 1982. Edition limited to 1000. $6.00 each or $5.00 in quantities of 10 or more.

*WORLD CONGRESS COMMEMORATIVE PRINT. Full-color print ($11\frac{1}{2}$ x 15 inches) of an Eastern Box Turtle (*Terrapene carolina*) in a natural setting, from a watercolor by David M. Dennis. Issued as part of SSAR's salute to the First World Congress of Herpetology, held at Canterbury, United Kingdom, in 1989. Edition limited to 1500. $6.00 each or $5.00 in quantities of 10 or more.

HERPETOLOGY AS A CAREER, by Henri C. Seibert, Ralph W. Axtell, Neil B. Ford, and Martin J. Rosenberg. 1985. Brochure developed as an aid to students and counselors. 4 p. Single copies free of charge; additional copies $0.25 each.

GUIDELINES FOR THE USE OF LIVE AMPHIBIANS AND REPTILES IN FIELD RESEARCH, by George R. Pisani, Stephen D. Busack, Herbert C. Dessauer, and Victor H. Hutchison, representing a joint committee of ASIH, HL, and SSAR. 1987. Brochure covers animal care, regulations, collecting, restraint and handling, marking, housing and maintenance in field, and final disposition of specimens. 16 p. $4.00 ($3.00 each in quantities of five or more copies).

PRODUCTION SPECIFICATIONS

WORD PROCESSING AND FORMATTING OF TEXT: University of Kansas, Lawrence, Kansas, USA (Joseph T. Collins) and Cornell University, Ithaca, New York, USA (Timothy D. Perry). Type was set in New Century Schoolbook face, using the Aldus PageMaker 4.2 program on a Macintosh IIci computer, and was printed on an Apple LaserWriter IIg printer.

PRINTING OF TEXT AND BINDING: Thomson-Shore, Inc., Dexter, Michigan, USA (Ned Thomson, Lana Paton, Merry Sumner). The text is printed on 60-pound Glatfelter Thor White paper, a recycled stock. The book is covered in Roxite C-1 cloth (vellum finish) with Multicolor Antique endpapers.

COLOR FRONTISPIECE: Glundal Color, Inc., East Syracuse, New York, USA (Douglass B. Selover). The plate was laser-scanned from the original watercolor and is printed on 80-pound Warren's Lustro Offset Enamel dull text stock.

PAPER: All paper in this book is acid- and groundwood-free. It meets the guidelines for permanence and durability of the Committee on Publication Guidelines for Book Longevity of the Council on Library Resources.

DATE OF PUBLICATION: 30 November 1994.

PLACE OF PUBLICATION: Ithaca, New York, USA.

NUMBER OF COPIES: 3,500.